A TEXT BOOK OF

NETWORK ANALYSIS

For
S.E. SEMESTER – III

SECOND YEAR DEGREE COURSES IN
ELECTRONICS & TELECOMMUNICATION ENGINEERING

As Per New Revised Syllabus of Shivaji University Kolhapur.
(Effective From, 2014)

Dr. Sachin D. Ruikar

M.E. (E & TC), Ph.D.
Associate Professor
Electronics Engg. Department
Walchand College of Engineering Sangli.
Formerly,
STES' Sinhgad Academy of Engineering
Kondhwa BK., Pune.

N 2214

NETWORK ANALYSIS (SE SEM - III E & TC - SU) ISBN : 978-93-5164-235-0
First Edition : August 2014

© :

The text of this publication, or any part thereof, should not be reproduced or transmitted in any form or stored in any computer storage system or device for distribution including photocopy, recording, taping or information retrieval system or reproduced on any disc, tape, perforated media or other information storage device etc., without the written permission of Authors with whom the rights are reserved. Breach of this condition is liable for legal action.

Every effort has been made to avoid errors or omissions in this publication. In spite of this, errors may have crept in. Any mistake, error or discrepancy so noted and shall be brought to our notice shall be taken care of in the next edition. It is notified that neither the publisher nor the authors or seller shall be responsible for any damage or loss of action to any one, of any kind, in any manner, therefrom.

Published By : **Printed at**
NIRALI PRAKASHAN **Repro Knowledgecast Limited**
Abhyudaya Pragati, 1312, Shivaji Nagar, **India**
Off J.M. Road, PUNE – 411005
Tel - (020) 25512336/37/39, Fax - (020) 25511379
Email : niralipune@pragationline.com

DISTRIBUTION CENTRES
PUNE

Nirali Prakashan
119, Budhwar Peth, Jogeshwari Mandir Lane
Pune 411002, Maharashtra
Tel : (020) 2445 2044, 66022708, Fax : (020) 2445 1538
Email : bookorder@pragationline.com

Nirali Prakashan
S. No. 28/25, Dhyari,
Near Pari Company, Pune 411041
Tel : (022) 24690204 Fax : (020) 24690316
Email : dhyari@pragationline.com
bookorder@pragationline.com

MUMBAI
Nirali Prakashan
385, S.V.P. Road, Rasdhara Co-op. Hsg. Society Ltd.,
Girgaum, Mumbai 400004, Maharashtra
Tel : (022) 2385 6339 / 2386 9976, Fax : (022) 2386 9976
Email : niralimumbai@pragationline.com

DISTRIBUTION BRANCHES

NAGPUR
Pratibha Book Distributors
Above Maratha Mandir, Shop No. 3, First Floor,
Rani Jhanshi Square, Sitabuldi, Nagpur 440012,
Maharashtra, Tel : (0712) 254 7129

BENGALURU
Pragati Book House
House No. 1, Sanjeevappa Lane, Avenue Road Cross,
Opp. Rice Church, Bengaluru – 560002.
Tel : (080) 64513344, 64513355,
Mob : 9880582331, 9845021552
Email:bharatsavla@yahoo.com

JALGAON
Nirali Prakashan
34, V. V. Golani Market, Navi Peth, Jalgaon 425001,
Maharashtra, Tel : (0257) 222 0395
Mob : 94234 91860

KOLHAPUR
Nirali Prakashan
New Mahadvar Road,
Kedar Plaza, 1st Floor Opp. IDBI Bank
Kolhapur 416 012, Maharashtra. Mob : 9855046155

CHENNAI
Pragati Books
9/1, Montieth Road, Behind Taas Mahal, Egmore,
Chennai 600008 Tamil Nadu, Tel : (044) 6518 3535,
Mob : 94440 01782 / 98450 21552 / 98805 82331, Email : bharatsavla@yahoo.com

RETAIL OUTLETS
PUNE

Pragati Book Centre
157, Budhwar Peth, Opp. Ratan Talkies,
Pune 411002, Maharashtra
Tel : (020) 2445 8887 / 6602 2707, Fax : (020) 2445 8887

Pragati Book Centre
Amber Chamber, 28/A, Budhwar Peth,
Appa Balwant Chowk, Pune : 411002, Maharashtra,
Tel : (020) 20240335 / 66281669
Email : pbcpune@pragationline.com

Pragati Book Centre
676/B, Budhwar Peth, Opp. Jogeshwari Mandir,
Pune 411002, Maharashtra
Tel : (020) 6601 7784 / 6602 0855

PBC Book Sellers & Stationers
152, Budhwar Peth, Pune 411002, Maharashtra
Tel : (020) 2445 2254 / 6609 2463

MUMBAI
Pragati Book Corner
Indira Niwas, 111 - A, Bhavani Shankar Road, Dadar (W), Mumbai 400028, Maharashtra
Tel : (022) 2422 3526 / 6662 5254, Email : pbcmumbai@pragationline.com

PREFACE

The book is written mainly for the second year students of Electronic and Telecommuncation course of Shivaji University, Kolhapur for the subject **"Network Analysis"**. It is written as per the new revised syllabus (2014) of Shivaji University, Kolhapur.

New text book is written, taking in to account all the new features that have been introduced. All the entrants to the engineering field will definitely find this book, complete in all respect. Students will find the subject matter presentation quite lucid. There are large number of illustrative examples and well graded exercises.

Salient features of this book are :

- **Written strictly according to revised syllabus of Shivaji University.**
- **Adequate emphasis on both Theory and Problems.**
- **Unnecessary Theory is avoided.**

My sincere hope is that the material presented in the book will be useful in understanding the subject as well as for attempting examination questions.

I take this opportunity to express my thanks to **Shri. Dineshbhai Furia** and **Shri. Jignesh Furia** and **Shri. M.P. Munde** for publishing this book in time.

I am also take this opportunity to express my thank all the staff members of Nirali Prakashan namely Mrs. Anita Kulkarni, Mrs. Shilpa Kale also Miss Sarika Shinde and Miss Mandakini Jadhvar for their tremendous dedication and hard work in bringing out this book in an excellent form.

I am also thankful to **Mr. Virdhaval Shinde**, Branch Manager, Kolhapur Office and **Mr. Ashok Nanaware**, Branch Manager, Sangli District for their valuable help and efforts for promotion of my book.

My special thanks to my family members, students and all those who directly or indirectly supported me in this project.

Any suggestions and feedback shall be appreciated and acknowledged.

August 2014   **Author**

Pune

SYLLABUS

Unit I : Network Fundamentals — 6 Hours

Basic Definitions: Passive Network, Active Network, Linear Element, nonlinear elements, Unilateral, bilateral, lumped & distributed elements. Representation of voltage & current sources.(Ideal & practical) , source transformation, series & parallel connection of passive elements(R,L,C), graph of network & its parts, loops & trees, linear graphs & incidence matrix, cutsets, planner & non-planner graph loop matrix. Star- Delta transformation, reduction of networks: Mesh analysis, Node analysis. Supermesh and supernode analysis.

Unit II : Network Theorems — 8 Hours

D.C. and A.C. network solution using dependent and independent sources : Superposition Theorem, Millman's Theorem, Norton's Theorem, Thevenin's Theorem, Maximum Power Transfer Theorem, Reciprocity Theorem, Duality theorem

Unit III : Two Port Network and Network Functions — 7 Hours

Two port network: Open circuit impedance (Z) parameters, Short circuit admittance (Y) parameters, Hybrid (H) parameter, Transmission parameters (ABCD), Interrelation of different parameters, Interconnections of two port network (Series, Parallel, Cascaded, Series- Parallel). Network Functions: Network functions for one port & two port networks, Driving point impedance and admittance of one port network, Driving point impedance, admittance and different transfer function of two port network (Z,Y,H & T parameters). Concept of complex frequency, significance of poles & zeros. Restrictions on poles & zeros for transfer and drawing points function, stability concept in passive circuit using Routh- Hurwitz criterion, pole zero diagram.

Unit IV : Resonance — 6 Hours

Defination , Types: series & parallel resonance. Series resonance- resonant frequency, variation of impedance, admittance, current and voltage across L and C with respect to. frequency, Effect of resistance on frequency response, Selectivity , B.W. and Quality factor. Parallel resonance – Anti resonance frequency, variation of impedance & admittance with frequency, Selectivity & B.W.

Unit V : Filters — 6 Hours

Definitions, classification & characteristics of different filters, filter fundamental such as attenuation constant (O) , phase shift (N) propagation constant (S) characteristic impedance (Zo) , decibel, neper. Design and analysis of constant K, M derived & composite filters (low pass, high pass, band pass & band stop filters): T & Pi sections.

Unit VI : Transient Response — 7 Hours

Network Solution using Laplace transforms, Initial Conditions of elements. Steady state and transient response (Voltage & Current). DC response of RL circuit. DC response of RC circuit DC response of RLC circuit. Sinusoidal response of RL, RC & RLC circuit.

CONTENTS

1. Network Fundamentals — 1.1 to 1.114

2. Network Theorems — 2.1 to 2.68

3. Two Port Network and Network Functions — 3.1 to 3.60

4. Resonance — 4.1 to 4.70

5. Filters — 5.1 to 5.78

6. Transient Response — 6.1 to 6.52

Unit - I
NETWORK FUNDAMENTALS

1.1 INTRODUCTION

Given an electrical network the network analysis involves various methods. The process of finding the network variables namely the voltage and currents in various parts of the circuit is known as network analysis. Before we carry out actual analysis it is very much essential to thoroughly understand the various terms associated with the network. In this chapter, we shall begin with the definition and understanding in detail some of the commonly used terms. Those terms includes a current source, voltage source, independent and controlled source, lumped and distributed network, active and passive networks, linear and non-linear circuits, open and short circuits.

Analysis becomes easier if we can simplify the given network. We will be discussing various simplifications techniques. These techniques involves combing series and parallel connections of R, L and C elements, series and parallel connection of every sources. Then source transformation and source shifting techniques are discussed. Star-Delta conversion of simplification is also briefly discussed.

KVL and KCL are the two basic electrical laws that can be used to analyse the given network when a network is complex containing many loops and nodes then loop analysis and nodal analysis techniques can be used for analysis. Various theorems are there which can be used to simplify and then analyse the network. Some of the theorem discussed in this chapter includes superposition theorem, Maximum Power Transfer (MPT) theorem, Thevenin's theorem, Norton's theorem, Millman's theorem.

1.2 DEFINITIONS OF NETWORK VARIABLES

Charge, current, follow voltage, power and energy are network variables which can be defined as given below.

1.2.1 Charge

This electrical quantity is the basic property of an atom. There are two types of charges positive and negative. Each atom consist of nucleus with a positive charge and is surrounded by negatively charged particles called electrons. Charge can be neither created nor destroyed. It can be only transferred. This is known as law of conservation of charges.

Basic SI unit of charge is Coulomb and is represented by symbol C. The quantity symbol is Q for constant charge and q for charge that varies with time.

1.2.2 Current

Electric current is produced because of movement of charge. SI unit for current is Ampere with unit symbol A. Quantity symbol is I for constant current and i for variable current.

If a steady flow of 1 C of charge passes a given point in a conductor in 1 second then the resultants current is 1 A.

Time rate of change of transfer of charge is called as current. Thus, we have,

$$i(t) = \frac{dq(t)}{dt} \quad \text{... (1.1 a)}$$

$$q(t) = \int_{-\infty}^{t} i(t)\, dt \quad \text{... (1.1 b)}$$

1.2.3 Voltage

"Voltage difference also called potential difference between two points is the work in joules required to move 1C of charge from one point to other. The SI unit for voltage is Volt with unit symbol V. The quantity symbol is V or v although E or e is also used. Thus, we have

$$V(\text{volts}) = \frac{W\,(\text{jowles})}{Q\,(\text{coloumbs})} \text{ or } v(t) = \frac{dw}{dq} \quad \text{... (1.2)}$$

1.2.4 Power

Power is defined as the time rate at which energy is transferred. Thus, we have

$$p = \frac{dw}{dt} \quad \text{... (1.3 a)}$$

$$p(t) = v(t)\, i(t) \quad \text{... (1.3 b)}$$

Also $\quad P(\text{watts}) = V(\text{volts}) \times I(\text{amps})$

If P is positive then component absorbs power i.e. it is a consumer of power (or load). If P is negative then the component produces power i.e. it is a source of energy. Positive and negative powers are explained in the Fig. 1.1.

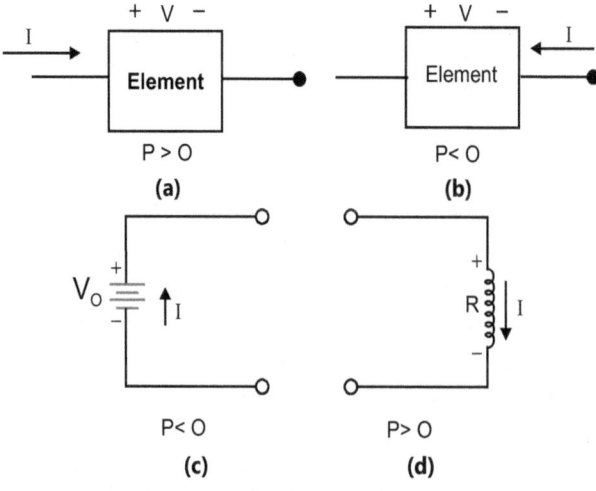

Fig. 1.1 : Positive and negative power

1.2.5 Energy

"Electrical energy used or produced is the product of electric power input or output and the time over which this input or output occurs."

Thus, (N/Joules) = P (watts) × t (seconds)

A.C. energy is given by the relation,

$$w = w(t) = \int_0^t P(t)\, d(t) = \int_0^t v(t)\, i(t)\, dt \qquad \ldots (1.4)$$

Joule is a small energy unit. Hence, commercially much large unit called kilowatt hour (kWh). is used.

$$W \text{ (kilowatt hours)} = P \text{ (kilowatts)} \times t \text{ (Hours)}$$

1.3 SOME CIRCUIT DEFINITIONS

In this section, we shall study some of the commonly used terms associated with the circuit.

1.3.1 Circuit Element

Any individual circuit element (such as inductor, capacitor, resistor, generator) with two terminals by which it may be connected to other circuit elements.

1.3.2 Electric Circuit or Network

An electric network or circuit is an interconnection of circuit elements or branches. It may be two terminals, three terminals or multiterminal network containing active and passive elements.

1.3.3 Branch

A group of elements connected in series or parallel and having two terminals is called a branch.

1.3.4 Mesh or Loop

Mesh or loop is a set of branches forming a closed path in a network such that if one of the branches is removed then the remaining branches do not form a closed path.

Consider Fig. 1.2 which is a electric circuit the closed paths forming loops are a-b-d-a, b-c-d-b and a-b-c-d-a.

An **Independent loop** is a loop that contains at least on new element in its path which is not there in other loop.

An **Non - independent** loop is one which do not contains at least one element which is not in the other loop.

In the Fig. 1.2, the loops a-b-d-a and b-c-d-b are independent loops. Then loop a-b-c-d-a becomes non - independent loop.

If we choose L_1 (a-b-d-a) and L_3 (a-b-c-d-a) as independent then L_2 (b-c-d-b) becomes non-independent loop.

Note : Selection of independent loops is very important while analyzing network using loop analysis which will be discussed later on.

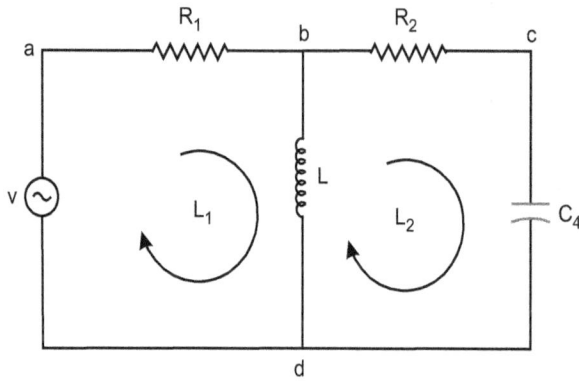

Fig. 1.2: An electric circuit

1.3.5 Node or Junction

It is the common terminal in a network at which one or more branches meets. In the circuit of Fig. 1.2 the nodes are a, b, c and d.

1.4 BASIC CIRCUIT ELEMENTS

There are only three basic circuit elements used. In this section we shall study basic voltage-current relationships of these basic elements.

1.4.1 Resistor

Resistor has the basic property of opposing flow of current. This property is known as resistance. The resistance is denoted by symbol R. It has the unit of ohms Ω. The symbol of resistor is shown in Fig. 1.3.

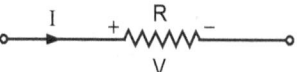

Fig. 1.3: A resistor of 'R' ohms

The voltage and current relationship is given by

$$V = RI \qquad \ldots (1.5\ a)$$

$$I = \frac{V}{R} \qquad \ldots (1.5\ b)$$

Resistor dissipates energy in the form of heat. The power consumed (absorbed) by a resistor is

$$P = VI = I^2 R = \frac{V}{R} \qquad \ldots (1.5\ c)$$

Using relationship (1.3 a) amount of energy dissipated into loop is given by

$$W = Pdt = I^2 R.t. = V.I.t. \text{ (joules)} \quad \ldots (1.5\ d)$$

The resistance of a material is proportional to length and is inversely proportional to cross section area and is given by:

$$R = \frac{\rho}{A}$$

Where ρ is called resistivity which is constant for a given material.

1.4.2 Capacitor

Capacitor is the element that stores electrical energy in the form of electrostatic field. The capacitance of a capacitor is denoted by symbol 'c'. It has basic unit of Farads (F). Farad being bigger unit, smaller unit of micro farads (µF) or milli farads (mF) are used. The symbol of a capacitor is shown in Fig. 1.4.

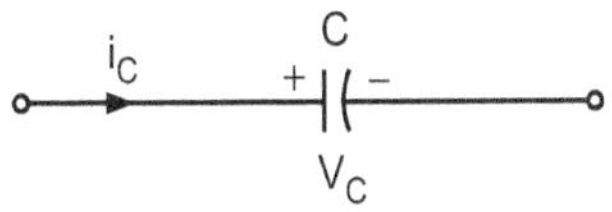

Fig. 1.4: A capacitor of 'C' Farads

The basic voltage and current relationship is given by

$$V_c = \frac{1}{C} \int_{-\infty}^{t} i\, dt \quad \ldots (1.6\ a)$$

$$i_c = \frac{C dv_c}{dt} \quad \ldots (1.6\ b)$$

The capacitor if already stored by a charge q_0 then voltage on capacitor is given by relation

$$V_c = V_0 + \frac{1}{C} \int_{-\infty}^{t} i_c\, dt \quad \ldots (1.6\ c)$$

Where V_0 is called Initial voltage. The electric energy stored in a capacitor is given by,

$$W_c = \frac{1}{2} C V_c^2 \quad \ldots (1.6\ d)$$

1.4.3 Inductor

Inductor is the element that stores magnetic energy in the form of electromagnetic field. The inductance of an inductor is denoted by symbol 'L'. It has basic unit of Henry (H). Henry being bigger unit, smaller unit of milli Henry (mH)) or micro Henry (µH) are used. The symbol of a Inductor is shown in Fig. 1.5.

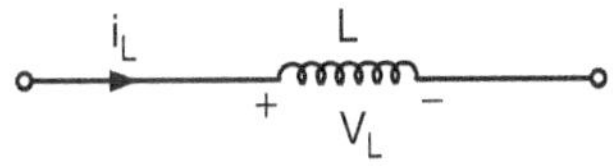

Fig. 1.5 : An inductor of 'L' Henry

The basic voltage and current relationship is given by

$$i_L = \frac{1}{L} \int_{-\infty}^{t} V_L \, dt \qquad \ldots (1.7\ a)$$

$$V_L = L \frac{di_L}{dt} \qquad \ldots (1.7\ b)$$

The inductor if already energized, then the current is given by

$$i_L = I_0 + \frac{1}{L} \int_{0}^{t} V_L \, dt \qquad \ldots (1.7\ c)$$

Where I_0 is the initial current due to initial energy stored.

The magnetic energy stored in the inductor is given by

$$W_m = \frac{1}{2} L i_L^2 \qquad \ldots (1.7\ d)$$

Note: In addition to basic elements of inductor, capacitor, and resistor, the network can contain other elements such as energy sources and transformer. Energy sources will be discussed later on while transformer is not used at all in this book.

1.5 NETWORK CLASSIFICATION

Based on the characteristics of elements used, some of the types of networks are discussed below.

1.5.1 Linear and Non-linear Networks

A linear element is one in which current and voltage relation is a Linear Differential Equation (LDE) with constant coefficients.

A resistor (R) is a linear element as it is governed by linear equation V = RI. Similarity uncharged capacitor with current $(i_c) = C \frac{dv_c}{dt}$ and unenergised inductor with voltage $v_L = L\frac{di_L}{dt}$ are also linear elements.

"A circuit containing only linear elements is called as linear circuit."

"If the circuit contain at least one non - linear element then it is called as Non-linear circuit".

Examples of non - linear circuit are one containing non - linear elements such as charged capacitor, energized inductor, diode, transistor etc.

Reciprocity and superposition theorems are valid for only linear circuit. Thus, alternatively. "A linear circuit is defined as the circuit for which superposition theorem and reciprocity theorem is valid."

1.5.2 Unilateral and Bilateral Networks

An bilateral element is one in which the voltage current relationship do not alters if we interchange the two terminals. The bilateral elements are resistor, capacitor and inductor.

An unilateral element is one in which the voltage - current relationship changes if we interchange the two terminals. The best example of two terminal bilateral element is diode.

"A circuit whose characteristic and behavior do not change irrespective of direction of current flow through various elements is called "Bilateral Network."

"A circuit whose characteristic and behavior does change with the direction of current flow through various elements is called unilateral network."

Thus, network containing at least one element as diode is definitely a unilateral network. But if it contains only R-L-C elements and energy sources then it may be unilateral or bilateral.

1.5.3 Lamped and Distributed Networks

"An Lumped network is one in which all the circuit elements are physically identifiable and separable." If a network is formed by interconnecting energy sources, resistors, inductor, and capacitors then it is a lumped circuit. Most of the'electronic circuits are lumped circuits.

"An distributed network is one in which circuit elements such as resistor, capacitor, inductor can not be isolated and physically separable."

Best example for distributed network is transmission lines. In the later chapter, we shall understand that in a transmission line such as telephone lines, power cables or coaxial cables/TV cable, the circuit elements (Resistor, capacitor, inductor) can not be identified and physically separated. But they exists through the wire length.

Note : All the network theorems, basic laws such as KCL, KVL or even Ohm's law are valid only for the distributed networks. They are not valid for the transmission line which is a lumped network.

1.5.4 Active and Passive Networks

"If an network contains only passive circuit elements (R, L, C) and, do not contains any energy sources then it is said to be a passive network."

"If an network contains energy sources or generators in addition to other circuit elements then it is said to be an active network."

A passive network neither absorbs nor dissipate any power unless it is used as an load. Hence, most of the electronic circuits are active networks.

1.6 ENERGY SOURCES

Voltage source and current source are said to be energy sources because they supply energy to the linear circuit. Let us study these sources in detail.

1.6.1 Voltage Source

An voltage source provides potential to the circuit. "An ideal voltage source is an energy unit that gives constant voltage across its terminal irrespective of the current drawn through its terminals."

Symbol for an ideal voltage source and its V-1 characteristic is shown in Fig. 1.6.

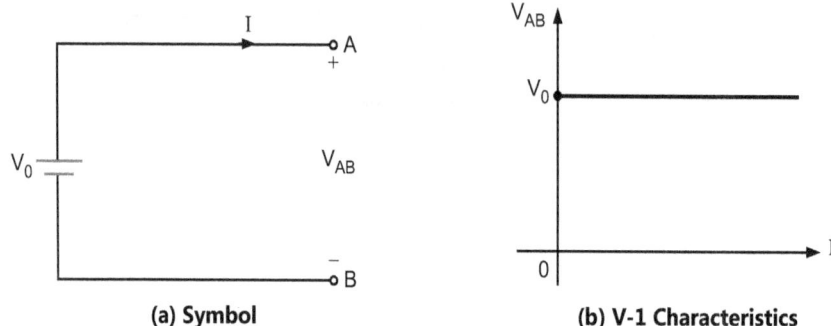

(a) Symbol   (b) V-1 Characteristics

Fig. 1.6 : Ideal voltage source

Practical Voltage Source :

Every voltage source has some series resistance across its terminals know as "source resistance" and is represented as R_s. For ideal voltage source $R_s = 0$. But in a practical [Non-Ideal] voltage source value of R_s is not zero but may have small value. Because of this R_s voltage across terminal decreases with increase in current. This is shown in Fig. 1.7.

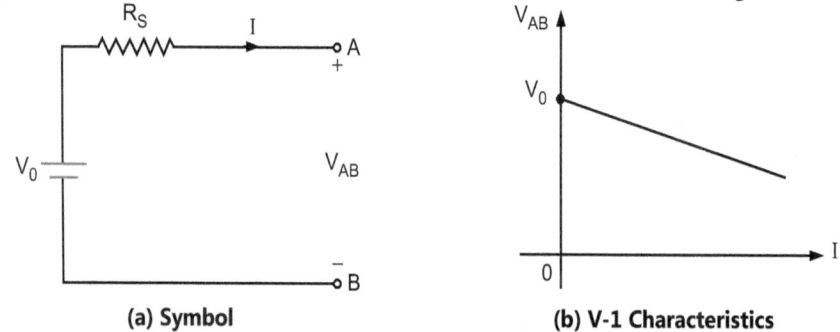

(a) Symbol   (b) V-1 Characteristics

Fig. 1.7 : Practical (Non-Ideal) voltage source

Terminal voltage of an practical voltage source is given by

$$V_{AB} = V_0 - R_s I \qquad \text{... (a)}$$

By above equation it is obvious that as the terminal current increases terminal voltage will be decreasing slightly. It is practically impossible to obtain ideal voltage source. Some of the practical voltage sources are battery cells. Battery eliminators and regulated power supply.

Note: Unless otherwise specified all the voltage sources in a given network are assumed to be ideal sources ($R_s = 0$).

1.6.2 Current Source

An current source provides current through terminal in a network. "Ideal current source is an energy unit that will give constant current through its terminals irrespective of the voltage appearing across its terminals."

Symbol for ideal current source and its V-1 characteristic is shown in Fig. 1.8.

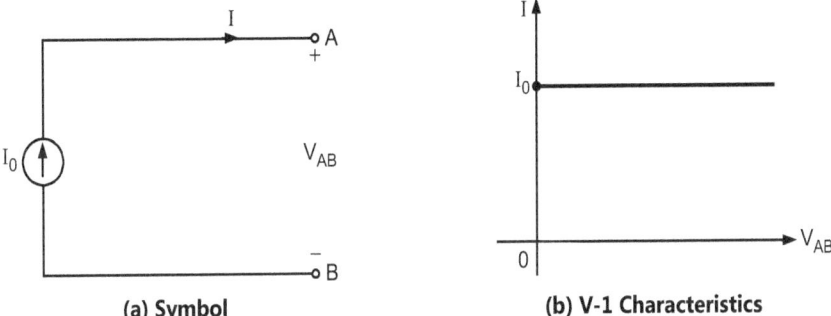

(a) Symbol (b) V-1 Characteristics

Fig. 1.8 : Ideal current source

Practical Current Source :

Every current source have some resistance in parallel across its terminals known as source resistance and is represented as R_p. For ideal current source value of R_p is infinity (∞). But in practical (Non-ideal) Current source R_a is not infinity but may have a large value. Thus, because of this large R_p current through its terminals slightly decreases as voltage across terminals increases. This is shown in Fig. 1.9.

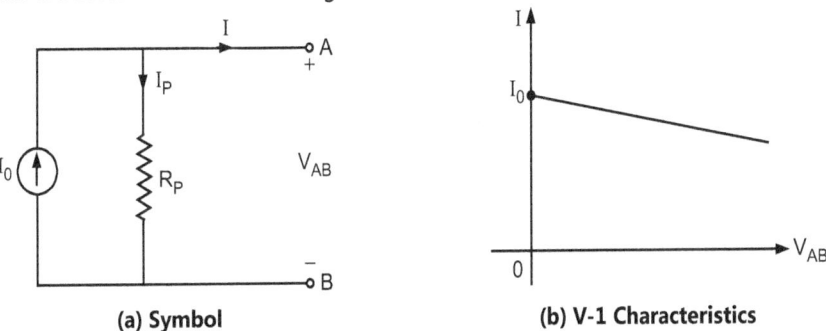

(a) Symbol (b) V-1 Characteristics

Fig. 1.9

Terminal current of a practical current source is given by

$$I = I_0 - I_p = I_0 = \frac{V_{AB}}{R_p} \qquad \ldots (b)$$

From equation (b) it is obvious that as V_{AB} increased from zero current (I) goes on decreasing. Current sources are formed using complex electronic circuits that uses OP - AMP or transistor as active elements. These are non-ideal current sources. It is practically impossible to obtain an ideal current source.

Note : Unless or otherwise specified all the current sources given in the circuit are assumed to be ideal sources ($R_p = \infty$).

1.7 INDEPENDENT AND CONTROLLED (DEPENDENT) SOURCES

In general in a electric circuit we use capital letters to designate quantities which are time invariant (Do not vary with time). Thus V or V_0 designate time invariant (or constant) or D.C. voltage; Similarly, I or I_0 represent D.C. (or constant) current. The symbol for them are shown in Fig. 1.10. (a).

If a quantity does vary with time then it will be represented by lower case letters such as v or v'(f) and i or i(t) for current source. Symbol for such time variant sources is shown in Fig. 1.10.

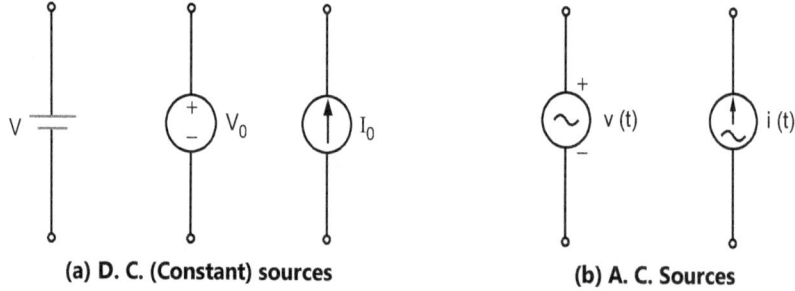

(a) D. C. (Constant) sources   (b) A. C. Sources

Fig. 1.10 : Independent energy sources

(a) Independent Energy Sources:

"Independent energy source is a voltage or current source whose value does not depend upon other voltages or currents or the circuit to which these sources are connected."

Independent sources are represented by circle with internal polarity marked. All the sources represented in Fig. 1.10 are independent energy sources. These sources can be time invariant (D.C.) or time variant (A.C.)

(b) Dependent (controlled) Energy Source

"Dependent energy source is a voltage or current source whose value depends upon some other voltage or current in the circuit. These sources are also called as controlled energy sources." Such sources are common in electronic circuits and are indicated by diamond shaped symbols as in Fig. 1.11 controlled sources are always associated with some equations such as $v = k i_1$, $i_1 = k_1 v_2$, $i_2 = k_2 i_2$ etc. where i_1, i_2, v_2 are currents or voltage in some other parts of circuit. KVL, KCL and other circuit laws are valid for circuit containing both independent and controlled energy sources.

Dependent (or controlled) Energy sources are of the following four types

1. Voltage controlled voltage sources (VCVS)
2. Current controlled voltage source (CCVS or ICVS)
3. Voltage controlled current source (VCIS or VCCS)
4. Current controlled current source (ICIS or CCCS)

All these sources are shown in Fig. 1.11.

In Fig. 1.11 (a) and Fig. 1.11 (b) terminal voltage is specified as a function of some variable x which is a current or voltage i.e. $i = f(x)$.

In Fig. 1.11 (c) and Fig. 1.11 (d) the terminal currents is specified as a function of some variable x which again is a voltage or current i.e. $I = f(x)$.

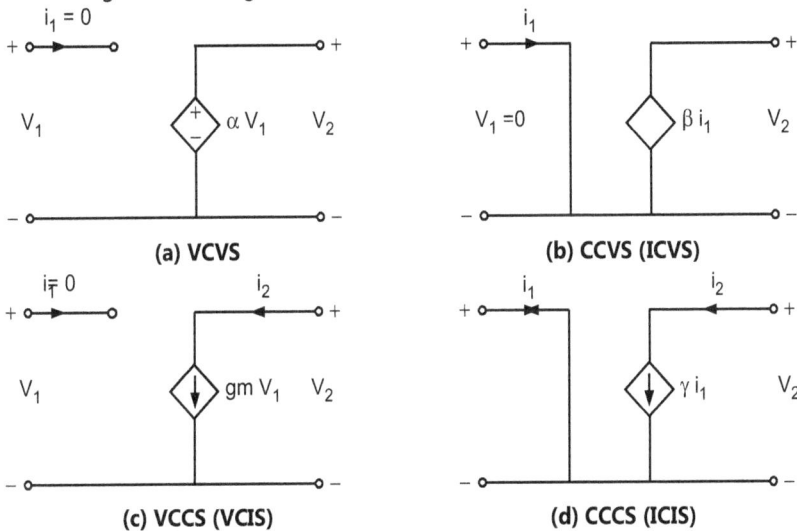

Fig. 1.11 : Dependent (Controlled) sources

1.8 POWER

The total work done in a time (t) in an electric circuit is called as energy

$$P = \frac{\text{Work (E)}}{\text{Time (t)}}$$

$$= \frac{W}{t}$$

The power can be written as

$$\text{Power (P)} = \text{Voltage (V)} \times \text{Current (I)}$$

$$P = V \times I \quad \text{watts (W)}$$

From Ohm's law

$$V = I \cdot R$$

$$I = \frac{V}{R}$$

∴

$$P = I^2 R$$

$$= \frac{V^2}{R}$$

1.9 OPEN AND SHORT CIRCUIT

Open and short circuits are two circuit connections that have special importance in the network analysis.

1.9.1 Open Circuit

Two points in a circuit are open circuited if there is no circuit element or a direct connection between them as shown in Fig. 1.12 (b).

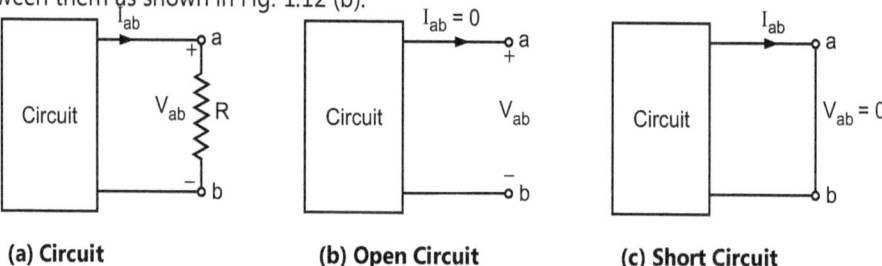

(a) Circuit   (b) Open Circuit   (c) Short Circuit

Fig. 1.12 : Open and short circuit

In open circuit since there is no connection between a and b current $I_{ab} = 0$ while voltage (V_{ab}) is determined by rest of the circuit. Consider circuit shown in Fig. 1.13. The current $I_{ab} = 0$. But voltage (V_{ab}) = $10 \times \dfrac{5}{10}$ = + 5V.

Thus, "two points with arbitrary voltage between them and zero current between them represents an open circuit (OC)".

Since, $I_{ab} = \dfrac{V_{ab}}{R}$, If $V_{ab} \neq 0$ but $I_{ab} = 0$ then $R = \infty$

Thus, in a open circuit resistance between two points is infinity.

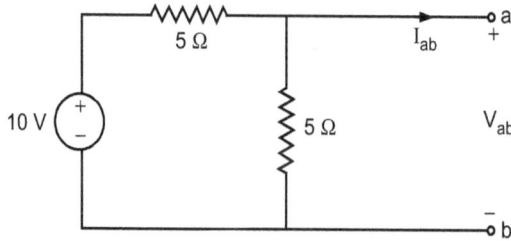

Fig. 1.13 : Circuit to explain open circuit (OC)

1.9.2 Short Circuit (SC)

Two points in a circuit are said to be short circuited when two points are connected by a good conducting wire as shown in Fig. 1.12 (c).

In a short circuit (SC) voltage between two points is zero (V_{ab}) = 0 but current between two points is determined by rest of the circuit.

Consider circuit shown in Fig. (1.14).

The voltage V_{ab} is zero while current $(i_{ab}) = 2 \times \dfrac{5}{10} = +1A$

Thus, "two points with arbitrary current through its terminals but zero voltage between is called as short circuit (SC)".

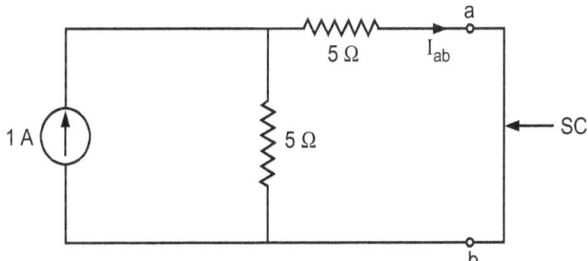

Fig. 1.14 : Circuit to explain short circuit (SC)

Since $V_{ab} = RI_{ab}$ if $I_{ab} = 0$ but $V_{ab} = 0$ this means $R = 0$. "Thus in a short circuit the resistance two points is zero."

Thus, the terms "Zero resistance" and "Short circuit" can be used interchangeably. Similarly the terms "Infinite resistance" and "Open circuit" are interchangeably used.

1.10 VOLTAGE DIVIDER AND CURRENT DIVIDER CIRCUITS

Voltage and current divider circuits are most commonly used in the analysis. Let us study two circuits in detail.

1.10.1 The Voltage Divider Circuit

Consider an voltage divider circuit shown in Fig. 1.15.

Here two series resistors R_1 and R_2 are driven by a voltage source V_0.

The current(I) is given by $\quad I = \dfrac{V_0}{R_1 + R_2}$

Hence, voltage V_1 is $\quad V_1 = IR_2 = \dfrac{V_0 R_2}{R_1 + R_2}$ ... (1.8)

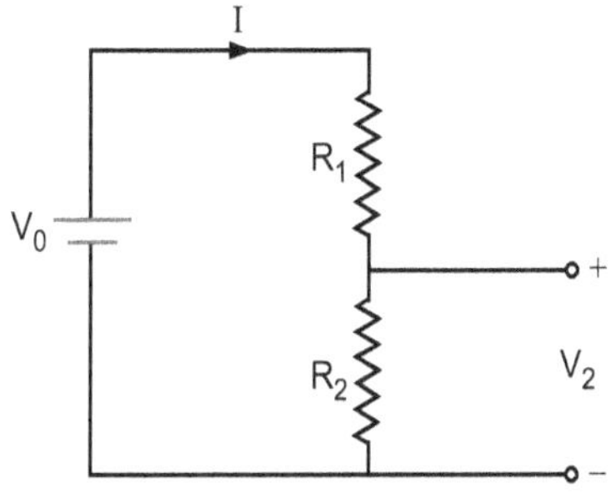

Fig. 1.15 : Voltage divider circuit

Equation (1.8) gives output voltage in terms of input voltage (V_0) and two resistors (R_1, R_2) and is called voltage divider equation. This principle can be extended to many number of voltage divider points as explained in Example (1.1) below.

Example 1.1 :

Design the resistors in Fig. 1.16 to provide the following voltage on the taps. $V_2 = 2V$, $V_3 = 6V$ and $V_4 = 10V$. Assume that taps are unloaded. All voltages are measured with respect to ground. Assume that $R_4 = 4$ ohms.

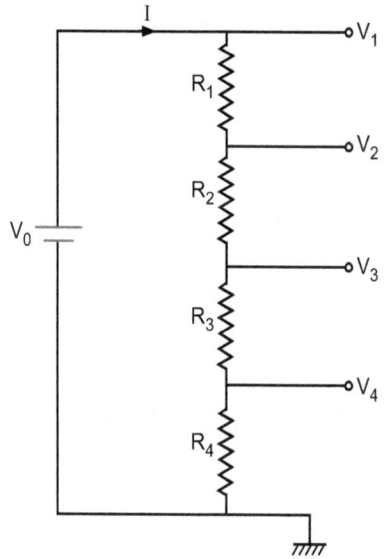

Fig. 1.16 : Figure for ex. (1.1)

Solution : Since, taps are unloaded no current flows through the tap terminal. Hence, all resistors are in series. The current in the circuit is given by

$$I = \frac{V_0}{R_1 + R_2 + R_3 + R_4}$$

$$= \frac{12}{R_1 + R_2 + R_3 + R_4}$$

Now $V_2 = R_4$, $V_2 = 2V$ (given), $R_4 = 4\Omega$

Hence, circuit current I = 0.5A

$$V_3 = (R_4 + R_3) I$$
$$= (4 + R_3) \times 0.5$$
$$= 6$$

Hence, $R_3 = 8\Omega$

Finally, $V_4 = 12V$
$$= (R_1 + R_2 + R_3 + R_4) \times 0.5$$
$$= (R1 + 20) \times 0.5$$

Solving this given $R_1 = 4\Omega$

Thus, designed values are $R_2 = 8\Omega$, $R_3 = 8\Omega$, $R_1 = 4\Omega$

1.10.2 The Current Divider Circuit

Consider circuit shown in Fig. 1.15 in which two resistors R_1, R_2 are in parallel across Vo. The total current (I) through battery is $I = I_1 + I_2$.

$$I_1 = \frac{V_0}{R_1} \text{ and } I_2 = \frac{V_0}{R_2}$$

Hence,
$$I_1 = \frac{V_0}{R_1} + \frac{V_0}{R_2} = V_0 \left[\frac{R_1 + R_2}{R_1 R_2}\right]$$

$$\text{Current } (I_1) = \frac{V_0}{R_1} = \frac{1}{R_1}\left[\frac{R_1 R_2}{R_1 + R_2}\right] I = \frac{R_2 I}{R_1 + R_2} \quad \text{... (1.9 a)}$$

$$\text{Current } (I_2) = \frac{V_0}{R_2} = \frac{1}{R_2}\left[\frac{R_1 R_2}{R_1 + R_2}\right] I = \frac{R_1 I}{R_1 + R_2} \quad \text{... (1.9 b)}$$

If $R_1 = R_2$ then $I_1 = I_2 = \frac{I}{2}$.

From equations (1.8) and (1.9) it is obvious that the voltage division is directly related to the resistor across which voltage is measured. While for current divider the division is related to other resistor also. The current division principles are explained in the Example (1.2) given below.

Example 1.2 :

A battery of 10 V carries a current of 10 mA. Design a current divider circuit such that the current in one of the resister is 1/3 of other resister current.

Solution : The current divider circuit is shown in Fig. 1.17.

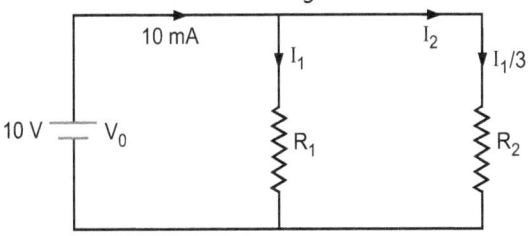

Fig. 1.17 : Circuit for Ex. (1.2)

We have, $\quad 10 = I_1 + \frac{I_1}{3} = \frac{4}{3}I_1$

Hence we have, $\quad I_1 = 7.5$ mA

Also, $I_1 \quad = \frac{10}{R_1} = 7.5$ mA gives $\boxed{R_1 = \frac{4}{3} k\Omega}$

Also $\frac{I_1}{3} \quad = 2.5$ mA $= \frac{10}{R_2}$ gives $\boxed{R_2 = 4 k\Omega}$

1.11 KIRCHOFF'S VOLTAGE LAW (KVL)

This is one of the fundamental laws used in network analysis.

Statement : "The algebraic sum of the voltage around a closed loop in a circuit must be equal to zero"

OR $\quad \sum_{Loop}$ Voltage across elements $= 0 \qquad$ ... (1.10 a)

The term algebraic is used since there are both positive and negative voltage around the loop. The positive (+ve) voltages are termed as "voltage rise" while negative (-ve) voltages are termed as "voltage fall" or 'voltage drop'.

Sign conventions for KVL :

The positive and negative voltages while using KVL is shown in Fig. (1.18).

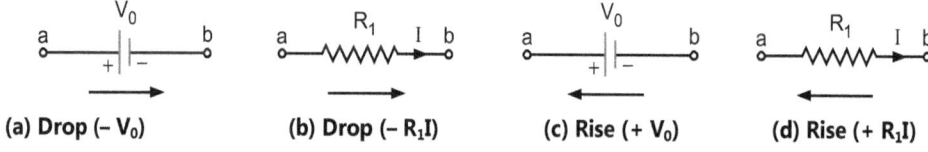

(a) Drop (– V_0)   (b) Drop (– R_1I)   (c) Rise (+ V_0)   (d) Rise (+ R_1I)

Fig. 1.18 : Sign conventions for KVL

Arrow indicates the direction in which we are moving. In Fig. 1.18 (a), we are moving from higher potential to lower potential [i.e. +ve to –ve of battery] hence take this as Voltage drop i.e. $V_{ab} = V_0$. In Fig. 1.18 (b) we are moving in the direction of current hence take the voltage $V_{ab} = -IR$, which is again a voltage drop.

In Fig. 1.18 (c) we are moving from lower potential to higher potential in the battery. Hence take voltage between a and b as $V_{ab} = + V$. which is a voltage rise. In Fig. 1.18 (d), we are moving against the current hence take $V_{ab} = + R_1 I$ which is again a voltage rise.

Note : Some books take exactly opposite conventions for voltages. But to avoid confusion stick to above conventions only which is used in this text book.

Now consider equation (1.10 a) in which all the voltages appears either as a voltage rise with positive sign OR they appear as voltage drop with negative sign. Hence equation (1.10 a) can be written as

$\quad \sum_{Loop}$ Voltage drops $- \sum_{Loop}$ Voltage rises $= 0$

OR $\quad \sum_{Loop}$ Voltage drops $= \sum_{Loop}$ Voltage rises $\qquad$ ... (1.10 b)

The alternatively KVL can be defined as "sum of all the voltage rises is equal to the sum of all the voltage drops around a closed loop in a circuit"

Now let us study how we can use the KVL in analyzing single loop circuit. The steps involved in a single loop analysis are:

1. Identify and assign loop current with direction and voltage polarities across all elements in the loop.

2. Apply Kirchoff's Voltage Law (KVL) across the loop, use Ohm's law for the resistors.
3. Solve the equation obtained above to get the loop current (I). If the current is negative then the assumed current direction is wrong.

Example 1.3 :

For the single loop circuit of Fig. 1.19 use KVL to find the current (I).

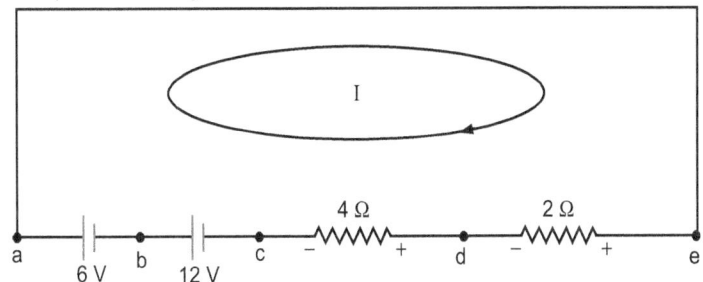

Fig. 1.19 : Circuit for ex. (1.3)

Solution : Loop current (I) with direction is already given. Also the polarities across resistor is given.

Using KVL across loop (a-e-d-c-b-a), we get,

$$V_{ae} + V_{ed} + V_{dc} + V_{cb} + V_{ba} = 0$$
$$0 - 2I - 4I + 12 + 6 = 0$$
$$6I = 18 \quad \text{OR} \quad I = +3A$$

Since, current is positive the assumed direction of current is correct. If we assume opposite direction then only sign of current (I) would be negative. But the magnitude remains 3Amp.

1.11.1 Ground (Datum) Node and Node-Node Voltages

Ground or Reference or Datum node in a circuit is a node whose voltage we assume to be 0V (zero) and the voltages of all other nodes are expressed with respect to this node. Please note that no current sinks into ground.

Consider the circuit of Fig. 1.20. Even though any node can be taken as ground generally the bottom most node is considered as a ground for our convenience. Here node d is considered as datum node i.e. we assume voltage $V_d = 0V$

Node voltage V_a, V_b and V_c are known as node-datum voltages.

For example, $\quad V_{ad} = V_a - V_d = V_a - 0 = V_a$

If $V_a = +8V$ this means that voltage of node 'a' is at higher potential than ground by 8V. If $V_b = -5V$ or $V_c = -2V$ this means voltages of nodes b and c are at lower potentials than ground voltage. Now V_{ab}, V_{bc}, V_{ac} are known as Node–Node voltages. With the above assumed values for V_a, V_b, V_c, we have

$$V_{ab} = V_a - V_b = 8 - (-5) = +13V$$
$$V_{bc} = V_b - V_c = -5 - (-2) = -3V$$
$$V_{ac} = V_a - V_c = +8 - (-2) = +10V$$

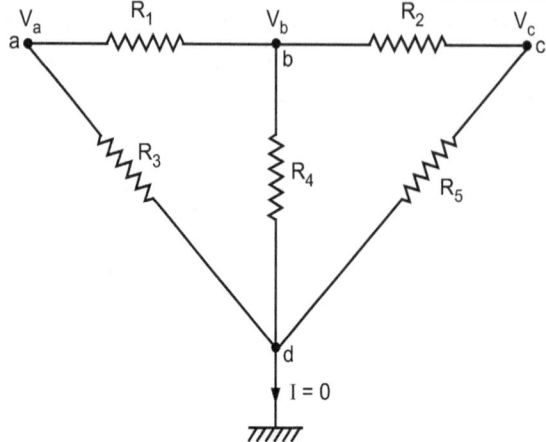

Fig. 1.20 : Ground (Reference) node

Note : When voltage is expressed with respect to the reference (or ground) erode then single suffix is used as in V_a, V_b and V_c. If voltages between two nodes neither of which is ground node, then two suffixes are used. For example V_{ab}, V_{bc}, V_{ac} etc.

1.12 KIRCHOFF'S CURRENT LAW (KCL)

This is also most fundamental law along with KVL used in the network analysis.

Statement : "The algebraic sum of currents at a node (or Junction) in a circuit is zero". Alternatively "The sum of currents directed into any node in a circuit is equal to the sum of the currents coming out of same node in a circuit".

$$\sum_{\text{node 'n'}} \text{Current in} = \sum_{\text{node 'n'}} \text{Current out} \quad \ldots (1.11\ a)$$

OR $\sum_{\text{node}} \text{Algebraic current} = 0 \ldots (1.11\ b)$

Sign Convention for KCL :

Generally, current leaving an node is taken as having positive sign. The currents entering an node is taken as having negative sign. We can assume other way also without any error being committed. But always stick to the convention given which we use in this text.

Consider a portion of circuit given as in Fig. 1.21. The dotted line indicates remaining part of the circuit.

Using the above sign convention given, the KCL at node 'a' as given by equation (1.11 b) is

$$-I_1 - I_2 + I_3 + I_4 = 0$$

OR $\qquad\qquad I_1 + I_2 = I_3 + I_4$

This also verify the equation (1.11 a).

While analyzing a given circuit KCL at a node enables us to determine node voltage. The following example explain this.

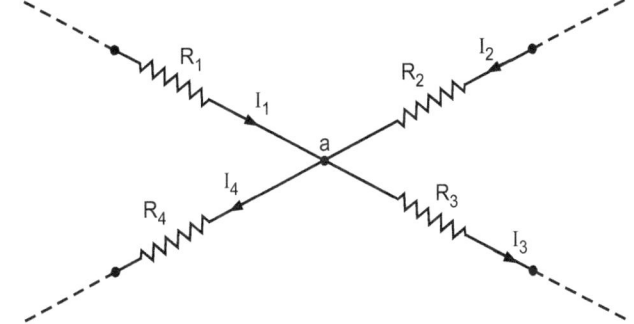

Fig. 1.21 : A node of a circuit used to explain KCL

Example 1.4 :

Using Kirchoff's current law find the currents in the resistors of 5Ω, 10Ω and 2Ω.

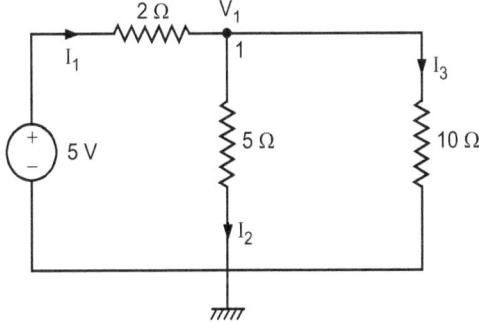

Fig. 1.22

Solution : All the branch currents are given, along with ground (reference) node. Now applying KCL at node '1' we get,

$$+ I_3 - I_1 + I_2 = 0$$

$$+ \frac{V_1}{10} - \left(\frac{5 - V_1}{2}\right) + \frac{V_1}{5} = 0 \quad \text{OR} \quad \frac{V_1}{10} + \frac{V_1}{5} = \left(\frac{5 - V_1}{2}\right)$$

Given
$$5(5 - V_1) = 2V_1 + V_1$$

OR
$$V_1 = +\frac{25}{8} \text{ Volts}$$

Current in 5Ω resistor $= I_2 = \frac{V_1}{5} = \frac{+5}{8}$ Amp.

Current in 10Ω resistor $= I_3 = \frac{V_1}{10} = \frac{5}{10}$ Amp.

Current in 2Ω resistor $= I_1 = \left(\frac{5 - V_1}{2}\right) = +\frac{15}{16}$ Amp.

Thus, $I_1 = \frac{15}{16} = I_2 + I_3 = \frac{5}{8} + \frac{5}{16} + \frac{15}{16}$ Amp.

1.13 PROBLEMS BASED ON KCL AND KVL ONLY

Two fundamental laws of KVL and KCL together forms a powerful tool in a circuit analysis. Following examples explain how they can be used effectively.

Example 1.5 :
Determine variables I_1, I_2 and V_A in the circuit using KVL and KCL.

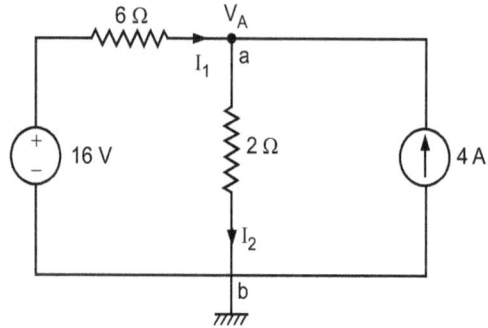

Fig. 1.23

Solution : KCL at node a gives $I_2 = 4 + I_1$ ... (a)
KVL across loop (a – b – c – a) gives $V_{ab} + V_{bc} + V_{ca} = 0$
$$-2I_2 + 16 - 6I_1 = 0v \quad\quad \text{OR} \quad 3I_1 + I_2 = 8 \quad ...(b)$$
Solving equation (a) and (b) gives
$$I_1 + 4 = 8 - 3I \quad\quad \text{OR} \quad I_1 = +1A$$
Hence $\quad I_2 = 4 + 1 = 5A \quad$ i.e. $\quad I_2 = +5A$
Thus, $\quad V_A = 2I_2 + 10 \text{ V} \quad$ i.e. $\quad V_A = +10V$

Example 1.6 :
Using Kirchoff's laws, determine current I_1 in the circuit shown.

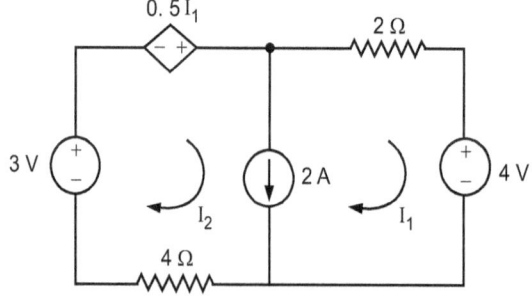

Fig. 1.24

Solution : The circuit can be redrawn as in Fig. (1.25) where nodes are taken as a, b, c. d and e.
Now KCL at b gives $\quad I_2 = I_1 + 2$ ... (a)
There are two unknown variables I_1 and I_2 for this we need two equations. The other equation

can be obtained by applying KVL across outer loop (a - b - c - d - e - a).

$$+0.5I_1 - 2I_1 - 4 - 4I_2 + 3 = 0$$

OR $\qquad 1.5 I_1 + 4 I_2 = -1 \qquad$ ... (b)

Solving (a) and (b) we get,

$$1.5 I_1 + 4 (I_2 + 2) = -1$$

OR $\qquad I_1 = \dfrac{-9}{5.5} = 1.636$ Amp.

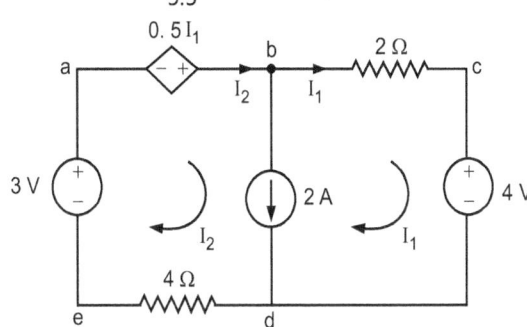

Fig. 1.25

Example 1.7 :

For the circuit shown determine I and V, use KCL and KVL.

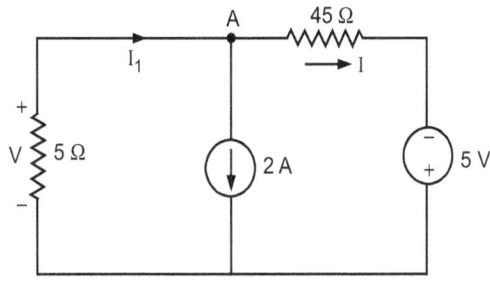

Fig. 1.26

Solution : KCL at A gives

$$I_1 = I + 2 \qquad ... (a)$$

We have $\qquad V = -5I_1 = -5 (I + 2) \qquad$ ... (b)

Applying KVL across outer loop gives

$$-5I_1 - 45I + 5 = 0$$
$$-5 (I + 2) - 45I = -5$$

OR $\qquad I = -0.1$ A ... from (a)

Hence by (b) $\qquad V = -5 (-0.1 + 2) = -9.5$ volts.

Example 1.8 :

Calculate V_1 and V_2 in the circuit shown by using only KVL and KCL.

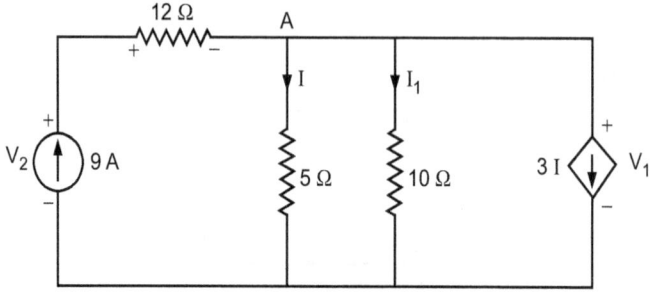

Fig. 1.27

Solution : Current $\quad I = \dfrac{V_1}{5} A \quad$ and $\quad I_1 = \dfrac{V_1}{10} A$

Now KCL at A given, $\quad I + I_1 + 3I = 9$

$$4I + I_1 = 9$$

$$4\left[\dfrac{V_1}{5}\right] + \dfrac{V_1}{10} = 9$$

Gives, $\quad V_1 = +10\ V$

Thus, voltage drop across 9A current source is V_2 where,

$$V_2 = +12 \times 9 + V_1$$
$$= 108 + 10$$
$$= +118\ \text{volts}$$

Example 1.9 :

Find the value of R in the circuit such that the voltage across resistor (R) $V_R = +2V$. Find power in the controlled source. Specify whether power is absorbed or delivered by the source. Use KVL and KCL only.

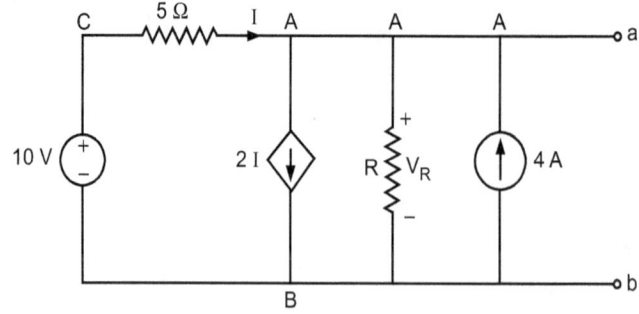

Fig. 1.28

Solution : Applying KCL at node A the circuit can be redrawn as shown in Fig. (1.29).

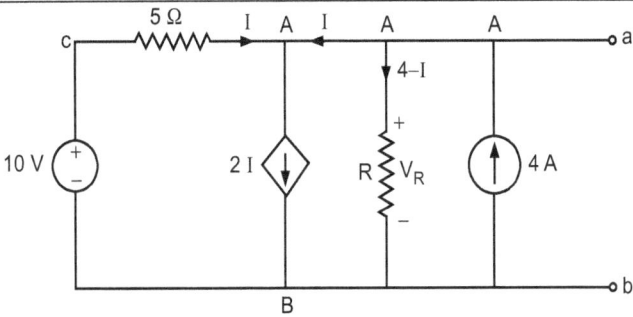

Fig. 1.29

KVL across loop (A-B-C-A) gives,

$$-V_R + 10 - 5I = 0$$

OR $\qquad V_R = 10 - 5I = +2V$

Hence $\qquad I = \dfrac{8}{5}$ Amp.

Now, $\qquad V_R = +2 = R[4 - I]$

$$= R\left[4 - \dfrac{8}{5}\right] = +\dfrac{12}{5} R$$

Hence, Resistor $\qquad (R) = \dfrac{5}{6}$ ohms

Power in the controlled source = $V_R \cdot 2I = 2 \times 2 \times \dfrac{8}{5} = 6.4$ W

Since, sign of the power is positive (P > 0) the power of 6.4 W is absorbed by controlled sources.

1.14 ENERGY SOURCES IN SERIES AND PARALLEL

Last section we have seen how to combine R, L, C element when they are in series or parallel. In this section, we will consider equivalent value when two or move voltages or currents in series and parallel.

1.14.1 Series Connection of Voltage Sources

Various types of series connections and their equivalents are shown in Fig. (1.30).

From the Fig. 1.30 it is obvious that if positive terminal of a voltage source is connected to the negative (–ve) terminal of other voltage source [Fig. 1.30 (a) and (b)] then two voltages are added to get equivalent voltage sources.

If the positive (+ve) terminal of one voltage source is connected to negative (–ve) terminal of other voltage source [Fig. 1.30 (c) and (d)] then equivalent voltage source is the difference between individual voltages.

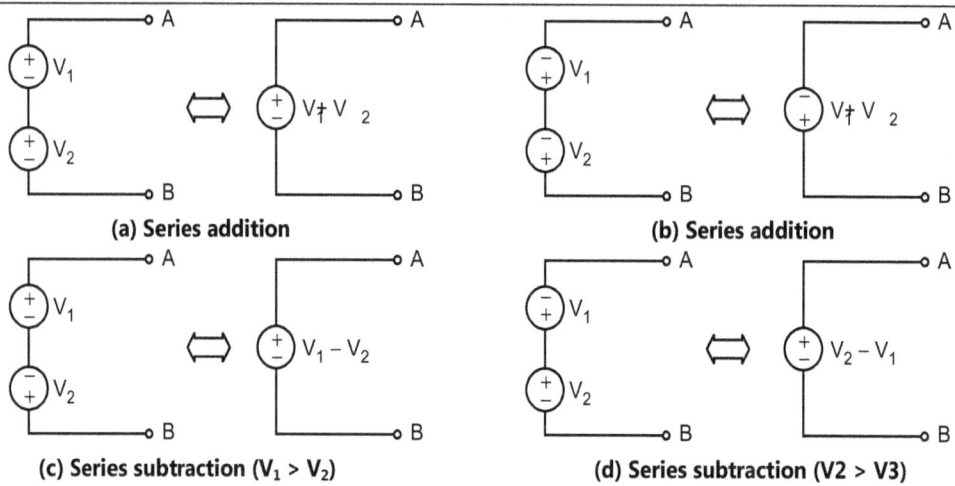

(a) Series addition (b) Series addition

(c) Series subtraction ($V_1 > V_2$) (d) Series subtraction ($V_2 > V_3$)

Fig. 1.30 : Voltage Sources in Series

To explain why voltage sources are connected in series we shall consider a practical situation. Suppose that we have many batteries with 1.5 V and 0.1 A ratings. Now we have a circuit that needs 12V and a current of 0.1 A maximum. Then 8 of such batteries can be connected in series. "Thus, to get the higher voltage with same current rating we are connecting voltage sources in series".

Note: To connect voltage sources in series all the sources must have same current ratings, but they may have same or different current ratings.

1.14.2 Parallel Connection of Voltage Sources

Two voltage sources connected in parallel is shown in Fig. (1.35) unlike series connection there are not many ways in which sources can be connected in parallel.

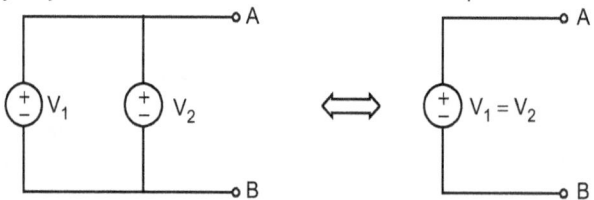

Fig. 1.31 : Voltage sources in parallel

To explain why voltage sources are connected parallel, let us consider an practical situation. As before suppose we have a lot of batteries with 1.5 V and 0.1 A ratings. Now suppose we have a circuit that needs an supply of 1.5V and 1A rating. Then we can well connect 10 such batteries in parallel. "Thus, to get the higher current rating with same voltage rating the voltage sources are connected in parallel".

Note: While connecting two or more voltage sources in parallel all the voltage sources must be having same voltage rating but can have different current ratings. If two voltage sources of unequal voltage ratings are connected in parallel then heavy current will flow through both the sources and can damage them.

1.14.3 Current Sources In Series

Series connection of two current sources is shown in Fig. (1.32).

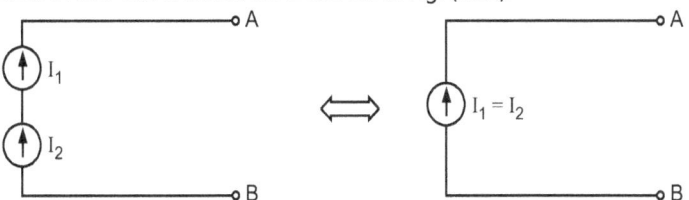

Fig. 1.32 : Current sources in series

To explain why current sources are connected in series consider a practical situation. Suppose we have many current sources with 2A and 10V ratings. Now if a circuit needs a current source with 2A and 30V rating then three such sources can be connected in series. "Thus, to get higher voltage rating with same current rating two or more current sources are connected in series."

Note: While connecting the current sources in series all the current sources must have same current ratings but their voltage ratings can be different.

1.14.4 Current Sources In Parallel

Various ways in which current sources can be parallel connected is shown in Fig. 1.37.

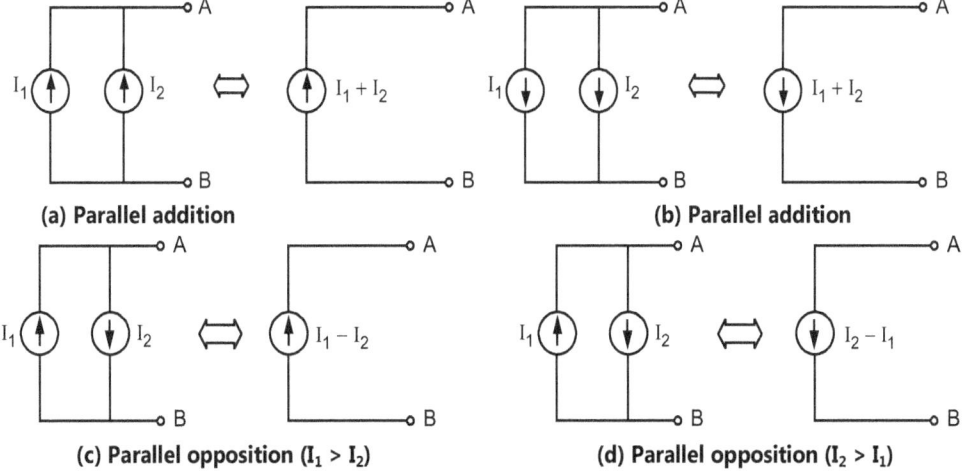

Fig. 1.33 : Current sources in parallel

To explain why current sources are parallel connected again consider a practical situation. As before we had many current sources of 2A and 10V rating each. Now if a circuit needs an current source of 6A and 10V rating then three such current "sources can be connected in parallel. Thus, to get higher current rating with same voltage rating two or more current sources are connected in parallel.

Note: While current sources are connected in parallel, all the sources must have same voltage rating but they can have same or different current ratings.

Now let us consider a peculiar situation in which voltage and current sources together are connected in series and parallel as shown in Fig. (1.34).

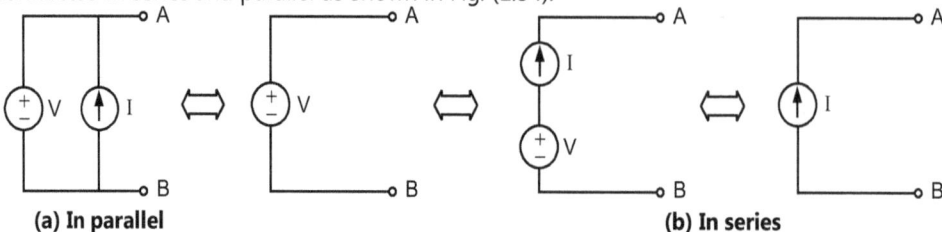

(a) In parallel   (b) In series

Fig. 1.34 : Voltage and current sources

In Fig. 1.34 (a), since internal resistance of the voltage source is zero, the output current from the current source flows through voltage source without any effects on its output voltage. Hence, the configuration has exactly the same properties as that of a voltage source alone.

In Fig 1.34 (b), since voltage rating of the current source is undefined addition of voltage of voltage source still leaves the quantity undefined. Thus, the combination will have same properties as that of current source alone.

1.15 SOURCE TRANSOFMRATION

Some times while analyzing an network we want all the sources to be same type either current sources or voltage sources. For example in "Loop analysis" all the sources preferably must be voltage sources while in "Nodal analysis" all the sources preferably must be current sources. Thus, conversion of one type of source into other type is very much essential in many network analysis. This conversion can be accomplished by source transformation equation which is discussed below.

1.15.1 Source Transformation Equation

If an voltage source has a series resistor then it can be converted into an current source. Similarly if an current source has a resistor in parallel with it then it can be converted into a equivalent voltage source. The conversion should not a effect the terminal property. Source transformation equation can be used for this purpose. Let us now derive this equation.

Consider the circuit shown in Fig. 1.35 (a) across terminal a-b there is a voltage source (V_0) in series with resistor (R). The equivalent circuit which converts the voltage source into a current source (I_0) is shown in Fig. 1.35 (b). The two circuits must have same terminal voltage (V_x) and terminal current (I_x).

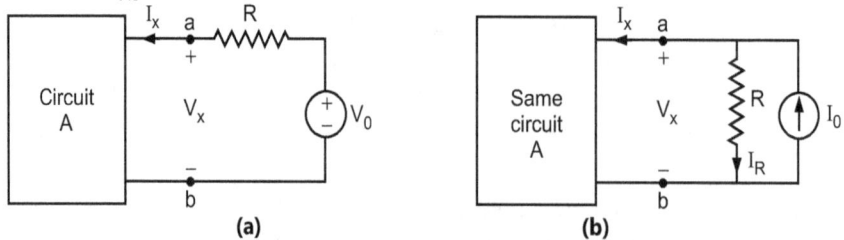

(a)   (b)

Fig. 1.35 : Source transformation

In Fig. 1.35 (a) KVL across a-b-a gives,

$$+ RI_x - V_0 + V_x = 0 \quad \text{or} \quad V_0 = V_x + RI_x \qquad \ldots(1.12)$$

In Fig. 1.35 (b) KCL at node a gives

$$I_R + I_x = I_0 \quad \text{or} \quad \frac{V_x}{R} + I_x = I_0$$

Hence, we have $\quad V_x + RI_x = RI_0 \qquad \ldots(1.13)$

For the two circuits to be equivalent (that is one can be replaced by the other) the two equations must be same.

Thus, we have $\quad \boxed{V_0 = RI_0} \qquad \ldots(1.14\ a)$

or $\quad \boxed{I_0 = \frac{V_0}{R}} \qquad \ldots(1.14\ b)$

Equation (1.14) is known as "Source transformation equation."

Thus, we conclude that "A voltage source V_0 in series with an resistor (R) can be converted into a current source (I_0) of value $\frac{V_0}{R}$ which is in parallel with resistor (R)".

Conversely "A current source (I_0) in parallel with the resistor (R) can be converted into a voltage source (V_0) of value (V_0) = RI_0 in series with resistor (R).

Note: In equation (1.14) (a) and (b) if R = 0 then I_0 will be infinite and if R = ∞ then V_0 = ∞. Thus source transformation has no meaning if R= 0 or R = ∞.

Following examples explains how source transformation is useful in circuit analysis.

Example 1.10 :

Using source transformation find voltage (V) in the circuit shown below.

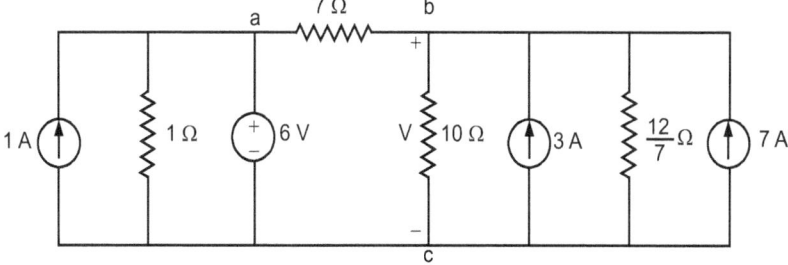

Fig. 1.36 (a)

Solution : Now $3\Omega \parallel 4\Omega = \frac{12}{7}\Omega$. This is in series with 12 V source. This can be converted into a current source of $12 \times \frac{7}{12} = 7A$ in parallel with $\frac{12}{7}\Omega$. The circuit can be redrawn as shown in Fig. 1.36 (a).

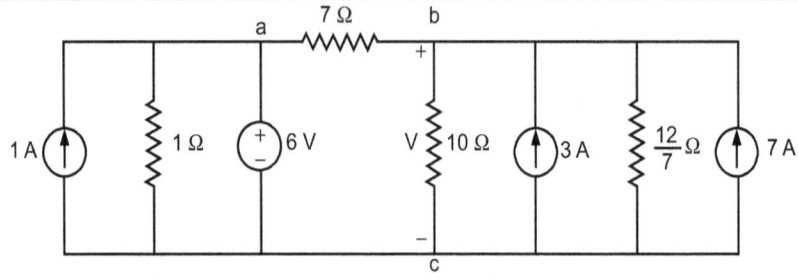

(i) Equivalent circuit of Fig. 1.36 (a)

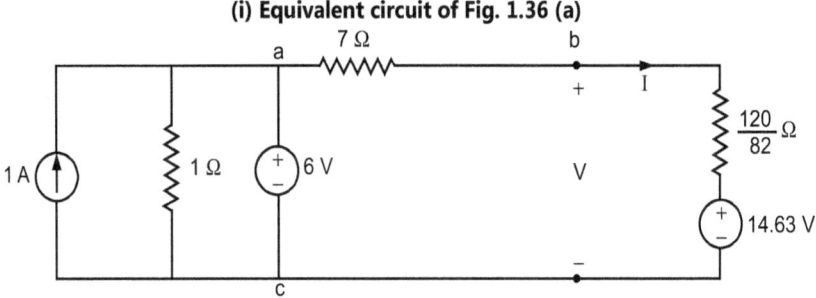

(ii) Simplified equivalent circuit of Fig. 1.36 (a)

Fig. 1.36 (b): Equivalent circuits

Now 7A and 3A are in parallel addition that gives 10A current source. $10\,\Omega$ and $\dfrac{12}{7}\,\Omega$ resistors are in parallel to give equivalent resistance (R_{eq}) of

$$R_{eq} = \dfrac{\dfrac{12}{7} \times 10}{\dfrac{12}{7} + 10} = \dfrac{120}{82}\,\Omega$$

With this simplification and after source transformation the circuit can be redrawn as in Fig. 1.36 (b). KVL across right loop (a-b-c-a) given

$$-7I - \dfrac{120}{82} I - 14.63 + 6 = 0$$

Or
$$I\,[7 + 1.463] = 6 - 14.63$$
$$= -8.63$$

Hence,
$$I = -1.02 \text{ Amp.}$$

Thus,
$$V = +\dfrac{120}{8} I + 14.63$$
$$= -1.492 + 14.63$$

Thus,
$$V = +13.137 \text{ volts.}$$

Example 1.11 :

Using source transformation find voltage VA in the circuit shown.

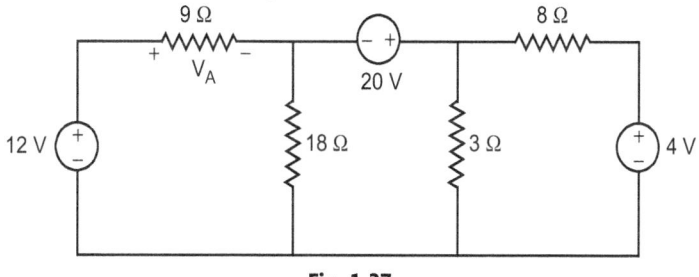

Fig. 1.37

Solution : Various steps involved in the simplification of the circuit are shown in Fig. 1.37. Let a, b, c, d be the nodes.

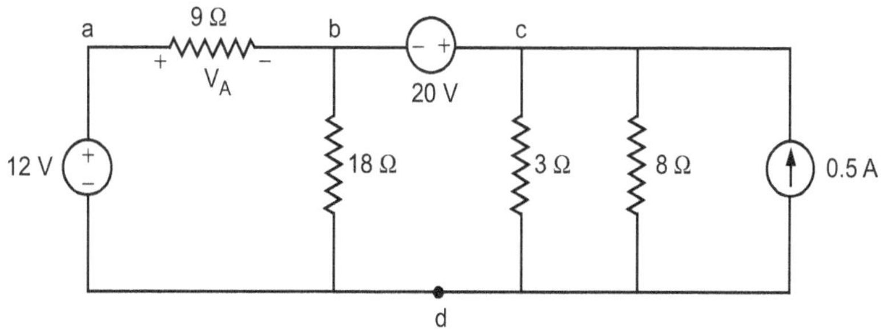

Fig. 1.38 (a)

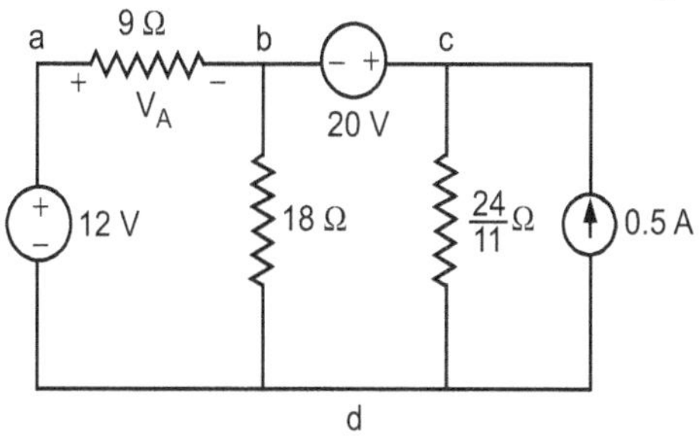

(b) 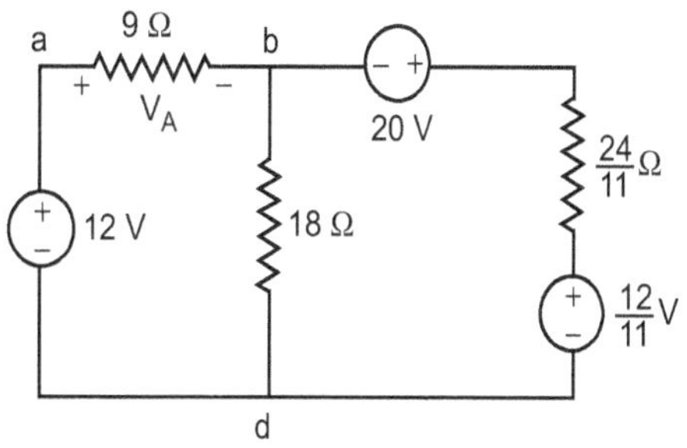　　　　　　　　　　(c)

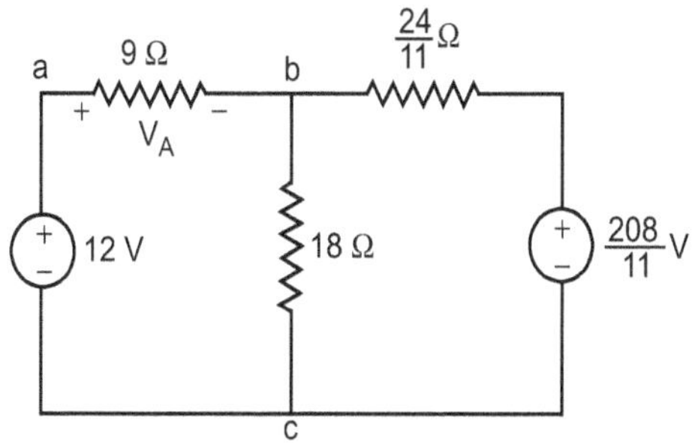

(d) 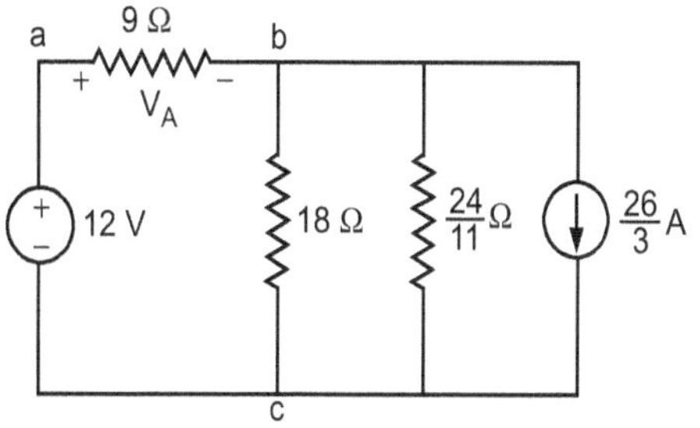　　　　　　　　　　(e)

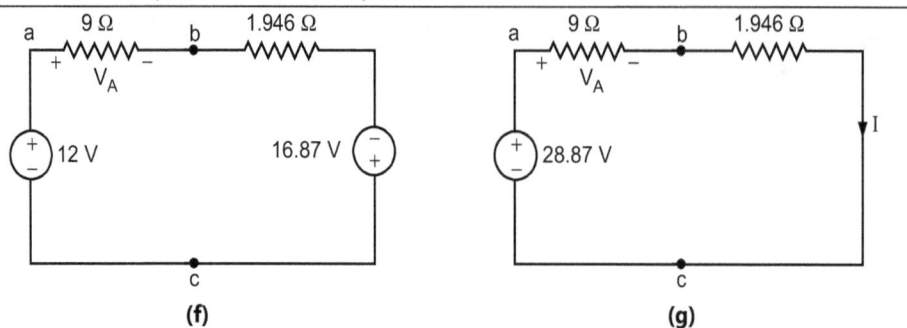

Fig. 1.38 : Various steps involve in simplification of Fig. 1.37

Converting 4V in series with 8Ω into a current source we get the circuit of Fig. 1.38 (a)

Now 8Ω parallel with 3Ω gives $\frac{24}{11}$ Ω as in Fig. (1.38 b).

$\frac{24}{11}$ Ω in parallel with 0.5 A is converted into a voltage source of $\frac{12}{11}$ Volts in series with $\frac{24}{11}$ Ω as in Fig. 1.38 (c).

Now 20V and $\frac{12}{11}$ Ω sources can be added into a voltage of $\left(20 - \frac{12}{11}\right) = \frac{208}{11}$ V as shown in Fig. 1.38 (d).

Convert $\frac{208}{11}$ V in series with $\frac{24}{11}$ Ω into a current source of $\frac{208}{11} \times \frac{11}{24} = \frac{26}{3}$ A in parallel with $\frac{24}{11}$ Ω as in Fig. 1.38 (e).

Now 18 Ω || $\frac{24}{11}$ Ω gives 1.946 Ω. This resistor is in series with voltage source of 1.946 × $\frac{26}{3}$ = 16.87 V as in Fig. 1.38 (f).

Finally, 12V and 16.87V can be added as shown in Fig. 1.38 (g).

Assume loop current (I) in the simplified single loop equivalent circuit. KVL across the loop gives.

$$I (9 + 1.946) = 28.87V$$

or $\quad I = + 2.637$ Amp.

Hence voltage $\quad (V_A) = + 9I$

$= 9 \times 2.637$

$= + 23.74$ volts.

Example 1.12 :

Using source transformation, find I_1 that gives $V_2 = 6.5V$ in the circuit shown.

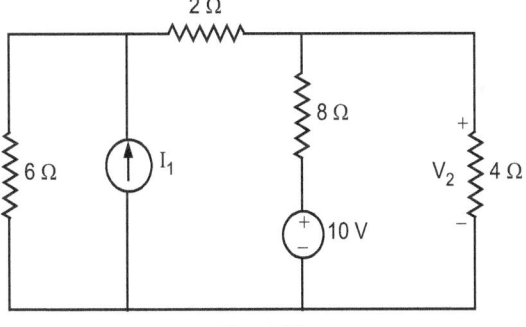

Fig. 1.39

Solution : 10V in series with 8Ω can be converted into a current source of $\frac{5}{4}$ in parallel with 8Ω as in Fig. 1.40 (a).

Now 8Ω and 4Ω in parallel gives equivalent resistance of $\frac{8 \times 4}{8 + 4} = \frac{24}{12} = \frac{8}{3}$ Ω as shown in Fig. 1.40 (b).

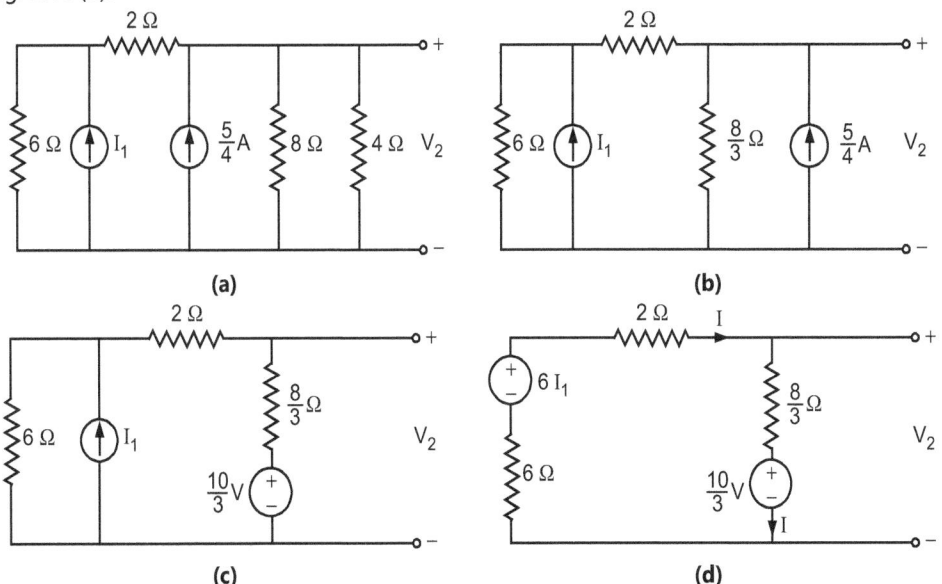

Fig. 1.40 : Various steps involved in simplification of Fig. 1.39

Thus, $\frac{5}{4}$ A current source and $\frac{8}{3}$ Ω resistor in parallel can be converted into voltage source of $\frac{10}{3}$ V in series with $\frac{8}{3}$ Ω as shown in Fig. 1.40 (c).

The final circuit after current source transformation is shown in Fig. 1.40 (d). Assume loop current (1) and using Ohm's across outer branch gives,

$$V_2 = 6.5$$

$$= \frac{8}{3}I + \frac{10}{3}$$

Solving this gives, $\quad I = \frac{19}{16} A$

Now KVL across the whole loop gives,

$$-6I + 6I_1 - 2I - V_2 = 0$$

i.e. $\quad -8I + 6I - 6.5 = -0$

or $\quad 6I_1 = 6.5 + 8I$

$$= 6.5 + 9.5 = 16$$

Hence $\quad I_1 = \frac{16}{6} = \frac{8}{3} A$

Thus, a current source of $\frac{8}{3}$ A in the circuit of Fig. 1.39 gives a voltage of V_2 6.5 V.

Example 1.13 :

Using source transformation, find current I in the circuit shown.

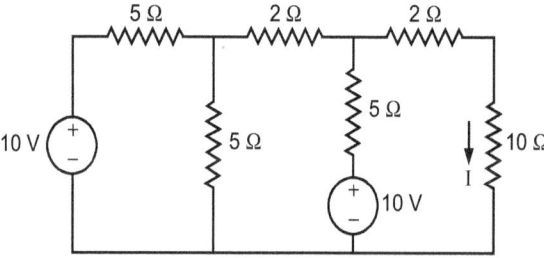

Fig. 1.41

Solution : Various steps involved in the simplification of the circuit given are shown in Fig. (1.42).

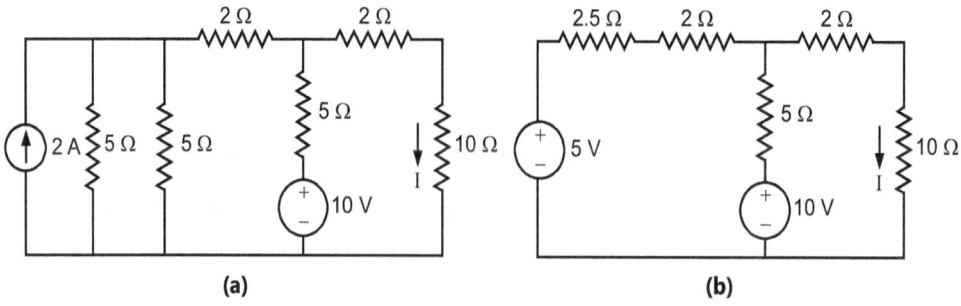

(a)   (b)

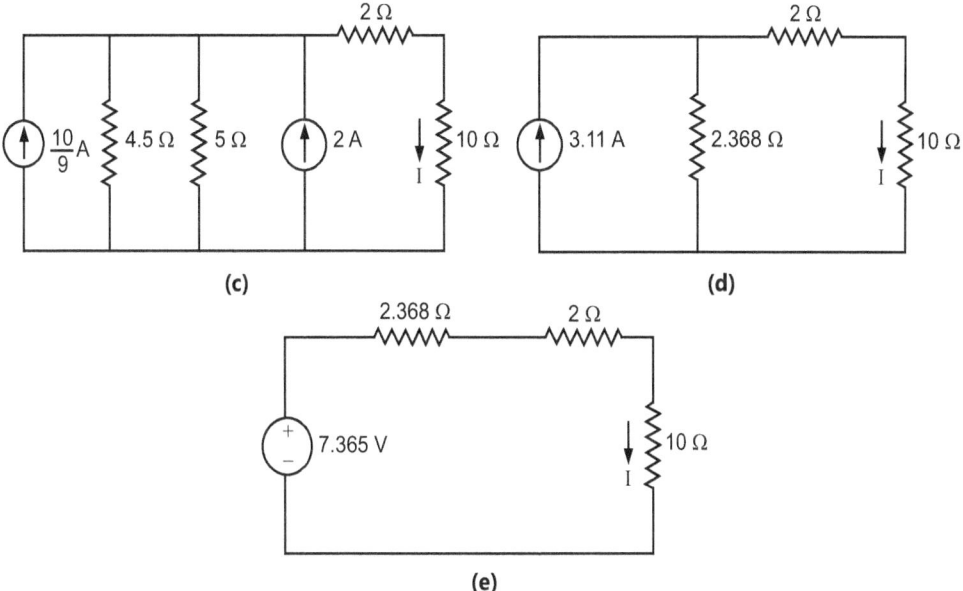

(c)   (d)

(e)

Fig. 1.42 : Various step involved in simplification of Fig. 1.41

Convert 10V in series with 5Ω into a current source of 2A parallel with 5Ω as in Fig. (1.42 a).

5Ω || 5Ω gives 2.5Ω resistor. This resistor is parallel with 2A current source. This combination is converted into an voltage source of 5V in series with 2.5Ω as shown in Fig. 1.42 (b).

Convert the two voltage sources in series with resistors into current sources in parallel as in Fig. 1.42 (c). Two current sources of two parallel resistors are combined to get circuit of Fig. 1.42 (d), where 4.5Ω || 5Ω gives 2.368 Ω resistor.

Finally, converting 3.11 A in parallel with 2.368Ω into voltage source of 3.11 × 2.368 = 7.365V in series with resistor 2.368Ω as shown in Fig. 1.42 (e).

Using KVL gives   7.365 = (2 + 10 + 2.368)
Or   I = 0.512 Amp.

Example 1.14 :

Use source transformation to find load current I_L in the circuit shown below.

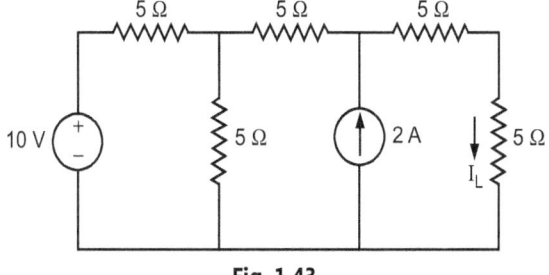

Fig. 1.43

Solution : This problem is similar to one in Ex. (1.13). The various steps involved in simplification are shown in Fig. 1.44. All these steps are self explanatory.

Now consider final simplified equivalent circuit of Fig. 1.44 (e) where I_L is the loop current using KVL across the loop gives:

$$20 = I_L [7.5 + 5 + 5]$$

or

$$I_L = \frac{20}{17.5} = +1.142 \text{ Amp.}$$

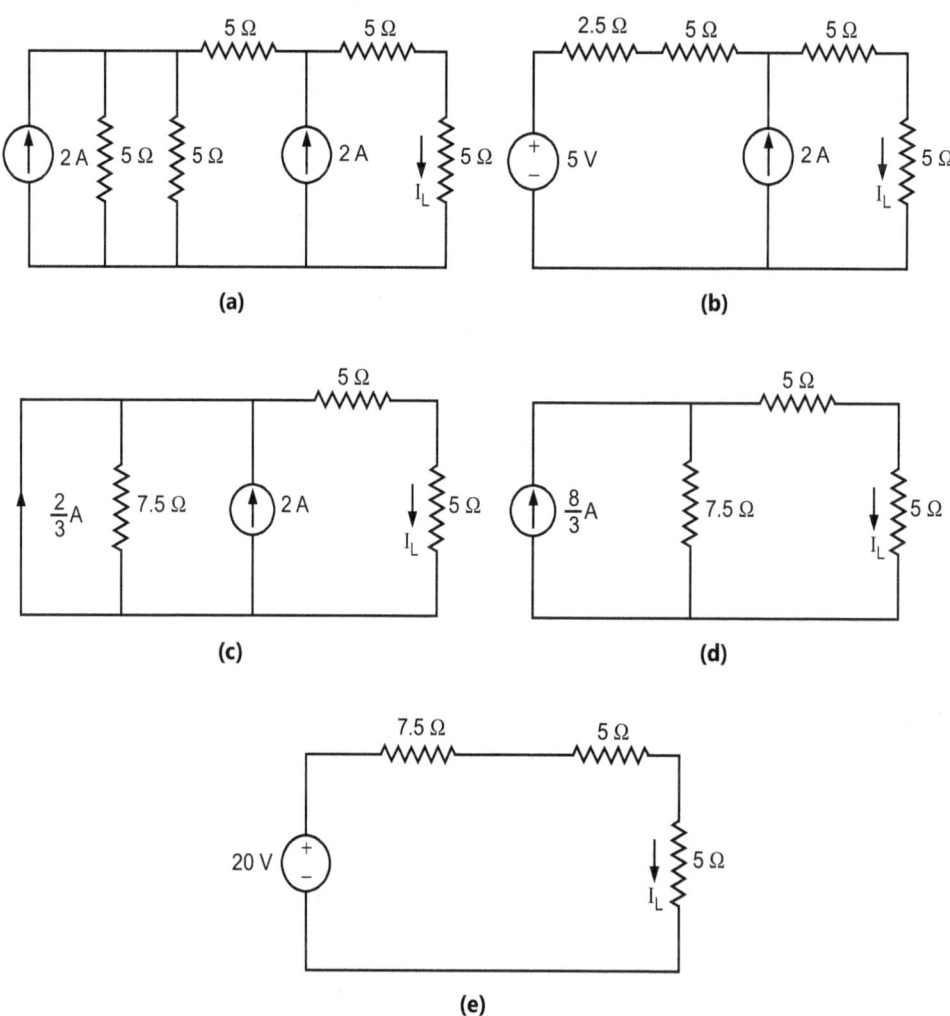

Fig. 1.44 : Various steps involved in simplification of Fig. 1.43

Example 1.15 :

Make use of source transformations to determine values of V and I in the circuit shown.

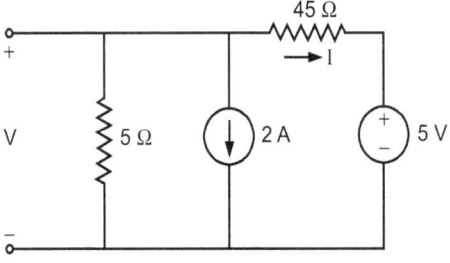

Fig. 1.45

Solution : In the given circuit 2A is in parallel with 5Ω. This can be converted into a voltage source of 2 x 5 = 10V in series with 5Ω. This conversion makes the circuit into a single loop as shown in Fig. 1.50.

KVL across the loop gives + 5 + 45I + 5I + 10 = 0

50I = −15   or I = − 0.3A

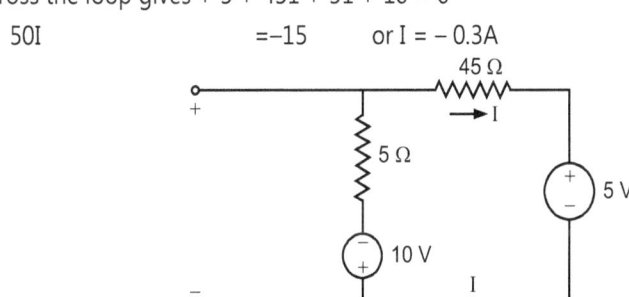

Fig. 1.46 : Equivalent circuit of Fig. (1.45)

Now,   V = − 10 − 5I = − 10 − 5 (− 0.3) = − 8.5 V
Also,   V = + 45I + 5 = 45 × − 0.3 + 5 = − 8.5 V

Example 1.16 :

Make use of source transformation to suppress the nodes and then obtain node voltages V_1 and V_2 in the circuit shown.

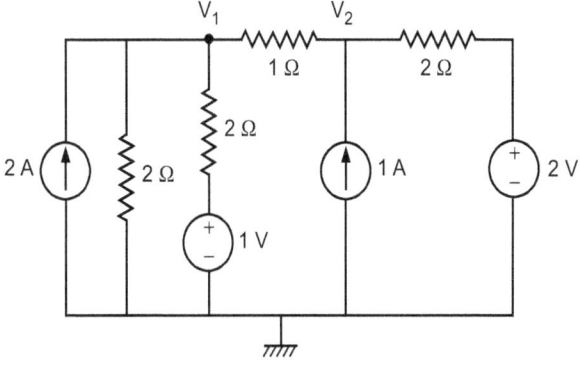

Fig. 1.47

Solution : Various step involved in simplifying the circuit into a single loop using source transformation is shown in Fig. 1.48.

KVL across loop in Fig. 1.48 (c) gives,

$$+4 + 2I + I + I - \frac{5}{2} = 0$$

or

$$4I = \frac{-3}{2} \text{ or } I = \frac{-3}{8} A$$

Hence, we have

$$V_1 = \frac{5}{2} - 1 = \frac{5}{2} + \frac{3}{8} = \frac{23}{8} V$$

$$= + 2.815 \, V$$

$$V_2 = 4 + 2I = 4 - 2 \times \frac{3}{8}$$

$$= \frac{26}{8} V = +3.25 \, V$$

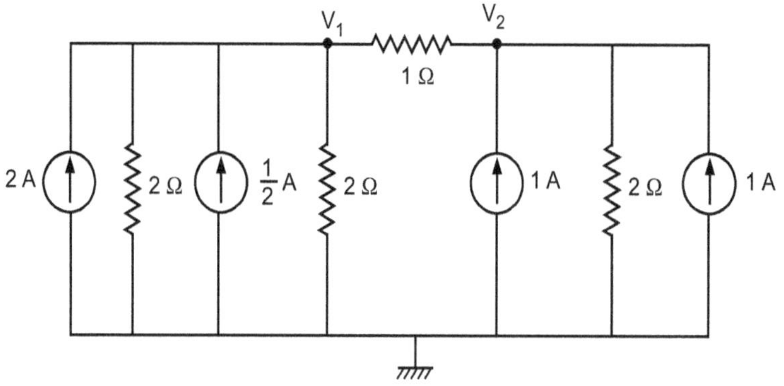

(a)

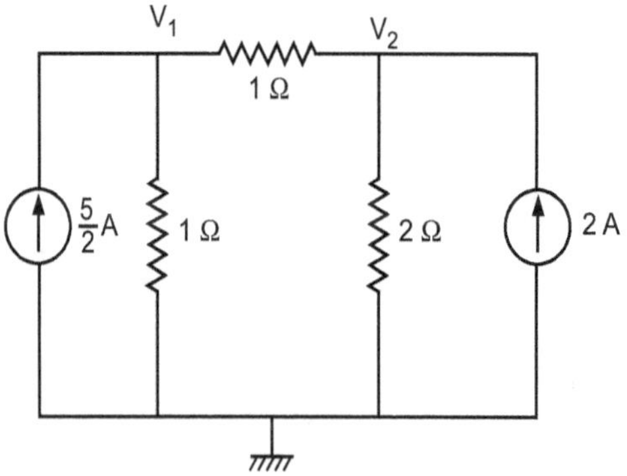

(b)

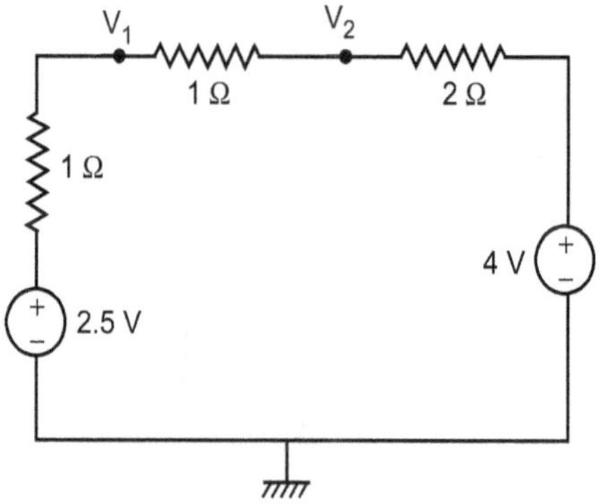

(c)

Fig. 1.48 : Various steps involved in simplifying the Fig. 1.47

Unit I | 1.36

1.16 MESH (OR LOOP) OR KVL ANALYSIS

When a network is complex containing many energy sources and impedances than KVL and KCL are not enough to analyze the circuit. In such cases we can use loop analysis or nodal analysis. In this section, we shall study how Mesh analysis can be used for analyze a complex circuit. Since, this analysis makes use of KVL this is also called KVL analysis.

Consider the circuit of Fig. (1.49). The circuit has two independent loops. These loops are L_1 (a-b-d-a) with loop current I_1 and L_2 (b-c-d-b) with loop current I_2. There is also a loop L_3 (a-b-c-d-a) but it is not an-independent loop (It does not contain any new element which are not in loop L_1 and Loop L_2). The assumption of loop current for this non-independent loop does not yield any new equations of variables.

There are two unknown currents (I_1, I_2) hence, we need two equations to obtain their values. These two equations can be obtained by applying KVL across two independent loops.

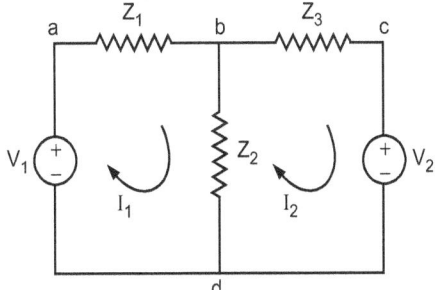

Fig. 1.49 : Circuit to explain loop (or Mesh) analysis

KVL across loop L_1 (a-b-d-a) gives,

$$-Z_1 I_1 + Z_2(I_2 - I_1) + V_1 = 0 \quad \ldots \text{(a)}$$

Or $\quad I_1(Z_1 + Z_2) - I_1 I_2 = V_1$

KVL across loop L_2 (b-c-d-b) gives

$$-Z_3 I_2 - V_2 - Z_2 (I_2 - I_1) = 0$$

Or $\quad -Z_2 I_1 + (Z_1 + Z_3) I_2 = -V_2 \quad \ldots \text{(b)}$

Above equations can be written in matrix form as

$$\begin{bmatrix} (Z_1 + Z_2) & -Z_2 \\ -Z_2 & (Z_2 + Z_3) \end{bmatrix} \begin{bmatrix} I_1 \\ I_2 \end{bmatrix} = \begin{bmatrix} V_1 \\ -V_2 \end{bmatrix} \quad \ldots \text{(c)}$$

These equations can be solved to obtain loop currents I_1 and I_2. Once these currents are obtained then the branch currents can be calculated.

It is not absolutely necessary that the loop currents (I_1, I_2 ...) should be clockwise always. These can be both clockwise and anticlockwise currents. But, for our convenience, the loop currents are always assumed in clockwise direction. These current directions are as shown in Fig. 1.50 below.

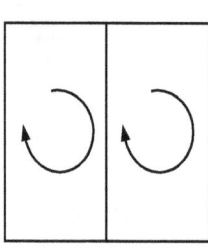 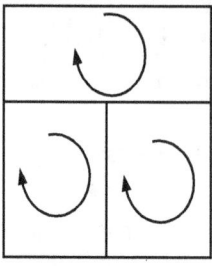 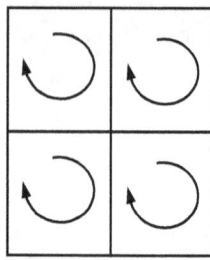

Fig. 1.50 : General loop current directions

If all loop currents are clockwise and V_1, V_2, V_3 etc. are sum of the voltage drop (– ve) in the current direction, then for 3 loop circuit the equation will be in the form of.

$$\begin{bmatrix} V_1 \\ V_2 \\ V_3 \end{bmatrix} = \begin{bmatrix} Z_{11} & -Z_{12} & -Z_{13} \\ -Z_{21} & Z_{22} & -Z_{23} \\ -Z_{31} & -Z_{32} & Z_{33} \end{bmatrix} \begin{bmatrix} I_1 \\ I_2 \\ I_3 \end{bmatrix} \qquad \ldots (1.15)$$

Where,

Z_{11} = sum of all impedances in loop L_1 i.e. self impedance of Loop L_1.

Z_{12} = sum of impedances common to L_1 and L_2 i.e. mutual impedance of loop L_1 or L_2.

Cramer's rule can be used to solve variable I_1, I_2 and I_3 in equations (1.15).

Analysis Procedure for Mesh (or loop) Analysis:

In general following steps can be used to carry out Mesh analysis.

Step I : First of all chose the independent loops (L_1, L_2, L_3 etc.) in the given circuit.

Step II : Assume all loop currents (I_1, I_2, I_3 etc.) in clockwise direction for convenience (even though currents can be anticlockwise).

Step III: Apply KVL across each loop in the circuit. Write equations in standard form interms of loop currents. Make use of Ohm's law.

Step IV: Solve simultaneous algebraic equations obtained in step III to obtain loop currents (I_1, I_2, I_3 etc. etc).

Step V : Once loop currents are obtained then branch currents and node voltages can be obtained.

Things to be remembered for Loop (Mesh) Analysis:

1. Always choose independent loops, which gives minimum but sufficient number of loops for analysis.
2. Convert all current sources into voltage source if possible. This is because mesh analysis makes use of KVL.
3. When current in a particular branch is required then choose loop current in such a way that only one loop current links with the branch.

Following examples explain the mesh analysis method.

Example 1.17 :

Use loop analysis for the circuit of Fig. 1.51 to obtain branch currents and node voltage at node A.

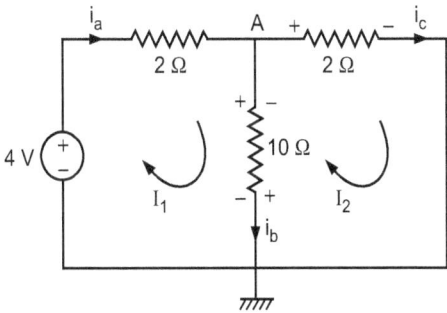

Fig. 1.51

Solution : Here two independent loops and their loop currents are already given. Hence, we can start with step III. KVL across loop I_1 gives,

$$-1(I_1 - I_2) + 4 - 2I_1 = 0 \quad \text{or} \quad 3I_1 - I_2 = 4 \quad \ldots (a)$$

KVL across loop I_2 gives

$$-2I_2 + 1(I_1 - I_2) = 0 \quad \text{or} \quad 3I_2 - I_1 = 0 \quad \ldots (b)$$

Solving equation (a) and (b) gives I_1 and I_2 as

$$I_2 = \frac{1}{2}A \quad \text{and} \quad I_1 = \frac{3}{2}A$$

Thus,
$i_a = I_1 = 1.5$ Amp.
$i_c = I_2 = 0.5$ Amp.
$i_b = (I_1 - I_2) = (1.5 - 0.5) = +1$ Amp.
$V_A = 1[I_1 - I_2] = 1 \times 1 = +1$ Volts

Also,
$V_A = +2I_2 = 2 \times 1 = +1$ Volts

Example 1.18 :

Make use of loop analysis to find current i_1 and i_2 and from this information determine voltages V_x in the circuit shown in Fig. 1.52.

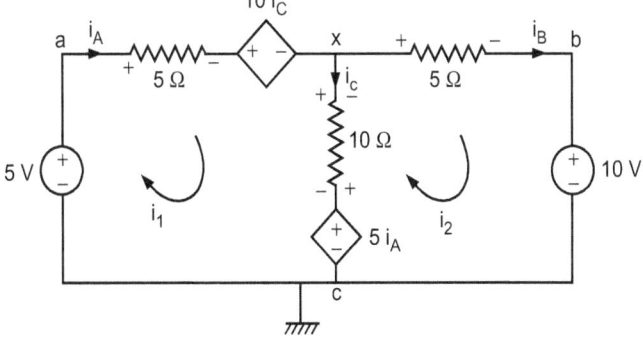

Fig. 1.52

Solution : Here two independent loops and their loop currents are already given. Hence, we can start with step III. KVL across loop i_1 (c – x – a – c) gives,

$$+ 5i_A + 10(i_1 - i_2) + 10 i_c + 5iA = 5$$

But $\qquad i_A = i_1, i_c = i_1 - i_2$ and $i_B = i_2$

Hence, we have $+ 5i_1 + 10(i_1 - i_2) + 10(i_1 - i_2) 5i_1 = 5$

Or, $\qquad\qquad 30i_1 - 20i_2 = 5$

i.e. $\qquad\qquad 6i_1 - 4i_2 = 1$ ... (a)

KVL across loop i_2 (c – b – x – c) gives

$$+ 10 + 5i_B + 10(i_2 - i_1) - 5i_A = 0$$
$$10 + 5i_2 + 10(i_2 - i_1) - 5i_1 = 0$$

Or $\qquad\qquad 15i_1 - 15i_2 = 10$

i.e. $\qquad\qquad 3i_1 - 3i_2 = 2$ ... (b)

From (a) and (b) solve for current i_1 and i_2

By (b) $3i_1 = 2 + 3i_2$, putting this in equation (a) gives,

$\qquad\qquad 2 \times [2 + 3i_2] - 4i_2 = 1$ or $\quad i_2 = -1.5$ Amp.

Hence, by (a) $\qquad\qquad 6i_1 = 1 + 4i_2 = 1 - 4 \times 1.5 = -5$

Thus, we have $\qquad\qquad i_1 = -\dfrac{5}{6}$ Amp.

The branch currents are: $\quad i_A = i_1 = \dfrac{-5}{6}$ A, $i_B = i_2 = -1.5$ A, $i_c = (i_1 - i_2) = +\dfrac{2}{3}$ Amp.

$$V_x = 10 + 5i_B = 10 - 5 \times 15 = + 2.5 \text{ V}$$

Also $\qquad\qquad V_x = 10i_c + 5i_A = 10 \times \dfrac{2}{3} - 5 \times \dfrac{5}{6} = + 2.5$ V

Example 1.19 :

Write mesh current equation for the network shown and solve them to obtain Current in 7Ω resistor.

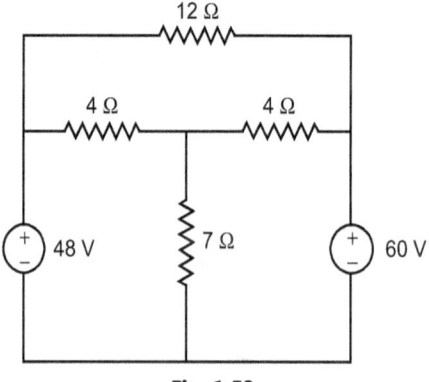

Fig. 1.53

Solution : There are three loops which are independent. These loops with loop currents I_1, I_2 and I_3 are shown in Fig. (1.54) KVL across loop with loop current I_1 (a – b – c – a) gives,

$$-4[I_1 - I_3] - 7[I_1 - I_2] + 48 = 0$$

or $\quad 11I_1 - 7I_2 - 4I_3 = 4 \quad$ ... (a)

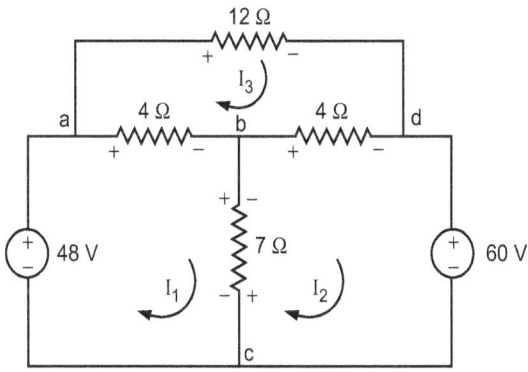

Fig. 1.54 : Redrawn circuit with loop current

KVL across loop with loop current I_2 (b – d – c – b) gives,

$$-4(I_2 - I_3) - 60 + 7(I_1 - I_2) = 0$$

Or $\quad -7I_1 + 11I_2 - 4I_3 = -60 \quad$ ... (b)

KVL across loop with loop current 13 (a – d – b – a) gives,

$$-12 I_3 + 4(I_2 - I_3) + 4(I_1 - I_3) = 0$$

Or $\quad -4I_1 - 4I_2 + 20I_3 = 0$

i.e. $\quad -I_1 - I_2 + 5I_3 = 0 \quad$ ... (c)

From equation (a), (b), (c) solve loop currents I_1, I_2, I_3 using Cramer's law. The above equation can be put into a standard form as given by equation (1.15).

$$\begin{bmatrix} 11 & -7 & -4 \\ -7 & 11 & -4 \\ -1 & -1 & 5 \end{bmatrix} \begin{bmatrix} I_1 \\ I_2 \\ I_3 \end{bmatrix} = \begin{bmatrix} 48 \\ -60 \\ 0 \end{bmatrix} \quad \text{... (d)}$$

By Cramer's rule $I_1 = \dfrac{\Delta_1}{\Delta}$, $I_2 = \dfrac{\Delta_2}{\Delta}$ and $I_3 = \dfrac{\Delta_3}{\Delta}$

Thus, $\quad I_1 = \dfrac{\begin{bmatrix} 48 & -7 & -4 \\ -60 & 11 & -4 \\ 0 & -1 & +5 \end{bmatrix}}{\begin{bmatrix} 11 & -7 & -4 \\ -7 & 11 & -4 \\ -1 & -1 & 5 \end{bmatrix}} = \dfrac{48(+55-4) + 7(-300) - 4(60-0)}{11(55-4) + 7(-35-4) - 4(7+11)}$

$$= \frac{108}{216} = +0.5 \text{ Amp.}$$

$$I_2 = \frac{\begin{bmatrix} 11 & 48 & -4 \\ -7 & -60 & -4 \\ -1 & 0 & 5 \end{bmatrix}}{\Delta} = \frac{11(-300) - 48(-35-4) - 4(0-60)}{216}$$

i.e. $I_2 = \frac{-1188}{216} = -5.5 \text{ Amp.,}$

Using (c) $\quad 5I_3 = I_1 + I_2 = 0.5 + (-5.5) = -5.0$

Thus, $\quad I_3 = \frac{-5}{5} = -1 \text{ Amp.}$

Now current in 7Ω resistor = $I_{7\Omega} = I_1 - I_2 = 0.5 - (-5.5) = 6A$.

Example 1.20 :
Set up the mesh equations for the circuit and use them to find voltage drop from point a to point b in the circuit shown below.

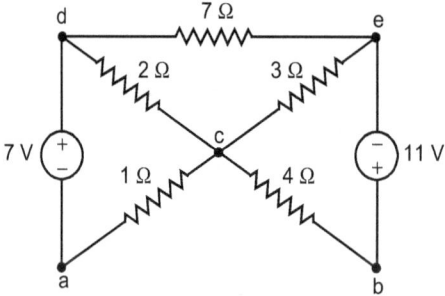

Fig. 1.55

Solution : There are three independent loops. These loops with loop currents I_1, I_2 and I_3 are shown below.

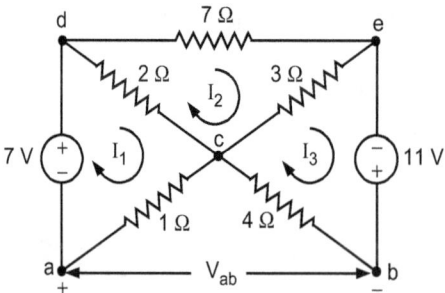

Fig. 1.56 : Redrawn circuit with loop current

KVL across loop with current I_1 (d - c - a - d) gives,

$$-2(I_1 - I_2) - I_1 + 7 = 0$$

Or $\qquad 3I_1 - 2I_2 + 0I_3 = 7$ ... (a)

KVL across loop with loop current I_2 (a – e – c – d) gives

$\qquad -7I_2 - 3(I_2 - I_3) + 2(I_1 - I_2) = 0$

Or $\qquad -2I_1 + 12I_2 - 3I_3 = 0$ ... (b)

KVL across loop with loop current I_3 (e – b – c – e) gives

$\qquad +11 - 4I_3 + 3(I_2 - I_3) = 0$

Or $\qquad 0I_1 - 3I_2 + 7I_3 = 11$ ... (c)

Above three equation can put into a standard form as given by equation. (1.15).

$$\begin{bmatrix} 3 & -2 & 0 \\ -2 & 12 & -3 \\ 0 & -3 & +7 \end{bmatrix} \begin{bmatrix} I_1 \\ I_2 \\ I_3 \end{bmatrix} = \begin{bmatrix} 7 \\ 0 \\ 11 \end{bmatrix}$$ ... (d)

Now voltage between a – b is given by applying KVL across outer loop.

$\qquad -11 + 7I_2 - 7 - V_{ab} = 0$

Or $\qquad V_{ab} = 7I_2 - 18$ ... (e)

From (e) it is obvious that only I_2 need to be found to calculate V_{ab}. Hence, solve for I_2 from equation (d) using Cramer's law,

$$I_2 = \frac{\Delta_2}{\Delta} = \frac{\begin{bmatrix} 3 & 7 & 0 \\ -2 & 0 & -3 \\ 0 & 11 & 7 \end{bmatrix}}{\begin{bmatrix} 3 & -2 & 0 \\ -2 & 12 & -3 \\ 0 & -3 & 7 \end{bmatrix}} = \frac{3(0 + 33) - 7(-14)}{3(84 - 9) + 2(-14 - 0)}$$

$$= \frac{197}{197} + 1 \text{ Amp.}$$

Hence, by (e) $\qquad V_{ab} = 7 \times 1 - 18 = -11$ Volts.

Thus, voltage between a – b is – 11 V which means 'b' is at higher potential than a by 11 V.

1.17 SUPER MESH ANALYSIS

While using mesh analysis preferably we requires all the voltage sources in the circuit. If there is a current source in the loop we choose, We can not use KVL since the voltage across the current source is not known directly. Consider the circuit shown in Fig. 1.57.

Here there are two loops which contains a current source (I_0) within loop. We cannot use KVL across loops since voltage between the current source is not known. There are two unknowns and hence two equations are needed in terms of currents I_1 and I_2.

The first equation can be obtained by the current source itself. Since, current in the branch is equal to source current (I_0), the first equation is given by,

$$I_1 - I_2 = I_0 \quad \ldots \text{(a)}$$

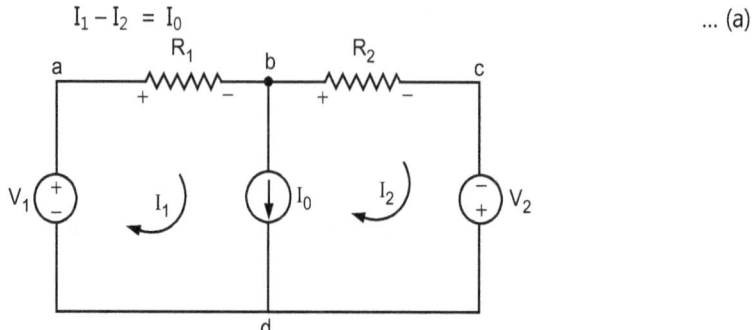

Fig. 1.57 : Circuit to explain super mesh

If we assume that current source (I_0) is removed temporarily then mesh (a - b - c - d - a) is formed that contains R_1, R, and two voltage sources. This mesh is known as super mesh. Thus, as super mesh is mesh formed when current source is assumed to be temporarily removed.

Now KVL across super mesh (a - b - c - d - a) gives the second equation, which is as shown below.

$$-R_1 I_1 - R_2 I_2 + V_2 + V_1 = 0$$

Or
$$R_1 I_1 + R_2 I_2 = V_1 + V_2 \quad \text{(b)}$$

Thus, these two equations can be solved to get the two unknown currents (I_1, I_2).

Example 1.21 :

Find mesh currents in the circuit given. Use loop analysis method.

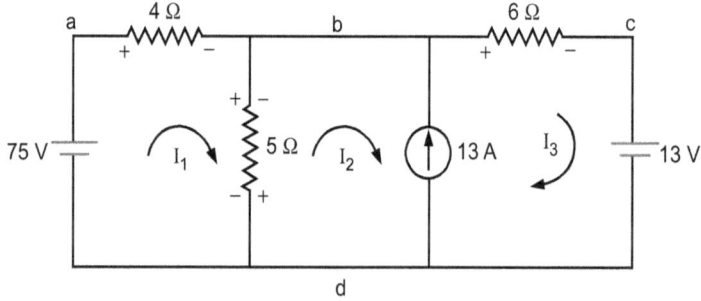

Fig. 1.58

Solution : One method to analyze this circuit is to convert current source of 13A parallel with 5Ω into an voltage source with a 5Ω series resistor across b – d. This will convert the circuit into two loops and make the loop current (I_2) zero. Therefore we cannot use this method.

Hence, we can make use of super mesh analysis. Super mesh (b - c - d - b) is formed if current source assumed to be temporarily removed. KVL across this super mesh (b - c- d - b) gives.

$$-6I_3 - 13 + 5(I_1 - I_2) = 0$$
$$5I_1 - 5I_2 - 6I_3 = 13 \quad \ldots (a)$$

KVL across loop I_1 (a - b - d - a) gives,
$$-4I_1 - 5(I_1 - I_2) + 75 = 0$$
$$9I_1 - 5I_2 + 0I_3 = 75 \quad \ldots (b)$$

The third equation can be obtained by current source of 13A it self and is given as,
$$I_3 - I_2 = 13 \quad \text{or} \quad 0I_1 - I_2 + I_3 = 13 \quad \ldots (c)$$

These three equations can be put into standard form of equation (1.15) as below.

$$\begin{bmatrix} 5 & -5 & -6 \\ 9 & -5 & 0 \\ 0 & -1 & 1 \end{bmatrix} \begin{bmatrix} I_1 \\ I_2 \\ I_3 \end{bmatrix} = \begin{bmatrix} 13 \\ 75 \\ 13 \end{bmatrix}$$

I_1, I_2 and I_3 can be solved using Cramer's law, gives,
$$I_1 = +5A, \ I_2 = -6A \ \text{and} \ I_3 = +7A$$

Example 1.22 :

Using mesh analysis find current through the branch c – d consisting of 3Ω resistor.

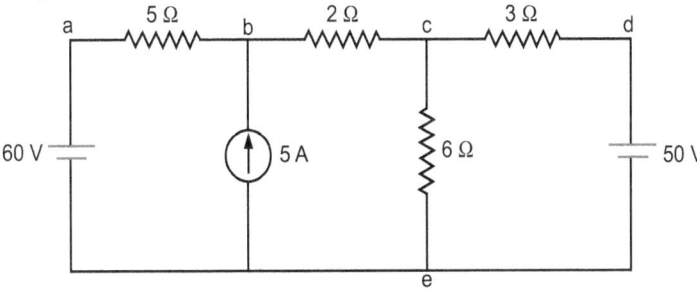

Fig. 1.59

Solution : There are three independent loops. These three loops and their loop currents I_1, I_2, I_3 are shown in Fig. (1.60).

First equation is given by current source itself.

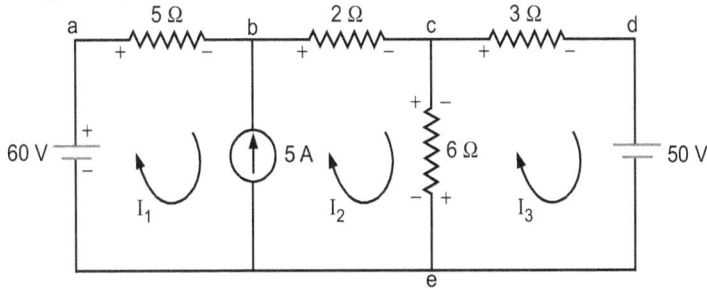

Fig. 1.60 : Redrawn circuit with loop currents

Thus, $\quad I_2 - I_1 = 5 \quad \text{Or} \quad -I_1 + I_2 + 0I_3 = 5 \quad \ldots (a)$

Assuming current source (5A) is temporarily removed an super mesh (a – b – c – e – a) consisting of 5Ω, 3Ω, 6Ω and 60V is formed. KVL across this super mesh (a – b – c – e – a) gives,

$$-5I_1 - 2I_2 - 6(I_2 - I_3) + 60 = 0$$

Or $\qquad 5I_1 + 8I_2 - 6I_3 = 60 \qquad$ ... (b)

Third equation can be obtained by applying KVL across loop I_3 (c – d – e – c)

$$-3I_3 - 50 + 6(I_2 - I_3) = 0$$

Or $\qquad 0I_1 + 6I_2 - 9I_3 = 50 \qquad$ ... (c)

These equations can be put into standard form as,

$$\begin{bmatrix} -1 & 1 & 0 \\ 5 & 8 & -6 \\ 0 & 6 & -9 \end{bmatrix} \begin{bmatrix} I_1 \\ I_2 \\ I_3 \end{bmatrix} = \begin{bmatrix} 5 \\ 60 \\ 50 \end{bmatrix}$$

Solve I_1, I_2 and I_3 using Cramer's law. But as we need current through 3Ω resistor which is loop current I_3 solve only I_3 for this problem.

$$I_3 = \frac{\Delta_3}{\Delta} = \frac{\begin{bmatrix} -1 & 1 & 5 \\ 5 & 8 & 60 \\ 0 & 6 & 50 \end{bmatrix}}{\begin{bmatrix} -1 & 1 & 0 \\ 5 & 8 & -6 \\ 0 & 6 & -9 \end{bmatrix}} = \frac{140}{-81} = -1.73 \text{ Amp.}$$

Hence, a current of 1.73 A flow from d – c in 3Ω resistor.

Example 1.23 :

Use mesh analysis to find voltage V_0 in the circuit shown below.

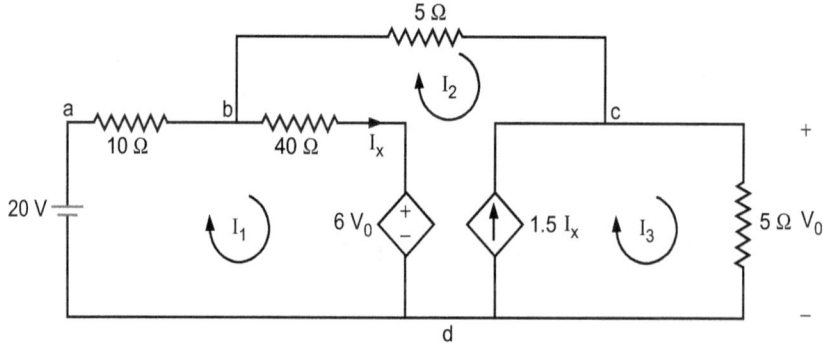

Fig. 1.61

Solution : We have $\qquad I_x = I_1 - I_2 \qquad$ ... (a)

And $\qquad V_0 = 5I_3 \qquad$ ... (b)

We need three equations in terms of I_1, I_2, I_3 to solve for these currents. We cannot use KVL for loop 2 and loop 3 since they contains current source in between. When current source is temporarily removed a super mesh is formed (b – c – d – b) containing 5Ω, 5Ω, 40Ω and $6V_0$ source. KVL across this super mesh (b – c – d –b) gives.

$$-5I_2 - 5I_3 + 6V_0 + 40(I_1 - I_2) = 0$$

Or
$$-5I_2 - 5I_3 + 6 \times 5I_3 + 40(I_1 - I_2) = 0$$
$$-40 I_1 + 45 I_2 - 25 I_3 = 0 \quad \ldots (c)$$

KVL across loop with current I_1 (a – b – d – a) gives,

$$-10I_1 - 40(I_1 - I_2) - 6V_0 + 20 = 0$$
$$-10I_1 - 40I_1 + 40I_2 - 6 \times 5I_3 + 20 = 0$$
$$50I_1 - 40I_2 + 30I_3 = 20 \quad \ldots (d)$$

The third equation can be obtained by applying KCL at node V which is $1.5 I_x = I_3 - I_2$. Using equation (a) for I_x we get $1.5 \times (I_1 - I_2) = I_3 - I_2$.

Hence,
$$1.5I_1 - 0.5I_2 - I_3 = 0 \quad \ldots (e)$$

These three equations can be put into standard form as,

$$\begin{bmatrix} -40 & 45 & -25 \\ 50 & -40 & 30 \\ 1.5 & -0.5 & -1 \end{bmatrix} \begin{bmatrix} I_1 \\ I_2 \\ I_3 \end{bmatrix} = \begin{bmatrix} 0 \\ 20 \\ 0 \end{bmatrix} \quad \ldots (f)$$

Solving for current I_3 using Cramer's law, we get

$$I_3 = \frac{\begin{bmatrix} -40 & 45 & 0 \\ 50 & -40 & 20 \\ 1.5 & -0.5 & 0 \end{bmatrix}}{\begin{bmatrix} -40 & 45 & -25 \\ 50 & -40 & 30 \\ 1.5 & -0.5 & -1 \end{bmatrix}} = 0.792 \text{ Amp.}$$

Hence, by (b)
$$V_0 = 5I_3 = 5 \times 0.792 = + 3.96 \text{ V.}$$

Example 1.24 :

Write loop equations for the circuit shown and find power absorbed by 3Ω resistor.

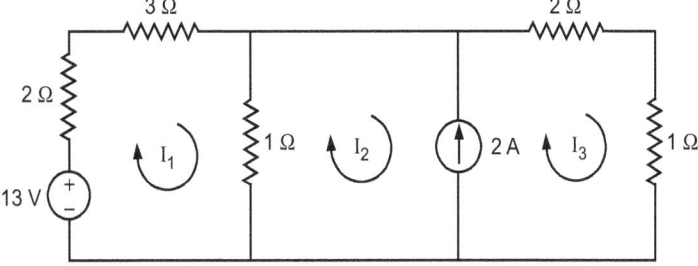

Fig. 1.62

Solution : The circuit can be redrawn as shown in Fig. 1.63. Power absorbed by 3Ω resistor = $I_1^2 \times 3$. Hence, we need to find current loop current I_1. First equation is obtained by 2A current source itself.

Thus,
$$I_3 - I_2 = 2A$$
Or
$$0I_1 - I_2 + I_3 = 2 \quad \ldots (a)$$

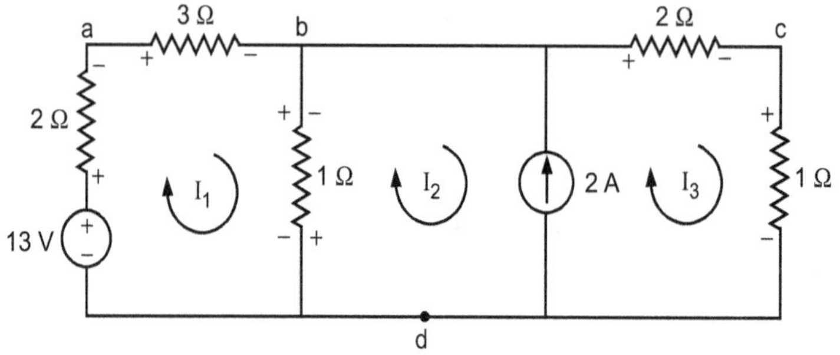

Fig. 1.63 : Redrawn circuit

KVL across loop I_1 (a – b – d – a) gives.
$$-3I_1 - 1(I_1 - I_2) + 13 - 2I_1 = 0$$
Or
$$6I_1 - I_2 + 0I_3 = 13 \quad \ldots (b)$$

Now we can not apply KVL across loop 2 and loop 3 as it contains current source in between. With 2A current source temporarily assumed removed super mesh (b – c – d – b) consisting of 1Ω, 1Ω and 2Ω resistors formed.

KVL across this super mesh (b – c – d – b) gives.
$$-2I_3 - I_3 + 1(I_1 + I_2) = 0$$
$$I_1 - I_2 - 3I_3 = 0 \quad \ldots (c)$$

These three equations can be put into standard form as.
$$\begin{bmatrix} 0 & -1 & 1 \\ 6 & -1 & 0 \\ 1 & -1 & -3 \end{bmatrix} \begin{bmatrix} I_1 \\ I_2 \\ I_3 \end{bmatrix} = \begin{bmatrix} 2 \\ 13 \\ 0 \end{bmatrix}$$

Solve for current I_1 using Cramer's rule.

$$I_1 = \frac{\Delta_1}{\Delta} = \frac{\begin{vmatrix} 2 & -1 & 1 \\ 13 & -1 & 0 \\ 0 & -1 & -3 \end{vmatrix}}{\begin{vmatrix} 0 & -1 & 1 \\ 6 & -1 & 0 \\ 1 & -1 & -3 \end{vmatrix}} = \frac{-46}{-23} = +2A$$

Thus, power absorbed by 3Ω = $P_3 = (2)^2 \times 3 = +12$ watts.

1.18 NODAL (KVL) ANALYSIS

This is another technique to analysis a complicated electrical circuit. Nodal analysis make use of KCL. Hence, it is also known as KCL analysis. To explain this analysis consider the circuit shown in Fig. (1.64). Node '0' is taken as reference (ground) node and voltages of node 1 and 2 is taken as V_1 and V_2 respectively with respect to ground. Choose unknown branch currents as i_1, i_2 and i_3 arbitrarily.

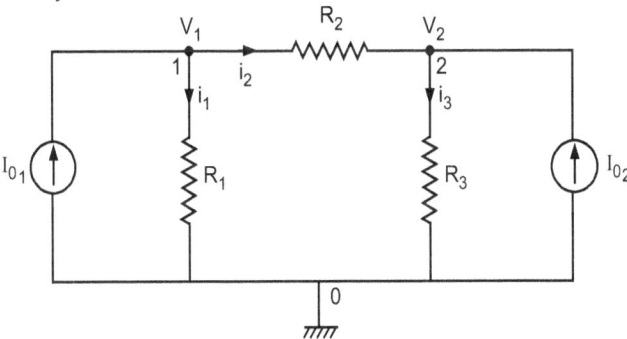

Fig. 1.64 : Circuit to explain nodal analysis

Our aim is to find voltages V_1 and V_2. Once these are known, then branch currents can be found out. KCL at node 1 gives,

$$I_1 + I_2 = I_{01}$$

Or
$$\frac{V_1}{R_1} + \left[\frac{V_1 - V_2}{R_2}\right] = I_{01}$$

Hence
$$V_1 + \left[\frac{1}{R_1} + \frac{1}{R_2}\right] - \frac{V_2}{R_2} = I_{01} \qquad \ldots (a)$$

KCL at node 2 gives $I_3 - I_2 = I_{02}$

Or
$$\frac{V_2}{R_3} - \left[\frac{V_1 - V_2}{R_2}\right] = I_{02}$$

$$-\frac{V_1}{R_2} + \left[\frac{1}{R_2} + \frac{1}{R_3}\right] V_2 = I_{02}$$

If R_1, R_2, R_3 and I_{01}, I_{02} are known then voltages V_1, V_2 can be found out. For example, if $R_1 = 5\Omega$, $R_2 = 10\Omega$, $R_3 = 10\Omega$ and $I_{01} = 5A$, $I_{02} = 10$ A then.

By (a)
$$\frac{V_1}{5} + \left[\frac{V_1 - V_2}{10}\right] = 5$$

Or
$$3V_1 - V_2 = 50 \qquad \ldots (c)$$

By (b)
$$\frac{-V_1}{10} + \left[\frac{1}{10} + \frac{1}{10}\right] V_2 = 10$$

Or
$$2V_2 - V_1 = 100 \qquad \ldots (d)$$

Solving (c) and (d) gives $V_1 = 40V$ and $V_2 = 70V$.

Hence,
$$I_1 = \frac{40}{5} + 8A$$

$$I_2 = \frac{40-70}{10} - \frac{30}{10} = -3A$$

and
$$I_3 = \frac{70}{10} = +7A$$

Thus, nodal analysis enables to find us currents in various branches of a circuit by finding various node voltages.

Analysis Procedure for Nodal Analysis

In general following steps can be used to carry out nodal analysis.

Step I : Simplify the circuit by combining impedances in parallel or series and combining current sources in parallel.

Step II : Choose a reference (or ground) node. Any node can be choosen as ground but preferably for convenience, we choose bottom node as reference. Assign unknown node voltages as V_1, V_2, V_3 etc. With respect to the ground (0V).

Step III : Assign arbitrarily currents in various branches of the circuit where current is not known.

Step IV : Apply KCL at each node except at ground Node. Make use of ohm's law to obtain branch currents.

Step V : Simplify the equations algebraically to put them in standard form in terms of V_1, V_2, V_3.

Step VI : Solve the above simultaneous equations for the unknown node voltages V_1, V_2, V_3 etc.

Step VII : Using these node voltages, current in all or any required branch can be determined.

In general the standard form of nodal equations will be as below.

$$\begin{bmatrix} I_{01} \\ I_{02} \\ I_{03} \end{bmatrix} = \begin{bmatrix} Y_{11} & -Y_{12} & -Y_{13} \\ -Y_{21} & Y_{22} & -Y_{23} \\ -Y_{31} & -Y_{32} & -Y_{33} \end{bmatrix} \begin{bmatrix} V_1 \\ V_2 \\ V_3 \end{bmatrix} \qquad \text{... (1.16)}$$

Where, V_1, V_2, V_3 are unknown node voltages. I_{01}, I_{02}, I_{03} are known current sources.
Y_{11} = Sum of admittances connected to node V_1 = Self admittance.
Y_{12} = Admittance connected between nodes 1 and 2 = mutual admittance.

Things to be Remembered for Nodal (KCL) Analysis:

1. Nodal analysis prefers all sources to be current sources. If there are any voltage sources convert them into current sources.
2. Do not apply KCL at ground (or reference) node.
3. Currents in unknown branches can be choosen arbitrarily with arbitrary direction. Following examples explains node analysis in detail.

Example 1.25 :

Find branch currents I_1, I_2, and I_3 and node voltages by using nodal analysis.

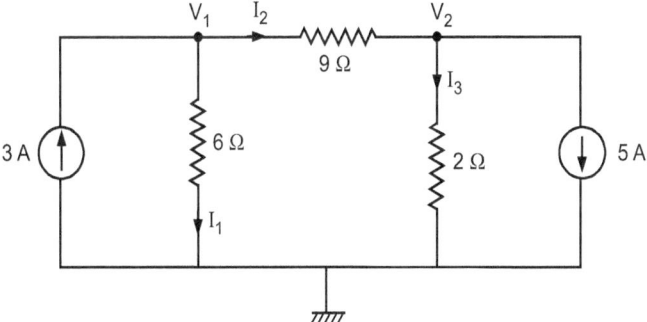

Fig. 1.65

Solution : First three steps of analysis are already included in the circuit given. Hence, we can start with step IV. Using KCL at node V, gives $I_1 + I_2 = 3$.

$$\frac{V_1}{6} + \frac{(V_1 - V_2)}{9} = 3$$

or
$$5V_1 - 2V_2 = 54 \quad \ldots (a)$$

Using KCL at node V_2 gives $I_2 - I_3 = 5$

$$\frac{V_1 - V_2}{9} - \frac{V_2}{2} = 5$$

Or
$$2V_1 - 11V_2 = 90 \quad \ldots (b)$$

These equations can be put into standard form of equation (1.16) as below.

$$\begin{bmatrix} 5 & -2 \\ 2 & -11 \end{bmatrix} \begin{bmatrix} V_1 \\ V_2 \end{bmatrix} = \begin{bmatrix} 54 \\ 90 \end{bmatrix}$$

Solve V_1 and V_2 by using Cramer's law.

$$V_1 = \frac{\Delta_1}{\Delta} = \frac{\begin{bmatrix} 54 & -2 \\ 90 & -11 \end{bmatrix}}{\begin{bmatrix} 5 & -2 \\ 2 & -11 \end{bmatrix}} = \frac{-594 + 180}{-55 + 4} = +8.118 \text{ Volts.}$$

By (a) $\quad 2V_2 = 5V_1 - 54 = -13.41$

Hence, $\quad V_2 = -6.7$ Volts

$$I_1 = \frac{8.12}{6} + 1.35 \text{ Amps}$$

$$I_2 = \frac{V_1 - V_2}{9} = \frac{8.12 + 6.7}{9} = +1.645 \text{ Amp.}$$

$$I_3 = \frac{V_2}{2} = \frac{-6.7}{2} = -3.35 \text{ Amp.}$$

Negative sign of V_2 indicates that voltage node V_2 is less than reference (0 V).

Example 1.26 :

Determine Node to Datum voltages for the circuit shown, use nodal analysis method.

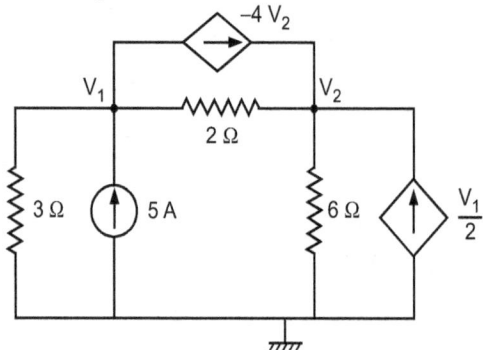

Fig. 1.66

Solution : Assume currents in various branches arbitrarily as shown in redrawn circuit of Fig. (1.67).

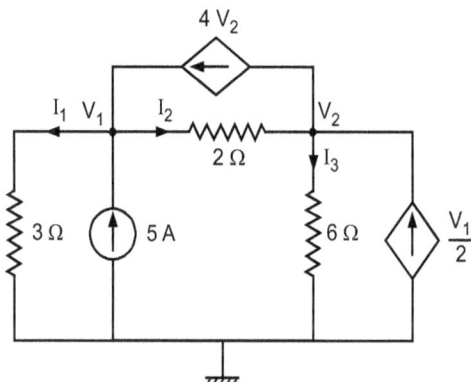

Fig. 1.67 : Redrawn circuit

KCL at V_1 gives $I_1 + I_2 = 5 + 4V_2$.

Or $\quad \dfrac{V_1}{3} + \left(\dfrac{V_1 - V_2}{2}\right) - 4V_2 = 5$

Hence, $\quad 5V_1 - 27 V_2 = 30$ ... (a)

KCL at V_2 gives, $I_3 + 4V_2 = I_2 + \dfrac{V_1}{2}$

Or $\quad I_3 - I_2 + 4V_2 \dfrac{-V_1}{2} = 0$

$\dfrac{V_2}{6} \left(\dfrac{V_1 - V_2}{2}\right) + 4V_2 - \dfrac{V_1}{2} = 0$

Hence, $6V_1 = 28V_2$, OR $V_2 = \dfrac{3}{14} V_1$ ... (b)

By (a), $5V_1 - 27 \times \dfrac{3}{14} V_1 = 30$. Solving this gives $V_1 - 38.12$ V.

Hence, by (b) $\qquad V_2 = \dfrac{3}{14} \times (-38.12) = -8.18$ V

Thus both nodes are at less potential than ground node.

Example 1.27 :

Using nodal analysis find node voltage V_b in the circuit.

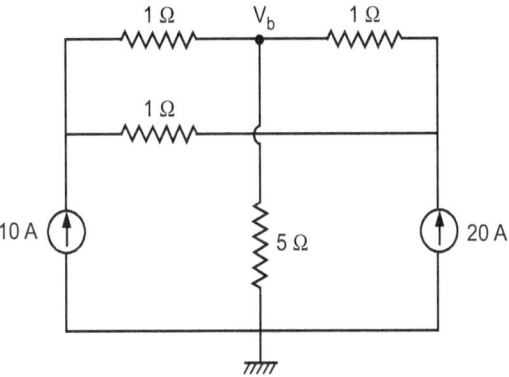

Fig. 1.68

Solution : Let other two unknown node voltages be V_a and V_c. Assume arbitrarily currents in various branches. The redrawn circuit is shown in Fig. (1.69).

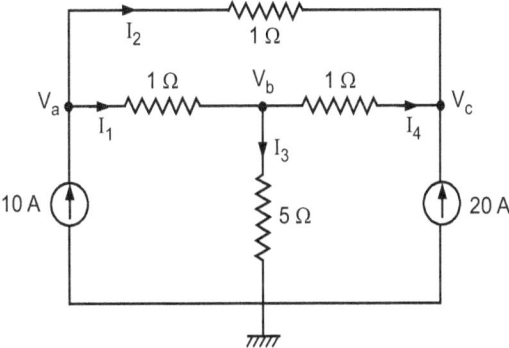

Fig. 1.69 : Redrawn circuit

KCL at node 'a' with voltage V_a gives $I_1 + I_2 = 10$

$$\left(\dfrac{V_a - V_b}{1}\right) + \left(\dfrac{V_a - V_c}{1}\right) = 10$$

Or $\qquad 2V_a - V_b - V_c = 10 \qquad \ldots$ (a)

KCL at node 'b' with voltage V_b gives $I_3 + I_4 = I_1$

$$\dfrac{V_b}{5} + \left(\dfrac{V_b - V_c}{1}\right) = \left(\dfrac{V_a - V_b}{1}\right)$$

Or $\quad V_a - 2.2 V_a + V_c = 0 \quad$ ... (b)

KCL at node 'c' with voltage V_c gives $I_4 + I_2 + 20 = 0$

$$\left(\frac{V_b - V_c}{1}\right) + \left(\frac{V_a - V_c}{1}\right) + 20 = 0$$

$$V_b + V_a - 2V_c = -20 \quad \text{... (c)}$$

In matrix form these can be written as:

$$\begin{bmatrix} 2 & -1 & -1 \\ 1 & -2.2 & 1 \\ 1 & 1 & -2 \end{bmatrix} \begin{bmatrix} V_a \\ V_b \\ V_c \end{bmatrix} = \begin{bmatrix} 10 \\ 0 \\ -20 \end{bmatrix} \quad \text{... (d)}$$

Solve for V_b using Cramer's law

$$V_b = \frac{\begin{vmatrix} 2 & 10 & -1 \\ 1 & 0 & 1 \\ 1 & -20 & -2 \end{vmatrix}}{\begin{vmatrix} 2 & -1 & -1 \\ 1 & -2.2 & 1 \\ 1 & 1 & -2 \end{vmatrix}} = \frac{2(20) - 10(-3) - 1(-20)}{2(-5.4) + 1(-3) - 1(3.2)} = \frac{90}{-17} = -5.3 \text{ Volts}$$

Example 1.28 :
Using nodal analysis to find voltage V_y in the circuit shown in the Fig. 1.70.

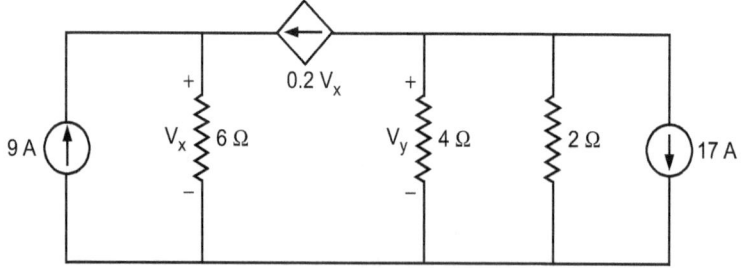

Fig. 1.70

Solution : Let bottom node be at ground (0V). Then two unknown node voltages will be V_x and V_y. Combine 2Ω || 4Ω into a single resistor of $\frac{4}{3}$ ohms. The redrawn circuit is shown in Fig. (1.71).

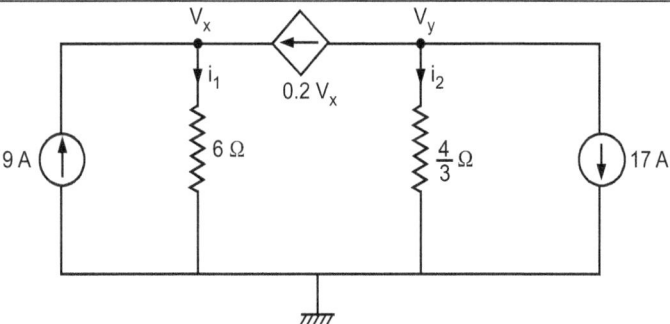

Fig. 1.71 : Redrawn equivalent circuit

KCL at node 'x' with voltage V_x gives $i_1 = 9 + 0.2\, V_x$.

Or $\quad \dfrac{V_x}{6} - 0.2\, V_x = 9$

Hence, $\quad V_x[1 - 1.2] = 54$

Thus, $\quad$ Voltage $V_x = \dfrac{54}{-0.2} = -270\text{ V}$

KCL at node 'y' with voltage V_y gives $i_2 + 0.2\, V_x + 17 = 0$.

Or $\quad \dfrac{V_y}{4/3} + 0.2 \times [-270] + 17 = 0$

Hence, $\quad V_y = \dfrac{4}{3}[54 - 17] = +49.33\text{ V}$

Thus, voltage of node y is $V_y = +49.33\text{ V}$.

Example 1.29 :

Use nodal analysis to find voltage V_{AB} in the circuit of Fig. (1.72).

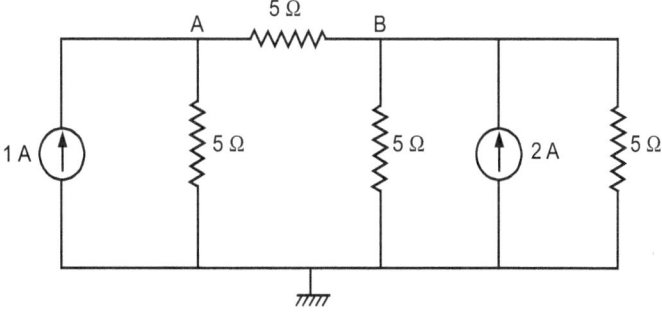

Fig. 1.72

Solution : Combine $5\Omega \parallel 5\Omega$ resistor into 2.5Ω resistor. Take the bottom most node at ground (0V). Let V_A and V_B be unknown node voltages. Assume arbitrarily currents in various branches. The revised simplified equivalent circuit is shown in Fig. (1.73).

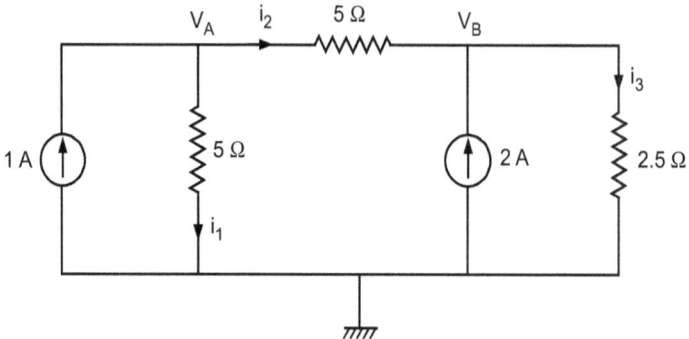

Fig. 1.73 : Redrawn equivalent circuit

KCL at node A with voltage V_A gives, $i_1 + i_2 = 1$

$$\frac{V_A}{5} + \left(\frac{V_A - V_B}{5}\right) = 1$$

$$2V_A - V_B = 5 \quad \text{... (a)}$$

KCL at node B with voltage V_B gives, $i_3 - i_2 = 2$

$$\frac{V_B}{2.5} - \left(\frac{V_A - V_B}{5}\right) = 2$$

$$3V_A - V_B = 10 \quad \text{... (b)}$$

Solve equations (a) and (b) to get V_A and V_B where.

$$V_A = +5V \text{ and } V_B = +5V$$

Thus, voltage between A and B = $V_{AB} = V_A - V_B = 5 - 5 = 0V$

Note: Two points A and B are effectively at same potential. Hence, no current flows in 5Ω resistor between A and B. Thus, path between A and B acts as a open circuit.

Example 1.30 :

Use nodal analysis to find currents, I_1, I_2, I_3 and node. Voltages V_1 and V_2 in the circuit shown.

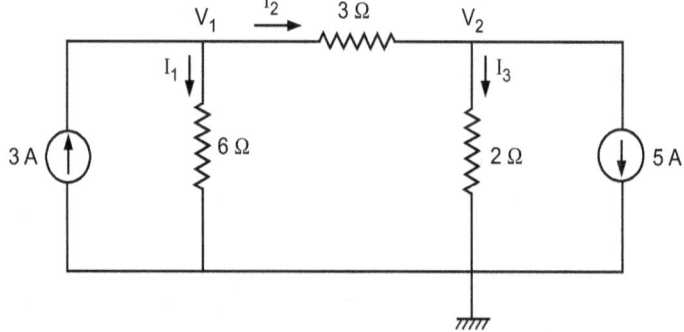

Fig. 1.74

Solution : Branch currents, reference node and unknown node voltages (V_1, V_2) are already given. We can start the analysis by using KCL at nodes V_1 and V_2.

KCL at node 1 with voltage V_1 gives $I_1 + V_2 = 3$.

$$\frac{V_1}{6} + \left(\frac{V_1 + V_2}{3}\right) = 3 \quad \text{Or} \quad 3V_1 - 2V_2 = 18 \quad \ldots \text{(a)}$$

KCL at node 2 with voltage V_2 gives $I_2 - I_3 = 5$

$$\left(\frac{V_1 - V_2}{3}\right) - \frac{V_2}{2} = 5 \quad \text{Or} \quad 2V_1 - 5V_2 = 30 \quad \ldots \text{(b)}$$

Solve (a) and (b) to obtain V_1 and V_2.

$$V_1 = \frac{\Delta_1}{\Delta} = \frac{\begin{vmatrix} 18 & -2 \\ 30 & -5 \end{vmatrix}}{\begin{vmatrix} 3 & -2 \\ 2 & -5 \end{vmatrix}} = \frac{-30}{-11} + 2.72 \text{ V}$$

$$V_2 = \frac{\Delta_2}{\Delta} = \frac{\begin{vmatrix} 3 & 18 \\ 2 & 30 \end{vmatrix}}{\begin{vmatrix} 3 & -2 \\ 2 & -5 \end{vmatrix}} = \frac{54}{-11} = -4.91 \text{ V}$$

$$I_1 = \frac{2.72}{6} = +0.453 \text{ A,}$$

$$I_2 = \frac{V_1 - V_2}{3} = \frac{2.72 + 4.91}{3} = +2.54 \text{ A}$$

$$I_3 = \frac{V_2}{2} = \frac{-4.91}{2} = -2.45 \text{ Amp.}$$

Example 1.31 :

Determine voltage V_{23} in the circuit shown using the nodal analysis method.

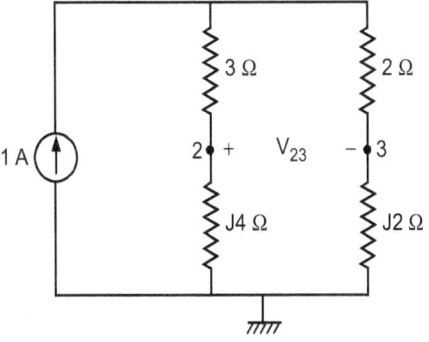

Fig. 1.75

Solution : The circuit contains only two external nodes out of which one is ground (Reference) Node. Let V_1 be the unknown voltage with respect to ground. Let I_1 and I_2 be branch currents as shown in Fig 1.76.

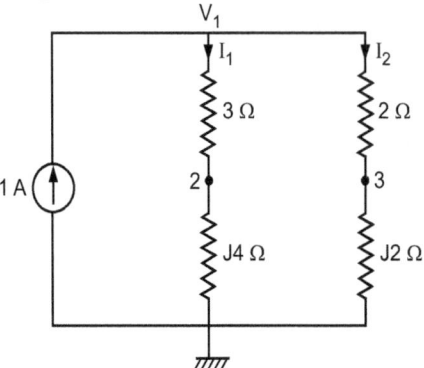

Fig. 1.76 : Redrawn equivalent circuit

KCL at node 1 with voltage V_1 gives

$$\frac{V_1}{(3+J4)} + \frac{V_1}{(2+J2)} = 1 \quad \text{or} \quad V_1 \left[\frac{5+J6}{-2+J14}\right]$$

Solving this gives

$$V_1 = \left[\frac{-2+J14}{5+J6}\right] \text{Volts}$$

Now,

$$I_1 = \frac{V_1}{(3+J4)} = \frac{(2+J2)}{(5+J6)}$$

Hence, Voltage V_2

$$= J4I_1 = \frac{-8+J8}{(5+J6)} = \frac{8(J-1)}{(5+J6)} \text{ Volts}$$

Also

$$I_2 = \frac{V_1}{2+J2} = \frac{3+J4}{5+J6}$$

Hence, Voltage

$$V_3 = J2 \times 12 = J2 \times \frac{(3+J4)}{(5+J6)} = \frac{-8+J6}{5+J6} \text{ Volts}$$

Thus,

$$V_{23} = V_2 - V_3 = \left[\frac{-8+J8}{5+J6}\right] - \left[\frac{-8+J8}{5+J6}\right] = \frac{J2}{(5+J6)}$$

$$= \frac{2/90°}{7.81/50.2°} = 0.256/39.8° \text{ Volts}$$

1.19 SUPER NODE ANALYSIS

Consider the circuit shown in Fig. 1.77 in which there is a voltage source between two unknown nodes V_1 and V_2 with many other circuit elements. The region (shown by dotted line) connecting two nodes by a voltage source directly are known as **super node**. Thus, V_1, V_2 along with voltage source V_x form a **super node**.

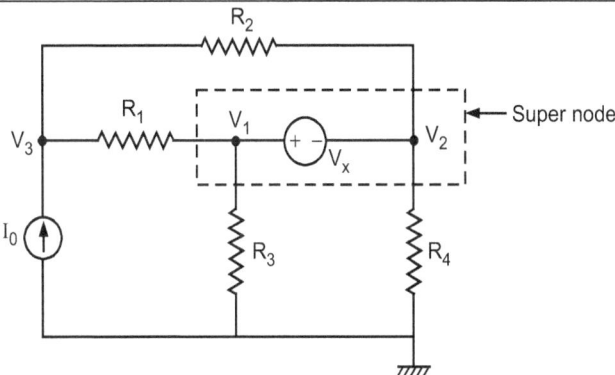

Fig. 1.77 : Circuit to explain super node

One of the equation can be obtained by the super node itself where $V_1 - V_2 = V_x$ ... (a)

Since, we do not know what is current flowing in voltage sources, we cannot apply KCL at nodes V_1 and V_2 directly. The current through voltage source connecting super nodes must be expressed in terms of the branch currents and hence node voltage of other nodes.

Following few examples explains how super node circuit analysis can be achieved.

Example 1.32 :

In the circuit shown find node voltage V, using nodal analysis.

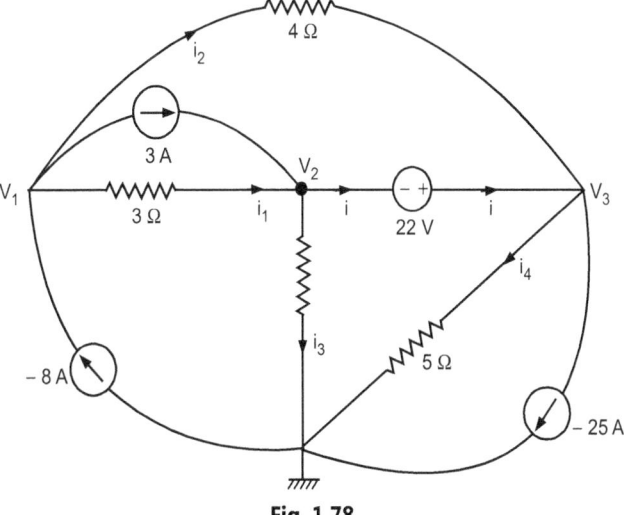

Fig. 1.78

Solution : In the circuit V_2, V_3 and 22V source together forms a super node. There are three unknown voltages and hence we need three equations in terms of V_1, V_2 and V_3. One of the equations is given by super node itself. Thus, $V_3 - V_2 = 22$ or $0V_1 - V_2 + V_3 = 22$ ... (a)

Current i leaving node V_2 must be equal to current entering the node V_3. This current can be expressed in terms of other branch current. Thus,

$$i = 3 + i_1 - i_3 = i_4 - 25 - i_2$$

Or $\quad 3 + 3(V_1 - V_2) - V_2 = 5V_3 - 25 - 4(V_1 - V_3)$

Hence, we get second equation as

$\quad\quad\quad\quad -7V_1 + 4V_2 + 9V_3 = 28$ ... (b)

The third equation can be obtained by applying the KCL at node V_1 as $i_1 + i_2 + 3 + 8 = 0$

$\quad\quad\quad\quad 3(V_1 - V_2) + 4(V_1 - V_3) + 11 = 0$

Or $\quad\quad\quad +7V_1 - 3V_2 - 4V_3 = -11$ ... (c)

These equations can be put into matrix form as below.

$$\begin{bmatrix} 0 & -1 & 1 \\ -7 & +4 & 9 \\ 7 & -3 & -4 \end{bmatrix} \begin{bmatrix} V_1 \\ V_2 \\ V_2 \end{bmatrix} = \begin{bmatrix} 22 \\ 28 \\ -11 \end{bmatrix} \quad\quad ... (d)$$

Solve for V_1 using Cramer's rule as

$$V_1 = \frac{\Delta_1}{\Delta} = \frac{\begin{vmatrix} 22 & -1 & 1 \\ 28 & 4 & 9 \\ -11 & -3 & -4 \end{vmatrix}}{\begin{vmatrix} 0 & -1 & 1 \\ -7 & 4 & 9 \\ 7 & -3 & -4 \end{vmatrix}} = \frac{22(-16 + 27) + 1(-112 + 99) + 1(-84 + 44)}{0 + 1(28 - 63) + 1(21 - 28)}$$

$$= \frac{242 - 13 - 40}{-35 - 7} = \frac{189}{-42} = -4.5 \text{ volts.}$$

Example 1.33 :
Find node voltages in the circuit shown using nodal analysis.

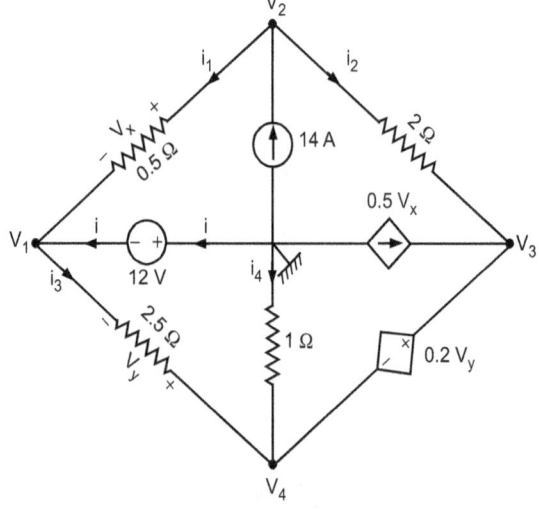

Fig. 1.79

Solution : In this circuit central node is grounded (0V) instead of bottom most node (V_4). Node V_1 and the reference (0V), along with 12V battery source represents a super node. Hence, we get voltage of node (V_1) as

$$V_1 = -12 \text{ V} \quad \ldots \text{(a)}$$

KCL at node (V_2) gives

$$\frac{V_2 - V_1}{0.5} + \frac{V_2 - V_3}{2} = 14$$

Or $\quad 2.5 V_2 - 2V_1 - 0.5 V_3 = 14 \quad \ldots \text{(b)}$

Since current i is flowing through 12V source we have,

$$i = i_1 + i_3 = -14 - 0.5 V_x - i_4$$

$$i = \left(\frac{V_1 - V_4}{2.5}\right) - \left(\frac{V_2 - V_1}{0.5}\right)$$

$$= -14 - \frac{(0 - V_4)}{1} - 0.5 (V_2 - V_1)$$

Solving this gives

$$1.9 V_1 - 1.5 V_2 + 0 V_3 - 1.4 V_4 = -14 \quad \ldots \text{(c)}$$

The fourth equation required can be obtained as below, from another super node consisting of V_3, V_4 and 0.2 Vy.

We have, $\quad 0.2 Vy = V_3 - V_4 = 0.2 (V_4 - V_1)$

Hence, $0.2 V_1 + 0 V_2 + V_3 - 1.2 V_4 = 0 \ldots \text{(d)}$

Solving these equations gives $\quad V_2 = 4V, V_3 = 0V, V_4 = -2V \text{ and } V_1 - 12V$

Example 1.34 :

Using nodal analysis find node voltages V_1, V_2 and V_3.

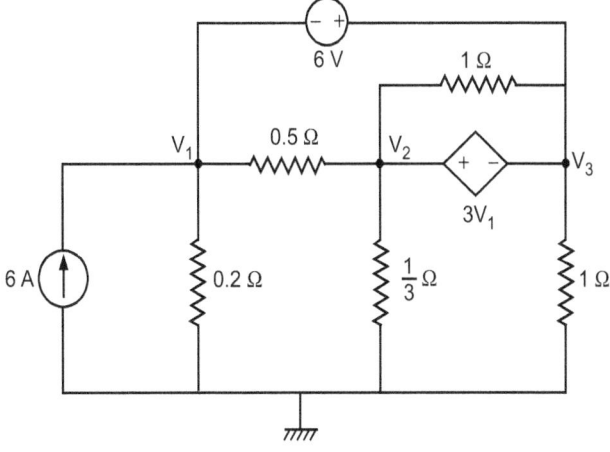

Fig. 1.80

Solution : There are two super nodes in the circuit. The dependent source ($3V_1$) along with V_2, V_3 forms a super node.

Hence, $V_2 - V_3 = 3V_1$ or $3V_1 - V_2 + V_3 = 0$ ... (a)

Second super node is formed by V_1, V_3 and 6V source.

Hence $V_3 - V_1 = 6, -V_1 + 0V_2 + V_3 = 6$ ... (b)

Assuming current through various branches the redrawn circuit is shown in Fig. 1.81.

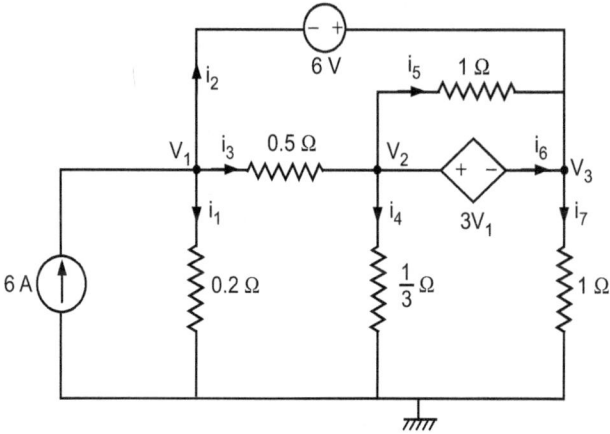

Fig. 1.81 : Redrawn circuit

Now third equation can be formed by calculating the current through voltage sources (6V and $3V_1$) forming the super node.

Current through $\quad 6V = i_2 = 6 - i_1 - i_3 = 6 - \dfrac{V_1}{0.2} - \left(\dfrac{V_1 - V_2}{0.5}\right)$

i.e. $\quad i_2 = 6 - 7V_1 + 2V_2$

Current through $3V_1$ source is given by $(i_6) = i_3 - i_4 - i_5$

i.e. $\quad i_6 = \dfrac{V_1 - V_2}{0.5} - 3V_2 - \left(\dfrac{V_2 - V_3}{1}\right)$

Thus $\quad i_6 = 2V_1 - 6V_2 + V_3$

Now KCL at V_3 gives the third equation required and is given by equation $i_2 + i_6 + i_5 - i_7 = 0$
Using (a) and (b) in above equation gives

$(6 - 7V_1 + 2V_2) + (2V_1 - (6V_2 + V_3) + (V_2 - V_3) - V_3 = 0$

Or $\quad -5V_1 - 3V_2 - V_3 + 6 = 0$ ... (c)

Equation (a), (b), (c) can be solved to get V_1, V_2, V_3

Using (a) and (b) in equation (c), we get,

$-5V_1 - 3[4V_1 + 6] - [V_1 + 6] + 6 = 0$

Or $\quad [V_1 = -1V]$

By (b) $\quad V_3 = 6 + V_1 = +5V$

By (a) $\quad V_2 = 3V_1 + V_3 = +2V$

Example 1.35 :

Using nodal analysis solve for voltages of all the nodes with reference to node 'e' in the circuit shown.

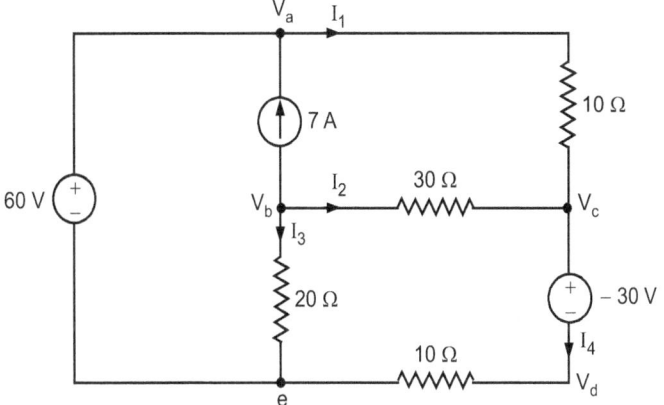

Fig. 1.82

Solution : Choose 'e' node as references. Let V_a, V_b, V_c and V_d be the other node voltages with reference to ground. Assume arbitrarily currents in various branches. The redrawn circuit is shown below in Fig. 1.83.

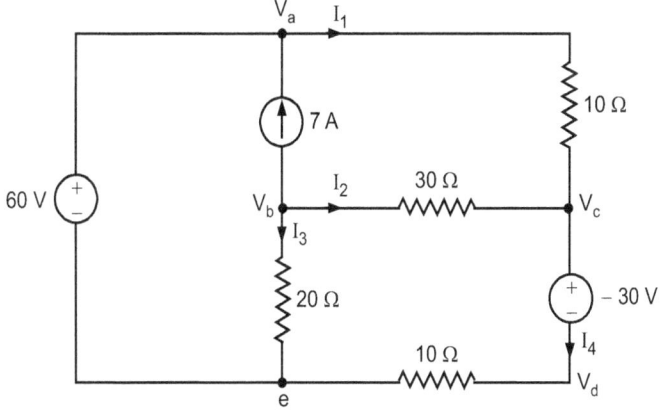

Fig. 1.83

There are four nodes. Hence we need four equations. Now V_a, reference node and 60V source together form a super node.

This gives first equation as $V_a = + 60V$ ... (a)

The voltage source of 30V, V_c and V_d nodes together forms another super node. This gives second equation as $V_a - V_c = 30$ ... (b)

KCL at node 'b' with voltage V_b gives third equation and is given by equation,

$$I_3 + I_2 + 7 = 0$$

$$\frac{V_b}{20} + \left(\frac{V_b - V_c}{30}\right) + 7 = 0$$

Or $\qquad 2V_c - 5V_b = 420 \qquad \ldots$ (c)

The fourth equation can be obtained by applying the KCL at node c and is given by equation,

$$I_1 + I_2 - I_4 = 0$$

$$\left(\frac{60 - V_c}{10}\right) + \left(\frac{V_b - V_c}{30}\right) - \left(\frac{V_c + 30}{10}\right) = 0$$

Or $\qquad 3(60 - V_c) + (V_b - V_c) - 3(V_c + 30) = 0$

Or $\qquad 7V_c - V_b = 90 \qquad \ldots$ (d)

[Current I_4 is given by equation $V_c = 10 \times I_4 - 30$]

Source equations (a), (b), (c) and (d) to get required node voltages. Putting equations (d) into equation (c) gives

$$2 V_c - 5 [7 V_c - 90] = 420$$

Hence $\qquad V_c = + 0.91$ V

By (d) $\qquad V_b = 7 V_c - 90 = -83.64$ V

By (d) $\qquad V_d = 30 + V_c = + 30.91$ V

1.20 ANALYSIS OF CIRCUITS WITH MIXED SOURCES

In section (1.17) we have studied mesh analysis where all energy sources uses voltage sources. Thus, mesh (KVL) analysis preferably requires all energy sources as voltage sources. Similarly in section (1.17) we have studied nodal (KCL) analysis in which all the energy sources were current source. But generally networks consists of both the voltage as well as current sources. Such circuits are called as the circuits with mixed sources. Analysis of such circuits can not be carried out directly. If the circuit is to be analysed on loop basis then all the current sources must be converted into voltage sources. Similarly if the circuit is to be analysed on nodal basis then all the voltage sources are to be converted into current sources. Following few examples explains the analysis of circuits with mixed sources.

Example 1.36 :

Using nodal analysis find the node voltages V_1 and V_2 in the circuit of Fig. 1.84.

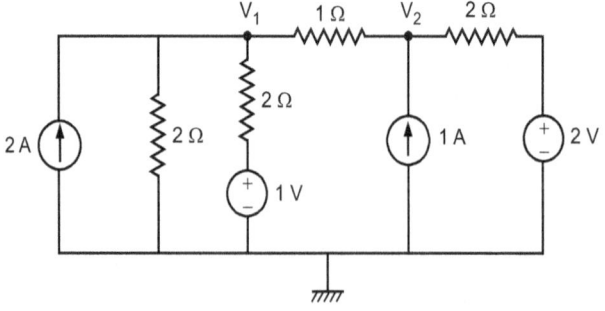

Fig. 1.84

Solution : Since, the circuit is to be analysis in nodal basis all the voltage sources need to be inverted into the current sources. The circuit after conversion is shown in Fig. 1.85 (a). The resistors are combined and so also are current sources. The simplified final equivalent circuit with all the assumed branch currents is shown in Fig. 1.85 (b).

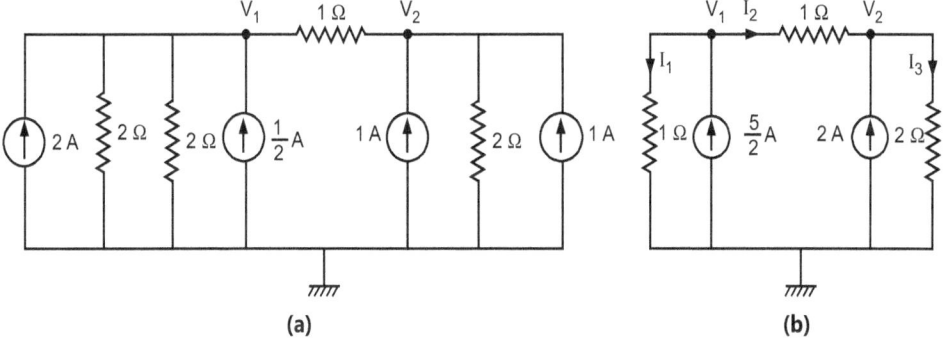

(a)   (b)

Fig. 1.85 : Equivalent circuits

Now KCL at node with voltage V_1 gives $I_1 + I_2 = \dfrac{5}{2}$

$$\dfrac{V_1}{1} + \left(\dfrac{V_1 - V_2}{1}\right) = 2.5 \text{ or } 2V_1 - V_2 = 2.5 \qquad \ldots \text{(a)}$$

KCL at node with voltage V_2 gives $I_3 - I_2 = 2$

$$\dfrac{V_2}{2} - \left[\dfrac{V_1 - V_2}{1}\right] = 2 \text{ or } -2V_1 - 3V_2 = 4 \qquad \ldots \text{(b)}$$

Solve (a) and (b) to get voltages V_1 and V_2

Adding (a) and (b) gives $2V_2 = 6.5$ hence $V_2 = +\,3.25\text{V}$

By (a) $2V_1 = 2.5 + V_2 = 5.75$ hence $V_1 = 2.875\text{V}$

Example 1.37 :

The circuit contains both the voltage and current sources. Analyse the circuit on loop basis to find the value of current I_a.

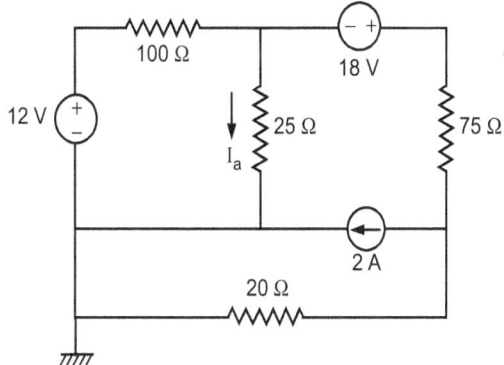

Fig. 1.86

Solution : Since, the circuit is to be analysed on loop basis convert the current source (2A) parallel with 20Ω into the voltage source of 40V in series with 20Ω. The modified equivalent circuit with loop currents I_1 and I_2 is shown in Fig. (1.87). Source conversion converts the three loops circuits into a two loops circuit.

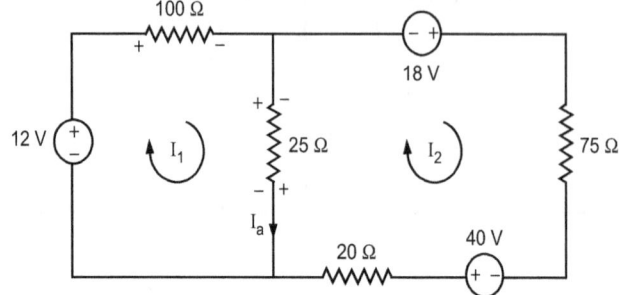

Fig. 1.87 : Modified equivalent circuits

KVL across loop I_1 gives
$$-100 I_1 - 25 (I_1 - I_2) + 12 = 0$$
Or $\qquad 125 I_1 - 25 I_2 = 12 \qquad$ ... (a)

KVL across loop I_2 gives $+18 - 75 I_2 + 40 - 20 I_2 + 25 (I_1 - I_2) = 0$
$$-25 I_1 + 120 I_2 = 58 \qquad \text{... (b)}$$

From (a) and (b) solve for I_1 and $_2$

Thus, $I_1 = \dfrac{\Delta_1}{\Delta} = \dfrac{\begin{vmatrix} 12 & -25 \\ 58 & 120 \end{vmatrix}}{\begin{vmatrix} 125 & -25 \\ -25 & 120 \end{vmatrix}} = \dfrac{1440 + 1450}{15000 - 625} = 0.2$ Amp.

By (a) $\qquad 25 I_2 = 125 I_1 - 12 = 13.13$
$\qquad\qquad I_2 = + 0.5252$ Amp

Hence, $\qquad I_a = I_1 - I_2 = 0.2 - 0.5252 = -0.325$ Amp.

Example 1.38 :

Write the node equations for the circuit and solve them to find the node voltages V_A and V_B.

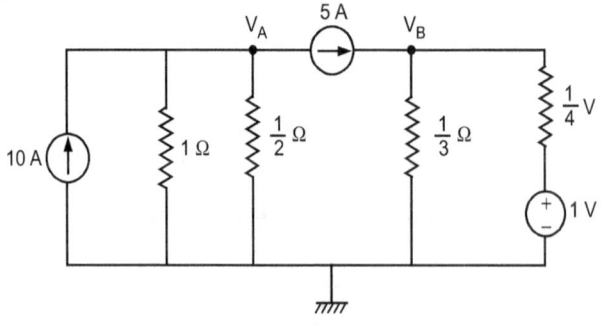

Fig. 1.88

Solution : Since, the circuit is to be analysed on nodal basis, the voltage source of 1V in series with $\frac{1}{4}\Omega$ is converted into a current sources of 4A in parallel with $\frac{1}{4}\Omega$. Now we have $\frac{1}{4}\Omega$ in parallel with $\frac{1}{3}\Omega$ that gives equivalent resistance of $\frac{1}{7}\Omega$. The simplified final equivalent circuit with all branch currents is shown in Fig. 1.89 (b).

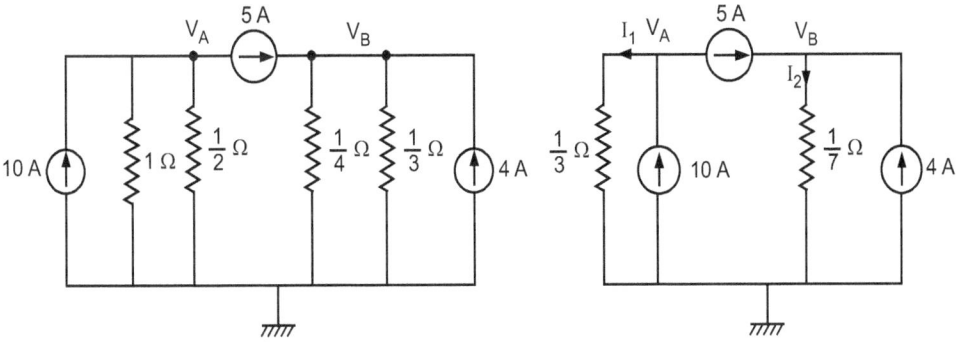

Fig. 1.89 : Modified equivalent circuit

KCL at node V_a gives $I_1 + 5 = 10$ or $I_1 = 5 = 3V_A$

Hence, $V_A = +\frac{5}{3}$ volts

KCL at node V_B gives, $I_2 = 5 + 4 = 9A = 7V_B$

Hence, $V_B = +\frac{9}{7}$ volts

Example 1.39 :

For the circuit of Fig. 1.90 find the current (I) flowing through 2Ω resistance.

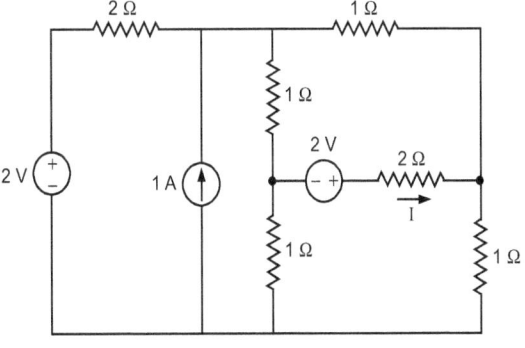

Fig. 1.90

Solution : We have to use loop analysis which is more easier for this problem than using nodal analysis. Convert 2V in series with 2Ω into a current source of 1A parallel with 2Ω. And two parallel current sources of 1A each into 2A current source. Again convert 2A in parallel with 2Ω into a voltage source of 4V in series with 2Ω. The final simplified circuit with assumed loop currents is shown in Fig. 1.91.

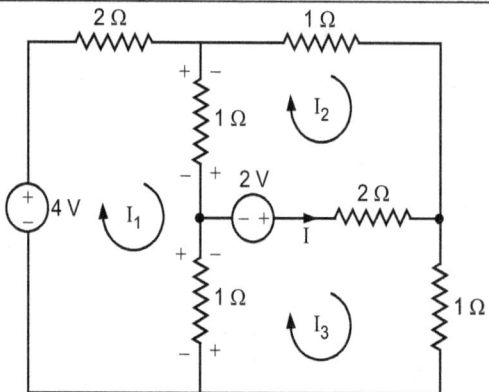

Fig. 1.91 : Modified equivalent circuit

KVL across loop with loop current I_1 gives:
$$-2I_1 - (I_1 - I_2) - (I_1 - I_3) + 4 = 0$$
Or
$$4I_1 - I_2 - I_3 = 4 \qquad \ldots (a)$$

KVL across loop with loop current I_2 gives.
$$-2 - I_2 + 2(I_3 - I_2) - (I_2 - I_1) = 0$$
Or
$$-I_1 - 4I_2 - 2I_3 = -2 \qquad \ldots (b)$$

KVL across loop with loop current I_3 gives:
$$+2 - 2(I_3 - I_2) - I_3 - (I_3 - I_1) = 0$$
Or
$$-I_1 - 2I_2 + 4I_3 = 2 \qquad \ldots (c)$$

Since, current in 2Ω resistor $= I = I_3 - I_2$, solve for I_2 and I_3

Thus, $I_2 = \dfrac{\Delta_2}{\Delta} = \dfrac{\begin{vmatrix} 4 & 4 & -1 \\ -1 & -2 & -2 \\ -1 & 2 & 4 \end{vmatrix}}{\begin{vmatrix} 4 & -1 & -1 \\ -1 & 4 & -2 \\ -1 & -2 & 4 \end{vmatrix}} = \dfrac{12}{36} = +\dfrac{1}{3}$ Amp.

Thus, $I_3 = \dfrac{\Delta_3}{\Delta} = \dfrac{\begin{vmatrix} 4 & -1 & 4 \\ -1 & 4 & -2 \\ -1 & -2 & 2 \end{vmatrix}}{36} = \dfrac{36}{36} = +\dfrac{1}{3}$ Amp.

Hence, $I = I_3 - I_2 = 1 - \dfrac{1}{3} = +\dfrac{2}{3}$ Amp.

Example 1.40 :

For the circuit shown determine voltage ratio $\dfrac{V_o}{V_S}$ and resistance $\dfrac{V_S}{I_S}$.

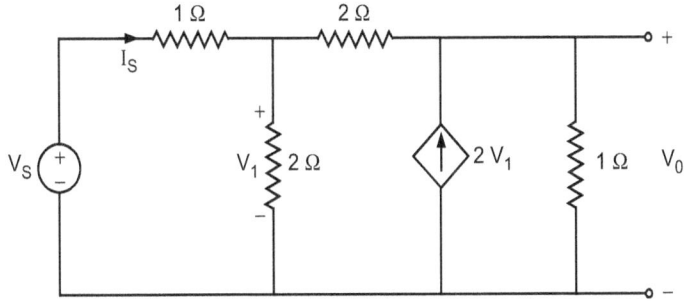

Fig. 1.92

Solution : The circuit consists of mixed sources. To carry out the mesh analysis convert the current source into an voltage source. The circuit is converted into two meshes as shown in Fig. 1.93. Choose I_1, I_2 as loop currents.

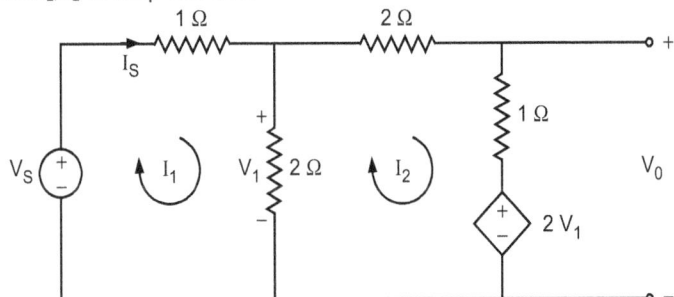

Fig. 1.93 : Equivalent circuit

Solve loop currents I_1 and I_2 in terms of V_S

KVL across loop I_1 gives

$$-I_1 - 2(I_1 - I_2) + V_S = 0$$
$$3I_1 - I_2 = V_S \quad\quad \text{... (a)}$$

Now, $V_1 = 2(I_1 - I_2)$ KVL across I_2 gives,

$$-2I_2 - I_2 - 2V_1 - 2(I_2 - I_1) = 0$$
$$-3I_2 - 2 \times 2(I_1 - I_2) - 2I_2 + 2I_1 = 0 \quad\quad \text{... (b)}$$

Solving this gives $I_2 = -2I_1$

Now put (b) into (a) gives $3I_1 + 2I_1 = V_S$

Or $\quad\quad I_1 = \dfrac{V_S}{7}$

Since, $\quad\quad I_1 = I_S$

We have $\quad\quad R_{in} = \dfrac{V_S}{I_S} = +7\,\Omega$

By (b) $\quad I_2 = -2I_1 = \dfrac{-2V_S}{7}$

$V_0 = I_2 + 2V_1 = I_2 + 2 \times 2\,(I_1 - I_2) = 4I_1 - 3I_2$

$\quad = \dfrac{4V_S}{7} - 3 \times \left(\dfrac{-2V_S}{7}\right) = \dfrac{4V_S}{7} + \dfrac{6V_S}{7} = \dfrac{10V_S}{7}$

Hence, voltage ratio $\left(\dfrac{V_0}{V_S}\right) = +\dfrac{10}{7}$

Note: Some times it is not possible in a circuit to have transformations to attain all sources of same type. In such cases some different techniques such as super node analysis or super mesh analysis or both combined need to be used. Following example explains this special technique.

Example 1.41 :

In the circuit shown use nodal analysis to find node voltages V_1, V_2 and V_3.

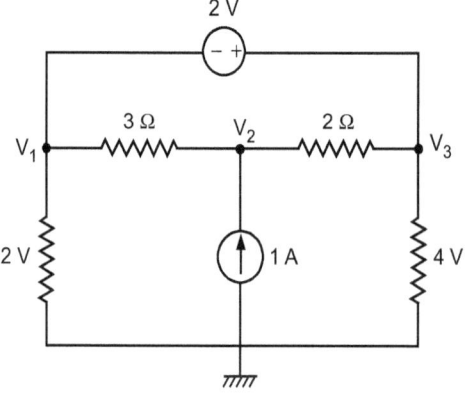

Fig. 1.94

Solution : Here voltage source has no series resistance and current source has no parallel resistance. Hence, the source transformation is not possible. We have to solve for V_1, V_2 and V_3 without transformation.

Now we have $\quad V_3 - V_1 = 2$ or $-V_1 + 0V_2 + V_3 = 2$ ... (a)

KCL at node V_2 gives second equation

$\quad\quad\quad I_4 - I_2 = 1$

$\quad\quad 2(V_2 - V_3) - 3(V_1 - V_2) = 1$

$\quad\quad -3V_1 + 5V_2 - 2V_3 = 1$ ... (b)

Now currents through 2V source (I_3) is given by

$\quad\quad I_3 = -I_1 - I_2 = I_5 - I_4$

$\quad\quad I_3 = -2V_1 - 3(V_1 - V_2) = 4V_3 - 2(V_2 - V_3)$ ... (c)

Hence $\quad V_1 - V_2 + V_3 = 0$

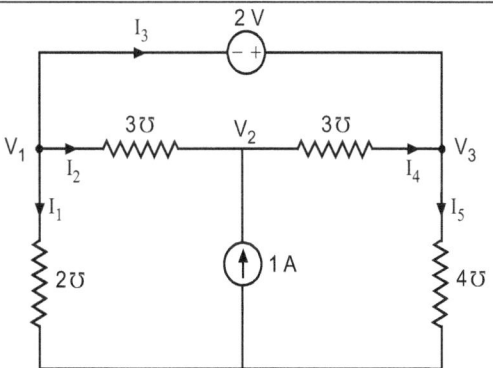

Fig. 1.95 : Circuit with branch currents

From (a), (b) and (c) solve V_1, V_2 and V_3

$$V_3 = \frac{\Delta_3}{\Delta} = \frac{\begin{vmatrix} -1 & 0 & 2 \\ -3 & 5 & 1 \\ 1 & -1 & 0 \end{vmatrix}}{\begin{vmatrix} -1 & 0 & 1 \\ -3 & 5 & -2 \\ 1 & -1 & 1 \end{vmatrix}}$$

$$= \frac{-1(1) + 0 + 2(3-5)}{-1(5+2) + 0 + 1(3-5)} = \frac{-5}{-5} = 1V$$

By (a) and (b)

$$V_1 = V_3 - 2 = -1V$$
$$V_2 = V_1 + V_3 = 0V$$

1.21 STAR (T) – DELTA (π) CONERSIONS

"One passive network is said to be the equivalent of the other network if the second passive network can be substituted for the first without change in current or voltage appearing at the terminals."

To understand T or π network equivalent of a circuit, consider any complicated network (N) containing many impedance (But no energy sources) as shown in Fig. 1.96 (a).

There are four variable as far as terminals are concerned. They are V_1, I_1, V_2 and I_2, out of these one variable is determined by external by external load i.e. $I_2 = \dfrac{V_2}{Z_L}$. Thus, there are only 3 variables V_1, I_1 and V_2 that are circuit dependent.

To get these variables we need three adjustable impedances. Two ways in which these three impedances can be connected are shown in Fig. 1.96 (b) and (c) which represent the T and π networks respectively. This is the basis of the star (T) or Delta (π) networks.

Many times star (T) or delta (π) connections are part of a complicated network. In order to simplify we need to convert a T into π network or vice versa. In the following section we shall consider these conversion.

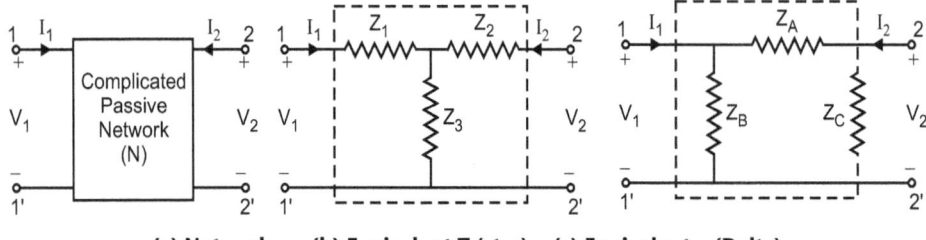

(a) Network (b) Equivalent T (star) (c) Equivalent π (Delta)

Fig. 1.96 : T and π equivalent circuits

1.21.1 Conversion of π (Delta) to T (star) Network

Given a π network with elements value Z_A, Z_B and Z_C as in Fig. 1.96 (c). The element values of equivalent T network (Z_1, Z_2 and Z_3) of Fig. 1.222 (c) are given by

$$Z_1 = \frac{Z_A Z_B}{Z_A + Z_B + Z_C} = \frac{Z_A Z_B}{\Sigma Z} \qquad \ldots 1.17\,(a)$$

$$Z_2 = \frac{Z_B Z_C}{Z_A + Z_B + Z_C} = \frac{Z_B Z_C}{\Sigma Z} \qquad \ldots 1.17\,(b)$$

$$Z_3 = \frac{Z_A Z_C}{Z_A + Z_B + Z_C} = \frac{Z_A Z_C}{\Sigma Z} \qquad \ldots 1.17\,(c)$$

where $\quad \Sigma Z = Z_A + Z_B + Z_C =$

Summation of network elements. It can be noted that π (Delta) to T (Star) conversion will create an additional node (O) as shown in Fig. 1.97.

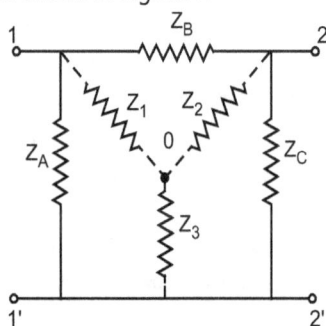

Fig. 1.97 : Conversion of π (Delta) to T (Star) Network

1.21.2 Conversion of T (Star) to π (Star) Network

Given a T network with elements value Z_1, Z_2 and Z_3 as in Fig. 1.96 (c). The element values equivalent π network (Z_A, Z_B and Z_C) of Fig. 1.222 (c) are given by

$$Z_A = \frac{Z_1 Z_2 + Z_2 Z_3 + Z_3 Z_1}{Z_2} = \frac{\Sigma Z}{Z_2} \qquad \ldots 1.18\,(a)$$

$$Z_B = \frac{Z_1 Z_2 + Z_2 Z_3 + Z_3 Z_1}{Z_3} = \frac{\Sigma Z}{Z_3} \qquad \text{...1.18 (b)}$$

$$Z_C = \frac{Z_1 Z_2 + Z_2 Z_3 + Z_3 Z_1}{Z_1} = \frac{\Sigma Z}{Z_1} \qquad \text{...1.18 (c)}$$

where $\Sigma Z = Z_1 Z_2 + Z_2 Z_3 + Z_3 Z_1$ = Sum of intermultiplication of T-network elements.

It can be noted that T (Star) to π (Delta) network conversion suppress a node as shown in Fig. 1.98.

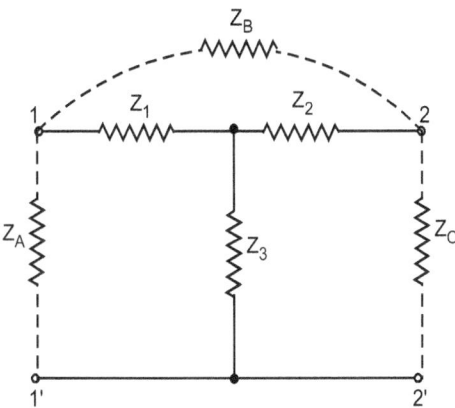

Fig. 1.98 : Conversion of p (Delta) network to T (Star) Network

Following examples explain Star-Delta conversions.

Example 1.42 :

By successive 'T' to 'π' conversions or vice versa, convert the network given into equivalent π-network.

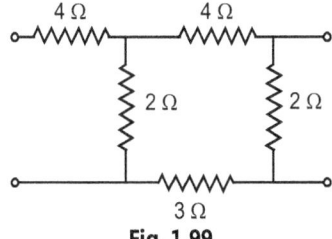

Fig. 1.99

Solution : We can add 3Ω and 4Ω resistor to give 7Ω which can be connected in place of 4Ω resistor. The resulting circuit is shown in Fig. 1.100 (a).

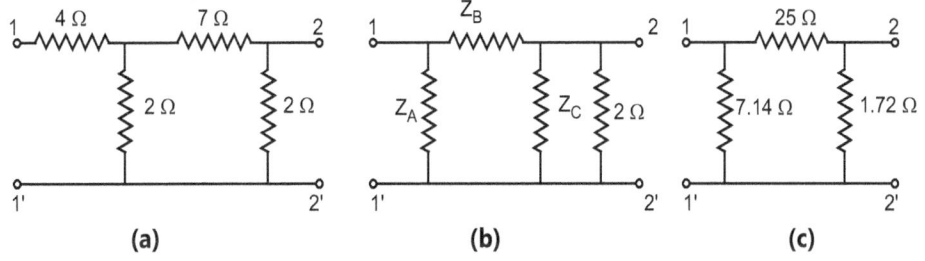

Fig. 1.100 : Equivalent Circuits

Now T (2Ω, 7Ω, 2Ω) is converted into π (Z_A, Z_B, Z_C) as shown in Fig. 1.100 (b) using formulae of equation (1.18).

$$Z_A = R_A = \frac{4 \times 2 + 2 \times 7 + 7 \times 4}{7} = \frac{50}{7} = 7.143 \, \Omega$$

$$Z_A = R_B = \frac{50}{2} = 25 \, \Omega$$

$$Z_C = R_C = \frac{50}{4} = 12.5 \, \Omega$$

Now Z_C and 2Ω are in parallel to give equivalent impedance of 12.5 ∥ 2 = 1.72 Ω
The resultant (equivalent) π-network is shown in Fig. (1.100) (c).

Example 1.43 : Convert the network into an equivalent π-network by use of successive T or π conversion or vice versa.

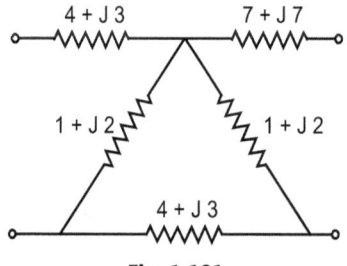

Fig. 1.101

Solution : Convert the π-network formed by (1 + J2), (1+ J2) and (4 + J3) into T-network. The resultant equivalent network is shown in Fig. 1.102 (a). Making use of equation (1.17) we get

$$Z_1 = \frac{(1 + J2)(1 + J2)}{(1 + J2) + (1 + J2) + (4 + J3)} = \frac{4.47 \angle 126.9°}{(6 + J7)}$$

$$= \frac{4.47 \angle 127°}{\angle 49.5°}$$

$$= 0.49 \angle 77.5° = (0.105 + J\,0.473) \text{ ohms}$$

$$Z_3 = Z_2 = \frac{(1 + J2)(4 + J3)}{(6 + J7)} = \frac{3 \angle 36.9° \times 2.23 \angle 63.4°}{9.22 \angle 49.5°}$$

$$= 1.126 \angle 51° = (0.763 + J0.942) \text{ ohms}$$

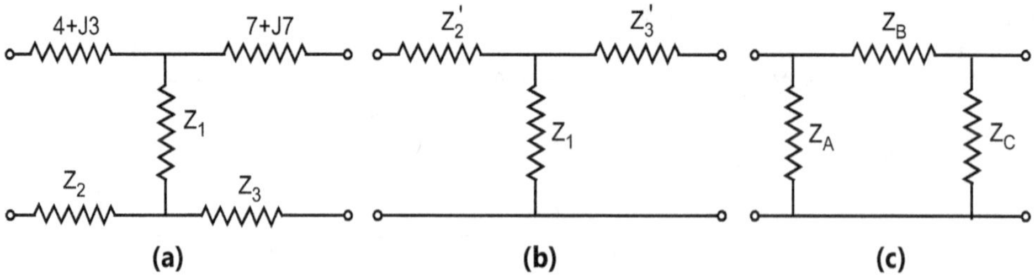

(a) (b) (c)

Fig. 1.102 : Equivalent Circuits

Now lower elements can be added with upper elements to give resultant T-network as shown

where

$$Z_2' = (4 + J3) + Z_2 = (4.763 + J3.942) \text{ ohms}$$

$$Z_3' = (7 + J7) + Z_3 = (7.763 + J7.942) \text{ ohms}$$

Now by use of equation (1.18) convert the T (Z_2', Z_1, Z_3') into π-network (Z_A, Z_B, Z_C) as shown in Fig. 1.102 (c) (calculation of this conversion is left to the readers of this book.

Example 1.44 :

Using Δ–T and T –Δ conversions, find current I in the network shown.

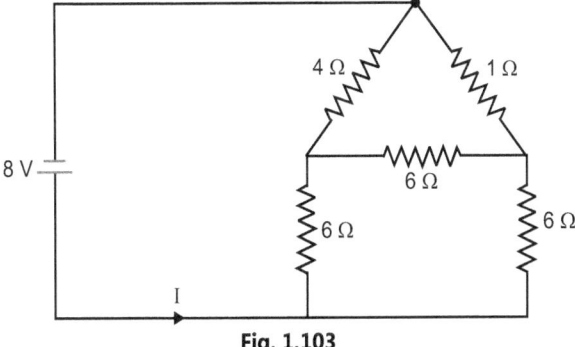

Fig. 1.103

Solution : We have to find equivalent resistance across the 8V battery to find current (I), convert π-network of the element (6Ω, 6Ω, 6Ω) into T-network as shown in the Fig. 1.104 (a) using equations (1.17). we get

$$Z_1 = Z_2 = Z_3 = \frac{6 \times 6}{6 + 6 + 6} = \frac{36}{18} = 2 \text{ ohms}$$

Now two arms of 6Ω (4 + 2) each are in parallel to give equivalent of 3Ω. This is in series with 2Ω to give equivalent resistance of 5Ω across battery.

Thus, Current (I) $= \dfrac{8}{2 + 3} = \dfrac{8}{5} = 16 \text{ Amp.}$

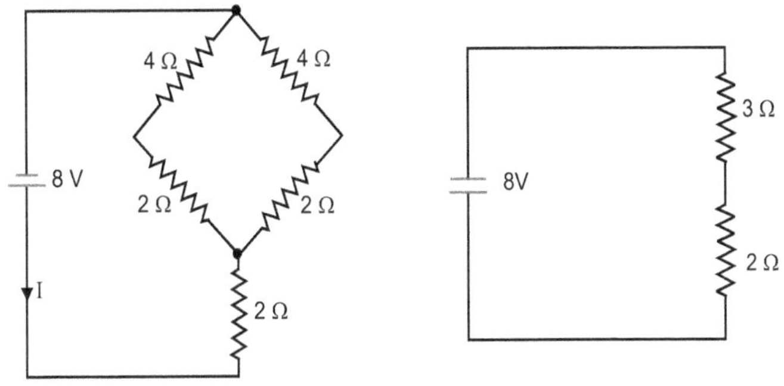

Fig. 1.104 : Equivalent Circuits

Example 1.45 :

Use a Δ to T transformation to find currents I_1, I_2 and I_3 in the circuit shown

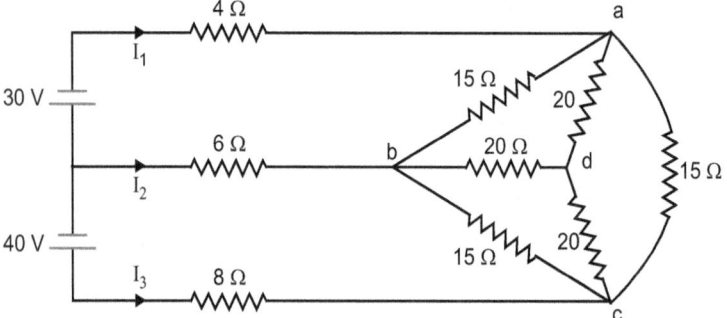

Fig. 1.105

Solution : Convert the Δ of (15Ω, 15Ω, 15Ω) into 'T' network. The value of each element is $= \dfrac{15 \times 15}{45} = 5\,\Omega$. The resultant simplified network is shown in Fig. 1.106 (a) across the terminals a, b and c.

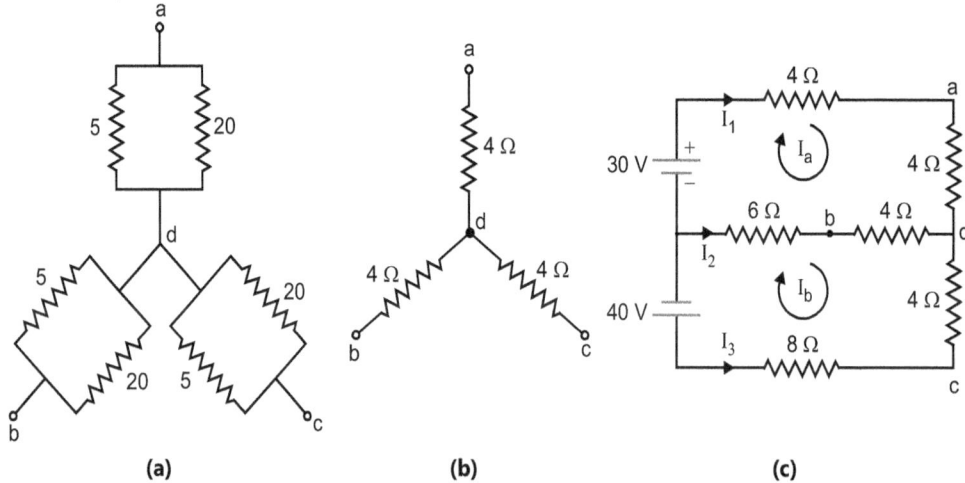

(a) (b) (c)

Fig. 1.106 : Equivalent Circuits

Now 5Ω and 20Ω are in parallel to give the equivalent of 4Ω. The resultant simplified T-network across a, b, c is shown in Fig. 1.106 (b). The complete resultant equivalent circuit is shown in Fig. 1.106 (c). Let I_a, I_b be the two loops currents. The KVL across two loop gives,

$$18 I_a - 10 I_b = 30 \qquad \text{...(a)}$$
$$-10 I_a + 22 I_b = -40 \qquad \text{...(b)}$$

Solve (a) and (b) to give two currents as $I_a = +0.88$ A and $I_b = -1.42$ A

Now,
$$I_1 = I_a = 0.88 \text{ Amp.}$$
$$I_2 = (I_b - I_a) = -1.42 - 0.88 = -2.3 \text{ Amp.}$$
$$I_3 = -I_b = 1.42 \text{ Amp.}$$

Example 1.46 :

Find equivalent T-network of the bridged T-network shown in Fig. 1.107. Make use of T to π conversion. Also find equivalent π-network.

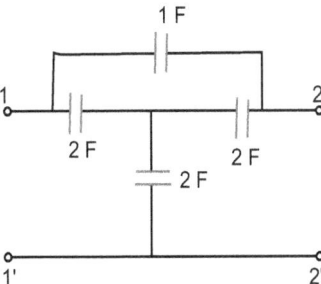

Fig. 1.107 : Bridged T-Equivalent

Solution : The reactance of a capacitor is $\dfrac{-j}{wC}$. Using this basic relation the given network can be redrawn as shown in Fig. 1.108 (a).

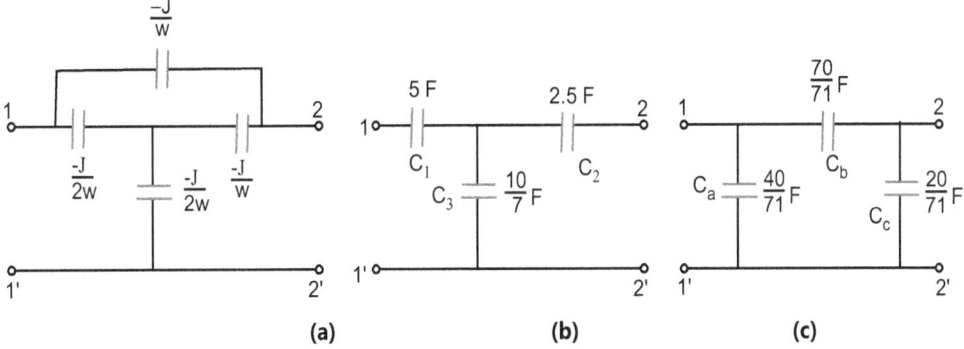

(a)　　　　　　　(b)　　　　　　　(c)

Fig. 1.108 : Equivalent circuits

Convert π-network of impedance $\left(\dfrac{-j}{2w}, \dfrac{-j}{w}, \dfrac{-j}{w}\right)$ into T-network whose values of impedances of element is given by,

$$Z_1 = \dfrac{\dfrac{-j}{2w} \times \dfrac{-j}{w}}{\dfrac{-j}{w} \dfrac{-j}{w} \dfrac{-j}{w}} = \dfrac{\dfrac{-j}{2w^2}}{\dfrac{-j5}{2w}} = \dfrac{-j}{5w}$$

Thus,　　　$C_1 = 5F$

$$Z_1 = \dfrac{\dfrac{-j}{w} \times \dfrac{-j}{w}}{\dfrac{-j5}{2w}} = \dfrac{\dfrac{-1}{w^2}}{\dfrac{-j5}{2w}} = \dfrac{-j2}{5w}$$

This impedance corresponds to $C_2 = 2.5$ F

$$Z_3 = \frac{\frac{-J}{w} \times \frac{-J}{w}}{\frac{-J5}{2w}} = \frac{-J}{5w}$$

This impedance is in series with $\frac{-J}{2w}$ to give equivalent impedance of

$$Z_3' = \frac{-J}{5w} - \frac{J}{2w} = -J\frac{7}{10w}$$

This impedance corresponds to $C_3 = \frac{10}{7}$ F

The T-network is shown in Fig. 1.234 (b). To obtain equivalent π-network.

Convert T-network of impedance $\left(\frac{-J}{5w}, \frac{-J2}{5w}, \frac{-J7}{10w}\right)$ into π-network as shown in Fig. 1.108 (c) where the element values are given by equation (1.32).

$$Z_n = \frac{\left[\left(\frac{-J}{5w} \times \frac{-J2}{5w}\right) + \left(\frac{-J2}{5w} \times \frac{-J7}{10w}\right) + \left(\frac{-J7}{10w} \times \frac{-J7}{2w}\right)\right]}{\frac{-J2}{5w}}$$

$$= \frac{\frac{-2}{25w^2} - \frac{14}{50w^2} - \frac{7}{20w^2}}{\frac{-J2}{5w}} = \frac{\frac{-71}{100w^2}}{\frac{-J2}{5w}} = \frac{-J71}{40w}$$

This corresponds to capacitor $C_a = \frac{40}{71}$ F

$$Z_b = \frac{\frac{-71}{100 w^2}}{-J\frac{7}{10w}} = -J\frac{71}{70w}$$

This corresponds to capacitor

$$C_b = \frac{70}{71} \text{ F}$$

$$Z_c = \frac{\frac{-71}{100w^2}}{\frac{-J}{5w}} = -J\frac{71}{20w}$$

This corresponds to capacitor $C_c = \frac{20}{71}$ F

1.22 NETWORK GRAPH

A graph is a collection of nodes and branches. In a graph each component of an electric network represented by a in line segment called as branch. The branches are connected at nodes. The basic elements of this graph theory are branches, nodes, loops and meshes.

Branch is a line segment representing an single element. It is connection between two nodes. Node is a point at which two or more elements are connected commonly. It is also called junction between two or more elements. Loop is a path between the two nodes. It forms a closed circuit. Mesh is a loop which does not contain any other loops within it. A graph of a network can be easily drawn with the help of basic elements. The network shown in Fig. 1.109 has four nodes and six branches.

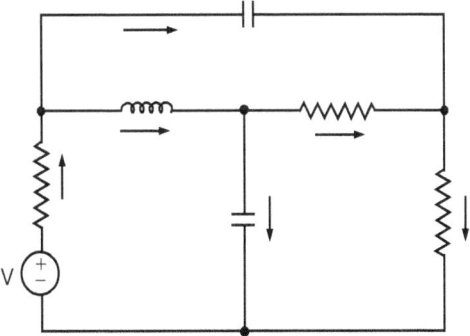

Fig. 1.109 : Electrical network

The graph of network can be drawn by replacing the element with line segment. These line segment with line segment. These line segment are joining at the nodes. The energy sources such as voltage source and current source are replaced by their internal resistances. The voltage sources are short circuited and the current sources are open circuited. The internal impedance of voltage source and current sources are zero and infinite respectively.

In a Electrical network each branches and nodes are numbered as shown in Fig. 1.110 (a) and its graph is shown in Fig. 1.110 (b).

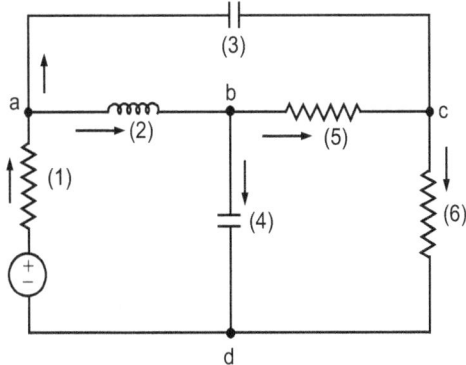

Fig. 1.110 (a) : Electrical network assigned with node and branch number

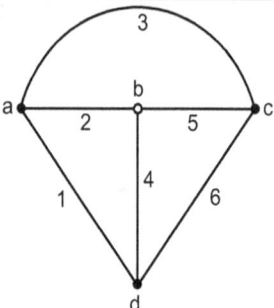

Fig. 1.110 (b) : Network group of electrical network (undirected graph)

The graph shown in Fig. 1.110 (b) has size branches and four nodes. This graph is called as undirected graph. If each branch or line segment has a direction then this type of graph is called as directed graph. The directed graph of Fig. 1.110 (a) is shown in Fig. 1.111.

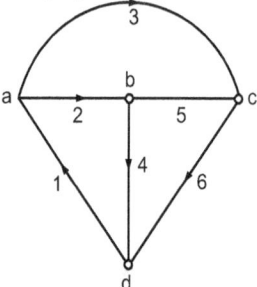

Fig. 1.111 : Directed graph of electrical network Fig. 1.110 (a)

1.22.1 Planer and Non-planar Graph

A graph is divided into two category such as planar and non-planar graph. A graph is drawn on a plane surface with a no crossing in branches called as planar graph. In a planar graph two branches are not cross each other. A non planar graph drawn on a two dimensional surface with two or more branches are crosses. A planar and non planar graph is shown in Fig. 1.112.

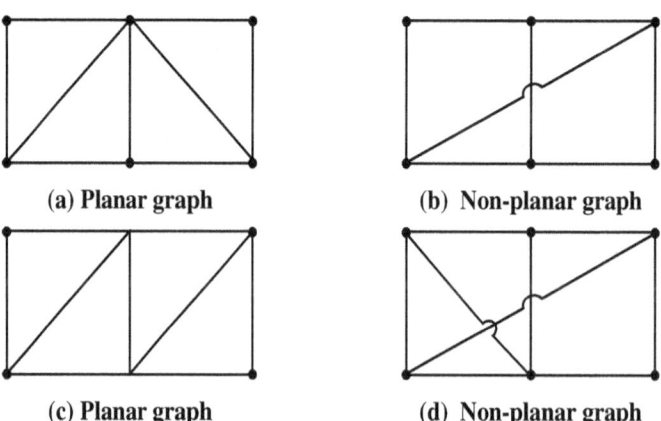

(a) Planar graph (b) Non-planar graph

(c) Planar graph (d) Non-planar graph

Fig. 1.112 : Planar and non planar graph

1.22.2 Elements of Network Graph

The network graph are independent of the type of components that make the branches. The network graph consists of elements such as branch, nodes, loop, meshes, path, rank of graph, subgraph, connected graph. A branch is a line segment representing an single element. A node is a point at which two or more elements are connected coming.

Loop is a closed path between two nodes.

A path is a sequence of branches in an subgraph having following properties.

(i) At the internal nodes, two branches are incident of the subgraph.

(ii) At the terminal nodes, there is incident one branch of the subgraph.

A rank of graph is $(n-1)$, where n is the number of nodes or vertices of the network graph.

The subset of nodes and branches of a graph is called as subgraph. A subgraph is said to be proper subgraph if it consists of less than total branches and nodes. A subgraph is shown in Fig. 1.113.

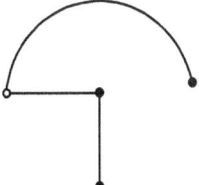

Fig. 1.113 : Subgraph of the graph of Fig. 1.110 (b)

In connected graph at least one path is exists between two nods.

1.23 TREES

A tree is connected sub graph of connected graph with all nodes of the graph without any loop. The graph of a network have more number of trees. In a graph theory the number of nodes in a graph is equal with the number of nodes in a tree. In a tree branches are called as twigs. A tree contain $(n-1)$ branches, where n is the number of nodes or vertices in the graph. i.e. A tree has $(n-1)$ twigs. Fig. 1.114 (a) shows that the graph of a network and Fig. 1.114 (b) shows the tree of a graph (G).

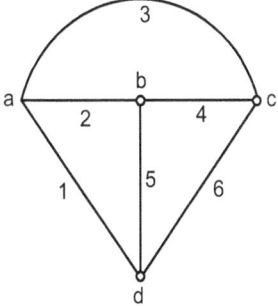

Fig. 1.114 (a) : Graph of a network

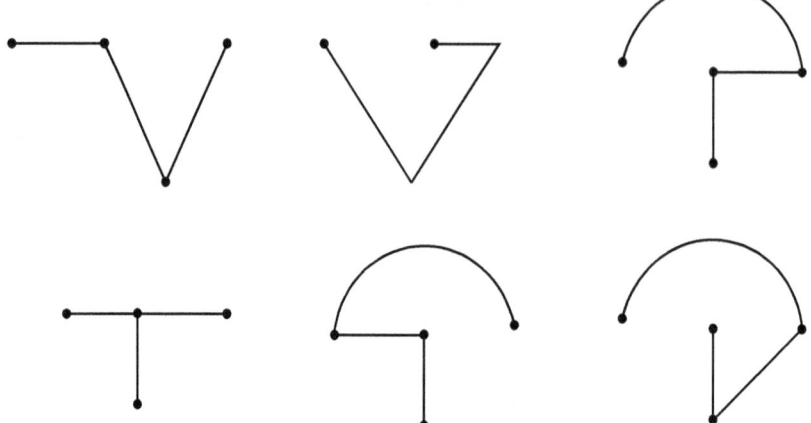

Fig. 1.114 (b) : Trees of a network Fig. 1.114 (a)

A tree has following properties
(i) It must contains all the nodes in a graph.
(ii) The graph of a tree have (n – 1) branches where 'n' is the number nodes of a graph.
(iii) A tree doesn't have any closed path.

In a graph theory, for a given graph there are many possible trees and it depends on the number of branches and nodes. The branches of the tree are called as twigs. The branches removed from the tree are termed as links. The links are as good as complement of twig. The number of twigs are (n – 1). If b be the number of branches then the total number of links are b – n + 1 or b – (n – 1).

1.24 COTREE

The branches of the graph which are not in the tree form the cotree or complement of the tree. For a given graph it is possible to draw numerous tree. The branches of the tree are called as twigs. The remaining branches of the tree are called as links or chords. The branches which are not on a tree are called as links or chords. All links of a given tree is called as the co tree of the graph. The graph is obtained from combining the links and twigs. The cotree of the graph is shown in Fig. 1.115.

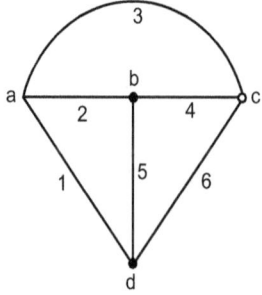

Fig. 1.115 (a) Graph of a network

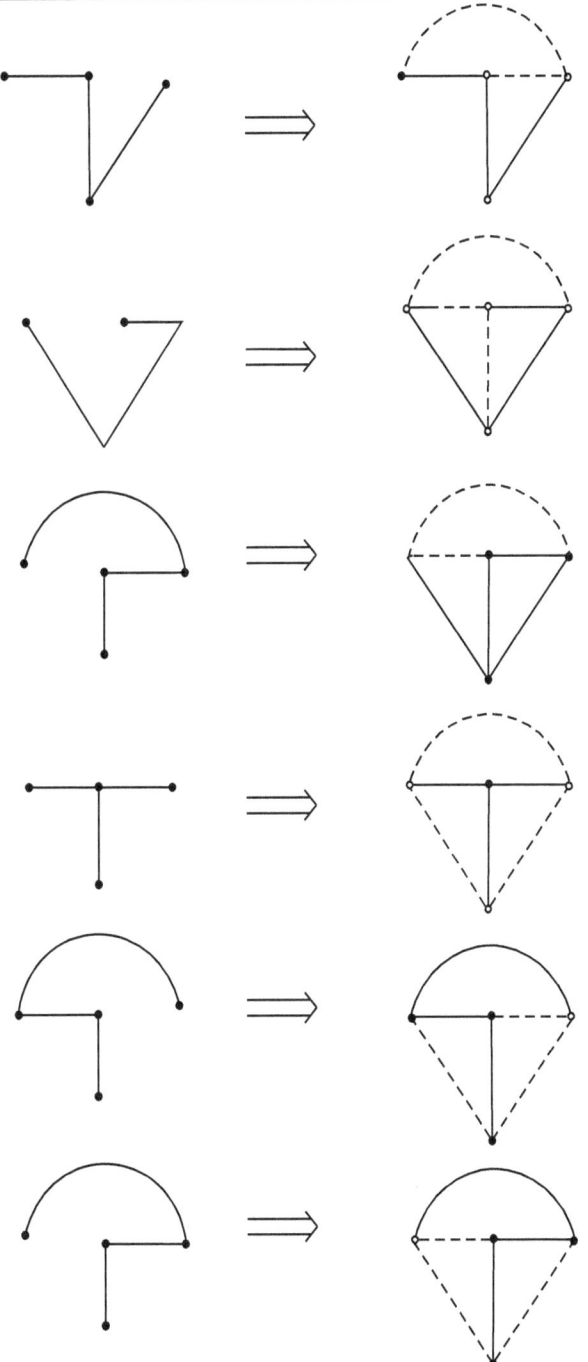

Fig. 1.115 (b) Tree and corresponding cotree of graph

In Fig. 1.115 (b), the tree of a graph and its corresponding cotree is shown. The dotted line in the cotree is called as links or chords. The number of twigs in a tree is (n – 1), where n is the number of nodes. The number of links 'l' in the graph are b-twigs. i.e. b − (n − 1) or b − n + 1. It means that the number of links in a cotree are b − n + 1 or b − (n − 1). The links are called as branches of the cotree. The concept of tree is applicable to only a connected graph. The concept of unconnected graph is called as Forest. A set of trees are called as Forest, which is one for each separate part of the graph. The rank of the connected graph is equal to the sum of the ranks of the connected subgraph.

1.25 LOOP OR CIRCUIT

In a graph theory of tree, a link is connected or added to a tree form a closed path a graph called as loop (or a circuit). If path are coincide at the terminate, it will form loop. A loop of the graph in a network is closed path of the subgraph. The loop of the graph has following properties.

(a) There are minimum two branches in the loop.

(b) There are exactly two paths between any pair of nodes in the Graph.

(c) In a loop, the maximum number of possible branches are equal to the number of nodes in the graph.

The loops of the graph are:

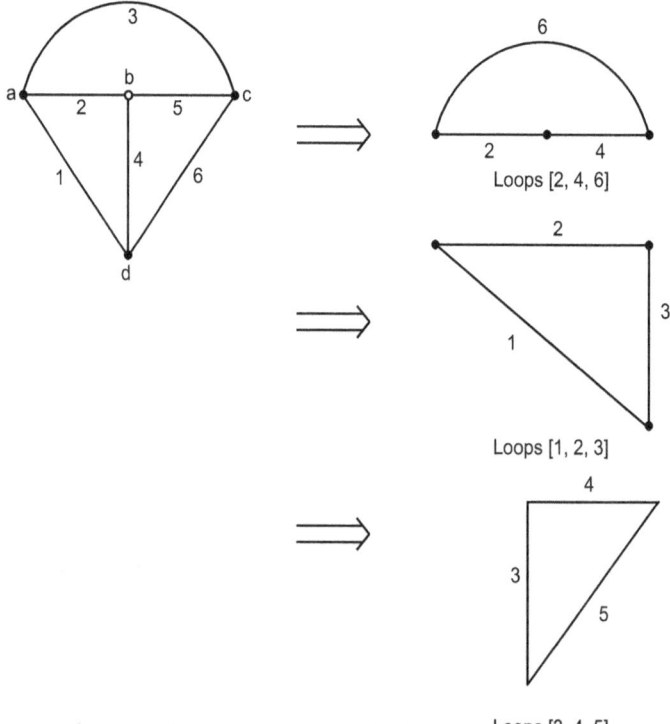

(a) Graph of network   (b) Loops of the graph

Fig. 1.116 : Loops of the given graph

1.26 INCIDENCE MATRIX

When a graph is given, it is possible to tell, which branches are joined to which node and whether the orientation of a branch is toward a node or away from the node. This information is given in coincise mathematical form by an array, in which the nodes of the graph result in the rows and the branches results in the columns as shown in Fig. 1.117.

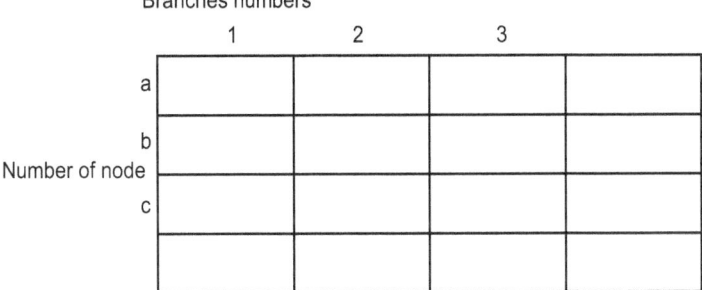

Fig. 1.117 : Incidence matrix

The nodes in the incidence matrix are numbered a, b, c, ... etc. The branches in the incidence matrix are numbered in 1, 2, 3, ... etc. Numbers are used in spaces to represent the graph is connected. These numbers are called as the elements of the matrix or incidence matrix. These elements of the matrix are represented by the symbol a with two subscript, the first subscript denoting row and the second column that the element is present. i.e. a_{12} means the branch two is joined to node 1. In other way we can express elements in terms of a_{ij}.

where j is the branch of the graph.

i is the node of the graph.

If a j branch is not joined, (incident) to a i node, the corresponding element in the matrix is given the value 0.

If aj branch is joined (incident) to a i node, it has one of two possible orientation due to arrow placed in a graph. If the orientation of the j branch is away from the i node, the corresponding matrix element value is written as + 1. If the orientation of the j branch is towards the i node, the corresponding matrix element value is written as – 1. The representation of the elements of the matrix have the following value.

 $a_{ij} = 1$, if branch j is jointed (incident) at node i and its orientation is away from node i.

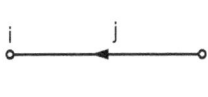 $a_{ij} = -1$, if branch j is jointed (incident) at node i and its orientation is towards node i.

 $a_{ij} = 0$, if branch j is not joined (incident) at node i.

The complete incidence matrix for a given graph shown in Fig. 1.118 is as given below

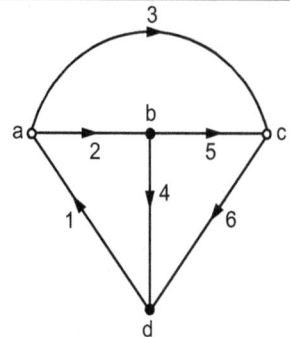

Fig. 1.118 : General graph of a network

Nodes	Branches					
	1	2	3	4	5	6
a	−1	1	1	0	0	0
b	0	−1	0	1	1	0
c	0	0	−1	0	−1	1
d	1	0	0	−1	0	−1

i.e.

$$A_a = \begin{bmatrix} -1 & 1 & 1 & 0 & 0 & 0 \\ 0 & -1 & 0 & 1 & 1 & 0 \\ 0 & 0 & -1 & 0 & -1 & 1 \\ 1 & 0 & 0 & -1 & 0 & -1 \end{bmatrix}$$

The complete incidence matrix is represented by A_a for a given graph shown in Fig. 1.118. It is observed that the sum of the elements in any column is zero. The order of the complete column is zero. The order of the complete incidence matrix is n × b, when n = nodes of a network graph and b is the number of branches of a network graph.

1.26.1 Reduced Incidence Matrix

The matrix obtained from the complete incidence matrix by eliminating one of the row is called as reduced incidence matrix. It is also called as incidence matrix. The order of reduced incidence matrix is (n − 1) × b.

To obtained reduced incidence matrix, select a tree of a graph. The incidence matrix is obtained by a arranging a columns in reduced incidence matrix such that the first column of a matrix corresponding to the twigs of a selected tree and the last column (b − n + 1). Corresponding to the links of the selected tree.

Table 1.1: Twigs, links and tree of a given graph shown in Fig. 1.118

Twigs	Tree	Links
(2, 4, 6)	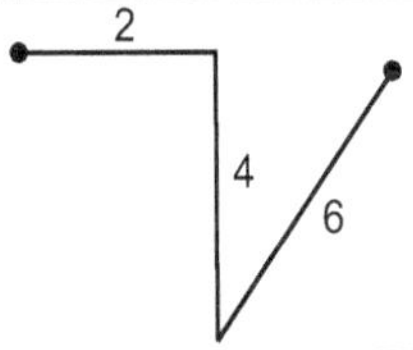	(1, 3, 5)
(2, 4, 5)	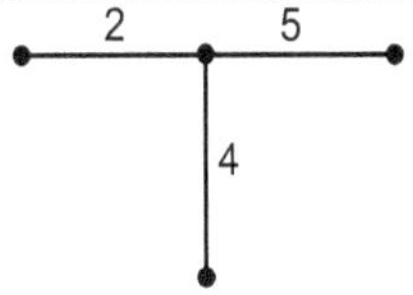 **Fig.**	(1, 3, 6)
(1, 5, 6)	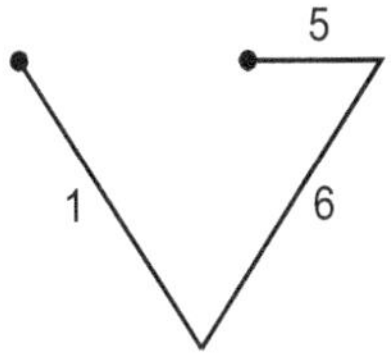 **Fig.**	(2, 3, 4)
(1, 3, 4)	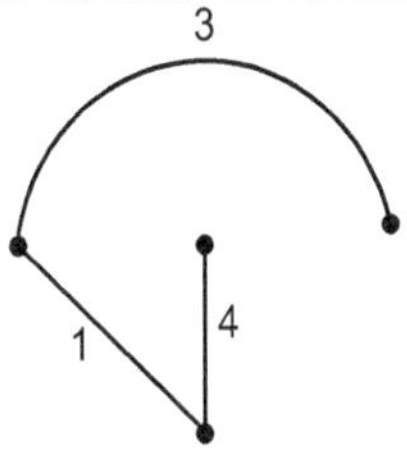 **Fig.**	(2, 5, 6)
(3, 4, 5)	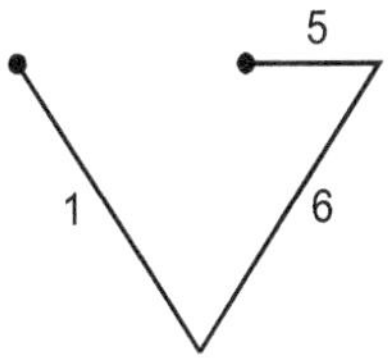 **Fig.**	(1, 2, 6)
(1, 3, 5)		(2, 4, 6)

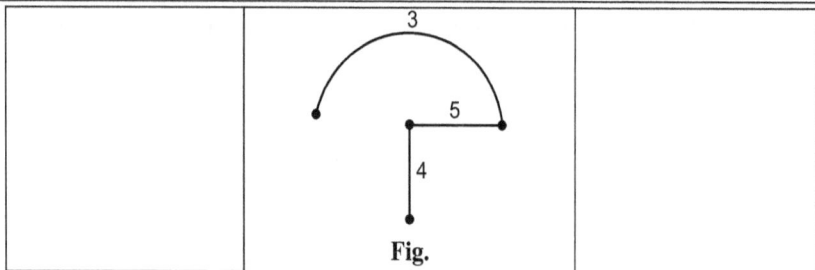

Fig.

Now select a tree as shown in Fig. 1.119.

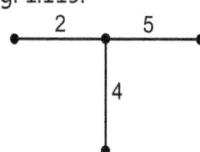

Fig. 1.119 : Tree of a given showing in Fig. 1.118

The reduced incidence matrix for a given tree can be arranged in Twigs and Links wise in the matrix, by eliminating the last row.

$$A = \begin{matrix} & \overbrace{2\ 4\ 5}^{\text{Twigs}} & \overbrace{1\ 3\ 6}^{\text{Links}} \\ & \begin{bmatrix} 1 & 0 & 0 & -1 & 1 & 0 \\ -1 & 1 & 1 & 0 & 0 & 0 \\ 0 & 0 & -1 & 0 & -1 & 1 \end{bmatrix} \end{matrix}$$

The matrix is subdivided in twigs matrix and links matrix i.e.

$$A = [A_t : A_L]$$
$$A_t = \text{twigs matrix}$$
$$A_L = \text{links matrix}$$

The order of the A_t matrix is $(n-1) \times (n-1)$ and the order of A_L matrix is $(n-1) \times (b-n+1)$. The rank of reduced incidence matrix is $(n-1)$.

1.26.2 Number of Possible Trees of a Graph

The number of possible trees obtained using transpose of the reduced incidence matrix A be A^T.

Number of possible trees = $|A\,A^T|$

The reduced incidence matrix is given by $\begin{bmatrix} 1 & 0 & 0 & -1 & 1 & 0 \\ -1 & 1 & 1 & 0 & 0 & 0 \\ 0 & 0 & -1 & 0 & -1 & 1 \end{bmatrix}$

Then transpose of this matrix will be

$$A^T = \begin{bmatrix} 1 & -1 & 0 \\ 0 & 1 & 0 \\ 0 & 1 & -1 \\ -1 & 0 & 0 \\ 1 & 0 & -1 \\ 0 & 0 & 1 \end{bmatrix}$$

The number of all possible trees of the graph = AA^T

$$= \begin{bmatrix} 1 & 0 & 0 & -1 & 1 & 0 \\ -1 & 1 & 1 & 0 & 0 & 0 \\ 0 & 0 & -1 & 0 & -1 & 1 \end{bmatrix} \begin{bmatrix} 1 & -1 & 0 \\ 0 & 1 & 0 \\ 0 & 1 & -1 \\ -1 & 0 & 0 \\ 1 & 0 & -1 \\ 0 & 0 & 1 \end{bmatrix}$$

$$= \begin{bmatrix} 3 & -1 & -1 \\ -1 & 3 & -1 \\ -1 & -1 & 3 \end{bmatrix}$$

= 3 (9 – 1) + 1 (–3 – 1) – 1 (1 + 3) = 24 – 4 – 4

[A A^T] = 16

For the given graph there are 16 trees can be drawn.

1.26.3 Properties of Incidence Matrix

(i) The algebraic sum of the column entries are zero.

(ii) The rank of the incidence matrix is (n – 1).

(iii) The determinant of the incidence matrix of a closed loop is zero.

The incidence matrix represents the number of nodes and branches. The nodes of the graph has two entries i.e. ± 1, it means that each branch is associated with that node. Every column has two entries i.e. + 1 and – 1.

Let us consider closed path of a given graph shown in Fig. 1.120. Obtain the incidence matrix for a given graph of a closed loop shown in Fig. 2.12

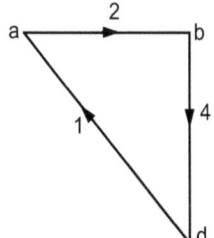

Fig. 1.120 : Closed loop of a graph shown in Fig. 1.118

Nodes	Branches		
	1	2	4
a	−1	1	0
b	0	−1	1
d	1	0	−1

The complete incidence matrix of a closed loop is

$$A = \begin{bmatrix} -1 & 1 & 0 \\ 0 & -1 & 1 \\ 1 & 0 & -1 \end{bmatrix}$$

$$A = -1 \begin{vmatrix} -1 & 1 \\ 0 & -1 \end{vmatrix} - 1 \begin{vmatrix} 0 & 1 \\ 1 & -1 \end{vmatrix} + 0 \begin{vmatrix} 0 & -1 \\ 1 & 0 \end{vmatrix}$$

$$A = -1 + 1 + 0$$
$$A = 0$$

Hence proved.

The determinant of the incidence matrix of a closed loop is zero.

Example 1.48 : Draw the oriented graph from the complete incidence matrix.

$$A = \begin{bmatrix} -1 & 1 & 0 & -1 & 0 & 0 \\ 0 & 0 & -1 & 1 & 0 & -1 \\ 1 & 0 & 0 & 0 & -1 & 1 \\ 0 & -1 & 1 & 0 & 1 & 0 \end{bmatrix}$$

Solution : First identify the number of nodes as rows of the network graph, from given incidence matrix n = 4. The number of branches are equal to number of column of the incidence matrix. i.e. b = 6. Jot down the nodes a, b, c, d as shown in Fig. 1.121. New consider the branch and find its orientation and incidence to nodes. If branch is between two nodes then according is between two nodes then according to the rule it will be assign the direction according to the value 1 or −1.

	1	2	3	4	5	6
a	−1	1	0	−1	0	0
b	0	0	−1	1	0	−1
c	1	0	0	0	−1	−1
d	0	−1	1	0	1	0

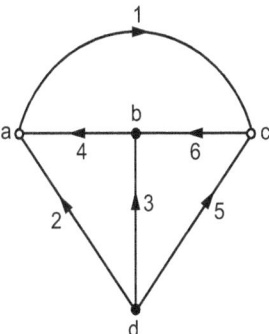

Fig. 1.121

1.26.4 The KCL Equation for Incidence Matrix

Consider a branch 1 it shows that at node a it has −1 and at node c it has value of 1, it means that branch oriented from node c to node a. Similarly we can obtain the oriented graph from the incidence matrix. The incidence matrix A is used in writing the KCL equations for the oriented graph. Let us consider the oriented graph shown in Fig. 1.122. The branches of the oriented graph are represented by currents.

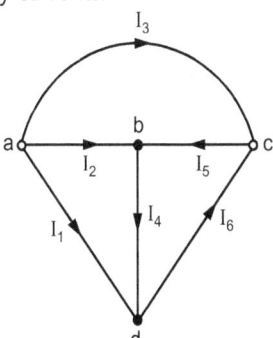

Fig. 1.122 : Oriented graph

The oriented graph represented by four nodes as a, b, c, d. Consider the reference direction of the branch currents corresponding to the orientation of the branches. Apply KCL at each nodes, we get

At node a, $\quad I_1 + I_2 + I_3 = 0$

At node b, $\quad -I_2 + I_4 - I_5 = 0$

At node c, $-I_3 + I_5 - I_6 = 0$

At node d, $-I_1 - I_4 + I_6 = 0$

Above equations are combined in matrix form which can be written as

$$\begin{bmatrix} 1 & 1 & 1 & 0 & 0 & 0 \\ 0 & -1 & 0 & 1 & -1 & 0 \\ 0 & 0 & -1 & 0 & 1 & -1 \\ -1 & 0 & 0 & -1 & 0 & 1 \end{bmatrix} \begin{bmatrix} I_1 \\ I_2 \\ I_3 \\ I_4 \\ I_5 \\ I_6 \end{bmatrix} = \begin{bmatrix} 0 \\ 0 \\ 0 \\ 0 \end{bmatrix}$$

Or $A\, I_b = 0$

Where A is incidence matrix of graph and I_b is column matrix or branch current vector.

The reduced incidence matrix can be obtained by considering one node as a reference node and writing equation of all remaining node. In our example of oriented graph there are four nodes. Out of which one node is considered as reference node or datum node. Then write the KCL expression for node a, b, and c. These equation can be written in matrix form which is called as reduced incidence matrix of the oriented graph.

1.27 LOOP MATRIX OR CIRCUIT MATRIX

It path are coincide at the terminal it will form loop. A loop of the graph in a given oriented graph. The way in which the loop or circuit equation written in matrix form which is called as loop matrix or circuit matrix. In the matrix form of loop equation an orientation is specified for each loop. The orientation can be arbitrary for a given graph. The elements in the loop matrix are valued as ± 1. The loop matrix is represented as B of a graph of their elements are b_{lb}. The subscript 'l' is used for loop number and subscript 'b' is used for the branches. If the branch is in that loop of their orientation coincide marked as + 1. If the branch is in that loop and its orientation doesnot coincide mark as -1 in loop matrix. If the branch is not in the loop then that element is marked as '0'.

The matrix elements are expressed as follows.

b_{lb} = 1: if the branch 'b' is in that loop 'l' and its orientation coincide

b_{lb} = -1: if the branch b is in that loop 'l' and its orientation does not coincide.

b_{lb} = 0: Branch 'b' is not in that loop 'l'

The branches in the loop are written as + 1 or –1 according the orientation. These are more loops in the circuit. The oriented graph is shown in Fig. 1.123.

The loops for the oriented graph are

Loop 1: (1, 2, 4)

Loop 2: (4, 5, 6)

Loop 3: (2, 3, 5)

Loop 4: (1, 3, 6)

Loop 5: (1, 3, 4, 5)
Loop 6: (2, 3, 4, 6)

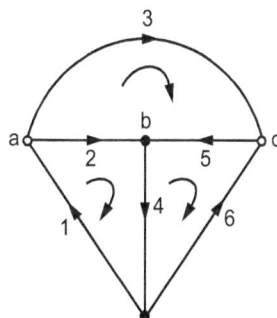

Fig. 1.123 : Orient graph representing loops

These loops equation are obtained by taking the clockwise orientation. These loops equation are written in the matrix form using orientation which is called as Loop matrix.

$$B = \begin{matrix} & \text{Branches} \\ \text{Loops} \begin{matrix}1\\2\\3\\4\\5\\6\end{matrix} & \begin{matrix}1 & 2 & 3 & 4 & 5 & 6\end{matrix} \\ & \begin{bmatrix} 1 & 1 & 0 & 1 & 0 & 0 \\ 0 & 0 & 0 & -1 & -1 & -1 \\ 0 & 1 & 1 & 0 & 1 & 0 \\ 1 & 0 & 1 & 0 & 0 & -1 \\ 1 & 0 & 1 & 1 & 1 & 0 \\ 0 & -1 & 1 & -1 & 0 & -1 \end{bmatrix} \end{matrix}$$

The loop matrix or circuit matrix can be expressed as letter B.

$$B = \begin{bmatrix} 1 & 1 & 0 & 1 & 0 & 0 \\ 0 & 0 & 0 & -1 & -1 & -1 \\ 0 & 1 & 1 & 0 & 1 & 0 \\ 1 & 0 & 1 & 0 & 0 & -1 \\ 1 & 0 & 1 & 1 & 1 & 0 \\ 0 & -1 & 1 & -1 & 0 & -1 \end{bmatrix}$$

The rank of the loop matrix or circuit matrix or circuit matrix is $nl = b - nt$ or $b - n + 1$. Then nl loops are the minimal required to describe the oriented graph. Where nl is the number of loops of the circuit and nt is the number of links of the graph.

1.28 FUNDAMENTAL LOOPS (F-LOOPS) OR F-CIRCUIT OR TIESET

The Fundamental loops are obtained from the selected tree of graph. In any tree, a link is connected which forms the loop or circuit this loop is called as fundamental loop or F-loop.

Consider a oriented graph shown in Fig. 1.124 (a). It has 4 nodes and 6 branches. Let, select a tree of oriented graph which is shown in Fig. 1.124 (b). It has three branches which is called as twigs. 2, 4 and 5. The link of the tree are branches 1, 3 and 6. The f-loop 1 is formed by adding branch 3 to the tree as shown in Fig. 1.124 (c). The F-loop 2 is formed by adding branch 6 to the tree as shown in Fig. 1.124 (d).

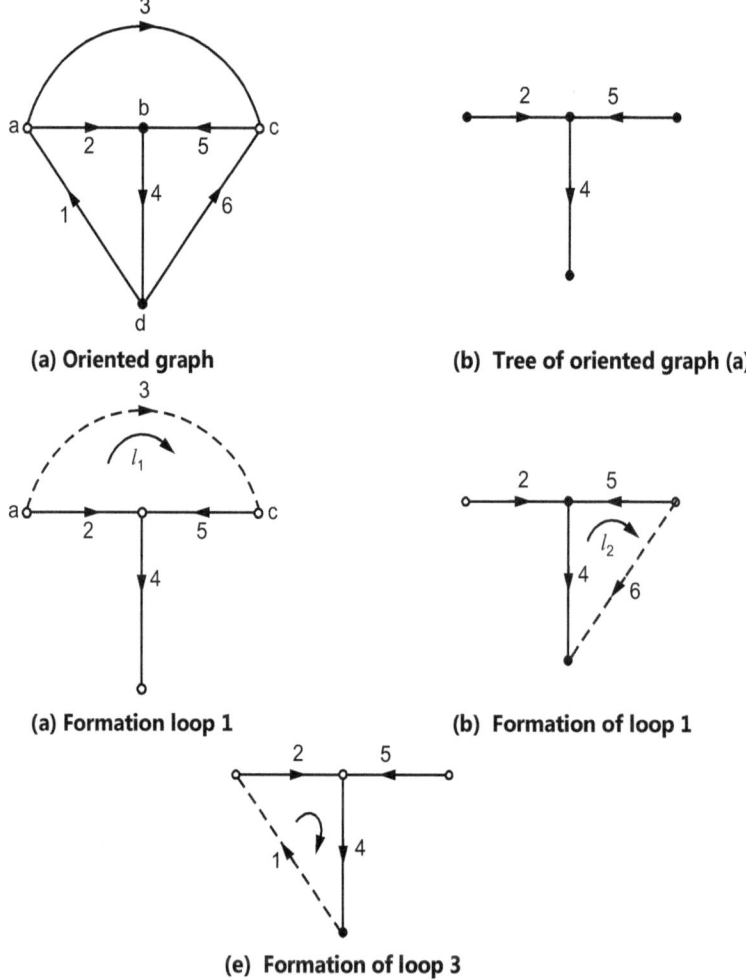

(a) Oriented graph

(b) Tree of oriented graph (a)

(a) Formation loop 1

(b) Formation of loop 1

(e) Formation of loop 3

Fig. 1.124 : Formation of F-loops of the given oriented graph

The loop 3 is formed by adding branch 1 to the tree as shown in Fig. 1.124 (e). The F-loop 1 is formed by adding links 3 to the tree whose branches are [2, 3, 5]. The F-loop 3 is formed by adding links 6 to the tree whose branches are [4, 5, 6]. The F-loop 3 is formed by adding link 1 to the three, whose branches are [1, 2, 4]. The fundamental loops are formed by adding links to the tree which is called as tieset. The number of tiesets is equal to nl, the number links. The orientation of the loop is consider as the orientation of the corresponding link. The number of F-loops or the tieset of the given graph is equal to the number of the links of the selected tree, i.e. the number of F-loops = $b - (n - 1) = b - n + 1 = nl$. The F-loops or tiesets of the given graph is written as

Tieset: [2, 3, 5] or F-loop: [2, 3, 5]

Tieset: [4, 5, 6] or F-loop: [4, 5, 6]

Tieset: [1, 2, 4] or F-loop: [1, 2, 4]

In writing the Tiesets or F-loops, the link the underlined. The Tiesets or F-loop matrix can be written in the form of loops, twigs and the links. In a given graph, branches 2, 4, 5 are the twigs of tree. Branches 1, 3, 6 are the links of the given tree. The loop 1 has link 3 the loop 2 has link 6 the loop 3 has link 1. The tieset or F-loop matrix can be written as

$$B_F = \begin{array}{c} \text{loops} \\ 1 \\ 2 \\ 3 \end{array} \begin{array}{c} \text{twigs} \quad\quad \text{links} \\ \begin{bmatrix} 2 & 4 & 5 & 1 & 3 & 6 \\ -1 & 0 & 1 & 0 & 1 & 0 \\ 0 & -1 & -1 & 0 & 0 & -1 \\ 1 & 1 & 0 & 1 & 0 & 0 \end{bmatrix} \end{array}$$

$$[B_F] = [B_t : B_l]$$

where, B_t = Submatrix of B_F which corresponds to the twigs of the select tree

B_l = Submatrix of B_F which corresponds to the links of the select tree

From the tie sets matrix, it is observed that the submatrix is a unity matrix.

$$B_l = \begin{bmatrix} 0 & 1 & 0 \\ 0 & 0 & 1 \\ 1 & 0 & 0 \end{bmatrix}$$

or

$$B_l = \begin{bmatrix} 1 & 0 & 0 \\ 0 & 1 & 0 \\ 0 & 0 & 1 \end{bmatrix}$$

Therefore the fundamental loop or tieset matrix equation can be written as

$$[B_F] = [B_t : B_l] = [B_t \; U]$$

The rank of the BF is $b - n + 1 = nl = b - nt$ i.e. in a given graph the rank is $b - n + 1 = 6 - 4 + 1 = 3$.

Example 1.49 :

Draw the oriented graph of a given network shown in figure, obtain the incidence and tieset matrix.

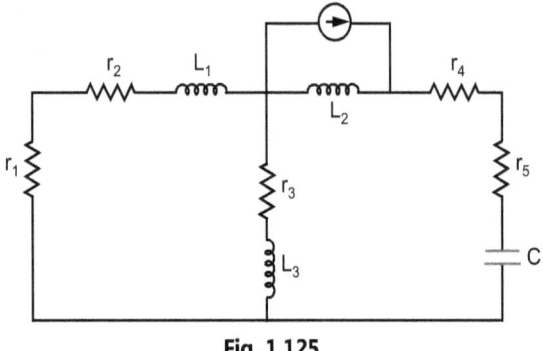

Fig. 1.125

Solution : (i) Replace all elements of network by line segments. Rep.
  (ii) Replace voltage source by short circuiting and current source by open circuit.
  (iii) Assume direction to branches arbitrarily
  (iv) Number the nodes and branches.

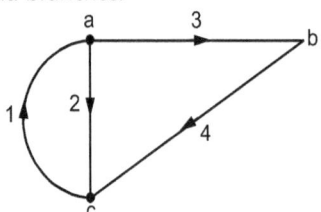

Fig. 1.126 : Network oriented graph

(a) Complete incidence matrix (A)

$$A = \begin{array}{c|cccc} \text{Nodes} & 1 & 2 & 3 & 4 \\ \hline a & -1 & 1 & 1 & 0 \\ b & 0 & 0 & -1 & 1 \\ c & 1 & -1 & 0 & -1 \end{array}$$

$$A = \begin{bmatrix} -1 & 1 & 1 & 0 \\ 0 & 0 & -1 & 1 \\ 1 & -1 & 0 & -1 \end{bmatrix}$$

(b) Tieset matrix (B)

Twigs: [2, 3]

Links: [1, 4]

Tieset 1: [1, 2]

Tieset 4: [2, 3, 4]

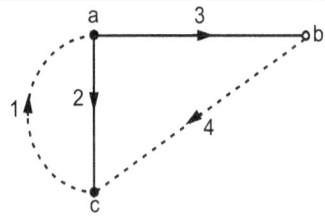

Fig. 1.127

Tieset   Branches

$$B = \begin{matrix} 1 \\ 4 \end{matrix} \begin{bmatrix} 1 & 2 & 3 & 4 \\ 1 & 1 & 0 & 0 \\ 0 & -1 & 1 & 1 \end{bmatrix}$$

$$B = \begin{bmatrix} 1 & 1 & 0 & 0 \\ 0 & -1 & 1 & 1 \end{bmatrix}$$

1.28.1 The KVL Equations for F-loops

The linear independent equations can be obtained by applying KVL to the fundamental loops. Consider the oriented graph shown in Fig. 1.123 (a). The tree of the graph is shown in Fig. 1.123 (b). The F-loop formed for the oriented graph is shown in Fig. 1.123 (c), (d), (e). There are three F-loops of the oriented graph, the loops I_1, I_2 and I_3 corresponds to the links 1, 3 and 6 respectively. The KVL equations. For the corresponding loops with the branch voltages are written as.

I_1 : $V_1 + V_2 + V_4 = 0$ since F-loop [1, 2, 4]
I_2 : $-V_2 + V_3 + V_5 = 0$ since F-loop [2,3,5]
I_3 : $-V_4 - V_5 + V_6 = 0$ since F-loop [4, 5, 6]

In writing the KVL equations for the loop, if the branch orientation coincides with the F-loop, then the branch voltage is written with a positive sign. In the case of the opposite branch orientation of the F-loop it is assigned a negative sign. The above equation can be written in matrix as

$$\begin{bmatrix} 1 & 1 & 0 & 1 & 0 & 0 \\ 0 & -1 & 1 & 0 & 1 & 0 \\ 0 & 0 & 0 & -1 & -1 & 1 \end{bmatrix} \begin{bmatrix} V_1 \\ V_2 \\ V_3 \\ V_4 \\ V_5 \\ V_6 \end{bmatrix} = \begin{bmatrix} 0 \\ 0 \\ 0 \end{bmatrix}$$

or $B_F V_b = 0$

where, B_F is an $l \times b$ matrix called Fundamental loop matrix or tie set matrix where V_b is the branch voltages.

$$[B_F] = [b_{ij}]$$

where b_{ij} is the element of B_F in i^{th} row and j^{th} column. The rows of B_F correspond to the F-loops and the columns to the branches. The element bij has value as follows

$b_{ij} = 1$: where branch j included in the ith F-loop and their orientation coincide.

$b_{ij} = -1$: where the branch j is included in the ith F-loop and their orientation are opposide.

$b_{ij} = 0$: where branch j is not the part of the ith F=loop.

The equation of Fundamental loop matrix or F-circuit has $l = b - n + 1$ number of linearly independent equations. Here the ve are $l = b - n + 1 = 6 - 4 + 1 = 4$ linearily independent equations.

1.29 CUT SET MATRIX

A cut set is a minimal set of branches of a connected graph. It can be obtained by removing a set of branches from a linear graph without affecting the nodes, two connected sub graphs are obtained and the original graph becomes unconnected. The removal of these set of branches from a connected graph which result in cutting the graph into two parts are known as cut-set. The cutest separate the nodes of the connected graph into two groups. Therefore the rank of the original graph decreased by one.

Consider the graph shown in Fig. 1.128.

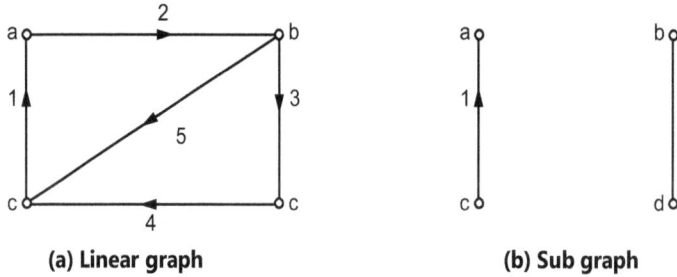

(a) Linear graph (b) Sub graph

Fig. 1.128

The rank of the original graph is $n - 1 = 4 - 1 = 3$. By removing the branches 2, 4 and 5 the graph is reduces into two connected sub graph as shown in Fig. 1.128 (b). The rank of the sub graph is $n - 1 = 2 - 1 = 1$. The addition of the rank of the sub graph is $1 + 1 = 2$. The rank of the graph is reduces by one so that this graph can be treated as cut set of the graph shown in Fig. 1.129 (a). The branches 2, 4, and 5 are called cut sets.

Consider the graph shown in Fig. 1.129. This connected graph has 6 branches and 4 nodes. The cutest of the graph obtained by removing the branches of the graph, so it can be divided into two sub graph.

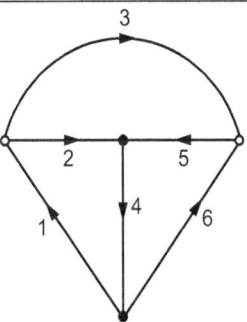

Fig. 1.129 : Oriented graph of a network

The cut set of the graph shown in Fig. 1.130 are obtained by removing the branches as shown in Fig. 1.130 (a), (b), (c), (d), (e), (f).

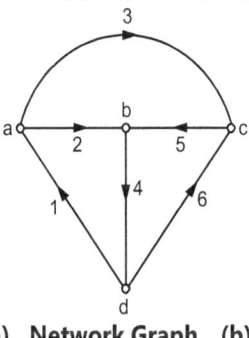

(a) **Network Graph**   (b) Cut set 1, C_1 : [1, 2, 3]

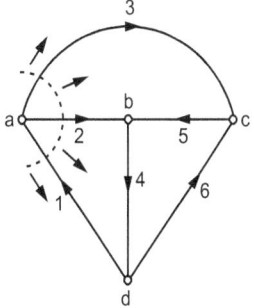

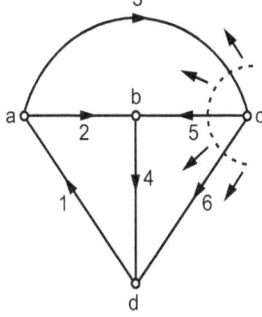

(c) Cut set 2 C_2 : [3, 5, 6]   (d) Cut set 3 C_3 : [2, 4, 5]

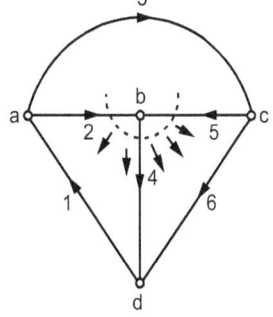

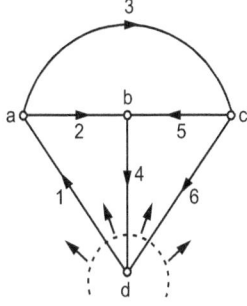

(e) Cut set 4 C_1 : [1, 4, 6]   (f) Cut set 5 C_1 : [1, 2, 3, 4, 5]

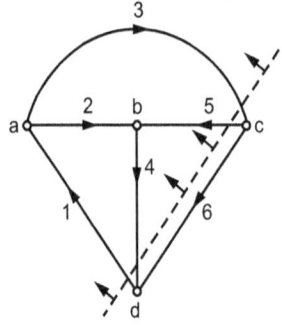
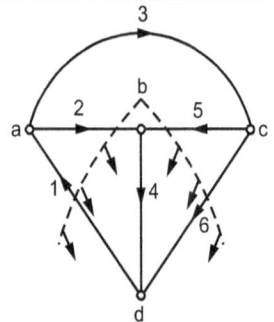

(g) Cut set C_1: [3, 4, 5, 1]   (h) Cut set C_7: [1, 2, 5, 6]

Fig. 1.130 : Cut set formation of network graph

C_1 : [1, 2, 3] C_4 : [1, 4, 6] C_7 : [1, 2, 5, 6]
C_2 : [3, 5, 6] C_5 : [2, 3, 4, 6]
C_3 : [2, 4, 5] C_6 : [3, 4, 5, 1]

A cut set divides the graph into exactly two sub graph. A cut set is shown on graph by a dashed line and indication of arrow. The line passing through all branches which defines the cut set. Every graph can have more than one cut set. The network graph is shown in Fig. 1.130 (a). which has four nodes (a, b, c, d) and six branches [1, 2, 3, 4, 5, and 6]. The cut set 1 shows in Fig. 1.130 (b) it has [1, 2, 3] branches. Each branches in cut set has one of its incident at node in one group and its other terminal incident at other node in the other group. The orientation of the cut set is arbitrary. The cut set 2 has [3, 5, 6] branches as shown in Fig. 1.130 (c). The cut set three 3 has [2, 4, 5] as shown in Fig. 1.130 (d). The cut set 4 has [1, 4, 6] branches as shown in Fig. 1.130 (e). The cut set 5 has [2, 3, 4, 6] branches, as shown in Fig. 1.130 (f). The cut set 6 has [1, 3, 4, 5] branches as shown in Fig. 1.130 (g). The cut set has [1, 2, 5, 6] branches as shown in Fig. 1.130 (h). The cut set of network graph can be written in matrix form. The element in the cut set has assigned as 1 or 0 according to the branches present or absent in cut set respectively.

$Q_{ij} = 1$ where branch j is included in cutest i and the branch orientation coincides with that of the cut set.

$Q_{ij} = -1$ where the branch j is included in the cut set i and the branch orientation does not coincide with the of the cut set.

$Q_{ij} = 0$ where the branch j is not included in the cut set i.

The complete cut set matrix Q_c of network graph is given as

Cut set	Branch					
	1	2	3	4	5	6
C_1	-1	1	1	0	0	0
C_2	0	0	-1	0	1	1
C_3	0	-1	0	+1	-1	0

$$Q_c = \begin{matrix} & C_4 & 1 & 0 & 0 & -1 & 0 & -1 \\ & C_5 & 0 & 1 & 1 & -1 & 0 & -1 \\ & C_6 & 1 & 0 & -1 & -1 & 1 & 0 \\ & C_7 & -1 & 1 & 0 & 0 & 1 & 1 \end{matrix}$$

There for the cut set matrix Q_c can be written as

$$Q_c = \begin{pmatrix} -1 & 1 & 1 & 0 & 0 & 0 & 0 \\ 0 & 0 & -1 & 0 & 0 & 1 & 1 \\ 0 & -1 & 0 & 1 & 1 & -1 & 0 \\ 1 & 0 & 0 & -1 & -1 & 0 & -1 \\ 0 & 1 & 1 & -1 & -1 & 0 & -1 \\ 1 & 0 & -1 & -1 & -1 & 1 & 0 \\ -1 & 1 & 0 & 0 & 0 & 1 & 1 \end{pmatrix}$$

The rank of the cutest matrix Q_c is nt = n − 1. The linear graph of n-nodes can be described using nt cutest containing minimal set.

Example 1.50 :

The network shown in Fig. 1.131 draw the oriented graph and write cut set matrix.

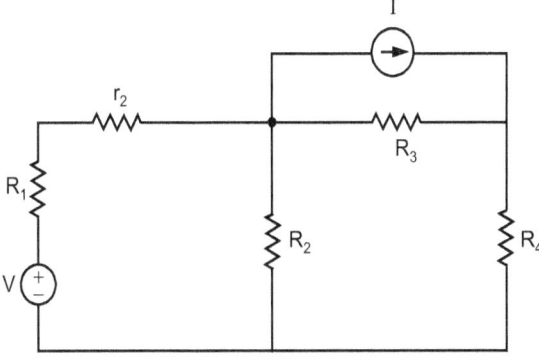

Fig. 1.131

Solution : Draw the oriented graph of a given network. Replace all the elements by line segments. Replace voltage source by short circuit and current source by an open circuit. Assume direction of branch currents arbitrarily. Assign the branch and node number to graph.

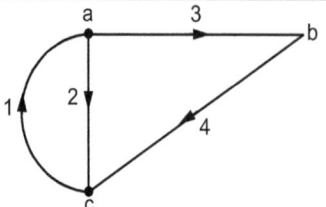

Fig. 1.132 : Oriented graph

The cut sets are

Cut set 1 : [1, 2, 3]

Cut set 2 : [3, 4]

Cut set 3 : [1, 2, 4]

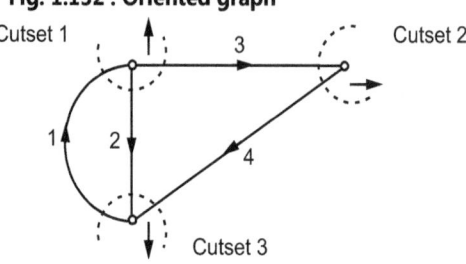

Fig. 1.133

Cut setBranches

$$Q = \begin{matrix} 1 \\ 2 \\ 3 \end{matrix} \begin{bmatrix} 1 & 2 & 3 & 4 \\ 1 & -1 & -1 & 0 \\ 0 & 0 & 1 & -1 \\ -1 & -1 & 0 & 1 \end{bmatrix}$$

$$Q = \begin{bmatrix} 1 & -1 & -1 & 0 \\ 0 & 0 & 1 & -1 \\ -1 & 1 & 0 & 1 \end{bmatrix}$$

1.30 FUNDAMENTAL CUT SETS (F-CUT SET)

The fundamental cut-set obtained for a given graph by using tree of a linear graph. Consider a network graph as shown in Fig. 1.134 (a). The tree of a graph is shown in Fig. 1.134 (b). A tree of a graph has nt twigs. By removing a twig from tree, the tree separates into two parts and nodes of the tree into two groups. Let all the links are joined to a node in one set which forms the cut set called as fundamental cut set.

The orientation of F-cut set is assumed to be the orientation of the corresponding twig. In Fig. 1.134 (b) there are 3 twigs of the tree [2, 5, 4]. The F-cut set formed by removing a twig 2 as shown in Fig. 1.134 (c). The F-cut set has [1, 2, 3] branches. The twigs of the F-cut set is underlined. The second set of F-cut set formed by removing 5 twig which result in F-cut set [3, 5, 6] as shown in Fig. 1.134 (d). The third set of 8 F-cut set formed by removing 4 twig which results in F-cut set [1, 4, 6] as shown in Fig. 1.134 (e). Each F-cut set contain only one and one twig and the remains elements of the graph are links.

The F-cut set obtained for a graph are n-1.

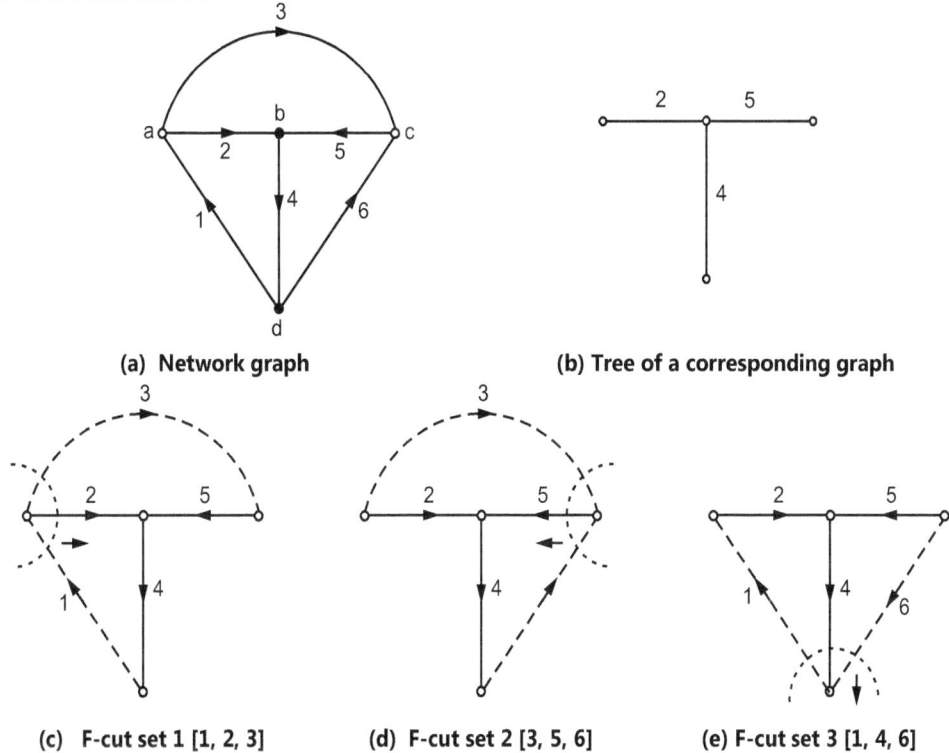

(a) Network graph (b) Tree of a corresponding graph

(c) F-cut set 1 [1, 2, 3] (d) F-cut set 2 [3, 5, 6] (e) F-cut set 3 [1, 4, 6]

Fig. 1.134 : Fundamental cut set of a given graph

The F-cut set matrix of the tree is given below.

Twigs	Branches					
	1	2	3	4	5	6
2	−1	1	1	0	0	0
4	−1	0	0	1	0	1
5	0	0	−1	0	1	1

$$Q_F = \begin{array}{c} \\ 2 \\ 4 \\ 5 \end{array} \begin{array}{c} \text{Twigs} \\ \overbrace{2 \ 4 \ 5} \\ \left[\begin{array}{ccc|ccc} 1 & 0 & 0 & -1 & 1 & 0 \\ 0 & 1 & 0 & -1 & 0 & 1 \\ 0 & 0 & 1 & 0 & -1 & 1 \end{array} \right] \end{array} \begin{array}{c} \text{Links} \\ \overbrace{1 \ 3 \ 6} \end{array}$$

Unit matrix

The rank of the F-cut set matrix is $n_t = n - 1 = 4 - 1 = 3$.

$$(Q_F) = [Q_{Ft} : Q_{Fl}]$$

where
- (Q_F) = $(U \Pi : Q_{Fl})$
- Q_{Fl} : sub matrix for twigs
- Q_{Fl} : sub matrix for links
- U : identity matrix

1.30.1 Relation Between Branch Voltages and Tree Twig Voltages

The fundamental cut set can be obtained by voltage relationship between branch voltage in terms of tree twig voltages. All the nodes are connected with twigs of the tree. The branch voltage are obtained using twigs voltages. The potential difference obtained between two nodes can be determined in terms of voltage is obtained using node pair voltage. The link voltages can be expressed in terms of tree-twig voltages. Consider a network graph shown in Fig. 1.135 (a).

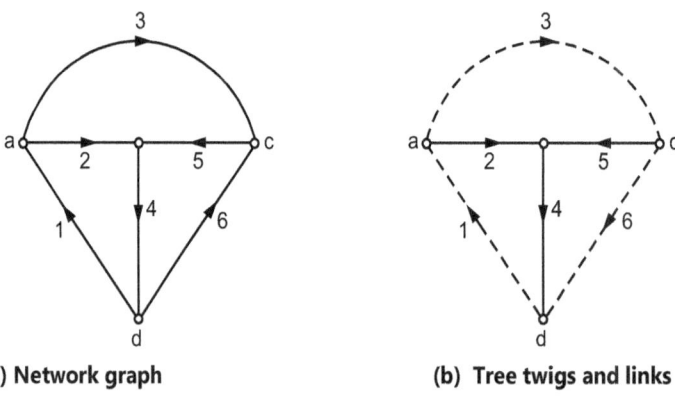

(a) Network graph (b) Tree twigs and links

Fig. 1.135 : Tree twigs and link of the graph

Let the branch voltages are denoted as V_1, V_2, V_3, V_4, V_5 and V_6. The network graph has a tree is shown in Fig. 1.135 (b). It has 2, 4, 5 branches are the twigs. The twig voltages are denoted as V_{t_2}, V_{t_4} and V_{t_5}. Now the branch voltages can be written in terms of twig voltages as given below.

$$V_2 = V_{t_2}$$
$$V_4 = V_{t_4}$$
$$V_5 = V_{t_5}$$
$$V_1 = -V_{t_4} - V_{t_2}$$
$$V_3 = V_{t_2} - V_{t_5}$$
$$V_6 = V_{t_5} + V_{t_4}$$

The above equation of branch voltage and twigs voltage can be written in matrix form as

$$\begin{bmatrix} V_1 \\ V_2 \\ V_3 \\ V_4 \\ V_5 \\ V_6 \end{bmatrix} = \begin{bmatrix} -1 & -1 & 0 \\ 1 & 0 & 0 \\ 1 & 0 & -1 \\ 0 & 1 & 0 \\ 0 & 0 & 1 \\ 0 & 1 & 1 \end{bmatrix} \begin{bmatrix} V_{t_2} \\ V_{t_4} \\ V_{t_5} \end{bmatrix}$$

We can arrange twig voltage in first row and link voltages in remaining rows so we rearrange as

$$\begin{bmatrix} V_2 \\ V_4 \\ V_5 \\ V_1 \\ V_3 \\ V_6 \end{bmatrix} = \begin{bmatrix} 1 & 0 & 0 \\ 0 & 1 & 0 \\ 0 & 0 & 1 \\ -1 & -1 & 0 \\ 1 & 0 & -1 \\ 0 & 1 & 1 \end{bmatrix} \begin{bmatrix} V_{t_2} \\ V_{t_4} \\ V_{t_5} \end{bmatrix}$$

$$V_b = Q_F^T \cdot V_t$$

where V_b = branch voltage of the network graph

Q_F^T = transpose of the F-cut set matrix of network graph

V_t = the column matrix of twig voltages corresponding to the selected tree

Example 1.51 :

Draw the oriented graph of a given network shown in Fig. 1.136 Write the fundamental cut set for a given network.

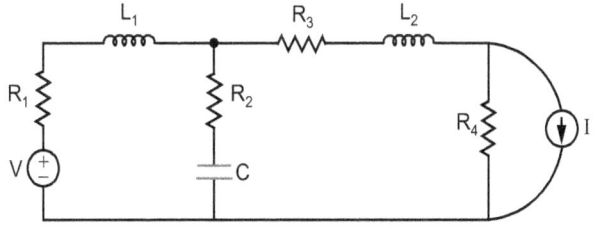

Fig. 1.136

Solution : To draw the oriented graph, replace the all the elements by line segments. Replace the voltage source by short circuit and current source by an open circuit. Assume direction of branch current arbitrarily and assign number nodes and branches.

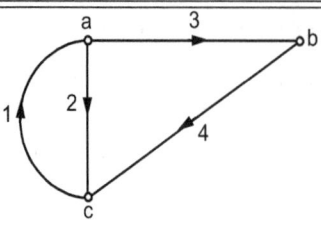

Oriented graph

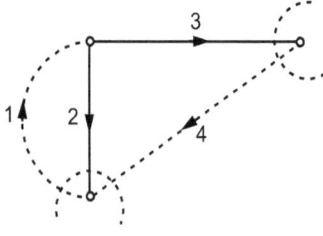

Fig. 1.137 : Tree of graph

F-cut set matrix obtained by considering twigs of the tree.

Fig. 1.138

F-cut set 2: [2, 1, 3]
F-cut set 3: [3, 4]

$$Q_c = \begin{array}{c} \text{cuts} \\ 2 \\ 3 \end{array} \begin{array}{c} \text{Branches} \\ \begin{array}{cccc} 1 & 2 & 3 & 4 \end{array} \\ \begin{bmatrix} -1 & 1 & 0 & 1 \\ 0 & 0 & 1 & -1 \end{bmatrix} \end{array}$$

$$Q_c = \begin{bmatrix} -1 & 1 & 0 & 1 \\ 0 & 0 & 1 & -1 \end{bmatrix}$$

1.31 INTER-RELATION AMONG THE VARIOUS MATRICES

In network graph theory, we have learned three different matrices for a graph. They are incidence matrix A, F-loop matrix B_F and F-cutset matrix Q_F. These matrices are not independent matrices. But these are interrelated with some relation such that one of these is known, the other two can be obtained. This conversion of one matrices to another matrices may be complicated. There relationship among these matrices are formulated in next section.

1.31.1 Relation between Incidence Matrix A and F-loop Matrix B_F

From a graph theory, it is observed that the column of both matrices, A and B_F are related to the branch of the graph. If the column of the incidence matrix A and F-loop matrix are arranged in the first twig and then the links, therefore these matrices are orthogonal to each other.

$$AB_F^T = 0$$

To prove this relation, we have to write these two matrices in terms of their submatrices corresponding to twigs first and the links. Therefore,

$$A = [A_t : A_l]$$

$$B_F^T = \begin{bmatrix} B_{Ft}^T \\ \cdots \\ U \end{bmatrix}$$

There relationship can be written as

$$[A_t : A_l] \begin{bmatrix} B_{Ft}^T \\ \cdots \\ U \end{bmatrix} = $$

or $\quad A_t B_{Ft}^T + A_l = 0$

$$B_{Ft}^T = -A_t^{-1} A_l$$

or $\quad B_{Ft} = [-A_t^{-1} A_l]$

It shows that the column of B_{Ft} are a linear complination of the rows of A.

Hence we can obtain B_F, if matrix A for a tree is known using above equations.

1.31.2 Relationship Between Incidence Matrix A and F-Cut set Matrix Q_F

In a graph theory, the KCL equations can be obtained by using incidence matrix as well as F-cut set matrices as

$$A I_b = 0 \quad \ldots(a)$$
$$Q_F I_b = 0 \quad \ldots(b)$$

where

$$I_b = \begin{bmatrix} I_t \\ \cdots \\ I_l \end{bmatrix} \text{; Branch current matrix of } b \times 1$$

I_F = the set of twig current
I_l = the set of link current

Therefore, the above equation can be written as

$$[A_t : A_l] \begin{bmatrix} I_t \\ \cdots \\ I_l \end{bmatrix} = 0$$

$$A_t I_t + A_l I_l = 0$$

$$I_t = -A_t^{-1} A_l I_l \qquad \ldots(c)$$

Similarly, the F-cut set matrix equation as

$$[U : Q_{Fl}] \begin{bmatrix} I_t \\ \cdots \\ I_l \end{bmatrix} = 0$$

$$I_t + Q_{Fl} \cdot I_l = 0$$

$$I_t = -Q_{F_l} I_l \qquad \ldots(d)$$

From equation (c) and (d), we can write

$$Q_{Fl} = A_t^{-1} A_l \qquad \ldots(e)$$

The above equation (2) shows that the rows of F-cut of matrix Q_{Fl} are linear combination of the rows incidence matrix A.

Hence, for a given incidence matrix A, the F-cut set matrix can be obtained using the above equation.

1.31.3 Relationship between F-loop matrix B_F and F cut set matrix Q_F

In a graph theory, the relation between F-loop matrix B_F and F-cut set matrix Q_F can be written as

$$Q_{Fl} = -B_{Ft}^T \qquad \ldots(a)$$

Therefore,
$$B_F = [B_t : U]$$
$$= [-Q_{-l}^T : U] \qquad \ldots(b)$$

$$Q_F = [U : Q_l]$$
$$= [U : -B_t] \qquad \ldots(c)$$

From equation (b) and (c)

$$B_F Q_F^T = [-Q_l^T : U] \begin{bmatrix} U \\ \vdots \\ Q_l^T \end{bmatrix}$$

$$= -Q_l^T + Q_l^T = 0 \qquad \ldots(d)$$

and
$$Q_F B_F^T = [U : Q_t] \begin{bmatrix} -Q_l \\ \vdots \\ U \end{bmatrix} = -Q_l + Q_l = 0 \qquad \ldots(e)$$

The above equation (d) and (e) shows that the F-cut set and F-loop matrices are orthogonal to each other.

1.32 RELATIONSHIP BETWEEN VOLTAGE AND CURRENT

From a graph theory, we can write

KVL	$B_F \cdot V_b = 0$	...(a)
KCL	$A I_b = 0$	...(b)
And	$Q_F I_b = 0$	...(c)

where,
$$V_b = \begin{bmatrix} V_t \\ \vdots \\ V_l \end{bmatrix} \text{; i.e. branch voltage matrix of } b \times 1 \text{ order.}$$

$$I_b = \begin{bmatrix} I_t \\ \vdots \\ I_l \end{bmatrix} \text{; i.e. branch current matrix of } b \times 1 \text{ order}$$

1.32.1 Twig voltage Transformation

For a graph theory equation (a), we can write

$$[B_{Ft} : U] \begin{bmatrix} V_t \\ \vdots \\ V_l \end{bmatrix} = 0$$

$$B_{Ft} V_t + V_l = 0$$
$$V_l = -B_F V_t$$

or
$$V_l = Q_{Ft}^T V_t$$

The above equation can be written as $V_t = U V_t$

$$V_b = \begin{bmatrix} V_t \\ \vdots \\ V_l \end{bmatrix} = \begin{bmatrix} UV_t \\ \vdots \\ Q_{Fl}^T V_t \end{bmatrix} = \begin{bmatrix} U \\ Q_{Fl}^T \end{bmatrix} V_t$$

$$V_b = Q_F^T V_t$$

The above equation shows that the branch voltage V_b are linear combination of twig voltages.

1.32.2 Node Voltage Transformation

The set of node voltage can be used to express the branch voltages. The branch voltages can be obtained using node voltage through the use of incidence matrix. Therefore,

$$V_b = A^T V_n$$

where V_n = node voltages vector

1.32.3 Link Current Transformation

The branch current can be expressed in terms of link current in graph theory. We know that,

$$Q_F I_b = 0 \qquad \ldots(a)$$

where Q_F = F-cut set matrix
I_b = branch current vector

Above equation (a) can be written in terms of Q_t and Q_l i.e. twig and link respectively.

$$[Q_t \; Q_l] \begin{bmatrix} I_t \\ I_l \end{bmatrix} = 0$$

Since, $\qquad I_t = B_t^T I_l = -A_t^{-1} A_l I_l = -Q_{Fl} I_l$

$\therefore \qquad I_t = [B_t^T I_l] \qquad \ldots(b)$

writing above equation (b) in terms of

$$I_l = UI_l$$

$$\begin{bmatrix} I_t \\ I_l \end{bmatrix} = \begin{bmatrix} B_t^T \\ U \end{bmatrix} [I_l]$$

or $\qquad [I_b] = B_F^T I_l$

It shows that the branch current are expressed as linear combination of link currents.

1.33 FORMULATION OF NETWORK EQUILIBRIUM EQUATION IN MATRIX FORM

The network equilibrium equation are set of equations that completely and uniquely determine the state of the network at any instant. These network variables or voltage variables. In general, for a given network the branch voltages and branch current can be written as

$$V_b = V_s + Z_b (I_b - I_s)$$
$$I_b = I_s + Y_b (V_b - V_s)$$

where,
- V_b = branch voltage matrix of $b \times 1$
- I_b = branch current matrix of $b \times 1$
- V_s = source voltage matrix of $b \times 1$
- I_s = source current matrix of $b \times 1$
- Z_b = branch impedance matrix of $b \times b$
- Y_b = branch admittance matrix of $b \times b$

The KCL equations for graph theory can be written as

$$A I_b = A I_s$$
$$Q I_b = Q I_s$$

The KVL equation can be written as

$$B V_b = B V_s$$

where
- I_s = source current matrices of $b \times 1$
- V_s = source voltage matrices of $b \times 1$

The transformation form branch voltages if branch currents to loop currents or node voltages are written as

$$I_b - I_s = B^T I_L$$
$$V_b - V_s = Q^T V_t$$
$$V_b - V_s = A^T V_n$$

The branch relationship of the network in matrix form can be written as

$$V_b = Z_b I_b$$
$$I_b = Y_b V_b$$

1.34 LOOP ANALYSIS

The branch voltages of a general network are written as

$$V_b = V_s + Z_b (I_b - I_s) \qquad \ldots(a)$$

Multiply B_F to both sides, we have

$$B_F V_b = B_F V_s + B_F Z_b (I_b - I_s) \qquad \ldots(b)$$

From the KVL equation of tree for the F-cutset we can write

Substitute equation (c) in equation (b), we have

$$0 = B_F V_S + B_F Z_b (I_b - I_s)$$
$$0 = B_F V_S + B_F Z_b (B_F^T I_l - I_s)$$

Since,
$$I_b = B_F^T I_l$$

$$B_F V_S = B_F Z_B B_F^T I_l - B_F Z_b I_s$$

$$B_F Z_b I_s - B_F V_S = B_F \cdot B_F^T Z_b I_l$$

Let,
$$B_F Z_b I_s - B_F V_S = V_l$$

and
$$B_F Z_b B_F^T = Z_l$$

Therefore,
$$V_l = Z_l I_l$$

where
$$Z_l = \text{loop impedance}$$
$$I_l = \text{loop current}$$

This is called as matrix loop equation.

The loop current I_l can be written as

$$I_l = Z_l^{-1} V_l$$

This equation is called loop current equation

2.13.2 Nodal Analysis

The nodal equation for a given network can be written as

$$I_b = I_s + Y_b (V_b - V_s)$$

multiply incidence matrix A to both side

$$A I_b = A I_s + A Y_b (V_b - V_s)$$
$$0 = A I_s + A Y_b (A^T V_b - V_s)$$

Since
$$A I_b = 0 \text{ and } V_b = A^T V_n$$

Simply above equation

$$0 = A I_s + A Y_b A^T V_b - A Y_b - V_s$$
$$A Y_b V_s - A I_s = A Y_b A^T V_b$$

Let
$$A Y_b V_s - A I_s = I_n$$

and
$$A Y_b A^T = Y_n$$

Therefore,
$$I_n = Y_n V_n$$

This equation is called nodal equation in matrix form.

where
$$Y_n = \text{node admittance matrix}$$
$$V_n = \text{node voltage matrix}$$

The node voltages can be written as

$$V_n = Y_n^{-1} I_n$$

This equation is called as nodal voltage equation in matrix form.

EXERCISE

1. Distinguish between independent and dependent energy sources.
2. Define following terms:
   (a) Capacitor (b) Current (c) Voltage (d) Power (e) Energy
3. Explain voltage-current (V-I) relationship between following circuit elements:
   (a) Capacitor (b) Resistor (c) Inductor
4. Explain the difference between short circuit (SC) and open circuit (OC) with an example.
5. What you mean by a lumped network and a distributed network?
6. Explain why voltage sources are connected in series and parallel. Give the requirement of voltage sources when they are to be connected in series or parallel.
7. Explain why current sources are connected in series and parallel. Give the requirements of current sources when they are to be connected in parallel or series.
8. What is source transformation? State and prove state transformation equation.
9. State and explain KVL and KCL.
10. With an example explain the general procedure to analyse a network using mesh (loop) analysis.
11. With an example explain the general procedure to the analysis of the given network using nodal (KCL) analysis.
12. Write short note on: (a) Mutual inductance; (b) Dual networks; (c) Coupling circuits
13. Determine current I_2. Use source shifting and the KVL analysis.

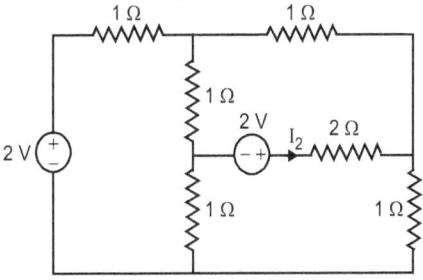

Fig. 1.139

14. Using KCL and KVL, find voltage V_1 in the circuit.

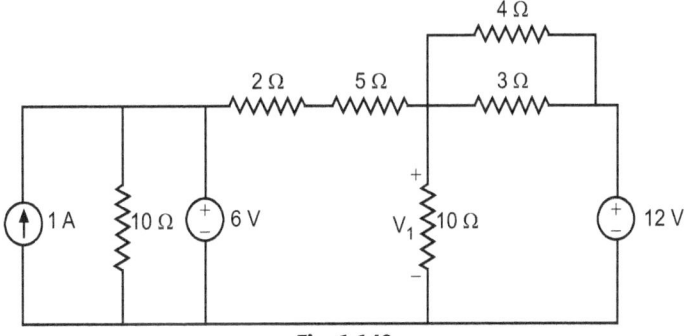

Fig. 1.140

15. Find I_1, I_2, V_1, V_2 and V_3 in the circuit shown. Make use of loop analysis.

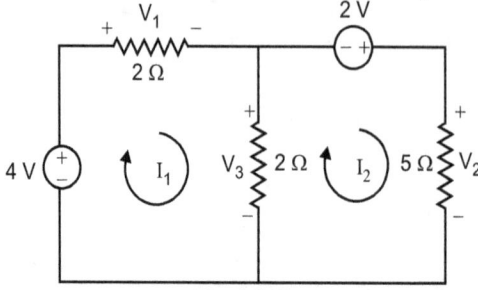

Fig. 1.141

16. Write Node equation for the circuit shown, solve for the voltage V_2 and V_3.

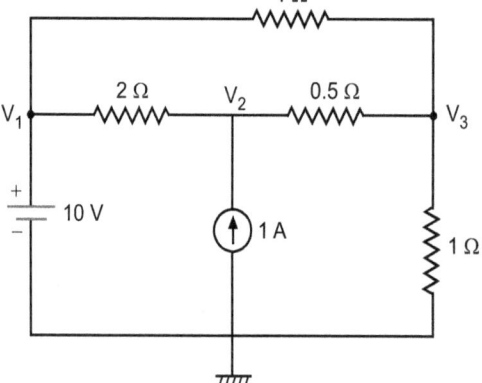

Fig. 1.142

17. Use nodal analysis to find V_1, V_2 and V_x in the circuit shown.

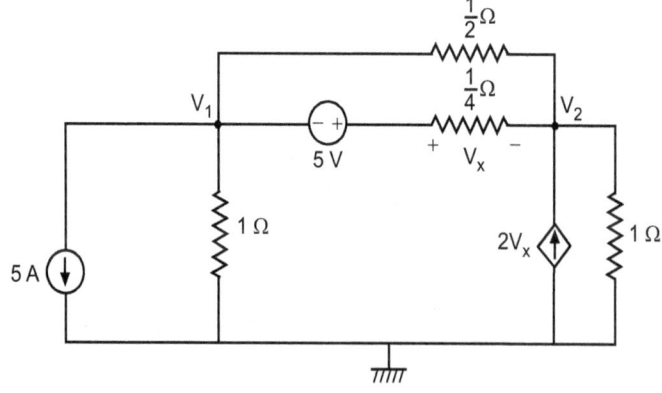

Fig. 1.143

Unit - II

NETWORK THEOREMS

2.1 SUPERPOSITION THEOREM

In the last sections, we have studied two powerful technique of mesh and nodal analysis to find the network variables. Network variable can also be out by using network theorems. In this section, we shall discuss one of the most basic theorem called superposition theorem. Remaining theorems are discussed in the subsequent sections.

Utility of Theorem :

Superposition theorem is used to find voltage across any (or all) branches and current through any (or all) branches in a circuit containing impedances and more than one independent energy source.

Statement :

"In a linear circuit containing linear and bilateral elements and energy sources. voltage across any branch or current in any branch is given by algebraic sum of voltage or current due to each energy sources considered separately (with other sources turned off)".

While turning off energy sources they are replaced by their internal impedances. The voltage source is replaced by short circuit and current source is replaced by open circuit across the two terminals where they are connected.

Proof :

To prove this theorem, we can consider a simple two loops circuit with voltage and current sources as shown in Fig. 2.1.

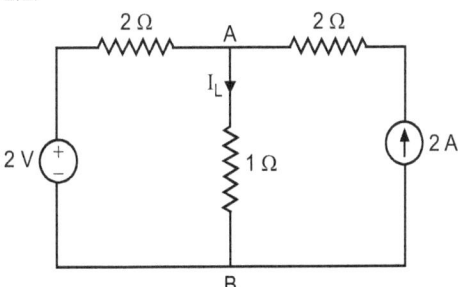

Fig. 2.1 : Circuit to prove superposition theorem

Let us find current (I_L) in 1 Ω across A-B by KVL and KCL and then verify the current by using superposition theorem.

Current (I_L) by use of KCL and KVL :

Using KCL current in 2Ω resistor is ($I_L - 2$) Amp. as shown in Fig. 2.2.
Now KVL across loop (B-A-C-B) gives

$$I_L + 2(I_L - 2) - 2 = 0 \text{ or } 3I_L = 6 \text{ or } I_L = 3A$$

Current (I_L) by using superposition theorem :

Current (I_L) can be found out by considering one source at a time.

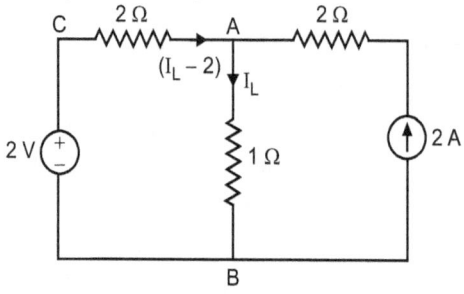

Fig. 2.2

Step I :
Consider 2V source alone. Make current source zero (Open the terminal since current source has infinite resistance between terminals). The circuit will be as shown in Fig. 2.3 (a).

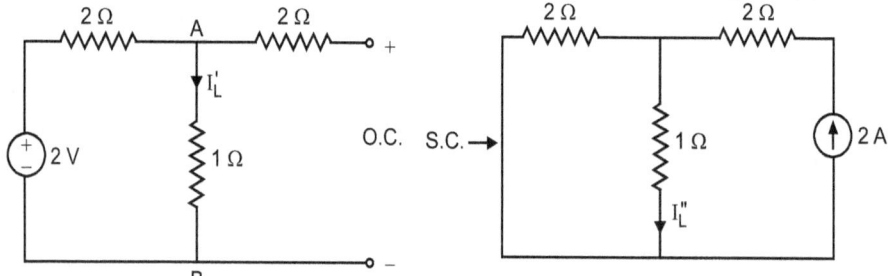

(a) Current to explain (b) Voltage Source Zero

Fig. 2.3 : Circuits to explain superposition theorem

Now current in $2\Omega = I_L' = \dfrac{2}{2+1} = \dfrac{2}{3}$ Amp.

Step II :
Consider 2A source alone. Make voltage source zero (short the terminals since ideal voltage source has zero resistance between terminals). The circuit will be as shown in Fig. 2.3 (b).

Now by current divider equation

$$I_L'' = \dfrac{2 \times 2}{3} = \dfrac{4}{3} \text{ A}$$

Step III : By superposition theorem

$$I_L = I_L' + I_L''$$
$$= \dfrac{2}{3} + \dfrac{4}{3} = 3A$$

Conclusion :

Since, current (I_L) found out by using superposition theorem is same as that by using KCL and KVL, the superposition theorem is proved.

Note :

Superposition theorem is valid for circuit with linear impedances. It is not applicable to circuit containing at least one or more nonlinear elements such as charged capacitor, energized inductor, diodes, transistors, incandescent lamp, vacuum tube or gas tubes.

Superposition theorem can also be used in a network supplied by generators with several different frequencies to compute currents as a sum of individual currents due to each frequency. Change in reactances to different frequencies should be considered while computing the currents.

Following examples explains principles of superposition theorem

Example 2.1 :

Using superposition theorem determine node voltages V_1 and V_2 in the circuit shown.

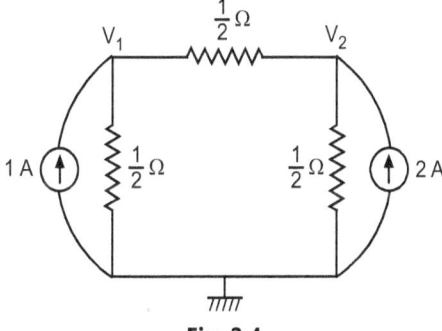

Fig. 2.4

Proof : Step I :

Consider 1A current source alone 2A source is made by opening terminals as in Fig. 2.5 (a).

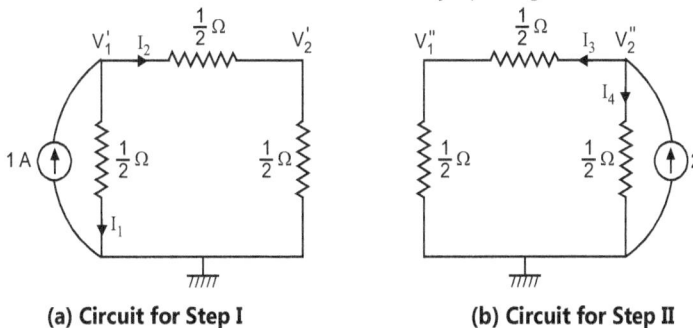

(a) Circuit for Step I (b) Circuit for Step II

Fig. 2.5 : Circuit to find required at variables

NETWORK THEOREMS

Current $\quad I_1 = \dfrac{1 \times 1}{1 + \dfrac{1}{2}} = \dfrac{2}{3}$ and current $I_2 = \dfrac{1}{3}$ A

Hence $\quad V_1' = \dfrac{1}{2} \times \dfrac{2}{3} = \dfrac{1}{3}$ V and $V_2' = \dfrac{1}{2} \times \dfrac{1}{3} = \dfrac{1}{6}$ V

Step II :
Consider 2A current source alone. A current source is made zero by opening its terminals as shown as in Fig. 2.5 (b).

Current $\quad I_3 = \dfrac{2 \times 1/2}{1 + 1/2} = \dfrac{2}{3}$ A current $I_4 = \left(2 - \dfrac{2}{3}\right) = \dfrac{4}{3}$ A

Hence $\quad V_2'' = \dfrac{1}{2} \times I_4 = \dfrac{2}{3}$ V

$\quad V_1'' = \dfrac{1}{2} \times I_3 = \dfrac{1}{2} \times \dfrac{2}{3} = \dfrac{1}{3}$ V

Step III :
By applying superposition theorem, we have

$$V_1 = V_1' + V_1'' = \dfrac{1}{3} + \dfrac{1}{3} = \dfrac{2}{3} V$$

$$V_2 = V_2' + V_2'' = \dfrac{1}{6} + \dfrac{2}{3} = \dfrac{5}{6} V$$

Example 2.2 :
Make use of superposition theorem to determine the voltage V in the circuit shown.

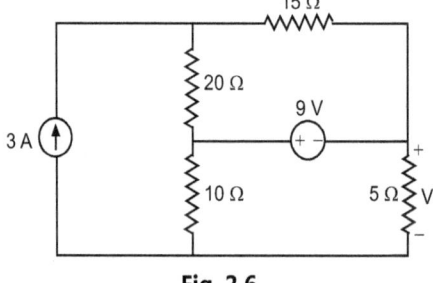

Fig. 2.6

Solution : Step I :
Consider 3A current source alone. Make the 9V source zero as in Fig. 2.7 (a).

We have 10Ω and 5Ω resistors in parallel to give equivalent resistance of $\dfrac{10}{3}$ Ω. Current of 3A flows through it.

Hence, we have $V' = \dfrac{10}{3} \times 3 = 10V$

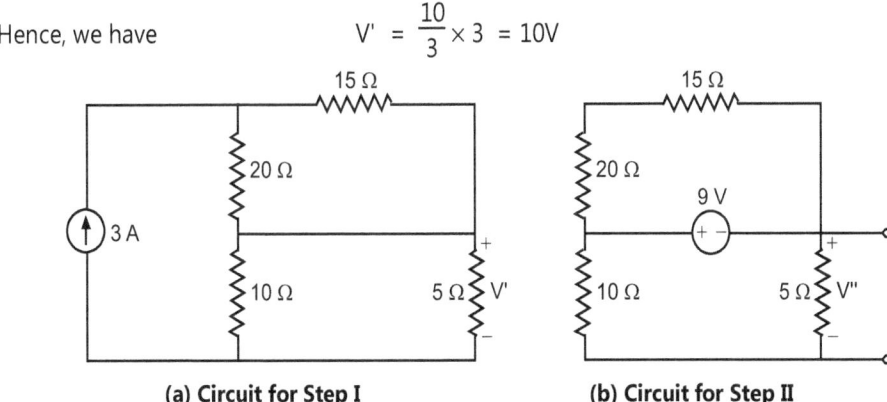

(a) Circuit for Step I (b) Circuit for Step II

Fig. 2.7 : Circuit to find required variables

Step II :

Consider 9V source alone. Make the 3A current source zero as shown in Fig. 2.7 (b).

Now 10Ω and 5Ω are in series and this series combination is in parallel with the 9V source. Hence, by voltage divider, we have

$$V'' = -5 \times \dfrac{9}{15} = -3V$$

Step III :

By superposition theorem, we have

$$V = V' + V'' = 10 - 3 = 7 \text{ Volts.}$$

Example 2.3 :

In the circuit shown find the open circuit voltage (V_{Th}) across a-b using superposition theorem.

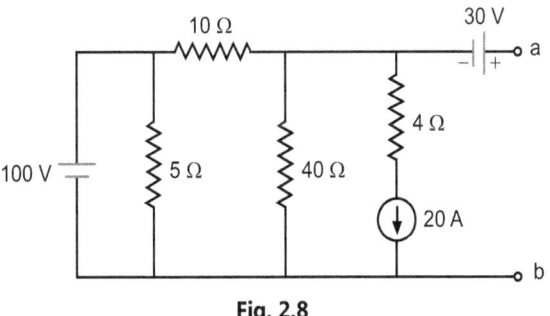

Fig. 2.8

Solution : Step I :

Consider 30V source alone. Make other sources zero i.e. short 100V source and open 20A source. As no current flows through circuit the open circuit voltage (V_{Th}) will be $V_{Th} = 30$ V.

Step II :

Consider 100 V source only make other sources zero. The circuit will be as shown in Fig. 2.9 (a)

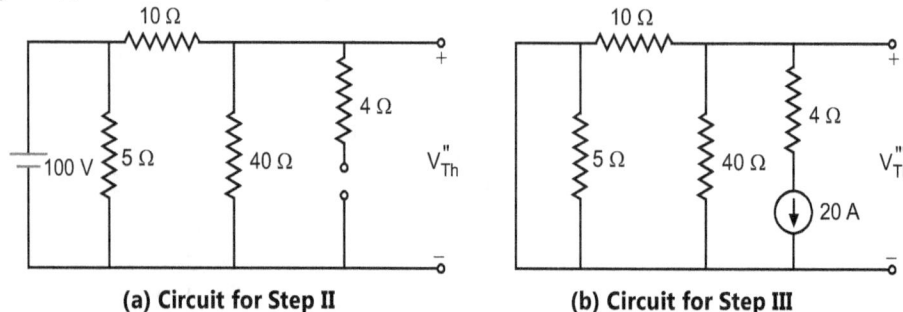

(a) Circuit for Step II   (b) Circuit for Step III

Fig. 2.9

Voltage across 40Ω resistor is the output voltage (V_{Th}). By voltage divider circuit, we have,

$$V_{Th}'' = \frac{40 \times 100}{40 + 10} = 80V$$

Step III :

Consider 20Ω current source alone make other sources zero as shown in Fig. 2.9 (b). 40Ω and 10 Ω are in parallel to give equivalent resistance of 8Ω. 20A current will flow through this combination to give output voltage (V_{Th}) of

$$V_{Th}''' = -8 \times 20$$
$$= -160V$$

Step IV: Hence by superposition theorem, we have

$$V_{Th}' + V_{Th}'' + V_{Th}''' = 30 + 80 - 160$$
$$= -50 \text{ Volts}$$

Example 2.4 :

Using superposition theorem determine voltage V_{AB} in the circuit, shown

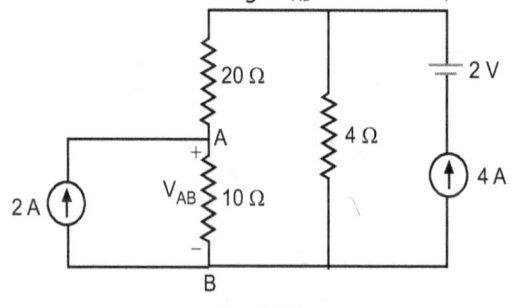

Fig. 2.10

Solution : Step I : Consider only 2V source. Open the two current sources. Then voltage source is open circuited. Hence, no current flows through the circuit resistors. Thus, we have

$$V'_{AB} = 0V.$$

Step II :

Consider 2A source only. Make the other two sources zero. The circuit will be as shown in Fig. 2.10 (a).

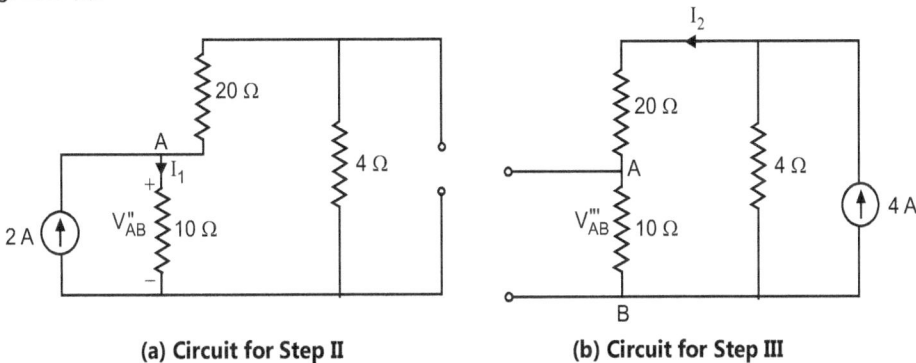

(a) Circuit for Step II   (b) Circuit for Step III

Fig. 2.10 : Circuit to find required variable

Now, Current $I_1 = 2 \times \dfrac{24}{24 + 10}$

$= 1.41$ Amp.

Thus we have, $V''_{AB} = I_1 \times 10$

$= 14.12$ V

Step III: Consider 4A source only. Make other two sources as shown in Fig. 2.10 (b). By current divider action the current,

$$I_2 = 4 \times \dfrac{4}{4 + 30} = \dfrac{16}{34} = \dfrac{8}{17} \text{ Amp}$$

Hence, $V'''_{AB} = 10 \, I_2 = + \dfrac{80}{17}$

$= 4.7$ Volts

Step IV: Hence by superposition theorem we have

$$V_{AB} = V'_{AB} + V''_{AB} + V'''_{AB}$$

$= 0 + 14.12 + 4.7$

$= 18.82$ V

Example 2.5 :

Using superposition theorem find I_1 that gives voltage $V_2 = 6.5$ V in the circuit shown.

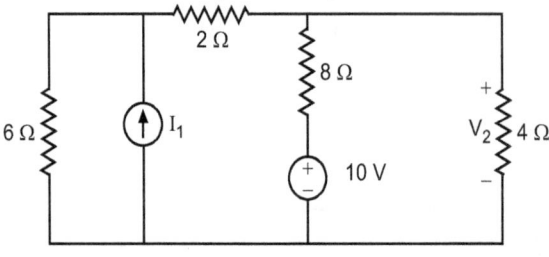

Fig. 2.11

Solution : Step I : Consider current source I_1 alone. Make the voltage source of 10V zero as shown in Fig. 2.12 (a).

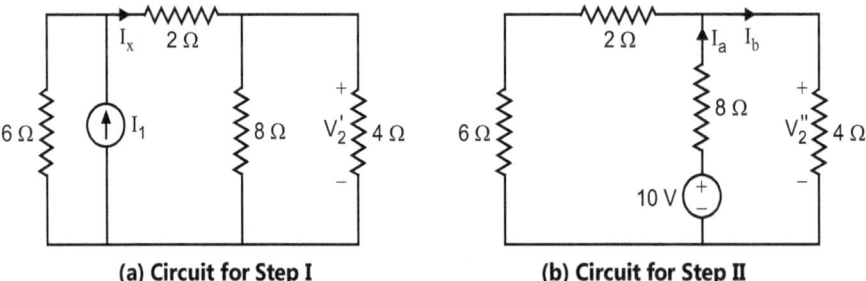

(a) Circuit for Step I (b) Circuit for Step II

Fig. 2.12 : Circuits to find required variables

$8\Omega \parallel 4\Omega$ gives 2.67Ω resistor. This is in series with 2Ω resistor. Now by current divider circuit, we have the current.

$$I_x = \frac{I_1 \times 6}{6 + 2 + 2.67} = \frac{6 I_1}{10.67}$$

$$= 0.562 \, I_1$$

This current flows through equivalent 2.67Ω resistor. Hence, we get V_2' as

$$V_2' = 2.67 \times I_x$$

$$= 1.5 \, I_1 \text{ volts}$$

Step II :

Consider 10V source alone. Make the current source zero as shown in Fig. 2.12 (b).

Now $(6 + 2) = 8\Omega$ resistor is in parallel with 4Ω resistor.

The   Total current $= I_a = \dfrac{10}{8 + 8 \parallel 4} = \dfrac{10}{8 + 2.67}$

$$= 0.937 \text{ Amp.}$$

Now by current divider action, we have,

$$I_b = I_a \times \frac{8}{8+4} = \frac{2}{3} \times I_a = 0.625 \text{ A}$$

Hence   Output voltage $= V_2'' = 4I_b = 2.5$ V

Step III :

By superposition theorem, we have,

$$V_2 = 6.5 = V_2' + V_2'' = 1.5I_1 + 2.5$$

Hence, $1.5I_1 = 4$ or $I_1 = \frac{8}{3}$ Amp.

Thus, an current of $I_1 = \frac{8}{3}$ A produces $V_2 = 6.5$ Volts

Example 2.6 :

Use superposition theorem to find current I in the circuit shown.

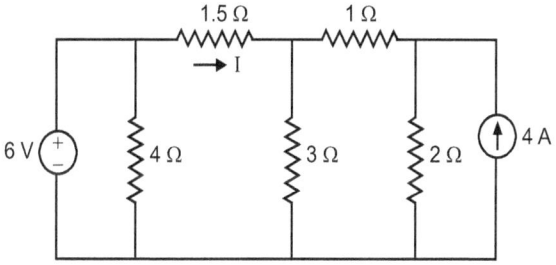

Fig. 2.13

Solution : Consider one source at a time to find the total current as a summation of two currents.

Step I : Consider 6V source alone. Make the 4A current source zero as shown in Fig. 2.14 (a). Now 1Ω and 2Ω are in series. This 3Ω is in parallel with 3Ω resistor to give 1.5Ω across a-b. This is in series with 1.5 Ω resistor. This total resistance of 3Ω is in parallel with 6V source.

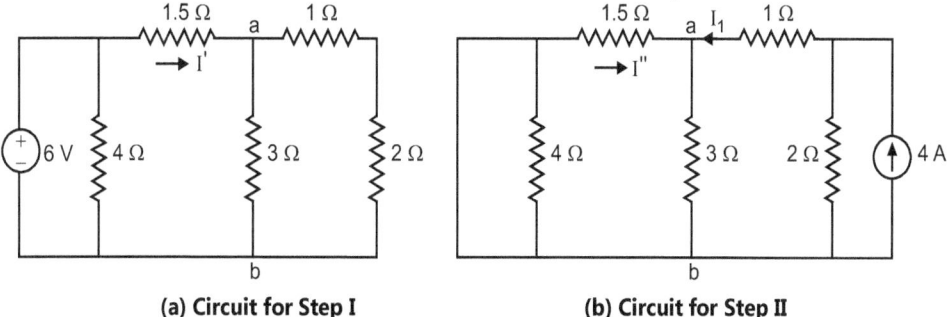

(a) Circuit for Step I   (b) Circuit for Step II

Fig. 2.14 : Circuits to find required variables

Thus, Current (I') = $\dfrac{6}{(1.5 + 1.5)} = \dfrac{6}{3} = 2A$

Step II :
Now consider 4A current source alone. Make the 6V voltage source zero as shown in Fig. 1.126 (b). Because of short 4Ω resistance becomes zero. Now 1.5 Ω and 3Ω are in parallel to give an equivalent of 1Ω. Now by current divider action

$$I_1 = \dfrac{4 \times 2}{2 + 1 + 1} = 2A$$

Now again using divider action, we have,

$$I" = -I_1 \times \dfrac{3}{3 + 1.5} = -I_1 \times \dfrac{3}{4.5} = -2 \times \dfrac{2}{3} = \dfrac{-4}{3} \text{ A}$$

Step III: By superposition theorem we have I = I' + I"

$$I = 2 - \dfrac{4}{3} = \dfrac{2}{3} \text{ Amp.}$$

Example 2.7 :
Determine the voltage V_1 in the circuit by using Superposition Theorem.

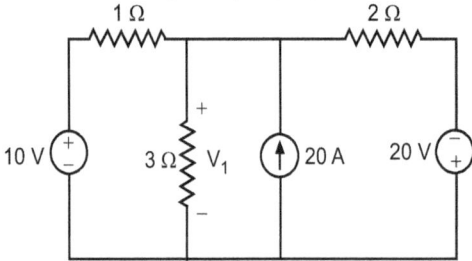

Fig. 2.15

Solution : Step I :
Consider 10V source alone. Make other two sources zero as in Fig. 2.16 (a).

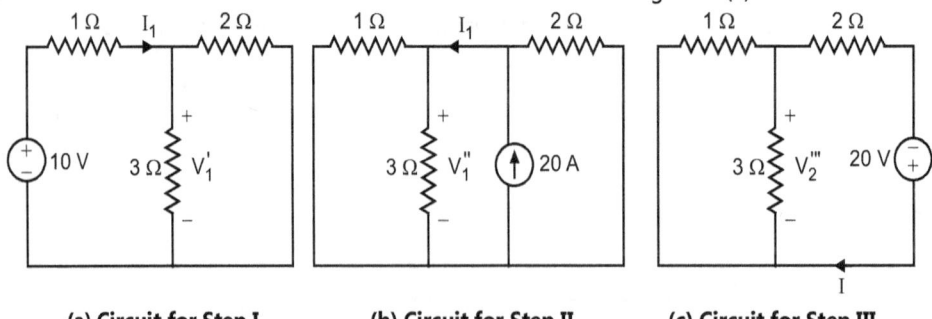

(a) Circuit for Step I   (b) Circuit for Step II   (c) Circuit for Step III

Fig. 2.16 : Circuit to find required variables

Now 3Ω and 2Ω in parallel gives $\frac{6}{5}$ Ω resistor. The voltage V_1' is across this resistor.

Hence, by voltage divider action.

$$V_1' = \frac{10 \times \frac{6}{5}}{1 + \frac{6}{5}} = 10 \times \frac{6}{11} = 5.45 \text{ V}$$

Step II :

Consider 20A current source alone. Make other two sources zero as shown in Fig. 2.15 (b). Now 1Ω || 3Ω gives an equivalent resistance of 0.75Ω. By current divider action, we have,

$$I_2 = 20 \times \frac{2}{2 + 0.75} = 14.545 \text{ Amp.}$$

Hence, $V_1'' = 0.75 \times I_1$

$= 10.9 \text{ V}$

Step III :

Consider 20V source alone. The other two sources are zero as shown in Fig. 2.16 (c). 1Ω || 3Ω gives an equivalent of 0.75Ω. Now by voltage divider action.

We have $V_1''' = -20 \times \frac{0.75}{0.75 + 2} = -5.45 \text{ V}$

Step IV :

By superposition theorem we have

$$V_1 = V_1' + V_1'' + V_1''' = 5.45 + 10.9 - 5.45 = 10.9 \text{ V}$$

Example 2.8 :

Find current I using superposition Theorem.

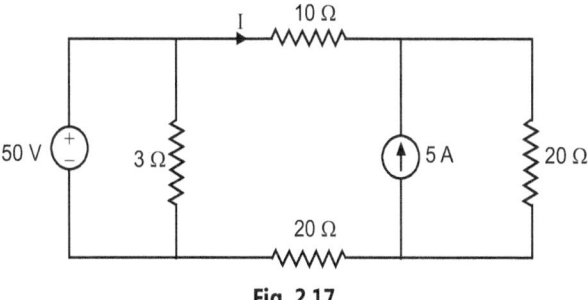

Fig. 2.17

Solution : Step I :

Consider 50V source alone. Make current source zero as shown in Fig. 2.18 (a).

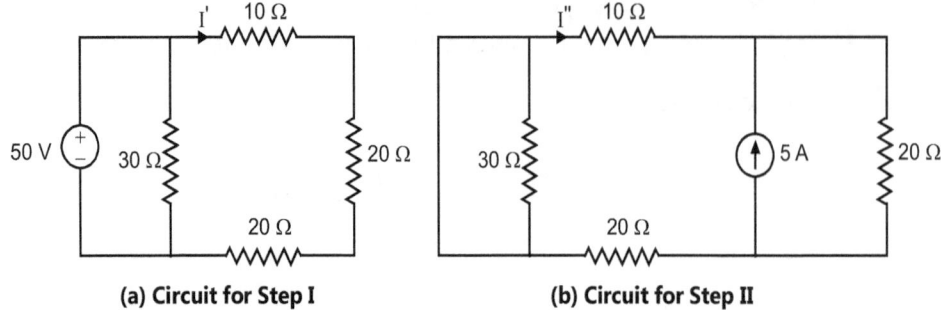

(a) Circuit for Step I   (b) Circuit for Step II

Fig. 2.18 : Circuits to find required variables

Now 10Ω, 20Ω and 20Ω all in series to give a total resistance of 50Ω. This 50Ω resistor is in parallel with 50V source.

Hence,
$$I' = \frac{50}{50} = 1 \text{ Amp.}$$

Step II :

Consider 5A current source alone. Make the voltage source zero as shown in Fig. 2.18 (b). Now 30Ω resistor becomes zero. 10Ω and 20Ω resistors are in series. By current divider action we have,

$$I'' = -5 \times \frac{20}{20 + 30} = -5 \times \frac{2}{5}$$

$$= -2 \text{Amp.}$$

Step III : By superposition theorem $I = I' + I'' = 1 - 2 = 1$ Amp.

Example 2.9 :

Find current through capacitor branch in the circuit by superposition theorem.

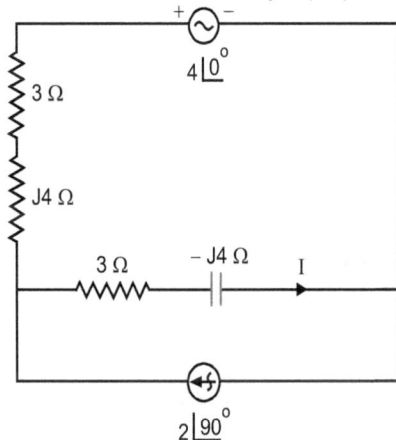

Fig. 2.19

Solution : Superposition theorem can also be applied to AC circuits. This example explain how A.C. circuits are analysed using superposition theorem.

Step I :

Consider voltage source alone. Make current source zero as shown in Fig. 2.20 (a).

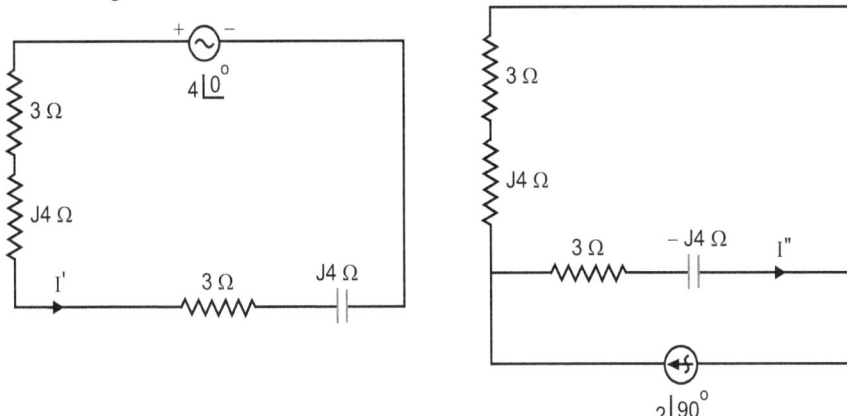

(a) Circuit for Step I   (b) Circuit for Step II

Fig. 2.20 : Circuits to find required variables

Current $\quad I' = \dfrac{4\angle 0°}{(3+J4)+(3-J4)} = \dfrac{4\angle 0°}{6} = \dfrac{2}{3}\angle 0°$ Amp.

Step II :

Consider current source alone. Make voltage source zero as shown in Fig. 2.20 (b). Now by current divider action.

We have $\quad I'' = 2\angle 90° \times \dfrac{(3+J4)}{(3+J4)+(3-J4)} = \dfrac{2\angle 90° \times (3+J4)}{6}$

$\qquad = \dfrac{1}{3} \angle 90° \times 5 \angle 53.13° = 1.65 \angle 143.3°$

$\qquad = (-1.33 + J1)$ Amp.

Step III: By superposition theorem $I = I' + I''$

$\qquad I = (0.67 + J0) + (-1.33 + J1)$

$\qquad = (-0.66 + J1)$ Amp.

$\qquad = 1.20 \angle 124.4°$ Amp.

Note : Many times controlled sources are also present in the circuit along with independent energy sources. While applying steps to Superposition Theorem the controlled sources are not to be considered as a separate source. Only independent energy source need to be considered.

Following examples explain this.

Example 2.10 :

Use superposition theorem to find current (I) in the circuit shown.

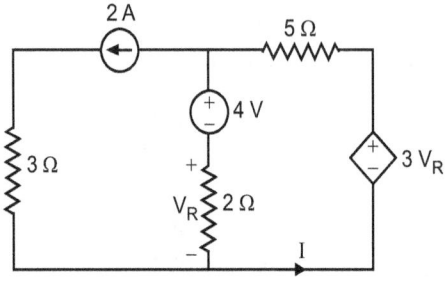

Fig. 2.21

Solution : There are two independent source. Hence, only two step to find current I. The controlled source of $3V_R$ is not separately considered.

Step I :

Consider 2A current source alone. Make 4V sources zero as shown in Fig. 2.22 (a).

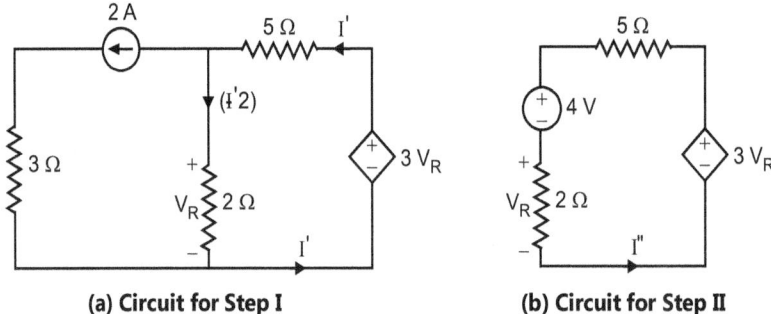

(a) Circuit for Step I   (b) Circuit for Step II

Fig. 2.22 : Circuits to find required variables

By KCL current in 2Ω branch is $(I' - 2)$. Hence, $V_R = 2(I' - 2)$
KVL across right side loop gives

$$3V_R - 5I' - 2(I' - 2) = 0$$

OR $\quad 3 \times 2 (I' - 2) - 5I' - 2I' + 4 = 0$

Solving this gives $\quad I' = -8$ Amp.

Step II :

Consider 4V source alone. Make current source zero as shown in Fig. 2.22 (b). Now there is a single loop with loop current I". We have $V_R = 2I"$. KVL across the loop gives

$$3V_R - 5I" - 4 - V_R = 0$$

i.e. $\quad\quad 2V_R - 5I" - 4 = 0$

$\quad\quad\quad 2 \times 2I" - 5I" - 4 = 0$

Hence $\quad I" - RA$

Step III :

By superposition theorem $I = I' + I" = -8 - 4 = -12$ Amp.

Example 2.11 :

By superposition theorem find current I in the circuit.

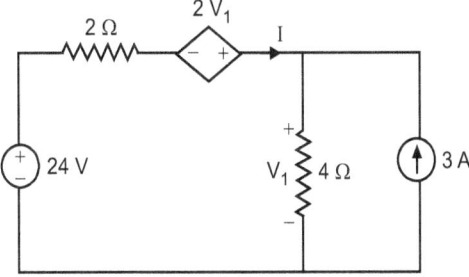

Fig. 2.23

Solution : Consider 24V and 3A only. Do not consider controlled source of $2V_1$ separately.

Step I :

Consider 24V alone. Make 3A source zero as shown in Fig. 2.24 (a). Now there will be a single loop with loop current I'. Now $V_1 = 4I'$ and hence KVL across whole loop gives,

$$+ V_1 - 2V_1 + 2I' - 24 = 0 \text{ or } -V_1 + 2I' - 24 = 0$$
$$-4I' + 2I' - 24 = 0 \text{ gives, } I" = -12 \text{ A}$$

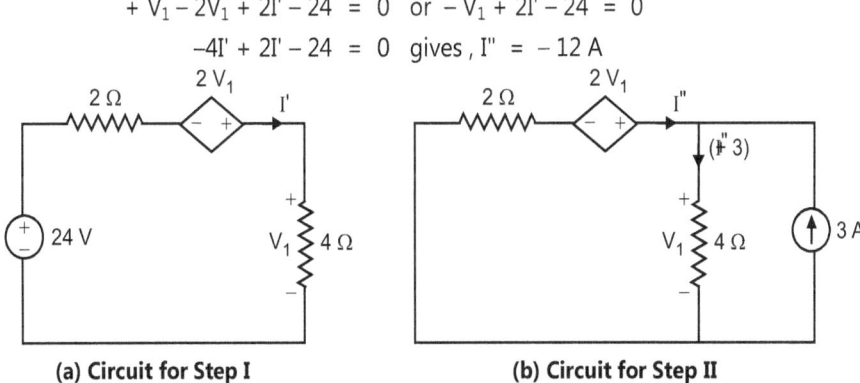

(a) Circuit for Step I (b) Circuit for Step II

Fig. 2.24 : Circuit to find required variables

Step II: Consider 3A source alone. Make voltage source zero as shown in Fig. 2.24 (b). KCL gives current in 4Ω resistor as (I" + 3) Amps. Hence, voltage $V_1 = 4 (I" + 3)$, and KVL across the left side the loop gives

$$+ V_1 + 2I" - 2V_1 = 0$$

or $\qquad 2I" - V_1 = 0$ i.e. $2I" - 4 (I" + 3) = 0$

Solving this gives $\qquad I" = -6A$

Step III: By superposition theorem

$$I = I' + I" = -12 - 6$$
$$= -18A$$

Current (I) from KVL and KCL:

To verify the superposition theorem for this circuit let us find current I directly for circuit of Fig. 1.135. By KCL current in 4Ω resistor is $(I + 4)$ Amp. The voltage $V_1 = 4(I + 4)$, and KVL across left loop as before gives

$$V_1 - 2V_1 + 2I - 24 = 0 \text{ or } -V_1 + 2I - 24 = 0$$

i.e. $\quad -4(I + 4) + 2I - 24 = 0 \text{ or } -2I = -36$

Hence, $\quad I = -18$

This is the same current we found out using superposition theorem. Thus superposition theorem is verified for this circuit.

Example 2.12 :

Find current in 6Ω resistor (I_L) by using the superposition theorem.

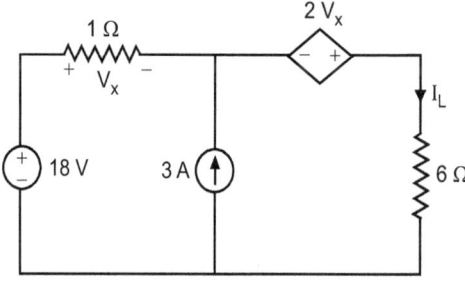

Fig. 2.25

Solution : Step I: Consider 18V only. Make current source zero as shown in Fig. 2.26 (a). The circuit is converted into a single loop with loop current I_L'. Now $V_x = I_L'$ and KVL across whole loop gives

$$+ 6I_L' - 2V_x + V_x - 18 = 0 \text{ or } 6I_L' - V_x = 18$$

i.e. $\quad 6I_L' - I_L' = 18 \text{ or } I_L' = +\dfrac{18}{5} = 3.6 \text{ Amp.}$

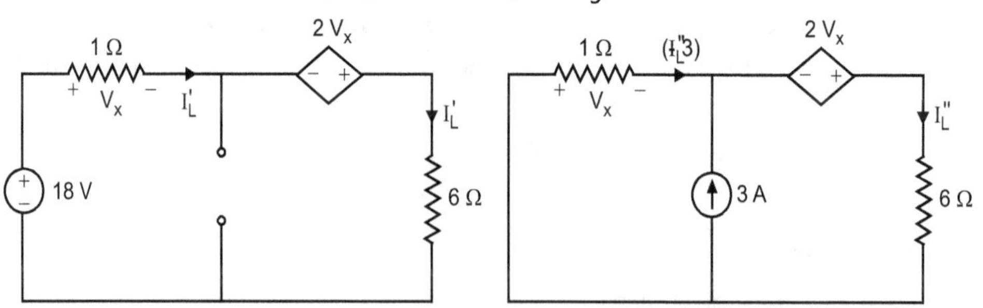

(a) Circuit for Step I (b) Circuit for Step II

Fig. 2.26 : Circuits to find required variables

Step II :

Consider 3A current source alone. Make the voltage source zero as shown in Fig. 2.26 (b). Now KCL gives current in 1Ω resistor branch as $(I_L'' - 3)$. Now applying KVL to outer loop (loop without 3A source in between) gives,

$$6I_L'' - 2V_x + V_x = 0 \text{ or } V_x = 6I_L'' = I(I_L'' - 3) \quad \text{where } V_x = (I_L'' - 3)$$

Solving this gives
$$I_L'' = \frac{-3}{5} = -0.6 \text{ Amp.}$$

Step III :

By superposition theorem $I_L = I_L' + I_L'' = (3.6 - 0.6)$

i.e. $I_L = 3.0$ Amp.

Example 2.13 :

Find current in 3Ω resistor (I) by using the superposition theorem.

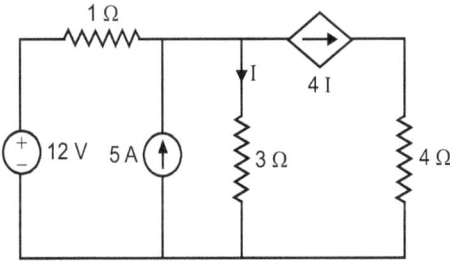

Fig. 2.27

Solution : Step I : Consider 12V source alone. Make 5A current source zero as shown in Fig. 2.27 (a). By KCL the current in 1Ω branch is + 5I'. KVL across the input loop gives

$$3I' + 5I' - 12 = 0 \text{ or } I' = + 1.5A$$

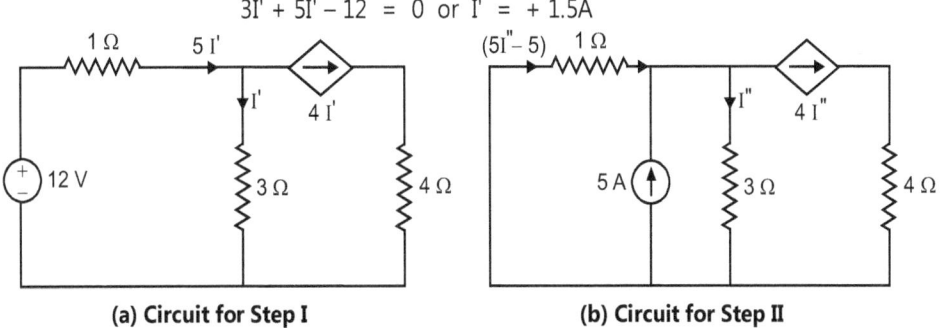

(a) Circuit for Step I   (b) Circuit for Step II

Fig. 2.28 : Circuits to find required variables

Step II :

Now consider 5A source make voltage source zero as shown in Fig. 2.28 (b). KCL at node gives current in 1Ω resistor as (5I" − 5). KVL across loop formed by the 3Ω and 1Ω resistor is

$$+3I'' + 1(5I'' - 5) = 0 \text{ or } I'' = \frac{5}{8} \text{ Amp.}$$

Step III :

By superposition theorem $I = I' + I'' = \frac{3}{2} + \frac{5}{8} = \frac{17}{8}$

Thus, current (I) = 2.125 Amp.

Example 2.14 :

By using superposition theorem find current (I) in the circuit shown.

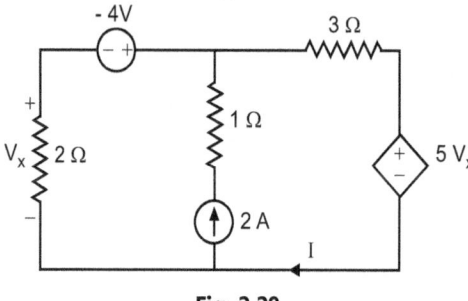

Fig. 2.29

Solution : There are only two independent energy sources. Consider 4V source alone. Make current source zero as shown in Fig. 2.30 (a). The circuit is converted into a single loop with loop current (I'). We have $V_x = -2I'$ and KVL across loop is gives $5V_x + 3I' + 4 - V_x = 0$.

i.e. $\quad\quad\quad 4V_x + 3I' + 4 = 0$

i.e. $\quad\quad\quad 4(-2I') + 3I' + 4 = 0$ or $I' = 0.8$ Amp.

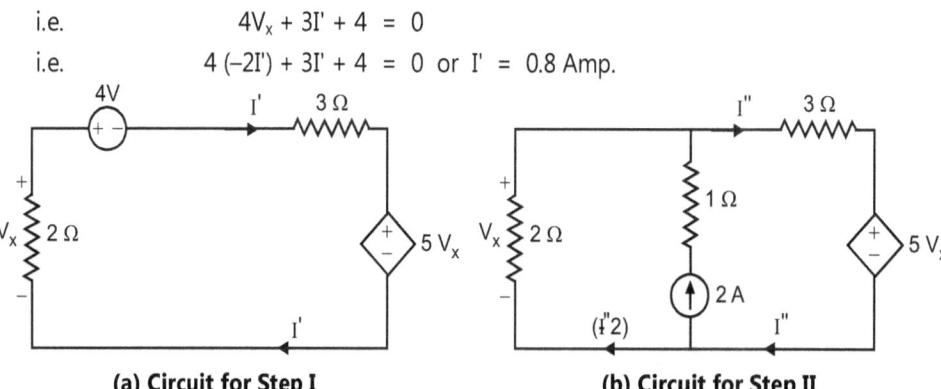

(a) Circuit for Step I (b) Circuit for Step II

Fig. 2.30 : Circuit to find required variables

Step II : Now consider current source only. Make voltage source zero as shown in Fig. 2.30 (b). KCL gives the current in 2Ω resistor as $(I'' - 2)$. Now $V_x = -2(I'' - 2)$ and KVL across outer loop gives

$$+ 5V_x + 3I'' - V_x = 0$$

OR $\quad\quad\quad 4V_x + 3I'' = 0$

i.e. $\quad\quad\quad 4 \times -2(I'' - 2) + 3I'' = 0$

gives, $\quad I'' = \dfrac{16}{5} = 3.2\,A$

Step III: By superposition theorem $I = I' + I'' = 0.8 + 3.2 = 4A$

Hence, $\quad$ current $(I) = 4A$

Example 2.15 : Using superposition theorem find current I in the circuit shown.

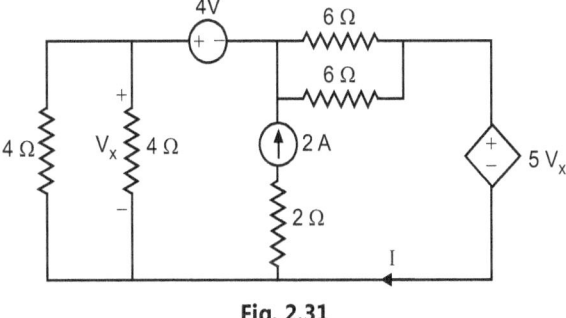

Fig. 2.31

Solution : Two 4Ω resistors are in parallel. Effective resistance is 4Ω || 4Ω = 2Ω. Also 6Ω in parallel with 6Ω gives equivalent of 3Ω. This will reduce the circuit which is same as that is given in Fig. 2.29 except that this has 2Ω resistor in series with 2A source of 1Ω.

Since, any resistor in series with current source do not change current through that branch and hence is of no meaning (Similarly resistor in parallel directly across the voltage source). The analysis will be exactly same as given for Ex. (2.14).

Thus, $\quad$ current $(I) = (0.8 + 3.2) = 4.0$ Amp.

2.2 TEVENIN'S THEOREM

Thevenin's theorem and Norton's theorem are two important network theorems used for the analysis of the electrical networks.

Utility of Thevenin's Theorem :

Thevenin's theorem is used when we want to find current (or voltage) across a particular branch of the given complicated circuit consisting of many energy sources and impedances. It cannot be used to find current (or voltage) across all the branches in the circuit.

Thevenin (voltage source) Equivalent Circuit :

Before we study Thevenin's theorem let us consider Thevenin Equivalent circuit by considering following problem. Suppose that we had a complicated network (N) containing many impedance (R, L, C) and energy sources (Independent or dependent or both). Let Z_L be the load Impedance across any two terminals a-b as shown in Fig. 2.32 (a).

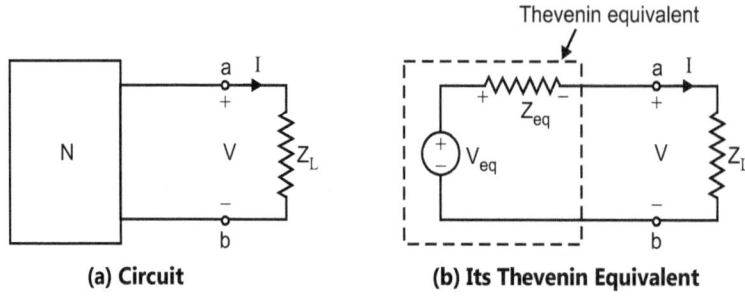

(a) Circuit   (b) Its Thevenin Equivalent

Fig. 2.32 : Circuit to explain Thevenin (Voltage source) Equivalent

Our aim is to replace whole the circuit across a-b by equivalent circuit consisting of a voltage source (V_{eq}) in series with a impedance (Z_{eq}). This is known as Thevenin Equivalent Circuit. The two circuits are equivalent regardless of whatever load (Z_L) connected. This means voltage across terminal a-b (V) and current through terminal (I) must be same in both the circuits.

For Fig. 2.32 (b) $V_{eq} = Z_{eq} I + V$ ...(a)

Value of V_{eq} and Z_{eq} can be found out by considering two simple loads.

(a) To find the voltage V_{eq}: Consider Z_L being temporarily removed by open circuiting as shown in Fig. 2.33.

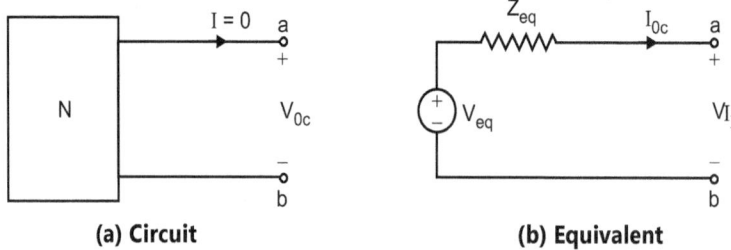

(a) Circuit   (b) Equivalent

Fig. 2.33 : Circuit used to find V_{eq}

As a-b are open ($Z_L = \infty$) we have $I = I_{oc} = 0$

and $V = V_{oc} = V_{eq}$ ...(2.1)

"Thus, V_{eq} is the open circuit voltage (V_{oc}) between the two terminals"

(b) To find value of equivalent Impedance (Z_{eq}): There are two methods by which Z_{eq} can be determined.

Method I: Consider Load (Z_L) is replaced by a short circuit (SC) as shown in Fig. 2.34.

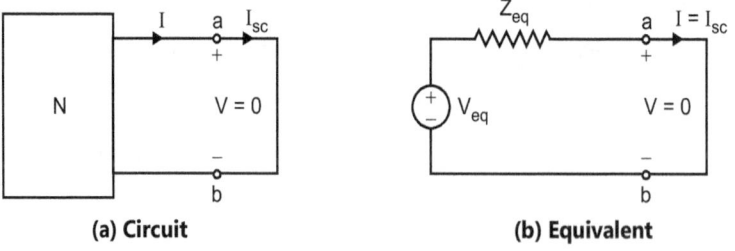

(a) Circuit   (b) Equivalent

Fig. 2.34 : Circuits to find Z_{eq}

As a-b is short V = 0 and $Z_L = 0$

By equation (a) $V_{eq} = Z_{eq} I_{sc} + 0 = Z_{eq} I_{sc}$

Hence $Z_{eq} = \dfrac{V_{eq}}{I_{sc}} = \dfrac{V_{oc}}{I_{sc}}$ ...(2.2)

"**Thus the Z_{eq} is obtained by taking ratio of open circuit voltage (V_{oc}) and short circuit current (I_{sc})**".

Method II: If the network (N) contains only independent energy (voltage or current) sources then Z_{eq} is the impedance seen between terminals a-b of the network with all sources made zero (replace voltage source by short circuit and current source by open circuit).

This is explained in Fig. 2.35.

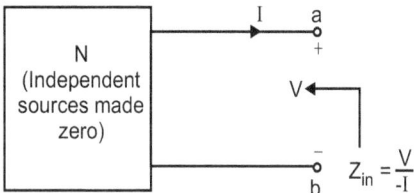

Fig. 2.35 : Alternate method to find Z_{eq}

Thus, $Z_{eq} = Z_{in} = \dfrac{V}{-I}$ ...(2.3)

Z_{eq} is called as "Thevenin equivalent impedance".

Note :

(1) To find Z_{eq} by method II [equation (2.1)] the network (N) should not contain any controlled (dependent) energy sources, and must contain only independent energy sources.

(2) If the network (N) contains controlled energy sources then to find Z_{eq} method – I must be used. Infact method I is general that can be used to find Z_{eq} when network contains both independent and controlled energy sources.

Summary : Thevenin Equivalent circuit can be obtained by using the following steps:

Step I Remove load (Z_L) leaving network (N) with terminals a-b open. Find open circuit voltage (V_{oc}).

Step II : Short terminals a-b ($Z_L = 0$). Find short circuit current (I_{sc})

Then $Z_{eq} = \dfrac{V_{oc}}{I_{sc}}$

Step III : Thevenin equivalent circuit of N is obtained by a voltage source (V_{oc}) in series with impedance (Z_{eq}).

With the study of Thevenin Equivalent circuit now we can define the Thevenin's Theorem and prove it.

Statement of Thevenin's Theorem :

"In a linear circuit containing energy sources and linear, bilateral elements, across any two terminals in the circuit the whole circuit can be replaced by a equivalent voltage source (V_{eq}) in series with equivalent impedance (Z_{eq}) where V_{eq} is the open circuit voltage between the terminals and Z_{eq} is the input impedance seen between the terminals with all the energy sources are replaced by their internal impedances".

Proof :

To prove the above Theorem let us consider a simple circuit shown in Fig. 2.36 (a).

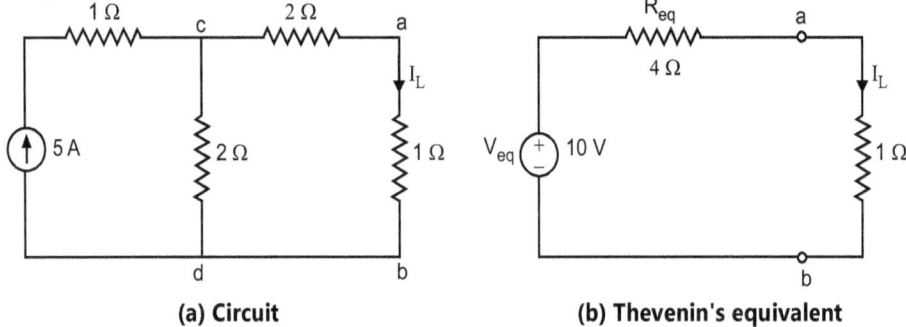

(a) Circuit (b) Thevenin's equivalent

Fig. 2.36 : Circuits used to prove Thevenin's theorem

To prove the theorem let us find out load current (I_L). By current divider action this current is given by

$$I_L = 5 \times \frac{2}{2 + 2 + 1} = 5 \times \frac{2}{5} = 2A$$

Now we have to prove that current I_L as found from using Thevenin Theorem is also equal to 2A. The equivalent circuit is as shown in Fig. 2.36 (b).

With terminal a-b opened the open circuit voltage is the voltage across 2Ω resistor connected between c-d. This voltage is $V_{eq} = V_{oc} = 2 \times 5 = 10V$.

Now to find R_{eq} between a-b make the current source zero (open the two terminals). Then two 2Ω resistors will be in series across a-b. Hence we have $R_{eq} = 2\Omega + 2\Omega = 4$ ohms. Hence the load current (I_L) from Fig. 2.36 (b) is given by

$$I_L = \frac{10}{4 + 1} = \frac{10}{5} = 2A$$

Since, this current is same as the current obtained from current divider action the Thevenins theorem is proved.

Following few examples explains how the Thevenin's theorem can be used effectively in network analysis.

Example 2.16 :

Determine load current (I_L) in 4Ω resistor connected across a-b in the circuit using Thevenin's theorem.

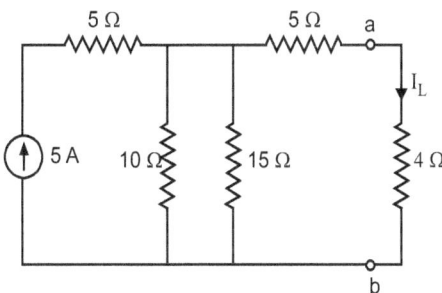

Fig. 2.37

Solution : Let us find Thevenin equivalent across a-b.

Step I : To find open circuit voltage (V_{oc}): With a-b opened the circuit is shown in Fig. 2.38 (a). Then open circuit voltage = $V_{oc} = V_{eq} = 5 \times [6\Omega] = 30V$ where 6Ω resistor is parallel equivalent of 10Ω and 15Ω.

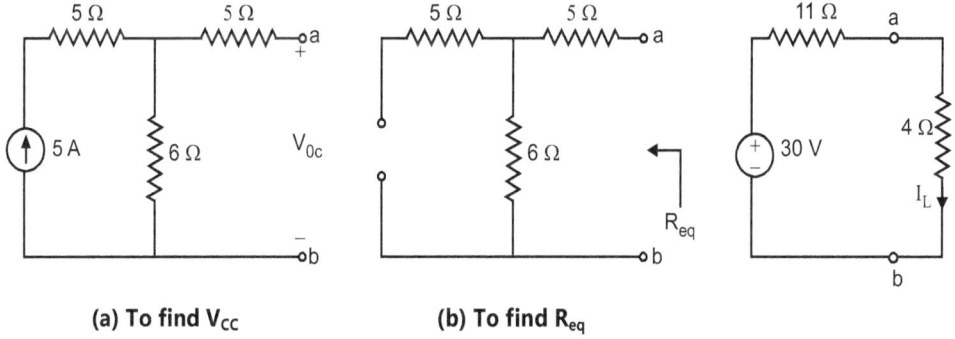

(a) To find V_{cc} (b) To find R_{eq}

Fig. 2.38 : Steps to find Thevenin equivalent circuits

Step II : To find Thevenin equivalent Impedance (R_{eq}) : Open the current source as in Fig. 2.38 (b). Then resistance between

$$a - b = R_{eq} = (5 + 6) = 11 \Omega$$

Step III : Thevenin equivalent circuit: This is shown in the Fig. 2.38 (c). The load current (I_L) is given by

$$(I_L) = \frac{30}{11 + 4} = \frac{30}{15}$$

$$= 2A$$

Example 2.17 :

Find Thevenin equivalent across terminal a-b in the circuit shown below and find current (I_L).

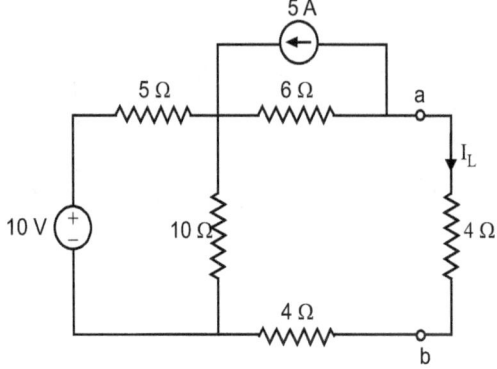

Fig. 2.39

Solution : Let us find Thevenin's equivalent across a-b.

Step I : To find V_{oc} : Open terminal a-b. Make source transformation of 3A current source the resultant circuit is shown in Fig. 2.40 (a). Current (I) = $\dfrac{10}{5+10} = \dfrac{2}{3}$ Amp.

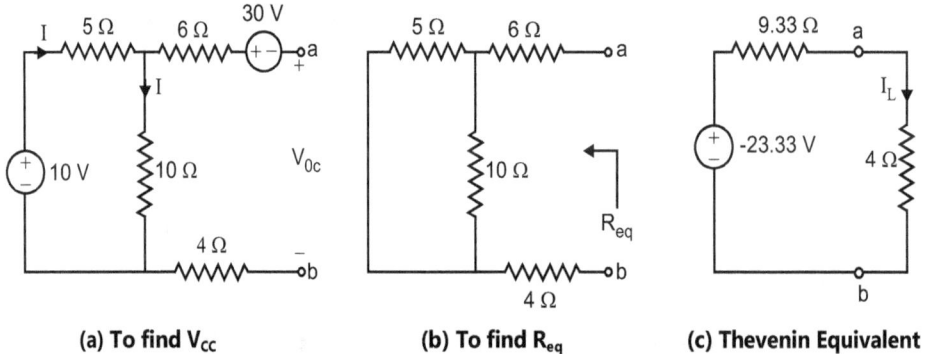

(a) To find V_{cc} (b) To find R_{eq} (c) Thevenin Equivalent

Fig. 2.40 : Steps to find Thevenin equivalent circuits

Open circuit (OC) voltave = V_{oc} = –30 + 10I = –30 + 6.67 = –23.33 V

Step II: To find R_{eq}: Open the current source and short the voltage source the equivalent circuit to find R_{eq} is shown in Fig. 2.40 (b).

$$R_{eq} = 6 + 5 \| 10 = 6 + \dfrac{10}{3} = 9.33 \, \Omega$$

Step III: Thevenin equivalent circuit: This is shown in Fig. 2.40 (b).

$$\text{The load current } (I_L) = \dfrac{-23.33}{9.33 + 4} = -1.75 \text{ Amps.}$$

Example 2.18 :

Find current (I_L) in 10 Ω resistance across a-b. Make use of Thevenin's theorem.

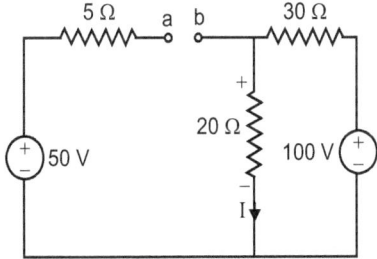

Fig. 2.41

Solution : Let us find the Thevenin equivalent across a-b.

Step I : To find V_{oc}: As it is terminals a-b are open in the given circuit.

The current

$$I = \frac{100}{20 + 30} = \frac{100}{50} = 2.0 \text{ Amp.}$$

Hence voltage between

$$a - b = V_{ab} = V_{oc} = 50 - 20I = 10 \text{ Volts}$$

Step II : To find R_{eq}: Short the two voltage sources. The equivalent circuit is shown in Fig. 2.42 (a). The two resistors of 30Ω || 20 Ω gives equivalent of 12Ω. Thus, equivalent resistance between a – b = R_{eq} = 5 + 12 = 17 Ω.

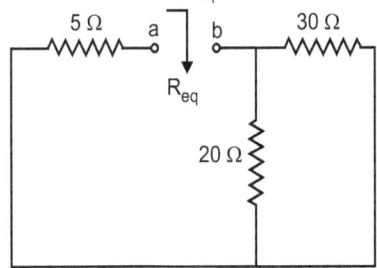
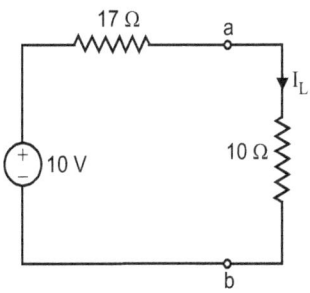

(a) To find R_{eq} (Method II)　　　　(b) Thevenin's equivalent

Fig. 2.42 : Steps to find Thevenin equivalent circuits

Step III: The Thevenin equivalent circuit is shown in Fig. 2.42 (b).

$$\text{The load current } (I_L) = \frac{10}{17 + 10} = \frac{10}{27}$$

$$= 0.37 \text{ Amp.}$$

Example 2.19:
Find current in 20Ω resistor across a-b in the circuit. Make use of Thevenin's theorem.

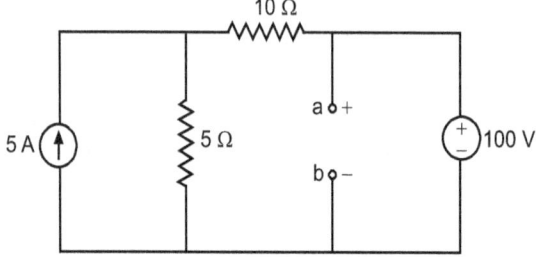

Fig. 2.43

Solution : Let us find Thevenin equivalent across a-b.

Step I : To find V_{oc}: As it is terminals a-b opened. Since 100V is directly across terminals a-b. The voltage across a-b = V_{ab} = V_{oc} = 100V (Fixed)

Step II : To find R_{eq}: Open the current source and short the voltage source as in Fig. 2.44 (a). As terminals a-b are directly shorted R_{ab} = 0. Thus, R_{eq} = 0 ohms.

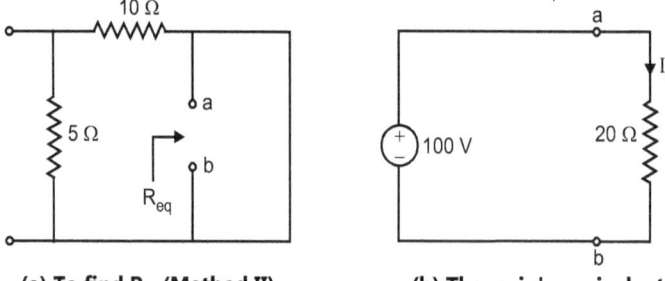

(a) To find R_{eq} (Method II)   (b) Thevenin's equivalent

Fig. 2.44 : Thevenin's equivalent circuits

Step III : Thevenin's equivalent circuit: This is shown in Fig. 2.44 (b). The current in 20Ω is given as

$$(I_L) = \frac{100}{20} = 5A$$

Example 2.20:
Find Thevenin's equivalent circuit across a-b and then find current in 10Ω resistor connected between a-b.

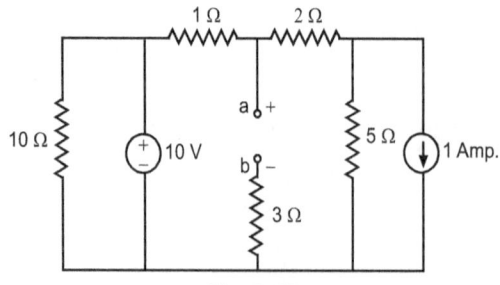

Fig. 2.45

Solution : Let us find Thevenin equivalent circuit across a-b.

Step I : To find open circuit voltage: Convert current source of 1A into voltage source as shown in Fig. 2.46 (a). The loop current I is given by applying KVL across the loop.

i.e.

$$+ 10 - I - 2I - 5I + 5 = 0 \text{ or } I = \frac{15}{8} \text{ Amp.}$$

With terminals a-b open no current flows in 3Ω resistor.

Hence, $V_{ab} = V_{oc} + 7I - 5 = 8.125 \text{ V}$

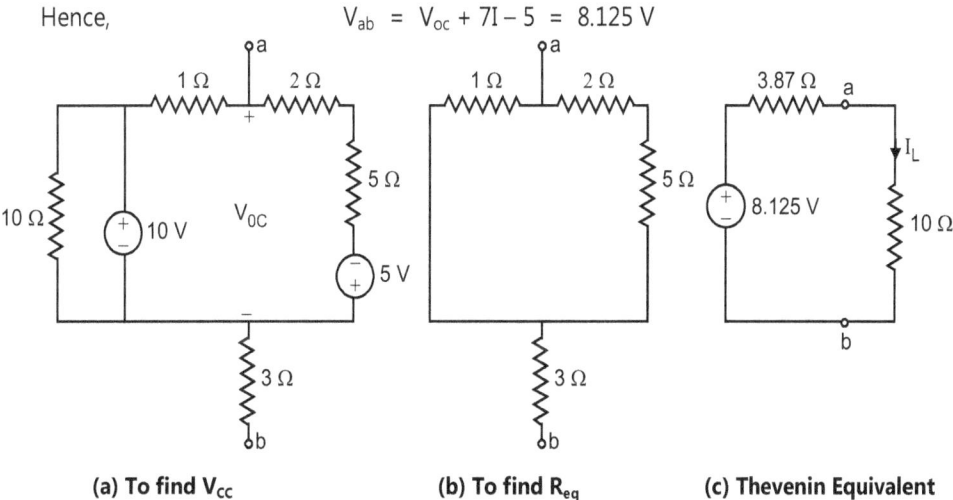

(a) To find V_{cc} (b) To find R_{eq} (c) Thevenin Equivalent

Fig. 2.46 : Thevenin's equivalent circuits

Step II: To f_in R_eq: Open the current sources. Short the voltage sources. The resultant circuit is shown in Fig. 12.46(b). 1Ω is in parallel with (2 + 5) = 7Ω resistor. Hence the equivalent resistance between a-b is

$$R_{eq} = 3 + 1 \| 7$$
$$= 3 + \frac{7}{8}$$
$$= 3.87 \, \Omega$$

Step III: The Thevenin equivalent circuit is shown in Fig. 2.46 (c).

The current between resistor of $10\Omega = I_L = \dfrac{8.125}{10 + 3.87} = 0.585 \text{ A}$

Example 2.21:
In the circuit shown find I_L when $R_L = 5\,\Omega, 10\,\Omega, 20\,\Omega$.

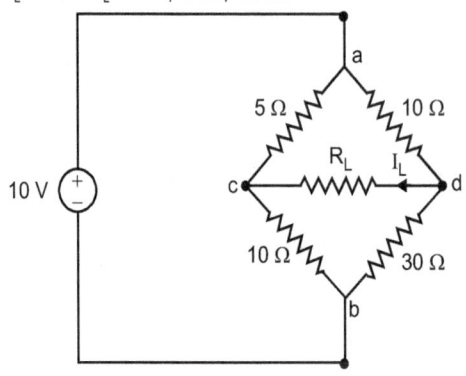

Fig. 2.47

Solution: Since, we have to find load current (I_L) for three different R_L, it is very laborious to calculate the currents by repeating calculations for different values of R_L. Hence, this problem can be solved by using the Thevenin equivalent across load (R_L). For the time being assume R_L is removed.

Step I: To find Thevenin's voltage (V_{oc}): With R_L removed circuit is shown in Fig. 2.48 (a). The currents I_1 and I_2 are $I_1 = \dfrac{10}{10+5} = \dfrac{2}{3}$ A and $I_2 = \dfrac{10}{10+30} = 0.25$ A

$$V_{oc} = \text{Voltage between d and c} = V_{dc} = 30\,I_2 - 10\,I_1$$
$$= 30 \times 0.25 - 10 \times 0.667 = 0.83\text{ V}$$

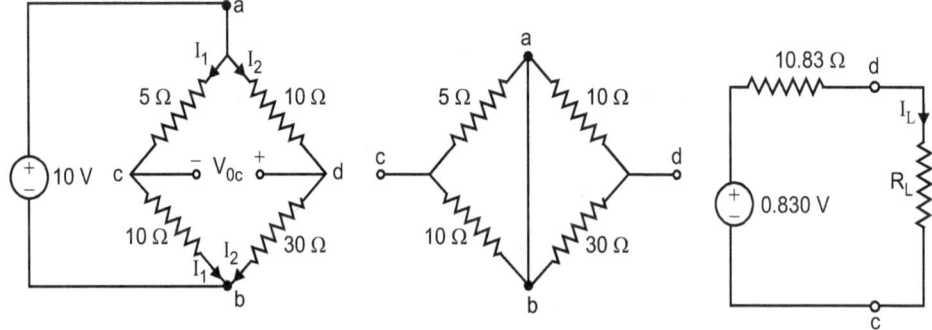

Fig. 2.48 : Thevenin's equivalent circuits

Step II: To find R_{eq}: Short the voltage source with R_L being removed the circuit is shown in Fig. 2.48 (b). Now a-b being shorted $10\,\Omega$ is paralle with $5\,\Omega$ and $10\,\Omega$ is parallel with $30\,\Omega$. This parallel combination is in series across terminals c and d. Thus, we have,

$$R_{eq} = [5 \| 10] + [10 \| 30] = \dfrac{10}{3} + 7.5 = 10.83\,\Omega$$

Step III: Thevenin equivalent circuit is shown in Fig. 2.48 (c).

$$\text{Load current } (I_L) = \frac{0.83}{10.83 + R_L}$$

For $R_L = 5\,\Omega$ we have $I_{L1} = 52.43$ mA
For $R_L = 10\,\Omega$ we have $I_{L2} = 39.85$ mA
For $R_L = 20\,\Omega$ we have $I_{L3} = 26.92$ mA

Note :

In last few examples we have seen that the Thevenin equivalent circuit is very convenient and easy to find current (or voltage) across a particular branch of the circuit. It is more convenient especially when load is variable like the one in Ex. 2.21 Thus, the Thevenin's theorem simplify the network analysis to a greater extent. In fact the Thevenin Theorem is considered to be major break through in the circuit analysis.

Example 2.22 :

For the circuit shown find Thevenin's equivalent circuit across terminal a-b.

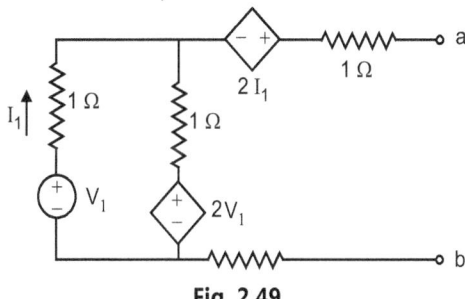

Fig. 2.49

Solution : Step I: To find V_{oc}: As its terminals are opened current I_1 is given by

$$I_1 = \frac{V_1 - 2V_1}{1 + 1} = \frac{-V_1}{2} \text{ Amp.}$$

$$V_{ab} = V_{co} = 2I_1 + I_1 + 2V_1 = 3I_1 + 2V_1$$

$$= \frac{-3V_1}{2} + 2V_1 = \frac{V_1}{2} \text{ Amp.}$$

Step II : To find R_{eq} : Since, circuit contains controlled sources the impedance is to be determined by using the equation (2.3).

i.e. $$R_{eq} = \frac{V_{oc}}{I_{sc}} \qquad \qquad \ldots(2.3)$$

To find I_{sc} use circuit of Fig. 2.50 (a)
KVL across first (Input) loop gives $2V_1 + (I_1 - I_{sc}) + I_1 - V_1 = 0$

$$2I_1 - I_{sc} + V_1 = 0 \text{ or } I_{sc} - 2I_1 = V_1 \qquad \ldots(a)$$

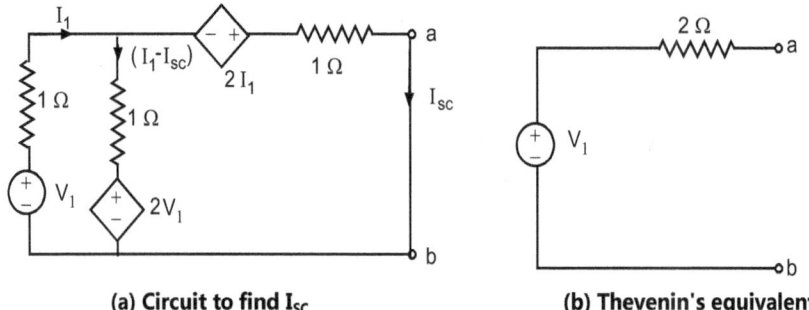

(a) Circuit to find I_{sc} (b) Thevenin's equivalent

Fig. 2.50 : Steps to find Thevenin equivalent

KVL across second (output) loop[gives

$$I_{sc} - 2 I_1 (I_1 - I_{sc}) - 2V_1 = 0$$

OR $\quad -3I_1 + 2I_{sc} = 2V_1 \quad$ ...(b)

From (a) and (b) solve for I_{sc}

$$I_{sc} = \frac{\begin{vmatrix} -2 & V_1 \\ -3 & 2V_1 \end{vmatrix}}{\begin{vmatrix} -2 & 1 \\ -3 & 2 \end{vmatrix}} = \frac{-4V_1 + 3V_1}{-4 + 3} = \frac{-V_1}{-1} = V_1$$

Hence by equation (2.3) $\quad R_{eq} = \dfrac{V_1}{V_1/2} = 2\Omega$

Step III : Thus, Thevenin equivalent across a-b is shown in Fig. 2.50 (b).

Example 2.23 :

Replace the portion within dotted line by Thevenin's equivalent circuit and then find voltage V_1.

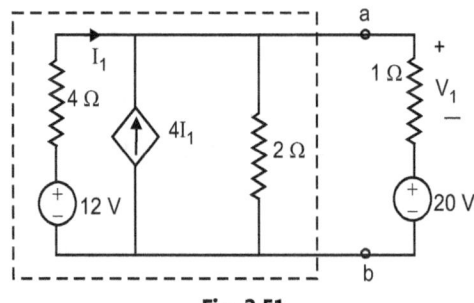

Fig. 2.51

Solution : We have to find Thevenin equivalent across a-b. For the time being assume that a-b is open circuited.

Step I : To find V$_{OC}$: The circuit is shown in Fig. 2.52 (a).

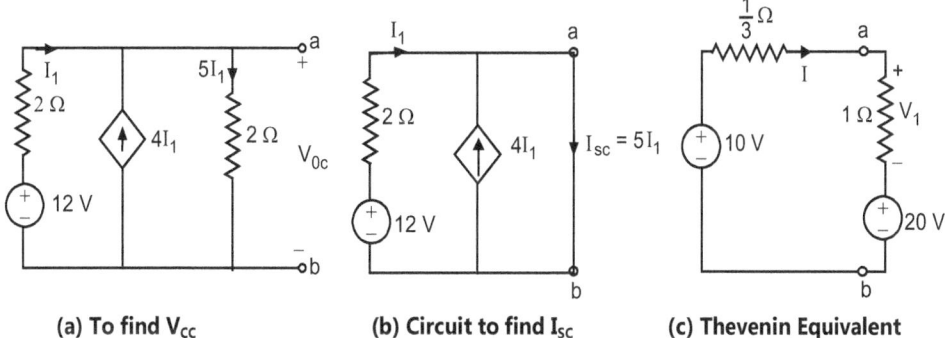

(a) To find V$_{CC}$ (b) Circuit to find I$_{SC}$ (c) Thevenin Equivalent

Fig. 2.52 : Steps to obtain Thevenin equivalent circuits

KVL across outer loop gives $2 \times 5I_1 + 2I_1 - 12 = 0$ or $I_1 = 1$ Amp.

Hence $\quad V_{eq} = V_{OC} = 2 \times 5I_1 = 10V$

Step II : To find R$_{eq}$: Since, circuit contains controlled sources we have to use equation $R_{eq} = \dfrac{V_{OC}}{I_{SC}}$. To find I$_{SC}$ consider the circuit shown in Fig. 2.52 (b).

KVL, across outer loop gives $0 + 2I_1 - 12 = 0$ OR $I_1 = 6A$. Thus I_1 is different from one found in Step I because here I_1 is found by short circuiting a-b while it was found by open circuiting in step I.

Thus, $\quad\quad\quad\quad\quad\quad I_{SC} = 5I_1 = 5 \times 6 = 30A$

Therefore $\quad\quad\quad\quad R_{eq} = \dfrac{V_{OC}}{I_{SC}} = \dfrac{10}{30} = \dfrac{1}{3} \Omega$

Step III : Thevenin equivalent is shown in Fig. 2.52 (c). KVL across whole loop gives current (I).

Thus $20 + I + \dfrac{I}{3} - 10 = 0$. Solving this gives current $(I) = \dfrac{30}{4}$ Amp. -7.5 A.

Hence $\quad\quad\quad\quad V_1 = 1 \times I = I = -75$ Volts

Example 2.24 : Find current in 9Ω resistor by using Thevenin's Theorem.

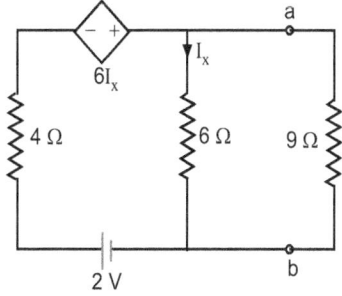

Fig. 2.53

Solution : Let us first find Thevenin equivalent across a- b.

Step I : To find V_{OC}: Open the terminal a-b by removing the 9Ω resistor as shown in Fig. 2.54 (a). There will be a single loop with loop current I_x.

KVL gives $\quad 6I_x - 6I_x + 4I_x - 2 = 0 \quad$ or $\quad I_x = 0.5$ A

Hence $\quad\quad\quad\quad\quad V_{OC} = V_{ab} = V_{eq} = 6I_x = 3V$

Step II : To find R_{eq}: Use $R_{eq} = \dfrac{V_{OC}}{I_{SC}}$ to find the R_{eq}. Now short a-b find I_{SC} as shown in Fig. 2.54 (b).

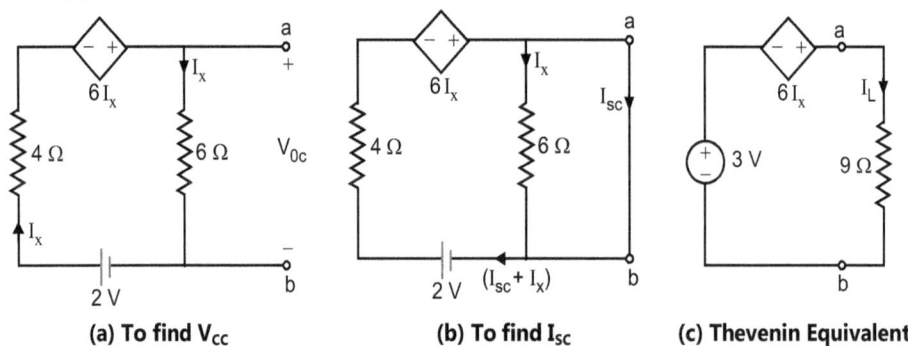

(a) To find V_{CC} (b) To find I_{SC} (c) Thevenin Equivalent

Fig. 2.54 : Step to find Thevenin's equivalent

KVL across input loop gives $\quad 6I_x - 6I_x + 4(I_{SC} + I_x) - 2 = 0 \quad$ ...(a)

OR $\quad\quad\quad\quad\quad\quad (I_{SC} + I_x) = 0.5$

KVL across output loop gives $6I_x = 0$ or $I_x = 0$

Hence, we have $\quad\quad\quad I_{SC} = 0.5$ A

Thus, $\quad\quad\quad\quad R_{eq} = \dfrac{V_{OC}}{I_{SC}} = \dfrac{3}{0.5} = 6 \, \Omega$

Step III : Thevenin equivalent circuit is shown in Fig. 2.54 (c).

The current through 9Ω resistor $= I_L = \dfrac{3}{6+9} = \dfrac{3}{15} = 0.2$ A

Example 2.25 :

Find current in 10Ω resistor across a-b in the circuit shown. Make use of voltage source equivalent across terminals a-b.

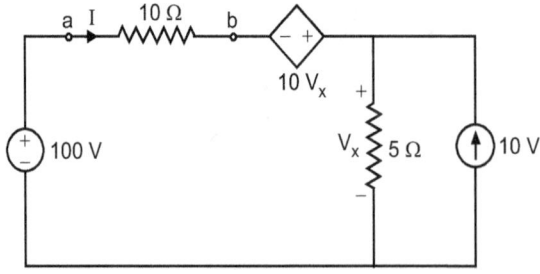

Fig. 2.55

Solution : We have to find voltage source (Thevenin's) equivalent circuit across terminals a-b.

Step I: To find V_{OC}: Open the terminals a-b as shown in Fig. 2.56 (a). 10 A current flows through 5Ω resistor. Hence $V_x = 50$ V.

Now, $V_{OC} = V_{ab} = 100 - V_x + 10V_x = 100 + 9V_x = 550V$

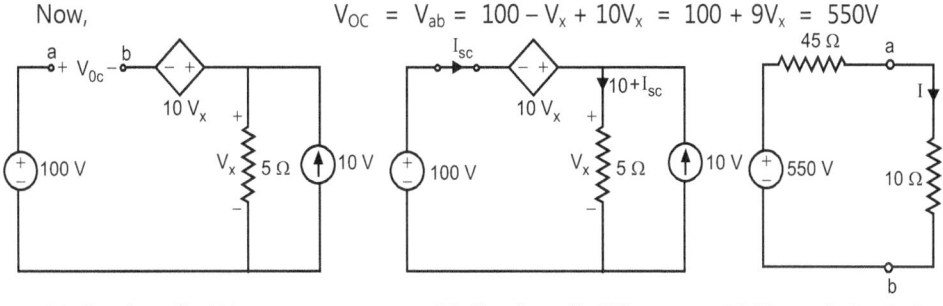

(a) Circuit to find V_{CC} (b) Circuit to find V_{OC} (c) Thevenin Equivalent

Fig. 2.56 : Steps to find voltage source equivalent

Step II : To find R_{eq}: Use the formula $R_{eq} = \dfrac{V_{OC}}{I_{SC}}$. To get I_{SC} short terminals a-b as shown in Fig. 2.56 (b). We have $V_x = 5(10 + I_{SC})$. Where $(10 + I_{SC})$ is the current in 5Ω resistor. KVL across input loop gives $V_x - 10 V_x - 100 = 0$ OR $-9V_x = 100$

i.,e. $\qquad -9[10 + I_{SC}] \times 5 = 100$

Solving this gives $\qquad I_{SC} = \dfrac{500}{45}$ A

Hence, $\qquad R_{eq} = \dfrac{V_{OC}}{I_{SC}} = 45\ \Omega$

Step III: Thevenin's (Voltage source) equivalent is shown in Fig. 2.56 (c).

2.3 NORTON'S THEOREM

Like Thevenin Theorem, Norton's Theorem is also used to analyse the given network.

Utility of Theorem :

It is used when current (or voltage) across a particular branch in a circuit consisting of many sources and impedance is to be found out. However it cannot be used when more than one branch currents (or voltages) are to be found out.

Norton's (Current Source) Equivalent Circuit :
Consider a network (N) consisting of impedances and energy sources is shown in Fig. 2.32 (a). Some time the whole network (N) is to be replaced across a-b by equivalent circuit shown in Fig. (2.57). This is an current source equivalent and is called Norton's equivalent circuit.

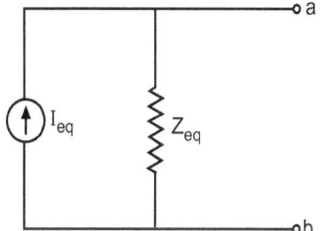

Fig. 2.57 : Norton's (Current source) Equivalent circuit

This equivalent can be obtained by source transformation of Thevenin's equivalent circuit of Fig. 2.32 (b) where

$$I_{eq} = I_N = \frac{V_{OC}}{Z_{eq}} \qquad ...(2.4)$$

This is the value of equivalent current source. Since,

$$Z_{eq} = \frac{V_{OC}}{I_{SC}}$$

We have,
$$I_{eq} = I_N = \frac{V_{OC}}{V_{OC}/I_{SC}} = I_{SC} \qquad ...(2.5)$$

Thus, Norton's equivalent current source is the short circuit current across terminals in the circuit.

Thus, **"Norton's equivalent circuit is obtained by the source Transformation of Thevenin equivalent circuit or vice versa".**

Statement of Norton's Theorem: "In a linear circuit containing energy sources and linear and bilateral element across any two terminals in the circuit the whole circuit can be replaced by equivalent current source (I_{eq}) in parallel with equivalent impedance (Z_{eq}) where, I_{eq} is the short circuit current (I_{SC}) between the terminals and Z_{eq} is the input impedance the terminals with all the energy sources replaced by their internal impedances."

Proof: To prove above theorem let us consider again the same circuit as shown in Fig. 2.36 (a) and is reproduced in Fig. 2.58 (a) below.

Let us find the load current (I_L) to prove this theorem. As before current divider action I_L:

$$= \frac{5 \times 2}{2 + 2 + 1} = 2A \text{ for the circuit of Fig. 2.58 (a)}$$

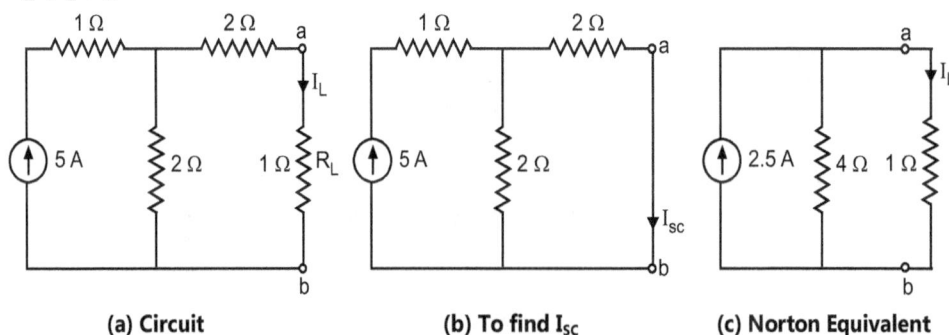

(a) Circuit   (b) To find I_{SC} (c) Norton Equivalent

Fig. 2.58 : Circuits to prove Norton's Theorem

Now we shall prove that I_L = 2A by Norton's theorem. Now short terminals a-b as shown in Fig. 2.58 (b). Then short circuit current (I_{SC}) which is equivalent current (I_{eq}) is given by

$$I_{eq} = I_{SC} = 5 \times \frac{2}{2 \times 2} = 2.5 \text{ A}$$

As before Z_{eq} is the impedance between a-b with current source made zero (open the terminals). Thus, we have $Z_{eq} = 4\Omega$.

Hence, the Norton's equivalent is shown in Fig. 2.58 (c). For this circuit the current in load (I_L) is given by current divider action as,

$$I_L = 2.5 \times \frac{4}{1+4} = 2A$$

Since, this current is same as that obtained by the current divider action the Norton's theorem is proved.

[**Note:** Norton's equivalent circuits is also called as the current source equivalent circuit.]
Following examples explains the use of the Norton's theorem in circuit analysis.

Example 2.26 :

Find current in 2Ω resistor across a-b by using Norton's theorem.

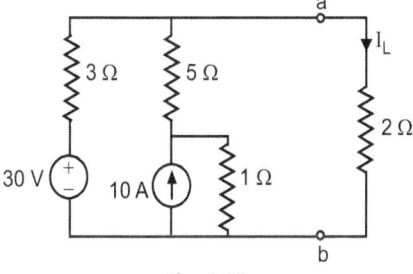

Fig. 2.59

Solution : Let us find Norton equivalent circuit across a-b.

Step 1 : To find I_{eq} (or I_N): To find I_{eq} short a-b as shown in Fig. 2.60 (a). Convert the current source into voltage source. Current I_1 and I_2 together added to get I_{SC}. We have $I_1 = \frac{30}{3} = 10$ A, $I_2 = \frac{10}{6} = \frac{5}{6}$ A. Hence $I_{SC} = I_1 + I_2 = 10 + \frac{5}{3} = 11.67$ Amp.

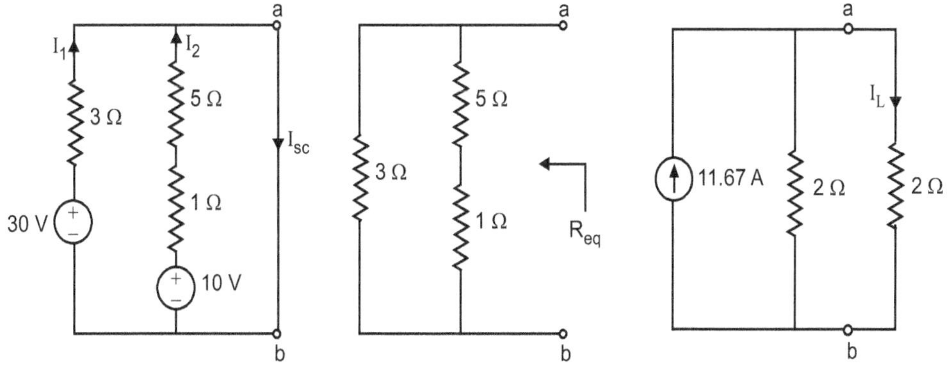

(a) To find I_{SC} (b) To find (Method II) (c) Norton Equivalent

Fig. 2.60 : Steps to obtain Norton's equivalent

Step II : To find R_{eq}: Remove load of 2Ω resistor. Short the voltage source V. Open the current source. The resultant circuit is shown in Fig. 2.60 (b). Hence, we have

$$R_{eq} = 3\Omega \parallel 6\Omega = \frac{3 \times 6}{3+6} = \frac{18}{9} = 2\Omega$$

Step III : The Norton equivalent circuit is shown in Fig. 2.60 (c). By current divider action the load current (I_L) is given by

$$I_L = 11.67 \times \frac{2}{2+2} = 5.835 \text{ A}$$

Example 2.27 : Find current in 1 ohm resistor by Norton equivalent circuit.

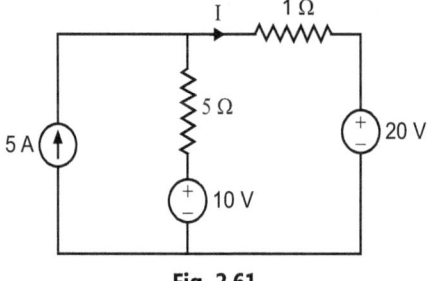

Fig. 2.61

Solution : Let a-b be the terminals where 1Ω resistor is connected. Let us find Nortons' equivalent circuit across terminals a-b.

Step I : To find I_{eq} (Or I_N): Short the terminals a-b as shown in Fig. 2.62 (a). Let I_{SC} be the short circuit current.

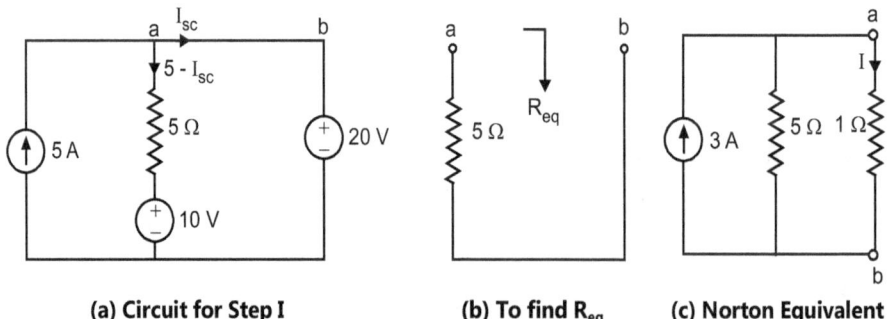

(a) Circuit for Step I   (b) To find R_{eq} (c) Norton Equivalent

Fig. 2.62 : Steps to obtain Norton's equivalent

By KCL current in 5Ω resistor is (5 –I_{SC}). Using KVL across output loop given

$$10 + 5(5 - I_{SC}) - 20 = 0$$

OR $I_{SC} = 3A$

Thus, $I_{eq} = I_N = 3A$

Step II: To find R_{eq}: Open the current source short the voltage sources. Remove the 1Ω resistor. The circuit is shown in Fig. 2.62 (b). The equivalent resistance between a-b is given by $R_{eq} = 5Ω$.

Step III: The Norton's Equivalent circuit is shown in Fig. 2.62 (c). By current divider action, the current in 1Ω reisistor is $I = 3 \times \dfrac{5}{5+1} = 2.5A$

Note: Many times we need to find both Thevenin's and Norton equivalent for the given circuit. Then we can first find any one of them and then the other equivalent can be obtained by using source transformation. Following few examples explains this.

Example 2.28 :

Find Thevenin's and Norton's equivalent across a-b in the circuit shown.

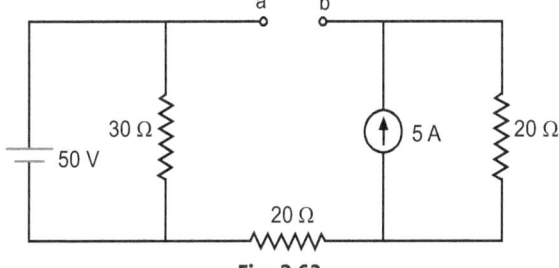

Fig. 2.63

Solution : Let us find Thevenin's equivalent circuit.

Step I: To find V_{OC}: The circuit is shown n Fig. 2.64 (a). Convert 5A current source into a voltage source. The voltage between a – b = V_{OC} = 50 –100 = –50V

Step II: To find R_{eq}: Open the current source and short the voltage source. Then resistance between a – b = R_{eq} = 20 + 20 = 40 Ω.

Step III: Thevenin equivalent circuit is shown in Fig. 2.64 (b).

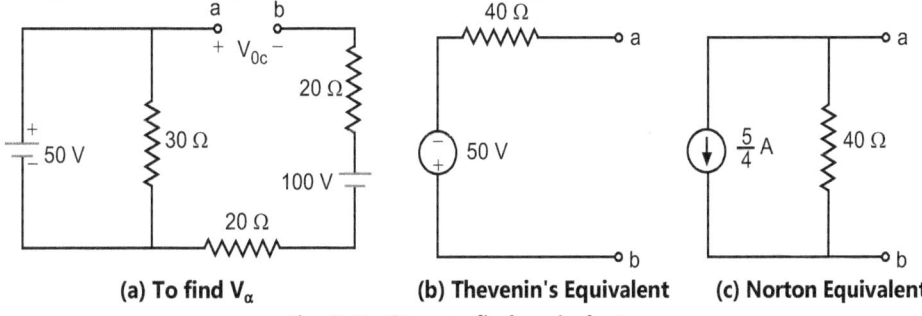

(a) To find $V_α$ (b) Thevenin's Equivalent   (c) Norton Equivalent

Fig. 2.64 : Steps to find equivalent

Since V_{OC} is – V_e (Negative), the polarity of 50V source is shown reversed.

The Norton's equivalent is obtained by source transformation of Thevenin's equivalent and is shown in Fig. 2.64 (c)

Example 2.29 :

Find Thevenin's and Norton's equivalent circuits across terminal pair a-b in the circuit shown below.

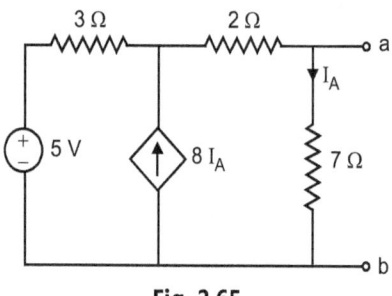

Fig. 2.65

Solution : Let us first find Thevenine equivalent circuit and then use source transformation to get Norton's equivalent.

Step I : To find V_{OC} : The circuit can be written as shown in Fig. 2.66 (a) KCL gives current in 3Ω resistor as $7I_A$.

KVL across loop b-a-c-d-b gives

$$7I_a + 2I_A - 7I_A \times 3 = 5$$

Solving this gives $\quad I_A = \dfrac{-5}{12}$ Amp.

Hence, $\quad V_{OC} = V_{ab} = 7I_A = \dfrac{-35}{12} = -2.917$ Volts

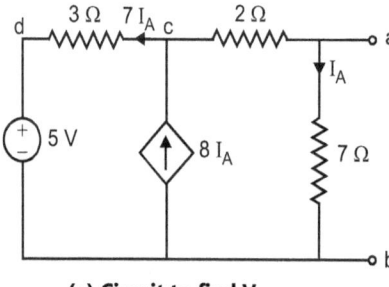
(a) Circuit to find V_α

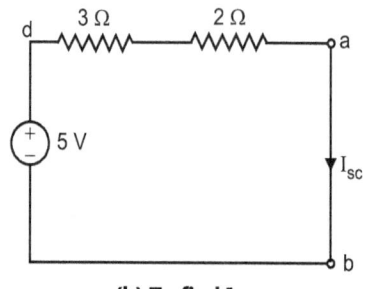
(b) To find I_{SC}

Fig. 2.66 : Steps to find equivalent

Step II: To find R_{eq}: Use method I and equation (2.1) to find R_{eq}. Since the circuit contains controlled sources. When a-b are shorted current I_A will be zero. The current source $8I_A$ KVL across loop gives $(2 + 3) I_{SC} = 5$ or $I_{SC} = 1$ Amp.

Thus, $\quad R_{eq} = \left| \dfrac{V_{OC}}{I_{SC}} \right| = \dfrac{35}{12} = 2.917\,\Omega$

NETWORK ANALYSIS (S.E. SEM. III. E & TC. SU)   NETWORK THEOREMS

Step III: The resultant Thevenin equivalent circuit is shown in Fig. 2.67 (a). By making use of source transformation Norton equivalent of Fig. 2.67 (b) is obtained.

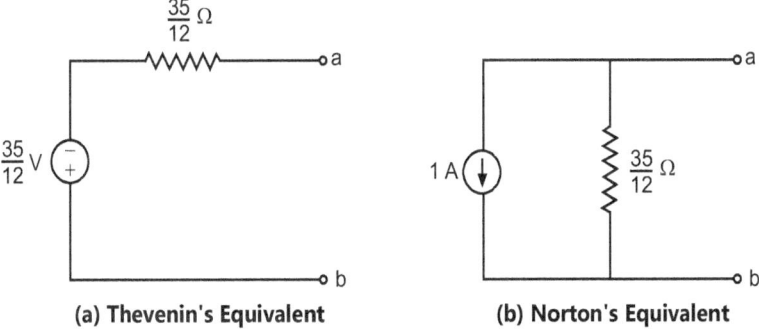

(a) Thevenin's Equivalent   (b) Norton's Equivalent

Fig. 2.67 : The equivalent circuits

Note: Since V_{OC} is negative the polarity of V_{OC} in the equivalent circuit is reversed.

Example 2.30 :

Find Thevenin's and Norton's equivalent circuits across terminals a-b in the circuit shown.

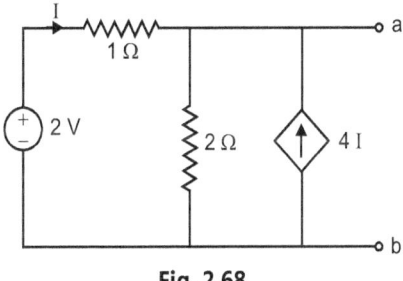

Fig. 2.68

Solution : Let us first find Thevenin's equivalent circuit.

Step I : To find V_{OC}: With terminal a-b opened as given, KCL gives current in 2Ω resistor as 5I. The circuit is as shown in Fig. 2.69 (a).

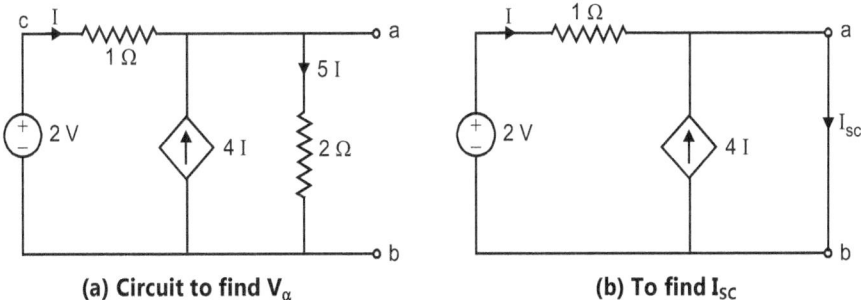

(a) Circuit to find V_α (b) To find I_{SC}

Fig. 2.69 : Steps to find equivalent

KVL across loop gives (b-a-c-b)

Unit II | 2.39

$$2 \times 5I + I - 2 = 0 \text{ OR } I = \frac{2}{1} \text{ Amp.}$$

Hence, $V_{OC} = V_{ab} = 2 \times 5I = 10I = \frac{20}{11}$ Volts

Step II : To find R_{eq}: Here method I is to be used where $R_{eq} = \frac{V_{OC}}{I_{SC}}$, Now short terminals a-b, then the resultant circuit is as shown in Fig. 2.69 (b). The current $(I_{SC}) = 5I$

Now KVL gives $I \times 1 = 2$ OR $I = 2$ Amp.

Hence, short circuit current $(I_{SC}) = I_{eq} = 10A$.

Therefore, $R_{eq} = \frac{20/11}{10} = \frac{20}{11} \times \frac{1}{10} = \frac{2}{11} \Omega$

Step III : Thevenin equivalent circuit is shown in Fig. 2.70 (a). The Norton's equivalent is shown in Fig. 2.70 (b).

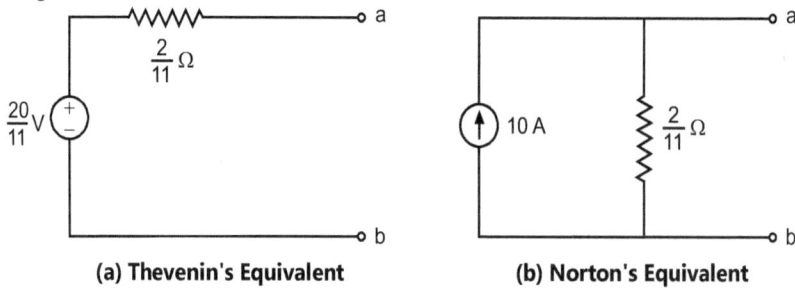

(a) Thevenin's Equivalent (b) Norton's Equivalent

Fig. 2.70 : Equivalent circuits

Example 2.31 :

Find Thevenin's and Norton's equivalent circuits across AB in the circuit shown.

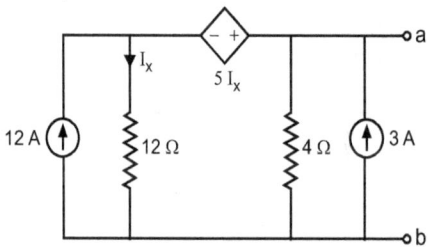

Fig. 2.71

Solution : Let us first find Thevein equivalent circuit.

Step I : To find V_{OC}: With terminal a-b open the currents in various branches are shown in Fig. 2.72 (a).

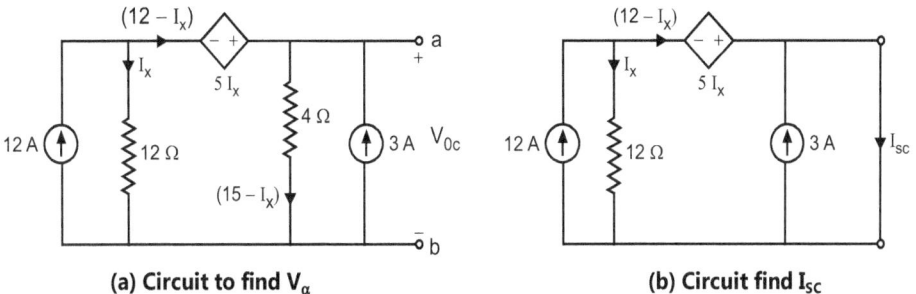

(a) Circuit to find V_α (b) Circuit find I_{SC}

Fig. 2.72 : Steps to find equivalents

There is only one unknown (I_x). KVL across the loop gives,.

$$4(15 - I_x) - 5I_x - 12(I_x) = 0 \text{ i.e. } I_x = \frac{60}{21} = \frac{20}{7} \text{ Amp.}$$

Hence,
$$V_{OC} = V_{ab} = 4(15 - I_x)$$
$$= 4\left[15 - \frac{20}{7}\right] = 48.57 \text{ Volts}$$

Step II : To find R_{eq} ; Use method I where $R_{eq} = \dfrac{V_{OC}}{I_{SC}}$. I_{SC} can be found out by shorting a-b as shown in Fig. 2.72 (b).

where $\qquad I_{SC} = (3 + 12 - I_x) = 15 - I_x$

Now KVL gives $-5I_x - 17I_x = 0$. Since, this equation cannot be satisfied the current $I_x = 0$.

Thus $\qquad I_{SC} = 15 - 0 = 15$ Amp.

Thus, $\qquad R_{eq} = \dfrac{V_{OC}}{I_{SC}} = \dfrac{48.57}{15}$

$\qquad = 3.23 \; \Omega$

Step III : Thevenin equivalent circuit is shown in Fig. 2.73 (a) while the Norton equivalent is shown in Fig. 2.73 (b).

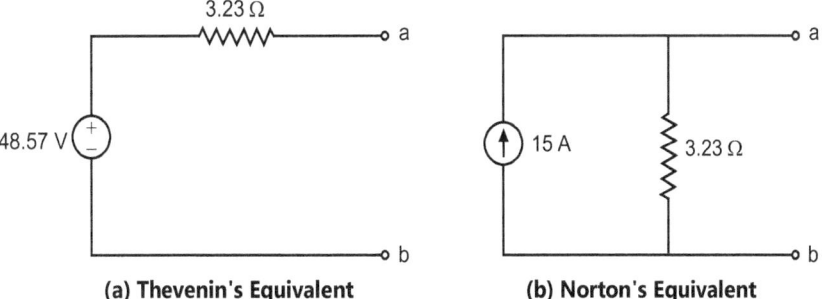

(a) Thevenin's Equivalent (b) Norton's Equivalent

Fig. 2.73 : The equivalent circuits

Example 2.32 :

Obtain current I_x for the circuit using the Thevenin's Theorem.

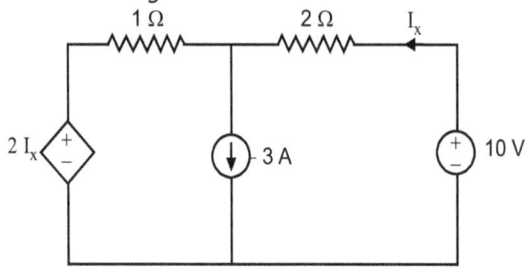

Fig. 2.74

Solution : Assume for the time being 2Ω removed. Then $I_x = 0$ and we shall find Thevenin equivalent across terminals a-b where 2Ω is connected.

Step I : To find V_{OC} : The circuit is as shown in Fig. 2.75 (a). The controlled source become inactive (0V).

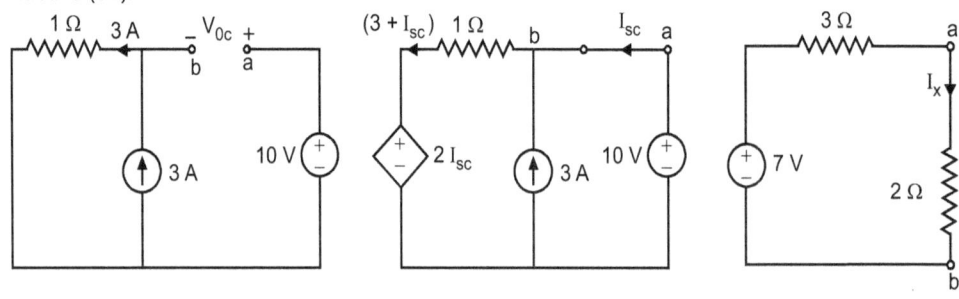

(a) Circuit for V_{CC} (b) Circuit to find I_{SC} (c) Thevenin Equivalent

Fig. 2.75 : Steps to find Thevenin equivalent

Step II : To find R_{eq}: We use $R_{eq} = \dfrac{V_{OC}}{I_{SC}}$. To find equivalent resistor short terminal a-b.

Let I_{SC} be the current flowing through the shorted terminals. By KCL current in 1Ω resistor is $(3 + I_{SC})$. The resultant circuit is shown in Fig. 2.75 (b). The KVL across loop gives $10 - (3 + I_{SC}) - 2I_{SC} = 0$. Hence $I_{SC} = \dfrac{7}{3}$ Amp.

Thus, $$R_{eq} = \dfrac{V_{OC}}{I_{SC}} = \dfrac{7}{7/3}$$
$$= 3\,\Omega$$

Step III : The Thevenin equivalent circuit is shown in Fig. 2.75 (c).

Thus, $$I_x = \dfrac{7}{3+2} = \dfrac{7}{5}$$
$$= 1.4\text{ A}$$

Example 2.33 :

Find Thevenin and Norton equivalent circuit across A-B in the circuit shown.

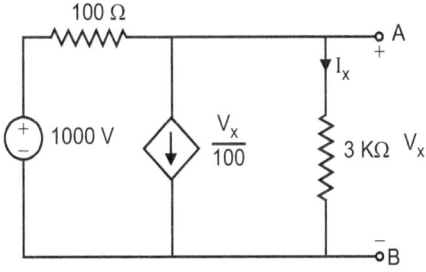

Fig. 2.76

Solution : Let us first find Thevenin equivalent circuit across A-B.

Step I : To find V_{OC}: As it is terminals are open

We have
$$I_x = \frac{V_x}{3000} = \left(\frac{V_x}{3}\right) mA$$

$$\text{Current (I)} = \left(\frac{V_x}{100} + I_x\right)$$

The KVL gives $V_x + 100I - 1000 = 0$

OR $V_x + 100\left(I_x + \frac{V_x}{100}\right) = 1000$

Solving this given $V_x = \frac{1000}{2.033} = 491.8 \text{ V} = V_{OC}$

The circuit is shown in Fig. 2.77 (a).

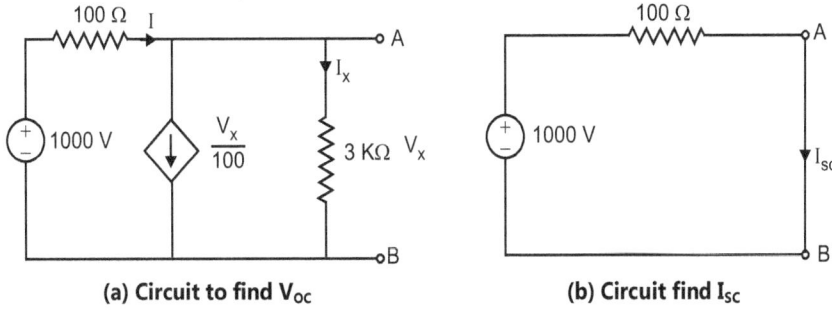

(a) Circuit to find V_{OC} (b) Circuit find I_{SC}

Fig. 2.77 : Steps to find equivalent

Step II: To find I_{SC}: Short the terminal A-B. Then $I_x = 0$ an controlled current source becomes zero. The resultant circuit will be as shown in Fig. 2.77 (b).

Now, $I_{SC} = \frac{1000}{100} = 10A$

Hence, $R_{eq} = \dfrac{V_{OC}}{I_{SC}} = 41.18$ ohms

Step III: The resultant Thevenin equivalent circuit is shown in Fig. 2.78 (a). The Norton equivalent circuit with $I_{eq} = I_{SC} = 10A$ is shown in Fig. 2.78 (b).

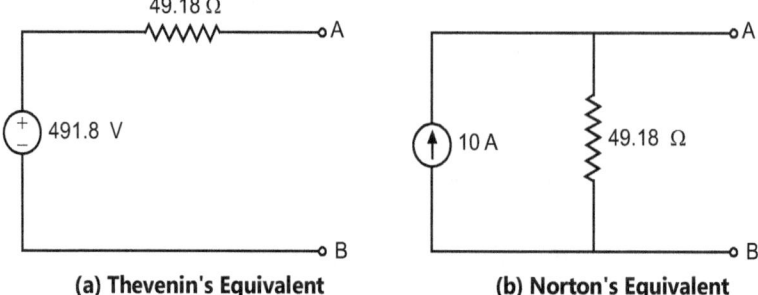

(a) Thevenin's Equivalent   (b) Norton's Equivalent

Fig. 2.78 : Equivalent circuits

Example 2.34 :

Find Thevenin and Norton's equivalent circuit across A-B in the circuit shown.

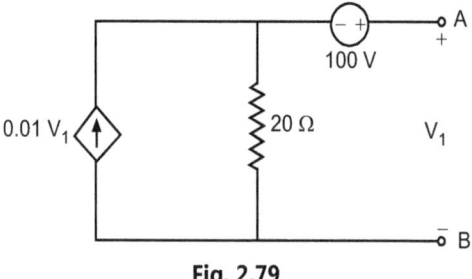

Fig. 2.79

Solution : Let us first find Thevenin equivalent circuit.

Step I : To find V_{OC}:

As it is terminals are opened. The voltage (V_1) is the V_{OC} between terminals. With A-B opened current of $0.01\ V_1$ flows through 20Ω resistor. KVL across the output loop gives

$$V_1 - 100 - 20 \times 0.02\ V_1 = 0 \quad \text{i.e.} \quad V_1 - 0.2\ V_s = 100$$

OR $\quad V_1 = 125V$ is the open circuit voltage

Step II : To find R_{eq}:

Use $R_{eq} = \dfrac{V_{OC}}{I_{SC}}$. To obtain Thevenin resistance short terminal A-B. Since $V_1 = 0$ the current source becomes zero. The resultant circuit is shown in fig. 2.80 (a).

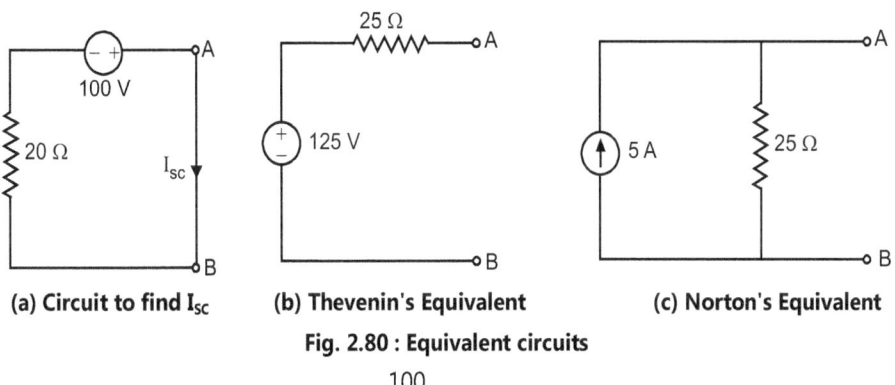

(a) Circuit to find I_{sc} (b) Thevenin's Equivalent (c) Norton's Equivalent

Fig. 2.80 : Equivalent circuits

Now, $\qquad I_{sc} = \dfrac{100}{20} = 5A$

Hence, $\qquad R_{eq} = \dfrac{V_{OC}}{I_{SC}} = \dfrac{125}{5}$

$\qquad \qquad \qquad = 25\Omega$

Step III: The resultant Thevenin equivalent circuit is shown in Fig. (2.80) (b).

As $\qquad I_{SC} = I_{eq} = 5A$

the Norton equivalent is shown in Fig. 1.192 (c).

Example 2.35 :

Find Thevenin and Norton's equivalent circuits across AB in the circuits.

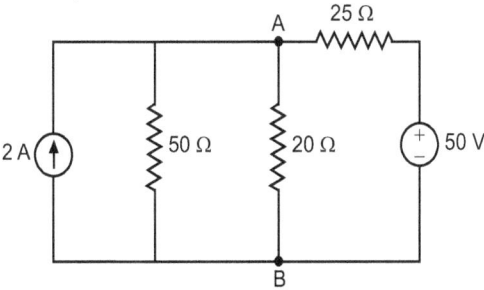

Fig. 2.81

Solution : Let us first find out Thevenin equivalent circuit.

Step I : To find V_{OC}: Open terminals A-B by removing 20Ω resistor temporarily. Convert 20A current source into a voltage source. The resultant circuit is shown in Fig. 2.82 (a). Let V_{OC} be voltage between A-B. Since, here is a single loop let I be loop current. Now KVL across loop gives.

$$50 + 25I + 50I - 100 = 0 \text{ OR } I = +\dfrac{2}{3} \text{ Amp.}$$

Voltage between $\qquad A - B = V_{AB} = 25I + 50 = 66.67 \text{ V}$

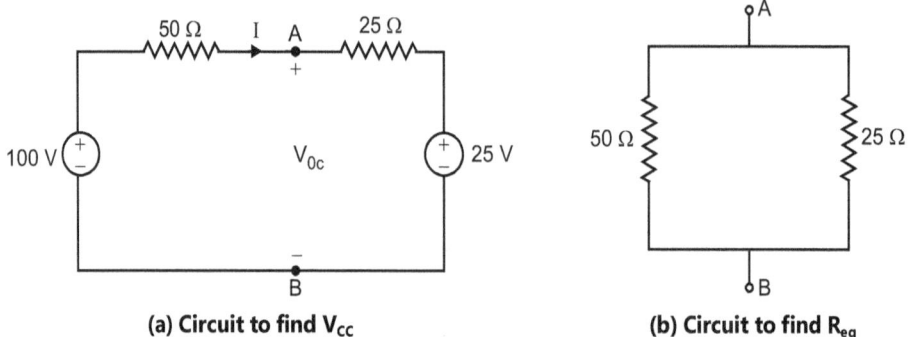

(a) Circuit to find V_{cc} (b) Circuit to find R_{eq}

Fig. 2.82 : Steps to find equivaqlent

Step II: Since circuit contains only independent source, use method – II to find R_{eq}, Open current source and short the voltage source the resultant circuit is shown in Fig. 2.82 (b).

Resistance between A-B = R_{eq} = $50 \| 25$ = $\dfrac{50 \times 25}{75}$ = $16.67\,\Omega$

Step III: The resultant Thevenin equivalent circuit in shown in Fig. 2.83 (a). By source transformation the resultant Norton equivalent circuit is shown in Fig. 2.83 (b).

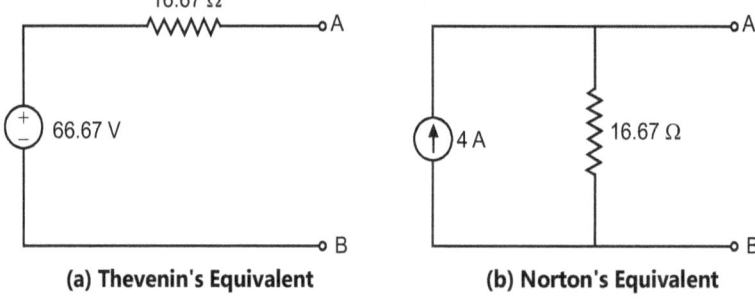

(a) Thevenin's Equivalent   (b) Norton's Equivalent

Fig. 2.83 : Equivalent circuits

2.4 MAXIMUM POWER TRANSFER (MPT) THEOREM

Sometimes it is necessary to determine the load impedance (Z_L) to be connected across two terminals of the circuit so that maxium power is transferred to load.

For example, consider a circuit (N) consisting of impedances and energy sources as shown n Fig. (2.84), where variable load (Z_L) is connected across A-B. We have to determine load (Z_L) so that maximum power is transferred (dissipated) in the load (Z_{-L}).

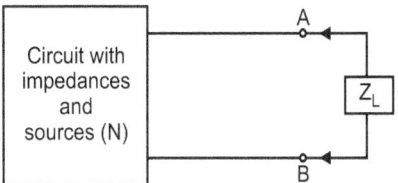

Fig. 2.84 : Circuit (N) with variable load

This is given by Maximum Power Transfer (MPT) theorem. There are three different cases depending upon type of network (N) and load (Z_L).

2.4.1 MPT Theorem for DC circuits

Consider the network contain in only "**DC source and resistance**". No reactive element (L or C) is present in the circuit. Now load Z_L will be purely resistive (R_L) as shown below in Fig. 2.85 (a).

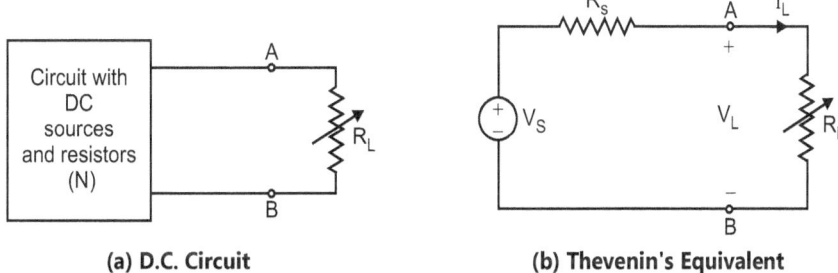

(a) D.C. Circuit (b) Thevenin's Equivalent

Fig. 2.85 : Circuit to explain MPT of DC circuits

Now according to Thevenin theorem the whole circuit (N) across A-B can be replaced by an open circuit voltage (V_S) in series with Thevenin resistor (R_S) as shown in Fig. 2.85 (b).

Load R_L is variable while source resistance (R_s) is fixed by the network. Our aim is to find value of R_L that will dissipate maximum power in R_L.

Applying KVL gives
$$I_L = \frac{V_S}{(R_S + R_L)} \quad \ldots(a)$$

Hence,
$$\text{Power in } R_L = P_L = I_L^2 \cdot R_L = \frac{V_S^2}{(R_S + R_L)^2} \times R_L \quad \ldots(2.6)$$

To find R_L for which P_L is maximum differentiate P_L with respect to R_L and equate it to zero (according to maxima minima theory). Thus we have,

$$\frac{dP_L}{dR_L} = V_S^2 \left[\frac{(R_S + R_L)^2 \cdot 1 - 2(R_S + R_L) \cdot R_L}{(R_S + R_L)^4} \right] = 0$$

Since, $V_S \neq 0$ and denominator is zero, the numerator must be zero. Equating numerator to zero we have

$$(R_S + R_L)^2 - (R_S + R_L) \cdot R_L = 0$$

OR $(R_S + R_L) - 2R_L = 0$

OR $R_S = R_L$ ...(2.7)

"Thus, for maximum power transfer across load (R_L), the load resistance must be equal to resistance (R_S)" with above condition of equation (2.7) which is known as matched condition, the maximum power (P_{Lmax}) is given by equation (2.6) as

$$P_{L\,max} = \frac{V_S^2 \cdot R_L}{(2R_L)^2} = \frac{V_S^2}{4R_L} = \frac{V_S^2}{4R_S} \qquad ...(2.8)$$

Since, $R_S = R_L$, same amount of power is dissipated in the internal resistances (i.e. R_S in this case). Hence maximum power efficiency is 50%.

Note: If R_L is fixed [fixed load] and internal resistance (R_S) is variable then by equation (2.6) maximum power will be in the load when $R_S = 0$. This maximum power is given by

$P_{L\,max} = \dfrac{V_S^2}{R_L}$ and the power efficiency in this case is 100%.

Thus, it is always advantageous to make source resistance (R_S) as small as possible in order to make the power efficiency larger. But if R_S is not zero, then maximum power efficiency is limited to 50% only. With the above proof the Maximum Power Transfer Theorem (MPT) for DC circuit can be stated as follows.

Statement of MPT for DC Circuit :

"In a linear circuit containing linear, bilateral resistance and DC energy sources the maximum power will be transferred in variable load resistance (R_L) connected between any two terminals when value of load resistance (R_L) is equal to source resistance (R_S) or Thevenin equivalent resistance".

The variation of load power (P_L) with variable load (R_L) and fixed source resistance (R_S) as given by equation (2.6) and circuit of Fig. 2.86 (b) is shown in Fig. 2.86 (c). Note that P_L is maximum when $R_L = R_S$.

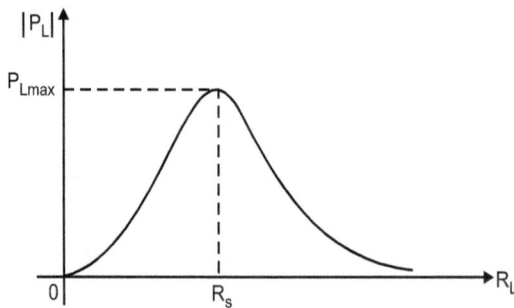

Fig. 2.86 (c): Variation of power (P_L) with load (R_L)

Following examples explain use of MPT for DC circuits.

Example 2.36 :

For the ladder circuit shown find R_L that will give maximum power to R_L and determine value of P_{Lmax}.

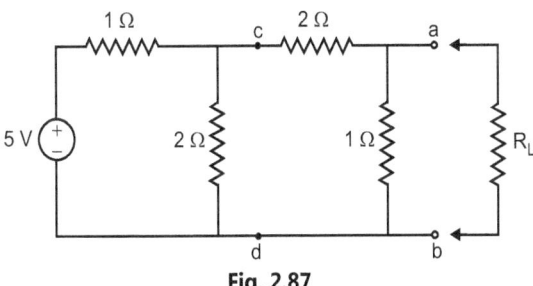

Fig. 2.87

Solution : Remove R_L and determine Thevenin equivalent circuit across a-b. The various steps involved are shown in Fig. 2.88.

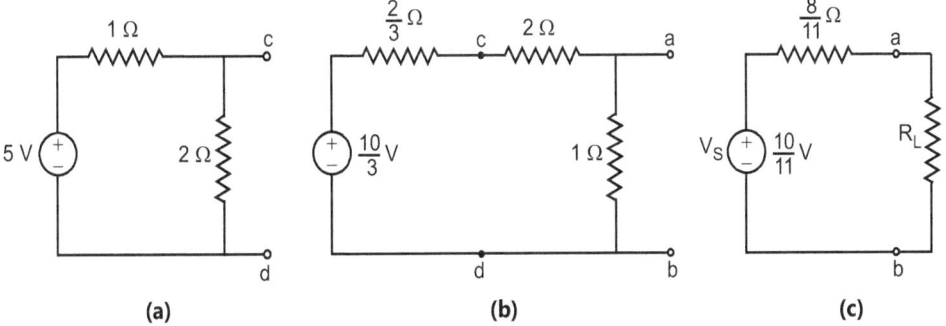

(a)   (b)   (c)

Fig. 2.88 : Various steps for Thevenin Equivalent circuit

Assume the network is broken at c-d as shown in Fig. 2.88 (a). First find Thevenin equivalent across c-d which is shown in Fig. 2.88 (b) where

$$V_{OC} = V_{cd} = \frac{2 \times 5}{2+1} = \frac{10}{3} \text{ volts and } R_{eq} = 2\Omega \parallel 1\Omega = \frac{2}{3}\Omega$$

Now add remaining part of network at c-d and then find Thevenin equivalent across R_L or a – b where $V_{OC} = V_{ab} = \dfrac{10/3 \times 1}{1 + 2 + 2/3} = \dfrac{10}{11}$ Volts

and $\qquad R_{eq} = 1\Omega \parallel \left(2 + \dfrac{2}{3}\right) = 1 \parallel \dfrac{8}{3} = \dfrac{1 \times 8/3}{1 + 8/3} = \dfrac{8}{11}\Omega$

The final equivalent is shown in Fig. 2.88 (c). By the MPT theorem we have by equation (2.7),

For maximum pwer transfer $R_L = R_S = \dfrac{8}{11}\Omega$

Using equation (2.8), we have

$$P_{Lmax} = \frac{V_S^2}{4R_L} = \frac{(10/11)^2}{4 \times 8/11} = \frac{100}{11 \times 8 \times 4} = 0.284 \text{ watts}$$

Example 2.37:

For the circuit shown in Fig. 2.89 (1) find R_L that will maximum the power delivered to R_L and find power in R_L for load under matched condition. (2) how much is power dissipated by 1kΩ resistor R_L is selected as matched load?

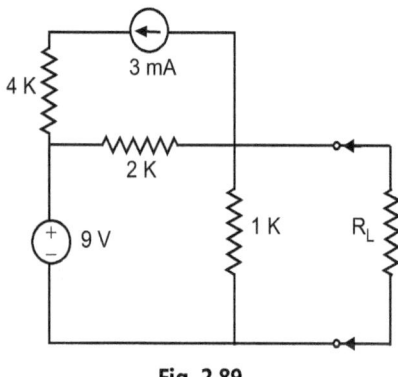

Fig. 2.89

Solution: Let us first find Thevenin equivalent circuit across R_L. Assume being removed from circuit for the time being. The redrawn circuit is shown in Fig. 2.90 (a).

Step I : To find V_{OC}: By KCL current in 1kΩ resistor is $(I_1 - 3)$ mA where I_1 is the current assumed in 2kΩ resistor. KVL across lower loop gives $(I_1 - 3) \times 1 + 2I_1 - 9 = 0$ solving this gives $3I_1 = 12$ or $I_1 = $ 4mA.

Thus, V_{OC} = Open circuit voltage = $1 \times (4 - 3)$ = 1 volts

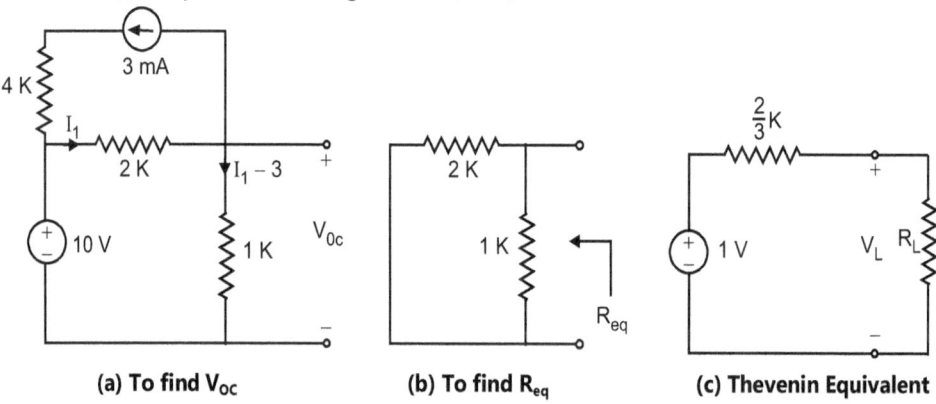

(a) To find V_{OC} (b) To find R_{eq} (c) Thevenin Equivalent

Fig. 2.90 : Steps to find Thevenin equivalents

Step II :

To find R_{eq}: Use method II where all sources are made zero as shown in Fig. 2.90 (b). We have 2k in parallel with 1k.

Hence the equivalent resistance = R_{eq} = 1k || 2k = $\frac{2}{3}$ kΩ

Step III : The final equivalent circuit is shown n Fig. 2.90 (c).

(1) For maximum power transfer $R_L = \dfrac{2}{3}$ kΩ

$$P_{Lmax} = \dfrac{V_S^2}{4R_L} = \dfrac{(1)^2}{4 \times \dfrac{2}{3}k} = \dfrac{3}{8} \text{ mW}$$

(2) When $R_L = \dfrac{2}{3}$ k is connected then voltage across R_L = 0.5 V. Since 1kΩ is directly in parallel with R_L the voltage across kΩ is also 0.5 V.

Hence, power in 1 kΩ $= \dfrac{(0.5)^2}{1k\Omega} = 0.25$ mW $= \dfrac{1}{4}$ mW

Example 2.38 :
In the circuit shown variable load absorbs power. Find current I [Magnitude and direction] so that it receives maximum power. Also find amount of power absorbed by R_L

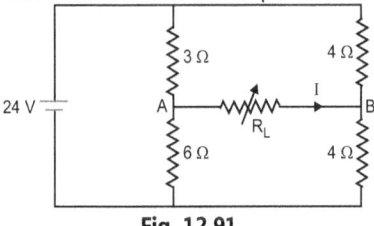

Fig. 12.91

Solution : Let us determine Thevenin equivalent across R_L assumes for the time being R_L is removed.

Step I : To find V_{OC}: With R_L removed circuit is as shown in the Fig. 2.92 (a). The currents I_1 and I_2 are given by $I_1 = \dfrac{24}{3+6} = \dfrac{8}{6}$ A and $I_2 = \dfrac{24}{4+4} = 3$A

$$V_{OC} = V_{AB} = 6I_1 - 4I_2 = 6 \times \dfrac{8}{3} - 12 = 4V$$

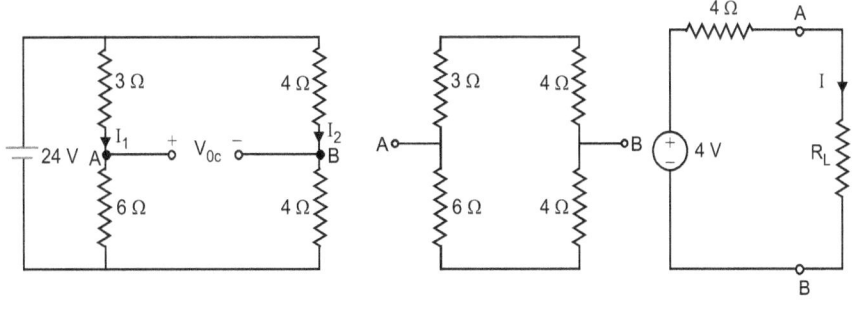

(a) To find V_{OC} (b) To find R_{eq} (c) Thevenin Equivalent

Fig. 2.92 : Steps to find Thevenin equivalent

2.4.2 MPT Theorem for AC Circuits

If a network is AC containing AC sources and impedances (R, L and C) then load (Z_L) should also be reactive then MPT Theorem for such circuit is stated as below.

Statement : "The maximum power will be delivered by a network to a load impedance (Z_L) if the impedance (Z_L) is the complex conjugate of impedance (Z_S) of the network measured looking back into terminals of the network".

Proof : To prove the Theorem consider a complex network (N) containing AC energy sources and impedances with a complex load (Z_L) as shown in Fig. 2.93 (a). The Thevenin equivalent across load is shown in Fig. 2.93 (b), where V_s is a phasor containing both magnitude and phase and $Z_S = R_S + JX_S$ is a complex Thevenin equivalent impedance. For maximum power transfer $Z_L = (R_L + JX_L)$ should also be complex in which R_L and X_L are both adjustable.

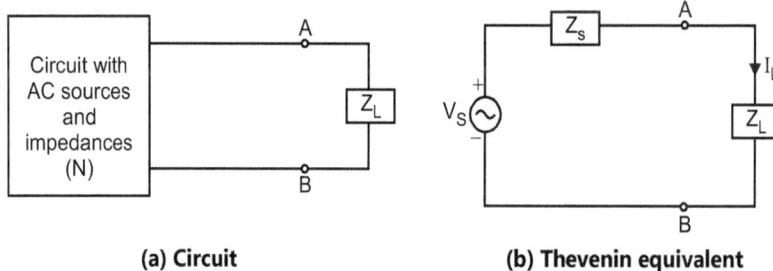

(a) Circuit (b) Thevenin equivalent

Fig. 2.93 : Circuit to explain MPT for AC circuits

Thus, we have $Z_S = R_S + JX_S$ = source (Internal) impedance

$$Z_L = R_L + JX_L = \text{Load impedance}$$

Then
$$I_L = \frac{V_S}{Z_S + Z_L} = \frac{V_S}{(R_S + R_L) + J(X_L + X_S)} \quad \ldots (a)$$

Power delivered in the load (P_L) is given by -

$$P_L = [I_L]^2 R_L = \frac{V_S^2 \cdot R_L}{(R_S + R_L)^2 + (X_S + X_L)^2} \quad \ldots (b)$$

In above power (P_L) expression R_L and X_L are variable while all other quantities (V_S, R_S, X_S) are fixed for a given circuit.

Case I: Keep R_L fixed and X_L as a variable. Then for maximum power $\frac{dP_L}{dX_L}$ must be zero.

$$\frac{dP_L}{dX_L} = \frac{-2V_S^2 R_L (X_L + X_S)}{[(R_L + R_S)^2 + (X_S + X_L)^2]^2} = 0$$

Hence, $(X_L + X_S) = 0$ **Or** $(X_L = -X_S)$ ... (2.9)

Thus, "Condition for maximum power when only reactance is varied is given by $X_L = -X_S$".

"Reactance of load must be equal to the reactance of source impedance but of opposite nature (sign)".

Now substituting equation (2.9) into equation (b) we have,

$$P_L = \frac{V_S^2 R_L}{(R_S + R_L)^2} \qquad \ldots (c)$$

Case II: Now vary R_L also. To get maximum power output we have $\dfrac{dP_L}{dR_L} = 0$.

Differentiating (c) with respect to R_L, we get,

$$\frac{dP_L}{dR_L} = \frac{V_S^2 (R_L + R_S)^2 - V_S^2 \cdot R_L (R_S + R_L)}{(R_L + R_S)^4} = 0$$

Hence, $(R_S + R_L)^2 - R_L(R_S + R_L) = 0$ Or $R_S = R_L$ ... (2.10)

'With $X_S = -X_L$ the condition for maximum power transfer is that load resistance must be equal to source resistance'.

Thus, a network of internal impedance of $Z_S = R_S + JX_S$ will delivers maximum power to load impedance (Z_L) when $Z_L = R_S - JX_S$".

Hence, **"Load impedance (Z_L) must be complex conjugate of source impedance (Z_S) for maximum power transfer in load".**

Hence the Theorem is proved.

Power efficiency: When matched load is used i.e. $Z_L = Z_S^*$ then maximum power transfer in load (P_{Lmax}) is given by the equation (b) as

$$P_L(max) = \frac{V_S^2 R_L}{4R_L^2} = \frac{V_S^2}{4R_L} \qquad \ldots (2.11)$$

This is same expression as equation (2.8). As equal amount of power is wasted in R_s the maximum power efficiency is 50% only. Following examples explains this Theorem in detail.

Example 2.39 :

In the network shown w = 200r/s. Determine load (Z_L) for maximum power transfer. Also determine energy delivered to load in 1 hour.

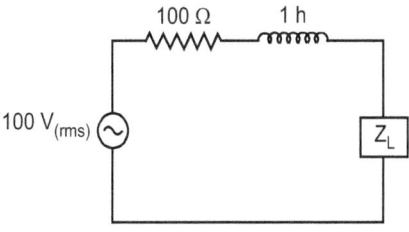

Fig. 2.94

Solution : We have $Z_S = 100 + JwL = (100 + J200)\ \Omega$

Now for maximum power transfer $Z_L = Z_S^* = (100 - J200)\ \Omega$

Where $R_L = 100\ \Omega$ and $X_L = X_C = 200 = \dfrac{1}{wC}$

Hence, $\quad C = \dfrac{1}{w \times 200} = \dfrac{1}{200 \times 200} = 25\ \mu F$

Thus load consists of 100Ω resistor in series with $25\mu F$ capacitor.

Power delivered to load $= \dfrac{V_{rms}^2}{4R_L} = \dfrac{(110)^2}{4 \times 100} = 25$ watts

Energy delivered in 1 hour $= \dfrac{25}{1000} \times 1 = 0.025$ kWh

Example 2.40 :

In the circuit w = 400 r/s. Find load impedance (Z_L) that maximizes power transfer and find power transferred when load is matched.

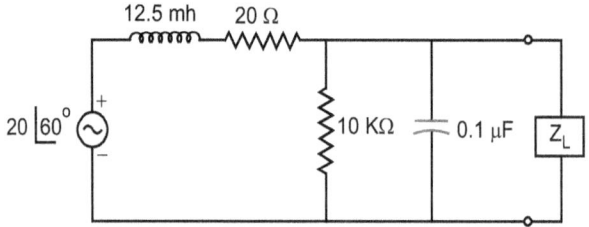

Fig. 2.95 : Circuit

Solution : Assume Z_L being removed for time being.

Let $\qquad Z_1 = 20 + JwL = (20 + J \times 400 \times 12.5 \times 10^{-3}) = (20 + J5)\ \Omega$

$\qquad Z_2 = 10k\Omega\ ||\ \dfrac{-J}{wC} = 10\ k\Omega\ ||\ -25\ k\Omega$

$\qquad\quad = \dfrac{-J250M\Omega}{(10 - J25)\ K\Omega}$

$\qquad\quad = \dfrac{250\ \angle -90°}{26.9\ \angle -68.2°}\ k\Omega = 9.285\ \angle -21.8°\ k\Omega$

Thus, $\qquad Z_2 = (8.62 - J3.44)\ k\Omega$

$\qquad V_{Th} = V_{OC} = \dfrac{20\angle 60° \times Z_2}{Z_2 + Z_1} = 20\angle 60°$

And $\qquad Z_{Th} = Z_2\ ||\ Z_1 = Z_1 \approx Z_1$

Thus, $\qquad Z_{Th} = (20 + J5)\ \Omega$

The Thevenin equivalent circuit is shown in Fig. 2.96.

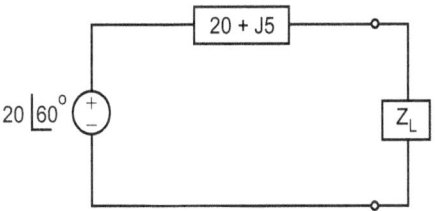

Fig. 2.96 : Thevenin equivalent circuit

For maximum power transfer $Z_L = (20 - J5)\ \Omega$

Thus load must consist of 20Ω resistor and a capacitor (C) of $\dfrac{1}{400 \times 5} = 500\ \mu F$

when matched load is used then maximum power is transferred and is given by.

$$P_{Lmax} = \dfrac{V_{rms}^2}{4R_L} = \dfrac{(20)^2}{4 \times 20} = 5\ \text{watts}$$

Example 2.41 :

In the circuit shown $V_1 = 2\sqrt{2}\ \sin 2t$. For the element values given find value of 'C' that will cause maximum power in 1 ohm load.

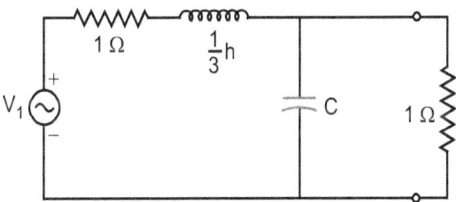

Fig. 2.97

Solution : With 1Ω load removed, Let us find Z_{Th} across load, $w = 2$

$$Z_{Th} = (1 + JwL)\ \|\ \dfrac{-J}{wC}$$

$$= \left(1 + J\dfrac{2}{3}\right)\ \|\ \dfrac{-J}{2C}$$

$$= \dfrac{\left(1 + J\dfrac{2}{3}\right)(-J/2C)}{1 + J\left(\dfrac{2}{3} - \dfrac{1}{2C}\right)} = \dfrac{\left(\dfrac{1}{3C} - \dfrac{J}{2C}\right)}{1 + J\left[\dfrac{2}{3} - \dfrac{1}{2C}\right]} \qquad \text{... (a)}$$

$$= \dfrac{\left(\dfrac{1}{3C} - \dfrac{J}{2C}\right)\left[1 - J\left(\dfrac{2}{3} - \dfrac{1}{2C}\right)\right]}{1 + \left[\dfrac{2}{3} - \dfrac{1}{2C}\right]^2}$$

For maximum power transfer in load $R_L = 1\Omega$ we must have $Z_{Th} = 1\Omega$. This means real part of Z_{Th} must be 1Ω and imaginary part must be zero.

Thus,
$$\frac{\frac{1}{3C} - \frac{1}{2C}\left[\frac{2}{3} - \frac{1}{2C}\right]}{1 + \left(\frac{2}{3} - \frac{1}{2C}\right)^2} = 1 \qquad ...(b)$$

And
$$\frac{1}{2C} + \frac{1}{3C}\left(\frac{2}{3} - \frac{1}{2C}\right) = 0 \qquad ...(c)$$

condition (c) gives,
$$\frac{-1}{3}\left(\frac{2}{3} - \frac{1}{2C}\right) = \frac{1}{2} \quad \text{Or} \quad \frac{-2}{3} + \frac{1}{2C} = 1.5$$

This gives C = 0.23F

Thus value of capacitor (C) must be 0.23F. Similarly, condition (b) gives another value of 'C' for which maximum power transfer occurs.

Example 2.42 :

In the circuit shown current source has a frequency of 1000 Hz. Find value of load for maximum power transfer also calculate power in load for matched condition and also calculate power efficiency.

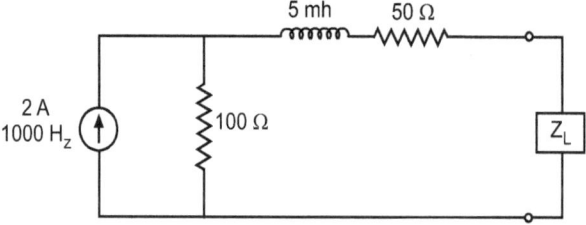

Fig. 2.98 : Circuit for Ex. (1.87)

Solution : Given $f = 1000$ Hz, $X_L = JwL = J2\pi \times 1000 \times 5 \times 10^{-3} = -J31.4\Omega$

Source transformation gives circuit shown in Fig. 2.99.

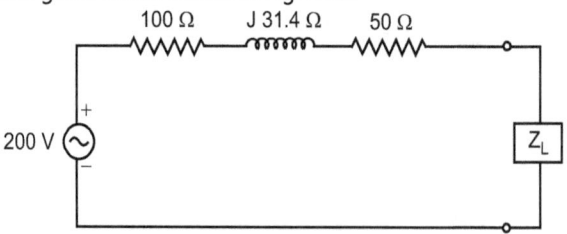

Fig. 2.99 : Equivalent circuit

Source impedance = $Z_S = (100 + 50 + J31.4) = (150 + J31.4)$

Hence, load must be $Z_L = (150 - J31.4)$ for MPT.

With this load connected maximum power delivered is

$$P_{Lmax} = \frac{V_S^2}{4R_L} = \frac{(200)^2}{4 \times 150}$$

$$= 66.66 \text{ watts}$$

Maximum power efficiency = 50%

Note: Load should consists of a resistor of 150Ω in series is with a Capacitor (C) = $\frac{1}{31.4w}$

$$= \frac{1}{3.14 \times 2 \pi \times 1000} = 5\mu F$$

Example 2.43 :

For the circuit shown find load impedance (Z_L) such that maximum power is transferred in load. Also find the power transferred to load under this condition.

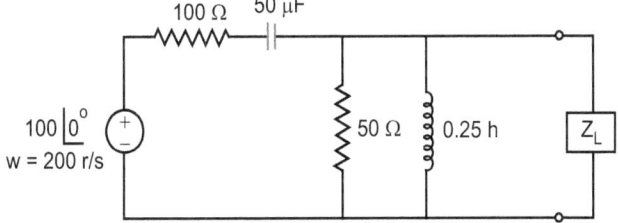

Fig. 2.100 : Circuit

Solution : Let $Z_S = 100 - JX_C = \left(100 - \frac{J}{wC}\right) = \left(100 - \frac{J}{50 \times 10^{-6} \times 200}\right)$

i.e $\quad Z_1 = (100 - J100) = 141.42 \angle -45°\Omega$

$$Z_2 = 50\Omega \parallel JwL = 50\|J50 = \frac{2500\angle 90°}{(50 + J50)}$$

i.e $\quad Z_2 = (25 + J25) = 35.35\angle 45°$

We have, $\quad V_{OC} = 100\angle 0° \times \frac{Z_2}{Z_1 + Z_2} = 100 \times \frac{35.35\angle 45°}{(125 - J75)}$

$$= \frac{3535\angle 45°}{145.77\angle -31°} = 24.25\angle 76° \text{ Volts}$$

$$Z_{Th} = Z_1\|Z_2 = \frac{141.42\angle -45° \times 35.35\angle 45°}{(125 - J75)}$$

$$= \frac{5000}{145.7\angle -31} = 34.3\angle 31 = (29.4 + J17.67)\Omega$$

Thus, for maximum power transfer $Z_L = Z_{Th}^*$.

The load impedance must be $Z_L = (29.4 - J17.67)\Omega$

The circuit under matched condition is shown in Fig. 2.101.

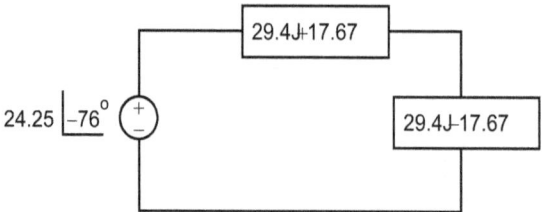

Fig. 2.101 : Matched load

Maximum power transferred to load $= \dfrac{(24.25)^2}{4 \times 29.4} = 5$ Watts.

Example 2.44 :

Find Z_L such that maximum power is transferred in Z_L. Also find maximum power transferred.

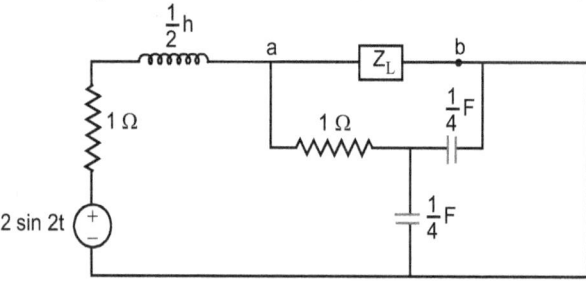

Fig. 2.102

Solution : Two capacitors are in parallel to given equivalent capacitance of $\dfrac{1}{2}$ F = 0.5 F. The reactance of this capacitor is X_C where, $X_C = \dfrac{1}{wC} = \dfrac{1}{2 \times 0.5} = 1\Omega$, reactance of inductor = $X_L = wL = 2 \times \dfrac{1}{2} = 1\Omega$. The resultant circuit is shown in Fig. 2.103 (a).

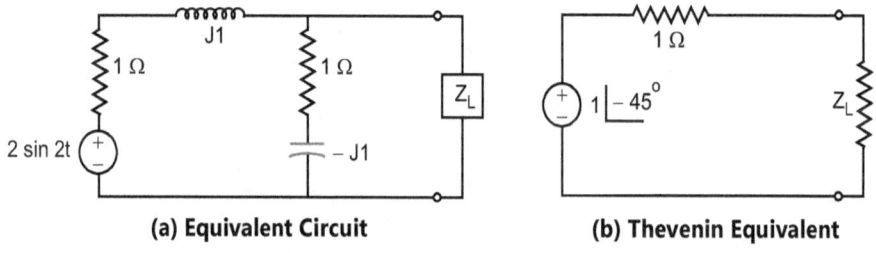

(a) Equivalent Circuit (b) Thevenin Equivalent

Fig. 2.103

With Z_L removed for the time being we shall find the Thevenin equivalent circuit across load.

$$(1 + J1) \parallel (1 - J1) = \dfrac{(1 + J1)(1 - J1)}{(1 + J1) + (1 - J1)}$$

We have $Z_{Th} = \dfrac{1+1}{1+1} = 1\,\Omega$

The r.m.s value of input voltage = $V_{rms} = \sqrt{2}$ Volts.

Hence, $V_{Th} = \dfrac{\sqrt{2}\times(1-J1)}{(1+J1)+(1-J1)} = \dfrac{\sqrt{2}(1-J1)}{2} = 1\angle -45°$

$= (1-J1)$ Volts

The Thevenin equivalent circuit is shown in Fig. 2.103 (b).

For maximum power transfer Z_L should be 1 ohm. With matched load the maximum power transferred is given by $P_{L(max)} = \dfrac{V_{rms}^2}{4R_L} = \dfrac{(1)^2}{4\times 1} = 0.25$ watts.

2.4.3 Corollary of Maximum Power Transfer (MPT)

If a network is AC containing AC sources and impedances (R, L, C elements) and load is resistive (not reactive) in which only magnitude of load and not the angle can be varied then corollary of maximum power transfer can be used to obtain the condition for maximum power transfer.

Statement:

If only the absolute magnitude and not the angle of the load impedance (Z_L) can be varied, then the greatest power is delivered from the network to load if the absolute magnitude of Z_L (i.e. $|Z_L|$) is made equal to absolute magnitude of source Impedance Z_S (i.e. $|Z_S|$)".

Proof: We have $Z_L = (R_L + JX_L) = |Z_L|\angle\theta = Z_L[\cos\theta + I\sin\theta]$

Hence, $R_L = |Z_L|\cos\theta$, $X_L = |Z_L|\sin\theta$

Hence, for the given AC circuit power delivered to load is given by expression (b) of section (2.4.2) as,

$$P_L = \dfrac{V_S^2\,|Z_L|\cos\theta}{[R_S + |Z_L|\cos\theta]^2 + [X_S + |Z_L|\sin\theta]^2} \quad \ldots(a)$$

As magnitude of impedance (Z_L) can be varied and not the angle, therefore we have $\dfrac{dP_L}{d|Z_L|} = 0$ for maximum power transfer, is given by equation,

$$R_S^2 + (X_S)^2 - |Z_L|^2[\sin^2\theta + \cos^2\theta] = 0$$

Or $\qquad R_S^2 + (X_S)^2 = |Z_L|^2 \qquad \ldots(2.12)$

Hence, $\qquad |Z_L| = \sqrt{R_S^2 - X_S^2} = |Z_S|$

Thus, if load angle cannot be varied but magnitude can be varied then load impedance ($|Z_L|$) should be made equal to the magnitude of source impedance ($|Z_S|$) for the greatest amount of power transfer. Hence, proved.

Following examples explains the principles of this theorem.

Example 2.45 :

A resistance variable between 0 to 500Ω is available as a load for the circuit shown in Fig. 2.13.

1. What should be the value of resistor (R_L) so as to develop maximum power in the resistor?
2. How much power is developed?
3. Draw the curve of power output versus resistance load (R_L) showing that selected value of resistance does develop maximum power.

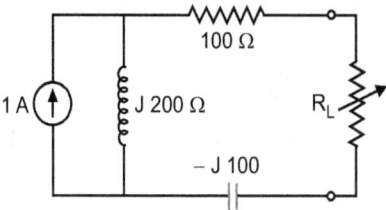

Fig. 2.104

Solution : Open circuit voltage = V_{OC} = J200 – × 1 = 200 ∠90° volts. Open the current source to find Z_{Th}. thus, we have Z_{Th} = 100 + J200 – J100 = 100 = 141.42∠45°

The Thevenins's equivalent circuit is shown in Fig. 2.105.

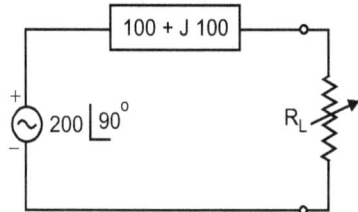

Fig. 2.105 : Thevenin equivalent circuit

1. By corollary of MPT and hence by equation (2.12) the value of $|R_L|$ that transfers maximum power in it is given by,

$$R_L = \sqrt{(R_S)^2 + (X_S)^2} = \sqrt{(100)^2 + (100)^2} = 141.4 \text{ ohms}$$

2. Maximum power developed = $P_{RL(max)} = \dfrac{V_S^2}{4R_L} = \dfrac{(200)^2}{4 \times 141.4} = 70.7$ watts.

3. Power developed by load = $P_L = \dfrac{V_S^2 |Z_L|}{[|Z_S| + |Z_L|]^2}$ ... (1)

Now, $|Z_S| = \sqrt{(100)^2 + (100)^2} = 141.4$ ohms

Hence, $P_L = \dfrac{V_S^2 \times |Z_L|}{[141.4 + |Z_L|]^2}$ ... (2)

Since, $|Z_L|$ is resistive (R_L), P_L versus R_L can be plotted by taking different values of R_L and using equation (2).

When
$R_L = 50\Omega$ then $P_L = 54.6$ watts.
$R_L = 200\Omega$ then $P_L = 68.64$ watts.
$R_L = 500\Omega$ then $P_L = 48.6$ watts.
$R_L = 141.4\Omega$ then $P_L = 70.7$ watts.
$R_L = 100\Omega$ then $P_L = 68.64$ watts.

From above values of P_L and R_L it is obvious that for $R_L = 141.4\Omega$ the power delivered to load is maximum and it reduces if $R_L > 141.4\Omega$ or $R_L < 141.4\Omega$.

The graph of P_L (watts) versus R_L is shown below in fig. 2.106.

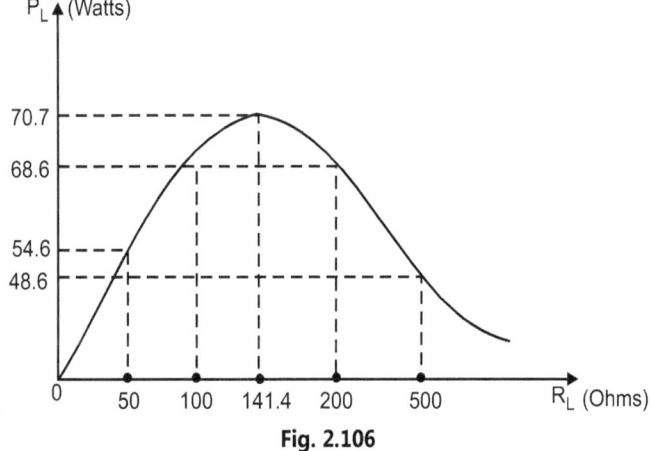

Fig. 2.106

Example 2.46 :

(1) In the circuit shown what is the load needed to obtain maximum power output at the terminals a-b?

(2) What is the generator current, load current, power generated and power delivered to load and matched load condition?

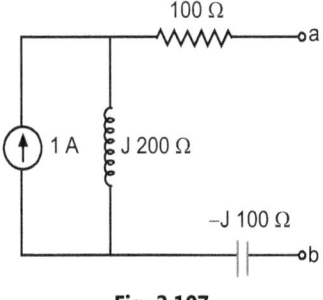

Fig. 2.107

Solution : Assume load (Z_L) being temporarily removed.

(1) Find Thevenin equivalent resistance between a-b. With current source made zero [open circuited]

We have, $Z_{Th} = Z_S = 100 + J200 - J100 = (100 + J100)$ ohms

For maximum power transfer $Z_L = Z_S = (100 - J100)$ ohms

(2) Circuit with matched load (Z_L) connected is as shown in Fig. 2.108.

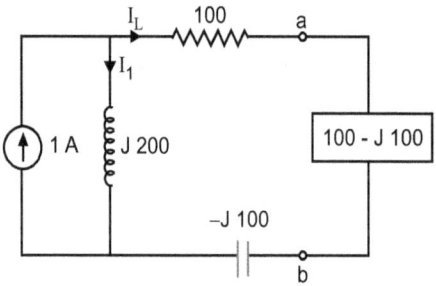

Fig. 2.108 : Circuit with matched load

Now current source $1 \angle 0°$ is divided into two currents I_1 and I_L. By current divider action.

$$I_L = I \times \frac{J200}{Z_L + Z_S} = \frac{1 \angle 0° \times 200 \angle 90°}{(100 + J100) + (100 - J100)}$$

$$= \frac{200 \angle 90°}{200}$$

Thus, $I_L = 1 \angle 90°$ Amp.

Power delivered in load $= |I_L|^2 \times R_L = 1 \times 100 = 100$ watts

Power generated $= VI \cos \theta$ where I is the generator current and V is the generator voltage. θ is angle between two. We have $I = 1 \angle 0°$ and V can be calculated by knowing. I_1 which is

$$I_1 = I - I_L = 1 \angle 0° - 1 \angle 90° = (1 - J1)$$

Thus, $I_1 = (1 - J1) = \sqrt{2} \angle -45°$ Amps.

Thus, voltage across generator (V) $= J200 \, J1 = 282.83 \angle + 45°$

Thus, power generated $= VI \cos \theta$

$$= 282.84 \times 1 \times \cos (45°)$$

$$= 200 \text{ watts}$$

Since, power efficiency for matched load is 50%, out of total power of 200 watts generated, 100 watts is supplied to load and remaining power of 100 watts is consumed by circuits itself.

2.5 MILLERS THEOREM AND ITS DUAL

Miller's theorem is used extensively to simplify the analysis of some two part network configurations. Millers theorem applies to the process of creating equivalent circuits. The general circuit theorem is useful in the high frequency analysis of transistor. It states that IF impedance is connected between the input and output terminal of a Linear network, then this impedance can be replaced by two equivalent impedances, one connected across the input and the other connected across the output terminals. Given any general network having a common terminal and two terminals whose voltage ratio, with respect to the common terminals is given by, $V_2 = AV$, where A = Gain of the network.

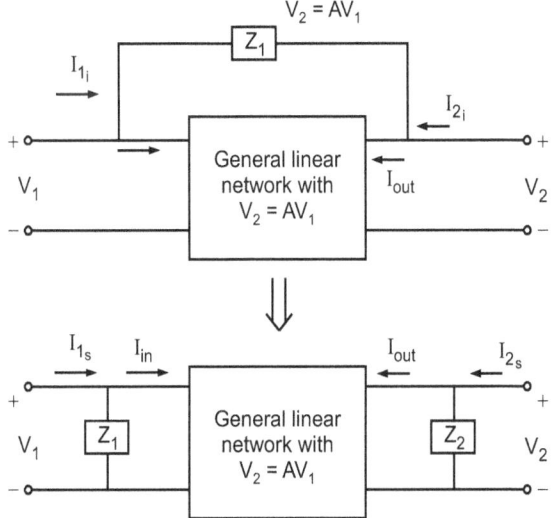

Fig. 2.109 : Miller equivalent circuits (a) Interconnecting impedance
(b) Part shunting impedance

i.e.
$$Z_1 = \frac{Z}{1-A} \quad \ldots (2.13)$$

$$Z_1 = \frac{AZ}{A-1} \quad \ldots (2.14)$$

Proof of Miller Theorem : If A is the gain of the network i.e. the ratio of the output voltage to the input voltage is called gain.

∴ $\quad V_2 = AV_1 \quad \ldots (1)$

The input current is given by

$$I_1 = \frac{V_1 - V_2}{Z}$$

$$I_1 = \frac{V_1 - AV_2}{Z}$$

$$I_1 = V_1\left(\frac{1-A}{Z}\right) \qquad \ldots (2)$$

The input impedance of the miller equivalent circuit is given by

$$Z_{in} = \frac{V_1}{I_1} \qquad \ldots (3)$$

∴ From equation (2) and (3), we can write

$$Z_{in} = \frac{Z}{1-A} = Z_1 \qquad \ldots (4)$$

The output current is given by

2.6 MILLER'S DUAL THEOREM

If there is a branch in a network with impedance z connecting a node, where two currents converge to ground, then this branch can be replace by two conducting branches with referred currents. The two impedances are equal to $(1 + \alpha)\, z$ and $\frac{(1+\alpha)^2}{\alpha}$.

i.e.
$$Z_1 = (1 + \alpha)\, z \qquad \ldots (2.15)$$

$$Z_2 = \frac{(1+\alpha)\, z}{\alpha} \qquad \text{where}, \ \alpha = \frac{I_2}{I_1} \quad \ldots (2.16)$$

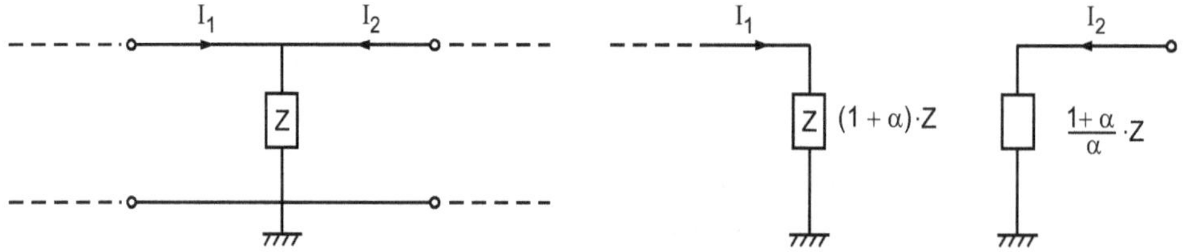

Fig. 2.110 : Miller dual and its equivalent

$$I_2 = \frac{V_2 - V_3}{z}$$

$$= \frac{V_2 - V_2/A}{z}$$

Since $V_2 = V_1 A$

$$I_2 = V_2 \frac{(A-1)}{Z \cdot A} \qquad \ldots (5)$$

The output impedance of the miller equivalent circuit is

$$Z_{out} = Z_2 = \frac{V_2}{I_1} \qquad \ldots (6)$$

From equation (5) and (6), we can write

$$Z_2 = \frac{ZA}{(A-1)} \quad \ldots(7)$$

Therefore, we can write z_1 and z_2 in the form of miller equivalent. i.e.

$$Z_1 = \frac{Z}{1-A}$$

and

$$Z_2 = \frac{ZA}{A-1}$$

Hence proved.

This theorem is applicable to the any circuit provided it ahs no independent circuit.

EXERCISE

1. State and prove Superposition theorem.
2. State and prove Maximum Power Transfer (MPT) as applied to DC circuit.
3. State and prove Maximum power Transfer (MPT) theorem as applied to AC circuit.
4. State and explain corollary of Maximum Power Transfer (MPT) theorem.
5. State and prove Thevenin's theorem.
6. State and prove Norton's theorem.
7. State and prove Millman's theorem.
8. State and prove dual of Millman's theorem.
9. Simplify following circuit into equivalent current source and a parallel resistor between A-B.

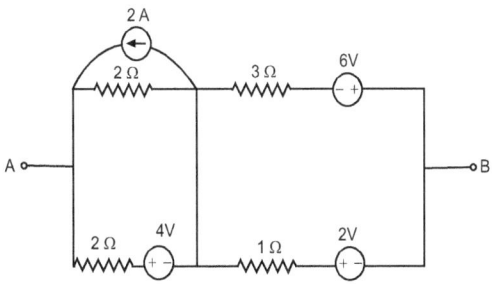

Fig. 2.111

10. Use superposition Theorem to find current in J3Ω across terminal a-b in the circuit shown.

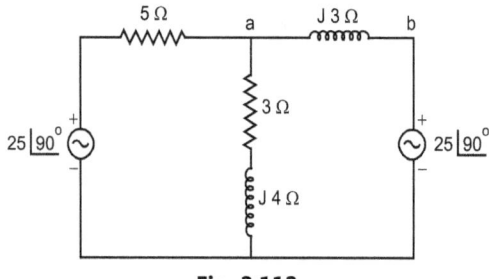

Fig. 2.112

11. Show that the equivalent Thevenin circuit consists of $R_{eq} = \dfrac{3-b}{2}$ and $V_{OC} = \dfrac{V_1}{2}[1 + a + b - ab]$ across R_L.

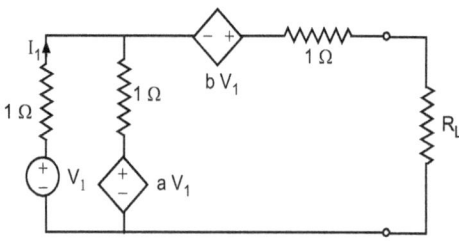

Fig. 2.113

12. For the ladder circuit shown determine R_L to be connected across a-b so that maximum power is transferred in R_L. Also determine maximum power when R_L is selected as a matched load.

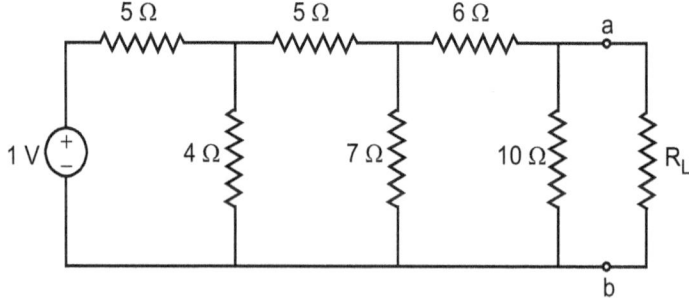

Fig. 2.114

13. What should be value of pure resistance load that is to be connected across terminals a-b in the circuit shown so that maximum power is transferred to the load? What is the maximum power.

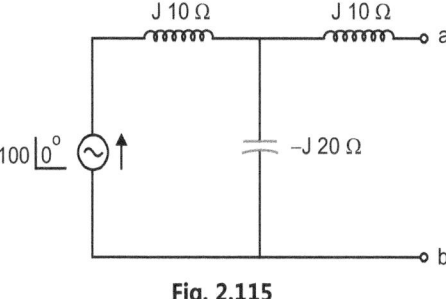

Fig. 2.115

14. In the network shown determine impedance Z_L for the maximum power transfer. Also calculate maximum power transferred to the load.

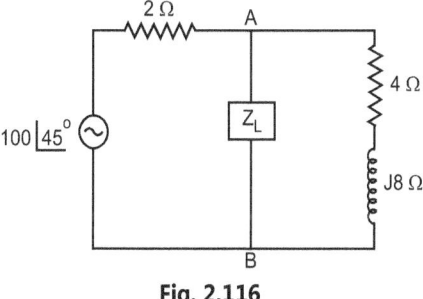

Fig. 2.116

15. Find current through capacitor. Make use of Superposition theorem

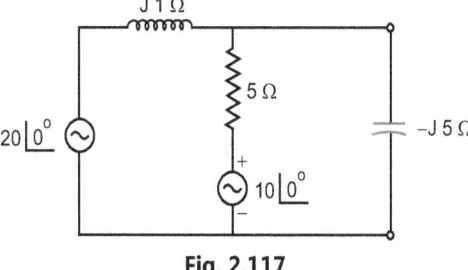

Fig. 2.117

16. Find current through 20Ω resister by (1) Superposition Theorem (2) Norton's theorem.

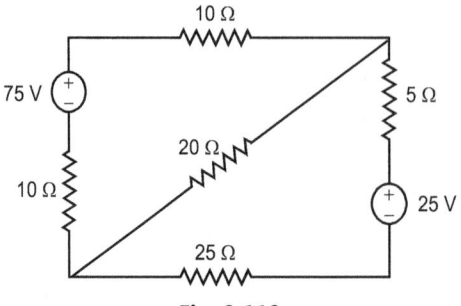

Fig. 2.118

17. Use Superposition theorem to find current through 5 ohm resistor.

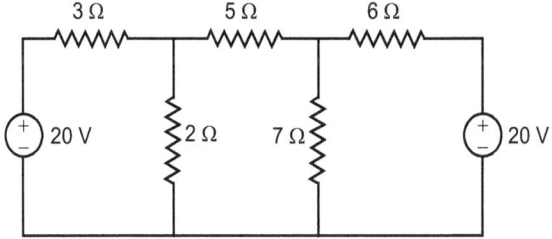

Fig. 2.119

18. Find current in resistor (R_L) across A-B by using (1) Thevenin's theorem (2) Norton's theorem.

Also determine R_L for maximum power transfer find maximum power transferred for matched load.

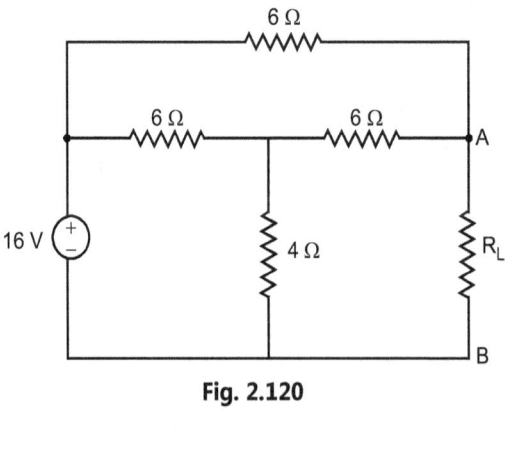

Fig. 2.120

Unit - III

TWO PORT NETWORK AND NETWORK FUNCTIONS

3.1 INTRODUCTION

A network containing two pairs of terminals is called as two port network. One of them is input port other one is output port. In total there are 4 variables. Taking two variables as independent and expressing other two variables in terms of these independent variables gives rise to six types of parameters. In this chapter we are going to study only 4 types of parameters viz z-parameter, y-parameter. H-parameter and ABCD parameters in detail. No detailed study is carried out about inverse transmission parameters and g-parameters.

Parameters of a network represents characteristic of that particular network. For example, H-parameters are extensively used to define characteristic of a transistor such as its input impedance, output impedance. Reverse voltage gain, current gain etc. By knowing parameter we can judge suitability of a particular network to some applications. Thus parameters represents electrical characteristic (quality) of a particular network.

In addition to defining various types of parameters, and calculation of parameters of various network, effect on parameters, when various networks are inter-connected is also studied in this chapter. Also characteristic of gyrator, transformer and negative impedance converters is studied.

3.1.1 Four-Terminal Network

Every network has some external terminals. One for entry and other for exit.

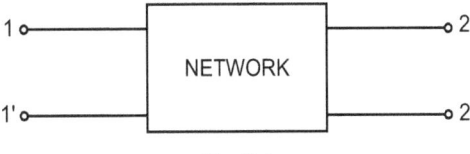

Fig. 3.1

A network having four such terminals is called as four terminal network.

3.1.2 Port

A pair of terminals at which an electrical signal may enter or leave a network is called as a port.

3.1.3 One Port Network

A network having only one pair of terminals is called as one port network.

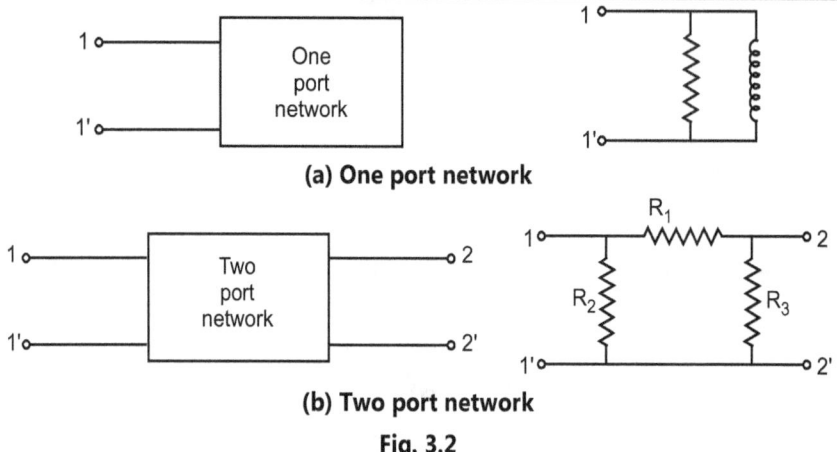

(a) One port network

(b) Two port network

Fig. 3.2

3.1.4 Two Port Network

A network having two pairs of terminals is called as two port network.

By analogy with transmission networks, one of the port (normally the port labelled with 1-1') is called as **input port.** While the other (labelled as 2-2') is called as output port.

3.1.5 Multiport Network

A network having multiple such ports is called as multiport network.

e.g.

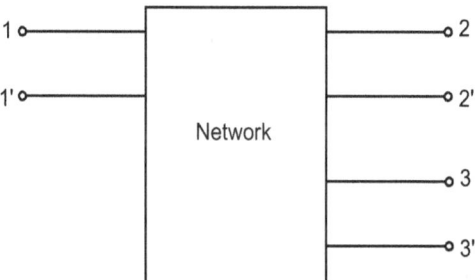

Fig. 3.3: 6-Terminal three port network

3.2 CHARACTERIZATION OF TWO PORT NETWORK

In the two port networks as shown in Fig. 3.4, we see four variables identified - two voltages (V_1 and V_2) and two currents (I_1 and I_2).

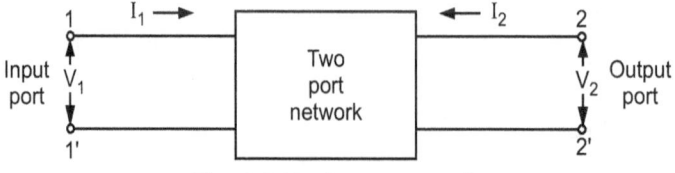

Fig. 3.4: Two port network

Here we assume that -

- There are other voltages and currents that might be identified inside the box. But they are not considered here for analysis.
- The box showing two port network is perfectly **linear** and **time invariant.**
- Only dependent sources may be present inside the box, no independent source is allowed.
- The direction of currents I_1 and I_2 is inside as shown in Fig. 3.4.

Here we assume that the variables V_1 and I_1 at input port and V_2 and I_2 at output port are transformed quantities. In order to describe the relationships among the port voltages and currents, as many linear equations are required as there are ports.

Thus, for a two port network, two linear equations are required among the four variables.

Out of the four variables - two are **independent** variables and remaining two are **dependent** i.e. by specifying any two we can calculate remaining two.

Here there are six possible ways of selecting two independent variables out of four variables. These six combinations and their different network parameters names are indicated in the Table 3.1.

Table 3.1

Network Parameter	Variable		Equation giving dependent variable
	Dependent	Independent	
Open-circuit impedance (Z)	$V_1\ V_2$	$I_1,\ I_2$	$\begin{bmatrix} V_1 \\ V_2 \end{bmatrix} = \begin{bmatrix} Z_{11} & Z_{12} \\ Z_{21} & Z_{22} \end{bmatrix} \begin{bmatrix} I_1 \\ I_2 \end{bmatrix}$
Short-circuit admittance (Y)	$I_1,\ I_2$	$V_1,\ V_2$	$\begin{bmatrix} I_1 \\ I_2 \end{bmatrix} = \begin{bmatrix} Y_{11} & Y_{12} \\ Y_{21} & Y_{22} \end{bmatrix} \begin{bmatrix} V_1 \\ V_2 \end{bmatrix}$
Transmission parameters (T) (A, B, C, D)	$V_1,\ I_1$	$V_2,\ I_2$	$\begin{bmatrix} V_1 \\ I_1 \end{bmatrix} = \begin{bmatrix} A & B \\ C & D \end{bmatrix} \begin{bmatrix} V_2 \\ -I_2 \end{bmatrix}$
Hybrid parameter (h)	$V_1,\ I_2$	$V_2,\ I_1$	$\begin{bmatrix} V_1 \\ I_2 \end{bmatrix} = \begin{bmatrix} h_{11} & h_{12} \\ h_{21} & h_{22} \end{bmatrix} \begin{bmatrix} I_1 \\ V_2 \end{bmatrix}$
Inverse transmission (T') (A', B', C', D')	$V_2,\ I_2$	$V_1,\ I_1$	$\begin{bmatrix} V_2 \\ I_2 \end{bmatrix} = \begin{bmatrix} A' & B' \\ C' & D' \end{bmatrix} \begin{bmatrix} V_1 \\ -I_1 \end{bmatrix}$
Inverse hybrid (g)	$I_1,\ V_2$	$V_1,\ I_2$	$\begin{bmatrix} I_1 \\ V_2 \end{bmatrix} = \begin{bmatrix} g_{11} & g_{12} \\ g_{21} & g_{22} \end{bmatrix} \begin{bmatrix} V_1 \\ I_2 \end{bmatrix}$

3.3 OPEN CIRCUIT IMPEDANCE OR Z-PARAMETER

In Z-parameter, voltages V_1 and V_2 are expressed in terms of current of I_1 and I_2.

$$(V_1, V_2) = f(I_1, I_2)$$
$$[V] = [Z][I]$$
$$\begin{bmatrix} V_1 \\ V_2 \end{bmatrix} = \begin{bmatrix} Z_{11} & Z_{12} \\ Z_{21} & Z_{22} \end{bmatrix} \begin{bmatrix} I_1 \\ I_2 \end{bmatrix}$$

∴ Z-parameter equations are

$$\left. \begin{array}{l} V_1 = Z_{11} I_1 + Z_{12} I_2 \\ V_2 = Z_{21} I_1 + Z_{22} I_2 \end{array} \right\} \quad \ldots (3.1)$$

To calculate the values of Z_{11}, Z_{12}, Z_{21} and Z_{22}, we have to make either $I_1 = 0$ or $I_2 = 0$. Thus we will get,

(i) When $I_2 = 0$, output is open circuited,

$$Z_{11} = \left[\frac{V_1}{I_1} \right]_{I_2 = 0} \quad \ldots (a)$$

$$Z_{21} = \left[\frac{V_2}{I_1} \right]_{I_2 = 0} \quad \ldots (b)$$

(ii) When $I_1 = 0$, input is open circuited,

$$Z_{12} = \left[\frac{V_1}{I_2} \right]_{I_1 = 0} \quad \ldots (c)$$

$$Z_{22} = \left[\frac{V_2}{I_2} \right]_{I_1 = 0} \quad \ldots (d)$$

where,
Z_{11} = Open circuit during point impedance
Z_{22} = Open circuit output impedance
Z_{12} = Open circuit forward transfer impedance
Z_{21} = Open circuit reverse transfer impedance

As per the conditions, $I_1 = 0$ or $I_2 = 0$ implies open circuit at port 1 or port 2. These parameters are called as open-circuit parameters.

The equivalent circuit for Z-parameters is as shown in Fig. 3.5.

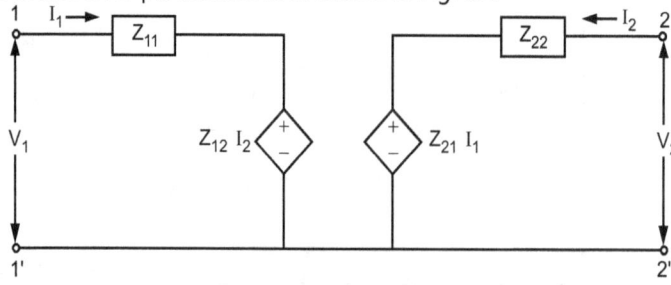

Fig. 3.5: Equivalent two port network in terms of Z-parameters

3.3.1 Condition for Reciprocity and Symmetry

(A) Symmetry condition:

The network is said to be symmetrical if impedance measured from one port with other port open circuit is equal to the impedance measured at other port with first port open circuited.

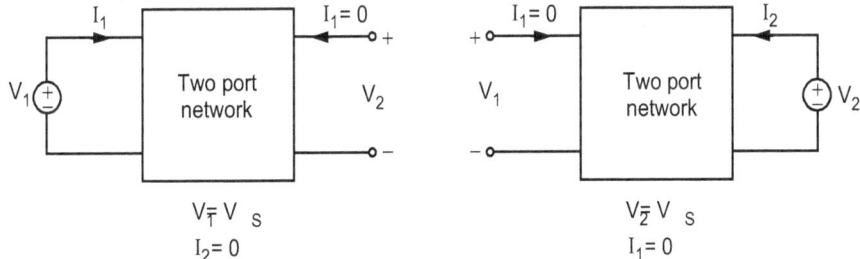

Fig. 3.6

To prove the condition of symmetry, let us consider,

Case I:
$$\left.\begin{array}{c} V_1 = V_s \\ I_2 = 0 \end{array}\right\} \qquad \ldots (a)$$

From equation (3.1),
$$V_1 = Z_{11} I_1 + Z_{12} I_2$$
$$V_2 = Z_{21} I_1 + Z_{22} I_2$$

Putting equation (a) in equation (3.1),
$$V_s = Z_{11} I_1$$

$$\therefore \quad \boxed{Z_{11} = \frac{V_s}{I_1}} \qquad \ldots (b)$$

Case II:
$$\left.\begin{array}{c} V_2 = V_s \\ I_1 = 0 \end{array}\right\} \qquad \ldots (c)$$

Putting equation (c) in equation (3.1),
$$V_s = Z_{22} I_2$$

$$\therefore \quad \boxed{Z_{22} = \frac{V_s}{I_2}} \qquad \ldots (d)$$

As per symmetry condition,
$$\text{Input impedance} = \text{Output impedance}$$
$$\frac{V_s}{I_1} = \frac{V_s}{I_2}$$

$$\therefore \quad \boxed{Z_{11} = Z_{22}} \qquad \ldots (3.2)$$

is the condition for symmetry.

(B) Reciprocity Condition:

A network is said to be reciprocal, if the ratio of voltage at one port to the current at other port is same to the ratio, if position of voltage and current are interchanged.

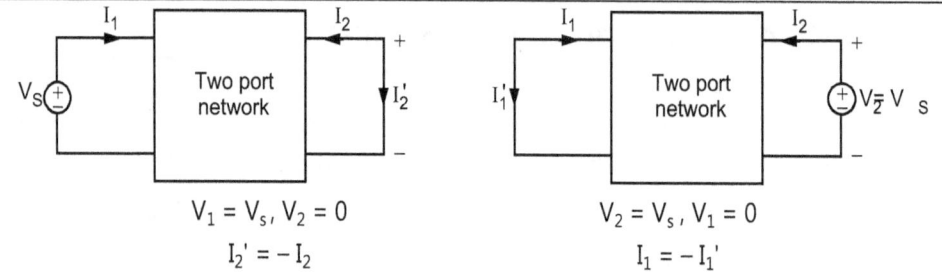

Fig. 3.7

For reciprocal network, $\boxed{\dfrac{V_s}{I_1} = \dfrac{V_s}{I_2}}$ ... (e)

For Z-parameter:

Case I: $\quad V_1 = V_s, V_2 = 0$
$\quad I_2 = -I_2'$

Putting these values in equation (3.1),

$$V_s = Z_{11} I_1 + Z_{12} (-I_2') \quad \text{... (f)}$$

and $\quad 0 = Z_{21} I_1 + Z_{22} (-I_2')$

$\therefore \quad Z_{21} I_1 = Z_{22} I_2'$

$\therefore \quad I_1 = \dfrac{Z_{22}}{Z_{21}} \cdot I_2'$ ... (g)

Putting in equation (f),

$$V_s = Z_{11} \left(\dfrac{Z_{22}}{Z_{21}}\right) I_2' - Z_{12} (I_2')$$

$$V_s = \dfrac{Z_{11} Z_{22}}{Z_{21}} \cdot I_2' - Z_{12} I_2' = I_2' \left(\dfrac{Z_{11} Z_{22} - Z_{12} Z_{21}}{Z_{21}}\right)$$

$$\boxed{\dfrac{V_s}{I_2'} = \left(\dfrac{Z_{11} Z_{22} - Z_{12} Z_{21}}{Z_{21}}\right)} \quad \text{... (h)}$$

Case II: $\quad V_2 = V_s, V_1 = 0$
$\quad I_1 = -I_1'$

Putting these values in equation (3.1),

$$0 = Z_{11} (-I_1') + Z_{12} I_2 \quad \text{... (i)}$$
$$V_s = Z_{21} (-I_1') + Z_{22} I_2 \quad \text{... (j)}$$

From equation (i),

$$\boxed{I_2 = \dfrac{Z_{11}}{Z_{12}} \cdot I_1'} \quad \text{... (k)}$$

Putting in equation (j),

NETWORK ANALYSIS (S.E. SEM III E & TC. SU) — TWO PORT NETWORK & NETWORK FUNCTIONS

$$V_s = Z_{21}(-I_1') + Z_{22}\left(\frac{Z_{11}}{Z_{12}}\right)I_1'$$

∴ $$\boxed{\frac{V_s}{I_1'} = \frac{Z_{11}Z_{22} - Z_{12}Z_{21}}{Z_{12}}}$$ ... (l)

From reciprocity condition,

$$\frac{V_s}{I_2'} = \frac{V_s}{I_1'}$$

∴ $$\frac{Z_{11}Z_{22} - Z_{12}Z_{21}}{Z_{21}} = \frac{Z_{11}Z_{22} - Z_{12}Z_{21}}{Z_{12}}$$

∴ $$\boxed{Z_{21} = Z_{12}}$$ ... (3.3)

is the condition for reciprocity.

Example 3.1 : Find the Z-parameters of the network shown in Fig. 3.8 and draw its equivalent circuit.

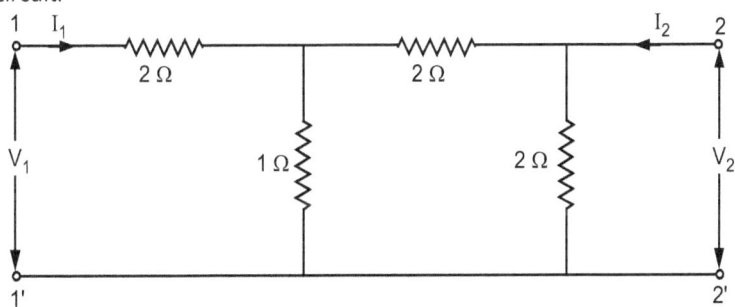

Fig. 3.8 (a)

Solution: From definitions,
(a) $I_2 = 0$
Output terminals 2 - 2' open circuit.

∴ $$Z_{11} = \left[\frac{V_1}{I_1}\right]_{I_2=0} \quad \text{and} \quad Z_{21} = \left[\frac{V_2}{I_1}\right]_{I_2=0}$$

Let us consider that a V_1 volt source is applied as input to 1 - 1'.

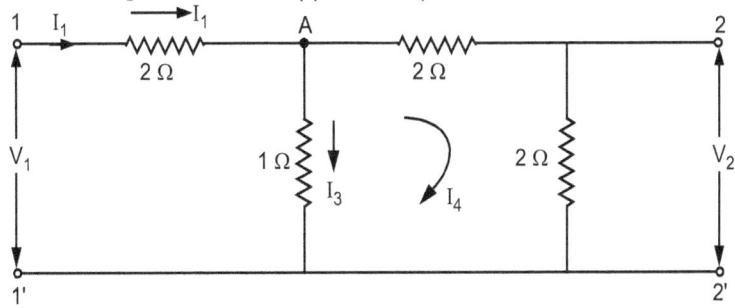

Fig. 3.8 (b)

Unit III | 3.7

By applying KCL at point A,
$$I_1 = I_3 + I_4$$

By current divider rule,
$$I_4 = \left(\frac{1}{1+4}\right) I_1$$

∴
$$\boxed{I_4 = \frac{1}{5} I_1} \quad \ldots \text{(a)}$$

and
$$I_3 = \frac{4}{(1+4) I_1}$$

∴
$$\boxed{I_3 = \frac{4}{5} I_1} \quad \ldots \text{(b)}$$

But
$$I_4 = \frac{V_2}{2}$$

∴ Putting into equation (a),
$$\frac{V_2}{2} = \frac{I_1}{5}$$

∴
$$\frac{V_2}{I_1} = \frac{2}{5}$$

∴
$$Z_{21} = \left[\frac{V_2}{I_1}\right]_{I_2 = 0} = \frac{2}{5} \, \Omega$$

∴
$$\boxed{Z_{21} = \frac{2}{5} \, \Omega}$$

Now by applying KVL to input loop,
∴ $$-2I_1 - I_3 + V_1 = 0$$
∴ $$V_1 = 2I_1 + I_3$$

But,
$$I_3 = \frac{4}{5} I_1$$

From equation (3.1)

∴
$$V_1 = 2I_1 + \frac{4}{5} I_1$$

$$V_1 = I_1 \left(2 + \frac{4}{5}\right)$$

$$\frac{V_1}{I_1} = \frac{14}{5}$$

∴
$$\boxed{Z_{11} = \frac{14}{5} \, \Omega}$$

(b) Now make $I_1 = 0$

Input terminals 1 - 1' open circuit.

$$\therefore \quad Z_{12} = \left[\frac{V_1}{I_2}\right]_{I_1 = 0}$$

$$Z_{22} = \left[\frac{V_2}{I_2}\right]_{I_1 = 0}$$

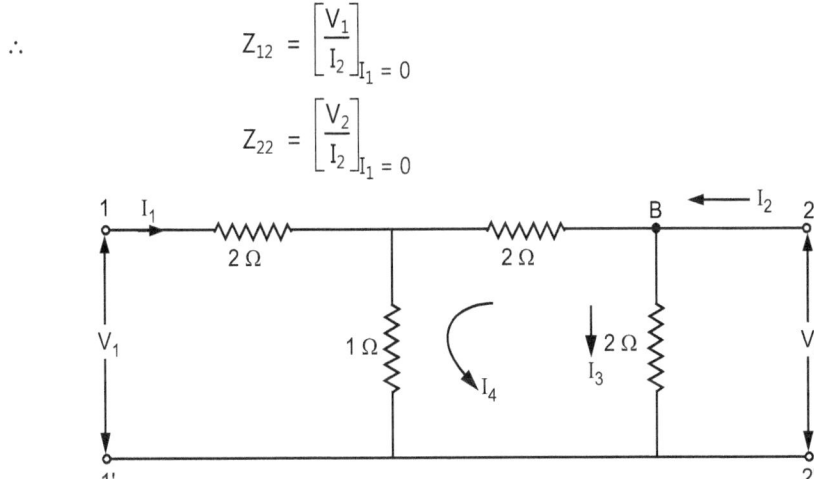

Fig. 3.8 (c)

By KCL at point B, $\quad I_2 = I_3 + I_4$

By current divider rule, $\quad I_4 = \dfrac{2 I_2}{(2 + 3)}$

$$I_4 = \frac{2}{5} I_2 \qquad \ldots \text{(c)}$$

and $\quad I_3 = \dfrac{3 \times I_2}{(3 + 2)}$

$$I_3 = \frac{3}{5} I_2 \qquad \ldots \text{(d)}$$

But $\quad I_4 = \dfrac{V_1}{1}$

$\quad I_4 = V_1$

$\therefore \quad V_1 = \dfrac{2}{5} I_2 \qquad \ldots$ From equation (c)

$\quad \dfrac{V_1}{I_2} = \dfrac{2}{5}$

$\therefore \quad \boxed{Z_{12} = \dfrac{2}{5} \Omega}$

By applying KVL to output side,

$$V_2 = 2 I_3$$

$$= 2 \times \frac{3}{5} I_2 \qquad \ldots \text{From equation (d)}$$

$$\therefore \quad \frac{V_2}{I_2} = \frac{6}{5}\,\Omega$$

$$\therefore \quad \boxed{Z_{22} = \frac{6}{5}\,\Omega}$$

$\therefore$ Z-parameters are: $[Z] = \begin{bmatrix} \dfrac{14}{5} & \dfrac{2}{5} \\ \dfrac{2}{5} & \dfrac{6}{5} \end{bmatrix} \Omega$

Equivalent circuit for Z-parameters is

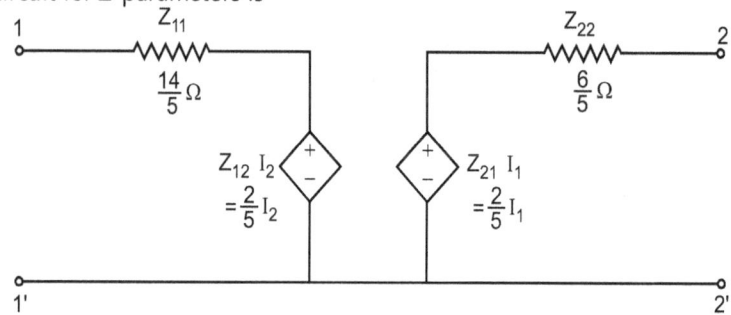

Fig. 3.8 (d)

3.4 SHORT-CIRCUIT ADMITTANCE OR Y-PARAMETERS

In Y-parameter, currents I_1 and I_2 are expressed in terms of voltage V_1 and V_2.

$$(I_1, I_2) = f(V_1, V_2)$$
$$[I] = [Y][V]$$

or

$$\begin{bmatrix} I_1 \\ I_2 \end{bmatrix} = \begin{bmatrix} Y_{11} & Y_{12} \\ Y_{21} & Y_{22} \end{bmatrix} \begin{bmatrix} V_1 \\ V_2 \end{bmatrix}$$

Y-parameter equation is

$$\left. \begin{array}{l} I_1 = Y_1 V_1 + Y_{12} V_2 \\ I_2 = Y_{21} V_1 + Y_{22} V_2 \end{array} \right\} \qquad \ldots (3.4)$$

To calculate Y_{11}, Y_{12}, Y_{21} and Y_{22}, we have to make either $V_1 = 0$ or $V_2 = 0$

Case I: $V_2 = 0$, i.e. output is short-circuited.

(i) Driving point admittance,

$$Y_{11} = \left[\frac{I_1}{V_1} \right]_{V_2 = 0}$$

(ii) Forward transfer admittance,

$$Y_{21} = \left[\frac{I_2}{V_1} \right]_{V_2 = 0}$$

Case II: $V_1 = 0$ i.e. input is short circuited.

(iii) Output driving point admittance,

$$Y_{22} = \left[\frac{I_2}{V_2}\right]_{V_1 = 0}$$

(iv) Reverse transfer admittance:

$$Y_{12} = \left[\frac{I_1}{V_2}\right]_{V_1 = 0}$$

As $V_1 = 0$ or $V_2 = 0$, input or output are short circuited. Hence it is called as **short circuit admittance parameters**.

The equivalent circuit for Y-parameter is shown in Fig. 3.9.

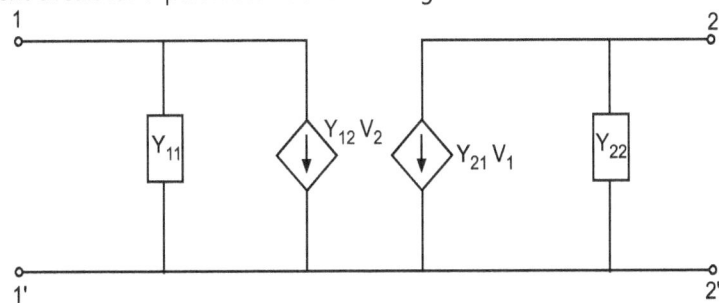

Fig. 3.9: Y-Parameters equivalent circuit

3.4.1 Condition for Symmetry and Reciprocity

(A) Symmetry Condition:

Similar to Z-parameters, Refer Fig. 3.9.

Case I: $V_1 = V_s$
$I_2 = 0$

From equation (3.4), $I_1 = Y_{11} V_s + Y_{12} V_2$ ... (a)
$0 = Y_{21} V_s + Y_{22} V_2$ ... (b)

$\therefore \quad V_2 = -\dfrac{Y_{21}}{Y_{22}} V_s$

Putting in equation (a) $I_1 = Y_{11} V_s + Y_{12} \left(-\dfrac{Y_{21}}{Y_{22}}\right) V_s$

$$I_1 = V_s \left[Y_{11} - \dfrac{Y_{12} Y_{21}}{Y_{22}} \right]$$

$$\boxed{\dfrac{V_s}{I_1} = \dfrac{Y_{22}}{Y_{11} Y_{22} - Y_{12} Y_{21}}} \quad \text{... (c)}$$

Case II: $V_2 = V_s$
and $I_1 = 0$

∴ From equation (3.4),

$$0 = Y_{11} V_1 + Y_{12} V_s \quad \text{... (d)}$$
$$I_2 = Y_{21} V_1 + Y_{22} V_s \quad \text{... (e)}$$

$$V_1 = -\frac{Y_{12}}{Y_{11}} \cdot V_s$$

Putting in equation (e),

$$I_2 = Y_{21} \left(-\frac{Y_{12}}{Y_{11}}\right) V_s + Y_{22} V_s$$

$$I_2 = V_s \left[-\frac{Y_{21} Y_{12}}{Y_{11}} + Y_{22}\right]$$

$$\boxed{\frac{V_s}{I_2} = \frac{Y_{11}}{Y_{11} Y_{22} - Y_{21} Y_{12}}} \quad \text{... (f)}$$

But by symmetry condition,

$$\frac{V_s}{I_1} = \frac{V_s}{I_2}$$

$$\frac{Y_{22}}{Y_{11} Y_{22} - Y_{21} Y_{12}} = \frac{Y_{11}}{Y_{11} Y_{22} - Y_{21} Y_{12}}$$

∴ $\boxed{Y_{22} = Y_{11}}$ ... (3.5)

That is the condition for symmetry.

Example 3.2 : Find y-parameters for the 'T' network shown. Is this a symmetrical and reciprocal network?

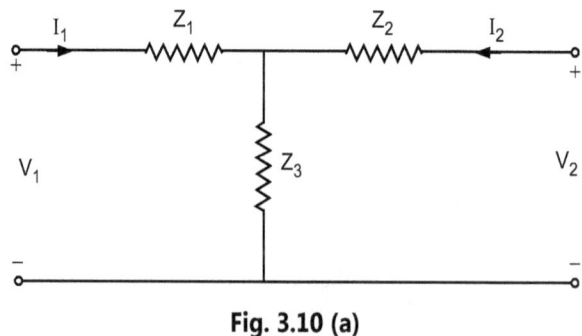

Fig. 3.10 (a)

Solution:
Step I : With $V_2 = 0$ we have,

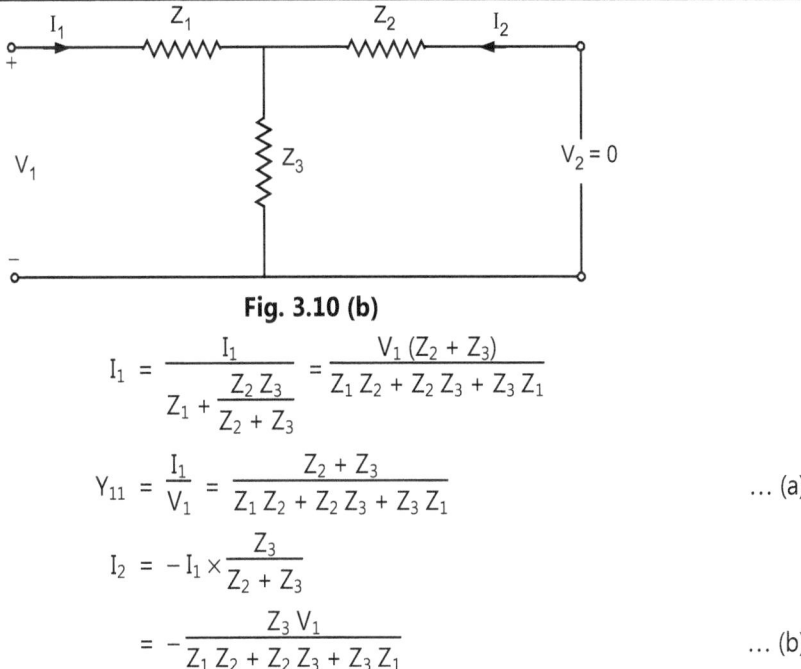

Fig. 3.10 (b)

$$I_1 = \frac{V_1}{Z_1 + \frac{Z_2 Z_3}{Z_2 + Z_3}} = \frac{V_1(Z_2 + Z_3)}{Z_1 Z_2 + Z_2 Z_3 + Z_3 Z_1}$$

$$\therefore \quad Y_{11} = \frac{I_1}{V_1} = \frac{Z_2 + Z_3}{Z_1 Z_2 + Z_2 Z_3 + Z_3 Z_1} \quad \ldots (a)$$

$$I_2 = -I_1 \times \frac{Z_3}{Z_2 + Z_3}$$

$$= -\frac{Z_3 V_1}{Z_1 Z_2 + Z_2 Z_3 + Z_3 Z_1} \quad \ldots (b)$$

Step II: With $V_1 = 0$.

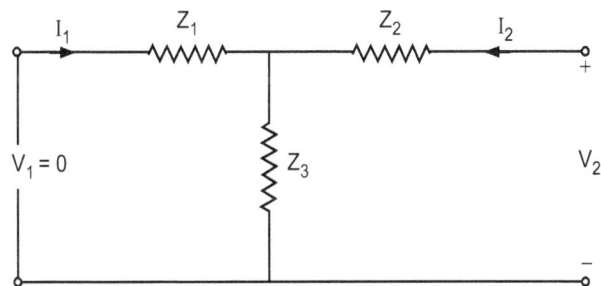

Fig. 3.10 (c)

$$I_2 = \frac{V_2}{Z_2 + \frac{Z_1 Z_3}{Z_1 + Z_3}} = \frac{(Z_1 + Z_3) V_2}{(Z_1 Z_3 + Z_1 Z_2 + Z_2 Z_3)}$$

$$Y_{22} = \frac{I_2}{V_2} = \frac{Z_1 + Z_3}{Z_1 Z_3 + Z_1 Z_2 + Z_2 Z_3} \quad \ldots (c)$$

$$I_1 = -I_2 \times \frac{Z_3}{Z_1 + Z_3} = \frac{Z_3 V_2}{Z_1 Z_3 + Z_2 Z_3 + Z_1 Z_2}$$

$$\therefore \quad Y_{12} = \frac{I_1}{V_2} = -\frac{Z_3}{Z_1 Z_3 + Z_2 Z_3 + Z_1 Z_2} \quad \ldots (d)$$

Since $Y_{11} \neq Y_{22}$ network is not symmetrical

$Y_{12} = Y_{21}$ network is reciprocal.

(B) Reciprocity Condition:

Similar to Z-parameters,

Case I: $\quad V_1 = V_s, V_2 = 0$

$$I_2 = -I_2'$$

Putting these values in equation (3.4),

$$I_1 = Y_{11} V_s + 0$$
$$-I_2' = Y_{21} V_s + 0$$
$$I_1 = Y_{11} V_s$$

and
$$\boxed{\frac{V_s}{I_2'} = \frac{-1}{Y_{21}}} \qquad \ldots \text{(a)}$$

Case II: $\quad V_2 = V_s, V_1 = 0$

$$I_1 = -I_1'$$

Putting in equation (3.14),

$$-I_1' = Y_{12} V_s$$
$$I_2 = Y_{21} V_s$$

$$\boxed{\frac{V_s}{I_1'} = \frac{-1}{Y_{12}}} \qquad \ldots \text{(b)}$$

But by reciprocity condition,

$$\frac{V_s}{I_2'} = \frac{V_s}{I_1'}$$

$\therefore \qquad Y_{21} = Y_{12}$ or $\boxed{Y_{12} = Y_{21}} \qquad \ldots \text{(3.6)}$

This is the condition for reciprocity.

3.5 TRANSMISSION OR ABCD PARAMETERS

In transmission or ABCD or chain parameters, voltage V_1 and current I_1 at input port is expressed in terms of voltage V_2 and current I_2 at output port.

$$V_1 = f(V_2, -I_2)$$
$$I_1 = f(V_2, -I_2)$$

Transmission parameters are generally used in the analysis of power transmission line, the input port is called as sending end and the output port is receiving end.

Here variable used is $-I_2$ instead of I_2. Negative sign indicates that current I_2 is considered outward i.e. leaving port 2 - 2'.

In matrix form,

$$\begin{bmatrix} V_1 \\ I_1 \end{bmatrix} = \begin{bmatrix} A & B \\ C & D \end{bmatrix} \begin{bmatrix} V_2 \\ -I_2 \end{bmatrix} \qquad \ldots (3.7)$$

∴ ABCD parameter equations are

$$\left. \begin{array}{l} V_1 = AV_2 + B(-I_2) \\ I_1 = CV_2 + D(-I_2) \end{array} \right\} \qquad \ldots (3.8)$$

∴ To calculate ABCD parameters, we have to make either $V_2 = 0$ or $I_2 = 0$.

Case I: $I_2 = 0$ i.e. output port 2 - 2' is open circuited.

(i) $$A = \left[\frac{V_1}{V_2} \right]_{I_2 = 0}$$

i.e. the reverse voltage ratio with receiving i.e. output port open circuited.

(ii) $$C = \left[\frac{I_1}{V_2} \right]_{I_2 = 0}$$

i.e. transfer admittance.

Case II: $V_2 = 0$ i.e. output or receiving end is short-circuited.

(iii) $$B = \left[\frac{V_1}{-I_2} \right]_{V_2 = 0}$$

i.e. transfer impedance with output short-circuited.

(iv) $$D = \left[\frac{I_1}{-I_2} \right]_{V_2 = 0}$$

i.e. reverse current ratio.

3.5.1 Condition for Symmetry and Reciprocity

(A) Symmetry Condition:
Similar to Z-parameters, refer Fig. 3.6.

Case I: $\qquad V_1 = V_s, I_2 = 0$

From equation (3.7),

$$V_s = AV_2 \qquad \ldots (a)$$
$$I_1 = CV_2 \qquad \ldots (b)$$

∴ $$V_2 = \frac{I_1}{C}$$

Putting in equation (a), we get

$$V_s = \frac{A}{C} I_1$$

∴ $$\frac{V_s}{I_1} = \frac{A}{C} \qquad \ldots (c)$$

Case II: $\qquad V_2 = V_s, I_1 = 0$

Putting in equation (3.7),

$$V_1 = AV_s + B(-I_2)$$
$$0 = CV_s + D(-I_2)$$

$$\therefore \quad CV_s = DI_2$$

$$\therefore \quad \frac{V_s}{I_2} = \frac{D}{C} \quad \ldots (d)$$

But from symmetry condition,

$$\frac{V_s}{I_1} = \frac{V_s}{I_2}$$

$$\therefore \quad \frac{A}{C} = \frac{D}{C}$$

$$\therefore \quad \boxed{A = D} \quad \ldots (3.9)$$

Symmetry condition.

(B) Reciprocity Condition:

Similar to Z-parameters,

Case I: $\quad V_1 = V_s, V_2 = 0$
and $\quad I_2' = I_2$

From equation (3.7),

$$V_s = B I_2'$$

$$\therefore \quad \frac{V_s}{I_2'} = B \quad \ldots (e)$$

Case II: $\quad V_2 = V_s, V_1 = 0$ and $I_1' = -I_1$

$\therefore$ Equation (3.7) becomes,

$$0 = AV_s + B(-I_2) \quad \ldots (f)$$
$$-I_1' = CV_s + D(-I_2) \quad \ldots (g)$$

$\therefore$ From equation (f), we get

$$I_2 = \frac{A}{B} \cdot V_s$$

Putting this in equation (g) gives

$$-I_1' = CV_s + D\left(-\frac{A}{B} \cdot V_s\right)$$

$$-I_1' = V_s\left(C - \frac{AD}{B}\right)$$

$$-I_1' = V_s\left(\frac{BC-AD}{B}\right)$$

$$\frac{V_s}{I_1'} = \frac{B}{AD-BC}$$

∴ From reciprocity condition,

$$\frac{V_s}{I_1'} = \frac{V_s}{I_2'}$$

$$\frac{B}{AD-BC} = B$$

∴ $\boxed{AD - BC = 1}$ Condition of reciprocity ... (3.10)

Example 3.3: Find ABCD parameters for the given R-C network.

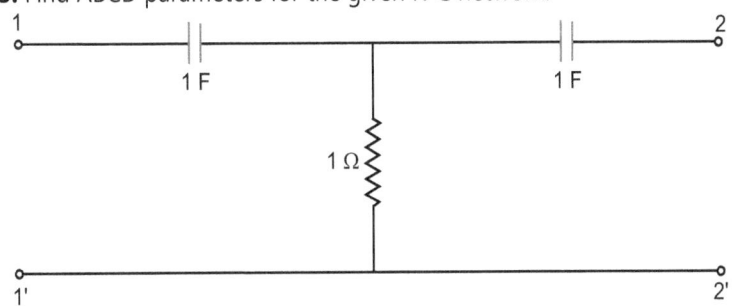

Fig. 3.11

Solution: ABCD parameter equations are

$$V_1 = AV_2 + B(-I_2)$$
$$I_1 = CV_2 + D(-I_2)$$

Case I: $I_2 = 0$ i.e. output is open circuited.

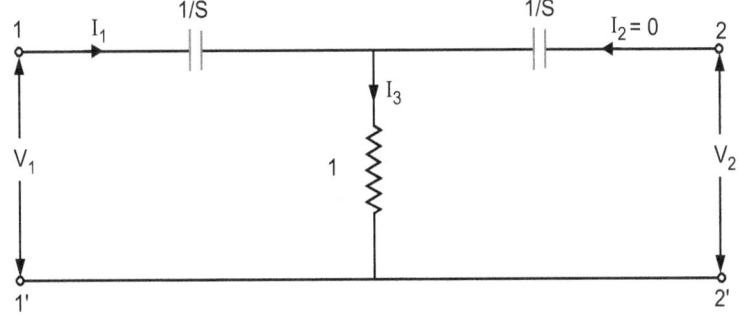

Fig. 3.11 (a): S-domain representation

∴ $$I_1 = \frac{V_1}{1+\frac{1}{S}} = V_1 \cdot \frac{S}{S+1}$$

But, $V_2 = I_1 \times 1\,\Omega$

∴ $A = \left[\dfrac{V_1}{V_2}\right]_{I_2 = 0} = \dfrac{\dfrac{s+1}{s} \cdot I_1}{I_1}$

∴ $\boxed{A = \dfrac{s+1}{s}}$

and $C = \left[\dfrac{I_1}{V_2}\right]_{I_2 = 0} = 1$

∴ $\boxed{C = 1}$

Case II: $V_2 = 0$ i.e. output is short-circuited.

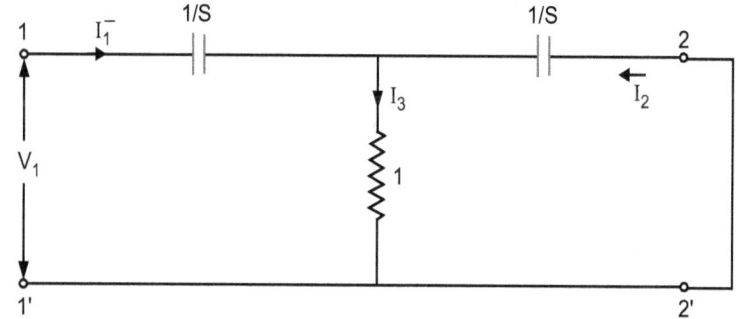

Fig. 3.11 (b)

$V_2 = 0$

∴ $I_3 = -I_2 \cdot \dfrac{1}{s}$

$I_1 = I_3 - I_2$

$= -\dfrac{I_2}{s} - I_2$

$I_1 = -I_2 \left[\dfrac{s+1}{s}\right]$

∴ $D = \left[-\dfrac{I_1}{I_2}\right]_{V_2 = 0}$

∴ $\boxed{D = \dfrac{s+1}{s}}$

Now, $V_1 = I_1 \cdot \dfrac{1}{s} + I_3 = -I_2 \cdot \dfrac{s+1}{s^2} - I_2 \cdot \dfrac{1}{s}$

$= -I_2 \left[\dfrac{2s+1}{s^2}\right]$

$$\therefore \quad B = \left[-\frac{V_1}{I_2}\right]_{V_2 = 0}$$

$$\therefore \quad \boxed{B = \frac{2s + 1}{s^2}}$$

∴ ABCD parameters are

$$[T] = \begin{bmatrix} \dfrac{s+1}{s} & \dfrac{2s+1}{s^2} \\ 1 & \dfrac{s+1}{s} \end{bmatrix}$$

3.6 HYBRID PARAMETERS OR H-PARAMETERS

The hybrid or h-parameters are used in constructing models of transistors. The parameter of transistor cannot be measured by short-circuit admittance or open circuit impedance parameter individually. Therefore, the combination of both short-circuit admittance and open-circuit impedance is called as hybrid or h-parameter.

In h-parameters, voltage at input port V_1 and the current of the output port I_2, are expressed in terms of the current at the input port I_1 and voltage at output port V_2.

$$(V_1, I_2) = f(I_1, V_2)$$

or
$$V_1 = f(I_1, V_2)$$
$$I_2 = f(I_1, V_2)$$

In matrix form,
$$\begin{bmatrix} V_1 \\ I_2 \end{bmatrix} = \begin{bmatrix} h_{11} & h_{12} \\ -h_{21} & h_{22} \end{bmatrix} \begin{bmatrix} I_1 \\ V_2 \end{bmatrix} \quad \ldots (3.11)$$

h-parameter equations are

$$\left. \begin{array}{l} V_1 = h_{11} I_1 + h_{12} V_2 \\ I_2 = h_{21} I_1 + h_{22} V_2 \end{array} \right\} \quad \ldots (3.12)$$

To calculate h-parameters,

Case I: $V_2 = 0$ i.e. output is short-circuited.

$$\therefore \quad h_{11} = \left[\frac{V_1}{I_1}\right]_{V_2 = 0}$$

which is input impedance with output short-circuited.

$$h_{21} = \left[\frac{I_2}{I_1}\right]_{V_2 = 0}$$

which is forward current gain.

Case II: $I_1 = 0$

$$h_{12} = \left[\frac{V_1}{V_2}\right]_{I_1 = 0}$$

Which is reverse voltage gain with input open-circuited.

$$h_{22} = \left[\frac{I_2}{V_2}\right]_{I_1 = 0}$$

Which is output admittance (℧).

The equivalent circuit for h-parameters are shown in Fig. 3.12.

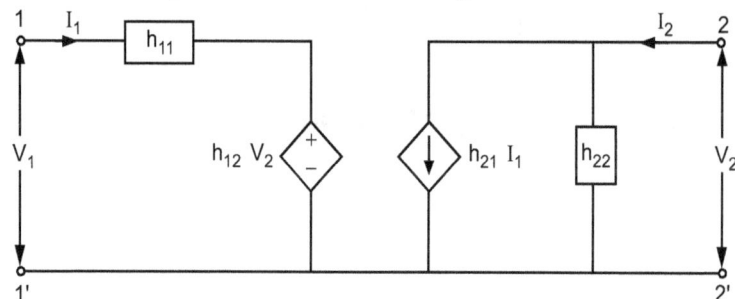

Fig. 3.12: h-parameters equivalent circuit

3.6.1 Condition for Symmetry and Reciprocity

(A) Symmetry Condition:

Similar to Z-parameters. Refer to Fig. 3.6.

Case I: $V_1 = V_s, I_2 = 0$

From equation (3.12),

$$V_s = h_{11} I_1 + h_{12} V_2 \quad \ldots \text{(a)}$$

and

$$0 = h_{21} I_1 + h_{22} V_2 \quad \ldots \text{(b)}$$

$$\therefore \quad -h_{22} V_2 = h_{21} I_1$$

$$V_2 = -\frac{h_{21}}{h_{22}} \cdot I_1$$

Substituting value of V_2 in equation (a) gives

$$V_s = h_{11} I_1 + h_{12} \left[\frac{-h_{21}}{h_{22}}\right] I_1$$

$$V_s = \left[h_{11} - \frac{h_{12} h_{21}}{h_{22}}\right] I_1$$

$$\frac{V_s}{I_1} = \frac{h_{11} h_{22} - h_{12} h_{21}}{h_{22}} \quad \ldots \text{(c)}$$

Case II: $V_2 = V_s$ and $I_1 = 0$

$$V_1 = h_{12} V_s \quad \ldots (d)$$
$$I_2 = h_{22} V_s \quad \ldots (e)$$
$$\frac{V_s}{I_2} = \frac{1}{h_{22}} \quad \ldots (f)$$

From symmetry condition,
$$\frac{V_s}{I_1} = \frac{V_s}{I_2}$$
$$\frac{h_{11} h_{22} - h_{12} h_{21}}{h_{22}} = \frac{1}{h_{22}}$$

∴ $\boxed{h_{11} h_{22} - h_{12} h_{21} = 1}$ ... (3.13)

which is condition of symmetry.

(B) Reciprocity Condition:

Similar to Z-parameter.

Case I: $\quad V_1 = V_s, V_2 = 0$
and $\quad I_2' = -I_2$

From equation (3.10),
$$V_s = h_{11} I_1 \quad \ldots (g)$$
and $\quad -I_2' = h_{21} I_1$

∴ $\quad I_1 = \frac{-1}{h_{21}} \cdot I_2'$

Putting in equation (g), we get
$$V_s = \frac{-h_{11}}{h_{21}} \cdot I_2'$$

∴ $\quad \dfrac{V_s}{I_2'} = \dfrac{-h_{11}}{h_{21}} \quad \ldots (h)$

Case II: $\quad V_2 = V_s, V_1 = 0$
$\quad I_1' = -I_1$

Putting in equation (3.10),
$$0 = -h_{11} I_1' + h_{12} V_s \quad \ldots (i)$$
and $\quad I_2 = -h_{21} I_1' + h_{22} V_s \quad \ldots (j)$

∴ $\quad I_1' = \dfrac{h_{12}}{h_{11}} V_s$

∴ $\quad \dfrac{V_s}{I_1'} = \dfrac{h_{11}}{h_{12}} \quad \ldots (k)$

By reciprocity condition,

$$\frac{V_s}{I_2'} = \frac{V_s}{I_1'}$$

$$-\frac{h_{11}}{h_{21}} = \frac{h_{11}}{h_{12}}$$

∴ $\boxed{h_{12} = -h_{21}}$ ... (3.14)

Reciprocity condition for h-parameters.

Example 3.4: The hybrid parameters of the network shown in Fig. 3.13 are $h_{11} = 2\,\Omega$, $h_{12} = 4$, $h_{21} = -5$, $h_{22} = 2\,\mho$.

Determine the supply voltage V_s if the power dissipated in the load resistor $R_L = 4\,\Omega$ is 25 W and $R_s = 2\,\Omega$.

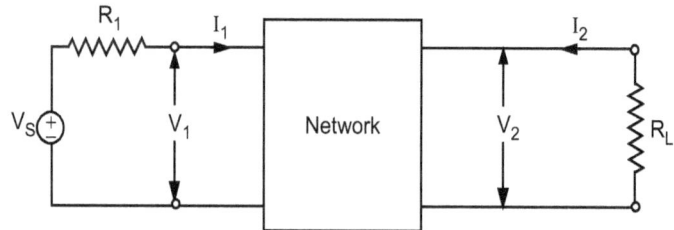

Fig. 3.13

The h-parameter equations are

$$V_1 = 2I_1 + 4V_2$$
$$I_2 = -5I_1 + 2V_2$$

Now power dissipated in R_L is

$$P_L = \frac{V_2^2}{R_L} = 25 \text{ watts}$$

∴ $V_2 = 10$ V

But $V_2 = -I_2 R_L$

∴ $I_2 = -2.5$ A

Putting these values in h-parameter equation,

$$V_1 = 2I_1 + 40$$

and $-2.5 = -5I_1 + 20$

Solving these two equations,

$I_1 = 4.5$ A

and $V_1 = 49$ V

Since, $I_1 = \dfrac{V_s - V_1}{2}$

$$4.5 = \frac{V_s - 49}{2}$$

$$9 = V_s - 49$$

∴ $V_s = 58$ V

∴ The supply voltage is $V_s = 58$ V

3.7 INTERRELATIONSHIPS BETWEEN THE PARAMETERS

Uptil now, we have studied four different parameters. Each has its own utility and is suited for certain specific application. But, we often find it necessary to convert from one set of parameters to another. Through simple mathematical manipulation, it is possible to convert from any one set to any of the remaining set.

3.7.1 Z-Parameter in Terms of Other Parameters

Let us first rewrite the equations of Z-parameters.

$$\left. \begin{array}{l} V_1 = Z_{11} I_1 + Z_{12} I_2 \\ V_2 = Z_{21} I_1 + Z_{22} I_2 \end{array} \right\} \quad \ldots \text{(a)}$$

(A) Z-Parameters in Terms of Y-Parameters

Now equations for Y-parameters are

$$\left. \begin{array}{l} I_1 = Y_{11} V_1 + Y_{12} V_2 \\ I_2 = Y_{21} V_1 + Y_{22} V_2 \end{array} \right\} \quad \ldots \text{(b)}$$

i.e. $\begin{bmatrix} I_1 \\ I_2 \end{bmatrix} = \begin{bmatrix} Y_{11} & Y_{12} \\ Y_{21} & Y_{22} \end{bmatrix} \begin{bmatrix} V_1 \\ V_2 \end{bmatrix}$

Let us solve this equation simultaneously for V_1 and V_2 from (b)

By Cramer's rule, $V_1 = \dfrac{\begin{vmatrix} I_1 & Y_{12} \\ I_2 & Y_{22} \end{vmatrix}}{\begin{vmatrix} Y_{11} & Y_{12} \\ Y_{21} & Y_{22} \end{vmatrix}} = \dfrac{Y_{22} I_1 - Y_{12} I_2}{Y_{11} Y_{22} - Y_{12} Y_{21}}$

$$V_1 = \frac{Y_{22}}{Y_{11} Y_{22} - Y_{12} Y_{21}} I_1 - \frac{Y_{12}}{Y_{11} Y_{22} - Y_{12} Y_{21}} I_2$$

Let $Dy = Y_{11} Y_{22} - Y_{12} Y_{21}$

$$V_1 = \frac{Y_{22}}{Dy} I_1 - \frac{Y_{12}}{Dy} I_2 \quad \ldots \text{(c)}$$

and
$$V_2 = \frac{\begin{vmatrix} Y_{11} & I_1 \\ Y_{21} & I_2 \end{vmatrix}}{\begin{vmatrix} Y_{11} & Y_{12} \\ Y_{21} & Y_{22} \end{vmatrix}} = \frac{Y_{11} I_2 - Y_{21} I_1}{Y_{11} Y_{22} - Y_{12} Y_{21}}$$

$$\therefore V_2 = \frac{Y_{11}}{Dy} I_2 - \frac{Y_{21}}{Dy} I_1$$

$$V_2 = \frac{-Y_{21}}{Dy} I_1 + \frac{Y_{11}}{Dy} I_2 \qquad \ldots (d)$$

Comparing equations (c) and (d) with Z-parameter equations, we get

$$Z_{11} = \frac{Y_{22}}{Dy}, \; Z_{12} = \frac{-Y_{12}}{Dy}$$

$$Z_{21} = \frac{-Y_{21}}{Dy}, \; Z_{22} = \frac{Y_{11}}{Dy}$$

$$[Z] = \begin{bmatrix} \frac{Y_{22}}{Dy} & \frac{-Y_{12}}{Dy} \\ \frac{-Y_{21}}{Dy} & \frac{Y_{11}}{Dy} \end{bmatrix} \qquad \ldots (3.15)$$

Thus Z-parameters matrix is obtained by inverse of y-parameters matrix. Similarly it can be proved that y-parameters matrix is obtained by inverse of z-parameters matrix.

(B) Z-Parameters in Terms of h-Parameters

The h-parameter equations are

$$V_1 = h_{11} I_1 + h_{12} V_2 \qquad \ldots (e)$$
$$I_2 = h_{21} I_1 + h_{22} V_2 \qquad \ldots (f)$$

$$\therefore h_{22} V_2 = I_2 - h_{21} I_2$$

$$V_2 = \frac{1}{h_{22}} I_2 - \frac{h_{21}}{h_{22}} I_1$$

$$V_2 = \frac{-h_{21}}{h_{22}} I_1 + \frac{1}{h_{22}} I_2 \qquad \ldots (g)$$

Putting this value in equation (e), we get

$$V_1 = h_{11} I_1 + h_{12} \left[\frac{1}{h_{22}} I_2 - \frac{h_{21}}{h_{22}} I_1 \right]$$

$$V_1 = h_{11} I_1 + \frac{h_{12}}{h_{22}} I_2 - \frac{h_{12} h_{21}}{h_{22}} I_1$$

$$V_1 = \left[h_{11} - \frac{h_{12} h_{21}}{h_{22}}\right] I_1 + \frac{h_{12}}{h_{22}} I_2$$

$$V_1 = \frac{h_{11} h_{22} - h_{12} h_{21}}{h_{22}} I_1 + \frac{h_{12}}{h_{22}} I_2 \qquad \ldots \text{(h)}$$

Comparing this equation with Z-parameter equation,

$$\boxed{Z_{11} = \frac{h_{11} h_{22} - h_{12} h_{21}}{h_{22}}} \qquad \boxed{Z_{12} = \frac{h_{12}}{h_{22}}}$$

Comparing equation (g) with Z-parameter equation.

$$\boxed{Z_{21} = -\frac{h_{21}}{h_{22}} \quad \text{and} \quad Z_{22} = \frac{1}{h_{22}}}$$

$$\therefore \quad [Z] = \begin{bmatrix} \dfrac{Dh}{h_{22}} & \dfrac{h_{12}}{h_{22}} \\ -\dfrac{h_{21}}{h_{22}} & \dfrac{1}{h_{22}} \end{bmatrix} \qquad \ldots \text{(3.16)}$$

(C) Z-Parameters in Terms of ABCD Parameters

ABCD parameter equations are

$$V_1 = AV_2 + B(-I_2) \qquad \ldots \text{(i)}$$
$$I_1 = CV_2 + D(-I_2) \qquad \ldots \text{(j)}$$

From equation (j), we get,

$$CV_2 = I_1 + DI_2$$
$$V_2 = \left(\frac{1}{C}\right) I_1 + \left(\frac{D}{C}\right) I_2 \qquad \ldots \text{(k)}$$

Comparing equation with Z-parameter equation,

$$\boxed{Z_{21} = \frac{1}{C}} \qquad \boxed{Z_{22} = \frac{D}{C}}$$

Putting value of V_2 in equation (j), we get

$$V_1 = A\left[\frac{1}{C} I_1 + \frac{D}{C} I_2\right] + B(-I_2)$$

$$V_1 = \frac{A}{C} I_1 + \frac{AD}{C} I_2 - BI_2$$

$$V_1 = \frac{A}{C} I_1 + \left[\frac{AD}{C} - B\right] I_2$$

$$V_1 = \frac{A}{C} I_1 + \frac{AD - BC}{C} I_2 \qquad \ldots \text{(l)}$$

Comparing with Z-parameter equation,

$$Z_{11} = \frac{A}{C} \qquad Z_{12} = \frac{AD - BC}{C}$$

$$\therefore \quad [Z] = \begin{bmatrix} \dfrac{A}{C} & \dfrac{AD - BC}{C} \\ \dfrac{1}{C} & \dfrac{D}{C} \end{bmatrix} \qquad \ldots (3.17)$$

In similar manner, we can express any one parameter in terms of remaining other parameters.

Table 3.2 gives the summary of all relationships between different sets of parameters. In this table matrices placed in each rows are equivalent. The equivalent table involves determinants Dz, Dy, Dh, ΔT, etc. where

$$Dz = Z_{11} Z_{22} - Z_{12} Z_{21}$$

$$Dy = Y_{11} Y_{22} - Y_{12} Y_{21}$$

$$Dh = h_{11} h_{22} - h_{12} h_{21}$$

$$\Delta T = AD - BC, \text{ etc.}$$

Table 3.2: Interrelationship between parameters

[Z]	[Y]	[T]	[h]
$\begin{bmatrix} Z_{11} & Z_{12} \\ Z_{21} & Z_{22} \end{bmatrix}$	$\begin{bmatrix} \dfrac{Y_{22}}{Dy} & \dfrac{-Y_{12}}{Dy} \\ \dfrac{-Y_{21}}{Dy} & \dfrac{Y_{11}}{Dy} \end{bmatrix}$	$\begin{bmatrix} \dfrac{A}{C} & \dfrac{DT}{C} \\ \dfrac{1}{C} & \dfrac{D}{C} \end{bmatrix}$	$\begin{bmatrix} \dfrac{Dh}{h_{22}} & \dfrac{h_{12}}{h_{22}} \\ \dfrac{-h_{21}}{h_{22}} & \dfrac{1}{h_{22}} \end{bmatrix}$
$\begin{bmatrix} \dfrac{Z_{22}}{Dz} & \dfrac{-Z_{12}}{Dz} \\ \dfrac{-Z_{21}}{Dz} & \dfrac{Z_{11}}{Dz} \end{bmatrix}$	$\begin{bmatrix} Y_{11} & Y_{12} \\ Y_{21} & Y_{22} \end{bmatrix}$	$\begin{bmatrix} \dfrac{D}{B} & \dfrac{-DT}{B} \\ \dfrac{-1}{B} & \dfrac{A}{B} \end{bmatrix}$	$\begin{bmatrix} \dfrac{1}{h_{11}} & \dfrac{-h_{12}}{h_{11}} \\ \dfrac{h_{21}}{h_{11}} & \dfrac{Dh}{h_{11}} \end{bmatrix}$

…Cont.

$$\begin{bmatrix} \dfrac{Z_{11}}{Z_{21}} & \dfrac{Dz}{Z_{21}} \\ \dfrac{1}{Z_{21}} & \dfrac{Z_{22}}{Z_{21}} \end{bmatrix} \quad \begin{bmatrix} \dfrac{-Y_{22}}{Y_{21}} & \dfrac{-1}{Y_{21}} \\ \dfrac{-Dy}{Y_{21}} & \dfrac{-Y_{11}}{Y_{21}} \end{bmatrix} \quad \begin{bmatrix} A & B \\ C & D \end{bmatrix} \quad \begin{bmatrix} \dfrac{-Dh}{h_{21}} & \dfrac{-h_{11}}{h_{21}} \\ \dfrac{-h_{22}}{h_{21}} & \dfrac{-1}{h_{21}} \end{bmatrix}$$

$$\begin{bmatrix} \dfrac{Dz}{Z_{22}} & \dfrac{Z_{21}}{Z_{22}} \\ \dfrac{-Z_{21}}{Z_{22}} & \dfrac{1}{Z_{22}} \end{bmatrix} \quad \begin{bmatrix} \dfrac{1}{Y_{11}} & \dfrac{-Y_{12}}{Y_{11}} \\ \dfrac{Y_{21}}{Y_{11}} & \dfrac{Dy}{Y_{11}} \end{bmatrix} \quad \begin{bmatrix} \dfrac{B}{D} & \dfrac{DT}{D} \\ \dfrac{-1}{D} & \dfrac{C}{D} \end{bmatrix} \quad \begin{bmatrix} h_{11} & h_{12} \\ h_{21} & h_{22} \end{bmatrix}$$

Table 3.3 gives the summary for condition of symmetry and reciprocity for different parameters.

Table 3.3: Condition for symmetry and reciprocity

Parameter	Condition of symmetry	Condition of reciprocity
[Z]	$Z_{11} = Z_{22}$	$Z_{12} = Z_{21}$
[Y]	$Y_{11} = Y_{22}$	$Y_{12} = Y_{21}$
{ABCD} or [T]	$A = D$	$AD - BC = 1$
[h]	$h_{11} h_{22} - h_{12} h_{21} = 1$	$h_{12} = -h_{21}$

SOLVED EXAMPLES OF PARAMETERS

Example 3.5: Find Z-parameters of the network shown in Fig. 3.14 (a).

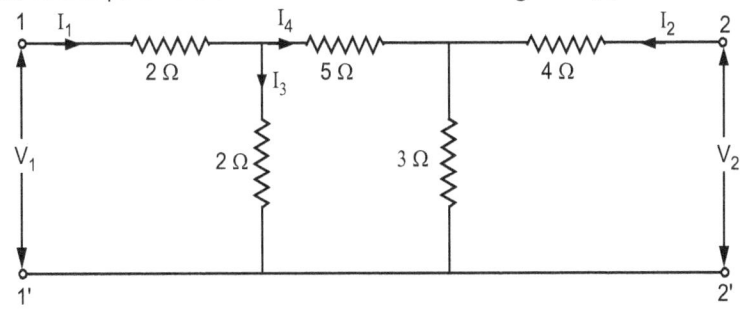

Fig. 3.14 (a)

Solution: Z-parameter equations are

$$V_1 = Z_{11} I_1 + Z_{12} I_2$$
$$V_2 = Z_{21} I_1 + Z_{22} I_2$$

Case I: $I_2 = 0$, output 2 - 2' open circuited.

$$I_1 = I_3 + I_4$$

$$I_4 = \left(\frac{2}{2+8}\right)I_1 = \frac{1}{5}I_1$$

and
$$I_3 = \frac{8\,I_1}{2+8} = \frac{4}{5}I_1$$

But
$$I_4 = \frac{V_2}{3}$$

∴ $$\frac{V_2}{3} = \frac{I_1}{5}$$

∴ $$\frac{V_2}{I_1} = \frac{3}{5}$$

∴ $$Z_{21} = \left[\frac{V_2}{I_1}\right]_{I_2 = 0} = \frac{3}{5}\,\Omega$$

By applying KVL to input loop,
$$-2I_1 - 2I_3 + V_1 = 0$$
$$V_1 = 2(I_1 + I_3)$$

But
$$I_3 = \frac{4}{5}I_1$$

$$V_1 = 2\left(I_1 + \frac{4}{5}I_1\right)$$

$$V_1 = 2I_1\left(\frac{9}{5}\right)$$

$$\frac{V_1}{I_1} = \frac{18}{5}$$

∴ $$\boxed{Z_{11} = \frac{V_1}{I_1} = \frac{18}{5} = 3.6\,\Omega}$$

Case II: $I_1 = 0$, Input 1 - 1' is open circuited.

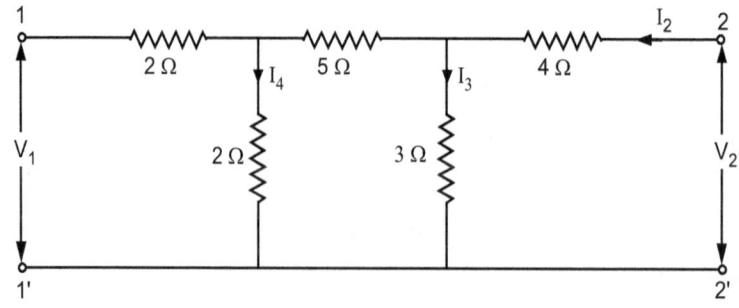

Fig. 3.14 (b)

$I_2 = {}_3 + I_4$

$I_3 = \dfrac{7 I_2}{(3 + 7)} = \dfrac{7}{10} I_2$

and $I_4 = \dfrac{3 I_2}{7 + 3} = \dfrac{3}{10} I_2$

By applying KVL to output loop,

$-4 I_2 - 3 I_3 + V_2 = 0$

$V_2 = 4 I_2 + 3 I_3$

$= 4 I_2 + 3 \times \dfrac{7}{10} I_2$

$V_2 = I_2 \left[4 + \dfrac{21}{10} \right]$

$Z_{22} = \dfrac{V_2}{I_2} = \dfrac{40 + 21}{10}$

$= \dfrac{61}{10} = 6.1$

∴ $\boxed{Z_{22} = 6.1 \, \Omega}$

$V_1 = 2 I_4$

$I_4 = \dfrac{V_1}{2}$

But $I_4 = \dfrac{3}{10} I_2 = \dfrac{V_1}{2}$

$\dfrac{V_1}{I_2} = \dfrac{6}{10} = 0.6$

∴ $\boxed{Z_{12} = 0.6 \, \Omega}$

∴ $[Z] = \begin{bmatrix} 3.6 & 0.6 \\ 0.6 & 6.1 \end{bmatrix}$ (ohms)

Example 3.6: Find transmission parameters of the following network shown in Fig. 3.15.

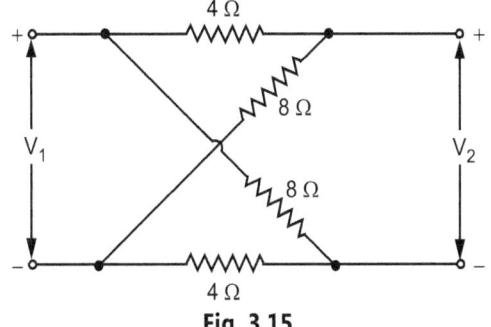

Fig. 3.15

NETWORK ANALYSIS (S.E. SEM III E & TC. SU) — TWO PORT NETWORK & NETWORK FUNCTIONS

Solution: Transmission parameters or ABCD parameters are given by equations:

$$V_1 = AV_2 + B(-I_2)$$
$$I_1 = CV_2 + D(-I_2)$$

The network shown in Fig. 3.15 can be redrawn as:

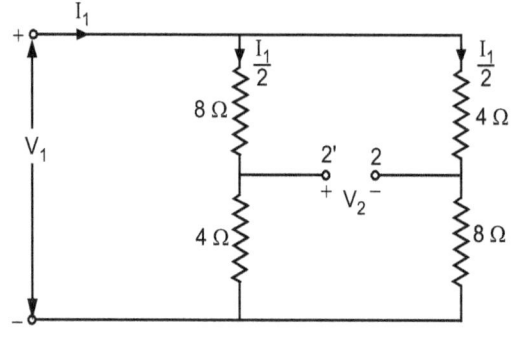

Fig. 3.15 (a)

Case I: Let $I_2 = 0$ i.e. 2 - 2' is open-circuited.

Voltage at terminal 2 is

$$V' = 8\left(\frac{I_1}{2}\right) = 4 I_1$$

Voltage at terminal 2' is

$$V'' = 4\left(\frac{I_1}{2}\right) = 2 I_1$$

$$V_2 = V' - V''$$
$$= 4 I_1 - 2 I_1$$

∴ $$V_2 = 2 I_1 \qquad \ldots \text{(a)}$$

∴ $$\boxed{C = \left[\frac{I_1}{V_2}\right]_{I_2 = 0} = \frac{1}{2}\,\mho}$$

Now, $$V_1 = I_1 \left[(8+4) \,\|\, (8+4)\right]$$
$$V_1 = I_1 \left[12 \,\|\, 12\right]$$

∴ $$V_1 = I_1 \times 6 \qquad \ldots \text{(b)}$$

Dividing equation (b) by equation (a),

$$\frac{V_1}{V_2} = \frac{6 I_1}{2 I_1} = 3$$

∴ $$\boxed{A = \left[\frac{V_1}{V_2}\right]_{I_2 = 0} = 3}$$

Unit III | 3.30

Case II: Let $V_2 = 0$. The circuit is shown in Fig. 3.15 (b).

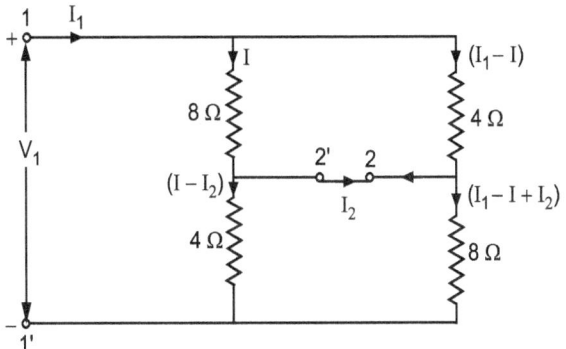

Fig. 3.15 (b)

Consider a closed path 1 - 2 - 2' - 1' - 1.
$$V_1 = 4(I_1 - I) + 4(I - I_2)$$
$$V_1 = 4I_1 - 4I + 4I - 4I_2$$
$$V_1 = 4I_1 + 4(-I_2) \qquad \ldots (c)$$

Consider a closed path 1 - 2' - 2 - 1' - 1.
$$V_1 = 8I + 8(I_1 - I + I_2)$$
$$V_1 = 8I_1 + 8I_2$$
$$V_1 = 8I_1 - 8(-I_2) \qquad \ldots (d)$$

Let us solve for I_2.
$$V_1 = 16(-I_2)$$

$$B = \left[\frac{V_1}{-I_2}\right]_{V_2 = 0} = 16\,\Omega$$

$$D = \left[\frac{I_1}{-I_2}\right]_{V_2 = 0} = 3\,\Omega$$

∴ $$[T] = \begin{bmatrix} 3 & 16\,\Omega \\ 1/2\,\mho & 3 \end{bmatrix}$$

Example 3.7: Determine Y-parameters of the network shown in Fig. 3.16.

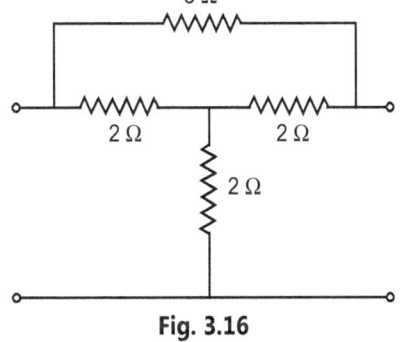

Fig. 3.16

Solution: The given network can be considered as parallel connection of two networks shown in Fig. 3.16 (a) and 3.16 (b).

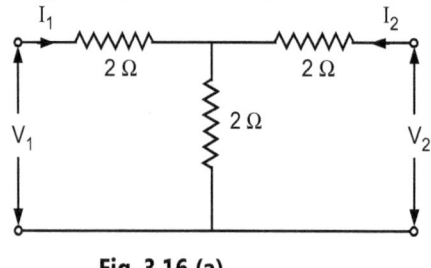

Fig. 3.16 (a)　　　　　　　　　　Fig. 3.16 (b)

Now, for Fig. 3.16 (a), Y-parameters can be written as

With $V_2 = 0$,　　　$I_1 = \dfrac{V_1}{3}$

∴　　　$Y_{11} = \left[\dfrac{I_1}{V_1}\right]_{V_2=0} = \dfrac{1}{3}\ \mho$

and　　　$I_2 = -\left(\dfrac{2}{4}\right) I_1 = \dfrac{-V_1}{6}$

∴　　　$Y_{21} = \left[\dfrac{I_2}{V_1}\right]_{V_2=0} = -\dfrac{1}{6}\ \mho$

As network is symmetric and reciprocal,

$$Y_{12} = Y_{21} = -\dfrac{1}{6}\ \mho$$

$$Y_{22} = Y_{11} = \dfrac{1}{3}\ \mho$$

Similarly Y-parameters of Fig. 3.16 (b) can be written as

$$Y_{11} = Y_{22} = \dfrac{1}{3}\ \mho$$

$$Y_{12} = Y_{21} = -\dfrac{1}{3}\ \mho$$

Here, these two networks are connected in parallel.

The overall Y-parameters of the combination can be written as:

$$[Y] = \begin{bmatrix} \dfrac{1}{3} & -\dfrac{1}{6} \\ -\dfrac{1}{6} & \dfrac{1}{3} \end{bmatrix} + \begin{bmatrix} \dfrac{1}{3} & -\dfrac{1}{3} \\ -\dfrac{1}{3} & \dfrac{1}{3} \end{bmatrix} = \begin{bmatrix} \dfrac{2}{3} & -\dfrac{1}{2} \\ -\dfrac{1}{2} & \dfrac{2}{3} \end{bmatrix}\ \text{(mho)}$$

Example 3.8: Find open-circuit impedance parameters of the circuit containing a controlled source shown in Fig. 3.17. Also find out its Y-parameters.

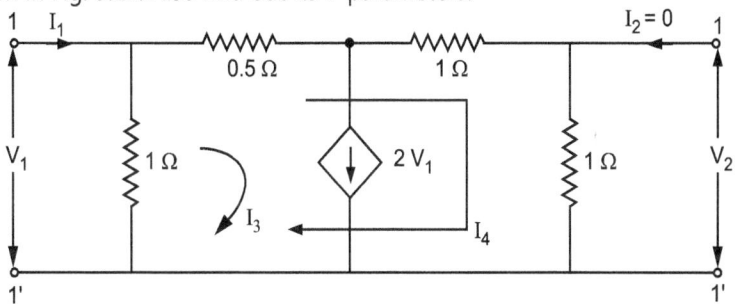

Fig. 3.17

Solution: For Z-parameters:
Case I: Port 2 - 2' is open-circuited.

i.e. $I_2 = 0$
and $I_3 = 2V_1$
Now, $V_1 = (I_1 - I_3) \times 1$
∴ $V_1 = I_1 - 2V_1$
∴ $3V_1 = I_1$
∴ $\dfrac{V_1}{I_1} = \dfrac{1}{3}$
∴ $Z_{11} = \left[\dfrac{V_1}{I_1}\right]_{I_2 = 0} = \dfrac{1}{3} \, \Omega$

Again, by KVL, $1.5 I_4 + 0.5 I_3 + V_2 = V_1$
or $1.5 (2V_2) + 0.5 I_3 + V_2 = V_1$
or $3V_2 + 0.5 (2V_1) + V_2 = V_1$
∴ $4V_2 = 0$
∴ $V_2 = 0$
∴ $Z_{21} = \left[\dfrac{V_2}{I_1}\right]_{I_2 = 0} = 0 \, \Omega$

Case II: $I_1 = 0$, the circuit is shown in Fig. 3.17 (a).

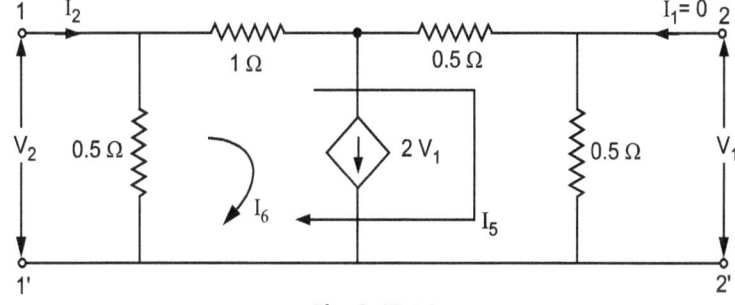

Fig. 3.17 (a)

For this circuit, $I_6 = 2V_1$
and $1 \times I_5 = V_1$

By KVL,
$$(I_2 - I_6 - I_5) \times 0.5 = V_2$$
and $I_6 \times 1 + I_5 (2.5) = V_2$
Thus, $(I_2 - I_5 - I_6) \times 0.5 = I_6 + 2.5 I_5$
∴ $I_2 = 3 I_6 + 6 I_5$

Putting the values of I_5 and I_6,
$$I_2 = 6V_1 + 6V_1 = 12 V_1$$

∴ $Z_{12} = \left[\dfrac{V_1}{I_2}\right]_{I_1 = 0} = \dfrac{1}{12} \Omega$

and $I_6 + 2.5 I_5 = V_2$
or $2V_1 + 2.5 V_1 = V_2$
∴ $4.5 V_1 = V_2$

But $V_1 = \dfrac{I_2}{12}$

∴ $4.5 \left(\dfrac{I_2}{12}\right) = V_2$

∴ $Z_{22} = \left[\dfrac{V_2}{I_2}\right]_{I_1 = 0} = \dfrac{4.5}{12} = \dfrac{3}{8} \Omega$

∴ Z-parameters are $[Z] = \begin{bmatrix} 1/3 & 1/12 \\ 0 & 3/8 \end{bmatrix} \Omega$

From conversion table, $Y_{11} = \dfrac{Z_{22}}{Dz}$

$$Dz = Z_{11} Z_{22} - Z_{12} Z_{21} = \dfrac{1}{8}$$

∴ $Y_{11} = \dfrac{3/8}{1/8} = 3 \mho$

$Y_{21} = \dfrac{-Z_{21}}{Dz} = 0$

$Y_{12} = \dfrac{-Z_{12}}{Dz} = -\dfrac{2}{3} \mho$

$Y_{22} = \dfrac{Z_{11}}{Dz} = \dfrac{8}{3} \mho$

∴ Y-parameters are $[Y] = \begin{bmatrix} 3 & -2/3 \\ 0 & 8/3 \end{bmatrix} \mho$

3.8 SYSTEM FUNCTION OR NETWORK FUNCTIONS

A network function F (s) is a function of 's' relating transform of voltage and currents. The network may contain passive component dependent sources, **but must not contain any independence energy sources and initial conditions**.

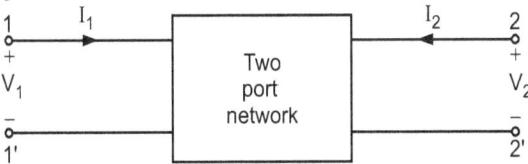

Fig. 3.18

In a linear network (system), excitation e (t) and response r (t) are related by linear differential equations. But when Laplace transform is used, then relation between E (s) and R (s) is algebraic.

Thus, $\qquad$ R (s) = F (s) E (s) $\qquad$ ... (3.8)

F (s) is called system function. It assume many forms depending on whether excitation E (s) is voltage or current and response (R) is voltage or current.

Driving Point Functions: If excitation and response are measured at same pair of terminals, then it is called driving point function.

$$Z_{11}(s) = \frac{V_1(s)}{I_1(s)} \qquad \text{... (a)}$$

is a driving point impedance function.

$$Z_{22}(s) = \frac{V_2(s)}{I_2(s)} \qquad \text{... (b)}$$

is also driving point impedance function.

Thus, $Z_{11}(s)$, $Z_{22}(s)$ are transform impedances which are ratio of voltage transform to current transform at a port.

Similarly, $\qquad Y_{22}(s) = \dfrac{I_2(s)}{V_2(s)}$

and $\qquad Y_{11}(s) = \dfrac{I_1(s)}{V_1(s)}$

are transform admittances. Here they are called driving point admittance function.

Transfer Functions: If excitation and response are measured at separate terminal pairs, then it is called transfer function. For two port network, there are four types of transfer function.

Voltage transfer function,

$$G_{21}(s) = \frac{V_2(s)}{V_1(s)} \qquad \text{... (c)}$$

Current transfer function,

$$\alpha_{21}(s) = \frac{I_2(s)}{I_1(s)} \quad \ldots (d)$$

Transfer impedance function,

$$Z_{21}(s) = \frac{V_2(s)}{I_1(s)} \quad \ldots (e)$$

Transfer admittance function,

$$Y_{21}(s) = \frac{I_2(s)}{V_1(s)} \quad \ldots (f)$$

Following examples explain various types of network functions.

This is series R–L–C circuit which has only one port. Driving point impedance function for this is

$$Z(s) = R_1 + L_1 s + \frac{1}{C_1 s}$$

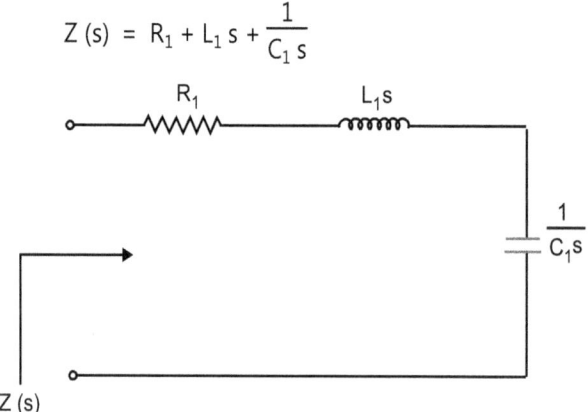

Fig. 3.19: One-port network

For this network, driving point admittance function is

$$Y(s) = Cs + \frac{1}{(R + sL)}$$

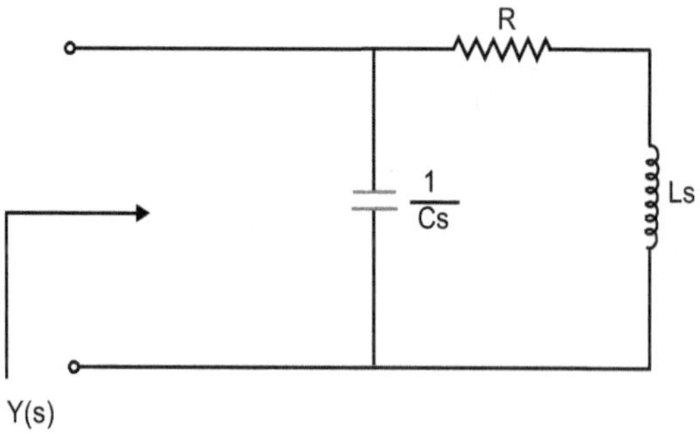

Fig. 3.20: One-port network

Thus for one port network only driving point impedance and admittance functions are define. Also $Z(s) = \dfrac{1}{Y(s)}$. But transfer functions are not defined.

Now consider two port network shown in Fig. 3.21.

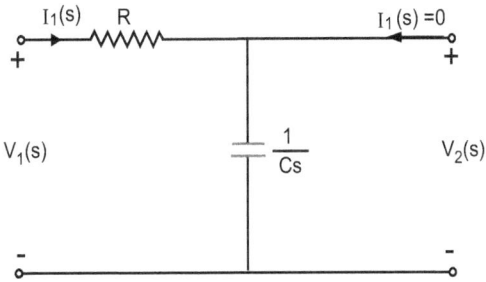

Fig. 3.21: Two port network

Driving point impedance function is

$$Z_{11}(s) = \dfrac{V_1(s)}{I_1(s)}$$

$$= R + \dfrac{1}{sC}$$

Transfer impedance function

$$Z_{21}(s) = \dfrac{V_2(s)}{I_1(s)}$$

$$= \dfrac{1}{sC}$$

Voltage ratio transfer function,

$$G_{21}(s) = \dfrac{\dfrac{1}{Cs} \cdot I_1(s)}{\left(R + \dfrac{1}{Cs}\right) I_1(s)}$$

i.e. $\quad G_{21}(s) = \dfrac{1}{1 + RCS}$

Current ratio transfer function,

$$\alpha_{21}(s) = \dfrac{I_2(s)}{I_1(s)} = 0$$

Impedance functions and admittance functions together are called as immittance functions. For one port networks,

$$Z(s) = \dfrac{1}{Y(s)},$$

While for two port networks, usually,

$$Z_{12}(s) \neq \frac{1}{Y_{12}(s)}$$

In general, all network functions are the ratio of polynomial in s. The general form is

$$F(s) = \frac{p(s)}{q(s)}$$

$$= \frac{a_0 s^n + a_1 s^{n-1} + \ldots + a_n}{b_0 s^m + b_1 s^{m-1} + \ldots + b_m} \quad \ldots (3.19)$$

where 'n' is the degree of numerator polynomial and 'm' is the degree of denominator polynomial.

3.9 POLES AND ZEROS

As said above, in general network function F (s) is ratio of two polynomials of 's' and is written as

$$F(s) = \frac{p(s)}{q(s)} = \frac{a_0 s^n + a_1 s^{n-1} + \ldots + a_n}{b_0 s^m + b_1 s^{m-1} + \ldots + b_m} \quad \ldots (3.20)$$

where a, b are coefficients with real positive value with p (s) having 'n' roots, q (s) having 'm' roots.

Hence F (s) is rewritten as

$$F(s) = H \cdot \frac{(s - Z_1)(s - Z_2) \ldots (s - Z_n)}{(s - P_1)(s - P_2) \ldots (s - P_m)} \quad \ldots (3.21)$$

where $H = \frac{a_0}{b_0}$ is a constant.

Zeros: When $s = Z_1, Z_2, Z_3, \ldots, Z_n$ then network function F (s) = 0. Hence complex frequencies, at which network function F (s) vanishes, are called as zeros of network function. Roots of numerator polynomial p (s) are zeros of network functions.

Poles: When $s = P_1, P_2, \ldots, P_m$, then network function F (s) = ∞. Hence complex frequencies at which value of network function F (s) becomes infinite are called as poles of network function. Roots of denominator polynomial q (s) are poles of network functions.

Significance of Poles and Zeros:

Poles and zeros together with scale factor (H) completely specifies a network function. When two or more poles or zeros have same value then those poles or zeros are said to be repeated. Poles or zeros which are not at s = 0 or ∞ are said to be finite poles or zeros. For any rational network function, if poles and zeros at 0 and at ∞ are taken into account in addition to finite poles and zeros. Then,

Total number of poles = Total number of zeros

Poles and zeros are critical frequencies because at poles network function becomes '∞' while at zero network function becomes 0. At any other frequency network function has finite non-zero value. For example, if

$$Z_{11}(s) = \frac{V_1(s)}{I_1(s)}$$

then a pole of $Z_{11}(s)$ implies zero current for finite value of driving voltage i.e. it signifies a open circuit. While zeros of $Z_{11}(s)$ implies zero voltage $V_1(s)$ for finite value of driving point current i.e. it signifies a short circuit.

Representation of Poles and Zeros:

Poles and zeros are represented on a complex 's' plane. Poles are marked 'X' while zeros are marked as '0'.

For example, if
$$F(s) = \frac{s^2(s+4)}{(s+1)(s^2+4s+5)}$$

then,
$$F(s) = \frac{s^2(s+4)}{(s+1)(s+2+j1)(s+2-j1)}$$

This is represented as

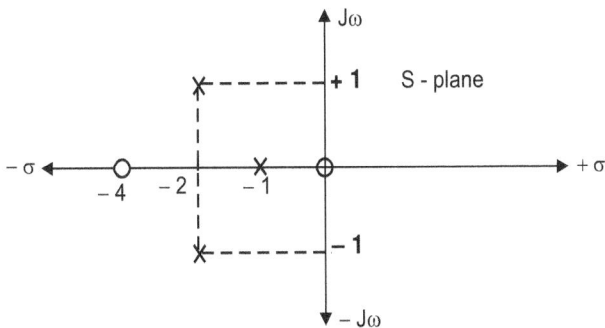

Fig. 3.22: Pole - zero locations

Note that there are two zeros at origin. Also complex poles and zeros always occur in conjugate.

3.10 NECESSARY CONDITIONS FOR TRANSFER FUNCTION AND DRIVING POINT FUNCTION

When given network is dissipationless (loss less) then network has only imaginary poles and zeros.

A network function having poles and zeros, which are real or complex, is stable if real part of poles and zeros are negative i.e. poles and zeros are lying in left half of s-plane.

Necessary condition for driving point function:

1. Coefficient in polynomial p(s) and q(s) of $F(s) = \frac{p(s)}{q(s)}$ must be real and positive.

2. Complex and imaginary poles and zeros occur in conjugate.
3. Polynomial p (s), q (s) must not have missing terms between highest and lowest degree unless all even or odd terms missing.
4. Real part of all poles and zeros must be negative and not positive. If real part is zero, then pole and zero must be simple.
5. p (s) and q (s) must differ at most by one in highest or lowest degree.

Necessary condition for transfer function:

For a given network function F (s) to be a transfer function,

1. Coefficients in polynomials p (s) and q (s) must be real and those of q (s) must be positive.
2. Imaginary or complex poles and zeros are conjugate.
3. Real part of poles must be negative. If it is zero, then it must be simple pole.
4. Polynomial q (s) must not have any missing term between highest and lowest degree unless all even or odd terms missing.
5. Polynomial p (s) may have terms missing between highest and lowest degree and some coefficient may be negative.
6. Degree of p (s) may be as small as zero independent of degree of q (s).
7. For G_{21} and α_{12}, p (s) and q (s) must have same highest degree.
8. For Z_{21} and Y_{21} highest degree of p (s) is greater than q (s) by unity.

Example 3.9: Poles and zeros plot of a voltage transfer function is as shown. D.C. gain is 10. Find transfer function.

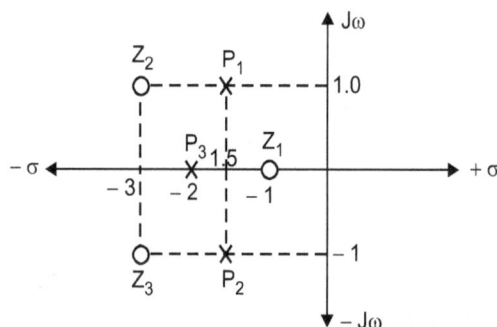

Fig. 3.23: Pole-zero plot for Example 3.1

Solution:

Zeros are at $\quad Z_1 = -1$
$Z_2 = -3 + j1$
$Z_3 = -3 - j1$

Poles are at $\quad P_1 = -1.5 + j1$

$$P_2 = -1.5 - j1$$
$$P_3 = -2$$

Hence transfer function is

$$T(s) = K \frac{(s+1)(s+3+j1)(s+3-j1)}{(s+2)(s+1.5+j1)(s+1.5-j1)}$$

$$= K \frac{(s+1)(s^2+6s+10)}{(s+2)(s^2+3s+3.25)}$$

Since d.c. gain is 10, i.e. T (s) = 10 for d.c. (s = 0),

$$\therefore \quad 10 = \frac{K \times 1 \times 10}{2 \times 3.25}$$

$$\therefore \quad K = 6.5$$

Hence required transfer function is

$$T(s) = \frac{6.5(s+1)(s^2+6s+10)}{(s+2)(s^2+3s+3.25)}$$

Example 3.10: For the network shown determine transfer function $Y_{21}(s)$ and plot the pole-zeros of $Y_{21}(s)$.

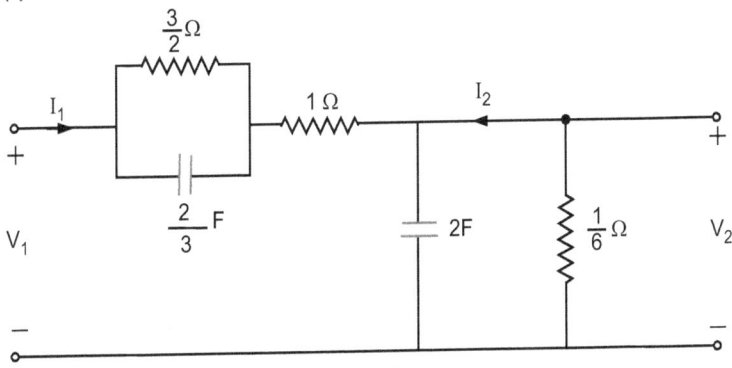

Fig. 3.24

Solution: Transformed circuit of the network given is

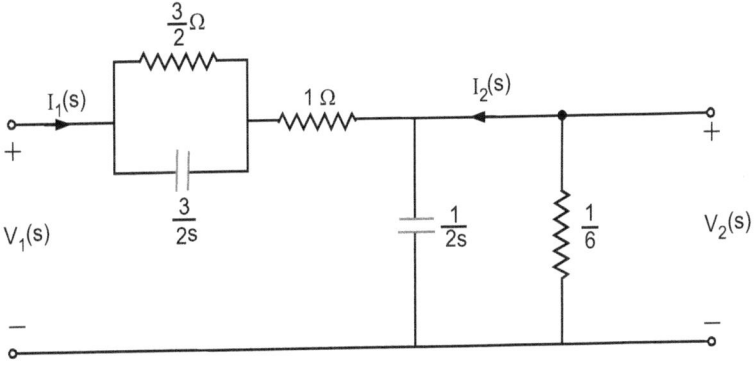

Fig. 3.25 (a): Transformed circuit

Now, $Y_{21}(s) = \dfrac{I_2(s)}{V_1(s)}$

$V_2(s) = \dfrac{\dfrac{1}{2s} \times \dfrac{1}{6}}{\dfrac{1}{2s} + \dfrac{1}{6}} \times I_1(s) = \dfrac{1}{6+2s} \times I_1(s)$

$V_1(s) = \dfrac{I_1(s)}{6+2s} + \left(\dfrac{\dfrac{3}{2} \times \dfrac{3}{2s}}{\dfrac{3}{2} + \dfrac{3}{2s}} + 1\right) I_1(s)$

$= \dfrac{I_1(s)}{6+2s} + \left(\dfrac{9}{6s+6} + 1\right) I_1(s)$

$= \dfrac{I_1(s)}{6+2s} + \dfrac{s+2.5}{(s+1)} I_1(s)$

$= \dfrac{I_1(s)}{1}\left[\dfrac{0.5}{(s+3)} + \dfrac{s+2.5}{(s+1)}\right]$

$= I_1(s)\left[\dfrac{0.5 + 0.5s + s^2 + 5.5s + 7.5}{(s+1)(s+3)}\right]$

$= I_1(s)\left[\dfrac{s^2 + 6s + 8}{(s+1)(s+3)}\right]$

$= I_1(s)\left[\dfrac{(s+4)(s+2)}{(s+1)(s+3)}\right]$

Also, $I_2(s) = -6V_2(s) = -6 \times \dfrac{I_1(s)}{2(s+3)} = -3 \times \dfrac{I_1(s)}{(s+3)}$

$Y_{21}(s) = \dfrac{I_2(s)}{V_1(s)} = -\dfrac{3}{(s+3)} \times \dfrac{(s+1)(s+3)}{(s+4)(s+2)}$

$= -3 \times \dfrac{(s+1)}{(s+4)(s+2)}$

Pole-zero plot is shown below.

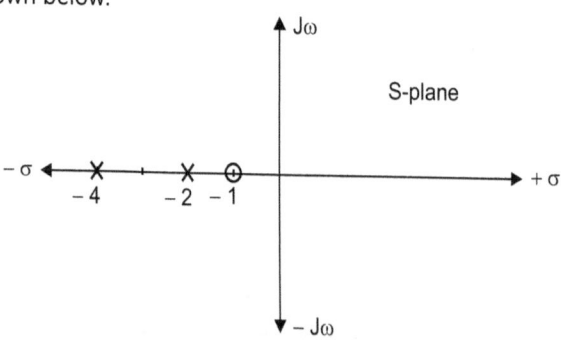

Fig. 3.25 (b): Pole-zero plot

Example 3.11: For the network determine voltage ratio $\dfrac{V_2}{V_1}$, current ratio $\dfrac{I_2}{I_1}$ and transfer impedance $\dfrac{V_2}{I_1}$.

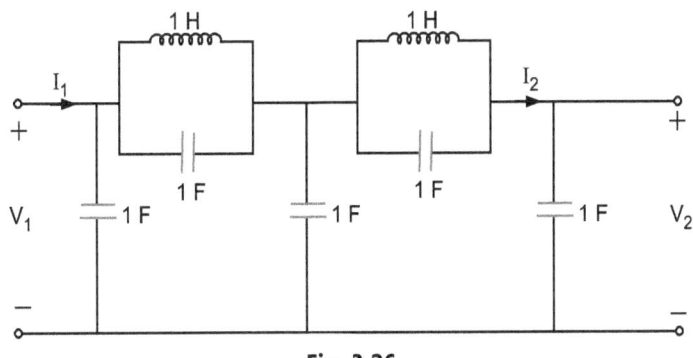

Fig. 3.26

Solution: Transformed circuit is as shown below.

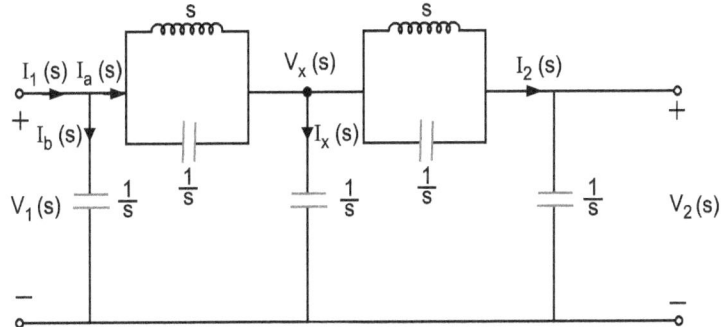

Fig. 3.27 (a): Transformed circuit

We have, $V_2(s) \times s = I_2(s)$

$$V_x(s) = V_2(s) + \left[\dfrac{s \times \dfrac{1}{s}}{s + \dfrac{1}{s}}\right] I_2(s)$$

$$= V_2(s) + \dfrac{s}{s^2 + 1} \times s \cdot V_2(s)$$

$$= V_2(s)\left[1 + \dfrac{s^2}{s^2 + 1}\right]$$

$$= V_2(s)\left[\dfrac{1 + 2s^2}{1 + s^2}\right]$$

$$I_x(s) = s\, V_x(s) = s\left[\dfrac{1 + 2s^2}{1 + s^2}\right] V_2(s)$$

$$I_a(s) = I_x(s) + I_2(s)$$

$$= \left[\frac{s(1+2s^2)}{1+s^2} + s\right] V_2(s)$$

$$= \left[\frac{s^3 + s + s + 2s^3}{(1+s^2)}\right] V_2(s)$$

$$= \frac{3s^3 + 2s}{(1+s^2)} \times V_2(s)$$

$$\therefore \quad I_a(s) = \frac{s(2+3s^2)}{(1+s^2)} \times V_2(s)$$

$$V_1(s) = V_x(s) + \left[\frac{s}{s^2+1}\right] \times I_a(s)$$

$$V_1(s) = V_2(s)\left[\frac{(1+2s^2)}{(1+s^2)} + \frac{s^2(3s^2+2)}{(1+s^2)^2}\right] \quad \ldots (2)$$

$$I_1(s) = I_a(s) + I_b(s)$$

$$= V_2(s)\left[\frac{s(3s^2+2)}{1+s^2}\right] + sV_1(s)$$

$$= V_2(s)\left[\frac{s(3s^2+2)}{(1+s^2)} + \frac{s(1+2s^2)}{(a+s^2)} + \frac{s^3(2+3s^2)}{(1+s^2)^2}\right]$$

$$I_1(s) = V_2(s)\left[\frac{s(3s^2+2)(1+s^2) + s(1+2s^2)(1+s^2) + s^3(2+3s^2)}{(1+s^2)^2}\right]$$

$$I_1(s) = V_2(s)\left[\frac{3s^5 + 5s^3 + 2s + 2s^5 + 3s^3 + s + 3s^5 + 2s^3}{(1+s^2)^2}\right] \quad \ldots (3)$$

Hence by (1), (2) and (3), we have,

$$\frac{V_2(s)}{V_1(s)} = \frac{(1+s^2)^2}{3s^4 + 2s^2 + 2s^4 + 3s^2 + 1} = \frac{(1+s^2)^2}{5s^4 + 5s^2 + 1}$$

$$\frac{I_2(s)}{I_1(s)} = \frac{s(1+s^2)^2}{8s^5 + 10s^3 + 3s}$$

$$\frac{V_2(s)}{I_1(s)} = \frac{(1+s^2)^2}{(8s^5 + 10s^3 + 3s)}$$

3.11 TIME DOMAIN BEHAVIOUR FROM POLE-ZERO PLOT

Time domain behaviour of a system can be determined from pole-zero plot of the system function on S-plane.

For example, let a driving voltage $V(s)$ be applied to a network having a impedance $Z(s)$ then,

Current, $\quad I(s) = \dfrac{V(s)}{Z(s)} = \dfrac{P(s)}{q(s)} = F(s)$

where $\quad \dfrac{P(s)}{q(s)} = \dfrac{H(s-Z_1)(s-Z_2)...(s-Z_n)}{(s-P_1)(s-P_2)...(s-P_m)} \quad\quad ... m > n$

$$= \dfrac{K_1}{(s-P_1)} + \dfrac{K_2}{(s-P_2)} + ...$$

K_1 and K_2 etc. are called residue at P_1 and P_2 etc.

The poles determine the time domain behaviour of $i(t)$. Scale factor H and zeros together with poles determine magnitude of each term of $i(t)$.

Graphical method for determination of residue:

Let $\quad F(s) = \dfrac{K_1}{(s-P_1)} + \dfrac{K_2}{(s-P_2)} + ... + \dfrac{K_m}{(s-P_m)} \quad\quad ...(1)$

Then residue K_i is given by

$$K_i = \left[(s-P_i)F(s)\right]_{s \to P_i} = H\dfrac{(P_i-Z_1)(P_i-Z_2)...(P_i-Z_n)}{(P_i-P_1)(P_i-P_2)...(P_i-P_m)} \quad ...(2)$$

From complex plane (s) point of view, equation (2) interprets that "Each term $(P_i - Z_i)$ represents a vector drawn from Z_i to pole in question i.e. P_i.

Also each term $(P_i - P_k)$, $i \neq k$, represents vector drawn from other poles to pole in question i.e. P_i.

Hence, $\quad K_i = \dfrac{\text{Product of vectors from each zero to } P_i}{\text{Product of vectors from other poles to } P_i} \times H$

For example: Given pole-zero diagram as below:

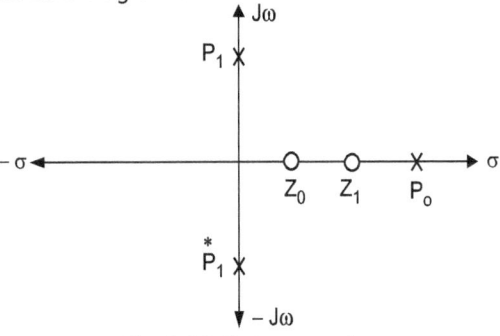

Fig. 3.28: Pole-zero plot

Now function representing above pole-zero plot is

$$F(s) = \dfrac{H(s+Z_0)(s+Z_1)}{(s+P_0)(s-P_1)(s-P_1^*)}$$

$$= \dfrac{K_0}{(s+P_0)} + \dfrac{K_1}{(s-P_1)} + \dfrac{K_1^*}{P_1^*}$$

Now to find residue at P_1:

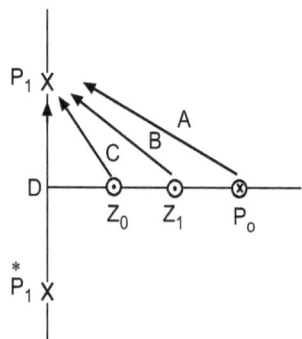

Fig. 3.29 (a): Residue at P_1

$$K_1 = \frac{CB}{AD} \times H$$

i.e.
$$K_1 = \frac{\text{(Vector from } Z_0 \text{ to } P_1\text{) (Vector from } Z_1 \text{ to } P_1\text{)}}{\text{(Vector from } P_0 \text{ to } P_1\text{) (Vector from } P_1^* \text{ to } P_1\text{)}} \times H$$

Note: Graphical method can be used if poles are simple and complExample But it cannot be used when there are multiple (repeated) poles.

Example 3.12: Voltage transform V (s) of a network is given by

$$V(s) = \frac{4s}{(s+2)(s^2+2s+2)}$$

Plot its poles and zeros. Calculate residue at poles graphically, Hence find V (t).

Solution: Pole-zero plot is as shown in Fig. 3.30 below.

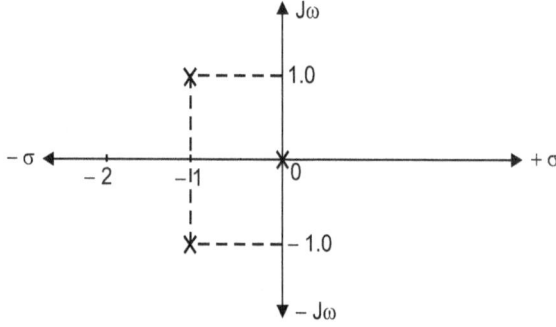

Fig. 3.30: Pole-zero plot

$$V(s) = \frac{4s}{(s+2)(s+1+j1)(s+1-j1)}$$

$$= \frac{K_0}{(s+2)} + \frac{K_1}{(s+1+j1)} + \frac{K_1^*}{(s+1-j1)}$$

(a) Residue at $s = -2$ is K_0

$$K_0 = \frac{4 \times 2 \angle -180°}{\sqrt{2} \angle -135° \times \sqrt{2} \angle +135°}$$

$$= \frac{4 \times 2}{2} \angle -180° = -4$$

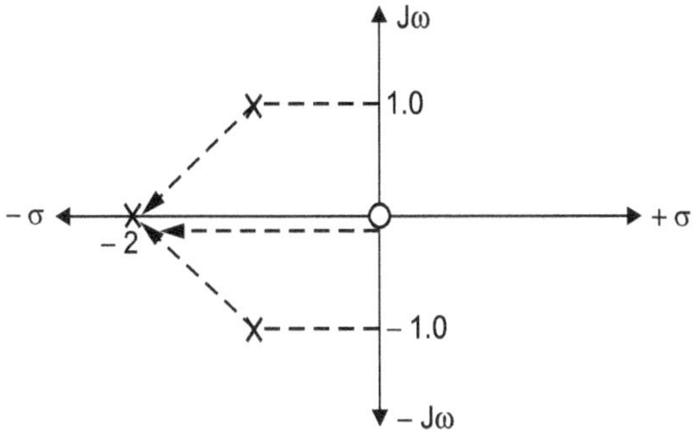

Fig. 3.31 (a): Residue at $s = -2$

(b) Residue at $s = -1 - j1$ is K_1

$$K_1 = \frac{4 \times \sqrt{2} \angle 135°}{\sqrt{2} \angle 45° \times 2 \angle +90°} = 2 \angle 0° = 2$$

(c) Residue at $s = -1 - 1 + j1$ is K_1^*

$$K_1^* = \frac{4 \times \sqrt{2} \angle -135°}{\sqrt{2} \angle 45° \times 2 \angle -90°} = \frac{4}{2} \angle 0° = 2$$

Hence given function is

$$V(s) = \frac{-4}{(s+2)} + \frac{2}{(s+1+j1)} + \frac{2}{s+1-j1}$$

$$= \frac{-4}{s+2} + 2\left[\frac{2s+2}{(s+1)^2+1}\right] = \frac{-4}{(s+2)} + \frac{4(s+1)}{(s+1)^2+1}$$

Hence, $V(t) = -4e^{-2t} + 4e^{-t} \sin t$

$$= 4\left[e^{-t} \sin t - e^{-2t}\right]$$

Example 3.13 : Graphically determine residue at poles of the following function

$$F(s) = \frac{s^2 + 4}{(s+2)(s^2+9)}$$

Solution: Given F (s) can be written as

$$F(s) = \frac{s^2+4}{(s+2)(s+j3)(s-j3)} = \frac{(s+j2)(s-j2)}{(s+2)(s+j3)(s-j3)}$$

$$= \frac{K_0}{s+2} + \frac{K_1}{(s+j3)} + \frac{K_1^*}{(s-j3)}$$

(a) To find residue at s = −2, plot is

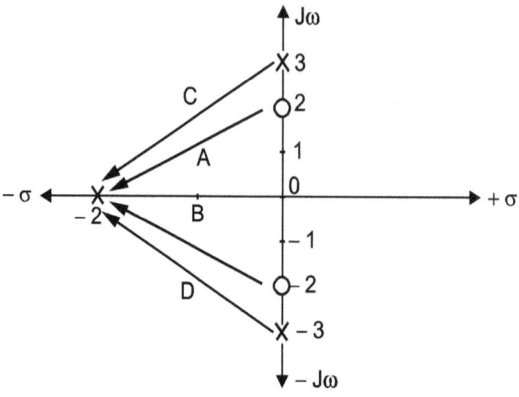

Fig. 3.32: Residue K_o

$$K_o = \frac{AB}{CD}$$

$A = \sqrt{8} \angle 225°$
$B = \sqrt{8} \angle 135°$
$C = \sqrt{13} \angle 236.4°$
$D = \sqrt{13} \angle 123.7°$

$$\therefore \quad K_o = \frac{\sqrt{8} \angle 225° \times \sqrt{8} \angle 135°}{\sqrt{13} \angle 236.4° \times \sqrt{13} \angle 123.7°}$$

$$= \frac{8}{13} \angle 360° - 360°$$

$$= \frac{8}{13}$$

(b) To find residue at s = j3.

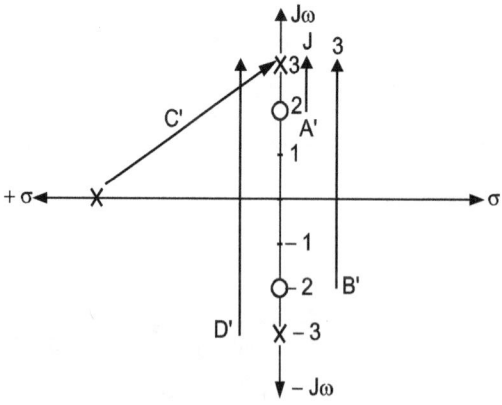

Fig. 3.33 (a): Residue K_1

$$K_1 = \frac{A'B'}{C'D'}$$

$$= \frac{1\angle 90° \times 5 \angle 90°}{\sqrt{13} \angle 56.31° \times 6 \angle 90°}$$

$$= \frac{5}{\sqrt{13} \times 6} \angle 33.69°$$

$$= 0.231 \angle 33.7°$$

$$= 0.192 + j\,0.128$$

(c) Similarly residue at $s = -j3$ can be found out which is complex conjugate of K_1.

i.e.
$$K_1^* = 0.231 \angle -33.7°$$
$$= 0.192 - j\,0.128$$

3.12 POLE POSITION AND STABILITY

Most important requirement of any system is stability. An unstable system usually is considered as a useless system.

Stability of the system can be classified as absolute stability and relative stability. Absolute stability is the condition where the system is stable or unstable. It is like yes or no type answer. Once a system is confirmed to be stable, then relative stability of the system determines degree of the stability.

As defined earlier, a system is said to be stable if bounded input excitation the output (response) does not go on increasing indefinitely.

Impulse response of the system can be used to determine the system stability.

A stable system is one in which impulse response will approach zero for sufficiently large time.

An unstable system is one in which impulse response grows without bound. i.e. it approaches to infinity for sufficient large time.

In marginally stable system, impulse response approaches a constant non-zero value or a constant amplitude oscillation for a sufficient large time.

The pole position and system stability is very closely related. The necessary and sufficient condition for the system to be stable is that the roots of the characteristic equation of the system must lie on negative half of the S-plane. Thus, if $T(s) = \frac{N(s)}{D(s)}$ is the transfer function, then roots of $D(s) = 0$ must lie on the negative half of S-plane. For any root (pole) on right half of S-plane the system will be unstable.

Let us now consider the relationship between pole positions and the corresponding impulse responses.

(a) Poles on the negative real axis: Consider a simple pole on negative real axis.

i.e.
$$F(s) = \frac{K}{(s+a)}$$

The corresponding impulse response is given by
$$f(t) = L^{-1}[F(s)] = Ke^{-at}$$

For large t, f (t) approaches to zero as shown in the Fig. 3.47. Thus it is a stable system. Suppose we have multiple poles in the system. For example, consider

$$F(s) = \frac{K}{(s+a)r}$$

Then the response will be
$$f(t) = K\,tr\,e^{-at}$$

This also approaches to zero as $t \to \infty$. Hence this is a stable system.

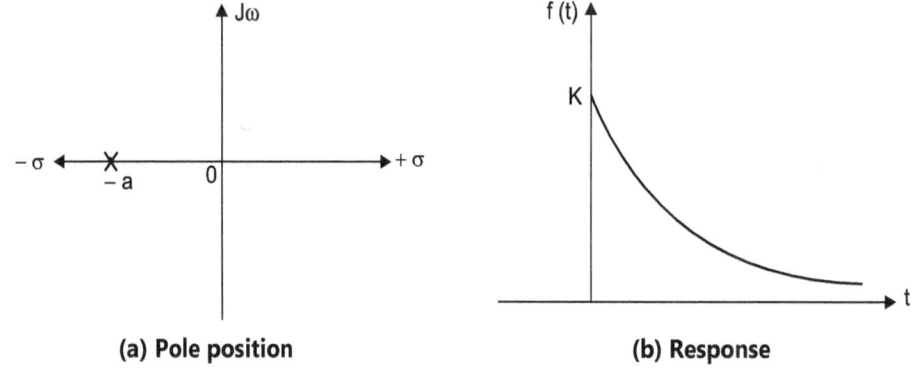

(a) Pole position (b) Response

Fig. 3.34: Poles on negative real axis and its response

Thus for all poles lying on the negative real axis, the system is stable.

(b) Complex poles on left half of S-plane: Consider an F (s) with poles at $s = -\sigma_1 \pm j\beta_1$ as in Fig. 3.35.

$$F(s) = \frac{K_1}{(s+\sigma_1-j\beta_1)} \pm \frac{K_2}{(s+\sigma_1+j\beta_1)}$$

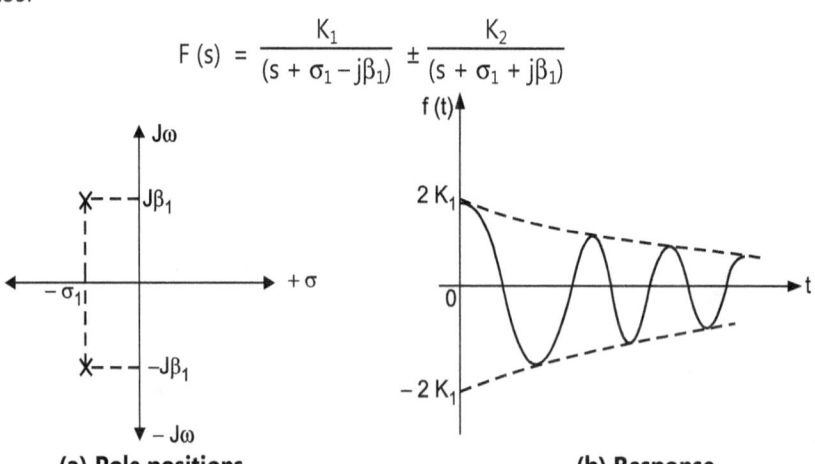

(a) Pole positions (b) Response

Fig. 3.35: Complex poles on left half of S-plane and its response

The corresponding time response is given by

$$f(t) = L^{-1}[F(s)] = L^{-1}\left[\frac{2K_1(s + \alpha_1)}{(s + \alpha_1)^2 + \beta_1^2}\right]$$

As t approaches infinity f(t) becomes zero. Thus the system becomes stable.

For multiple order of poles on left half of the S-plan, the response will be of the form

$$f(t) = 2t_1\, t^r\, e^{-\alpha_1 t} \cos \beta_1 t$$

This also approaches to zero as t → ×.

Thus "For all complex poles lying on left half of S-plane, the system is stable".

(c) Poles on positive real axis: Consider a function in which pole is on right half o S-plane i.e.

$$F(s) = \frac{K}{(s-a)}$$

Then response will be

$$f(t) = Ke^{+at}$$

This response increases exponentially to infinity as t → ∞. Thus the system is unstable. If there are multiple order of poles on +ve real axis, the system becomes more unstable.

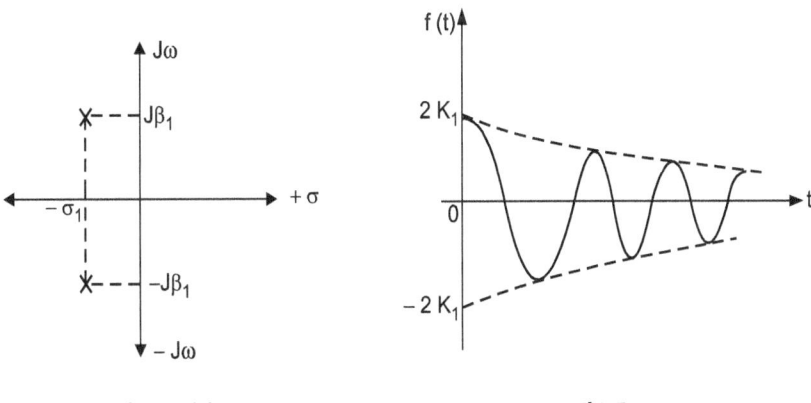

(a) Pole position　　　　　　　　　　　(b) Response

Fig. 3.36: Simple pole on positive real axis and its response

Thus "If the system has any pole on right half of S-plane then it is an unstable system".

(d) Complex poles on the right half of S-plane: Consider a system with complex poles at $s = \alpha_1 + j\beta_1$. i.e.

$$F(s) = \frac{K_1}{(s - \alpha_1 + j\beta_1)} + \frac{K_1}{(s - \alpha_1 - j\beta_1)}$$

The time response is given by

$$f(t) = L^{-1}[F(s)] = L^{-1}\left[\frac{2K_1(s-\alpha_1)}{(s-\alpha_1)^2 + \beta_1^2}\right] = 2K_1 e^{\alpha_1 t} \cos \beta_1 t$$

Thus, f (t) increases exponentially with damped oscillations as t → ∞ as shown in Fig. 3.37.

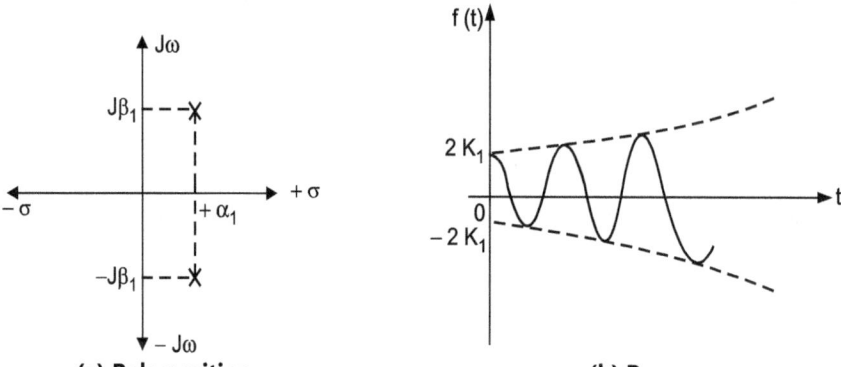

(a) Pole position (b) Response
Fig. 3.37: Complex poles on +ve real axis and its response

Thus "If the system has complex poles on right half of S-plane i.e. on +ve real axis then the system is an unstable system".

(e) Pole at the origin: Consider a system with the poles at origin. i.e. $F(s) = \frac{K}{s}$. Now the time domain response is given by

$$f(t) = L^{-1}[F(s)] = L^{-1}\left[\frac{K}{s}\right] = K u(t)$$

Thus, as t → ∞, f (t) remains constant at K. Hence it is a stable system.

Suppose there are multiple poles at the origin. If $F_1(s) = \frac{K}{s^2}$, then time response will be given by

$$f_1(t) = K t u(t)$$

This shows that if t → ∞, then f (t) → ∞ and hence it is a unstable system.

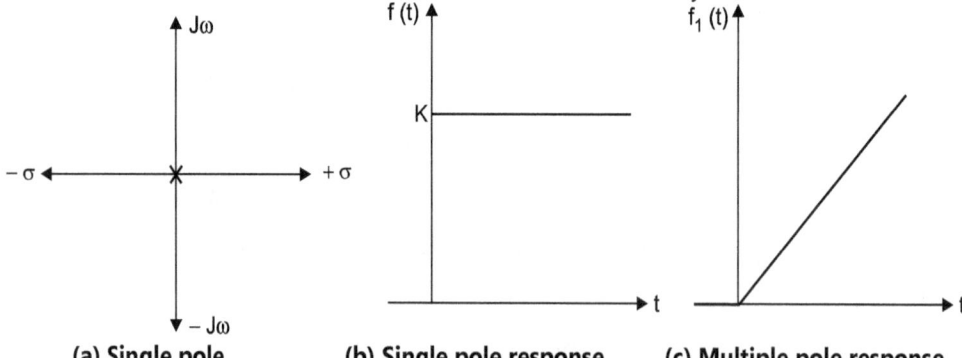

(a) Single pole (b) Single pole response (c) Multiple pole response
Fig. 3.38: Single and multiple pole at origin and its response

Thus "If there is single pole at origin, then the system is stable. If there are multiple poles at origin, then the system is unstable".

3.13 THE CONCEPT OF COMPLEX FREQUENCY

The Solution of the differential equations for networks gives rise to time domain function in the form

$$K_n e^{S_n t} \quad \text{... (a)}$$

where, $\quad S_n = \sigma_n + j\omega_n \quad$ ... (3.22)

is the complex number defined as the complex frequency,

ω_n is imaginary part of complex frequency interpreted as radian frequency (radians/sec.),

σ_n is real part of complex frequency defined as neper frequency (nepers/sec.).

The radian frequency ω_n appears in time domain equations in the forms $\sin \omega_n t$ or $\cos \omega_n t$.

σ_n appears as an exponential factor $I = I_0 e^{\sigma_n t}$ such that

$$\sigma_n = \frac{1}{t} \ln \frac{I}{I_0}$$

Case I: Let $\quad S_n = \sigma_n + j0$

The exponential function of equation (a) becomes $K_n e^{\sigma_n t}$. It is an exponential function which increases exponentially for $\sigma_n > 0$ and decays exponentially for $\sigma_n < 0$.

When $\sigma_n = 0$; $K_n e^{\sigma_n t} = K_n e^{0t} = K_n \quad$ ... (b)

A time invariant quantity which in terms of current and voltage is described as "direct current".

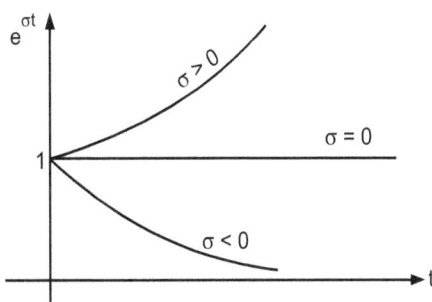

Fig. 3.39: Plot of $e^{\sigma t}$ for positive, negative and zero value of σ

Case II: Let $\quad S_n = 0 \pm j\omega_n$ (radian frequency only)

$$\therefore \quad K_n e^{\pm j\omega_n t} = K_n (\cos \omega_n t \pm j \sin \omega_n t) \quad \text{... (c)}$$

Case III: Let $\quad S_n = \sigma_n + j\omega_n$

$$K_n e^{(\sigma_n + j\omega_n)t} = K_n e^{\sigma_n t} e^{j\omega_n t}$$

$$= K_n e^{\sigma_n t} (\cos \omega_n t + j \sin \omega_n t) \quad \text{... (d)}$$

$$\text{Re}\left(e^{S_n t}\right) = e^{\sigma_n t} \cos \omega_n t$$

$$\text{Im}\left(e^{S_n t}\right) = e^{\sigma_n t} \sin \omega_n t$$

For $\sigma_n < 0$, waveform is damped sinusoid.

For $\sigma_n > 0$, oscillations increase exponentially.

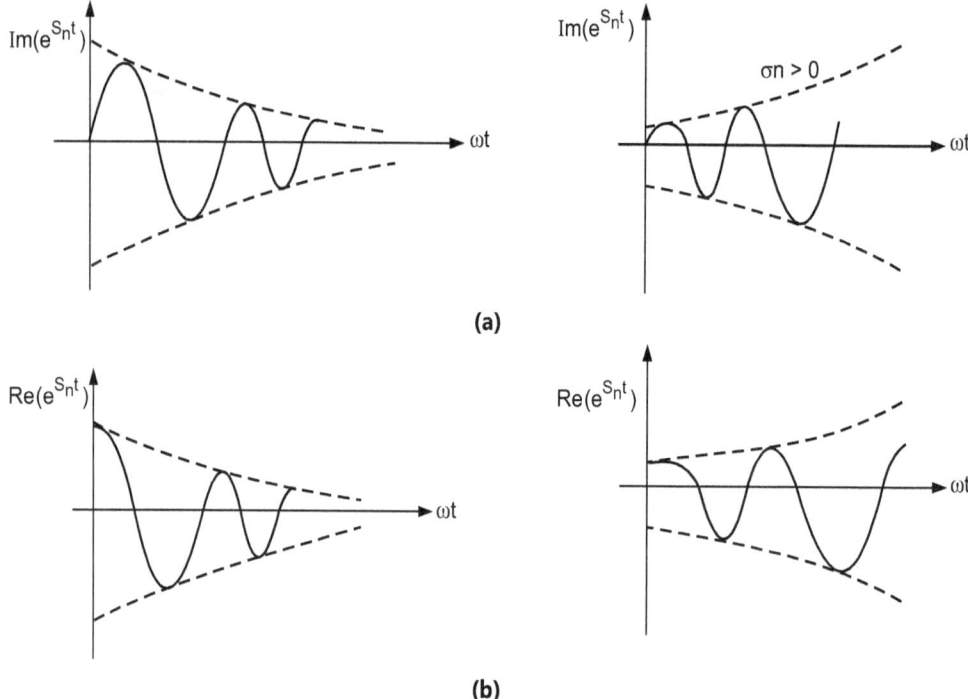

Fig. 3.40: Real and imaginary projections of rotating phasors ωt

3.14 THE ROUTH HURWITZ STABILITY CRITERION

Suppose we are given an n-th order homogeneous system of differential equations with constant coefficients:

$$X'(t) = AX(t),\ X(t) = \begin{bmatrix} x_1(t) \\ x_2(t) \\ \vdots \\ x x_1(t) \end{bmatrix},\ A = \begin{bmatrix} a_{11} & a_{12} & \vdots & a_{1n} \\ a_{21} & a_{22} & \vdots & a_{2n} \\ \ldots & \ldots & \vdots & \ldots \\ a_{x1} & a_{x2} & \vdots & a_{xn} \end{bmatrix}$$

where X(t) is an n-dimensional vector containing the unknown functions, A is a square matrix of size n × n.

A nonlinear autonomous system can be reduced to the linear system by performing a linearization around an equilibrium point. Then without loss of generality, we may assume that the equilibrium point is at the origin. It is always possible to reach by choosing a suitable coordinate system.

The stability or instability of the equilibrium state is determined by the signs of the real parts of the eigenvalues of A. To find the eigenvalues λ, it is necessary to solve the characteristic equation

$$\det(A - \lambda I) = 0$$

which is reduced to an algebraic equation of the nth degree

$$a_0\lambda^n + a_1\lambda^{n-1} + a_2\lambda^{n-2} + \ldots + a_{n-1}\lambda = 0$$

The roots of this equation can be easily calculated in the case $n = 2$, and in some cases when $n \geq 3$.

In other cases, solving the characteristic equation can be a difficult problem. Moreover, Norwegian mathematician Niels Henrik Abel (1802-1829) proved a theorem according to which the general algebraic equation of degree $n \geq 5$ cannot be solved using four basic arithmetical operations, i.e. there is no formula expressing the roots of the equation through its coefficients in the case $n \geq 5$.

In such a situation, methods allowing to determine whether all roots have negative real parts and establish the stability of the system without solving the characteristic equation itself, are of great importance. One of these methods is the Routh-Hurwitz criterion, which contains the necessary and sufficient conditions for the stability of the system.

Consider again the characteristic equation

$$a_0\lambda^n + a_1\lambda^{n-1} + a_2\lambda^{n-2} + \ldots + a_{n-1}\lambda + a_n = 0$$

describing the dynamic system. Note that the necessary condition for the stability is satisfied if all the coefficients $a_i > 0$. Therefore, we assume that the coefficient $a_0 > 0$. We write the so-called Hurwitz matrix. It is composed as follows. The main diagonal of the matrix contains elements $a_1, a_2, \ldots, a_n$. The first column contains numbers with odd indices $a_1, a_3, a_5, \ldots$.

In each row, the index of each following number (counting from left to right) is 1 less than the index of its predecessor. All other coefficients a_i with indices greater than n or less than 0 are replaced by zeros. The result is a matrix shown in Fig.

$$\begin{bmatrix} a_1 & a_0 & 0 & 0 & 0 & 0 & 0 \\ a_3 & a_2 & a_1 & a_0 & 0 & 0 & 0 \\ a_5 & a_4 & a_3 & a_2 & a_1 & a_0 & 0 \\ & & & & & & \\ 0 & 0 & 0 & 0 & 0 & 0 & a_n \end{bmatrix}$$

Fig. 3.41

The principal diagonal minors Δ_i of the Hurwitz matrix are given by the formulas

$$\Delta_1 = a_1, \quad \Delta_2 = \begin{vmatrix} a_1 & a_0 \\ a_3 & a_2 \end{vmatrix}, \quad \Delta_3 = \begin{vmatrix} a_1 & a_0 & 0 \\ a_3 & a_2 & a_1 \\ a_5 & a_4 & a_3 \end{vmatrix}, \quad \Delta_n = \begin{vmatrix} a_1 & a_0 & 0 & \cdots & 0 \\ a_3 & a_2 & a_1 & \cdots & 0 \\ a_5 & a_4 & a_3 & \cdots & 0 \\ \cdots & \cdots & \cdots & \vdots & \cdots \\ 0 & 0 & 0 & \cdots & a_x \end{vmatrix}$$

We now formulate the Routh-Hurwitz stability criterion : The roots of the characteristic equation have negative real parts if and only if all the principal diagonal minors of the Hurwitz matrix are positive provided that $a_0 > 0$: $\Delta_1 > 0$, $\Delta_2 > 0$, ..., $\Delta_n > 0$. Since $\Delta_n = a_n \Delta_{n-1}$, the last inequality can be written as $a_n > 0$.

For the most common systems of the 2nd, 3rd and 4th order, we obtain the following stability criteria:

For a second order system, the condition of the stability is given by

$$a_1 > 0, \Delta_1 = a_1 > 0, \Delta_2 = \begin{vmatrix} a_1 & a_0 \\ a_3 & a_2 \end{vmatrix} = a_1 a_2 > 0$$

or $a_0 > 0$, $a_1 > 0$, $a_2 > 0$.

that is, all coefficients of the quadratic characteristic equation must be positive. In other words, for a system of 2nd order, the necessary condition of the stability is also the sufficient one. We emphasize that we consider here the asymptotic stability of the zero solution.

For a 3rd order system, the stability criterion is defined by the inequalities

$$a_0 > 0, \Delta_1 = a_1 > 0, \Delta_2 = \begin{vmatrix} a_1 & a_0 \\ a_3 & a_2 \end{vmatrix} = a_1 a_2 - a_0 a_3 > 0, \Delta_3 = a_3 > 0$$

or $a_0 > 0$, $a_1 > 0$, $a_2 > 0$, $a_3 > 0$, $a_1 a_2 - a_0 a_3 > 0$

Similarly, for a 4th order system, we obtain the following set of inequalities:

$$a_0 > 0, \Delta_1 = a_1 > 0, \Delta_2 = \begin{vmatrix} a_1 & a_0 \\ a_3 & a_2 \end{vmatrix}$$

$$= a_1 a_2 - a_0 a_3 > 0, \Delta_3 = \begin{vmatrix} a_1 & a_0 & 0 \\ a_3 & a_2 & a_1 \\ 0 & a_4 & a_3 \end{vmatrix}$$

$$= a_1 a_2 a_3 - a_1^2 a_4 - a_0 a_3^2 > 0, \Delta_4 = a_4 > 0$$

or $a_i > 0$ ($i = 0, ..., 4$), $a_1a_2 - a_0a_3 > 0$, $a_1a_2a_3 - a_1^2a_4 - a_0^2a_3^2 > 0$

If all the $n - 1$ principal minors of the Hurwitz matrix are positive and the nth order minor is zero: $\Delta_n = 0$, the system is at the boundary of stability. Since $\Delta n = an \Delta n -1$, then there are two options:

The coefficient $a_n = 0$. This corresponds to the case when one of the roots of the characteristic equation is zero. The system is on the boundary of the aperiodic stability.

The determinant $\Delta_n -1 = 0$. In this case, there are two complex conjugate imaginary roots. The system is on the boundary of the oscillatory stability.

The Routh-Hurwitz stability criterion belongs to the family of algebraic criteria. It can be conveniently used to analyze the stability of low order systems. The computational complexity grows significantly with the increase of the order. In such cases, it may be preferable to use other criteria

such as the Lienard-Shipart theorem or the Nyquist frequency criterion.

Example 3.14 : Investigate the stability of the zero solution of the equation

$$x''' + 6x'' + 3x' + 2x = 0$$

Solution :

We write the characteristic equation:

$$\lambda^3 + 6\lambda^2 + 3\lambda + 2 = 0$$

The coefficients ai are

$a_0 = 1$, $a_1 = 6$, $a_2 = 3$, $a_3 = 2$.

Form the Hurwitz matrix

$$\begin{bmatrix} a_1 & a_0 & 0 \\ a_3 & a_2 & a_1 \\ 0 & 0 & a_3 \end{bmatrix} = \begin{bmatrix} 6 & 1 & 0 \\ 2 & 3 & 6 \\ 0 & 0 & 2 \end{bmatrix}$$

and find all its principal minors:

$$\Delta_1 = 6 > 0, \Delta_2 = \begin{vmatrix} 6 & 1 \\ 2 & 3 \end{vmatrix} = 18 - 2 = 16 > 0,$$

$$\Delta_3 = a_3\Delta_2 = 2 \cdot 16 = 32 > 0$$

As can be seen, all minors are positive. Therefore, the zero solution of the equation is asymptotically stable.

Example 3.15 : Investigate the stability of the zero solution of the differential equation

$$x^{iv} + 2x''' + 4x'' + 7x' + 3x = 0$$

Solution :

The characteristic equation is given by

$$\lambda^4 + 2\lambda^3 + 4\lambda^2 + 7\lambda + 3 = 0$$

The coefficients ai in this equation are

$a_0 = 1, a_1 = 2, a_2 = 4, a_3 = 7, a_4 = 3$.

We write the Hurwitz matrix and find its principal diagonal minors:

$$\begin{bmatrix} a_1 & a_0 & 0 & 0 \\ a_3 & a_2 & a_1 & a_0 \\ 0 & a_4 & a_3 & a_2 \\ 0 & 0 & 0 & a_4 \end{bmatrix} = \begin{bmatrix} 2 & 1 & 0 & 0 \\ 7 & 7 & 2 & 1 \\ 0 & 3 & 7 & 4 \\ 0 & 0 & 0 & 3 \end{bmatrix}$$

$\Delta_1 = 2 > 0, \Delta_2 = \begin{vmatrix} 2 & 1 \\ 7 & 4 \end{vmatrix} = 8 - 7 = 1 > 0$.

$$\Delta_2 = \begin{vmatrix} 2 & 1 & 0 \\ 7 & 4 & 2 \\ 0 & 3 & 7 \end{vmatrix} = -2 \begin{vmatrix} 2 & 1 \\ 0 & 3 \end{vmatrix} + 7 \begin{vmatrix} 2 & 1 \\ 7 & 4 \end{vmatrix}$$

$= -12 + 7 = -5 > 0$

In the course of calculations, we've got a negative minor Δ3 < 0. This means that the zero solution is unstable.

EXERCISE

1. Explain the disadvantages of a m derived filter. How are they corrected in a composite filter.
2. Define open circuit impedance parameters. Obtain the equivalent circuit in terms of Z-parameters.
3. Define short circuit admittance parameters. Obtain the equivalent circuit in terms of Y-parameters.
4. Define hybrid parameters. Obtain the equivalent circuit in terms of h-parameters. Explain why h-parameters are used for transistors.
5. Define Transmission (ABCD) parameters. Explain why ABCD parameters are also known as T-parameters.
6. Establish the relationship between Z and Y parameters.
7. What is the symmetrical network reciprocal network? Give relationship between parameters for symmetrical and reciprocal network.
8. Show that when two or more networks are cascaded, then their overall T-parameters is the multiplication of T-parameter matrix of individual networks.
9. Show that when two networks are series-series connected, then overall Z-parameter matrix is the addition of Z-parameters of the individual networks.

10. For the network shown below obtain Z and h parameters.

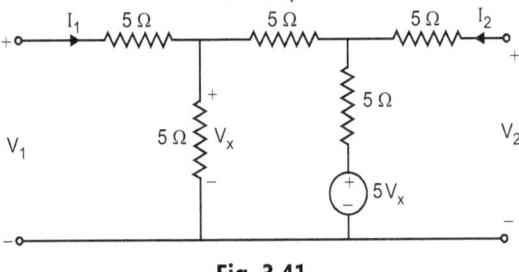

Fig. 3.41

16. Show that for the network given, following equation holds good.

$$\begin{bmatrix} V_2 \\ I_2 \end{bmatrix} = \begin{bmatrix} 1.5 & 6.5 \\ 0.25 & 1.25 \end{bmatrix} \begin{bmatrix} V_1 \\ -I_1 \end{bmatrix}$$

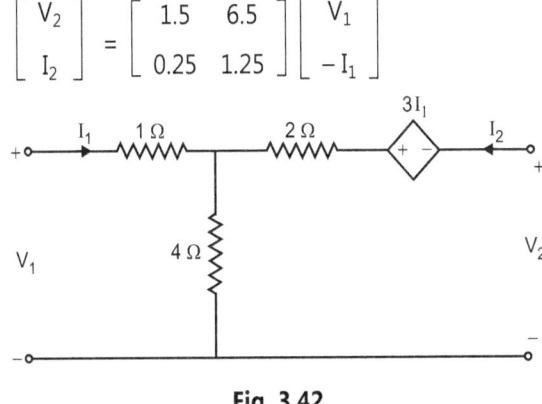

Fig. 3.42

17. Determine $\dfrac{V_2}{I}$ in terms of R_1, R_2 and Z-parameters of network.

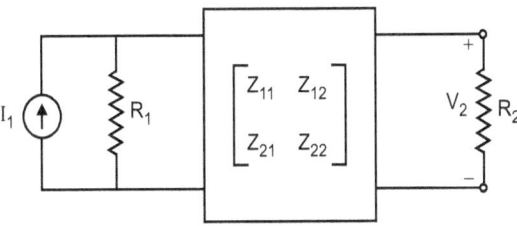

Fig. 3.43

18. Find Z and Y parameters.

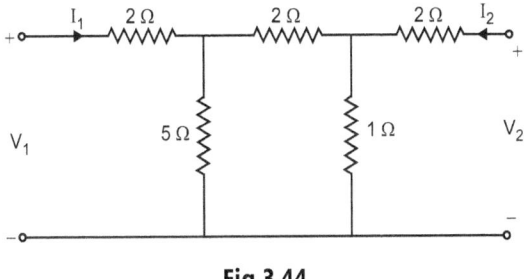

Fig 3.44

19. Show that ABCD parameters of the network is

$$\begin{bmatrix} A & B \\ C & D \end{bmatrix} = \begin{bmatrix} \left(\dfrac{1+s^2}{s^2}\right) & \left(\dfrac{1+2s^2}{s^3}\right) \\ \dfrac{1}{s} & \left(\dfrac{s^2+1}{s^2}\right) \end{bmatrix}$$

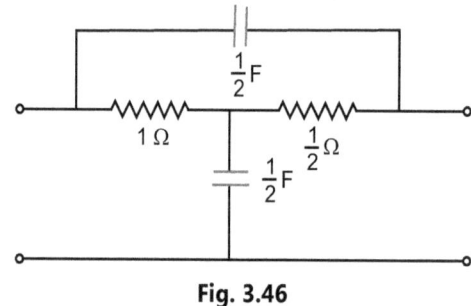

Fig. 3.45

20. For the bridged T, R-C network, determine Z and Y parameters.

Fig. 3.46

21. What is a network function? Explain various types of network functions for a one port network and a two port network.

22. Define poles and zeros of a network functions. What are the significance of a pole and zero in a network function?

23. Give the essential properties of driving point function.

24. Give the essential properties of transfer function.

25. Give the essential properties of an driving point function.

26. Explain how time domain behaviour can be obtained from pole-zero plot.

27. Explain how frequency domain behaviour (magnitude plot and phase plot) can be obtained from the pole-zero plot.

28. Explain what is meant by stable and unstable system. Explain how location of pole-zero on S-plane affect the system stability.

Unit - IV

RESONANCE

4.1 INTRODUCTION

- Frequency response of any system is the measure of system's output spectrum in response to the input signal. [Output spectrum is output voltage or gain of system].
- The concept of frequency response also called as frequency curve is extremely important in all the fields of science and engineering, forming the foundation for understanding factors that determine various important parameters of the particular system like its accuracy, stability etc.
- This is applicable to any type of system, be it a electrical, mechanical, chemical, biological etc.
- As seen in Fig. 4.1 (a) of the systems or components are ideally expected to have a flat frequency response (e.g. OP-AMP) i.e. a system or component must reproduce all the desired input signals at all the frequencies with no emphasis or attenuation of a particular frequency band.
- But in some cases, the frequency response of the system may be chosen deliberately to reject some frequency components of the forcing function or to emphasize on others.
- The networks designed to impart such a behaviour are called as frequency selective networks.
- Tuned circuits or resonant circuits, Twin T networks and wein bridge networks are all some of the most popular examples of a frequency selective networks.
- Even the hottest means of entertainment today, Radio Mirchi ... Radio city ... are also nothing but examples of frequency selective networks, where we select only one frequency (i.e. one individual radio station) in the complete available band.

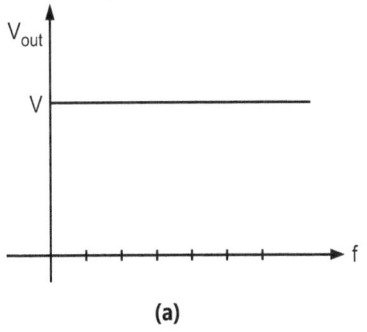
(a)
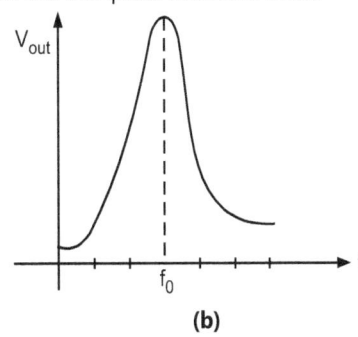
(b)

- Fig. 4.1 (a) shows flat frequency curve say for an ideal amplifier wherein the input at all the frequencies is equally amplified, thus giving a constant output voltage V at any frequency f. Fig. 4.1 (b) shows the frequency curve of a frequency selective network.

Observe that output voltage of the circuit at frequency f_0 is appreciably high, thus making f_0 easily and prominently distinguishable or separable from rest of the other frequencies at which the output is very less.

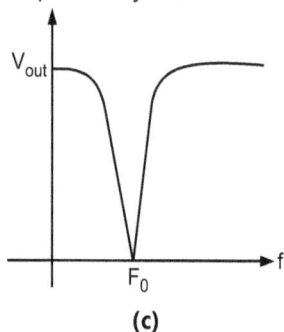

(c)

Fig. 4.1 : Ideal frequency response or frequency curve:
(a) An amplifier, (b), (c) Frequency selective network

- The other possibility as shown in Fig. 4.1 (c) is also very much possible in some frequency selective networks (like notch filters) i.e. having zero output voltage at f_0 and thus making it similarly distinguishable and separable from rest of the frequencies.
- We will discuss few such frequency selective networks in this unit.
- Inductors and capacitors are used along with resistors in the frequency selective networks.

4.2 QUALITY FACTOR Q

- We have seen that the frequency selective networks are made up of R, L and C components.
- The frequency responses of these frequency selective networks are not flat but are of a nature which makes one frequency prominently distinguishable from others. The frequency curves thus have a particular height and a width.
- The height of the curve depends only upon the value of R for constant amplitude excitation [This will be very clear in further section 4.4.6]. But the width of the curve, or steepness of the sides depends upon the other two element values i.e. L and C.
- Inductors and capacitors are basically energy storing devices. Various inductors or capacitors can be compared in the terms of efficiency of energy storage. Figure of merit or quality factor Q is such a measure of efficiency.
- The width of the response curve thus depends on a very important parameter, the quality factor i.e. Q.
- The higher the value of the Q, the narrower and the sharper is the peak of the response curve.

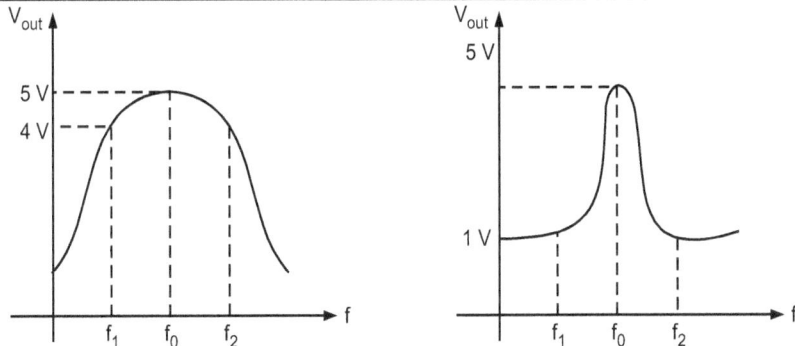

Fig. 4.2 : An example of frequency response of a frequency selective network having (a) Very low Q, (b) Very high Q

- Fig. 4.2 (a) shows the frequency response curve of a selective circuit having low value of Q. Observe that in this case it is very difficult to separate f from the band of frequencies between f_1 and f_2 because all these frequencies have more or less the same voltage less. So it is hard to identify only one frequency.
- Fig. 4.2 (b) on the other hand shows the frequency response curve of the same circuit but now having a very higher value of Q. In this case, selecting f_0 is very easy because it is almost the only frequency with very high output. So it can be easily distinguished from others.
- It is very difficult to find the tallest boy in a group of 5 students where each of the boy has a height of 5.4", 5.3", 5.5", 5.35", 5.45" individually. The same task can be very easily done at a glance in a group of boys where the boys have the height of 5.2", 5.1", 7.1", 5.1", 5.3".
- Note that height of both the curves in Fig. 4.2 (a) and (b) is same. But curve in Fig. 4.2 (b) is more selective than curve in Fig. 4.2 (a).
- Thus, any frequency selective network must always have a narrow and a sharp peak.
- This quality factor Q, can be defined in two ways:
  - Generally Q is defined in terms of the ratio of the peak energy stored in the circuit to that of the energy being lost in one cycle such that

$$Q = 2\pi \times \frac{\text{Peak energy stored}}{\text{Energy dissipated per cycle}}$$

The factor of 2π is used to keep this definition of Q consistent with the second definition.
$$Q = \frac{f_r}{\Delta f} = \frac{\omega_r}{\Delta \omega} \quad \text{...[This will be more clear in section 4.4.10]}$$

where,
f_r : Resonant frequency
Δf : Bandwidth
ω_r : Angular resonant frequency
$\Delta \omega$: Angular bandwidth

Let us now define the Q of a (coil) inductor and a capacitor.

4.2.1 Q of a Inductor or a Coil

Inductor is always associated with a series resistance (R_S) as shown in Fig. 4.3. Energy stored in the inductor is maximum when the current is maximum i.e. I_m.

Thus, Maximum energy stored $= \dfrac{1}{2} L I_m^2$

Average power dissipated in the inductor $= I_{rms}^2 \, R_S = \left(\dfrac{I_m}{\sqrt{2}}\right)^2 R_S = \dfrac{1}{2} I_m^2 \, R_S$

Energy dissipated per cycle $= \dfrac{I_m^2 \, R_S}{2f}$

Thus, $\therefore \quad Q_L = 2\pi \times \dfrac{\frac{1}{2} L I_m^2}{\dfrac{I_m^2 \, R_S}{2f}}$

$$Q_L = 2\pi \times \dfrac{L I_m^2}{2} \times \dfrac{2f}{I_m^2 \, R_S}$$

$$\boxed{Q_L = \dfrac{\omega L}{R_S}}$$

where, Q_L = Quality factor of an inductor
R_S = Series resistance
I_m = Peak or maximum value of current in the circuit
f = Frequency of operation
L = Value of the inductor

Comments on Q of the coil:
- Resistance and inductance of the coil and hence Q is effected by the length of the coil, its shape, number of turns and also the core on which the coil is wounded.
- At low frequencies, value of Q must obviously be low because Q of a coil is directly proportional to the frequency (ω).
- As the frequency increases, the Q of the coil also rises. But then, because of the skin effect and dielectric losses, at high frequency, the resistance R of the coil also increases and its comparatively increases more rapidly.
- Quality factor Q of the coil is inversely proportional to the resistance R. So as a net effect, eventually Q drops off.
- In general, Q versus frequency graph is as shown in Fig. 4.4.

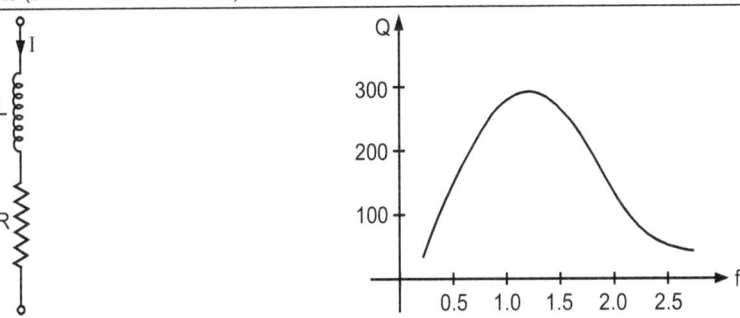

Fig. 4.3 : A practical inductor   Fig. 4.4 : Variation of Q as a function of frequency

- Q of a form coil be raised by adding a core of a magnetic material usually in compressed powdered form. Inductance and hence Q increases by using the core material of low eddy current and hysteresis losses.
- Q of the coil controls the effective Q of the circuit and is thus the controlling factor.

4.2.2 Quality Factor of a Capacitor

Capacitor is always associated with a resistor R_P as shown in Fig. 4.5. This is called as a leakage resistance. If E_m is the maximum voltage across the capacitor, then

$$\text{Maximum energy stored} = \frac{1}{2} C E_m^2 = \frac{1}{2} C \left[\frac{I_m}{C\omega}\right]^2$$

Average power lost in resistor

$$P_D = \left(\frac{I_m}{\sqrt{2}}\right)^2 R_P$$

$$= \frac{I_m^2}{2} R_P$$

$$\text{Energy lost per cycle} = \frac{I_m^2 R_P}{2f}$$

Thus,

$$Q_C = 2\pi \frac{\frac{1}{2} C \left[\frac{I_m}{C\omega}\right]^2}{\frac{I_m^2 R}{2f}}$$

$$Q = \frac{1}{2} C \left[\frac{I_m}{C\omega}\right]^2 \times \frac{2f}{I_m^2 R_P} = \frac{I_m^2 \cdot 2f \cdot C}{2 C^2 \omega^2 I_m^2 R_P}$$

$$\boxed{Q_C = \frac{1}{\omega C R_P}}$$

where, Q_C = Quality factor of a capacitor
 ω = Frequency of operation
 R_P = Leakage resistance
 E_m = Maximum voltage across capacitor
 C = Capacitor

Comments on Q of the capacitor:
- The leakage resistance R_P in case of capacitor is very large so the losses in a capacitor are usually very small and hence Q of the capacitor is large.
- Even if losses are small, they are still affected by the type of dielectric material used.
- Air has the lowest losses of the various materials frequently used and then followed by polystyrene, mica and paper.

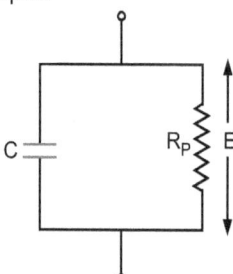

Fig. 4.5: A practical capacitor

4.3 RESONATING CIRCUITS

- Whenever, the natural frequency of oscillation of a system (would be electrical, mechanical or a civil structure) coincides with the frequency of the driving force (a voltage source in an electric circuit or a wind force in a civil structure) the two system resonate with respect to each other and the system has maximum response to a fixed magnitude of driving force. This phenomenon is known as Resonance.
- This phenomenon may be useful under certain conditions and sometimes it may prove to be disastrous for the system.
- There are many engineering applications of resonance. And so it is a very phenomenon, which must be taken into consideration when designing a system.
- For example: A suspension bridge in Washington showed tendencies to oscillate up and down during the construction and only a few months after construction, it began to build up oscillations under a moderate wind and within a hour the multibillion dollar bridge was reduced to pieces. This is a typical example of designing a bridge ignoring the possibility of phenomenon of resonance on the bridges.
- Thus in general resonance is defined as a phenomenon, in which

- o applied voltage and resulting current are in phase.
- o circuit exhibits unity power factor condition [cos φ = 1].
- o the reactance in an A.C. circuit gets cancelled if the inductive and capacitive reactances are in series or the susceptances get cancelled if the inductive and capacitive reactances are in parallel.
- o Complex impedance of the A.C. circuit consists of only the real resistive part.
- Resonance in series circuit i.e. when R, L and C are all connected in series is referred as series resonance or simply resonance. Similarly resonance in parallel circuits is referred as parallel resonance or antiresonance. In this unit, we will study series and parallel resonance in detail.

4.3.1 General Rules for Finding the Condition for Resonance

To find the condition for resonance, it is necessary to simplify and write down the impedance Z and to state the condition that the z will be resistive (i.e. only real part). This can be done in many ways depending upon the nature of z.

(a) If z is in the form of (r, φ), the resonant condition is φ = 0.

(b) If z is in the form of R + JX, the resonant condition is X = 0.

(c) If z is in the form of G + jB, the resonant condition is B = 0.

(d) If z is in the form of term $\frac{A + JB}{C + JD}$, then resonant conditions is $\frac{B}{A} = \frac{C}{D}$.

(e) This condition is equivalent to saying the numerator and denominator have equal angle and hence the angle of z is 0.

It may be noted that we will be using condition (b) to find the resonant frequency of a series R-L-C circuit and condition (c) to find condition of resonance for a parallel R-L-C circuit.

4.4 SERIES RESONANCE

- A series circuit of R, L and C is shown in Fig. 4.6, driven by a generator of V volts.
- The resistance R, which is connected in series with Inductor and Capacitor actually includes:
  - o Generator Resistance – R_g.
  - o Series Resistance R_S of an inductor.
  - o Leakage Resistance R_P of a capacitor.
  - o Any other resistance introduced into the circuit as load.

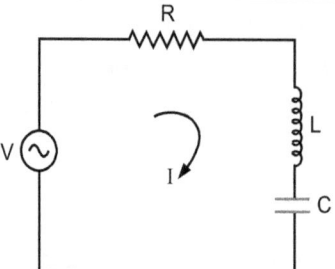

Fig. 4.6: Series R, L, C circuit

4.4.1 Resonating Frequency

Applying kVL to the series RLC circuit in Fig. 4.6,

$$V = R - I + Ij\omega L - \frac{jI}{\omega C}$$

$$V = I\left[R + j\left(\omega L - \frac{1}{\omega C}\right)\right]$$

Since, the resonance has been defined as a unity power factor, then at resonant frequency, f_r the reactive term must be zero.

∴ At resonance

$$\omega_0 L - \frac{1}{\omega_r C} = 0$$

ω is replaced by ω_r in the above equation is satisfied only and only at $\omega = \omega_r$.

$$\omega_r L = \frac{1}{\omega_R C}$$

$$\omega_r^2 LC = 1$$

$$\omega_r^2 = \frac{1}{LC}$$

$$\boxed{f_r = \frac{1}{2\pi\sqrt{LC}}} \qquad \ldots (4.1)$$

where, f_r is the resonating frequency of the series RLC circuit.

4.4.2 Quality Factor

- Quality factor depends on the energy stored by the elements.
- In series RLC circuit, inductor and capacitor are connected in series, so the same current will flow through them and the same energy will be stored by both the elements.

- Value of Q depends on frequency when Q of a resonant circuit is stated or specified value is by default the value of Q at the resonant frequency f_r.
- So the Q factor of a series resonant circuit is nothing but the Q factor of the used inductor or of capacitor at the resonant frequency.

$$\boxed{Q = \frac{\omega_r L}{R} = \omega_r RC} \quad \ldots(4.2)$$

where,
Q = Quality factor of the series RLC circuit at the resonant frequency
ω_0 = Resonant frequency
L = Inductor
C = Capacitor

Q in terms of circuit elements.

We have,

$$Q = \frac{\omega_r L}{R} = \frac{1}{\omega_r RC}$$

Substituting $\omega_0 = \frac{1}{\sqrt{LC}}$ in this equation

$$Q = \frac{L}{\sqrt{LC}\, R}$$

$$= \frac{\sqrt{LC}}{RC}$$

$$\boxed{Q = \frac{1}{R}\sqrt{\frac{L}{C}}} \quad \ldots(4.3)$$

where, R, L and C are the components of the series resonant circuit
Q is Quality factor of resonant circuit

4.4.3 Reactance Curves

- The graph of reactance of a reactive components versus the frequency is called as the reactance curve.
- Inductor and the capacitor are the reactive elements in series RLC circuit.
- It can be seen from definition

$$jX_L = j\, 2\pi f L$$

that inductive reactance X_L is a linear positive function of frequency which plots as a straight line through the origin.
- Similarly from the definition,

$$jX_C = \frac{-j}{2\pi f_C}$$

that the capacitive reactance, X_C appears as a negative hyperbola, asymptotic to the reactance and the frequency axes.

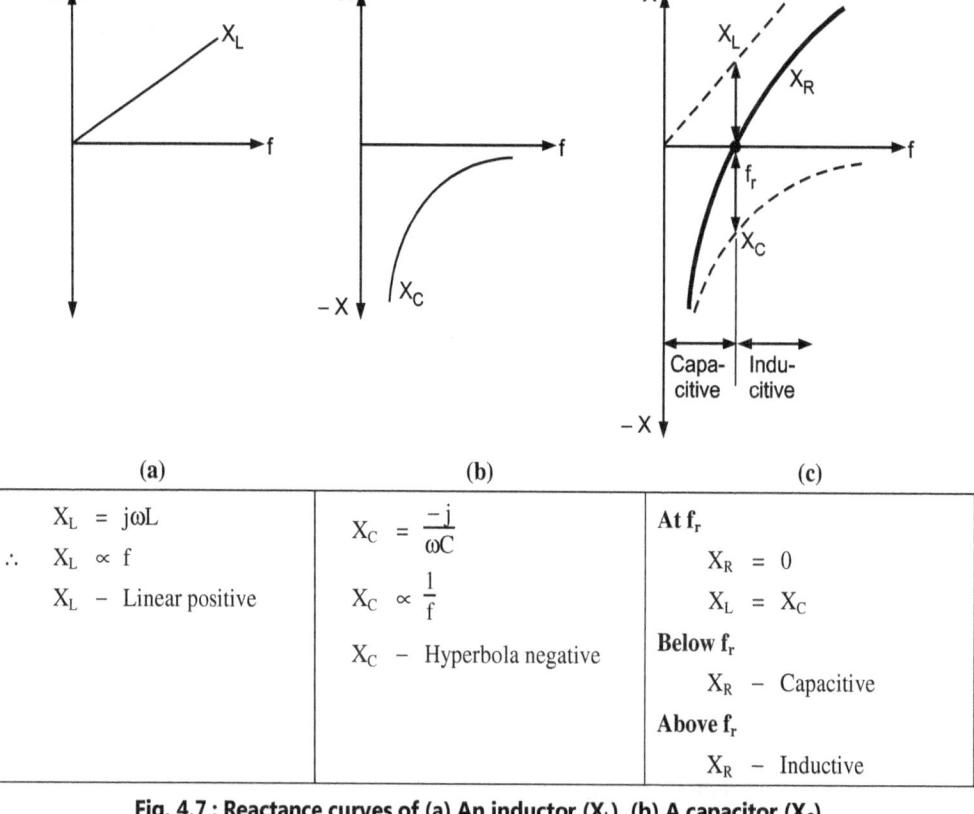

(a)	(b)	(c)
$X_L = j\omega L$ $\therefore \; X_L \propto f$ X_L − Linear positive	$X_C = \dfrac{-j}{\omega C}$ $X_C \propto \dfrac{1}{f}$ X_C − Hyperbola negative	At f_r $\quad X_R = 0$ $\quad X_L = X_C$ Below f_r $\quad X_R$ − Capacitive Above f_r $\quad X_R$ − Inductive

Fig. 4.7 : Reactance curves of (a) An inductor (X_L), (b) A capacitor (X_C), (c) Total reactance plot of series RLC circuit indicating f_r

- Curves X_L and X_C are added algebraically, as would be the case in a series resonant circuit, to give the resultant curve X_R which indicates the resonating frequency f_r.
- As seen in Fig. 4.7 (c) at f_r, $X_L = X_C$ and thus canceling each other to give zero reactance or a purely resistive circuit.
- The series resonating circuit is capacitive below the resonating frequency f_r and it is inductive above the resonating frequency.
- This can also be logically justified. At low frequencies,

$$\omega L < \frac{1}{\omega C}$$

i.e. $X_L < X_C$

Therefore, the circuit is capacitive. Similarly at high frequencies,

$$\omega L > \frac{1}{\omega C}$$

∴ $X_L > X_C$

Therefore, the circuit is inductive.

4.4.4 Phasor Diagrams

- A sinusoidal current and a given frequency is characterized by two parameters, an amplitude and a phase angle.
- The phasor diagrams are used to represent these parameters.

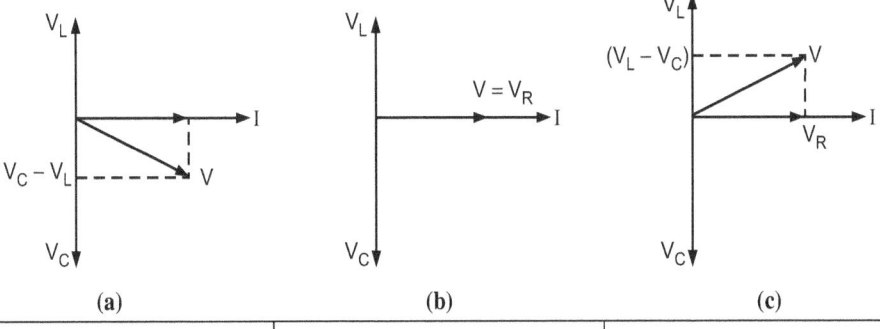

At f < f_r	At f < f_r	At f > f_r
$\omega L < \dfrac{1}{\omega C}$	$\omega L = \omega C$	$\omega L > \dfrac{1}{\omega C}$
∴ $V_L < V_C$	∴ $V_L = V_C$	∴ $V_L = V_C$
I leads V Capacitive Circuit	V and I in phase	V leads I
	Resistive Circuit	Resistive Circuit

Fig. 4.8 : Phasor diagrams of a series RLC circuit at frequency

(a) Below resonating frequency, (b) At resonating frequency, (c) Above resonating frequency

- For any frequency f, lower than resonant frequency f_r as already explained in reactance curves, the circuit is capacitive having X_C as the dominating reactance. The current leads the resultant supply voltage V.
- Similarly at f_r, X_L is equal to X_C and therefore when connected in series V_L is also equal to V_C. Thus, canceling each other. Current and the supply voltage are in phase and circuit behaves as a resistive circuit.

- For any frequency f, higher than the resonant frequency f_r, the inductive reactance is dominating with X_L greater than X_C and thus V_L greater than V_C. The current leads the supply voltage and circuit behaves as inductive.

4.4.5 Impedance of Series RLC Circuit

The impedance of series RLC circuit is given by

$$Z = R + j\left(\omega L - \frac{1}{\omega C}\right)$$

Hence, the magnitude of impedance is given by

$$|Z| = \frac{\sqrt{Z^2 + X^2}}{\sqrt{R^2 + \left(\omega L - \frac{1}{\omega C}\right)^2}} \quad \ldots X = X_L - X_C$$

Thus, total impedance it any frequency

$$\boxed{|Z| = \sqrt{R^2 + \left(\omega L - \frac{1}{\omega C}\right)^2}} \quad \ldots(4.4)$$

(a) Impedance of series RLC circuit at resonance:

At resonance $\omega L = \dfrac{1}{\omega C}$.

∴ Impedance at frequency f_r is

$$\boxed{Z = R} \quad \ldots(4.5)$$

... At resonating frequency f_r

(b) Impedance of series RLC circuit in the terms of Quality factor Q_0.

$$Z = R + j\left(\omega L - \frac{1}{\omega C}\right)$$

$$Z = R\left[1 + j\left(\frac{\omega L}{R} - \frac{1}{\omega CR}\right)\right]$$

$$Z = R\left[1 + j\left(\frac{\omega_r L}{R} \cdot \frac{\omega}{\omega_r} - \frac{1}{\omega_r CR} \cdot \frac{\omega_r}{\omega}\right)\right]$$

$$Z = R\left[1 + j\left(Q \cdot \frac{\omega}{\omega_r} - Q\frac{\omega_r}{\omega}\right)\right]$$

$$Z = R\left[1 + jQ\left(\frac{\omega}{\omega_r} - \frac{\omega_r}{\omega}\right)\right]$$

Thus, impedance at any frequency f in terms of quality factor Q is

$$\boxed{Z = R\left[1 + jQ\left(\frac{\omega}{\omega_r} - \frac{\omega_r}{\omega}\right)\right]} \quad \ldots(4.6)$$

(c) Impedance of series RLC circuit just near resonance:

Let δ be the fractional deviation of the actual frequency from the resonant frequency, such that this new variable δ may be defined as

$$\delta = \frac{f - f_r}{f_r}$$

$$= \frac{\omega - \omega_r}{\omega_r} = \frac{\omega}{\omega_r} - 1$$

Thus giving,

$$\frac{\omega}{\omega_r} = 1 + \delta$$

Substituting in equation (4.6),

$$Z = R\left[1 + jQ\left(1 + \delta - \frac{1}{1+\delta}\right)\right]$$

$$Z = R\left[1 + jQ\left(1 + \delta - (1+\delta)^{-1}\right)\right]$$

Using binomial theorem

$$(1+\delta)^{-1} \cong 1 - \delta + \delta^2$$

Thus, finally impedance of a series resonant circuit for small deviations from the resonant frequency, is given as

$$\boxed{Z = R[1 + jQ\delta(2-\delta)]} \qquad \ldots(4.7)$$

To summarise,

$$|Z| = \sqrt{R^2 + \left(\omega L - \frac{1}{\omega C}\right)^2}$$

$$Z = R \qquad \ldots \text{at resonance}$$

$$Z = R\left[1 + jQ\left(\frac{\omega}{\omega_r} - \frac{\omega_r}{\omega}\right)\right] \qquad \ldots \text{in terms of Q}$$

$$Z = R[1 + jQ\delta(2-\delta)] \qquad \ldots \text{just near } F_r$$

4.4.6 Current at Resonance

At resonant frequency, f_r

$$Z = R$$

$$\therefore \qquad \boxed{I_r = \frac{V}{R}} \qquad \ldots(4.8)$$

where,
I_r = Current at the resonating frequency f_r
V = Supply voltage
R = Resistance in the series RLC circuit

- This current I_r, at resonating frequency f_r will be the maximum current flowing through it.
- This is because the impedance of series RLC circuit is minimum at the resonance and it is equal to R.
- The value of the I_r and thus the nature of the frequency curve will be completely decided by R.
- Larger the value of R, small will be the current and so, steep slope with narrow and a sharp peak in the curve will not be achieved. Instead if the resistance is small, then the current at resonance rises sharply to a very high value. This is indicated in Fig. 4.9.

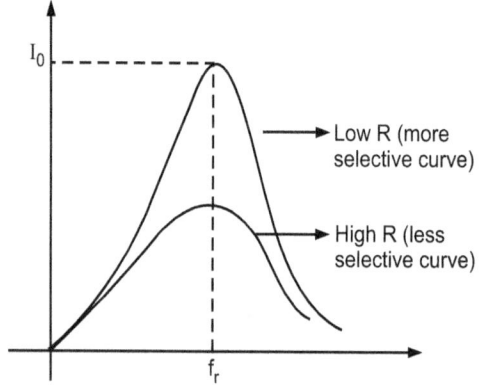

Fig. 4.9 : Variation of current with frequency

- In earlier section when discussing about the quality factor Q, a statement was mentioned saying.

  "Height of the frequency curve depends only upon the value of R for constant amplitude excitation".

- This statement must now be clear. The steepness of the curve can be varied by varying the resistance R.
- When value of R is low, I_0 is high thus increasing the height of the frequency curve and making it more selective and vice versa.
- So, when the input is of a constant amplitude, R in the series RLC circuit decides the height of the curve.
- It must be noted that current in RLC circuit at $\omega = 0$ is always zero, as the capacitor reactance is ∞. Therefore, the graph starts from origin and has some finite value at $f = \infty$.

4.4.7 Voltage Across R, L and C at Resonance

At resonance, current $I_r = \dfrac{V}{R}$.

Inductor, resistor and capacitor are all connected in series so the same current will be flowing through them.

$\therefore\quad$ Voltage across inductor $\quad V_L = I_r \cdot X_L$
$$= I_r (\omega_r L)$$
$$= I_r \cdot \omega_r L$$
$$= \dfrac{V}{R} \cdot \omega_r L$$

$$\boxed{V_L = Q \cdot V} \qquad \ldots(4.9)$$

Similarly, voltage cross capacitor
$$V_C = I_r \cdot X_C$$
$$= \dfrac{V}{R}\left(\dfrac{1}{\omega_r C}\right)$$

$$\boxed{V_C = Q \cdot V} \qquad \ldots(4.10)$$

Recollect equation (4.2) as per which
$$Q = \dfrac{\omega_r L}{R} = \dfrac{1}{\omega_r C R_p}$$

- Thus, V_L and V_C i.e. voltage across inductor and a capacitor is Q times the input voltage V.
- Q is always greater than one so the voltages developed across L and C are more than the applied voltage and are thus said to be amplified or magnified by a factor of Q.
- At resonance, series RLC circuit acts as a voltage amplifier and hence Q_0 is also referred as the magnification factor of the circuit.
- Through at resonance the voltages developed V_L and V_C are more than the applied voltage they actually cancel each other because they are equal in magnitude and opposite in phase.

4.4.8 Variation of Impedance, Admittance and Phase with Frequency

- At resonance, impedance is minimum and is equal to R. For Z at any other frequency will always be greater than R. This is indicated in Fig. 4.10 (a).
- Admittance is reciprocal of impedance so obviously if Z is minimum at f_r then at f_r Y will be maximum. So Fig. 4.10 (b) shows exact opposite nature of Y with respect to frequency.

- We have already seen, that below resonating frequency, the circuit is capacitive in nature (I leads V). Therefore, phase angle is negative. Above the resonant frequency circuit imparts inductive characteristics. Therefore, the phase angle tends to be positive (I lags V).

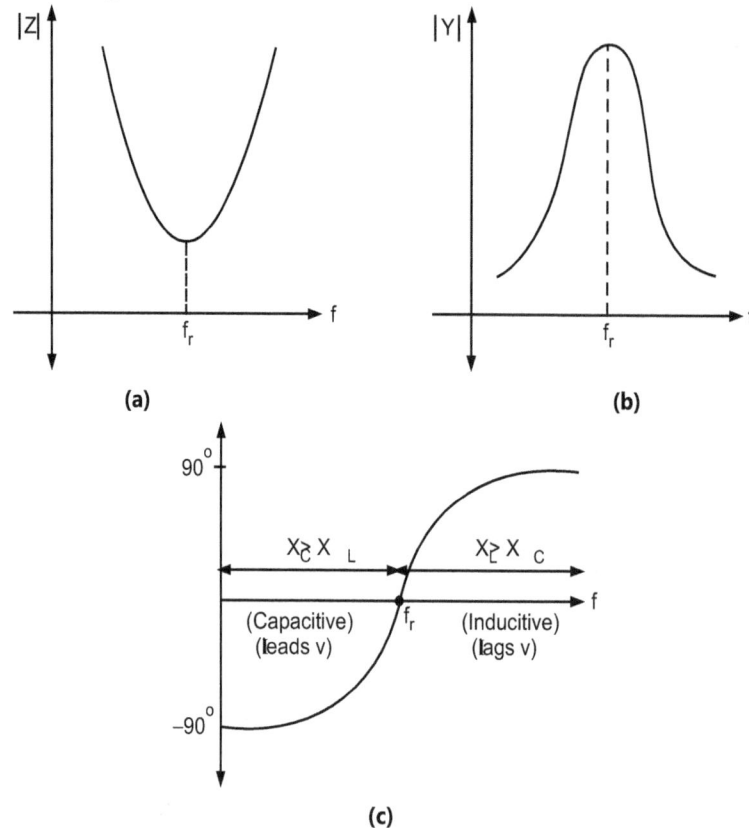

Fig. 4.10: Variation of (a) Z impedance, (b) Y admittance, (c) ϕ phase angle with frequency in a series resonating

- At the resonant frequency f_r, the circuit is purely resistive. So the phase angle ϕ is zero at resonance (cos ϕ = 1).
- This is indicated in Fig. 4.10 (c). However, it must be noted that the phase relations between the voltage and current in the individual elements R, L and C are not same. The current is inductor lags voltage by 90° and in the capacitor it leads the voltage by 90°.

4.4.9 Variation of V_L and V_C with Frequency

- We have seen that at resonance frequency ω_r, voltages across inductor and capacitor are equal but are of opposite signs and thus cancel each other. But these voltages are not the maximum voltages that can be appeared across them.

- Thus, the maximum voltage across inductor and capacitor appear the some other frequency and not the resonant frequency so the maximum values of V_L and V_C appear at some other frequency say f_L and f_C and not at f_r.
- This point can also be logically justified. Voltage will always depend on impedance. In this case, V_L and V_C will depend on reactance, X_L and X_C. Now at resonance, $X_L = X_C$. But this reactance of capacitor and inductor is definitely not the maximum reactance. In fact, the capacitive reactance is dominating below f_r and so obviously it must be some frequency f_C, below f_r where the capacitive reactance is maximum and therefore voltage V_C should be maximum. Similarly above f_r, the inductive reactance is dominating and circuit is inductive with higher value of X_L. So naturally, the voltage V_L will be maximum at some frequency f_L which must be above the resonating frequency f_r.
- This variation of V_L and V_C with frequency in a series resonating circuit is indicated in Fig. 4.11.

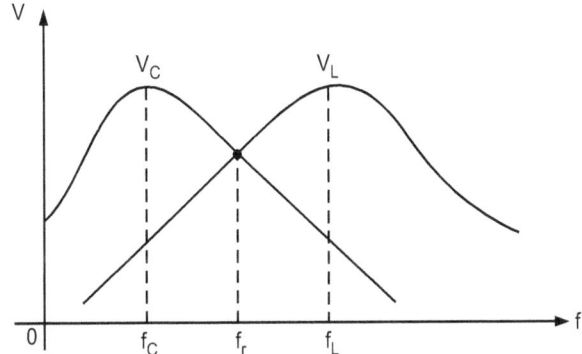

Fig. 4.11 : Variation of V_C and V_L with frequency

- Let us now attempt to find the expression to calculate f_C and f_L, the frequencies at which maximum voltage appears across a capacitor and an inductor.

(a) To calculate f_C: Voltage across capacitor

$$V_C = I \cdot X_C$$

$$V_C = I \cdot \left(\frac{1}{\omega C}\right)$$

$$V_C = \left(\frac{V}{Z}\right)\left(\frac{1}{\omega C}\right)$$

$$V_C = \frac{V}{\sqrt{R^2 + \left(\omega L - \frac{1}{\omega C}\right)^2}} \times \frac{1}{\omega C}$$

$$V_C = \frac{V}{\omega C \sqrt{R^2 + \left(\omega L - \frac{1}{\omega C}\right)^2}}$$

To find the frequency f_C, at which V_C is maximum, differentiate V_C with respect to ω, and equate it to zero.

We have,

$$V_C^2 = \frac{V^2}{\omega^2 C^2 \left[R^2 + \left(\omega L - \frac{1}{\omega C}\right)^2\right]}$$

$$\frac{d}{d\omega}[V_C^2] = \frac{d}{d\omega}\left[\frac{V^2}{\omega^2 C^2 \left(R^2 + \left(\frac{\omega^2 LC - 1}{\omega C}\right)^2\right)}\right]$$

$$= \frac{d}{d\omega}\left[\frac{V^2}{R^2\omega^2 C^2 + (\omega^2 LC - 1)^2}\right]$$

$$\frac{d}{d\omega}[V_C^2] = \frac{-V^2[2\omega R^2 C^2 + 2(\omega^2 LC - 1)\cdot 2\omega LC]}{[R^2\omega^2 C^2 + (\omega^2 LC - 1)^2]^2}$$

Since $V \neq 0$

$$2\omega C^2 R^2 + 2(\omega^2 LC - 1)\cdot 2\omega LC = 0$$
$$2\omega C^2 R^2 + (2\omega^2 LC - 2) 2\omega LC = 0$$
$$CR^2 + 2\omega^2 L^2 C\, 2L = 0$$
$$2\omega^2 L^2 C = 2L - CR^2$$
$$\omega^2 = \frac{1}{LC} - \frac{R^2}{2L^2}$$

Thus, frequency f_C at which V_C is maximum is given by,

$$\boxed{f_C = \frac{1}{2\pi}\sqrt{\frac{1}{LC} - \frac{R^2}{2L^2}}} = \boxed{f_r \sqrt{1 - \frac{R^2 C}{2L}}} \quad \ldots (4.11)$$

$f_r = \frac{1}{2\pi}\sqrt{\frac{1}{LC}}$, f_C is always less than [lower] f_r

(b) To calculate f_L: Voltage across inductor

$$V_L = I \cdot X_L$$
$$V_L = \frac{V}{Z} \cdot \omega L$$
$$V_L = \frac{V}{\sqrt{R^2 \rightarrow \left(\omega L - \frac{1}{\omega C}\right)^2}} \cdot \omega L$$

$$V_L = \frac{V \cdot \omega L}{\sqrt{R^2 + \left(\omega L - \frac{1}{\omega C}\right)^2}}$$

To find the frequency f_L at which V_L is maximum, differentiate V_L with respect to ω and equate it to zero.

We have,

$$V_L^2 = \frac{\omega^2 L^2 V^2}{R^2 + \frac{(\omega^2 LC - 1)^2}{\omega^2 C^2}}$$

$$V_L^2 = \frac{\omega^4 L^2 V^2 C^2}{R^2 \omega^2 C^2 + (\omega^2 LC - 1)^2}$$

$\frac{d}{d\omega}(V_L^2)$ and equating it to zero gives,

$$2\omega^2 LC - \omega^2 R^2 C^2 - 2 = 0$$
$$\omega^2 (2LC - R^2 C^2) = 2$$

$$\omega^2 = \frac{2}{2LC - R^2 C^2}$$

$$\omega^2 = \frac{1}{LC - \frac{R^2 C^2}{2}}$$

$$f_L = \frac{1}{2\pi \sqrt{LC - \frac{R^2 C^2}{2}}}$$

$$f_L = \frac{1}{2\pi \sqrt{LC} \times \sqrt{1 - \frac{R^2 C^2}{2L}}}$$

$$\boxed{f_L = \frac{f_r}{\sqrt{1 - \frac{R^2 C}{2L}}}} \qquad \ldots(4.12)$$

Thus, frequency f_L at which V_L is maximum is always higher than resonating frequency f_r.
To summarise maximum V_C at

$$f_C = f_r \sqrt{1 - \frac{R^2 C}{2L}} \qquad f_C < f_r$$

Maximum V_L at

$$f_L = \frac{f_r}{\sqrt{1 - \frac{R^2 C}{2L}}} \qquad f_L > f_r$$

4.4.10 Bandwidth of a Series Resonant Circuit

- Bandwidth is the measure of effectiveness with which a series resonant circuit selects given frequency and rejects all other frequencies.
- Bandwidth or frequency discrimination of a resonant circuit is defined as the width of a resonant wave in cycles at the frequency at which the power in the circuit is the half of the maximum power.
- Bandwidth requirement will depend upon the type of applications. It is about 400 Hz for telephone signals and about 6 MHz for the video (or television) signal. Example, in case of an op-amp, bandwidth should ideally be infinite and practically as large as possible where as contradictory to this in resonant circuit, this bandwidth must be as small as possible, which will make the circuit more and more selective. [Recall the example in Section 4.2].
- The bandwidth of series RLC circuit is defined as the band of frequencies over which the power in the circuit is half of its maximum value.

$$\text{Maximum power} = I_r^2 R \qquad I_r \text{ is maximum current}$$

At f_1,
$$\text{Half power} = \frac{1}{2} I_r^2 R = \left(\frac{I_r}{\sqrt{2}}\right)^2 R$$
$$= 0.707\, I_r^2 R$$

- Thus, at half power frequencies current becomes 0.707 times the maximum value as seen in Fig. 4.12.

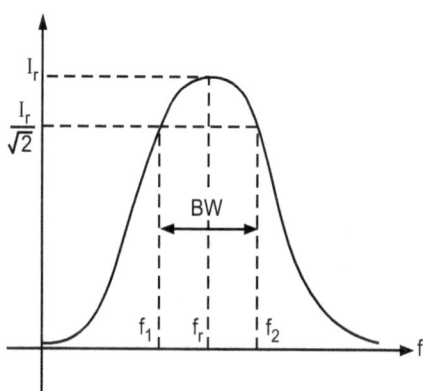

Fig. 4.12 : Frequency response of series RLC Circuit

- These half power frequencies are also referred are also referred as 3 dB frequencies. Let us determine these frequencies.

Thus, we have,

$$\text{Current in series RLC} = 0.707 \text{ or}$$

Circuit at f_1 and f_2 = $\dfrac{1}{\sqrt{2}} I_r$

(half power frequencies)

$$\dfrac{V}{\sqrt{R^2 + \left(\omega L - \dfrac{1}{\omega C}\right)^2}} = \dfrac{1}{\sqrt{2}} \dfrac{V}{R}$$

$$\therefore \quad \sqrt{R^2 + \left(\omega L - \dfrac{1}{\omega C}\right)^2} = \sqrt{2}\, R$$

Squaring both the sides.

$$R^2 + \left(\omega L - \dfrac{1}{\omega C}\right)^2 = 2R^2$$

$$\left(\omega L - \dfrac{1}{\omega C}\right)^2 = R^2$$

Taking square roots

$$\boxed{\left(\omega L - \dfrac{1}{\omega C}\right) = \pm R} \qquad \ldots(4.13)$$

Thus, at half power frequencies f_1 and f_2 in series RLC circuit,

$\boxed{\text{Reactive part of impedance = Resistive part of impedance}}$

At f_1 and ω_1 (Below resonance)

$$X_C > X_L$$

i.e. $\qquad \dfrac{1}{\omega C} > \omega L$

$\therefore \qquad \omega_1 L - \dfrac{1}{\omega_1 C} = -R \qquad \ldots(4.14\,(a))$

Similarly at f_2 or ω_2 (Above resonance)

$$X_L > X_C$$

i.e. $\qquad \omega L > \dfrac{1}{\omega C}$

$\qquad \omega_2 L - \dfrac{1}{\omega_2 C} = +R \qquad \ldots(4.14\,(b))$

Adding the above two equations (4.14 (a)) and (4.14 (b)).

$$\omega_1 L - \dfrac{1}{\omega_1 C} + \omega_2 L - \dfrac{1}{\omega_2 C} = 0$$

$$(\omega_1 + \omega_2) L - \left(\frac{1}{\omega_2} + \frac{1}{\omega_1}\right)\frac{1}{C} = 0$$

$$(\omega_1 + \omega_2) L - \left(\frac{\omega_1 + \omega_2}{\omega_1 \omega_2}\right)\frac{1}{C} = 0$$

$$(\omega_1 + \omega_2) L = \left(\frac{\omega_1 + \omega_2}{\omega_1 \omega_2}\right)\frac{1}{C}$$

$$\omega_1 + \omega_2 = \frac{1}{LC} \qquad \ldots(4.14\,(c))$$

$$\omega_1 + \omega_2 = \omega_r^2$$

$$\omega_r = \frac{1}{\sqrt{LC}}$$

$$\therefore \quad \boxed{\omega_r = \sqrt{\omega_1 \omega_2}} \qquad \ldots(4.14\,(d))$$

or

$$\boxed{f_r = \sqrt{f_1 f_2}}$$

Thus, resonating frequency f_r is geometric means of two half power frequencies f_1 and f_2.
Subtracting 4.14 (a) from 4.14 (b).

$$(\omega_2 + \omega_1) L - \left(\frac{1}{\omega_1} - \frac{1}{\omega_2}\right)\frac{1}{C} = 2R$$

$$(\omega_2 + \omega_1) L + \left(\frac{\omega_2 - \omega_1}{\omega_1 \omega_2}\right)\frac{1}{C} = 2R$$

From C we have $\omega_1 \omega_2 = \frac{1}{LC}$

$$\therefore \quad (\omega_2 + \omega_1) L + (\omega_2 - \omega_1) L = 2R$$

$$\omega_2 - \omega_1 = \frac{R}{L}$$

$$\boxed{BW = f_2 - f_1 = \frac{R}{2\pi L}} \qquad \ldots(4.15)$$

$$\boxed{\text{Bandwidth} = (f_2 - f_1) = \frac{R}{2\pi L}}$$

$$BW = \frac{R \cdot f_r}{2\pi L \, f_r}$$

$$BW = \frac{f_r}{\frac{\omega_r L}{R}}$$

$$\boxed{BW = \frac{f_r}{Q}} \quad \ldots (4.16)$$

where, $Q = \frac{\omega_r L}{R}$ i.e. the quality factor at the resonance of the circuit including generator, inductor, capacitor resistances and any load connected.

- Observe the BW is inversely proportional to the quality factor 'Q'. Q must be of a large value for the circuit to be very frequency selective. So if the circuit is frequency selective it will naturally have less bandwidth and vice versa.
- So, bandwidth is sometimes so also defined as means of comparing the selectivity of various designs.

4.4.11 Selectivity

- Frequency selective networks are designed to distinguish or select one particular frequency from the other frequencies in the given band.
- So 'selectivity' is one of the most important properties of any frequency selective network.
- Selectivity of any frequency selective network is defined as the ability of the circuit to discriminate or distinguish between the desired and the undesired frequencies.
- Selectivity is also, very often defined as the ratio of resonant frequency to the bandwidth of the resonant circuit.

$$\text{Selectivity} = \frac{\text{Resonant frequency}}{\text{Bandwidth}}$$

$$= \frac{f_r}{BW} = \frac{f_r}{(f_2 - f_1)}$$

$$\text{Selectivity} = \frac{f_r}{\frac{f_r}{Q}}$$

$$= Q$$

$$\boxed{\text{Selectivity} = Q} \quad \ldots (4.17)$$

Thus, selectivity of a series resonant circuit is directly proportional to the quality factor of a circuit. [This quality factor is always defined at f_r]. If quality factor Q is very high, the selectivity is high and the response curve becomes sharper and the bandwidth decreases. A smaller value of Q tends to make the curve flatter. This is indicated in Fig. 4.13.

Thus, to summarize in series RLC circuit.

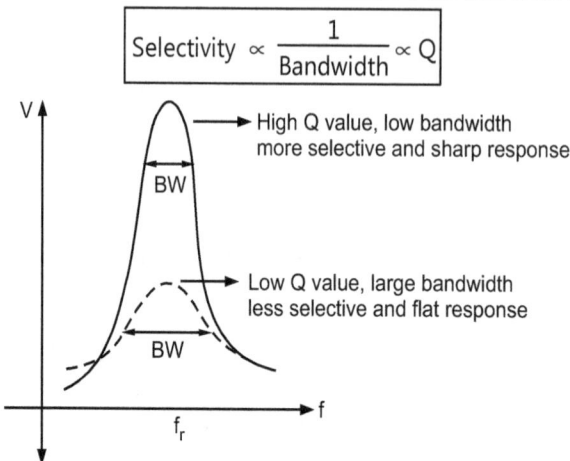

Fig. 4.13: Frequency response of a series RLC circuit for a high and low value of Q

4.4.12 Effect of R_g on Bandwidth and Selectivity

- An ideal current or a voltage source is non-existent in the real world. A practical current or a voltage source always has an internal resistance R_P or R_S in parallel or in series with the source, respectively. This resistance affects the behaviour of the circuit.
- This internal resistance is also referred to as generator resistance R_g'. Taking this into the series RLC circuit can be redrawn as:

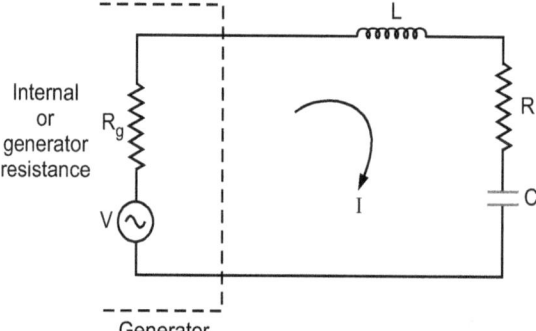

Fig. 4.14 : Series RLC circuit with R_g

- We have earlier defined bandwidth as

$$BW = \frac{f_r}{Q} = \left(\frac{R}{\omega L}\right) f_r$$

where, Q is that of the complete circuit including:
  - Generator resistance R_g
  - Inductor and capacitor resistances
  - Resistance of any connected load

So, in order to study the effect of the generator resistance R_g, let us separate this resistance from 'R'. Thus,

$$R = R_g + R'$$

where, R = Total circuit resistance
R_g = Generator resistance
R' = Resistance of capacitor, inductor and any connected load

Thus, rewriting the equation of BW in terms of R_g and R', we have,

$$BW = f_r \left(\frac{R}{\omega L} \right)$$

$$BW = f_r \left(\frac{R_g + R'}{\omega L} \right)$$

$$BW = f_r \left(\frac{R_g}{\omega L} + \frac{R'}{\omega L} \right)$$

$$\boxed{BW = f_r \left(\frac{R_g}{\omega L} + \frac{1}{Q_{circuit}} \right)} \quad \ldots (4.18)$$

$$Q_{circuit} = \frac{\omega L}{R'}$$

We have already studied that, the

1. $\quad Z = R \quad$ ... at resonating frequency f_r

   i.e. At resonance impedance of series circuit is equal to total resistance of the circuit

2. And the resistance must be small for the circuit to be very selective and have less bandwidth.

- So series resonant circuits should be used with voltage sources of low internal resistance.
- This is desirable and is advantageous as:
  1. Good frequency selectivity will be obtained, because BW is directly proportional to R i.e. ($R_g + R'$). So small value of R_g will give smaller Bandwidth and thus higher selectivity.
  2. The impedances can be matched to obtain maximum power transfer. This can be obtained by making

     $$R_g = R'$$

     i.e. Generator resistance = Circuit resistance

     Thus, in matched condition

     $$BW = \left(\frac{R_g}{\omega L} + \frac{R'}{\omega L} \right) f_r$$

$$\boxed{BW = \frac{2}{Q} f_r}$$ ... (4.19)

$$Q = \frac{\omega L}{R}$$

$$\boxed{\text{Selectivity} = \frac{Q}{2}}$$ ...(4.20)

- Thus, to summarise the effect of generator resistance on the bandwidth and selectivity it is clear that the generator resistance must be very low when a selective circuit is desired. A voltage source with higher value of R_g will increase the bandwidth making the frequency response curve flat and comparatively less selective.

4.4.13 Applications of Series RLC Circuit

- Series resonating circuit is used as an voltage amplifier.
- Series resonating circuits are used in m derived filters (to be discussed in next unit) because of their property of very low impedance at resonance. They are used to instantly increase the attenuation in filters to infinity.
- Series resonating circuits are also used in resonant converters.
- They are used to obtain high power output at specific frequency.

4.4.14 Summary of Series Resonating Circuit

The characteristics of series resonance circuit are:

1. At series resonating circuit, the input impedance is minimum or the admittance is maximum at resonating frequency f_r.
2. At resonance, circuit is purely resistive and hence the power factor is unity.
3. At f_{ar}, current in the circuit is maximum.
4. The circuit is capacitive for the frequencies below f_{ar} and it is inductive for the frequency below f_{ar}.
5. At reasonable, series RLC circuit acts as a voltage amplifier.

$$V_C = V \cdot Q$$
and $$V_L = Q \cdot V$$

They are equal in magnitude and opposite to each other.

6. Quality factor is given as,

$$Q = \frac{R}{\omega_r L} = \frac{1}{\omega_r CR}$$

7. The resonant frequency f_r is given as,

NETWORK ANALYSIS (S.E. SEM. III. E & TC. SU) — RESONANCE

$$f_r = \frac{1}{2\pi\sqrt{LC}}$$

9. R_g, generator resistance must be as small as possible for achieving high selectivity in series RLC circuit,

$$\text{Bandwidth} = \frac{f_r}{Q}$$

10. $f_r = \sqrt{f_1 f_2}$, where f_1 and f_2 are half power frequencies, f_r is geometric mean of f_1 and f_2.
11. At half power frequencies the resistive and reactive impedance are equal.

4.5 NUMERCIAL ON SERIES RLC CIRCUIT

Example 4.1:

A series R-L-C circuit consist of R = 10 Ω, L = 10 mH and C = 10 nF.

Find:

(i) Resonant frequency
(ii) Quality factor at resonance
(iii) Bandwidth

Solution : Given : R = 10 Ω, L = 10 mH and C = 10 nF.

To find: f_r, Q, BW.

(i) Resonating frequency:

$$f_r = \frac{1}{2\pi\sqrt{LC}}$$

$$= \frac{1}{2\pi\sqrt{10 \times 10^{-3} \times 10 \times 10^{-9}}}$$

$$\boxed{f_r = 15.915 \text{ kHz}}$$

(ii) Quality factor:

$$Q = \frac{\omega L}{R}$$

$$= \frac{2 \times \pi \times 15.915 \times 10^3 \times 10 \times 10^{-3}}{10}$$

$$\boxed{Q = 100}$$

(iii) Bandwidth Δf:

$$\Delta f = \frac{R}{2\pi L}$$

NETWORK ANALYSIS (S.E. SEM. III. E & TC. SU) — RESONANCE

$$= \frac{10}{2\times\pi\times 10\times 10^{-3}}$$

$$\boxed{\Delta f = 159.154 \text{ Hz}}$$

In the above numerical, Q can alternatively be calculated using

$$Q = \frac{1}{R}\sqrt{\frac{L}{C}}$$

$$= \frac{1}{10}\sqrt{\frac{10\times 10^{-3}}{10\times 10^{-9}}}$$

$$= 100$$

$$Q = \frac{1}{\omega_r RC}$$

$$= \frac{1}{2\times\pi\times 15.915\times 10^3\times 10\times 10\times 10^{-9}}$$

$$Q = 100$$

Thus, Q can be calculated using any of the above used methods.

Example 4.2 :

A circuit contains resistance of 200 Ω, a capacitance of 100 pF and inductance of 100 µH in series. Find fall in the current if the generator frequency is increased by 20 kHz above resonance of the circuit. (Generator has 50 Ω internal resistance with 10 V open circuit voltage). Also calculate the voltage across L and C at frequency of resonance. Find the maximum current in the circuit.

Solution : Given: R = 200 Ω, C = 100 pF, L = 100 µH, R_g = 50 Ω, V_{OC} = 10 V.

To find: I at f_r

I at (f_r + 20 kH)

V_L, V_C

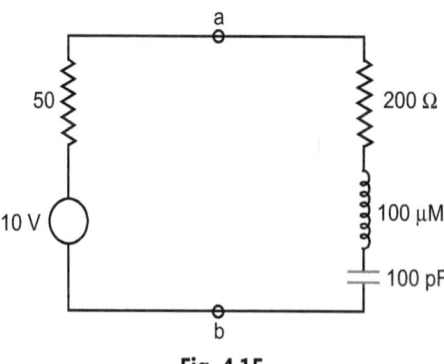

Fig. 4.15

V_{OC} = 10 V i.e. supply voltage = 10 V

Unit IV | 4.28

(i) Resonating frequency:

$$f_r = \frac{1}{2\pi\sqrt{LC}}$$

$$= \frac{1}{2\pi\sqrt{100 \times 10^{-12} \times 100 \times 10^{-6}}}$$

$$\boxed{f_r = 1.591 \text{ MHz}}$$

(ii) Current at resonating frequency:

$$I_r = \frac{V}{R} \quad (R = 200 + 50 = 250 \, \Omega)$$

$$I_r = \frac{10}{250} = 0.04 \text{ A}$$

$$\boxed{I_r = 0.04 \text{ A}}$$

(iii) Figure of merit i.e. Quality factor Q:

$$Q = \frac{\omega_r L}{R}$$

$$= \frac{2\pi \times 1.59 \times 10^6 \times 100 \times 10^{-6}}{250}$$

$$\boxed{Q = 4}$$

(iv) Voltage across L and C at resonance:

$$V_L = jQV$$
$$= j \times 4 \times 10$$
$$= j \, 40 \text{ V}$$
$$= \boxed{40 \angle 90° \text{ V}}$$

$$V_C = -jQV$$
$$= -j \times 4 \times 10$$
$$= -j \, 40 \text{ V}$$
$$= \boxed{40 \angle -90° \text{ V}}$$

(Recollect that Q in case of series RLC is a magnificent factor and circuit is voltage amplifier with V_L and $V_C > V$).

(v) Impedance of circuit 20 kHz above resonant.

Let us find δ $f = 1.591 \times 10^6 + 20 \times 10^3$

$$\delta = \frac{f - f_r}{f_r}$$

$$= \frac{20\,K}{1591\,K}$$

$$= 0.01257$$

$$Z_1 = R[1 + jQ\delta(2-\delta)]$$

$$Z_1 = 250[1 + j4(0.01257)(2)]$$

$$\boxed{Z_1 = 251.25\ \angle 57°\ \Omega}$$

I at 20 kHz above f_r = $\dfrac{V}{Z_1}$ = $0.0399\ \angle -5.7°$.

$$\boxed{I = 0.0399\ \angle -5.7°\ A}$$

i.e. voltage leads current. This is obvious as the impedance of the circuit is inductive above the resonant frequency.

Example 4.3 :

A series resonant circuit is in resonance at 8×10^6 Hz and it has coil of 35 µH and 10 Ω resistor.

(i) Find the current at resonance.
(ii) The value of the required capacitor.
(iii) Find the impedance at frequency of 8.1 MHz.
(iv) Find current at this frequency, applied voltage is sinusoidal 100 V_{rms}.

Solution : Given: $V = 100\ V_{rms}$, $f_r = 8 \times 10^6$ Hz, $L = 35$ µH, $R = 10\ \Omega$.

To find: I_r, C, Z at 8.1 MHz, I at 8.1 MHz.

(i) Current at resonance:

$$I_r = \frac{V}{R}$$

$$= \frac{100}{10} = 10\ A$$

$$\boxed{I_r = 10\ A}$$

(ii) Value of required capacitor:

$$f_r = \frac{1}{2\pi}\sqrt{\frac{1}{LC}}$$

$$8 \times 10^6 = \frac{1}{2\pi}\sqrt{\frac{1}{35 \times 10^{-6} \times C}}$$

$$\boxed{C = 11.3\ pF}$$

(iii) Impedance at frequency 8.1 MHz.:

Let us find $\delta = \dfrac{f - f_r}{f_r} = 0.0125$

$$Q = \dfrac{\omega L}{R}$$

$$= \dfrac{2\pi \times 8 \times 10^6 \times 35 \times 10^{-6}}{10} = 176$$

$$Z = R\left[1 + jQ\delta(2 - \delta)\right]$$

$$Z = 10\left[1 + j(176 \times 0.0125)(2 - 0.0125)\right]$$

$$\boxed{Z = 10 + j\,43.72\;\Omega \text{ at } 8.1 \text{ MHz}}$$

(iv) Current at f = 8.1 MHz:

$$I = \dfrac{V}{Z} = \dfrac{100}{10 + j\,43.72}$$

$$\boxed{I = 2.23\angle -77.11°\text{A at 8.1 MHz}}$$

The negative angle indicates current I is lagging voltage. Above f_r, the impedance is inductive as seen in (ii) and so voltage leads currents.

Example 4.4 : For a series RLC circuit

(i) Find the resonant frequency (ω_0)

(ii) Quality factor at resonance (Q_0)

(iii) Two half power frequencies (ω_1 and ω_2)

(iv) Bandwidth ($\Delta\omega$).

Assume circuit consists of R = 100 Ω, L = 100 mH and C = 10 nF. The applied voltage across the circuit is 100 V_{rms}.

Solution : Given: R = 100 Ω, L = 100 mH, C = 10 nF, V = 100 V_{rms}.

To Find: ω_r, Q_r, ω_1 and ω_2

(i) Resonant frequency ω_r:

$$\omega_r = \dfrac{1}{\sqrt{LC}}$$

$$= \dfrac{1}{\sqrt{100 \times 10^{-3} \times 10 \times 10^{-9}}}$$

ω_r = 31.6227 k rad/sec.

(ii) Quality factor:

$$Q_r = \dfrac{\omega_r L}{R}$$

$$= \frac{31.6227 \times 100 \times 10^{-3}}{100}$$

$$Q_r = 31.6227$$

(iii) Bandwidth $\Delta\omega$:

$$\Delta\omega = \frac{R}{L} = \frac{100}{100 \times 10^{-3}}$$

$$\Delta\omega = 1000 \text{ rad/sec.}$$

(iv) Half power frequencies:

Upper half power frequency, ω_2 is above ω_r

$$\omega_2 = \omega_0 + \frac{\Delta\omega}{2}$$

$$= 31.6227 \times 10^3 + \frac{1000}{2}$$

$$\omega_2 = 32.1227 \text{ k rad/sec.}$$

Lower half power frequency ω_1 is below ω_r

$$\therefore \quad \omega_1 = \omega_0 - \frac{\Delta\omega}{2} = 31.6227 \times 10^3 - \frac{1000}{2}$$

$$\omega_1 = 31.1227 \text{ k rad/sec.}$$

Example 4.5 :

A series circuit of negligible resistance and coil of 120 µH with 18 Ω resistance is resonated at 1 MHz. The circuit is driven by a generator of 1 V, 1 MHz frequency with $R_g = 0\Omega$.

(i) What will be the voltage across capacitor at resonance?
(ii) What current will flow at resonance and 10 kHz above resonance?

Solution : Given: L = 120 µH, R = 18 Ω, f_r = 1 MHz, V = 1 V, f_r = 1 MHz.
To find: V_C, I_r, I at 10 kHz above f_r, BW =?

(i) Quality factor:

$$Q = \frac{\omega_r L}{R} = \frac{2 \times \pi \times 10^6 \times 120 \times 10^{-6}}{18}$$

$$\boxed{Q = 41.888}$$

(ii) Voltage across the capacitor:

$$V_C = -jQV$$

$$= -j(41.88)(1)$$

$$V_C = -j\,41.88$$

$$\boxed{V_C = 41.88 \angle -90° \text{ V}}$$

(iii) Current at resonance:

$$I_r = \frac{V}{R} = \frac{1}{18}$$

$$= 55.55 \text{ mA}$$

$$\boxed{I_r = 55.55 \text{ mA}}$$

(iv) Current at 10 kHz above f_r:

We will have to calculate impedance.

So let us find δ

$$\delta = \frac{f - f_r}{f_r}$$

$$= \frac{10 \times 10^3}{1 \times 10^6} = 0.01$$

$$Z = R\left[1 + jQ\delta(2 - \delta)\right]$$

$$Z = 18\left[1 + j\, 41.888\,(0.01)(2 - 0.01)\right]$$

$$Z = 18\left[1 + j\, 0.8335\right]$$

$$\boxed{Z = (18 + j\, 15.003)\ \Omega}$$

$$\text{Current} = \frac{V}{Z}$$

$$= \frac{1}{18 + j\, 15.003}$$

$$= \frac{1}{23.43\ \angle\ 39.31°}$$

$$\boxed{I = 0.04267\ \angle -39.81°\text{A}}$$

(v) Bandwidth is given by

$$\Delta f = \frac{R}{2\pi L}$$

$$= \frac{18}{2\pi \times 120 \times 10^{-6}}$$

$$\boxed{\Delta f = 23.873\ \text{kHz}}$$

Example 4.6 :

A 20 Ω resistor is connected in series with an inductor, a capacitor and an ammeter across 25 V variable frequency supply when frequency is 400 Hz the current in maximum of 0.5°A and the potential difference across capacitor is 150 V. Find:

(i) Capacitance of the capacitor
(ii) Resistance and inductance.

Solution : Given: $R = 20\ \Omega$, $V = 25$ V, $I_r = 0.5$ A, $f_r = 400$ Hz, $V_C = 150$ V.
To find: C, R_L, L.

(i) Capacitance value:
- At 400 Hz, current is maximum, therefore the frequency $f = 400$ Hz is actually resonating f.
- At $f = f_r$, $V_C = X_C \cdot I_r$.
- At 400 Hz, $X_C = \dfrac{1}{\omega_r C}$

$$\dfrac{V_C}{I_r} = \dfrac{1}{\omega_r C}$$

$$\dfrac{150}{0.5} = \dfrac{1}{2\pi \times 400 \times C}$$

$$\boxed{C = 1.325\ \mu f}$$

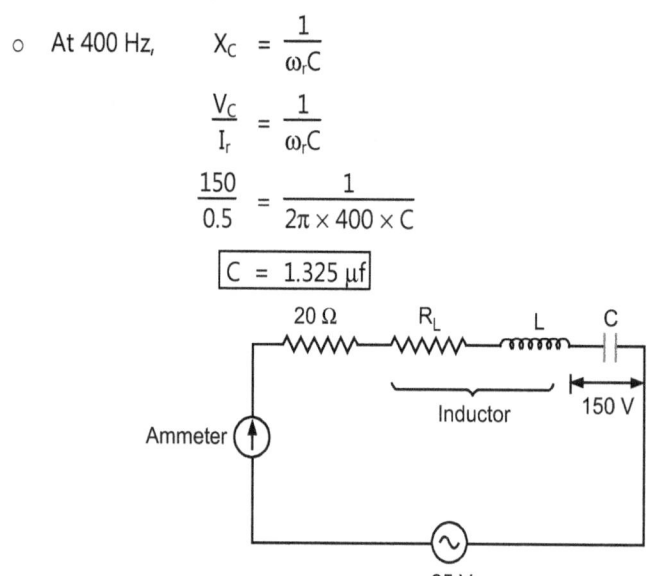

Fig. 4.16

(ii) Inductor value: At $f = f_r$,

$$X_L = X_C$$

$$\omega_r L = \dfrac{1}{\omega_r C}$$

$$2\pi \times 400 \times L = \dfrac{1}{2 \times \pi \times 400 \times 1.325 \times 10^{-6}}$$

$$\boxed{L = 0.119\ H}$$

(iii) Resistance of inductor:

$$I_r = \dfrac{V}{R}$$

$$\therefore \quad 0.5 = \dfrac{25}{R}$$

$$C = 20.2642\ \mu F$$
$$R = \frac{25}{0.5}$$
$$R = 50\ \Omega$$

This R is actually $20 + R_L$

$$\therefore \boxed{R_L = 30\ \Omega}$$

Example 4.7 :

A resistor and a capacitor are in series with a variable inductor. When this circuit is connected to 200 V, 50 Hz supply, 0.314 A is the maximum current obtained. At the instant $V_C = 300$ V. Find the circuit components.

Solution : Given: V = 200 V, F = 50 Hz, I_r = 0.314 A, V_C = 300 V.

To find: R, L, C.

(i) **To find the resistance:**

$$I_r = \frac{V}{R}$$

$$0.314 = \frac{200}{R}$$

$$\boxed{R = 636.95\ \Omega}$$

(ii) **To find the capacitor value:**

$$V_C = Q V$$
$$300 = Q\ 200$$
$$Q = 1.5$$

$$Q = \frac{1}{\omega_r R C}$$

$$1.5 = \frac{1}{2\pi \times 50 \times 636.59 \times C}$$

$$\boxed{C = 3.3\ \mu F}$$

(iii) **To find inductor value:**

$$Q = \frac{\omega_r L}{R}$$

$$1.5 = \frac{2 \times \pi \times 50 \times L}{636.59}$$

$$\boxed{L = 3.041\ H}$$

NETWORK ANALYSIS (S.E. SEM. III. E & TC. SU) — RESONANCE

Example 4.8 :

A circuit consisting of a resistance of 4 Ω and inductor of 0.5 H and a variable capacitor all in series connected across 100 V, 50 Hz supply. At resonance calculate:

(i) Capacitor
(ii) Voltage across inductor
(iii) Q factor
(iv) Current in the circuit
(v) Find current at 100 Hz.

Solution : Given: R = 4Ω, L = 0.5 H, V = 100 V, f_r = 50 Hz.

To find: C, Q, V_L, I_r, I at 100 Hz.

(i) Capacitor:

$$f_r = \frac{1}{2\pi\sqrt{LC}}$$

$$50 = \frac{1}{2\pi\sqrt{0.5 \times C}}$$

$$\boxed{C = 20.2642 \ \mu F}$$

(ii) Q factor:

$$Q = \frac{\omega_r L}{R}$$

$$= \frac{2 \times \pi \times 50 \times 0.5}{4}$$

$$\boxed{Q = 39.27}$$

(iii) Voltage across inductor:

$$V_L = jQV$$
$$V_L = j\, 39.27 \times 100$$
$$\boxed{V_L = j\, 3.927 \text{ kV}}$$

(iv) Current at resonance:

$$I = \frac{V}{R} = \frac{100}{4}$$

$$\boxed{I = 25 \text{ A}}$$

(v) Current at f = 100 Hz:

Let us first calculate Z and δ

$$\delta = \frac{f - f_r}{f_r}$$

$$= \frac{50}{50} = 1$$

$$Z = R[1 + jQ\delta(2-\delta)]$$
$$Z = 4[1 + j\,39.27]$$
$$Z = 4j\,157.08\,\Omega$$

$$\therefore\quad I = \frac{V}{Z} = \frac{100}{4 + j\,157.08}$$

$$I = \frac{100\angle 0}{157.13\angle 88.5}$$

$$\boxed{I = 0.636\angle -88.5\,A}$$

∴ Impedance above f_r is unductive. Therefore, voltage leads I.

$$\boxed{I\text{ at }100\text{ Hz} = 0.636\angle -88.5°\,A}$$

Example 4.9:

A circuit consisting of 5 Ω, an inductor of 0.4 H and a variable capacitor is connected across 230 V, 50 Hz supply. At resonance calculate:

(i) Capacitance
(ii) Voltage across inductor
(iii) Current in the circuit.

Solution : Given: R = 5 Ω, L = 0.4 H, V = 230 V, f = 50 Hz.

To calculate: C, V_L, I_r.

(i) To calculate C:

$$f_r = \frac{1}{2\pi\sqrt{LC}}$$

$$50 = \frac{1}{2\times\pi\sqrt{0.4\times C}}$$

$$\boxed{C = 25.33\,\mu F}$$

(ii) Quality factor:

$$Q = \frac{\omega_r L}{R}$$

$$= \frac{2\pi\times 50\times 0.4}{5}$$

$$\boxed{Q = 25.1327}$$

(iii) Voltage across inductor at resonance:

$$V_L = jQV$$
$$V_L = j\,25.1327 \times 230$$
$$\boxed{V_L = j\,5.78 \text{ kV} = 5.78 \angle 90° \text{ V}}$$

(iv) Current at resonance:

$$I_r = \frac{V}{R}$$
$$= \frac{230}{5}$$
$$\boxed{I_r = 46 \text{ A}}$$

Example 4.10 :

A current in series resonant circuit is maximum at 3 kHz and it is 5 amperes. If the coil is of 0.05 mH and R = 5 Ω, then calculate the value of 'C' to get the resonance. What will be the value of 'V'? Draw the phasor diagram of the circuit at resonance.

Solution : Given: f_r = 3 kHz, I_r = 5A, L = 0.05 mH, R = 5Ω.

To calculate: C, V, phasor diagrams.

(i) To calculate C:

Current is maximum at 3 kHz

∴ $$f_r = 3 \text{ kHz}$$

$$f_r = \frac{1}{2\pi\sqrt{LC}}$$

$$3 \times 10^3 = \frac{1}{2\pi\sqrt{0.05 \times 10^{-3} \times C}}$$

$$\boxed{C = 56.2895 \text{ μF}}$$

(ii) Value V:

$$I_r = \frac{V}{R}$$
$$5 = \frac{V}{5}$$
$$\boxed{V = 25 \text{ V}}$$

(iii) Phasor diagram at resonance:

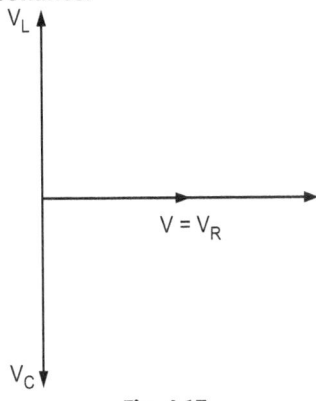

Fig. 4.17

4.6 PARALLEL RESONATING CIRCUIT

Consider circuit shown in Fig. 4.18

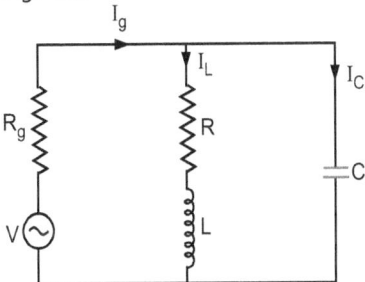

Fig. 4.18 : A parallel resonating circuit

- We have consider R_g i.e. the internal generator resistance in this circuit. Moreover, the capacitor is connected in parallel to an inductor and it is assumed to be a lossless element and hence its resistance is negligible. R in this case is the sum of the resistance of inductor and any other load resistance connected externally.
- This circuit is connected to the voltage source of V volts and generator resistance R_g ohms.
- It is also called as an antiresonating circuit.

4.6.1 Antiresonating Frequency

The admittance of the capacitive branch of the circuit is

$$Y_C = j\omega C$$

and that of the inductive branch is

$$Y_L = \frac{1}{R + j\omega L} = \frac{R - j\omega L}{R^2 + \omega^2 L^2}$$

Thus, Y i.e. total admittance

$$Y = Y_C + Y_L$$

$$Y = \frac{R - j\omega L}{R^2 + \omega^2 L^2} + j\omega C$$

$$Y = \frac{R}{R^2 + \omega^2 L^2} - j\left[\frac{\omega L}{R^2 + \omega^2 L^2} - \omega C\right]$$

- For antiresonance, the circuit must have unity power factor, therefore the j term must be zero. So setting the reactive term equal to zero at ω_{ar} i.e. antiresonant frequency.

∴ At $\quad \omega = \omega_{ar}$

$$\frac{\omega_{ar} L}{R^2 + \omega_{ar}^2 L^2} - \omega_{ar} C = 0$$

$$\boxed{R^2 + \omega_{ar}^2 L^2 = \frac{L}{C}} \quad \ldots (4.21)$$

This equation will be used in Section 4.5.3.

$$\omega_{ar}^2 = \left(\frac{L}{C} - R^2\right)\frac{1}{L^2}$$

$$\omega_{ar}^2 = \left(\frac{1}{LC} - \frac{R^2}{L^2}\right)$$

$$\boxed{f_{ar} = \frac{1}{2\pi}\sqrt{\frac{1}{LC} - \frac{R^2}{L^2}}} \quad \ldots (4.22)$$

f_{ar}, gives the frequency of resonance in a parallel R_{LC} circuit.

$$f_{ar} = \frac{1}{2\pi}\sqrt{\frac{1}{LC}}\sqrt{1 - \frac{1}{Q^2}}$$

$$\boxed{f_{ar} = f_r \sqrt{1 - \frac{1}{Q^2}}} \quad \ldots (4.23)$$

$$\boxed{\omega_{ar}^2 LC = 1 - \frac{1}{Q^2}} \quad \ldots (4.24)$$

which can be written as

$$\omega_{ar} L = \frac{1}{\omega_{ar} C}\left(1 - \frac{1}{Q^2}\right)$$

to give

$$\boxed{X_L = X_C \left(1 - \frac{1}{Q^2}\right)} \quad \ldots (4.25)$$

Equation (4.23) gives the expression for the antiresonating frequency. Equations (4.23), (4.24), (4.25) are the modified versions and need careful understanding.

Comments on Equations (4.21), (4.22), (4.23) and (4.24).

1. In series resonant circuit,

$$f_r = \frac{1}{2\pi\sqrt{LC}}$$

and thus resonance was possible for all the values of resistance present. In contrast to this, as clear from equation (4.22) in an antiresonant circuit, resonance is possible only when $\frac{1}{LC} > \frac{R^2}{L^2}$.

i.e. Resonance is impossible for all the values of R that makes

$$\frac{R^2}{L^2} > \frac{1}{LC}$$

This is clear from equation (4.22).

2. Equation (4.23) indicates that the antiresonant frequency, differs from that of a series resonant circuit with the same circuit elements only by the factor $\sqrt{1 - \frac{1}{Q^2}}$.

If Q > 10 then error < 10% and $f_{ar} = f_r$.

Another point indicated by equation (4.23) is that it shows the antiresonance is impossible for circuits with values of Q less than unity.

3. Equations (4.24) and (4.25) shows another interesting fact. We define resonance as a condition of a circuit when $X_L = X_C$ and unity power factor is achieved. But in an antiresonant circuit at f_{ar} the reactances of inductive and capacitive branches are not quite equal as they were incase of series resonating circuit.

4.6.2 Reactance Curves

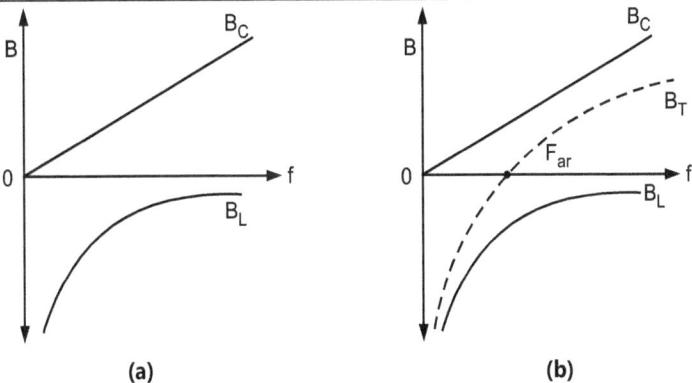

(a)   (b)

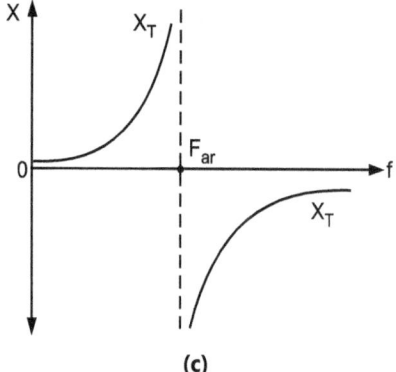

(c)

Fig. 4.19 : (a) Suspectance Vs Frequency plot for L and C, (b) Total Suspectance B_T Vs Frequency, (c) X_T plotted as reciprocal of B_T

- Inductive reactance is a linear positive function of frequency and is plotted as a straight line through origin. Capacitive reactance similarly, is plotted as a negative hyperbola the reason being it is an inverse negative function of frequency.
- In case of parallel resonating circuit we plot the susceptances, thus inductive susceptance is plotted as hyperbolic negative and capacitive susceptance is plotted as a linear positive plot.
- These plots are shown in Fig. 4.19 (a) and (b). Fig. 4.19 (c) shows the plot of total reactance X_T plotted as a reciprocal of total susceptance. Thus, at antiresonating frequency f_{ar}, susceptance B_T was zero and so X_T is therefore infinity. Below f_{ar}, B_T is capacitive and thus X_T is inductive. Similarly X_T is capacitive above f_{ar}. Even this is very contradictory to the reactance plot of series resonance.

4.6.3 Impedance of Parallel Resonance Circuit

The admittance of the capacitive branch of the circuit is

$$Y_C = j\omega C$$

Similarly,

$$Y_L = \frac{1}{R + j\omega L}$$

$$= \frac{R - j\omega L}{R^2 + \omega^2 L^2}$$

∴ Total admittance Y is

$$Y = \frac{R - j\omega L}{R^2 + \omega^2 L^2} + j\omega C$$

∴ $$Y = \frac{R}{R^2 + \omega^2 L^2} - j\left(\frac{\omega L}{R^2 + \omega^2 L^2} - \omega C\right)$$

(a) Impedance at antiresonating frequency:

With the condition of unity power factor imposed, admittance at f_{ar} is

$$Y_{ar} = \frac{R}{R^2 + \omega_{ar}^2 L^2}$$

∴ Antiresonant impedance is

∴ $$Z_{ar} = R_{ar} = \frac{R^2 + \omega_{ar}^2 L^2}{R}$$

$$Z_{ar} = R + \frac{\omega_{ar}^2 L^2}{R}$$

$$\boxed{Z_{ar} = R\left(1 + Q_{war}^2\right)} \qquad \ldots (4.26)$$

For the circuit with very high value of Q.

$$\boxed{Z_{ar} = R \cdot Q_{ar}^2} \qquad \ldots (4.27) \text{ high Q values}$$

This equation gives Z_{ar} in terms of Q_{ar}. Recollect equation (4.21) which we saw in Section 4.5.1. The equation is

$$R^2 + \omega_{ar}^2 L = \frac{L}{C}$$

Using this result in the equation

$$Z_{ar} = R + \frac{\omega_{ar}^2 L^2}{R}$$

i.e. $$Z_{ar} = \frac{R^2 + \omega_{ar}^2 L^2}{R}$$

Gives, $$\boxed{Z_{ar} = \frac{L}{CR}} \qquad \ldots (4.28)$$

This equation gives the expression for Z_{ar} in terms of circuit components.

(b) The impedance of parallel resonant circuit near resonance:

The impedance of parallel resonant circuit at any frequency is given by,

$$Z = (R + j\omega L) \parallel \left(\frac{1}{j\omega C}\right)$$

$$Z = \frac{(R + j\omega L) \times \frac{1}{(j\omega C)}}{R + j\omega L + \frac{1}{j\omega C}}$$

$$Z = \cfrac{R\left(1 + \cfrac{j\omega L}{R}\right)\left(\cfrac{1}{j\omega C}\right)}{R\left[1 + \cfrac{j\omega L}{R}\left(1 - \cfrac{1}{\omega^2 LC}\right)\right]}$$

$$Z = \cfrac{R\left(1 + \cfrac{j\omega L}{R}\right)\left(\cfrac{1}{j\omega C}\right)}{R\left[1 + \cfrac{j\omega L}{R}\left(1 - \cfrac{1}{\omega^2 LC}\right)\right]}$$

$$Z = \cfrac{\cfrac{L}{RC} + \cfrac{1}{j\omega C}}{1 + \cfrac{j\omega L}{R}\left(1 - \cfrac{1}{\omega^2 LC}\right)} \qquad \ldots (4.29)$$

Above equation gives general expression for the impedance of a parallel resonant circuit at any frequency ω.

Let δ be the fractional deviation

$$\delta = \frac{f - f_{ar}}{f_{ar}}$$

$$= \frac{\omega - \omega_{ar}}{\omega_{ar}} = \frac{\omega}{\omega_{ar}} - 1$$

$$\boxed{(1 + \delta) = \frac{\omega}{\omega_{ar}}} \quad \text{or} \quad \boxed{\frac{\omega_{ar}}{\omega} = \frac{1}{(1 + \delta)}}$$

Now let us consider the terms in the denominator of equation 4.29.

$$\frac{\omega L}{R} = \frac{\omega_{ar} L}{R} \cdot \frac{\omega}{\omega_{ar}} = Q(1 + \delta)$$

$$\frac{1}{\omega^2 LC} = \frac{\omega_{ar}^2}{\omega^2} \times \frac{1}{\omega_{ar}^2 LC}$$

$$= \frac{1}{(1 + \delta)^2} \qquad \ldots \text{when Q is high } \omega_{ar}^2 LC = 1$$

Substituting these values in equation 4.29.

$$Z = \cfrac{\cfrac{L}{CR}\left(1 + \cfrac{R}{j\omega L}\right)}{1 + j\cfrac{\omega L}{R}\left(1 - \cfrac{1}{\omega^2 LC}\right)}$$

$$Z = \frac{L}{CR} \frac{1 - j\frac{1}{Q_0(1+\delta)}}{1 + jQ(1+\delta)\left[1 + \frac{1}{(1+\delta)^2}\right]}$$

$$Z = \frac{L}{CR} \frac{1 - j\frac{1}{\theta(1+\delta)}}{1 + jQ\left[\frac{1 + \delta^2 + 2\delta - 1}{(1+\delta)}\right]}$$

$$Z = \frac{L}{CR} \frac{1 - j\frac{1}{Q(1+\delta)}}{1 + jQ\delta\frac{(2+\delta)}{(1+\delta)}} \quad \ldots (4.30)$$

At antiresonating frequency

$$Z_{ar} = \frac{L}{CR}$$

and $\delta \ll 1$. Therefore, neglecting it.
Substituting in equation 4.30.

$$Z = Z_{ar} \frac{1 - j\frac{1}{Q}}{1 + jQ\delta \cdot 2}$$

$\frac{1}{Q}$ is $\ll 1$. Therefore, neglecting it.

$$\boxed{Z = \frac{Z_{ar}}{1 + j2\delta Q}} \quad \ldots (4.31)$$

Equation (4.31) gives the value of impedance near resonance.

4.6.4 Currents in Antiresonant Circuits

At antiresonance, the power delivered by the generator to the circuit of Fig. 4.20.

$$P = I_g^2 R_{ar}$$

Power dissipated in the parallel circuit assuming negligible capacitor losses is

$$P = I_L^2 R$$

This power is equal to the power supplied by the generator, since there are no other power dissipating elements in the circuit.

∴   Input power = Delivered power

$$I_g^2 R_{ar} = I_L^2 R$$

RESONANCE

$$\frac{I_g^2}{I_L^2} = \frac{R}{R_{ar}}$$

Now, $R_{ar} = \dfrac{L}{CR}$

$$\frac{I_g^2}{I_L^2} = \frac{R}{\frac{L}{CR}}$$

$$\frac{I_g^2}{I_L^2} = \frac{CR^2}{L}$$

$$I_L^2 = \frac{L}{CR^2} I_g^2$$

As $Q = \dfrac{\omega L}{R} = \dfrac{1}{R}\sqrt{\dfrac{L}{C}}$ .... $\omega_{ar} = \dfrac{1}{\sqrt{LC}}$

$$I_L^2 = Q^2 I_g^2$$

$$\boxed{I_L = Q\, I_g}$$ ... (4.32)

At antiresonance:

Now current flowing through the capacitor is given by

$$I_C = \frac{V}{X_C} = \frac{V}{\left(\dfrac{1}{\omega_{ar} C}\right)}$$

$$I_C = \omega_{ar}\, C \cdot V$$
$$I_C = \omega_{ar}\, C\, [I_g \times Z_{ar}]$$
$$I_C = \omega_{ar}\, C\, I_g \left(\frac{L}{CR}\right)$$
$$I_C = \left(\frac{\omega_{ar} L}{R}\right) I_g$$

$$\boxed{I_C = Q\, I_g}$$ ... (4.33)

Equations (4.32) and (4.33) show that at f_{ar}, the currents through the inductor and the capacitor are amplified by a factor Q.

- Recollect the equation (4.22), which we saw in Section 4.5.1.

At antiresonance,

$$X_L = X_C \left(1 - \frac{1}{Q^2}\right)$$

i.e. the reactances of inductive and capacitive branches are not quite equal to units power factor.

- The current will always depend on reactance. So if reactances are not equal, the currents will obviously not be equal.

At antiresonance

$$\frac{I_C}{I_L} = \sqrt{1 - \frac{1}{Q^2}}$$

This is the ratio of magnitude of the currents in the capacitive branch to the inductive branch at unity power factor.

- The two currents are thus not equal if the resistance is appreciable, approaching equality as R is decreased.
- Higher the value of Q, the higher will I_C and I_L be and I_g will be low.
- At infinite Q, currents I_C and I_L will be infinite and I_g will be zero.

4.6.5 Bandwidth of Antiresonant Circuit

- We have already defined bandwidth for resonating circuits.
- Let us derive equation for bandwidth of a parallel resonant circuit shown in Fig. 4.20 (a).

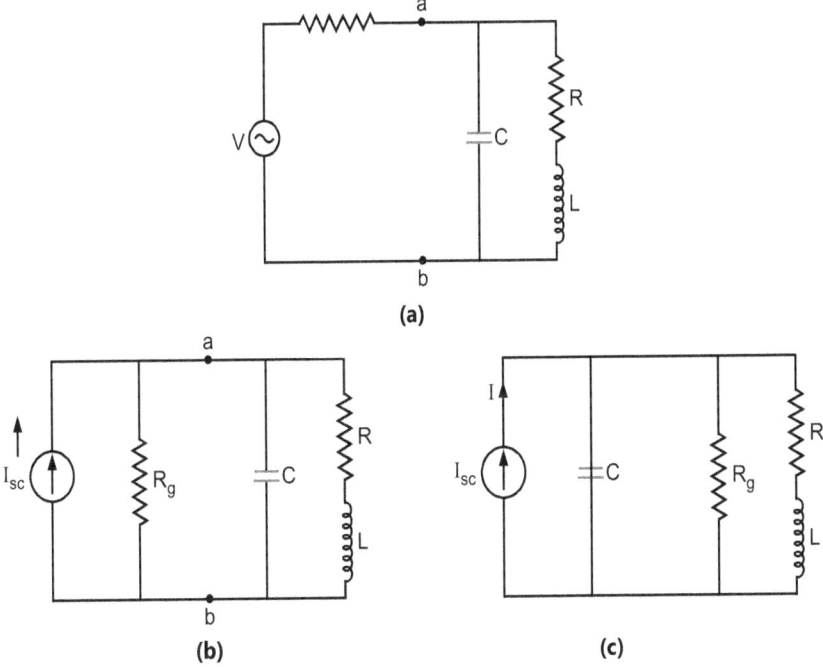

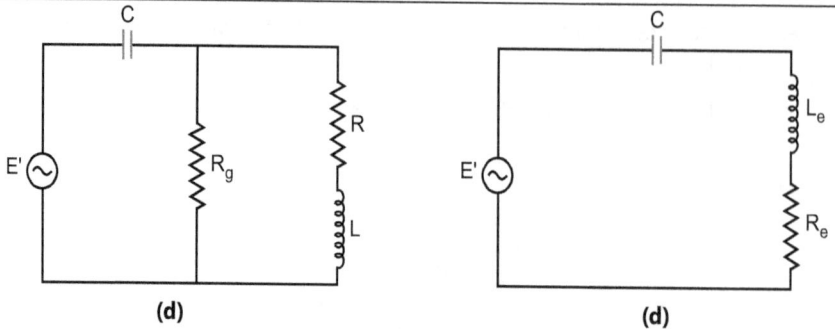

Fig. 4.20 (a) Parallel RLC circuit connected to a generator of internal resistance R_g
(b), (c), (d) Successive steps in reduction of (a) to (e)
(e) Series RLC equivalent of a

- Using voltage source transformation the circuit in Fig. 4.20 (a) is transformed to one in Fig. 4.20 (b). Since, all the branches are now in parallel we can interchange the positions of R_g and C. Using current source transformation circuit in Fig. 4.20 (c) can be drawn as in Fig. 4.20 (d). Finally, Fig. 4.20 (e) shows an equivalent of series RLC circuit the parallel RLC circuit in Fig. 4.20 (a) where

$$(R_e + X_{Le}) = R_g \,||\, (X_L + R)$$

- Now, in the equivalent series RLC circuit capacitor C is the internal impedance of a new generator E'.
- Let us now analyse Fig. 4.20 (e) where we have,

$$Z_e = R_e + L_e = R_g \,||\, (L + R)$$
$$Z_e = R_g \,||\, (j\omega L + R)$$
$$Z_e = \frac{R_g \times (j\omega L + R)}{R_g + R + j\omega L}$$

After rationalizing,

$$Z_e = \frac{R_g (j\omega L + R)(R_g + R - j\omega L)}{(R_g + R + j\omega L)(R_g + R - j\omega L)}$$

$$Z_e = \frac{(j\omega L R_g + R_g R)(R_g + R - j\omega L)}{(R_g + R)^2 + \omega^2 L^2}$$

$$Z_e = \frac{R_g^2 R + R_g R^2 - j\omega L R_g R + j\omega L R_g^2 + j\omega L R_g R + \omega^2 L_g^2}{(R_g + R)^2 + \omega^2 L^2}$$

$$Z_e = \frac{R_g^2 R + R_g R^2 + j\omega L R_g^2 + \omega^2 L^2 R_g}{(R_g + R)^2 + \omega^2 L^2}$$

$$Z_e = (R_e + X_{Le}) = \frac{R_g^2 R + R_g R^2 + R_g \omega^2 L^2 + j\omega L R_g^2}{(R_g + R)^2 + \omega^2 L^2}$$

Form which we have,

$$R_e = \frac{R_g^2 R + R_g R^2 + R_g \omega^2 L^2}{(R_g + R)^2 + \omega^2 L^2}$$

$$\omega L_e = \frac{\omega L R_g^2}{(R_g + R)^2 + \omega^2 L^2}$$

It has been shown that bandwidth of a series resonant circuit is given as

$$BW = \frac{f_r}{Q}$$

The parallel RLC circuit is proved to be equivalent to a series resonant circuit.

$$\therefore \quad BW \text{ of parallel RLC circuit } = \frac{f_{ar}}{Q}$$

where, $\quad Q$ must be $= \dfrac{\omega L_e}{R_e}$

$\therefore \quad$ Bandwidth (BW) $= \Delta f$

$$= f_2 - f_1$$

$$\Delta f = \frac{f_{ar}}{Q}$$

$$\Delta f = \frac{f_{ar}}{\frac{\omega L_e}{R_e}}$$

$$\Delta f = f_{ar} \cdot \frac{R_e}{\omega L_e}$$

$$\Delta f = \left(\frac{R_g R^2 + R R_g^2 + R_g \omega^2 L^2}{\omega L R_g^2}\right) f_{ar}$$

$$\Delta f = \left(\frac{R}{\omega L} + \frac{R_g (R^2 + \omega^2 L^2)}{\omega L R_g^2}\right) f_{ar}$$

$$\Delta f = \left[\frac{1}{Q} + \frac{R^2 \left(1 + \frac{\omega^2 L^2}{R^2}\right)}{\omega L R_g}\right] f_{ar}$$

$$\Delta f = \left[\frac{1}{Q} + \frac{R^2}{\omega L R_g}\left(\frac{R_{ar}}{R}\right)\right] f_{ar}$$

... equation (4.27) is section 4.6.3

$$Z_{ar} = R(1 + Q^2)$$

$$\Delta f = \left[\frac{1}{Q} + \frac{R \cdot R_{ar}}{\omega L \, R_g}\right] f_{ar}$$

$$\boxed{\Delta f = \frac{f_{ar}}{Q}\left[1 + \frac{R_{ar}}{R_g}\right]} \qquad \ldots(4.34)$$

- If it is desired to match the impedances, as to obtain the greatest possible power delivery from generator to load, then $R_g = R_{ar}$.

  ∴ Bandwidth for matched condition will be

$$\boxed{\Delta f = \frac{2}{Q} f_{ar}} \qquad \ldots(4.35)$$

- Above equation (4.34), can be modified slightly to explain the factors effecting bandwidth.

We have
$$\Delta f = \frac{f_{ar}}{Q}\left(1 + \frac{R_{ar}}{R_g}\right)$$

But
$$R_{ar} = \frac{L}{CR}$$

$$\boxed{\Delta f = \frac{f_{ar}}{Q}\left(1 + \frac{L}{CR \, R_g}\right)} \qquad \ldots(4.36)$$

Equations (4.34), (4.35) and (4.36) are the expressions of BW in terms of Q, R_{ar} and R_g and must be closely understood so need further clarification.

Comments on Bandwidth and Selectivity:

1. Equation (4.34) shows that as seen in series RLC circuit, even in parallel circuit the bandwidth is inversely proportional to the Q of the original parallel circuit modified by a factor dependent on R_g.

   Q of original parallel circuit $= \dfrac{\omega L}{R}$

   Q of equivalent series RLC circuit $= \dfrac{\omega L_e}{R_e}$

2. Equation (4.34), also shows that for smaller bandwidth or greater selectivity of the antiresonant circuit a generator of a very high internal resistance R_g, should be used. Thus, in case of parallel RLC circuit R_g must be of a very high value. This is indicated in Fig. 4.21.

3. Equation (4.35), indicates that for a matched conditions $R_g = R_{ar}$ [to have maximum power transfer]. Since, R_g must be high for high selectivity R_{ar} must also be very high for maximum power transfer in the circuit.

4. Equation (4.36), shows that L must be small and C must be large for designing a circuit with high frequency selectivity i.e. circuit with less bandwidth. But doing this will lower the value of Z_{ar} and R_{ar}.

$$Z_{ar} = R_{ar} = \frac{L}{CR}$$

Lowering the value of R_{ar} is highly undesirable if maximum power is needed to be transferred. So the designer must go for some engineering compromise between selectivity and maximum power to be transferred in a parallel resonating circuit.

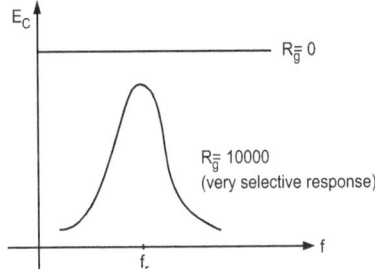

Fig. 4.21 : Frequency response indicating effect of internal resistance R_g

4.6.6 General Case: Resistance present in both the Branches

Let the capacitor be lossy hence there will be resistances in both the branches as shown in Fig. 4.22.

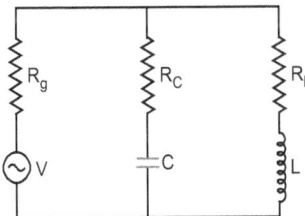

Fig. 4.22 : Antiresonant circuit with resistance in both the branches

In this case, admittance Y_L of an inductive branch is

$$Y_L = \frac{1}{R_1 + j\omega L}$$

$$Y_L = \frac{R_1 - j\omega L}{R_1^2 + \omega^2 L^2}$$

Similarly, admittance Y_C of a capacitive branch is

$$Y_C = \frac{1}{R_2 - \dfrac{j}{\omega C}}$$

$$Y_C = \frac{R_2 + \dfrac{j}{\omega C}}{R_2^2 + \dfrac{1}{\omega^2 C^2}}$$

Total admittance $Y_T = Y_C + Y_L$

$$Y_T = \frac{R_1 - j\omega L}{R_1^2 + \omega^2 L^2} + \frac{R_2 + \dfrac{j}{\omega C}}{R_2^2 + \dfrac{1}{\omega^2 C^2}}$$

$$Y_T = \frac{R_1}{R_1^2 + \omega^2 L^2} + \frac{R_2}{R_2^2 + \dfrac{1}{\omega^2 C^2}} - j\left(\frac{\omega L}{R_1^2 + \omega^2 L^2} - \frac{\dfrac{1}{\omega C}}{R_2^2 + \dfrac{1}{\omega^2 C^2}}\right) \quad \ldots(4.37)$$

For antiresonant condition, unity power factor must be achieved. Therefore, the reactive term must be zero, thus at $\omega = \omega_{ar}$.

$$\omega_{ar} L \left[R_2^2 + \frac{1}{\omega_{ar}^2 C^2} \right] - \frac{1}{\omega_{ar} C} \left[R_1^2 + \omega_{ar}^2 L^2 \right] = 0$$

$$\omega_{ar} L R_2^2 + \frac{L}{\omega_{ar} C^2} = \frac{R_1^2}{\omega_{ar} C} + \frac{\omega_{ar} L^2}{C}$$

$$\omega_{ar}^2 R_2^2 C^2 L + L = R_1^2 C + \omega_{ar}^2 L^2 C$$

$$\omega_{ar}^2 LC \left(R_2^2 C - L \right) = C R_1^2 - L$$

$$\omega_{ar}^2 = \frac{1}{LC} \left[\frac{C R_1^2 - L}{R_2^2 C - L} \right]$$

$$\boxed{f_{ar} = \frac{1}{2\pi} \sqrt{\frac{1}{LC} \left(\frac{L - R_1^2 C}{L - R_2^2 C} \right)}} \quad \ldots (4.38)$$

- Equation (4.38) gives the expression for f_{ar} when resistance is present in both the branches of the antiresonant circuit.
- If $R_2 = 0$, then the circuit will be same as in Fig. (4.37), and f_{ar} will be

$$f_{ar} = \frac{1}{2\pi} \sqrt{\frac{1}{LC}\left(1 - R_1^2 \frac{C}{L}\right)}$$

which is same as the one derived earlier.

(a) Antiresonance at all Frequencies:

- If two resistances R_1 and R_2 are equal and is $\sqrt{\dfrac{L}{C}}$

  i.e. $\quad R_1 = R_2 = \sqrt{\dfrac{L}{C}}$

Then the reactance associated with J terms in above Y_T equation (4.37), is

$$\dfrac{\omega L}{R_1^2 + \omega^2 L^2} - \dfrac{\dfrac{1}{\omega C}}{R_2^2 + \dfrac{1}{\omega^2 C^2}} = \dfrac{\omega L}{\dfrac{L}{C} + \omega^2 L^2} - \dfrac{\dfrac{1}{\omega C}}{\dfrac{L}{C} + \dfrac{1}{\omega^2 C^2}}$$

$$= \dfrac{\omega C}{1 + \omega^2 CL} - \dfrac{\omega C}{1 + \omega^2 CL} = 0$$

Thus, the reactance term is zero. The total admittance will be given by

$$Y_T = \dfrac{\sqrt{\dfrac{L}{C}}}{\dfrac{L}{C} + \omega^2 L^2} + \dfrac{\sqrt{\dfrac{L}{C}}}{\dfrac{L}{C} + \dfrac{1}{\omega^2 C^2}}$$

$$Y_T = \dfrac{\sqrt{\dfrac{L}{C}} \times C}{L(1 + \omega^2 LC)} + \dfrac{\sqrt{\dfrac{L}{C}} \times \omega^2 C^2}{C(1 + \omega^2 LC)}$$

$$Y_T = \sqrt{\dfrac{L}{C}}$$

The impedance $= \dfrac{1}{Y_T} = \sqrt{\dfrac{L}{C}} = R_1 = R_2$.

Thus, at all the frequencies impedance of the parallel circuit is

$$\boxed{Z = \sqrt{\dfrac{L}{C}}}$$

when $\quad R_1 = R_2 = \sqrt{\dfrac{L}{C}}$

So we say, the circuit is antiresonant at all the frequencies and thus the circuit is purely resistance (unity power factor) at all the frequencies.

(b) Variable Phase Angle Circuit:

Consider the circuit as shown in Fig. 4.23.

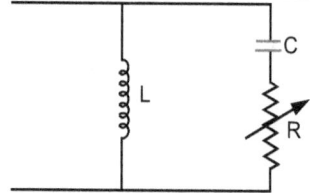

Fig. 4.23 : Variable phase and constant impedance circuit

Impedance of the circuit is

$$Z = j\omega L \parallel \left(R - \frac{j}{\omega C}\right)$$

$$Z = \frac{j\omega L \cdot \left(R - \frac{j}{\omega C}\right)}{j\omega L + R - \frac{j}{\omega C}}$$

If at a given frequency ω,

$$\omega L = \frac{2}{\omega C}$$

Then,

$$Z = \frac{j\left(\frac{2}{\omega C}\right)\left(R - \frac{j}{\omega C}\right)}{R + \frac{2j}{\omega C} - \frac{j}{\omega C}}$$

$$Z = \frac{2}{\omega C} \angle 90° - 2 \tan^{-1}\left(\frac{1}{\omega RC}\right)$$

As R is varied then the impedance magnitude $\left(\frac{2}{\omega C}\right)$ is constant but phase angle varies from $+30°$ at $R = \infty$ to $-90°$ at $R = 0$.

4.6.7 Applications of Parallel RCL Circuit

1. Parallel RLC circuit or an antiresonant circuit is used to achieve impedance transformation.

Impedance transformation is necessary to match the resistances of the generator and load in all the applications for the maximum power transfer. To mention a few applications, where impedance transform is required are radio transmitters and common emitter amplifier.

When a radio transmitter having output impedance of the order of few kilo ohms is coupled with an antenna having very small resistance (75 Ω – typical value) there is a mismatch, hence maximum power cannot be transferred.

Parallel resonant circuit offer a purely resistive impedance at antiresonance. At antiresonance

$$Z_{ar} = \frac{L}{CR_L}$$

R_L is negligible

$$Z_{ar} = \frac{L}{C}$$

∴ Thus, Z_{ar} depends on ratio $\frac{L}{C}$, so by varying the ratio $\frac{L}{C}$, the value of Z_{ar} can be varied.

2. Currents through the inductor and a capacitor are Q times the supplied current at antiresonance

$$I_L = QI$$
$$I_C = QI$$

Antiresonant circuit can be used as current amplifier.

4.6.8 Summary of Parallel Resonant Circuit

The characteristics of a parallel resonance are given as:

1. At antiresonance, the input impedance is maximum or the input admittance is minimum.
2. An antiresonance, circuit is purely resistive and hence the power factor is unity. Current is minimum at f_{ar}
3. The circuit is capacitive for frequencies above f_{ar}, (i.e. $f > f_{ar}$). It is inductive for frequency below f_{ar} (i.e. $f < f_{ar}$).
4. At antiresonance, parallel RLC circuit acts as a current amplifier where $I_L = QI$ and $I_C = QI$.
5. Quality factor is given as:

$$Q = \frac{R}{\omega_{ar} L} = \omega_{ar} CR$$

6. The resonant frequency is given

$$f_{ar} = \frac{1}{2\pi} \sqrt{\frac{1}{LC} - \frac{R^2}{L^2}} = f_r \sqrt{\frac{1-1}{Q^2}}$$

Antiresonance is possible when $\frac{1}{LC} > \frac{R^2}{L^2}$.

7. R_g, generator resistance must be very high for high selectivity in the parallel RLC circuit.
8. Bandwidth $= \frac{f_{ar}}{a}\left[1 + \frac{Z_{ar}}{R_g}\right]$. $f_{ar} = \sqrt{f_1 f_2}$
9. $f_{ar} = \sqrt{f_1 f_2}$ above f_1 and f_2 are half power frequencies and f_{ar} is geometric mean of f_1 and f_2.

4.7 NUMERICALS ON PARALLEL RESONANT CIRCUITS

Example 4.11 :

Find the bandwidth of the antiresonant circuit with the following conditions:

(i) Q of the circuits inductive branch is 100.
(ii) Frequency of unity power factors is 1 MHz.
(iii) Value of inductance = 100 μH.
(iv) Internal resistance of generator is 10 kΩ.

Solution : Given: Q of inductive branch = 100, f_r = 1 MHz, L = 100 μH, R_g = 10 kΩ.

To calculate: BW = To calculate bandwidth

$$BW = \frac{f_{ar}}{Q}\left[1 + \frac{Z_{ar}}{R_g}\right]$$

$$= f_{ar}\left[1 + \frac{1}{C R_L \cdot R_g}\right]$$

Let us calculate BW. We need to calculate C, R_L.

(i) To calculate capacitance value:

$$f_{ar} = \frac{1}{2\pi\sqrt{LC}}\sqrt{1 - \frac{1}{Q^2}}$$

$$1 \times 10^6 = \frac{1}{2\pi\sqrt{100 \times 10^{-6}}\sqrt{C}}\sqrt{1 - \frac{1}{100^2}}$$

$$C = \frac{1}{(2\pi)^2 (100 \times 10^{-6})(1 \times 10^6)^2}\sqrt{1 - \frac{1}{100^2}}$$

$$\boxed{C = 0.2533 \text{ nF}}$$

(ii) To calculate value of R_L:

$$Q = \frac{\omega_r L}{R}$$

∴ $$100 = \frac{2 \times \pi \times 1 \times 10^6 \times 100 \times 10^{-6}}{R}$$

$$\boxed{R = 6.2831 \, \Omega}$$

(iii) To calculate Z_{ar}:

$$Z_{ar} = \frac{L}{CR_L} = \frac{100 \times 10^{-6}}{0.2533 \times 10^{-9} \times 6.2831} = 62.833 \text{ k}\Omega$$

$$\boxed{Z_{ar} = 62.833 \text{ k}\Omega}$$

(iv) To calculate bandwidth:

$$BW = \frac{f_{ar}}{Q}\left[1 + \frac{Z_{ar}}{R_g}\right]$$

$$BW = \frac{1 \times 10^6}{100}\left[1 + \frac{62.833 \times 10^3}{10 \times 10^3}\right]$$

$$\boxed{BW = 72.833 \text{ kHz}}$$

In this example, Z_{ar} can alternatively be calculated using $Z_{ar} = R_L(1 + Q^2) = 6.2831 (1 + 100^2) = 62.83$ kΩ. So no need to calculate value of C.

Example 4.12:

For a parallel resonant circuit:

(i) Specify the value of the circuit capacitor.
(ii) Calculate the resistance of the circuit at parallel resonance.
(iii) What is the absolute bandwidth of the resonant circuit?
(iv) What is the bandwidth of the circuit when it is matched with the generator impedance?

Assume Q = 75, L = 120 µH and the resonating frequency of 1 MHz.

Solution : Given: L = 120 µH, Q = 75, f_{ar} = 1 × 10^6 Hz.

To calculate: C, R_L, Z_{ar}, BW, BW when R_g = Z_{ar}.

(i) To calculate value of capacitor:

$$f_{ar} = \frac{1}{2\pi\sqrt{LC}}\sqrt{1 + \frac{1}{Q^2}}$$

$$1 \times 10^6 = \frac{1}{2\pi\sqrt{120 \times 10^{-6}}\sqrt{C}}\sqrt{1 - \frac{1}{75^2}}$$

$$C = \frac{1}{(2\pi \times 1 \times 10^6)^2(120 \times 10^{-6})}\left[1 - \frac{1}{75^2}\right]$$

$$\boxed{C = 208.9 \text{ pF}}$$

(ii) Resistance of coil, R_{coil}:

$$Q = \frac{\omega_{ar} L}{R}$$

$$75 = \frac{2 \times \pi \times 1 \times 10^6 \times 120 \times 10^{-6}}{R}$$

$$\boxed{R_L = 10.05 \text{ Ω}}$$

(iii) The resistance of circuit at resonance:

i.e. Z_{ar} or R_{ar}

$$Z_{ar} = \frac{1}{CR_L}$$

or $$Z_{ar} = R_L(1+Q^2)$$

$$Z_{ar} = \frac{120 \times 10^{-6}}{(208.9 \times 10^{-12})(10.05)}$$

$$\boxed{Z_{ar} = 57.157 \text{ k}\Omega}$$

(iv) **Absolute bandwidth is given by:**

$$BW = \frac{f_{ar}}{Q} = \frac{1 \times 10^6}{75}$$

$$\boxed{BW = 13.33 \text{ k}\Omega}$$

(v) **When it is matched condition $R_g = Z_{ar}$:**

∴ $$BW = \frac{f_{ar}}{Q}\left[1 + \frac{Z_{ar}}{R_g}\right] = 2\frac{f_{ar}}{Q} = 26.66 \text{ k}\Omega$$

$$\boxed{BW = 26.66 \text{ k}\Omega}$$

Example 4.13:

In the circuit shown in Fig. 4.24 the inductance of 0.1 H having Q factor of 5 is in parallel with capacitor. Determine the value of capacitance and coil resistance at resonant frequency of 500 rad/sec.

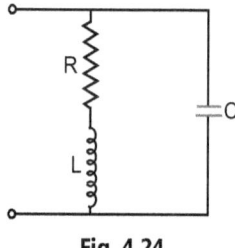

Fig. 4.24

Sol.: Given: $f_r = 500$ rad/sec., $L = 0.1$ H, $Q = 5$.

(i) **To calculate R_L:**

$$Q = \frac{\omega_{ar} L}{R}$$

$$5 = \frac{500 \times 0.1}{R}$$

$$\boxed{R_L = 10 \, \Omega}$$

(ii) To calculate value of capacitance:

$$f_{ar} = \frac{1}{2\pi}\sqrt{\frac{1}{LC} - \frac{R_L^2}{L^2}}$$

$$\omega_{ar}^2 = \left(\frac{1}{LC} - \frac{R_L^2}{L^2}\right)$$

$$500^2 = \frac{1}{(0.1)C} - \frac{10^2}{(0.1)^2}$$

$$\frac{1}{0.1\,C} = 250000 + 10000$$

$$C = 38.46 \times 10^{-6}\,F$$

$$\boxed{C = 38.46\,\mu F}$$

Example 4.14 :

A parallel resonant circuit has a coil of 150 µH with Q of 60 and resonated at 1 MHz.
(i) Specify the value of required capacitor.
(ii) What is the circuit impedance at resonance?
(iii) What is the resistance of inductor?
(iv) If Q is reduced to 4 by adding additional series resistance, then how much resistance is needed?

Solution : Given: $L = 150\,\mu H$, $Q = 60$, $f_{ar} = 1$ MHz. To calculate C, R_L, Z_{ar}, New Q, New f_{ar}.

(i) **The value of capacitance:**

$$f_{ar} = \frac{1}{2\pi\sqrt{LC}}\sqrt{1 - \frac{1}{Q^2}}$$

$$1 \times 10^6 = \frac{1}{2\pi\sqrt{150 \times 10^{-6}}\sqrt{C}}\sqrt{1 - \frac{1}{60^2}}$$

$$C = \frac{1}{(2\pi \times 1 \times 10^6)^2 \cdot (150 \times 10^{-6})}\left[1 - \frac{1}{3600}\right]$$

$$C = 168.821 \times 10^{-12}\,F$$

$$\boxed{C = 168.82\,pF}$$

(ii) **The resistance of coil:**

$$Q = \frac{\omega_{ar} L}{R_L}$$

$$60 = \frac{2\pi \times 1 \times 10^6 \times 150 \times 10^{-6}}{R_L}$$

$$\boxed{R_L = 15.7\,\Omega}$$

(iii) The impedance of the parallel circuit:

$$Z_{ar} = \frac{L}{CR_L} = \frac{150 \times 10^{-6}}{168.82 \times 10^{-12} \times 15.7}$$

$$\boxed{Z_{ar} = 56.593 \text{ k}\Omega}$$

(iv) New quality factor can be expressed in terms of additional resistance:

$$Q' = \frac{\omega'_{ar} L}{(R_L + R')}$$

We will thus, need to calculate ω'_{ar}.

$$\therefore \quad f'_{ar} = \frac{1}{2\pi \sqrt{LC}} \sqrt{1 - \frac{1}{Q^2}}$$

$$f'_{ar} = \frac{1}{2\pi \sqrt{150 \times 10^{-6} \times 168.82 \times 10^{-12}}} \sqrt{1 - \frac{1}{4^2}}$$

$$\boxed{f'_{ar} = 968.385 \text{ kHz}}$$

$$\therefore \quad Q' = \frac{\omega'_{ar} L}{(R_L + R')}$$

where R' is the additional resistance to be added.

$$(R_L + R') = \frac{2\pi f'_{ar} L}{Q'}$$

$$(15.7 + R') = \frac{2\pi \times 968.385 \times 10^3}{4}$$

$$\boxed{R' = 212.417 \, \Omega}$$

Example 4.15 :

Two impedances $Z_1 = 20 + 10j$ and $Z_2 = 10 - 30j$ are connected in parallel and this combination is connected in series with $Z_3 = 30 + XJ$. Find the value of X which will produce resonance.

Solution :

Given:
$Z_1 = 20 + 10j$
$Z_2 = 10 - 30j$
$Z_3 = 30 + XJ$

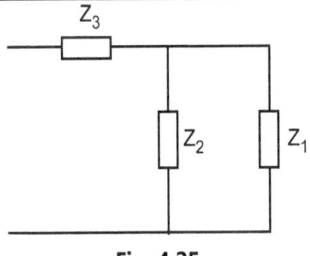

Fig. 4.25

To calculate X:
(i) To find the total impedance:

$$Z_T = Z_3 + (Z_1 \| Z_2) = Z_3 + \frac{Z_1 Z_2}{Z_1 + Z_2}$$

$$Z = Z_3 + \frac{Z_1 Z_2}{Z_1 + Z_2}$$

$$Z = (30 + jX) + \frac{(20 + j10)(10 - j30)}{(20 + j10) + (10 - j30)}$$

$$Z = 30 + jX + \frac{200 + j100 + j600 + 300}{30 - j20}$$

$$Z = 30 + jX + \frac{500 - j500}{30 - j20}$$

$$Z = 30 + jX + \frac{[500(1-j)][30 + j20]}{30^2 + 20^2}$$

$$Z = 30 + jX + \frac{500}{1300}[30 + j20 - 30j + 20]$$

$$Z = 30 + jX + \frac{5}{13}[50 - j10]$$

$$Z = 30 + \frac{250}{13} + j\left[X - \frac{50}{13}\right]$$

To circuit will resonate, if imaginary part is zero.

∴ $\quad X - \frac{50}{13} = 0$

$X = \frac{50}{13}$

$\boxed{X = 3.846 \, \Omega}$

Example 4.16 :

From the basics obtain the expression for the resonance frequency in the circuit shown in Fig. 4.26.

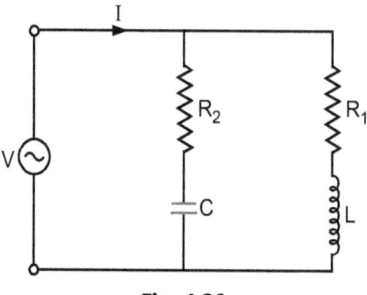

Fig. 4.26

Solution : The two branches connected in parallel will produce resonance when the resultant current through combination i.e. I, is in phase with voltage V. The condition of parallel resonance is that the impedance of the parallel combination is purely resistive.

The admittance of branch containing:

L is:

$$Y_L = \frac{1}{R_1 + j\omega L}$$

$$= \frac{R_1 - j\omega L}{(R_1 + j\omega L)(R_1 - j\omega L)}$$

$$Y_L = \frac{R_1 - jX_l}{R_1^2 + X_L^2}$$

where, $X_L = \omega L$

The admittance of branch containing C is

$$Y_C = \frac{1}{R_2 - \frac{j}{\omega C}}$$

$$= \frac{R_2 + jX_C}{R_2^2 + X_C^2}$$

Total admittance Y is given by

$$Y = Y_L + Y_C$$

$$Y = \frac{R_1 + jX_C}{R_1^2 + X_L^2} + \frac{R_2 + jX_C}{R_2^2 + X_C^2}$$

$$Y = \left(\frac{R_1}{R_1^2 + X_L^2} + \frac{R_2}{R_2^2 + X_C^2}\right) + \left(\frac{X_C}{R_2^2 + X_C^2} - \frac{X_L}{R_1^2 + X_L^2}\right)$$

Unit IV | 4.62

At resonance, we have unity power factor is zero condition

$$\therefore \quad \frac{X_C}{R_2^2 + X_C^2} - \frac{X_L}{R_1^2 + X_L^2} = 0$$

$$\frac{X_C}{R_2^2 + X_C^2} = \frac{X_L}{R_1^2 + X_L^2}$$

$$\frac{\frac{1}{\omega_{ar} C}}{R_2^2 + \left(\frac{1}{\omega_{ar} C}\right)^2} = \frac{\omega_{ar} L}{R_1^2 + \omega_{ar}^2 L^2}$$

$$\therefore \quad R_1^2 + \omega_{ar}^2 L^2 = \omega_{ar}^2 LC \left(R_2^2 + \frac{1}{\omega_{ar}^2 C^2}\right)$$

$$R_1^2 + \omega_{ar}^2 L^2 = \omega_{ar}^2 LC R_2^2 + \frac{L}{C}$$

$$\omega_{ar}^2 (L^2 - LCR_2^2) = \frac{L}{C} - R_1^2$$

$$(LC)\,\omega_{ar}^2 = \frac{\frac{L}{C} + R_1^2}{\frac{L}{C} - R_2^2}$$

$$\boxed{\omega_{ar} = \frac{1}{\sqrt{LC}} \sqrt{\frac{R_1^2 - \frac{L}{C}}{R_2^2 - \frac{L}{C}}}}$$

$$\boxed{f_{ar} = \frac{1}{2\pi\sqrt{LC}} \sqrt{\frac{R_1^2 - \frac{L}{C}}{R_2^2 - \frac{L}{C}}}}$$

where, f_{ar} : Antiresonating frequency
R_1 : Ohmic resistance of coil
R_2 : Leakage and dielectric loss resistance of capacitor

Example 4.17 :

In the circuit of Fig. 4.27 calculate resonant frequency (ω_{ar}). If R_1 is increased what is the maximum value of R_1 for which there is a resonant frequency?

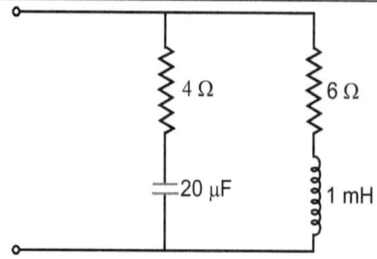

Fig. 4.27

Solution : $R_2 = R_L = 6\,\Omega$, $R_1 = R_C = 4\,\Omega$, $L = 1$ mH, $C = 20$ μF.

To calculate: ω_{ar} and maximum value of R_L

(i) To calculate ω_{ar}:

In case when resistance is present in both the branches:

$$\omega_{ar} = \frac{1}{\sqrt{LC}} \sqrt{\frac{R_L^2 - \frac{L}{C}}{R_C^2 - \frac{L}{C}}} = \frac{1}{\sqrt{1\times 10^{-3} \times 20\times 10^{-6}}} \sqrt{\frac{6^2 - \frac{1\times 10^{-3}}{20\times 10^{-6}}}{4^2 - \frac{1\times 10^{-3}}{20\times 10^{-6}}}}$$

$$= \frac{1}{\sqrt{20\times 10^{-9}}} \sqrt{\frac{36 - 50}{16 - 50}}$$

$$\boxed{\omega_{ar} = 2911.62 \text{ rad/sec.}}$$

(ii) To calculate $R_{1\,(max)}$ i.e. R_C maximum:

$$\omega_{ar} = \frac{1}{\sqrt{LC}} \sqrt{\frac{R_L^2 - \frac{L}{C}}{R_C^2 - \frac{L}{C}}}$$

So if $R_C^2 = \frac{L}{C}$, then denominator = 0 and $\omega_{ar} = \infty$

Therefore, maximum value should be selected as follows:

$$R_C = R_1 = \sqrt{\frac{L}{C}}$$

$$R_C = R_1 = \sqrt{\frac{10^{-3}}{20\times 10^{-6}}}$$

$$R_C = \sqrt{50} = 7.071\,\Omega$$

At this value of R_C, $f_{ar} = \infty$.

∴ Maximum value of R_C must be less than 7

∴ $\boxed{R_{C\,(max)} < 7}$

Example 4.18 :

Find exact resonant frequency of the network shown in Fig. 4.31. Also find 'Q_0' at that frequency.

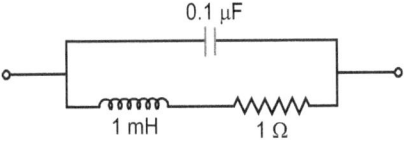

Fig. 4.28

Solution : Given: C = 0.1 µF, L = 1 mH, R = 10 Ω. To calculate f_{ar}, Q.

(i) To calculate f_{ar}:

$$f_{ar} = \frac{1}{2\pi}\sqrt{\frac{1}{LC} - \frac{R^2L}{L^2}}$$

$$= \frac{1}{2\pi}\sqrt{\frac{1}{1\times 10^{-3}\times 0.1\times 10^{-6}} - \frac{10\times 10\times 1\times 10^{-3}}{(1\times 10^{-3})^2}}$$

$$\boxed{f_{ar} = 15.835 \text{ kHz}}$$

(ii) To calculate Q:

$$Q = \frac{\omega_{ar}L}{R}$$

$$Q = \frac{2\times\pi\times 15.83\times 10^3\times 1\times 10^{-3}}{10}$$

$$Q = 9.95$$

$$\boxed{Q \approx 10}$$

Example 4.19 :

Find 'R_L' for resonance circuit of Fig. 4.29. Comment on R_L obtained.

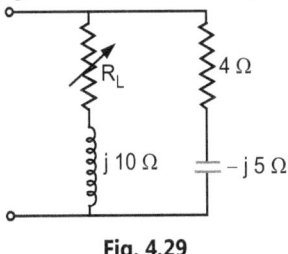

Fig. 4.29

Solution : For the resonance, the susceptance in admittance must be zero.

$$Y = \frac{1}{R+j10} + \frac{1}{4-j5}$$

$$Y = \frac{R-j10}{R^2+100} + \frac{4+j5}{(4)^2+5^2}$$

$$Y = \frac{R-j10}{R^2+100} + \frac{4+j5}{41}$$

$$Y = \left[\frac{R}{R^2+100} + \frac{4}{41}\right] + j\left[\frac{5}{41} - \frac{10}{R^2+100}\right]$$

Susceptance part must be zero.

$$\frac{5}{41} - \frac{10}{R^2+100} = 0$$

$$\frac{5}{41} = \frac{10}{R^2+100}$$

$$5R^2 + 500 = 410$$

$$R^2 = -\frac{90}{5} = -18$$

Ans.:

$$\boxed{R = \sqrt{18}\,\Omega}$$

Thus, for resonance, value of R is negative i.e. R is imaginary. This clearly shows that in the circuit, resonance is impossible for positive values of R.

Example 4.20 :

Find the value of 'L' for which the circuit in Fig. 4.30 is resonant at a frequency of $\omega_0 = 1000$ rad/sec.

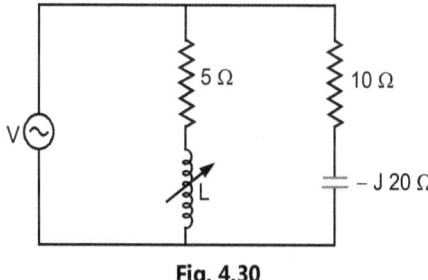

Fig. 4.30

Solution : Given: $R_L = 5$, $R_C = 10$, $C = -j20\,\Omega$.

To calculate :

Let the reactance offered by the inductance is jX_L. Then the total admittance of parallel resonant circuit looking from source side is given by

$$Y_T = Y_L + Y_C$$

$$Y_T = \frac{1}{5+jX_L} + \frac{1}{10-j20}$$

$$Y_T = \frac{5-jX_L}{5^2+X_L^2} + \frac{10+j20}{10^2+20^2}$$

$$Y_T = \frac{5}{25+X_L^2} - \frac{jX_L}{25+X_L^2} + \frac{10}{500} + \frac{j20}{500}$$

$$Y_T = \left[\frac{5}{25+X_L^2} + \frac{10}{500}\right] + j\left[\frac{20}{500} - \frac{X_L}{25+X_L^2}\right]$$

To have resonance, the imaginary term must be zero.

Hence, to obtain the condition of resonance, equate susceptance to zero.

$$\frac{20}{500} - \frac{X_L}{25+X_L^2} = 0$$

$$\frac{X_L}{25+X_L^2} = \frac{1}{25}$$

$$X_L^2 - 25X_L + 25 = 0$$

Solving quadratic equation for X_L,

$$X_L = \frac{+25 \pm \sqrt{25^2 - 4 \times 25 \times 1}}{2}$$

$$X_L = \frac{25 \pm \sqrt{0.525}}{2}$$

$$X_L = \frac{25 \pm 22.9128}{2}$$

$$X_L = 23.9564 \ \Omega$$

or $\quad X_L = 1.0436$

But $\quad X_L = \omega L$

∴ $\quad \omega L = 23.9564 \ \Omega$ or 1.0436

$\quad \omega = 1000$ rad/sec.

∴ $\boxed{L = 23.9564 \text{ mH or } 1.0436 \text{ mH}}$

4.8 COMPARISON OF SERIES AND PARALLEL RESONATING CIRCUITS

Series Resonating	Parallel Resonant
1. Fig. (a)	Fig. (b)
2. In series resonating circuit, resonance is possible at all values of R.	In parallel, resonating is possible only when $\frac{1}{LC} > \frac{R^2}{L^2}$.
3. Series resonating circuit acts as a voltage amplified at f_r.	Parallel resonating circuit acts a current amplifier at f_{ar}.
4. R_q must be for high selectivity.	R_q must be high for high selectivity.
5. At $f > f_r$ – Circuit is inductive $f = f_r$ – Resistive $f < f_r$ – Capacitive	$f > f_{ar}$ – circuit is capacitive $f = f_{ar}$ – resistive $f < f_r$ – inductive
6. At f_r: Impedance is minimum. Admittance is maximum. Current is maximum.	5. At f_{ar}: Impedance is maximum. Admittance is minimum. Current is minimum.

Important Formulae in Series and Parallel Resonating Circuit

	Series RLC Circuit	Parallel RLC Circuit
1. Diagram	Fig.	Fig.
2. Resonating frequency	$f_o = \dfrac{1}{2\pi\sqrt{LC}}$	$f_{ar} = \dfrac{1}{2\pi}\sqrt{\dfrac{1}{LC} - \dfrac{R^2}{L^2}}$ $f_{ar} = f_o\sqrt{1 - \dfrac{1}{Q^2}}$

3. Quality factor	$Q = \dfrac{\omega_r L}{C} = \dfrac{1}{\omega_r RC}$ $Q = \dfrac{1}{R}\sqrt{\dfrac{L}{C}}$		$Q = \dfrac{\omega_{ar} L}{C}$ $Q = \dfrac{1}{\omega_{ar} CR}$
4. Reactancy type	Above f_o : Inductive At f_o : Resistive Below f_o : Capacitive		Above f_{ar} : Capacitive At f_{ar} : Resistive Below f_{ar} : Inductive
5. Impedance	$Z_r = R$ at resonance $Z = R[1 + jQ\delta(2-\delta)]$ ... Near f_r $\delta = \dfrac{f - f_r}{f_r}$		$Z_{ar} = \dfrac{L}{CR_L}$ $= R(1 + Q^2)$ ... at F_{ar} $Z = \dfrac{Z_{ar}}{1 + j2\delta Q}$ ...near f_{ar}
6. Voltage or current at resonance	$V_L = Q \cdot V$ $V_L = Q \cdot V$		$I_C = Q \cdot I$ $I_L = Q \cdot I$
7. Frequencies of maximum voltage (V_L and V_C)	$f_L = \dfrac{f_r}{\sqrt{1 - \dfrac{R^2 C}{2L}}}$ $f_L > f_o$ $f_C = f_o \sqrt{1 - \dfrac{R^2 C}{2L}}$ $f_C < f_o$		
8. Bandwidth	$BW = \dfrac{R}{2\pi L} = \dfrac{f_r}{Q}$ BW match $= \dfrac{2 f_r}{Q}$		$BW = \dfrac{f_{ar}}{Q}\left[1 + \dfrac{R_{ar}}{R_g}\right] \quad R_{ar} = Z_{ar}$ $BW = \dfrac{f_{ar}}{Q_o}\left[1 + \dfrac{Z_{ar}}{R_g}\right]$

EXERCISE

1. Define and explain the figure of merit (Q) of an inductor and a capacitor on what factor does Q depend.
2. Draw reactance curve characteristics for series and a parallel resonant circuit illustrating condition of circuit at different frequencies.
3. Series resonant circuit acts a voltage amplifier. Justify.
4. The voltage across L and C at resonance is not the maximum voltage that can appear across it. Justify and derive the expression for frequency at which the voltage across L and C are maximum.
5. Derive the expression for an impedance of a series resonant circuit in terms of Q and δ.

6. Derive the expression for bandwidth of series resonating circuit and prove that resonant frequency is geometric mean of two half power frequencies.
7. Explain the effect of quality factor Q on the selectivity and the bandwidth of a series and a parallel resonating circuit
8. Explain the effect of the generator resistance R_g on the bandwidth and the selectivity of a series and a parallel resonating circuit.
9. Obtain an expression of the frequency of resonance of a series and a parallel resonating circuit.
10. Parallel resonant circuit is a current amplifier justify.
11. Derive the expression for the bandwidth of an antiresonant circuit.
12. Give important properties and applications of series and parallel resonant circuits.
13. Two impedances $Z_1 = a + Jb$ and $Z_2 = C - Jd$ are connected in : (a) series (b) parallel. Determine the condition of resonance in each case.
14. A series RLC circuit consists of a resistance R = 10 Ω, inductance L = 0.2 H and capacitance C = 0.2 µF. Calculate the frequency of resonance. A 10 volts sinusoidal voltage at the frequency of resonance is applied across the circuit. Draw the phasor diagram showing the value of each phasor. Also calculate values (i) current and (ii) voltage across R, C and L and draw the phasor diagram when 10 volt 850 Hz voltage is applied to the circuit.

Ans.: V_r = 10 V
V_C = 10^3 V
V_L = 10^3 V
I = 76.15 mA

15. A series RLC circuit consists of a resistance R = 20 Ω, inductance L = 0.01 H and capacitance C = 0.04 µF. Calculate the frequency of resonance. If a 10 volts voltage of frequency equal to the frequency of resonance is applied to this circuit, calculate the values of voltages V_C and V_L across C and L respectively. Find the frequencies at which these voltages V_C and V_L are maximum.

Ans.: F_r = 7960 Hz
V_L = 250 V
V_C = 250 V
f_C = 7955 Hz
f_L = 7960 Hz

16. A coil of R = 10 Ω, L = 0.5 H is connected in series with a capacitor. The current is maximum when f = 50 Hz. A second capacitor is connected in parallel with this circuit. What capacitance must it have so that the combination acts like a non-inductive resistor at 100 Hz. Calculate the total current supplied in each case if the applied voltage is 220 V. **Ans.:** I = 39.55 mA

Unit - V

FILTERS

5.1 INTRODUCTION

- Concept of "Filters" is very common in our day-to-day life. We use filters at many places. e.g. Paper filter is used to remove unwanted constituents such as suspended particles in water.

  Example: Breathing masks (Filters) are used when driving in a very polluted city, etc.

- These are all the examples of mechanical filters. Similarly electrical filters do exists and are used to remove unwanted constituents such as noise or some frequency band from a electrical signal.

- An electronic filter is an electronic circuit which performs signal processing functions, specifically to remove unwanted frequency components from the signal to enhance the wanted ones or both.

- An electronic filter may also be sometimes used in circuits with sinusoidal sources of constant frequency. Ex. L, C, LC filters used for ripple rejection in the various power supplies, just after the rectifier circuits. Filter are very commonly used in telephones, TV, radio receivers and almost in every electronic circuit. Any electronic filters can roughly be classified as under:

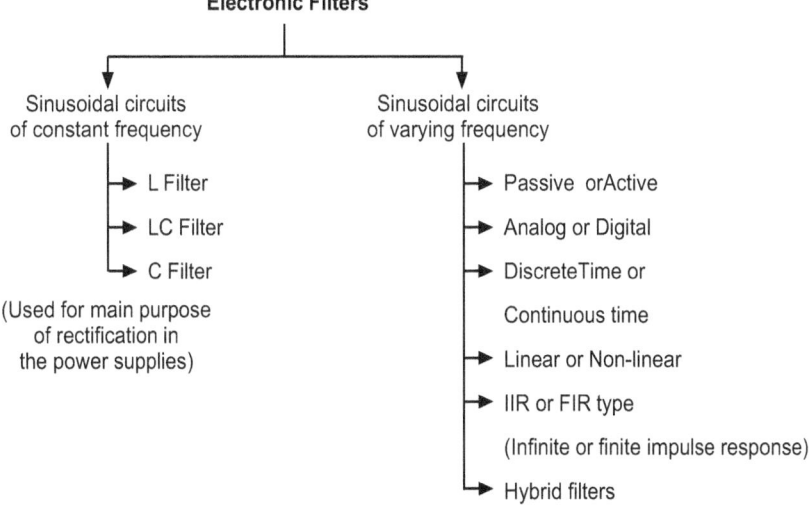

Fig. 5.1: Classification of Electronic Filters

In this chapter we will concentrate only on PASSIVE filters and analyse the effect on the o/p voltage due to the variation in the source frequency.

5.2 PASSIVE FILTERS

- Passive filters are the oldest forms of the electronic filters, which incorporates passive devices like resistors, capacitors and inductors.
- A passive filter does not have any active components like transistors or op-amps.
- Thus the output signal in case of passive filters can never have more power or amplitude than the applied that signal.
- Moreover use of inductors in the passive filters, make the circuit bulky and costly.
- The only advantage of using passive circuits is that they do not require additional power supplies for their operation.

  [op/amps need V_{cc}, V_{ee} supply for their operation. Even transistors have to be biased by V_{cc}, I_B etc. before their operation].

5.2.1 Basic Definitions

Let us now understand the basic terms associated with any filter circuit.

(a) Frequency Response:
- Filter networks are designed to separate different. Frequency bands available in an alternating input signal. Thus, when analyzing the filter network, we actually analyse the effect on voltage and current in different frequency bands, due to variation in the source frequency.
- That means we learn the response of the filter circuit (in terms of voltage, gain or current) to the changing i/p frequency. This is called as the frequency response of the circuit.

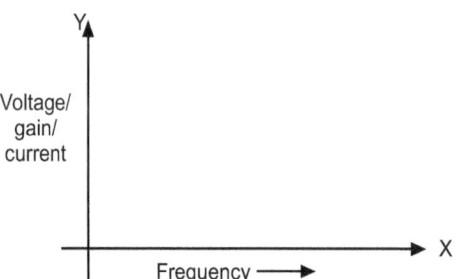

Fig. 5.2: Frequency Response: Plot of frequency Vs. Circuit parameter

- And the analysis of this behaviour is called as frequency response analysis.

(b) Cut-off Frequency:
- Speaking in terms of network filters, the cut-off frequency can loosely be defined as the frequency can loosely be defined as the frequency after which the circuit will show change in its behaviour and the response. It is the frequency which indicates the change in the band (pass band to stop band or vice versa) of the filter, thus separates the bands.
- It is actually the frequency at which the voltage gain equals 0.707 of its maximum value.

- This cut-off frequency is also referred to as the half power frequency because the load power is half of its maximum value at the this frequency.
- The output power is half of the maximum at the cut-off frequencies because:
  When the voltage gain is 0.707 of the maximum value, the output voltage is 0.707 of the maximum value. Now power = $\dfrac{(\text{Voltage})^2}{\text{Resistance}}$.
  So, when you square 0.707 we have 0.5 and so load power is half of its maximum value at the cut-off frequencies.
- Depending on the type of filter, the circuit may have one or two cut-off frequencies.
- Cut-off frequency is also referred as corner frequency.

(c) Pass Band:
- We have kept on defining a filter as the circuit which freely passes the desired band of the frequencies, while suppresses other band of frequencies. [Frequency discriminators].
- But in reality filters are not actually or physically separating the frequencies. It is the output voltage or current of the filter which prominently differs at different frequencies, thus enabling us to separate them.
- Thus, the pass band is defined as the range of frequencies for which the filter circuit responses to the input signal giving an considerable. Voltage at the output.
- In short it may be defined as the range of frequencies over which attenuation by the filter is zero, or the range of frequencies over which signals are passed from the input to the output.

(d) Stop Band or Attenuation Band:
- As the name indicates, a stop band can similarly be defined as the range of frequencies over which the filter circuit does not respond to the i/p signal giving almost no voltage at the output.
- In short it may be defined as the range of frequencies over which attenuation by the filter is infinite, or the range of frequencies over which the signals are blocked from input to the output.
- Depending on the type of the filter, the circuit may have one or two pass and stop bands.

Practically, we have one more band existing in the response of the filter circuit i.e. Transition Band. We will see this when discussing the ideal and practical filter.

5.2.2 Classification of Passive Filters

There are different types of filters existing in the electronics world. They are:
1. Low Pass Filter
2. High Pass Filter
3. Band Pass Filter
4. Band Stop Filter
5. All Pass Filter

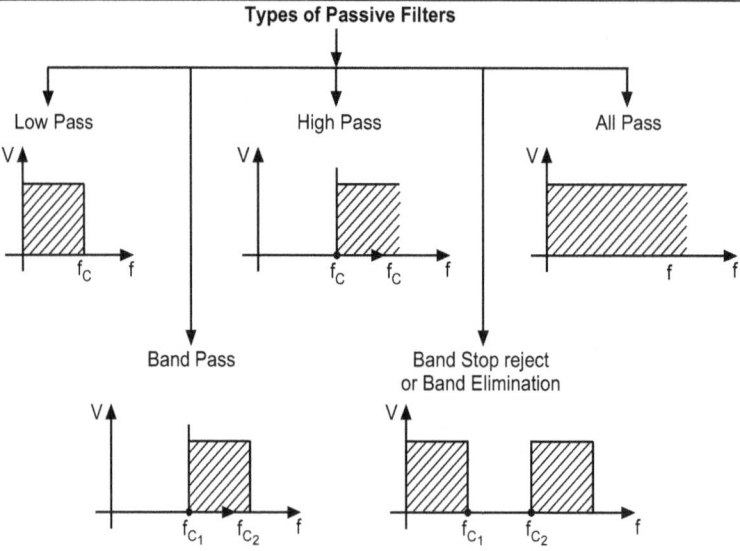

Fig. 5.3: Types of Passive Filters

1. Low Pass Filter:

A low pass filter is a circuit which responses to all the frequencies below the cut-off (f_c) frequency which attenuates or blocks the frequencies higher than the cut-off frequency. Thus, we say that low frequency signals are passed from input to the output with ideally zero and practically less attenuation. Signals falling in the band of frequencies ($0 < f < f_c$) have their magnitude ideally equal to the signal and are known as passband. Input voltage outside this band ($f_c < f < \infty$) of frequencies have their magnitude attenuated by the circuit. This band of frequencies is known as **stop band**.

Table 5.1: Low Pass Filter :
A filter that passes the frequencies lower than the cut-off frequency

Band	Frequency Range	O/P Voltage Ideal	Ideal Attenuation
Pass Band	$0 < f \leq f_c$	$V_{out} = V_{in}$	0
Stop Band	$f_c < f \leq \infty$	$V_{out} = 0$	∞

2. High Pass Filter:

- A High pass filter is a circuit which responses to all the frequencies above the cut-off (f_c). Frequency which attenuates or blocks the frequencies lower than the cut-off frequency.
- Thus, we Say that high frequency signals are passed from input to the output with ideally zero and practically less attenuation.
- Signals falling in this band of frequencies ($f_c < f$) have their magnitude ideally equal to the input signal and are known as **pass band**.

- Input voltage outside this band of frequencies (0 < f < f_c) have their magnitudes attenuated by the circuit. This band of frequencies is known as **stop band**.

3. **Band Pass Filter:**
   - A Band pass filter responses only to a particular band of frequencies and blocks the frequencies higher and lower than the desired hand.
   - It is a circuit with two cut-off frequencies f_L and f_H and has two stop hands.
   - The frequencies below f_L and above f_H are completely attenuated.
   - Only the frequencies between f_L and f_H are passed to the output.
   - This band of frequencies where ($f_L \leq f \leq f_H$) V_{out} is ideally equal to V_{in} is called as **pass band**.
   - The two bands of frequencies (f < f_L and f > f_H) i.e. below the lower cut-off and above the higher cut-off are **stop band** frequencies.

4. **Band Stop Filter:**
   - A Band stop filter rejects or blocks a particular band of frequencies and passes all the frequencies higher and lower than this band.
   - It is a circuit with two cut-off frequencies f_L and f_H and it has two pass bands.
   - The frequencies between f_L and f_H are completely blocked or attenuated by the circuit and the frequencies less than f_L and higher than f_H are passed to the output.
   - These band of frequencies where in ideally V_{out} = V_{in} [f $\leq f_L$ and f $\geq f_H$] is **stop band** frequency. [V_{out} = 0].
   - This filter is also called as **Band Stop** or **elimination** filter.

5. **All Pass Filter:**
   - All pass filter is a circuit with no stop band and has only a pass band. Because of it passes all the frequencies between zero and infinity.
   - It is strange that it still has to be called as filter. Since it zero attenuation for all the frequencies.
   - The reason it is so called is because of the effect it has on the phase of the signals passing thorough it.
   - This filter is useful when we want to produce a certain amount of phases shift for the signal being filtered without changing the amplitude.

We will however restrict our discussion and scope of analysis to only first four types of filters namely LPF, HPF, BPF, BSF. So let just summarise them:

Filter	Band	Frequency Range	Ideal output voltage	Ideal Attenuation	Ideal frequency Responses
Low Pass	Pass Stop	$0 < f \leq f_c$ $f_c < f < \infty$	$V_{out} = V_{in}$ $V_{out} = 0$	0 ∞	PB / SB at f_c
High Pass	Pass Stop	$f \leq f_c < \infty$ $0 < f < f_c$	$V_{out} = V_{in}$ $V_{out} = 0$	0 ∞	SB / PB at f_c
Band Pass	Pass Stop Stop	$f_L < f \leq f_H$ $0 < f < f_L$ $f_H < f < \infty$	$V_{out} = V_{in}$ $V_{out} = 0$ $V_{out} = 0$	0 ∞ ∞	SB / PB / SB at f_L, f_H
Band Stop	Pass Pass Stop	$0 < f < f_L$ $f_H < f < \infty$ $f_L < f < f_H$	$V_{out} = V_{in}$ $V_{out} = 0$ $V_{out} = 0$	0 0 ∞	PB / SB / PB at f_L, f_H

PB: Pass Band, SB: Stop Band

Fig. 5.4: Summary of Passive Filter

Low Pass : Passes the frequencies lower than the f_c.
High Pass : Passes the frequencies higher than the f_c.
Band Pass : Passes a band of frequencies between f_L and f_H.
Band Stop : Stops / Rejects a band of frequencies between f_L and f_H.

We have discussed one way of classifying the passive filters i.e. based on their functionality. Now each of these filters can be further classified as follows:

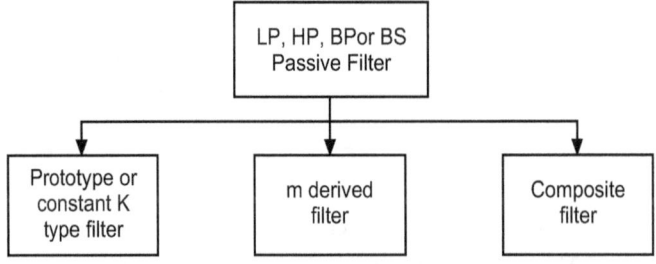

Fig. 5.5

We will be covering each of this type of filter in this chapter but at a later stage.

5.2.3 Ideal and a Practical Filter

You must have noticed that it all the discussions we had, there were always some terms like ideal and practical, may be related to voltages at the output or to the values of attenuation or frequency responses.

Now, let us understand these terms, considering an example.

Assume that you are on the sixth floor of a building and you want to reach the ground floor. Now this movement should ideally take absolutely no time. But practically even if you use an elevator with highest speed and latest technology it will still take some time (may be in ms) to reach the ground floor. So we need to understand that there is always some time elapsed in the change over of the states. No change can be sudden or instant. It will always take some time. That is the reason even the clock signal which ideally is drawn as in Fig. 5.6 (a) will in actual (practically) be as shown in Fig. 5.6 (b)

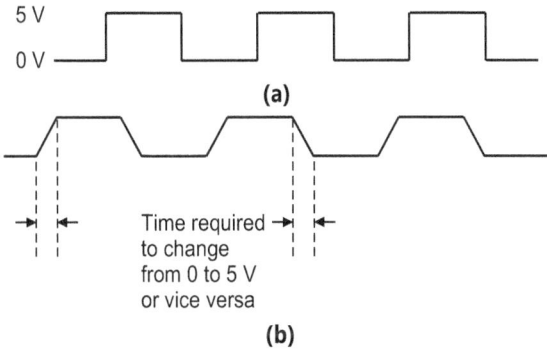

Fig. 5.6: Ideal and Practical Clock

- Now let us relate this concept with the filters.

  A filter circuit has two bands, pass band and stop band, following each other.

  Table 5.2

	Attenuation	V_{out}
Pass band	0	V_{in}
Stop band	∞	0

- Thus, it must now be clear that when the band changes from pass band to stop band, attenuation changes from 0 to ∞ and V_{out} change from V_{in} to 0.
- So this change over cannot be instant or sudden, as expected ideally. Practically it is gradual and takes time.
- As will be discussed in the point of filter fundamentals, filter is made up of reactive elements like inductors and capacitors, which oppose the change in current and voltage respectively. So change of voltage and current from 0 to maximum value cannot be instant.

- So an ideal frequency response, say for low pass filter is as shown in Fig. 5.7 (a) and a practical frequency curve would be as in Fig. 5.7 (b).

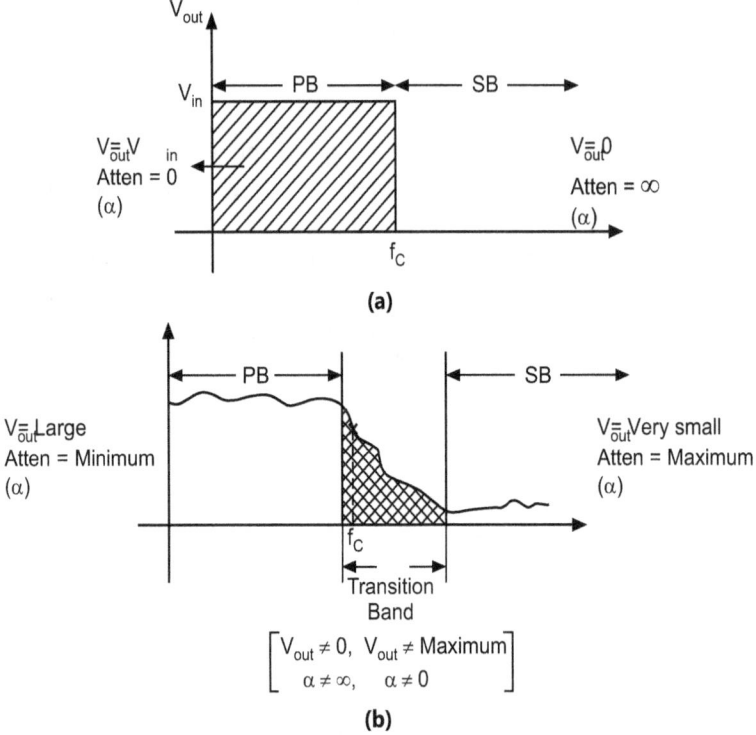

Fig. 5.7 : Ideal and Practical Frequency Response (LPF)

- As seen in the diagram, the roll-off region between the pass band and the stop band, where V_{out} is neither zero nor equal to V_{in} and even the attenuation is neither infinity nor-zero, is called as transition band.
- This transition band does not exist in the ideal response for a filter. It is sometimes called a **brick wall response**, because the right edge of the rectangle looks like a brick wall.

Summary:

Ideal frequency curves or response of any filter differ from the practical response in three ways:

	Ideal Filter Response	Practical Filter Response
1.	Attenuation α is zero in pass band infinite in stop band	Attenuation α is minimum is pass band maximum in stop band
2.	Output voltage is equal to V_{in} in pass band 0 is stop band	Output voltage is maximum ($\neq V_{in}$) in PB very less ($\neq 0$) in SB
3.	There exists no transition band in ideal response (vertical transition)	There exists a transition band in practical response.

5.3 FILTER FUNDAMENTALS

- We have discussed about the pass and the stop bands which every filter must have.
- Let us now discuss about the:
- Type of component [R, L or C] required to build any filter circuit.
- Necessary conditions which these components should satisfy so that filter operates in both bands.
- Frequency range of these bands.

  Filters are realized using symmetrical T or π sections as shown in Fig. 5.8.

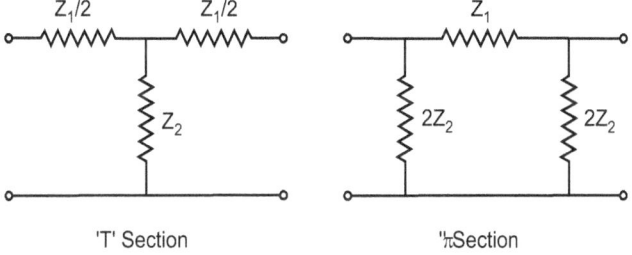

Fig. 5.8 : Symmetrical T and π Sections

- Now, as we are discussing passive filters in this chapter, so obviously we have to choose between R, L and C as the values of Z_1 and Z_2.
- So the possible combinations would be having a filter circuit consisting of

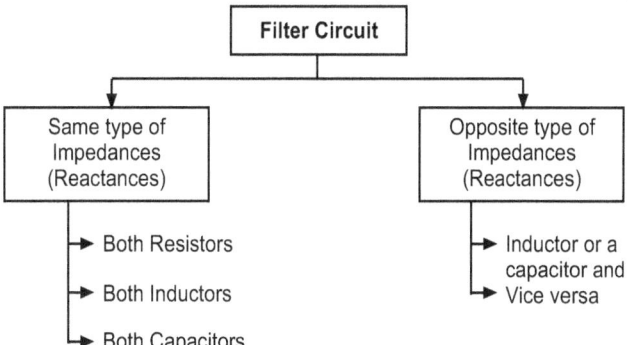

Fig. 5.9

- Before giving mathematical treatment or any analysis of all these possibilities, to reach a conclusion about the combination of Z_1 and Z_2, let us just logically think about the possible combination.

5.4 CONSTANT K / PROTOTYPE FILTERS

- Z_1 and Z_2 of a filter circuit are opposite type of reactance's than,

$$Z_1 \cdot Z_2 = R_K^2$$

where k is a constant and it is independent of frequency. It is also called as a design impedance.

Ex.: $Z_1 = j\omega L \quad Z_2 = -\dfrac{j}{\omega c}$

then,

$$Z_1 Z_2 = \dfrac{L}{C} = R_K^2$$

- Networks or filter sections for which this relation holds are called as **constant k filters**.
- These filters, either of T or π configuration are also known as **prototype** because more complex filters can be derived from them.

5.5 CONSTANT K LOW PASS FILTER

- A lowpass filter will ideally pass all the frequencies lower than (below) the cut-off frequencies. It will block the frequencies higher than the cut-off frequencies.
- We use inductor in the series arm and a capacitor in a shunt arm to achieve this kind of frequency response.
- (L) $\dfrac{Z_1}{2} + \dfrac{Z_1}{2} = Z_1$ series arm

  (C) $\dfrac{Z_2}{2} \| \dfrac{Z_2}{2} = Z_2$ shunt arm

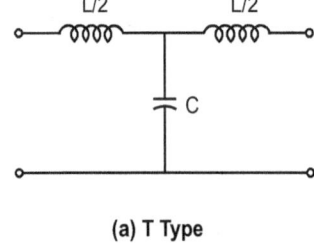
(a) T Type

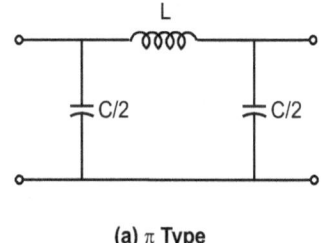
(a) π Type

Fig. 5.10 : Constant k LP filters

5.5.1 Operation of a Constant k LPF

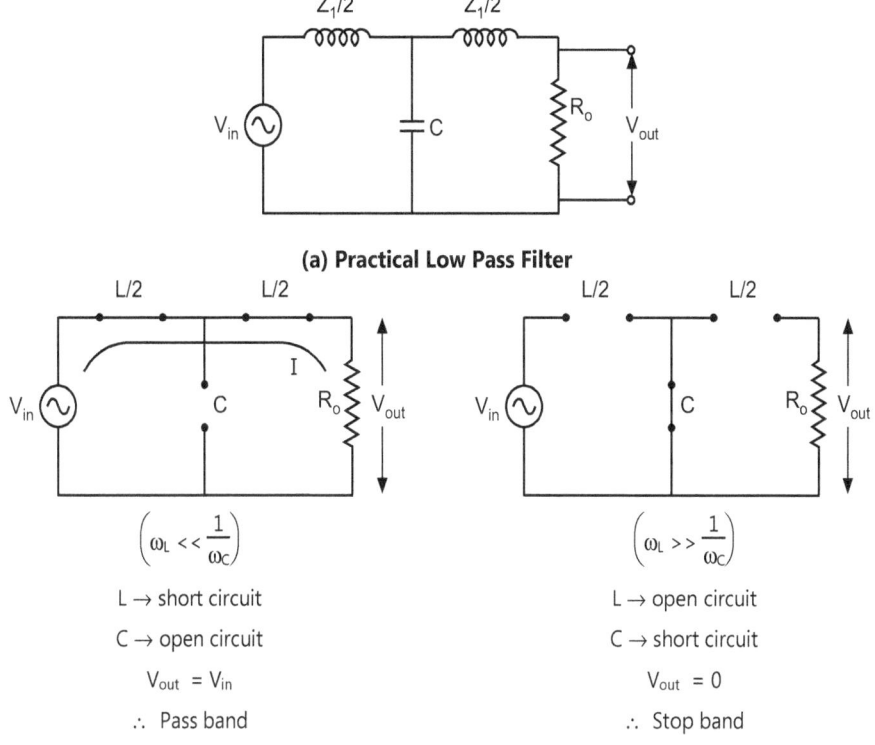

(a) Practical Low Pass Filter

(b) An approximate equivalent low frequency   (c) An approximate equivalent higher frequency

Fig. 5.11 : Operation of a low pass filter

- Though resistors on their own have no frequency selective property, they are still added and used in all the practical circuits [to the inductors and capacitors to determine the time constant of the circuit].
- At low frequencies the reactance (ωL) of an indicator is small when compared to reactance $\dfrac{1}{\omega C}$ of a capacitor and so effectively, L functions as a short circuit and passes input signal to the output and C functions as a open circuit.
- For low frequencies output voltage V_o taken across the resistance R is almost equal to the input sinusoidal voltage. This is pass band of the circuit.
- At higher frequencies, the reactance ωL of inductors starts increasing and becomes much larger than the reactance of a capacitor.

$$\omega L \gg \dfrac{1}{\omega C}$$

So, it is acts as open circuit and no current flows through the circuit. Therefore, V_{out} gradually decreases and ultimately becomes zero. This is the stop band of the circuit.

5.5.2 Design Impedance of a Constant K LPF

In low pass filters

Total series impedance

$$Z_1 = j\omega L$$

Shunt impedance

$$Z_2 = \frac{-j}{\omega C}$$

$$Z_1 Z_2 = j\omega L \times \frac{-j}{\omega C}$$

$$Z_1 Z_2 = \frac{L}{C} = R^2$$

$$\boxed{R_k = \sqrt{\frac{L}{C}}} \qquad \ldots(5.1)$$

5.5.3 Reactance curves and cut-off frequency of a constant K LPF

- The reactances of Z_1 (inductor) and Z_2 (capacitor) will vary as shown in Fig. 5.2 (a).
- The curve representing $-4Z_2$ is draw and is compared with the curve for Z_1.
- Recollect that the pass band starts at a frequency at which $Z_1 = 0$ and runs to a frequency at which $Z_1 = -4Z_2$.
- It is clear from reactance curve that as ideally expected, pass band starts from $f = 0$ and continues till $f = f_c$. Frequencies
- All frequencies above f_c lie in the stop band.
- Thus, the network is called as a low pass filter.
- $Z_1 = 0$ and $Z_1 = -4Z_2$ determine the cut-off frequencies.

$$Z_1 = -4Z_2 \qquad \text{This is the condition at cut-off frequency}$$

$$j\omega L = -4\left(\frac{-j}{\omega C}\right)$$

$$\omega^2 LC = 4 \qquad \qquad \therefore \omega = \omega_c$$

$$4\pi^2 f_c\ LC = 4$$

$$\boxed{f_c = \frac{1}{\pi\sqrt{LC}}} \qquad \text{Higher cut-off frequency} \ldots (5.2)$$

Cut-off frequency of LPF is sometimes called as f_H.

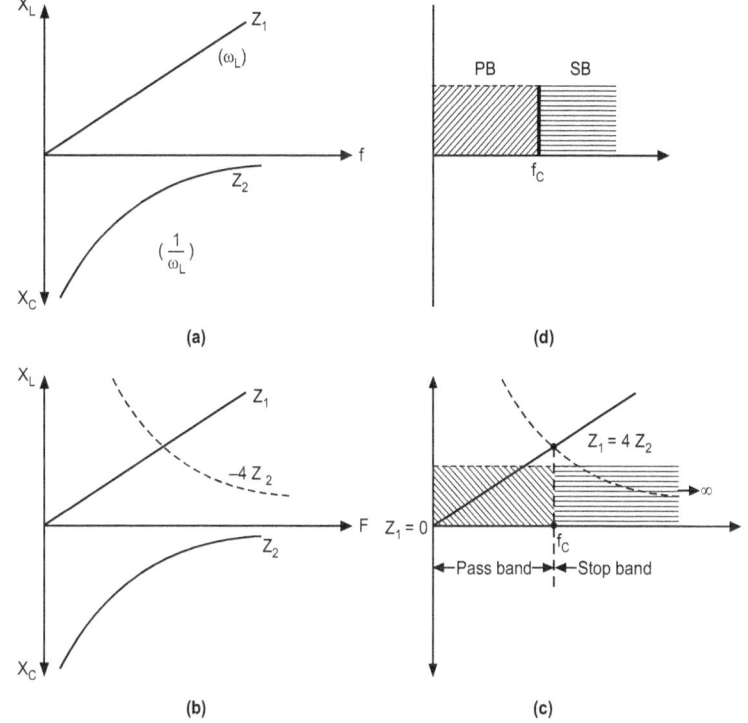

Fig. 5.12: Reactance curves for LPF

5.5.4 Design Equations of Constant K LPF

If the cut-off frequencies and the design impedance R_K for a filter are given we can design the filter components.

We have

$$f_C = \frac{1}{\pi\sqrt{LC}}$$

$$R_K = \sqrt{\frac{L}{C}}$$

Multiplying both the equations

$$f_C \cdot R_K = \frac{1}{\pi\sqrt{LC}} \times \sqrt{\frac{L}{C}}$$

$$f_C \cdot R_K = \frac{1}{\pi C}$$

$$\boxed{C = \frac{1}{\pi f_C R_K}} \quad \ldots(5.3)$$

Dividing equation of R_K by f_C

$$\frac{R_K}{f_c} = \sqrt{\frac{L}{C}} \Big/ \frac{1}{\pi\sqrt{LC}}$$

$$\frac{R_K}{f_c} = \sqrt{\frac{L}{C}} \times \pi\sqrt{LC}$$

$$\boxed{L = \frac{R_K}{\pi f_c}} \qquad \ldots (5.4)$$

These equations are called as design equations for prototype or constant K LPF.

5.5.5 Attenuation Constant and Phase Shift of a Constant K LPF

Recall the summary of the filter fundamentals.

β is pass band is

$$\beta = 2\sin^{-1}\sqrt{\frac{Z_1}{4Z_2}}$$

$$\beta = 2\sin^{-1}\sqrt{\frac{\omega L}{4 \cdot \frac{1}{\omega C}}}$$

$$\beta = 2\sin^{-1}\sqrt{\frac{\omega^2 LC}{4}}$$

$$\beta = 2\sin^{-1}\sqrt{\frac{\omega^2}{\omega_c^2}} \qquad \omega_c = \frac{4}{LC}$$

At $f = 0$, $\beta = 0$
At $f = f_c$ $\beta = 0$

Thus, $\boxed{\beta = 2\sin^{-1}\left(\frac{f}{f_c}\right)}$ ... (5.5)

As the frequency increases from 0 to f_c, β also increases from 0 to π radian.

β is stop band is $\boxed{\beta = \pi}$ radians. ... (5.6)

Attenuation of a constant K LPF.

α in pass band is

$\boxed{\alpha = 0}$ ...(5.7)

Recall the filter fundamentals

$$\alpha = 2\cosh^{-1}\sqrt{\frac{Z_1}{4Z_2}}$$

$$\alpha = 2\cosh^{-1}\sqrt{\dfrac{j\omega L}{4\dfrac{1}{\omega C}}}$$

$$\boxed{\alpha = 2\cosh^{-1}\left(\dfrac{f}{f_c}\right)} \quad \ldots (5.8)$$

In stop band as frequency f increases above f_c, α also increases.

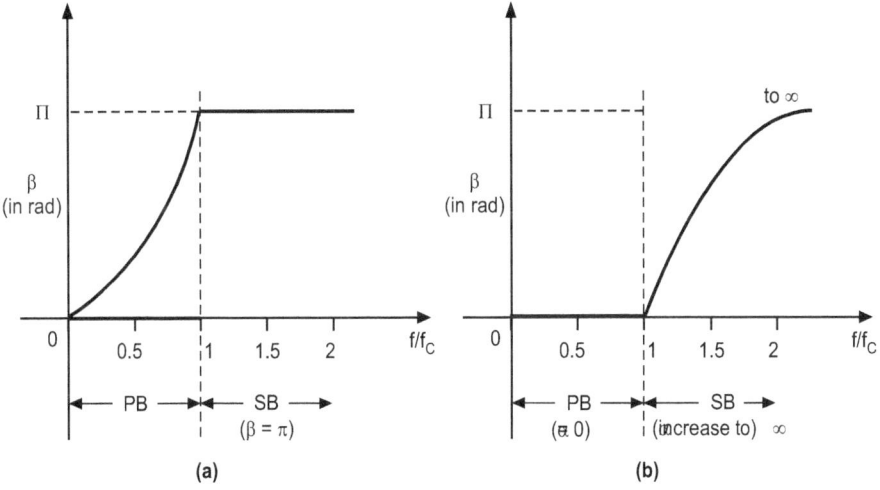

Fig. 5.13: Variation of (a) phase angle β and (b) attenuation α of a constant K LPF with frequency

5.5.6 Characteristics Impedance of Constant K LPF

- Any filter circuit is made up of symmetrical T or π type networks.
- Z_o, characteristics impedance is an important property of symmetrical network.

The characteristics impedance, of symmetrical T and π networks is given by,

$$Z_{0T} = \sqrt{\dfrac{Z_1^2}{4} + Z_1 Z_2}$$

$$Z_{0\pi} = \dfrac{Z_1 Z_2}{Z_{0T}}$$

Now, in case of LPF

$$Z_1 = j\omega L$$

$$Z_1 Z_2 = \dfrac{L}{C} = R_K^2$$

∴ $$Z_{0T} = \sqrt{\dfrac{(+j\omega L)^2}{4} + \dfrac{L}{C}} = \sqrt{\dfrac{-\omega^2 L^2}{4} + \dfrac{L}{C}}$$

$$= \sqrt{\frac{L}{C}} \sqrt{1 - \frac{\omega^2 LC}{4}}$$

$$Z_{OT} = \sqrt{\frac{L}{C}} \sqrt{1 - \frac{\omega^2}{\omega_c^2}} \qquad \omega_c = \frac{2}{\sqrt{LC}}$$

$$\boxed{Z_{OT} = R_K \sqrt{1 - \left(\frac{f}{f_c}\right)^2}} \qquad R_K = \sqrt{\frac{L}{C}} \qquad \ldots (5.9)$$

$$\boxed{Z_{0\pi} = \frac{R_K}{\sqrt{1 - \left(\frac{f}{f_c}\right)^2}}} \qquad \ldots (5.10)$$

Thus, for a T type LPF

when $f = 0$, $Z_{OT} = R_K$ }
$\quad\quad f = f_c$, $Z_{OT} = 0$

i.e. in T LPF as frequency increases from f to f_c Z_{OT} decreases from R_K to zero.

And, for a π type LPF

when $f = 0$, $Z_{0\pi} = R_K$
$\quad\quad f = f_c$, $Z_{0\pi} = \infty$

Similarly, here in π type LPF, when frequency increases from $f = 0$ and $f = f_c$, $Z_{0\pi}$ increases from R_K to ∞.

Characteristics impedance Z_0	Nature	Variation of Z_0 between frequencies		
		$f = 0$	to	$f = f_c$
Z_{OT}	Decreases	R_K	to	Zero
$Z_{0\pi}$	Increases	R_K	to	Infinity

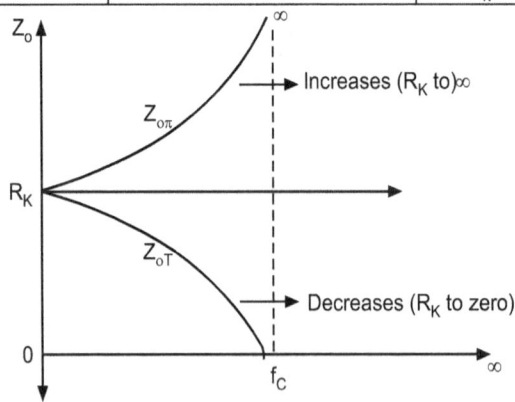

(f_c is sometimes called as F_H)

Fig. 5.14

5.6 SOLVED NUMERICALS ON CONSTANT K LPF

Example 5.1 :

Design a constant K π section LPF to be terminated into 600 Ω and having a cut-off frequency of 3 kHz.

Determine:

(i) The frequency at which filter offers at attenuation of 17.37 dB.

(ii) Attenuation of 6 kHz.

(iii) Characteristics impedance and a phase constant at 2 kHz.

Given $\qquad R_k = 600\ \Omega$
$\qquad\qquad f_C = 3$ kHz

To calculate:

(i) Filter elements
(ii) Frequency at which $\alpha = 17.372$ dB
(iii) Attenuation at $f = 6$ kHz
(iv) Z_0 and β at $f = 2$ kHz.

Solution : Given: $\qquad R_k = 600\ \Omega$
$\qquad\qquad f_C = 3$ kHz

(i) To calculate filter elements, design equations of LPF

$$L = \frac{R_0}{\pi f_C}$$

$$= \frac{600}{\pi \times 3 \times 10^3}$$

$$\boxed{L = 63.66\ \text{mH}}$$

$$C = \frac{1}{\pi f_C R_0} = \frac{1}{\pi \times 3 \times 10^3 \times 600}$$

$$\boxed{C = 0.176\ \mu F}$$

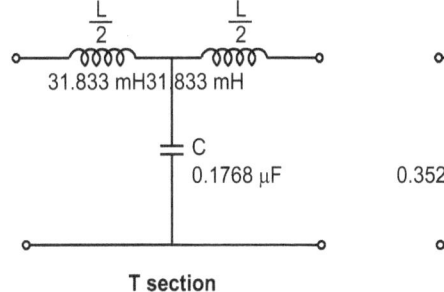
T section

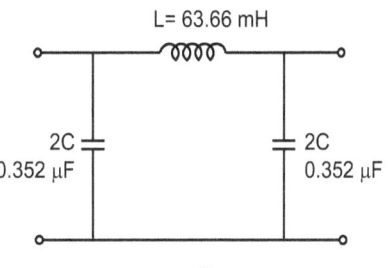
π section

Fig. 5.15

(ii) To calculate frequency at which $\alpha = 17.372$ dB

Let us express α in nepers

Attenuation in Nepers = $0.1151 \times$ Attenuation in dB
= 0.1151×17.372
= 1.9995 Nepers

For a prototype LPF

$$\alpha = 2\cosh^{-1}\left(\frac{f}{f_c}\right)$$

$$1.995 = 2\cosh^{-1}\left(\frac{f}{3000}\right)$$

$$\cosh\left(\frac{1.995}{2}\right) = \frac{f}{3000}$$

$$\boxed{f = 4.628 \text{ kHz}}$$

(iii) To calculate attenuation at $f = 6$ kHz.

F 6 kHz lies in stop band,

$$\alpha = 2\cosh^{-1}\left(\frac{f}{f_c}\right)$$

$$\alpha = 2\cosh^{-1}\left(\frac{6 \times 10^3}{3 \times 10^3}\right)$$

$$\alpha = 2.633 \text{ Nepers}$$

Attenuation in Neper = $0.1151 \times$ Attenuation in dB

$\therefore$ $\boxed{\alpha = 22.87 \text{ dB at } f = 6 \text{ kHz}}$

(iv) To calculate Z_0 and β at 2 kHz

$$Z_0 = R_k \sqrt{1 - \left(\frac{f}{f_c}\right)^2}$$

$$= 600\sqrt{1 - \left(\frac{2 \times 10^3}{3 \times 10^3}\right)^2}$$

$$\boxed{Z_0 = 447.213 \,\Omega \text{ at } f = 2 \text{ kHz}}$$

2 kHz lies in pass band, therefore the phase constant β in pass band is given by

$$\beta = 2\sin^{-1}\left(\frac{f}{f_c}\right)$$

$$\beta = 2\sin^{-1}\left(\frac{2 \times 10^3}{3 \times 10^3}\right) = 1.4594^C \text{ or}$$

$$\boxed{\beta = 83.62° \text{ at } f = 2 \text{ kHz}}$$

Example 5.2 :

Design a constant K LPF with $f_c = 1$ kHz and $R_0 = 600\ \Omega$. At what frequency α will be 10 dB ?

Given: $f_c = 1$ kHz
$R_K = 600\ \Omega$

To calculate (i) L, C (filter elements), (ii) Frequency at which $\alpha = 10$ dB.

Solution : (i) To calculate filter elements using the design equations derived for constant K LPF.

$$L = \frac{R_K}{\pi f_c} = \frac{600}{\pi \times 1 \times 10^3}$$

$$\boxed{L = 190.98\ \text{mH}}$$

$$C = \frac{1}{\pi f_c R_K} = \frac{1}{\pi \times 1 \times 10^3 \times 600}$$

$$\boxed{LC = 0.5305\ \mu F}$$

(ii) T and π sections

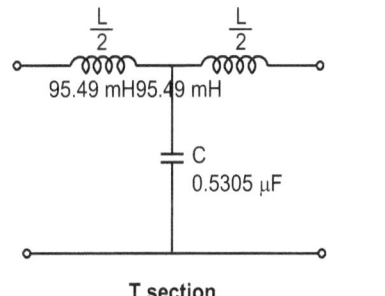
T section

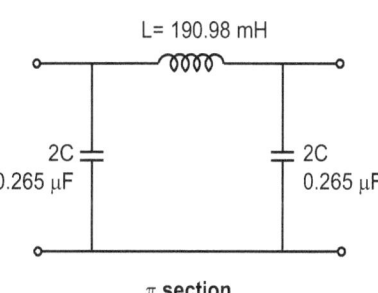
π section

Fig. 5.16

(iii) Frequency at which $\alpha = 10$ dB

$$\alpha = 2\cosh^{-1}\left(\frac{f_c}{f}\right)$$

Attenuation in nepers = $0.1151 \times \alpha$ in dB
$= 0.1151 \times 10$
$\alpha = 1.151$ Nepers

$$\alpha = 2\cosh^{-1}\left(\frac{f}{f_c}\right)$$

$$1.151 = 2\cosh^{-1}\left(\frac{f}{1000}\right)$$

$$\cosh\left(\frac{1.151}{2}\right) = \frac{f}{1000}$$

$$\boxed{f = 1.17\ \text{K}}$$

Example 5.3 :

Each of two series elements of T type LPF consists of an inductor of 60 mH and shunt element of 0.2 µF capacitor. Calculate cut-off frequency and design impedance at 1 kHz. Also find ratio of phase difference between the input and the output voltages of the filter at 1 kHz and 5 kHz.

Given: $\dfrac{L}{2} = 60 \text{ mH}$

$C = 0.2 \text{ µF}$

To calculate:
(i) R_K and f_C = ?
(ii) Z_0 at 1 kHz = ?
(iii) β at 1 kHz = ? and 5 kHz = ?

Solution : Each series element of T section is 60 mH.

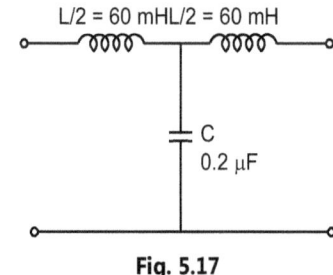

Fig. 5.17

∴ $L = 2 \times 60 = 120 \text{ mH}$

(i) To calculate cut-off frequency f_C

$$f_C = \dfrac{1}{\pi \sqrt{LC}}$$

$$= \dfrac{1}{\pi \sqrt{120 \times 10^{-3} \times 0.2 \times 10^{-6}}}$$

$\boxed{f_C = 2.054 \text{ kHz}}$

(ii) Design impedance

$$R_K = \sqrt{\dfrac{L}{C}} = \sqrt{\dfrac{120 \times 10^{-3}}{0.2 \times 10^{-6}}}$$

$\boxed{R_K = 774.59 \text{ }\Omega}$

(iii) Z_{OT} at 1 kHz

$$Z_{OT} = R_0 \sqrt{1 - \left(\dfrac{f}{f_C}\right)^2}$$

$$= 774.59 \sqrt{1 - \left(\frac{1 \times 10^3}{2.054 \times 10^3}\right)^2}$$

$$\boxed{Z_{OT} = 676.59 \, \Omega} \text{ at 1 kHz}$$

(iv) β at 1 kHz

$$\beta = 2 \sin^{-1}\left(\frac{f}{f_C}\right)$$

$$= 2 \sin^{-1}\left(\frac{1 \times 10^3}{2.054 \times 10^3}\right)$$

$$\boxed{\beta = 58.26°} \text{ at 1 kHz}$$

(v) β at 5 kHz

$$\beta = 2 \sin^{-1}\left(\frac{f}{f_C}\right)$$

For a LPF, when f_C = 2.05 kHz.

5 kHz lies in stop band. Therefore, β in stop band is 180° or π^C.

$$\boxed{\beta = 180°} \text{ at 5 kHz}$$

5.7 CONSTANT K HIGH PASS FILTER

- A High Pass Filter would ideally pass all the frequencies higher than the cut-off frequencies and will block the frequencies lower than the cut-off frequencies.
- We use capacitor in a series arm and a inductor in a shunt arm to achieve this characteristics.

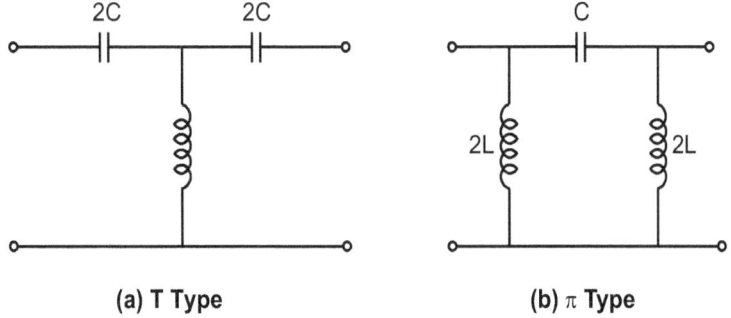

(a) T Type   (b) π Type

Fig. 5.18 : Constant k HP Filters

5.7.1 Operation of a Constant K HPF

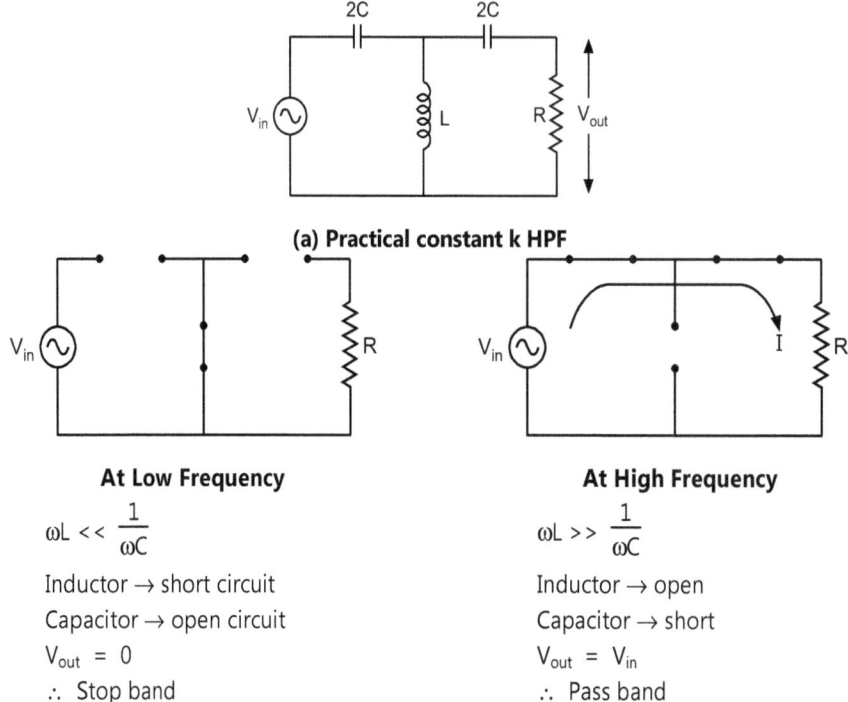

(a) Practical constant k HPF

At Low Frequency

$\omega L \ll \dfrac{1}{\omega C}$

Inductor → short circuit
Capacitor → open circuit
$V_{out} = 0$
∴ Stop band

At High Frequency

$\omega L \gg \dfrac{1}{\omega C}$

Inductor → open
Capacitor → short
$V_{out} = V_{in}$
∴ Pass band

(b) An approximate equivalent at low frequencies

(c) An approximate equivalent at higher frequency

Fig. 5.19 : Operation of Constant K HPF

- Though resistors on their own have no frequency selective property, they are still added and used in practical filters to determine the time constant of the circuit.
- At low frequencies the reactance of an inductor (ωL) will be very small, when compared to the reactance $\dfrac{1}{\omega C}$ of a capacitor. So effectively L functions as a short circuit and the input signal receives a path to ground. Thus, no signal reaches the output and it is completely blocked by the capacitor. Circuit is in stop band.
- But at higher frequencies the reactance $\dfrac{1}{\omega C}$ of a capacitor will be too less thus making it function almost like a short circuit and making inductor function as open circuit and giving a path to the input signal to reach output.
- Thus, at higher freqenices,

$$\omega L \gg \dfrac{1}{\omega C}$$

and V_{out} is almost equal to V_{in}. The circuit operates in pass band.

5.7.2 Design Impedance of a constant K HPF

In a high pass filter

Total series impedance $Z_1 = \dfrac{-j}{\omega C}$

shunt impedance $Z_2 = j\omega L$

∴ $Z_1 Z_2 = j\omega L \times \dfrac{-j}{\omega C}$

$Z_1 Z_2 = \dfrac{L}{C} = R_K^2$

$$\boxed{R_K = \sqrt{\dfrac{L}{C}}} \quad \ldots (5.11)$$

...[This is similar to one derived for LPF]

5.7.3 Reactance Curves and Cut-off frequency of a Constant K HPF

- The reactance's of Z_1 (capacitor) and Z_2 (inductor) will vary as shown in Fig. 5.20 (a). The curve representing $-4Z_2$ is drawn and is compared with the curve for Z_1.
- Recollect that the pass band lies between the frequencies where $Z_1 = 0$ and $Z_1 = -4Z_2$.
- It is clear from the reactance curve that $Z_1 = 0$ at infinite frequency. As ideally expected, pass band starts from f_C, the frequency where $Z_1 = -4Z_2$ and continues till the frequency where $Z_1 = 0$ i.e. infinity.
- All the frequencies above f_C lie in the pass band.
- Thus, the network is called as a high pass filter.
- Conditions $Z_1 = 0$ and $Z_1 = -4Z_2$ determine the cut-off frequency.

$Z_1 = -4Z_2$ ... This is the condition at cut-off frequency

$\dfrac{-j}{\omega_c C} = -4j\omega_c L$

$\omega_c^2 LC = \dfrac{1}{4}$ ∴ $\omega = \omega_c$

$$\boxed{f_c = \dfrac{1}{4\pi\sqrt{LC}}} \quad \ldots (5.12)$$

Cut-off frequency of HPF is sometimes called as f_L lower cut-of frequency.

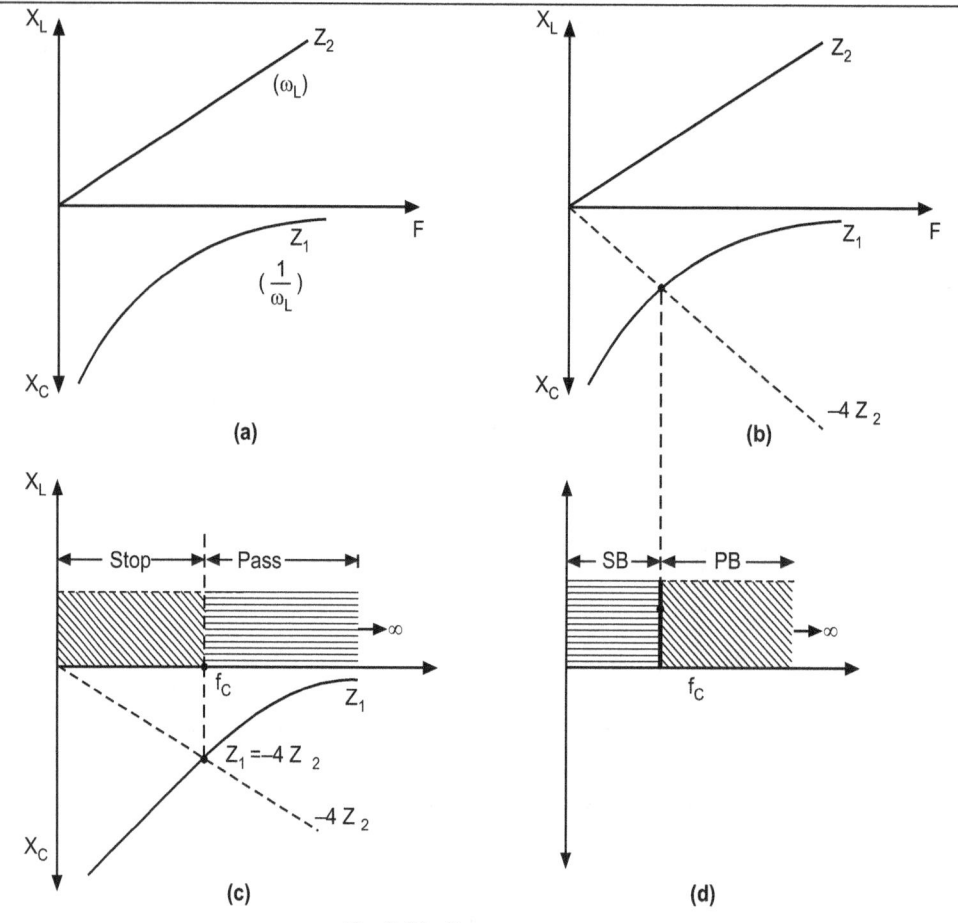

Fig. 5.20 : Reactance curves

5.7.4 Design Equations of Constant K HPF

If the cut-off frequencies and the design impedance R_K for a filter are given we can design the filter components.

We have,

$$f_C = \frac{1}{4\pi\sqrt{LC}}$$

$$R_K = \sqrt{\frac{L}{C}}$$

Multiplying both the equations

$$f_C \cdot R_K = \frac{1}{4\pi\sqrt{LC}} \times \sqrt{\frac{L}{C}}$$

$$f_C \cdot R_K = \frac{1}{4\pi\sqrt{C}\cdot\sqrt{C}}$$

$$\boxed{C = \frac{1}{4\pi f_C R_K}} \qquad \ldots (5.13)$$

Dividing equation of R_K by f_C

$$\frac{R_K}{f_C} = \sqrt{\frac{L}{C}} \Big/ \frac{1}{4\pi\sqrt{LC}}$$

$$\frac{R_K}{f_C} = \sqrt{\frac{L}{C}} \times 4\pi\sqrt{LC}$$

$$\frac{R_K}{f_C} = 4\pi L$$

$$\boxed{L = \frac{R_K}{4\pi f_C}}$$

These equations are called as design equations for prototype or constant K HPF.

5.7.5 Attenuation Constant and Phase Shift of a Constant K HPF

Recall the summary of the filter.

β in stop band is π. As will be clear later, in this case β will be $-\pi$.

In stop band

$$\boxed{\beta = -\pi} \qquad \ldots (5.14)$$

In pass band,

$$\beta = 2\sin^{-1}\sqrt{\frac{Z_1}{4Z_2}}$$

$$= 2\sin^{-1}\sqrt{\frac{\frac{-j}{\omega C}}{4j\omega L}}$$

$$= 2\sin^{-1}\sqrt{\frac{-1}{4\omega^2 LC}} = 2\sin^{-1}\frac{-j}{2\omega\sqrt{LC}}$$

$$\beta = 2\sin^{-1}\frac{-j}{2\omega\sqrt{LC}}$$

$$\beta = 2\sin^{-1}\frac{-j}{2\omega \times \frac{1}{4\pi f_C}} \quad \ldots f_C = \frac{1}{4\pi\sqrt{LC}}$$

$$\boxed{\beta = 2\sin^{-1}-j\left(\frac{f_C}{f}\right)} \text{ radians} \qquad \ldots (5.15)$$

Thus, phase angle β will be negative. As the frequency f increases from f_C to ∞, the band of frequencies will be pass band, so β will decrease from $-\pi$ to zero.

Attenuation of a constant K HPF

α in pass band is zero.

$$\boxed{\alpha = 0} \qquad \ldots(5.16)$$

Recall the filter fundamentals

$$\alpha = 2\cosh^{-1}\sqrt{\frac{Z_1}{4Z_2}}$$

$$\boxed{\alpha = 2\cosh^{-1} - j\left(\frac{f_C}{f}\right) \text{ Nepers}} \qquad \ldots(5.17)$$

Thus, in stop band attenuation α decreases from ∞ at f = 0 to zero at f = f_C.

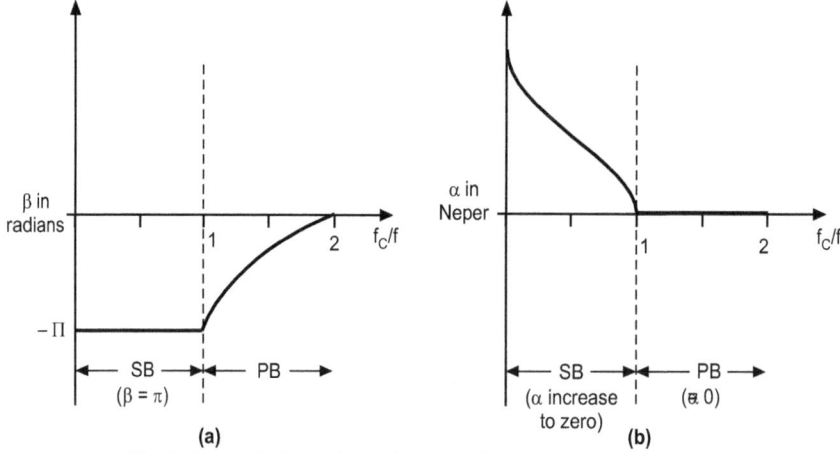

Fig. 5.21: Variation of (a) phase angle and (b) attenuation α

5.7.6 Characteristics Impedance of Constant K HPF

- Z_0, characteristics impedance is an important property of symmetrical network.
- Z_0 of a symmetrical T and π network is given by,

$$Z_{0T} = \sqrt{\frac{Z_1^2}{4} + Z_1 Z_2}$$

$$Z_{0\pi} = \frac{Z_1 Z_2}{Z_{0T}}$$

In case of HPF,

$$Z_1 = \frac{-j}{\omega C}$$

$$Z_2 = j\omega L$$

$$Z_1 Z_2 = \frac{L}{C} = R_K^2$$

$$Z_{OT} = \sqrt{\frac{\left(\frac{-j}{\omega C}\right)^2}{4} + \frac{L}{C}}$$

$$Z_{OT} = \sqrt{\frac{L}{C}} \sqrt{1 - \frac{1}{4\omega^2 LC}}$$

$$Z_{OT} = R_K \sqrt{1 - \frac{1}{4\omega^2 LC}}$$

$$\boxed{Z_{OT} = R_K \sqrt{1 - \left(\frac{f_c}{f}\right)^2}} \quad \ldots f_c = \frac{1}{4\pi \sqrt{LC}} \quad \ldots(5.18)$$

$$\boxed{Z_{0\pi} = \frac{R_K}{\sqrt{1 - \left(\frac{f_c}{f}\right)^2}}} \quad \ldots (5.19)$$

Thus, for a T type HPF
when
    $f = f_c$ $Z_{OT} = 0$
    $f = \infty$ $Z_{OT} = R_K$

As frequency f increases from f_c to ∞ in pass band, Z_{OT} also increases from 0 to R_K.
Similarly, for a π type HPF
when,
    $f = f_c$ $Z_{0\pi} = \infty$
    $f = \infty$ $Z_{0\pi} = R_K$

Table 5.5

Characteristics impedance	Nature	Variation of Z_0 between frequencies
Z_{OT}	Increases	zero to R_K
$Z_{0\pi}$	Decreases	Infinity to R_K

Note that this behaviour is exactly opposite to the behaviour of Z_0 in a LPF.

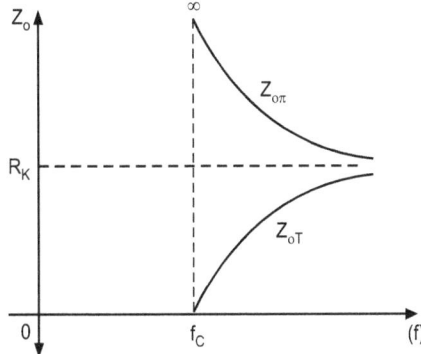

Fig. 5.22: Variation of characteristics impedance with frequency

5.8 SOLVED NUMERICALS ON CONSTANT K HPF

Example 5.4 :

A prototype HPF has cut-off frequency of 10 kHz and design impedance of 600 Ω. Find element values of L and C. Also find attenuation in dB and phase shift in degrees at a frequency of 8 kHz.

Given: (i) $f_C = 10$ kHz

(ii) $R_K = 600$ Ω

To calculate:

(i) Filter elements

(ii) α at 8 kHz

(iii) β at 8 kHz

Solution : (i) To calculate filter elements L and C

$$L = \frac{R_K}{4\pi f_C}$$

$$= \frac{600}{4\pi \times 10 \times 10^3}$$

$$\boxed{L = 4.77 \text{ mH}}$$

$$C = \frac{1}{4\pi f_C R_K}$$

$$= \frac{1}{4\pi \times 10 \times 10^3 \times 600}$$

$$\boxed{C = 13.26 \text{ nF}}$$

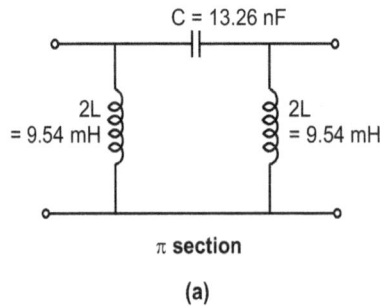
π section
(a)

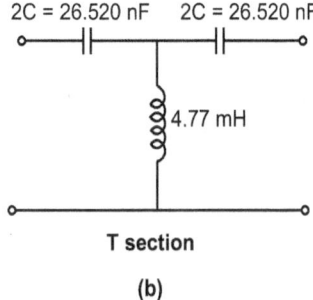
T section
(b)

Fig. 5.23

(ii) To calculate α At 8 kHz. For a HPF of prototype type, attenuation is given

$$\alpha = 2 \cosh^{-1}\left(\frac{f_C}{f}\right)$$

$$= 2 \cosh^{-1}\left(\frac{10 \times 10^3}{8 \times 10^3}\right)$$

$$\boxed{\alpha = 1.3862 \text{ N}} \text{ at 8 kHz}$$

$$\alpha \text{ in dB} = 8.68 \times \alpha \text{ in Neper}$$
$$= 8.68 \times 1.3862$$

$$\boxed{\alpha \text{ in dB} = 12.04 \text{ dB}} \text{ at 8 Hz}$$

(iii) β at 8 kHz.

For a high pass filter, with f_c = 10 kHz, f = 8 kHz lies in stop band.

∴ Phase shift in stop band is π^c or 180°.

$$\boxed{\beta = 180°} \text{ at 8 kHz}$$

Example 5.5 :

Design a constant K π section high pass filter to have a design impedance of 600 Ω. The filter must have attenuation of 8.11 dB at 4.5 kHz. For the above design filter calculate phase angle in degrees at f = 5.5 kHz.

Given: R_K = 600 Ω

α = 8.11 d_B at 4.5 kHz

To calculate: L = ?

C = ?

β = ? at f = 5.5 kHz

Solution : (i) To calculate f_C, we have

$$\alpha = 2 \cosh^{-1}\left(\frac{f}{f_c}\right)$$

$$\alpha \text{ in dB} = 8.6866 \times \alpha \text{ in neper}$$
$$8.11 = 8.6866 \times \alpha$$

$$\boxed{\alpha = 0.933 \text{ nepers}}$$

∴ $$0.933 = 2 \cosh^{-1}\left(\frac{4.5 \times 10^3}{f_C}\right)$$

$$\boxed{f_C = 5 \text{ kHz}}$$

(ii) To calculate L and C

$$L = \frac{R_K}{4\pi f_C} = \frac{600}{4 \times \pi \times 5 \times 10^3}$$

$$\boxed{L = 9.55 \text{ mH}}$$

$$C = \frac{1}{4\pi f_C \cdot R_K} = \frac{1}{600 \times 4 \times \pi \times 5 \times 10^3}$$

$$\boxed{C = 0.0265 \text{ μF}}$$

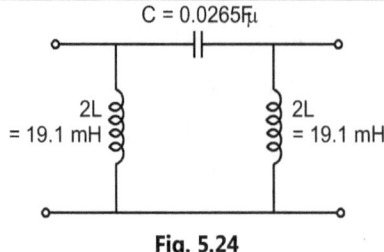

Fig. 5.24

(iii) To calculate phase angle β

$$\beta = 2 \sin^{-1}\left(\frac{f_c}{f}\right)$$

$$\beta = 2 \sin^{-1}\left(\frac{5 \times 10^3}{5.5 \times 10^3}\right)$$

$$\boxed{\beta = 130.76°}$$

5.9 CONSTANT K BAND PASS FILTERS

- The filter that passes the voltages in a band of frequencies and blocks or attenuates the frequencies outside this band of frequencies is known as a band pass filter.
- Such a band pass filter is obtained by connecting low pass filter section in cascade with high pass filter section, provided that the cut-off frequency of a low pass filter section must be selected higher than that of the high pass filter section.

5.9.1 Operation of a Constant K BPF

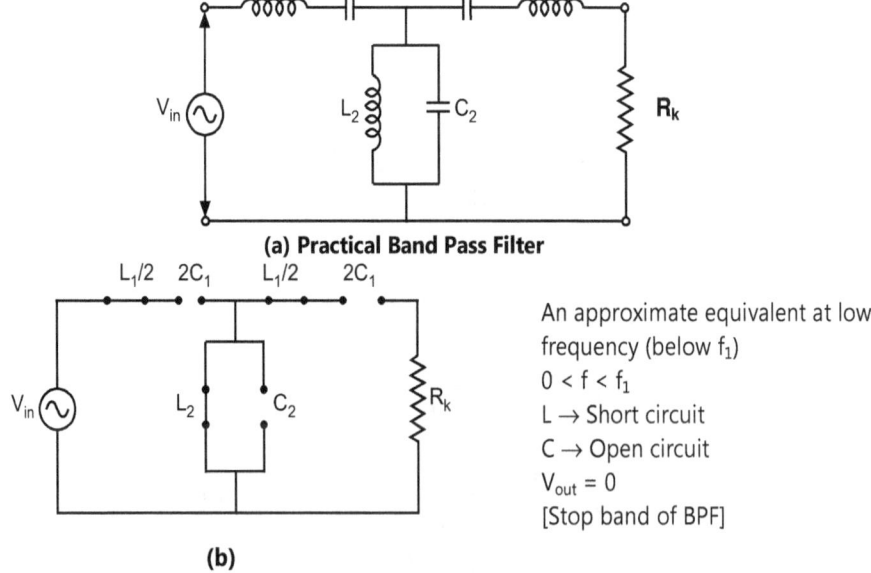

(a) Practical Band Pass Filter

(b)

An approximate equivalent at low frequency (below f_1)
$0 < f < f_1$
L → Short circuit
C → Open circuit
$V_{out} = 0$
[Stop band of BPF]

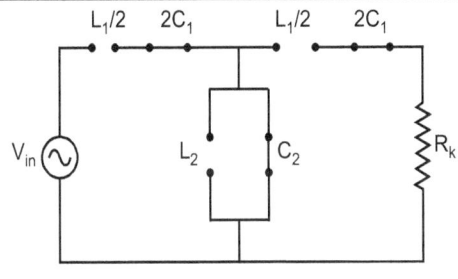

An approximate equivalent at high frequency (above f_2)

$f_2 < f < \infty$

L → Open circuit

C → Short circuit

$V_{out} = 0$

[Stop band of BPF]

(c)

Fig. 5.25

- As already discussed earlier, though resistors on their own have no frequency selective property, they are still added and used in all the practical circuits to determine the time constant of the circuit.
- For all the frequencies till f_1, i.e. lower cut-off frequency of BPF, the circuit operates in stop band giving V_{out} = 0V. LPF and HPF are in series. So far lower frequencies through LPF is operating in pass band, HPF actually is having its stop band therefore giving V_{out} = 0 V.
- Similarly at higher frequencies, i.e. frequency greater than f_2, the circuit operates in stop band giving V_{out} = 0V. LPF and HPF are in series. So for higher frequencies through HPF is operating in pass band. LPF actually is having its sop band therefore giving V_{out} = 0V.
- In the frequencies between f_1 and f_2 the band pass filter operates in pass band, giving V_{out} = V_{in}. Both, LPF and HPF having cut-off frequencies (f_H) f_2 and $f_1(f_L)$ respectively, operate in pass band region.
- These overlapping pass bands of LPF and HPF allow the corresponding BPF to operate in pass band, thus allowing only a band of frequencies to pass giving V_{out} = V_{in}.

5.9.2 Design Impedance of a Constant K BPF

In a BPF,

Total series arm impedance Z_1 is

$$Z_1 = j\omega L_1 + \left(\frac{-j}{\omega C_1}\right)$$

$$Z_1 = j\left[\frac{\omega^2 L_1 C_1 - 1}{\omega C_1}\right]$$

Total shunt arm impedance Z_2 is

$$Z_2 = j\omega L_2 \parallel \left(\frac{-j}{\omega C_2}\right)$$

Unit V | 5.31

$$Z_2 = \frac{j\omega L_2 \times \frac{-j}{\omega C_2}}{j\omega L_2 - \frac{j}{\omega C_2}}$$

$$Z_2 = \frac{\frac{L_2}{C_2}}{j\frac{(\omega^2 L_2 C_2 - 1)}{\omega C_2}}$$

$$Z_2 = \frac{-j\omega L_2}{\omega^2 L_2 C_2 - 1}$$

Now design impedance $R_K = \sqrt{Z_1 Z_2}$.

$$R_K = \sqrt{Z_1 Z_2}$$

$$R_K^2 = j\left[\frac{\omega^2 L_1 C_1 - 1}{\omega C_1}\right] \times \frac{-j\omega L_2}{\omega^2 C_2 C_L - 1}$$

$$R_K^2 = \frac{L_2}{C_1} \quad \ldots \quad L_2 C_2 = L_1 C_1$$

$$R_K^2 = \frac{L_1}{C_2}$$

$$\boxed{R_K = \sqrt{\frac{L_2}{C_1}} = \sqrt{\frac{L_1}{C_2}}} \quad \ldots (5.20)$$

$L_2 C_2 = L_1 C_1$ is another condition which must be satisfied by the filter elements of BPF. It is preassumed to the reason will be clear in the very next section of reactance curves.

5.9.3 Reactance curves and expression for cut-off frequency of a constant K BPF

- BPF is made up of series and a shunt resonating circuit.
- Before we directly plot the graphs and curves of BPF, let us first revise the reactance plots of series and shunt resonating circuits.
- Let us understand these plots.

Table 5.6

Series Resonance	X_L: Inductive Reactance	Linear positive
	X_C: Capacitive Reactance	Hyperbolic negative
Shunt Resonance	b_L: Inductive Susceptance	Hyperbolic negative
	b_C: Capacitive Susceptance	Linear positive

The reciprocal of a positive linear relation is a negative hyperbola.

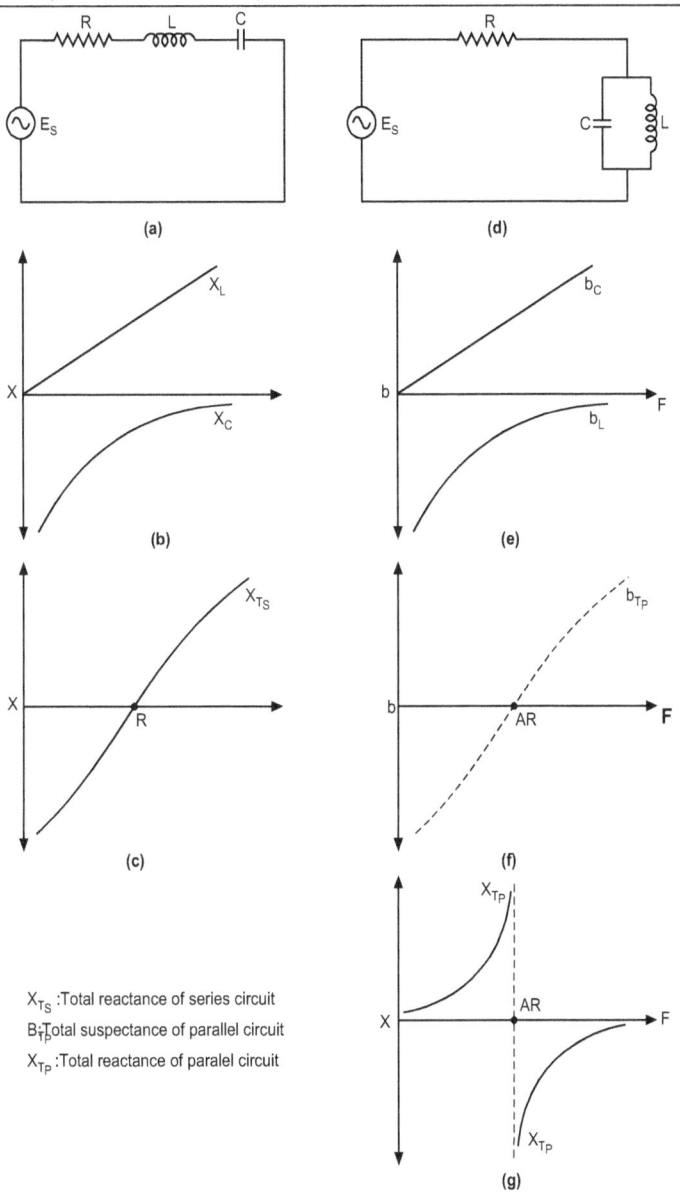

Fig. 5.26: Circuit diagram and reactance curves of

a, b, c: Series Resonance

d, e, f, g: Parallel Resonance

Series Resonance:
- Curves X_L and X_C in Fig. 5.26 (b) are the reactance plots of inductor and a capacitor.
- These curves are added algebraically as would be the case for the series resonant circuit to give the curve labelled X_{TS} in Fig. 5.26 (c).

- X_T gives the circuit performance as a frequency function.
- Point R is the resonant point showing zero reactance at that point.
- Series resonant circuit has capacitive reactance below the resonating frequency and inductive reactance at the frequencies above the resonanting frequency.

Parallel Resonance:

- Curves b_C and b_L in Fig. 5.26 (e) are the susceptance plots of inductor and a capacitor.
- These curves are added algebraically as would be the case for the parallel resonant circuit to give the curve labeled b_T in Fig. 5.26 (f).
- The reciprocal of b_{TP} is taken and plotted as x_{TP} in Fig. 5.26 (g) giving a curve of reactance Vs frequency for the parallel resonant circuit.
- At point "AR", b_{TP} is zero, so its reciprocal x_{TP} at that point will obviously theoretically go to infinity as shown in Fig. 5.26 (g).
- b_{TP} below point "AR" is capacitive and it is inductive above point "AR". So, x_{TP} i.e. reciprocal of b_{TP} is naturally inductive below "AR" and capacitive above AR.
- So Fig. 5.26 (c) and (g) are the final reactance plots of our interest.
- Fig. 5.27 (c) shows an existence of an additional stop band between two pass bands, which should not be the case, when compared with ideal response of BPF as shown in Fig. 5.27 (d).
- Fig. 5.27 (c) needs a through explanation which will help us in understanding a very important condition for BPF.
- Before understanding Fig. 5.27 (c) let us quickly revise the concepts we learned in section 5.27 i.e. filter fundamentals.

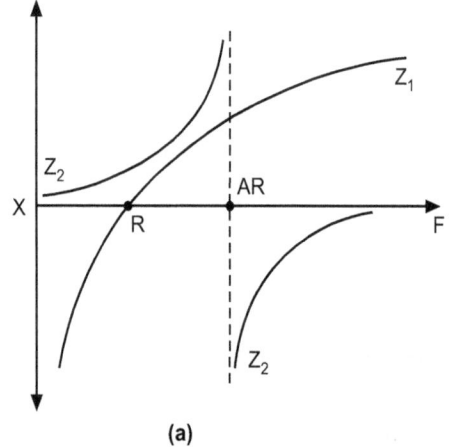

(a)

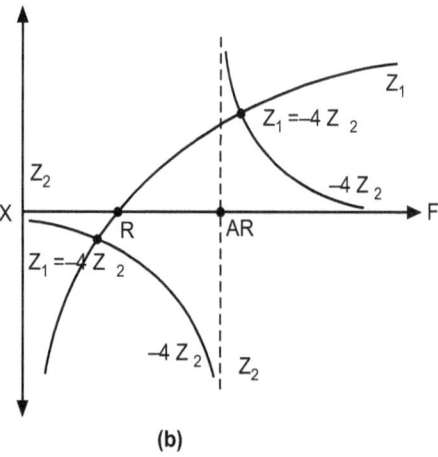

(b)

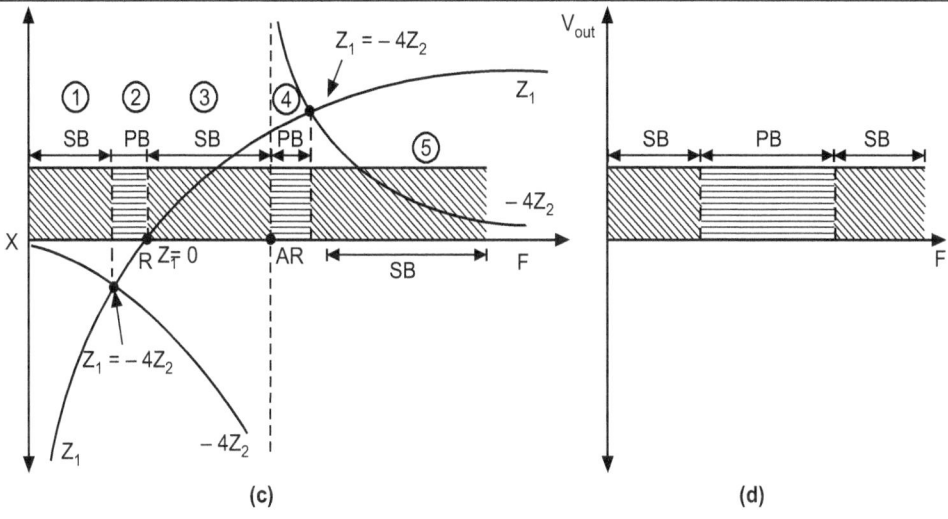

Fig. 5.27: Reactance curves

For a Filter circuit:
- Pass Band exists between Frequency $Z_1 = 0$ and $Z_1 = -4Z_2$.
- Stop Band exists between Frequency at which $Z_1 = -4Z_2$ and $-\infty$.
- And the most important concept Z_1 and Z_2 must always be opposite types of reactances.

- Concentrate on Fig. 5.27 (c).
  - Band 1 is a stop band existing between the frequency at which $Z_1 = -4Z_2$ and $Z_1 = \infty$. This matches the ideal Frequency curve of BPF.
  - Band 2 is a pass band existing between frequencies at which $Z_1 = 0$ and $Z_1 = -4Z_2$. Even this band matches the ideal Frequency curve of BPF.
  - Band 3 is marked as a stop band, irrespective of the fact that it is seen to be starting from $Z_1 = 0$. Now this stop Band should not have existed at all. And if at all existed should actually be considered as pass band [we know pass band exists between $Z_1 = 0$ and $Z_1 = -4Z_2$]. But the reason, that the circuit will definitely be in stop band for this slot is that, in this slot Z_1 and Z_2 are going to be the reactances of same type. See Fig. 5.27 (a). For the frequencies between the points R and AR, Z_1 and Z_2 are the reactances of same type. And so for the reactances of same type we are bound to get a stop band.
  - This is the reason for having the undesired stop band between the points R and AR.
- Now if a smooth operation of BPF is expected we must eliminate the existence of undesirable stop band in between the points R and AR on the frequency axis.
- Point R is actually the resonating frequency of series arm and point AR is the antiresonating frequency of the shunt arm.

- If the points 'R' and 'AR' overlap on the frequency axis, the undesirable stop band in between these points will not exists at all.
- Now making these points (R and AR) overlap means practically making the antiresonant frequency of the shunt arm to correspond to the resonant frequency of the series arm.

  i.e. $\qquad f_r = f_{ar}$

- Let us see the reactance curves when R = AR. i.e. $f_r = f_{ar}$

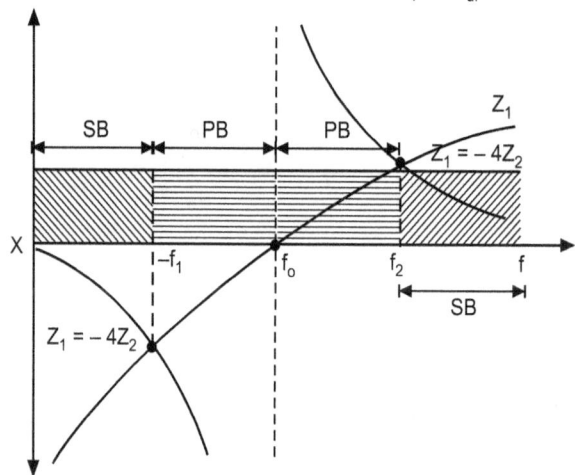

Fig. 5.28: Reactance curves for the band pass network when the resonant and antiresonant frequencies are equal

- Thus, when $f_r = f_{ar}$, the circuit behaves as expected for a BPF. We do not have any step band in between or do we have two different pass bands.
- Let us now derive the condition required for the filter elements (L_1, L_2, C_1, C_2) inorder to have $f_r = f_{ar}$.

$$f_r = \frac{1}{2\pi\sqrt{\frac{L_1}{2} \cdot 2C_1}}$$

$$= \frac{1}{2\pi\sqrt{L_1 C_1}}$$

$$\therefore \quad \omega_o = \omega_r = \frac{1}{\sqrt{L_1 C_1}}$$

$$f_{ar} = \frac{1}{2\pi\sqrt{\frac{L_1}{2} \cdot 2C_1}}$$

$$= \frac{1}{2\pi\sqrt{L_2 C_2}}$$

$$\therefore \quad \omega_0 = \omega_{ar} = \frac{1}{\sqrt{L_2 C_2}}$$

$$\omega_0^2 L_1 C_1 = \omega_0^2 L_2 C_2 = 1 \qquad \ldots (a)$$

We must have

$$f_0 = f_r = f_{ar}$$

$$\frac{1}{2\pi\sqrt{L_1 C_1}} = \frac{1}{2\pi\sqrt{L_2 C_2}}$$

$$\boxed{L_1 C_1 = L_2 C_2} \qquad \ldots(5.21)$$

This is the required condition for the filter elements in order to have $f_r = f_{ar}$.

Derivation of Cut-off Frequency

- BPF has two cut-off frequencies as seen earlier. At both the cut-off frequencies

$$Z_1 = -4 Z_2$$

Multiplying by Z_1 gives

$$Z_1^2 = -4 Z_1 Z_2$$
$$Z_1^2 = -4 R_K^2$$
$$= +4j^2 R_K^2$$
$$\therefore \quad Z_1 = \pm 2j R_K$$

Z_1 at lower cut-off frequency (f_1)

$$= -Z_1 \text{ at upper cut-off frequency } f_2$$

$-$ve sign in this equation (2), indicates that nature of Z_1 at f_1 and f_2 will be opposite.

$\therefore \quad Z_1$ at f_1 = opposite of Z_1 at f_2.

Below f_0, Z_1 is capacitive. So at lower cut-off frequency, f_1 capacitive reactance of Z_1 series resonating, is dominating. So naturally circuit

at f_1 $\qquad Z_1 = \dfrac{1}{\omega_1 C_1} - \omega_1 L_1 \ldots \left(\dfrac{1}{\omega_1 C_1} >> \omega_1 L_1\right) \qquad \ldots (b)$

Similarly, above f_0, Z_1 is inductive. So at higher cut-off frequency f_2, inductive reactance of Z_1 (series resonating circuit) is dominating,. So naturally

at f_2 $\qquad Z_1 = \omega_2 L_1 - \dfrac{1}{\omega_2 C_1} \ldots \left(\omega_2 L_1 >> \dfrac{1}{\omega_2 C_1}\right) \qquad \ldots(c)$

We had, Z_1 at f_1 $\qquad = -Z_1$ at f_2

$$\therefore \quad \frac{1}{\omega_1 C_1} - \omega_1 L_1 = \omega_2 L_1 - \frac{1}{\omega_2 C_1}$$

[writing $-$ve sign in the above equation is deliberately avoided because it has been taken care off when we wrote the equation (b) and (c) which are already opposite of each other].

$$\therefore \quad \frac{1}{\omega_1 C_1} - \omega_1 L_1 = \omega_2 L_1 - \frac{1}{\omega_2 C_1}$$

$$\frac{1 - \omega_1^2 L_1 C_1}{\omega_1 C_1} = \frac{\omega_2^2 L C_1 - 1}{\omega_2 C_1}$$

$$1 - \omega_1^2 L_1 C_1 = \frac{\omega_1 C_1}{\omega_2 C_1} \left[\omega_2^2 L_1 C_1 - 1 \right]$$

From equation (a), $L_1 C_1 = \dfrac{1}{\omega_0^2}$

$$1 - \frac{\omega_1^2}{\omega_0^2} = \frac{\omega_1}{\omega_2} \left[\frac{\omega_2^2}{\omega_D^2} - 1 \right]$$

$$1 - \frac{f_1^2}{f_0^2} = \frac{f_1}{f_2} \left[\frac{f_2^2}{f_0^2} - 1 \right]$$

$$f_2 \left(f_0^2 - f_1^2 \right) = f_1 \left(f_2^2 - f_0^2 \right)$$

$$f_2 f_0^2 - f_2 f_1^2 = f_1 f_2^2 - f_1 f_0^2$$

$$f_2 f_0^2 + f_1 f_0^2 = f_1 f_2^2 - f_2 f_1^2$$

$$f_0^2 (f_1 + f_2) = f_1 f_2 (f_1 + f_2)$$

$$f_0^2 = f_1 f_2$$

$$\boxed{f_0 = \sqrt{f_1 f_2}} \quad \ldots (5.22)$$

Equation (5.22) indicates that frequency of resonance of the individual arms is a geometric mean of two cut-off frequencies.

5.9.4 Design Equations for a Constant K BPF

Recollect the equations (b) and (c) of section 5.9.4.

We have,

At lower cut-off frequency

$$j\omega_1 L_1 - \frac{j}{\omega_1 C_1} = -j 2 R_K$$

$$\omega_1 L_1 - \frac{1}{\omega_1 C_1} = -2 R_K$$

$$\omega_1^2 L_1 C_1 - 1 = -2 R_K \omega_1 C_1$$

$$1 - \omega_1^2 L_1 C_1 = +2 R_K \omega_1 C_1$$

$$1 - \frac{\omega_1^2}{\omega_0^2} = 2\omega_1 C_1 \cdot R_K \qquad \ldots \omega_0 = \frac{1}{L_1 C_1}$$

$$1 - \frac{f_1^2}{f_0^2} = 4\pi f_1 C_1 R_K$$

$$1 - \frac{f_1^2}{f_1 f_2} = 4\pi f_1 C_1 R_K \qquad \ldots f_0 = \sqrt{f_1 f_2}$$

$$1 - \frac{f_1}{f_2} = 4\pi R_K f_1 C_1$$

$$\frac{f_2 - f_1}{f_2} = 4\pi R_K f_1 C_1$$

$$\boxed{C_1 = \frac{f_2 - f_1}{4\pi R_K f_1 f_2}}$$

Now, for constant K BPF,

$$\omega_0 = \frac{1}{\sqrt{L_1 C_1}}$$

$$\omega_0^2 = \frac{1}{\left(\sqrt{L_1 C_1}\right)^2} \qquad \therefore L_1 = \frac{1}{C_1 \omega_0^2}$$

Substituting value of C_1 and $\omega_0 = 2\pi f_0$

$$L_1 = \frac{1}{\frac{f_2 - f_1}{4\pi R_K f_1 f_2} \times 4\pi^2 f_0^2}$$

Substituting value of $f_0^2 = f_1 f_2$

$$L_1 = \frac{1}{\frac{f_2 - f_1}{4\pi R_K f_1 f_2} \times 4\pi^2 f_1 f_2} \qquad \boxed{L_1 = \frac{R_K}{\pi (f_2 - f_1)}} \quad \ldots (5.23)$$

We have already derived ...

that

$$R_K^1 = \sqrt{\frac{L_2}{C_1}} = \sqrt{\frac{L_1}{C_1}}$$

$$R_K^2 = \frac{L_2}{C_1} = \frac{L_1}{C_2}$$

which gives

$$L_2 = R_K^2 C_1 \qquad \text{and} \qquad C_2 = \frac{L_1}{R_K^2}$$

Substituting values of C_1 and L_1 in above equation

$$L_2 = \frac{R_K^2 (f_2 - f_1)}{4\pi R_K f_1 f_2} \qquad\qquad C_2 = \frac{R_K}{R_K^2 \pi (f_2 - f_1)}$$

$$\boxed{L_2 = \frac{R_K (f_2 - f_1)}{4\pi f_1 f_2}} \quad ...(5.24) \qquad \boxed{C_2 = \frac{1}{\pi R_K (f_2 - f_1)}} \quad ...(5.25)$$

Above equations are called the design equations of a constant K BPF.

5.10 SOLVED NUMERICALS ON CONSTANT K BAND PASS FILTERS

Example 5.6 :

Find the element value of L and C for a prototype band pass filter terminated with 500 Ω and cut-off frequency of 1 kHz and 5 kHz.

Given: $\quad R_K = 500\ \Omega$
$\quad\quad\quad\quad f_1 = 1\ \text{kHz}$
$\quad\quad\quad\quad f_2 = 5\ \text{kHz}$

To calculate: (i) L_1, C_1
(ii) L_2, C_2

Solution :

$$L_1 = \frac{R_K}{\pi (f_2 - f_1)}$$

$$= \frac{500}{\pi (5000 - 1000)}$$

$$\boxed{L_1 = 39.788\ \text{mH}}$$

$$C_1 = \frac{(f_2 - f_1)}{(4\pi f_1 f_2) R_K}$$

$$= \frac{5000 - 1000}{4\pi \times 1 \times 5 \times 10^3 \times 10^3 \times 500}$$

$$\boxed{C_1 = 0.1273\ \mu F}$$

$$L_2 = \frac{(f_2 - f_1) R_K}{4\pi f_1 f_2} = \frac{(5000 - 1000)(500)}{4\pi \times 5 \times 10^3 \times 1 \times 10^3}$$

$$\boxed{L_2 = 31.83\ \text{mH}}$$

$$C_2 = \frac{1}{\pi (f_2 - f_1) R_K}$$

$$= \frac{1}{\pi (5 \times 10^3 - 1 \times 10^3)\ 500}$$

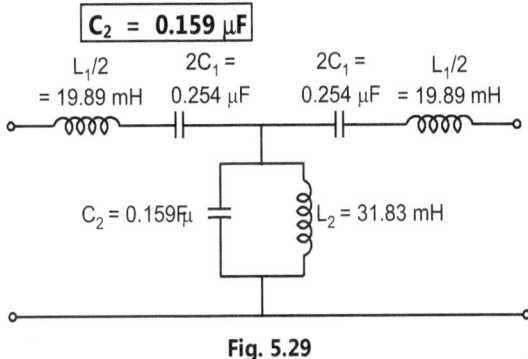

Fig. 5.29

Example 5.7 :

In a constant K bandpass filter, the ratio of the shunt arm capacitance to the total series arm capacitance is 100: 1. The frequency of resonance of both the arm is 1000 Hz. Calculate the bandwidth of the filter.

Solution : Given total series arm capacitance

$$C_1 = \frac{f_2 - f_1}{4\pi R_0 f_1 f_2}$$

Total shunt arm capacitance = C_2

$$C_2 = \frac{1}{\pi R_0 (f_2 - f_1)}$$

The ratio of C_2, C_1 is = 100: 1.

$$\frac{C_2}{C_1} = \frac{100}{1} = \frac{1}{\pi R_0 (f_2 - f_1)} \times \frac{4\pi R_0 f_1 f_2}{(f_2 - f_1)}$$

$$100 = \frac{4 f_1 f_2}{(f_2 - f_1)^2}$$

$$(f_2 - f_1)^2 = \frac{4 f_1 f_2}{100}$$

But

$$f_1 f_2 = f_0^2$$

$$(f_2 - f_1)^2 = \frac{4}{100} \times f_0^2$$

Taking square roots

$$f_2 - f_1 = \frac{2}{10} \times f_0$$

f_0 = Resonance frequency
    = 1000 Hz

∴ $$(f_2 - f_1) = \frac{2}{10} \times 1000$$

$$\boxed{f_2 - f_1 = 200 \text{ Hz}}$$

Example 5.8 :

The series arm Z_1 of a filter consists of 0.5 µF capacitor in series with an inductor of 0.35 H. If $R_0 = 500$ Ω determine the elements in the shunt arm. Also calculate frequency of resonance f_0 and pass band frequencies f_1 and f_2.

Solution : As the series arm consists of induction in series with capacitor, it is a band pass filter.

∴ Shunt arm will have an inductor and a capacitor connected in parallel.

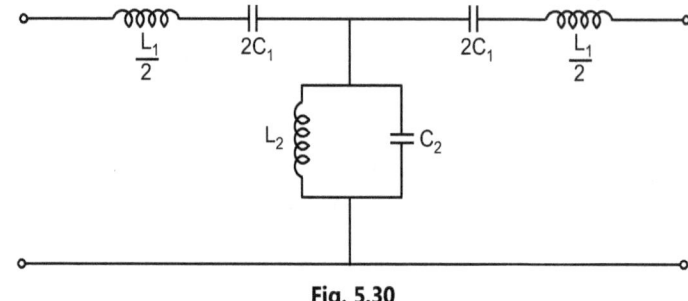

Fig. 5.30

1. To calculate L_2 and C_2:

$$\frac{L_2}{C_1} = \frac{L_1}{C_2} = R^2 = Z_1 Z_2$$

∴ $L_2 = C_1 R_K^2 = 0.5 \times 10^{-6} \times 500^2$

$$\boxed{L_2 = 125 \text{ mH}}$$

$$C_2 = \frac{L_1}{R_K^2} = \frac{0.35}{500^2} = 1.4 \text{ µF}$$

$$\boxed{C_2 = 1.4 \text{ µF}}$$

2. To calculate the frequency of resonance f_0:

$$f_0 = \frac{1}{2\pi \sqrt{L_1 C_1}}$$

$$= \frac{1}{2\pi \sqrt{0.35 \times 0.5 \times 10^{-6}}}$$

$$\boxed{f_0 = 380.453 \text{ Hz}}$$

3. To calculate pass band frequencies f_1 and f_2:

∴ $$L_1 = \frac{R_K}{\pi (f_2 - f_1)}$$

$$f_2 - f_1 = \frac{R_K}{L_1 \cdot \pi}$$

$$= \frac{500}{\pi \cdot 0.35}$$

$$f_2 - f_1 = 454.73 \text{ Hz} \qquad \ldots(1)$$

But
$$f_0 = \sqrt{f_1 f_2}$$

$$f_0^2 = f_1 f_2$$

$$= (380.45)^2$$

$$f_1 = \frac{144.744 \times 10^3}{f_2} \qquad \ldots(2)$$

Substituting value of 2 in 1.

$$f_2 - \frac{144.744 \times 10^3}{f_2}$$

$$= 454.73$$

$$f_2^2 - 454.73 f_2 - 144.744 \times 10^3 = 0$$

$$f_2 = \frac{-(-454.73) \pm \sqrt{454.73^2 - 4 \times 1 \times (-144.7 \times 10^3)}}{2(1)}$$

$$= \frac{454.73 \pm 886.43}{2}$$

$$\boxed{f_2 = 670.58 \text{ Hz}}$$

Substituting in equation (1)

$$f_1 = f_2 - 454.73$$

$$\boxed{f_1 = 215.85}$$

5.11 CONSTANT K BAND STOP FILTERS

- The filter that blocks or attenuates the frequencies in between two cut-off frequencies f_1 and f_2 and passes all the frequencies below f_1 and above f_2.

  f_1 : Lower cut-off frequency (f_L)

  f_2 : Higher cut-off frequency also called as f_H.

- Thus, in BSF all the frequencies between f_L and f_H are attenuated and all the frequencies outside this range are passed.

- Such a band stop filter is obtained by connecting low pass filter section in parallel with a high pass filter provided that the cut-off frequency of a low pass filter section must be selected lower than that of high pass filter section.

5.11.1 Operation of a Constant K BSF

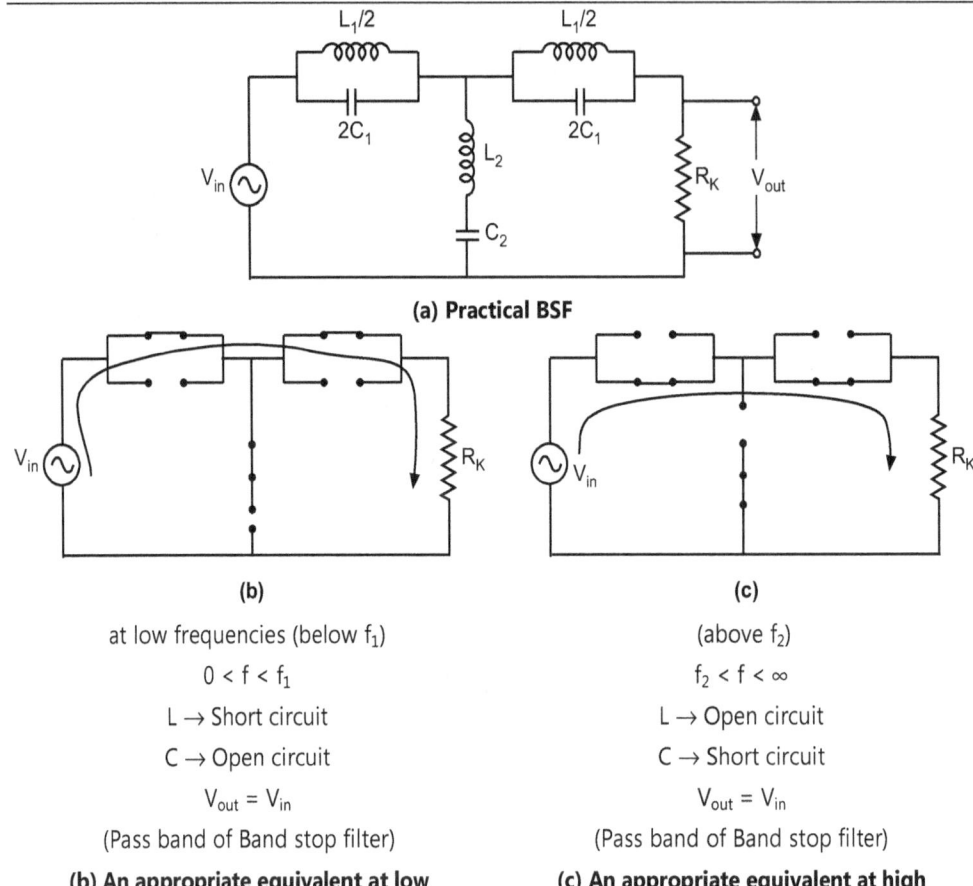

(a) Practical BSF

(b)

at low frequencies (below f_1)

$0 < f < f_1$

L → Short circuit

C → Open circuit

$V_{out} = V_{in}$

(Pass band of Band stop filter)

(b) An appropriate equivalent at low frequencies

(c)

(above f_2)

$f_2 < f < \infty$

L → Open circuit

C → Short circuit

$V_{out} = V_{in}$

(Pass band of Band stop filter)

(c) An appropriate equivalent at high frequencies

Fig. 5.31

- As already discussed earlier, though resistors can their own have no frequency selective property, they are still added and used in all the practical circuits to determine the time constant of the circuit.
- For all the frequencies till f_1, i.e. cut-off frequency of low pass filter, the circuit operates in pass band giving $V_{out} = V_{in}$. LPF and HPF are in parallel, so for lower frequencies though HPF is operating in stop band, LPF has its PB giving $V_{out} = V_{in}$.
- Similarly at higher frequencies, inductor acts as open circuit and capacitor acts as a short circuit. So even in this case current completes the path through capacitor making V_{in} available across the resistance. Thus, here the BSF is actually operating in the pass band of HPF.
- At frequencies between f_1 and f_2 ideally a stop band is expected. Practically the output is very small. The build BSF is said to operate in stop band.

5.11.2 Design Impedance of a Constant K BSF

In a BSF, total series arm is

$$Z_1 = j\omega L_1 \parallel \left(\frac{-j}{\omega C_1}\right)$$

$$Z_1 = \frac{j\omega L_1 \times \frac{-j}{\omega C_1}}{j\omega L_1 - \frac{j}{\omega C_1}}$$

$$Z_1 = \frac{\omega L_1}{j(\omega^2 L_1 C_1 - 1)} \qquad \ldots(a)$$

Similarly, total shunt arm is

$$Z_2 = j\omega L_2 - \frac{j}{\omega C_2}$$

$$Z_2 = j\left(\omega L_2 - \frac{1}{\omega C_2}\right)$$

$$Z_2 = +j\left(\frac{\omega^2 L_2 C_2 - 1}{\omega C_2}\right) \qquad \ldots(b)$$

Now, $\quad R_K^2 = Z_1 Z_2$

$\therefore \quad Z_1 Z_2 = \dfrac{\omega L_1}{j(\omega^2 L_1 C_1 - 1)} \times \dfrac{+j(\omega^2 L_2 C_2 - 1)}{\omega C_2}$

From (2), i.e. $\quad L_1 C_1 = L_2 C_2$

$\therefore \quad Z_1 Z_2 = \dfrac{L_1}{C_2} = \dfrac{L_2}{C_1} = R_K^2$

Thus, $\quad R_K^2 = Z_1 Z_2$

$$\boxed{R_K^2 = \frac{L_2}{C_1} = \frac{L_1}{C_2}} \qquad \ldots(5.26)$$

which is real and a constant. Hence above sections are a constant k filters.

5.11.3 Reactance Curves and Cut-off Frequency of BSF

As was already clear to us, the series and the shunt arm of the constant K BS filter are actually antiresonant and resonant circuits.

So we will reproduce the same reactance curves of series and parallel resonating circuits which we revised in the last section.

Z_1 : parallel resonating circuit

Z_2 : series resonating circuit

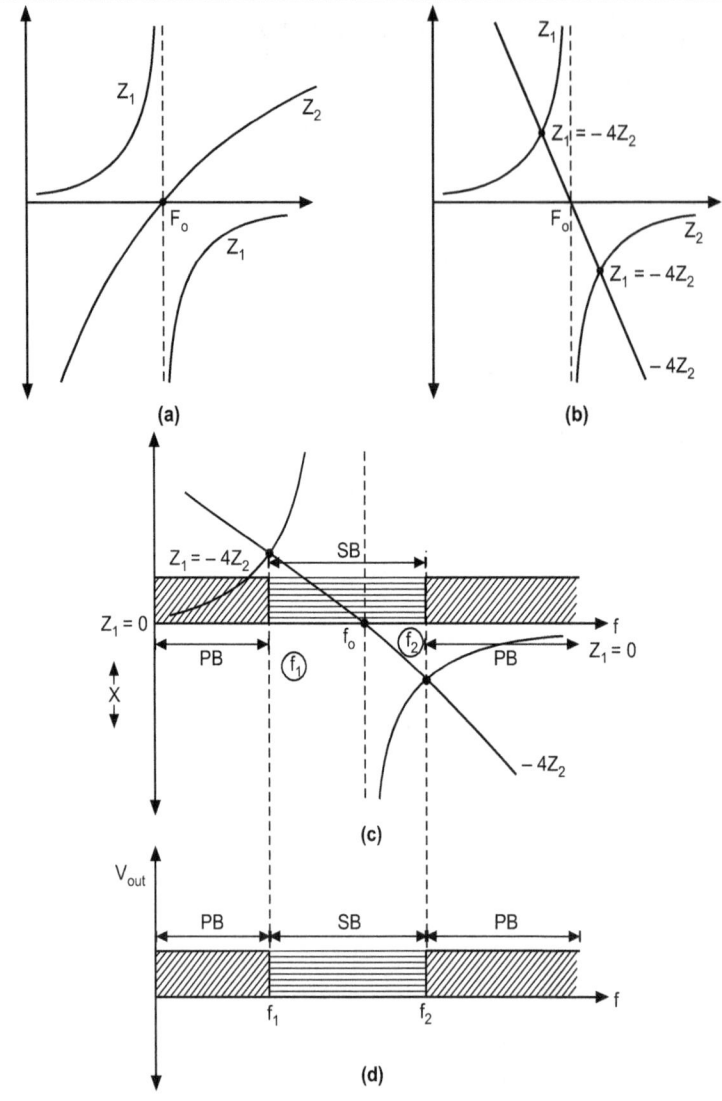

Fig. 5.32: a, b, c: Reactance curves
d: Ideal frequency curve

At both the cut-off frequencies

$$Z_1 = -4Z_2$$

Multiplying the equation by Z_1

$$Z_1^2 = -4Z_1Z_2$$
$$Z_1^2 = -4R_K^2 = +j^2 4R_K^2$$

∴ $\boxed{Z_1 = \pm j\,2\,R_K}$ ... (5.27)

This is also very clear from Fig. 5.32 (c).

Z_1 at lower cut-off frequency f_1 is equal and opposite to Z_1 at higher cut-off frequency f_2. [Z_1 is inductive at f_1 and capacitive at f_2].

$$Z_1 = \frac{\omega L_1}{j(\omega^2 L_1 C_1 - 1)}$$

$$Z_1 = \frac{j\omega L_1}{(1 - \omega^2 L_1 C_1)}$$

This value of Z_1 is equal and opposite at two different cut-off frequencies f_1 and f_2, therefore can be written as:

$$\frac{\omega_1 L_1}{1 - \omega_1^2 L_1 C_1} = -\frac{\omega_2 L_1}{1 - \omega_2^2 L_1 C_1}$$

$$\omega_1 L_1 (1 - \omega_2^2 L_1 C_1) = \omega_2 L_1 (\omega_1^2 L_1 C_1 - 1)$$

$$1 - \omega_2^2 L_1 C_1 = \frac{\omega_2}{\omega_1} (\omega_1^2 L_1 C_1 - 1)$$

We know that

$$\therefore \quad L_1 C_1 = \frac{1}{\omega_0^2}$$

$$\omega_0^2 = \frac{1}{L_1 C_1}$$

$$\therefore \quad 1 - \frac{\omega_2^2}{\omega_0^2} = \frac{\omega_2}{\omega_1}\left(\frac{\omega_1^2}{\omega_0^2} - 1\right)$$

$$1 - \frac{f_2^2}{f_0^2} = \frac{f_2}{f_1}\left(\frac{f_1^2}{f_0^2} - 1\right)$$

$$\frac{f_0^2 - f_2^2}{f_0^2} = \frac{f_2}{f_1}\left(\frac{f_1^2 - f_0^2}{f_0^2}\right)$$

$$f_1 f_0^2 - f_1 f_2^2 = f_2 f_1^2 - f_2 f_0^2$$

$$f_1 f_0^2 - f_2 f_0^2 = f_2 f_1^2 - f_1 f_2^2$$

$$f_0^2 (f_1 + f_2) = f_1 f_2 (f_1 + f_2)$$

$$f_0^2 = f_1 f_2$$

$$\boxed{f_0 = \sqrt{f_1 f_2}} \qquad \ldots (5.28)$$

This result matches the one derived for BPF. The frequency of resonance of the individual arms is the geometric mean of two cut-off frequencies.

5.11.4 Design Equations of a Constant K BSF

$$Z_1 = \pm j\, 2\, R_K$$

$$Z_1 = \frac{j\omega L_1}{(1 - \omega^2 L_1 C_1)}$$

At frequency f_1, Z_1 is inductive.

∴
$$Z_1 = +j\, 2\, R_K$$

$$\frac{j\omega_1 L_1}{(1 - \omega_1^2 L_1 C_1)} = j\, 2\, R_K$$

$$\frac{\omega_1 L_1}{1 - \omega^2 L_1 C_1} = j\, 2\, R_K \qquad \therefore \quad \omega_0^2 = \frac{1}{L_1 C_1}$$

$$\omega_0^2 = \omega_1 \omega_2$$

$$\omega_1 L_1 = 2 R_K \left(1 - \frac{\omega_1^2}{\omega_0^2}\right)$$

$$\omega_1 L_1 = 2 R_K \left(1 - \frac{\omega_1^2}{\omega_1 \omega_2}\right)$$

$$\omega_1 L_1 = 2 R_K \left(\frac{\omega_1 \omega_2 - \omega_1^2}{\omega_1 \omega_2}\right)$$

$$L_1 = 2 R_K \left(\frac{\omega_2 - \omega_1}{\omega_1 \omega_2}\right)$$

$$L_1 = \frac{2 R_K}{2\pi} \left(\frac{f_2 - f_1}{f_1 f_2}\right)$$

$$\boxed{L_1 = \frac{R_K (f_2 - f_1)}{\pi\, f_1 f_2}} \qquad \ldots (5.29)$$

For constant k BSF

$$\omega_0 = \frac{1}{\sqrt{L_1 C_1}}$$

$$\omega_0^2 = \frac{1}{L_1 C_1}$$

$$C_1 = \frac{1}{L_1 \omega_0^2}$$

Substituting value of L_1 and $\omega_0 = 2\pi f_0$

$$C_1 = \frac{1}{\dfrac{R_K (f_2 - f_1)}{\pi f_1 f_2} \times 4\pi^2 f_0^2}$$

$$\boxed{C_1 = \frac{1}{4\pi\, R_K\, (f_2 - f_1)}} \qquad \ldots (5.30)$$

We have already derived in equation (5.38).

$$R_K = \sqrt{\frac{L_2}{C_1}} = \sqrt{\frac{L_1}{C_2}}$$

$$R_K^2 = \frac{L_2}{C_1} = \frac{L_1}{C_2}$$

which gives

$$L_2 = R_K^2 C_1$$

and

$$C_2 = \frac{L_1}{R_K^2}$$

Substituting values of C_1 and L_1

$$\boxed{L_2 = \frac{R_K}{4\pi(f_2 - f_1)}} \quad \ldots (5.31)$$

$$\boxed{C_2 = \frac{(f_2 - f_1)}{\pi R_K (f_1 f_2)}} \quad \ldots (5.32)$$

Equations (5.31 to 5.32) are the design equations for BSF.

5.12 SOLVED NUMERICALS ON CONSTANT K BSF

Example 5.9 :

Compute the values of elements of a constant k band elimination or band stop filter so as to meet the following requirements.

(i) Cut-off frequencies: 350 kHz and 400 kHz.
(ii) Characteristics impedance: 300 Ω.

Given:
f_1 = 350 kHz
f_2 = 400 kHz
R_K = 300 Ω

To calculate: L_1, L_2, C_1, C_2.

Solution :

$$L_1 = \frac{R(f_2 - f_1)}{\pi f_1 f_2}$$

$$= \frac{300(400 - 350)}{\pi \cdot 350 \cdot 400}$$

$$\boxed{L_1 = 34 \ \mu H}$$

$$C_1 = \frac{1}{4\pi R_K (f_2 - f_1)} = \frac{1}{4 \times \pi \times 300 (400 - 350) \times 10^3}$$

$$\boxed{C_1 = 5.3 \text{ nF}}$$

$$L_2 = \frac{R_K}{4\pi(f_2 - f_1)} = \frac{800}{4\pi(400-350)\times 10^3}$$

$$\boxed{L_2 = 0.48 \text{ mH}}$$

$$C_2 = \frac{(f_2-f_1)}{4\pi R_K f_1 \cdot f_2} = \frac{(400-350)\times 10^3}{4\pi \cdot 300 \cdot 400 \cdot 350 \cdot 10^6}$$

$$\boxed{C_2 = 0.38 \text{ nF}}$$

The component values can also be calculated using the formula as under:

$$C_2 = \frac{1}{\pi R_K}\left[\frac{f_2-f_1}{f_1 f_2}\right]$$

$$= \frac{1}{\pi \cdot 300}\left[\frac{400-350}{350 \cdot 400}\right]\frac{10^3}{10^6}$$

$$\boxed{C_2 = 0.38 \text{ nF}}$$

$$L_2 = \frac{R_K}{4\pi(f_2-f_1)}$$

$$= \frac{300}{4\pi(400-350)\times 10^3}$$

$$\boxed{L_2 = 0.48 \text{ mH}}$$

$$L_1 = R_K^2 \cdot C_2$$
$$= 300^2 \times 0.38 \times 10^{-9}$$

$$\boxed{L_1 = 34 \text{ μH}}$$

$$C_1 = \frac{L_2}{R_K^2} = \frac{0.48\times 10^{-7}}{(300)^2}$$

$$\boxed{C_1 = 5.3 \text{ nF}}$$

T and π Sections of BSF are

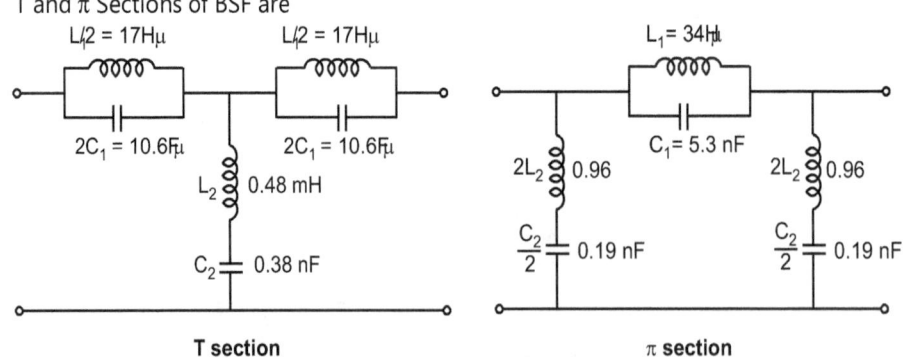

Fig. 5.33

Example 5.10 :

In a constant K band stop filter, the ratio of the shunt indicator to series capacitor is 100: 1. Calculate the ratio of the series inductor to shunt capacitance. Also calculate the value of design impedance. Find the frequency of resonance of both the arm if the bandwidth is 500 Hz and ratio of $\frac{L_1}{L_2}$ is 152.

Given: $\quad \frac{L_2}{L_1} = \frac{100}{1}, \quad (f_2 - f_1) = BW = 500 \text{ Hz}$

$$\frac{L_1}{L_2} = \frac{152}{1}$$

To calculate:

(i) $\frac{L_1}{C_2}$ (ii) R_K (iii) f_0

Solution : (i) To calculate $\frac{L_1}{C_2}$ and R_K.

We know that $\quad \frac{L_2}{C_1} = \frac{L_1}{C_2} = R_K^2$

$$\therefore \quad \boxed{\begin{array}{l}\frac{L_1}{C_2} = 100 \\ R_K = 10\end{array}}$$

(ii) To calculate $f_0 \qquad \frac{L_1}{L_2} = 152$

$$\frac{\frac{R_K (f_2 - f_1)}{\pi f_1 f_2}}{\frac{R_K}{4\pi (f_2 - f_1)}} = 152$$

$$\frac{R_K (f_2 - f_1)}{\pi f_1 f_2} \times \frac{4\pi (f_2 - f_1)}{R_K} = 152$$

$$4 (f_2 - f_1)^2 = 152 \, f_1 f_2$$

$$(f_2 - f_1)^2 = 38 \, f_1 f_2$$

$$\frac{500 \times 500}{38} = f_1 f_2$$

But $\qquad f_0^2 = f_1 f_2$

$$\frac{500 \times 500}{38} = f_0^2$$

$$f_0 = \frac{500}{\sqrt{38}}$$

$$\boxed{f_0 = 80.1}$$

5.13 'm' DERIVED FILTERS

- We need to completely eliminate the disadvantages of constant k or prototype section by designing a new section.
- For effective and appropriate working of the constant k section, the proposed new section must same satisfy the following conditions.
- The new section must have cut-off frequency as that of the constant k. Filter but different attenuation characteristics i.e. rapid rise in α at cut-off frequencies in stop band.
- The new section must have the same value of characteristic impedance Z_0 as that of prototype section at all the frequencies so that both the sections have identical pass bands.
- Such a filter section that satisfies all the above requirements is known as m-derived filter section. It is so called because the new section is actually derived from the original prototype, section with a slight modification.
- We have discussed T and π sections of LPF, HPF, BPF and BSF. On the similar grounds, we have m derived T and m derived π sections for each of the constant k filter.
- We will discuss m derived LPF and HPF in this chapter.

5.13.1 m Derived T Section

- A prototype T section is shown in Fig. 5.34 (a). Let the new section constructed from the prototype section be as shown Fig. 5.34 (b).

  1. Let this new section have the series arm impedance modified to $m\dfrac{Z_1}{2}$ where m is a constant. The shunt arm impedance also changes to some other value Z_2'.
  2. As will be clear later these two sections are connected in series.
  3. As already discussed, for satisfactory matching of several such types of sections in series, it is necessary that Z_0 of all be identical at all the points in the pass band. So Z_0 of both these sections must be equal $\dfrac{Z_2}{n}$.

- Now for Fig.5.48 (a). $Z_{OT} = \sqrt{\dfrac{Z_1^2}{4} + Z_1 Z_2}$

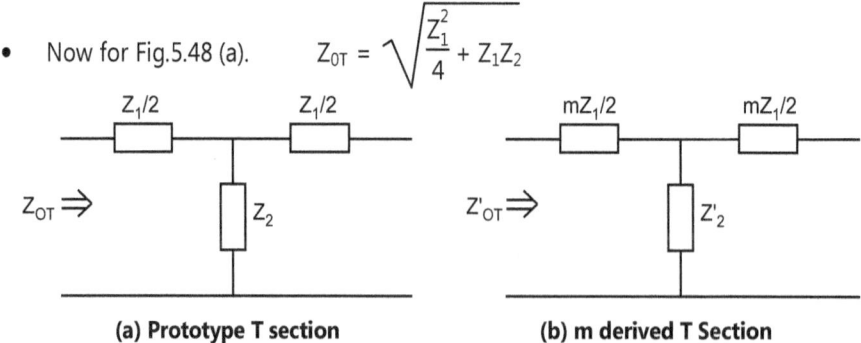

(a) Prototype T section (b) m derived T Section

Fig. 5.34

Similarly for m derived section i.e. Fig. 5.48 (b).

$$Z'_{OT} = \sqrt{\left(\frac{mZ_1}{2}\right)^2 + mZ_1 Z'_2}$$

To maintain same Z_0 we must have

$$Z_{OT} = Z^1_{OT}$$

$$\sqrt{\frac{Z_1^2}{4} + Z_1 Z_2} = \sqrt{\frac{m^2 Z_1^2}{4} + mZ_1 Z'_2}$$

$$\frac{Z_1^2}{4} + Z_1 Z_2 = \frac{m^2 Z_1^2}{4} + mZ_1 Z'_2$$

$$mZ_1 Z'_2 = \frac{Z_1^2}{4}[1 - m^2] + Z_1 Z_2$$

$$\boxed{Z'_2 = \left(\frac{1-m^2}{4m}\right) Z_1 + \frac{Z_2}{m}} \quad ...(5.33)$$

- Thus, impedance Z'_2 i.e. shunt arm of m derived section consists of two impedances in series.
- These two impedances are:
$\left(\frac{1-m^2}{4m}\right) Z_1$ and $\left(\frac{Z_2}{m}\right)$ connected in series.
- Note that the value of m can range from 0 to 1, when m = 1 the prototype and the m derived sections are identical.

    (Substitute m = 1 in equation (5.33) and you will get $Z'_2 = Z_2$)

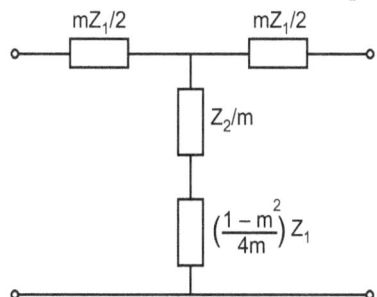

Fig. 5.35: m derived T section

5.13.2 m Derived π Section

- A prototype π section is shown in Fig. 5.36 (a). Let the new section constructed from the prototype section be as shown in Fig. 5.36 (b).

- Let this new section have the series arm Z_L' and the shunt impedance modified to $\dfrac{2Z_2}{m}$.
- As will be clear in the later part of the chapter, the prototype and m derived sections are connected in series.
- For satisfactory matching of several such type of sections in series it is very necessary that Z_0 of all the sections be identical at all points in the pass band. So Z_0 of both the sections must be equal.

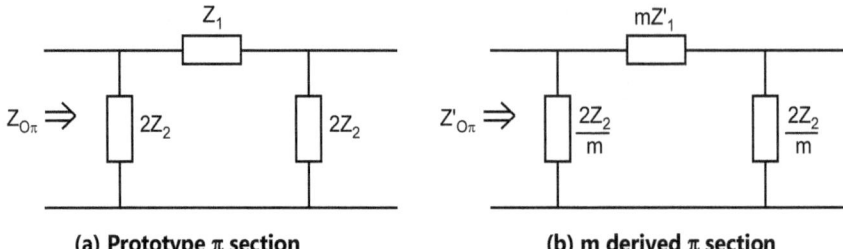

(a) Prototype π section (b) m derived π section

Fig. 5.36

$$Z_{0\pi} = \dfrac{Z_1 Z_2}{\sqrt{\dfrac{Z_1^2}{4} + Z_1 Z_2}}$$

Similarly for the m derived section of Fig. 5.107 (b).

$$Z'_{0\pi} = \dfrac{Z_1' \dfrac{Z_2}{m}}{\sqrt{\dfrac{(Z_1')^2}{4} + Z_1' \dfrac{Z_2}{m}}}$$

To maintain same Z_0 we must have

$$Z_{0\pi} = Z'_{0\pi}$$

$$\dfrac{Z_1 Z_2}{\sqrt{\dfrac{Z_1^2}{4} + Z_1 Z_2}} = \dfrac{Z_1' \dfrac{Z_2}{m}}{\sqrt{\dfrac{(Z_1')^2}{4} + Z_1' \dfrac{Z_2}{m}}}$$

$$\dfrac{Z_1^2}{\dfrac{Z_1^2}{4} + Z_1 Z_2} = \dfrac{\left(\dfrac{Z_1'}{m}\right)^2}{\dfrac{Z_1'^2}{4} + \dfrac{Z_1' Z_2}{m}}$$

$$\frac{Z_1^2 Z_1^{'2}}{4} + \frac{Z_1^2 Z_1^{'} Z_2}{m} = \frac{Z_1^2 Z_1^{'2}}{4m^2} + Z_1 Z_2 \frac{Z_1^{'2}}{m^2}$$

Multiplying throughout by $4m^2$.

$$m^2 Z_1^2 Z_1^{'2} + 4m Z_1^2 Z_1^{'} Z_2 = Z_1^2 Z_1^{'2} + 4 Z_1 Z_1^{'2} Z_2$$

dividing through by $Z_1^{'}$.

$$m^2 Z_1^2 Z_1^{'} + 4m Z_1^2 Z_2 = Z_1^2 Z_1^{'} + 4 Z_1 Z_1^{'} Z_2$$

$$Z_1^{'} \left[m^2 Z_1^2 - Z_1^2 - 4 Z_1 Z_2 \right] = -4m Z_1^2 Z_2$$

$$Z_1^{'} = \frac{4 m Z_1^2 Z_2}{Z_1^2 + 4 Z_1 Z_2 - m^2 Z_1^2}$$

Multiplying numerator and denominator by m.

$$Z_1^{'} = \frac{4 m^2 Z_1^2 Z_2}{m Z_1^2 + 4 m Z_1 Z_2 - m^3 Z_1^2}$$

$$Z_1^{'} = \frac{4 m^2 Z_1^2 Z_2}{4 m Z_1 Z_2 + m Z_1^2 (1 - m^2)}$$

$$Z_1^{'} = \frac{(4 m Z_2)(m Z_1^2)}{4 m Z_1 Z_2 + m Z_1^2 (1 - m^2)}$$

$$Z_1^{'} = \frac{\left(\frac{4 m Z_2}{1 - m^2} \right) m Z_1}{\frac{4 m Z_2}{1 - m^2} + m Z_1}$$

$$\boxed{Z_1^{'} = \left(\frac{4 m Z_2}{1 - m^2} \right) \| \, m Z_1} \qquad \ldots (5.34)$$

- Thus, importance $Z_1^{'}$ i.e. series arm of m derived section consists of two impedances in parallel.

- $Z_1^{'}$ is a parallel combination of $m Z_1$ and $\frac{4 m Z_2}{1 - m^2}$.

- Note that similar to m derived T section, even in this case value of m can range from 0 to 1. When m = 1 the prototype and the m derived sections are identical.

(Substitute m = 1 in equation (5.34) and we will have $Z_1^{'} = Z_1$).

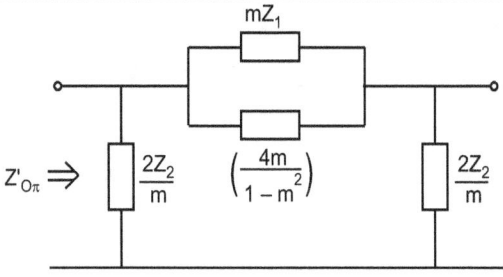

Fig. 5.37: m derived π sections

m derived T and π sections can be now designed for any of the constant k, filters, i.e. LPF, HPF, BSF and BPF. But here we will restrict our scope of discussion to m derived LPF and HPF.

5.14 m DERIVED LOW PASS FILTER

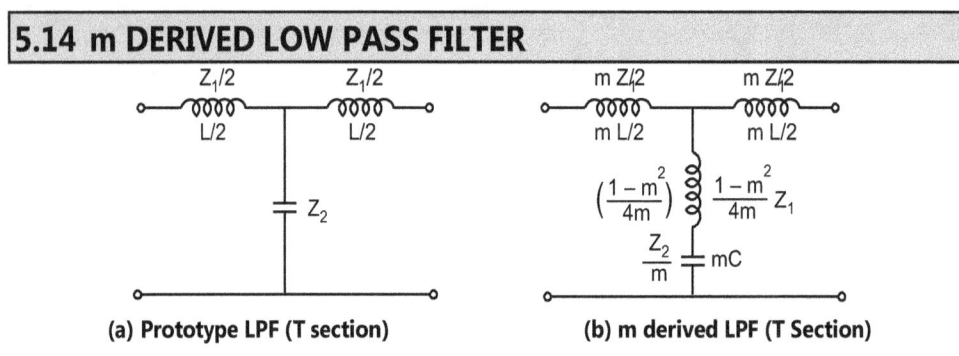

(a) Prototype LPF (T section)   (b) m derived LPF (T Section)

Fig. 5.38

- In the very last section we have seen that Z_2' in case of m derived section is a series combination of two impedances.

$$\frac{1-m^2}{4m} Z_1 \text{ and } \frac{Z_2}{m}$$

- **Note:** When an impedance of a condenser is divided by m then its capacitance must be multiplied by m.
- Now let us clearly understand that how such a small modification in the circuit will give us infinite attenuation near cut-off frequency or how do we get zero output voltage near f_c in case of m derived LPF.

5.14.1 Operation of m derived LPF

- As is clear from the Fig. 5.39 (b) shunt arm of m derived section is a series resonant circuit. [L in series with C].
- In a series resonant circuit i.e. in a circuit when inductive and capacitive reactances are in series the reactances cancel each other at resonant frequency.
- So, at this resonant frequency, the shunt arm appears as a short circuit on the network.

- As shown in Fig. 5.39 the short circuit provides ground path to the input signal, thereby making $V_{out} = 0V$ and thus attenuation is very high [as ideally expected] at this resonant frequency.
- This frequency of infinite or very high attenuation is called f_∞.

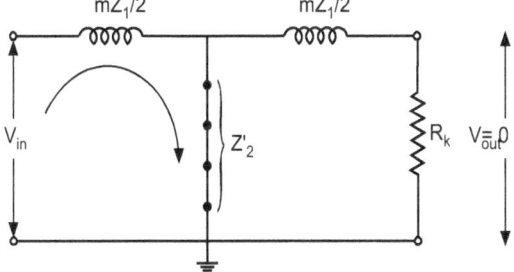

Fig. 5.39: An Approximate Model of m Derived LPF at f_∞, Where Shunt Arm Appears as Short circuit bypassing The Load

5.14.2 Reactance Curves

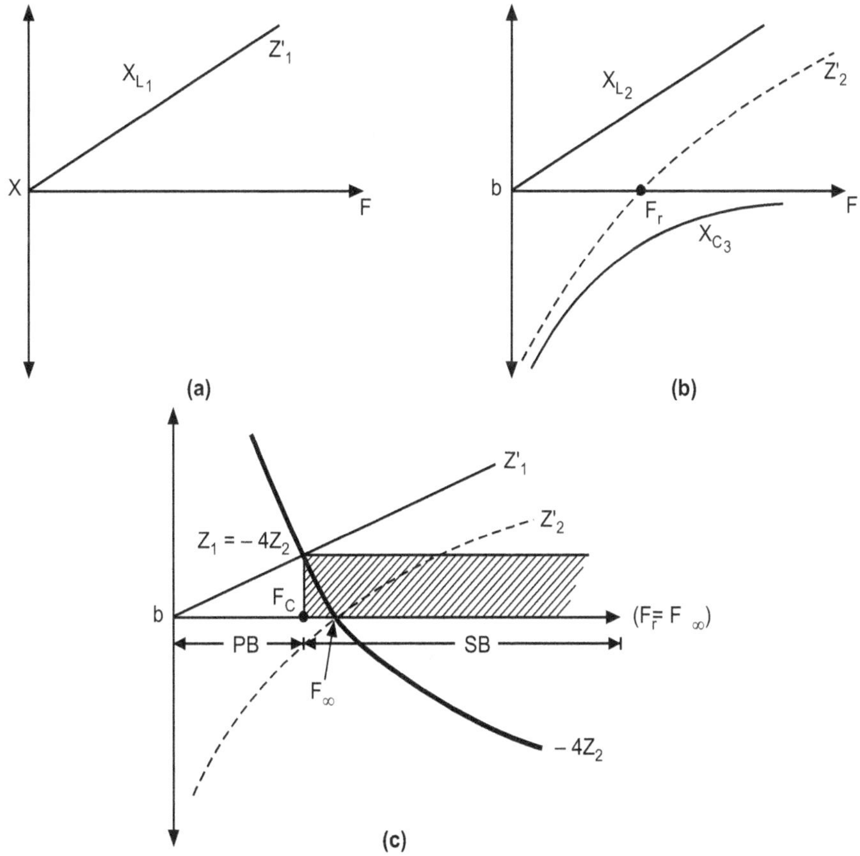

Fig. 5.40: Reactance plots of (a) series arm (b) shunt arm (c) reactance curve indicating PB and SB of m derived

Here,

$$Z_1' = \text{series arm having inductor } L_1$$

$$Z_2' = \text{shunt arm having inductor } L_2 \text{ capacitor } C$$

- Fig. 5.40 (a) is a plot of x_L against f. Fig. 5.40 (b) shows the plot of the individual components L_2 and C and also plot of Z_2' as a series resonating circuit.
- 'f_r' in Fig. 5.40 (b) is a resonating frequency at which $X_{L2} = X_C$.
  i.e. Reactances of inductor and capacitor present in the shunt arm of the m derived filter are equal, thus making it act as a short circuit at f_r.
- Fig. 5.40 (c) shows the reactance curves of Z_1' and Z_2' to indicate a pass band between the frequencies of which $Z_1' = -4Z_2'$ and $Z_1' = 0$.
- f_C and f_r are shown. f_r as discussed earlier is nothing but f_∞ i.e. the frequency at which shunt arm will act as short circuit making $V_{out} = 0$.
- **Note:** f_C and f_∞ are two different frequencies close to each other. This observation needs an explanation.

5.14.3 f_∞ and f_C in m Derived LPF

- We have designed m derived filters with an objective to have very high attenuation at cut-off frequency (f_C).
- To achieve this, a inductor is added in shunt arm making it function as series resonant circuit resonating at frequency f_∞ (i.e. f_r).
- At this frequency, f_∞, $V_{out} = 0$ and thus attenuation is very very high.
- Ideally we want this operation, this behaviour at f_C i.e. cut-off frequency.
- Practically we achieve it to f_∞ and not at f_C. f_∞ can be chosen arbitrarily close to f_C so the α near f_C is made high.
- We might end up thinking that why is f_∞ not made same as f_C.
- There are two reasons justifying that f_∞ and f_C can never be the same frequencies. $f_\infty \ne f_C$. And f_∞ will always and always be higher than f_C, in case of m derived LPF.
  1. At f_C we must have $Z_1' = -4Z_2'$.

     AT f_∞ we must have $Z_2' = 0$.

It is impossible to achieve or satisfy both these conditions at very same frequency. So f_C can never be equal to f_∞. They have to be two different frequencies.

2. Below f_C, Z_2' is capacitive.

   Below f_∞, Z_2' is capacitive

   Above f_∞, Z_2' is inductive.

So, if f_∞ is below f_C than these conditions will not be met. So f_∞ is always higher than f_C.

5.14.4 Derivations of f_∞ and m for a m Derived LPF

The shunt arm of m derived LPF (T section) resonates of frequency f_∞ (f_r).

$$f_r = \frac{1}{2\pi\sqrt{LC}} \quad \text{... expression for } f_r \text{ series reasonance}$$

Here,

$$f_\infty = \frac{1}{2\pi\sqrt{\left(\frac{1-m^2}{4m}\right)L(mC)}}$$

$$f_\infty = \frac{1}{\pi\sqrt{(1-m^2)LC}} \quad \text{... (a)}$$

But, for a low pass filter

$$f_C = \frac{1}{\pi\sqrt{LC}} \quad \text{... (b)}$$

∴ Substituting equation (b) in (a)

$$\boxed{f_\infty = \frac{f_C}{\sqrt{(1-m^2)}}} \quad \text{... (5.35)}$$

Simplifying equation (5.45) we have

$$\sqrt{1-m^2} = \frac{f_C}{f_\infty}$$

$$1 - m^2 = \left(\frac{f_C}{f_\infty}\right)^2$$

$$\boxed{m = \sqrt{1 - \left(\frac{f_C}{f_\infty}\right)^2}} \quad \text{... (5.36)}$$

This equation determines the value of m to be used for a particular f_∞.

5.15 M DERIVED HIGH PASS FILTER

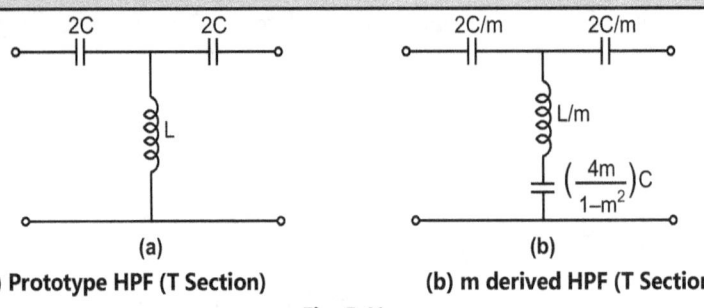

(a) Prototype HPF (T Section)   (b) m derived HPF (T Section)

Fig. 5.41

- Z_2' in case of m derived section in a series combination of two impedances.

$$\frac{1-m^2}{4m} Z_1 \text{ and } \frac{Z_2}{m}$$

Here Z_1 is a capacitor (C). Here Z_2 is an inductor (L)

$\therefore Z_2'$ is $\frac{L}{M}$ in series with $\frac{4m}{1-m^2}$ C.

- Note: When a impedance of a condenser is divided by m then its capacitance should be multiplied by m.

5.15.1 Operation

- It is clear From the Fig. 5.56 (b) shunt arm of m derived section is a series resonant circuit [L in series with C].
- In a series resonant circuit i.e. in a circuit when inductive and capacitive reactances are in series the reactances can cell each other at resonant frequency.
- So at this resonant frequency, the shunt arm appears as a short circuit on the network.
- As shown in Fig. 5.42, this short circuit provides ground path to the input signal thereby making V_{out} = 0V and thus the attenuation is very very high [as ideally expected] at this resonant frequency.
- This frequency of infinite or very high attenuation is called f_∞.

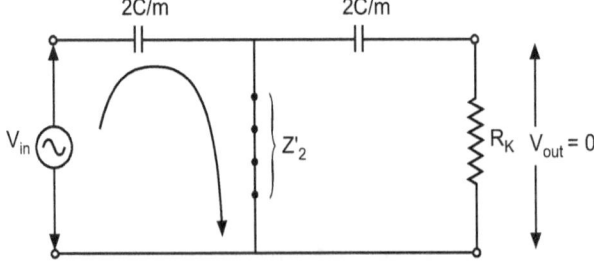

Fig. 5.42: An approximate model at f_∞
where shunt arm appears as short circuit (bypassing the load)

5.15.2 Reactance Curves

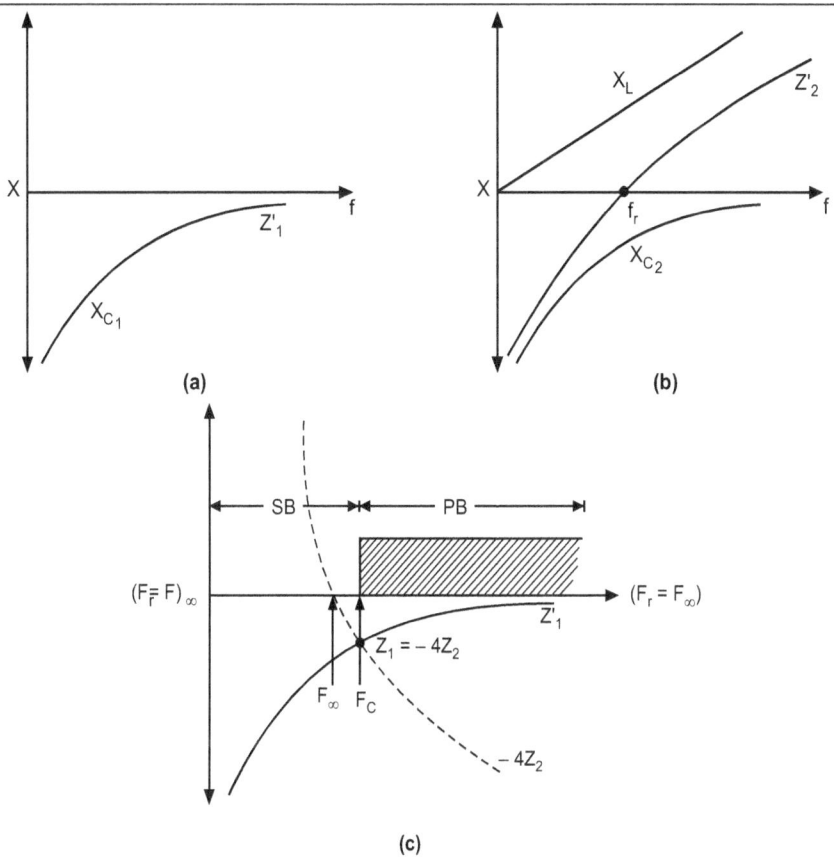

Fig. 5.43: Reactance plots of (a) series arm (b) shunt arm
(c) reactance curve indicate PB, SB

Here, Z_1' = Series arm having capacitor (C_1)

Z_2' = Shunt arm having inductor (L), capacitor (C_2)

- Fig. 5.58 (a) is a plot of X_{C_1} against f and 5.58 (b) shows the plot of the individual components L and C_2 and also plot of Z_2' as a series resonating circuit.
- f_r is Fig. 5.58 (b) is a resonating frequency at which

$$X_L = X_{C_2}$$

i.e. reactances of inductor and capacitor present in the shunt arm of m derived filter are equal, thus making it act as a short circuit at f_r.

- Fig. 5.58 (c) shows the reactance curves of Z_1' and Z_2' to indicate a pass band between the frequencies at which $Z_1' = -4Z_2'$ and $Z_1' = 0$.
- f_r and f_∞ are indicated. f_r as already discussed is nothing but f_∞, i.e. the frequency at which shunt arm will act as short circuit making $V_{out} = 0$.
- f_C and f_∞ are two different frequencies close to each other.

5.15.3 f_∞ and f_C in m derived HPF

- The discussion explaining the reasons of having f_C and f_∞ as two different frequencies is applicable in this case as well.

1. At f_C, we must have

$$Z_1' = -4Z_2'$$

At f_∞, we must have

$$Z_2' = 0$$

2. It is impossible to achieve or satisfy both these conditions at very same frequency. So f_C can never be equal to f_∞. They have to be two different frequencies.

   Above f_C Z_2' is inductive

   Below f_∞ Z_2' is capacitive

   Above f_∞ Z_2' is inductive

   So, if f_∞ is shifted above f_C, than these conditions will not be satisfied. So f_∞ is always lower than f_C.

5.15.4 Derivations of f_∞ and m

The shunt arm of m-derived HPF (T section) resonates at frequency f_∞ i.e. f_r.

$$f_\infty = \frac{1}{2\pi\sqrt{\left(\frac{L}{m}\right)\left(\frac{4m}{1-m^2}\right)C}}$$

$$f_\infty = \frac{1}{2\pi\sqrt{\frac{4LC}{(1-m^2)}}}$$

Substituting value of f_C in the equation for f_∞.

$$\boxed{f_\infty = f_C\sqrt{(1-m^2)}} \qquad \ldots (5.37)$$

Simplifying equation (5.92)

$$\frac{f_\infty}{f_c} = \sqrt{1-m^2}$$

$$\left(\frac{f_\infty}{f_c}\right)^2 = 1-m^2$$

$$m^2 = 1 - \left(\frac{f_\infty}{f_c}\right)^2$$

$$\boxed{m = \sqrt{1 - \left(\frac{f_\infty}{f_c}\right)^2}} \qquad \ldots (5.38)$$

This equation determines the value of m to be used for a particular f_∞.

5.16 SOLVED NUMERICALS ON M DERIVED FILTERS

Example 5.11 : Design a m-derived low pas filter to match a line having characteristic impedance of 500 Ω and to pass signals upto 1 kHz with infinite attenuation at 1.2 kHz.

Solution : Given R_0 = 500 Ω, f_C = 1 kHz, f_∞ = 1.2 kHz.

1. **Design of prototype low pass filter section (T Type)**

   Using design equations,

   $$L = \frac{R_0}{(\pi f_C)}$$

   $$L = \frac{500}{\pi \times 1000}$$

   $$\boxed{L = 159.155 \text{ mH}}$$

   $$C = \frac{1}{(\pi f_C) R_0}$$

   $$C = \frac{1}{(\pi \times 1000)(500)}$$

   $$\boxed{C = 0.6366 \text{ }\mu F}$$

Thus, prototype low pass filter (T type) is as shown in the Fig. 5.60 (a).

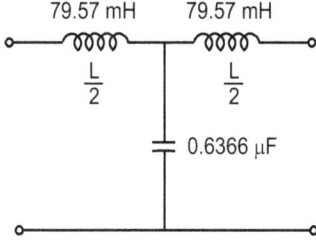

Fig. 5.44 (a)

2. **Design of m-derived low pass filter:**

The value of m is given by,

$$m = \sqrt{1 - \left(\frac{f_c}{f_\infty}\right)^2}$$

$$m = \sqrt{1 - \left(\frac{1000}{1200}\right)^2}$$

$$\boxed{m = 0.552}$$

The elements in the series and shunt arms of m-derived filter section are given by,

$$\frac{mL}{2} = \frac{(0.5527)(159.155 \times 10^{-3})}{2}$$

$$\boxed{\frac{mL}{2} = 43.976 \text{ mH}}$$

$$mC = (0.5527)(0.6366 \times 10^{-6})$$

$$\boxed{mL = 0.3518 \text{ µF}}$$

$$\left(\frac{1-m^2}{4m}\right)L = \left[\frac{1-(0.5527)^2}{4(0.5527)}\right](159.133 \times 10^{-3})$$

$$\boxed{\left(\frac{1-m^2}{4m}\right)L = 50 \text{ mH}}$$

Hence m-derived low pass filter is as shown in the Fig. 5.60.

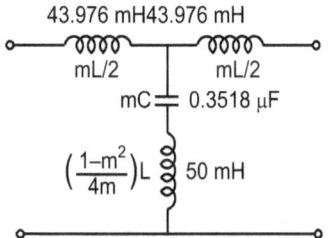

Fig. 5.44 (b): m-derived low pass filter T type section

Example 5.12 :

Design m-derived LPF having cut-off frequency of 5 kHz and impedance of 600 Ω. The frequency of infinite attenuation is 1.25 times the cut-off frequency.

Solution : Given: $R_0 = 600 \text{ Ω}$, $f_c = 5$ kHz, $f_\infty = (1.25 \times 5) = 6.25$ kHz.

$$L = \frac{R_0}{\pi f_c} = \frac{600}{\pi \times 5 \times 10^3}$$

$$\boxed{L = 38.197 \text{ mH}}$$

$$C = \frac{1}{(\pi f_c) R_0} = \frac{1}{\pi \times 5 \times 10^3 \times 600}$$

$$\boxed{C = 0.106 \ \mu F}$$

For m derived LPF m is given by,

$$m = \sqrt{1 - \left(\frac{f_c}{f_\infty}\right)^2} = \sqrt{1 - \left(\frac{5 \times 10^3}{6.25 \times 10^3}\right)^2}$$

$$\boxed{m = 0.6}$$

The actual values of components in series and shunt arms of m-derived filter are

$$\frac{mL}{2} = \frac{0.6 \times 38.197 \times 10^{-3}}{2}$$

$$\boxed{\frac{mL}{2} = 11.459 \ mH}$$

$$mC = 0.6 \, (0.106 \times 10^{-6})$$

$$\boxed{mC = 0.0636 \ \mu F}$$

$$\left(\frac{1-m^2}{4m}\right) L = \left(\frac{1-(0.6)^2}{4(0.6)}\right) (38.197 \times 10^{-3})$$

$$\boxed{\left(\frac{1-m^2}{4m}\right) L = 10.18 \ mH}$$

∴ The low pass filter is as shown below.

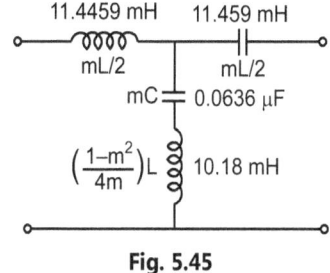

Fig. 5.45

5.17 DISADVANTAGES OF M DERIVED FILTER

- In constant k or prototype section, sharp rise in attenuation in the stop band was a limitation.

  i.e. In LPF, high α was needed in stop band after f_c.

  In HPF, high α was needed in stop band before f_c.

  and this was not achieved.

- So a m-derived. Filter was designed which gave very very high attenuation at frequency f_∞, very close but not equal to f_C.
- Thus, at f_∞ (which is located in stop band in LPF and HPF) the rise in the attenuation is very sharp.
- But the limitation is that this increase in α is only at f_∞. After f_∞ the value of α again decreases.
- Ideally α should be very large (infinite) throughout the stop band for any filter. But in the case of m derived filters the desired high attenuation is only at one frequency in stop band. It does not last for the entire stop band as actually expected and is clear. From Fig. 5.61.
- The reason for such a behaviour of α is because of f_∞, the shunt arm of LPF and HPF acts as good as a short circuit. X_L cancels X_C at f_∞, which is the resonating frequency.
  But if we recollect the concepts of resonance, it is very clear that only at resonating frequency, $X_L = X_C$ i.e. only the resonance the total reactance is zero. In series resonance for any frequency above or below f_r, there is some reactance existing (may be inductive or capacitive respectively), so the output will not be completely zero. A finite voltage will appear across the load.
- The attenuation α is said to be infinite or very large only when V_{out} is zero. So, in case of m derived filter this is achieved only at f_∞, value of α drops for other frequencies in stop band.
- This happens to be a major limitation in m derived filters.
- However, this limitation can be overcomed by two ways:
    1. Use of composite filter.
    2. Use as many m derived sections as desired to:
        - Produce a high attenuation over the entire stop band.
        - Supress the signal components at only at some particular frequencies.

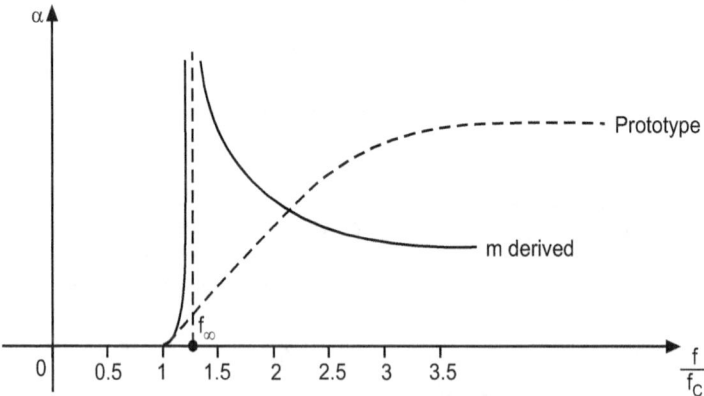

Fig. 5.46: Variation of α in prototype and m derived section

5.18 COMPOSITE FILTER

- In this unit of filters, we started our discussion with prototype filters. We realized that the attenuation characteristics is not very sharp in the attenuation band as it is ideally expected. Due to this it was very difficult to distinguish the frequencies after and before cut-off frequency.
- So, to overcome this drawback in prototype filters, we designed m derived filters which gave very large attenuation at a frequency f_∞, very close to f_C. But even m derived filters had a limitation. It was observed that in the stop band though α is very high at f_∞, it drastically reduces after f_∞ in case of LPF and before f_∞ in case of HPF.
- Constant k or prototype filter is a good choice if high attenuation is needed in deeper stop band, at frequencies far away from f_0.
- Similarly a m-derived filter should be a preferable choice if very high attenuation is needed at a frequency close to f_c.
- But none of these filters are ideal filters because none of them give you high attenuation through out the stop band as ideally desired.
- So a wise choice is to use a prototype section in series with a m derived section. As indicated in Fig. 5.71. This assembly would definitely give appreciably high attenuation through out the stop band.
- Such a combination along with terminating half sections is called as a composite filter.

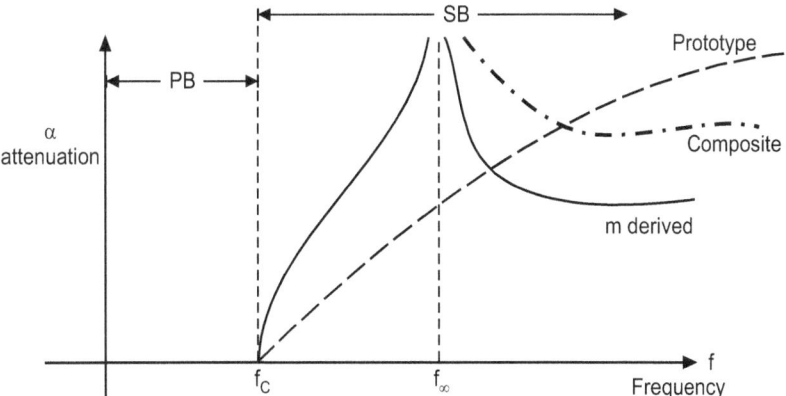

Fig. 5.47: Variation of α in Constant k, m Derived and Composite Filter

- Thus a general block schematic of the composite filter will have:
  1. One or more prototype sections.
  2. One or more m derived sections
  3. Terminating half sections (with m = 0.6).
- Thus to summarize.

	Filter	Attenuation Near f_C	Attenuation after f_C
1.	Constant K	Very low	Very high
2.	m derived	Very high	Low
3.	Composite	High	High

- The block schematic of composite filter is shown in Fig. 5.48.

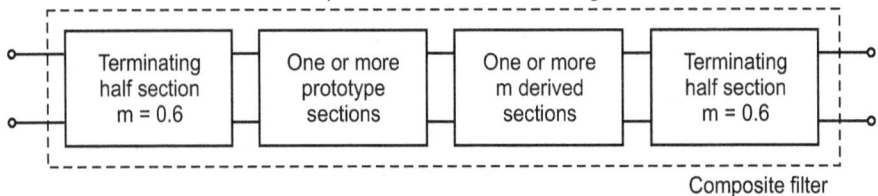

Composite filter

Fig. 5.48: Block Schematic of the Composite Filter

- Terminating half sections with m = 0.6 are inserted to achieve proper impedance matching and constant characteristics impedance through out the pass band.
- If it is desired to have very large attenuation at few particular frequencies in the stop band, corresponding number of m derived filter section must be used in cascade with the desired value of f_∞.
- In cases, where an impedance match is not important, the attenuation may be built-up near cut-off by cascading or connecting a number of constant k prototype sections in series.
- Thus, the number of various sections in any composite filter would totally depend on the desired attenuation characteristics.
- In any case, design impedance R_K, the cut-off frequency f_C and infinite frequency f_∞ are some important design specification in a composite filter.

5.19 SOLVED NUMERICALS ON COMPOSITE FILTERS

Example 5.13 :

Design a composite low pass filter to work into 500 Ω resistance with cut-off at 1000 Hz. It should have very high attenuation at 1065, 1250 and ∞ kHz.

Given: f_C = 1000 Hz, $f_{\infty 1}$ = 1065, $f_{\infty 2}$ = 1250 Hz, $f_{\infty 3}$ = ∞, R_k = 500 Ω.

Solution : (i) Prototype Section:

$$L = \frac{R_K}{\pi f_C}$$

$$= \frac{500}{\pi \times 1000}$$

$$L = 159 \text{ mH}$$

$$\boxed{\frac{L}{2} = 0.079\ H}$$

$$C = \frac{1}{\pi f_C R}$$

$$= \frac{1}{\pi \times 1000 \times 500}$$

$$\boxed{C = 0.636\ \mu F}$$

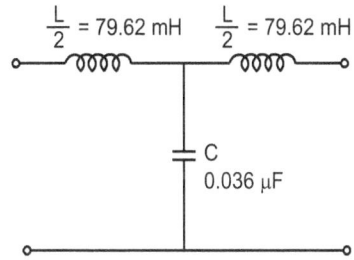

Fig. 5.49 (a)

(ii) m derived section

We know, $m = \sqrt{1 - \left(\frac{f_c}{f_\infty}\right)^2}$

(a) For $f_\infty = \infty$ (infinity) Hz

$\boxed{m = 1}$, which is nothing but the prototype as shown above in Fig. 5.133 (a)

(b) For $f_\infty = 1065$ Hz

$$m = \sqrt{1 - \left(\frac{1000}{1065}\right)^2}$$

$$\boxed{m = 0.344}$$

$$\left(\frac{1-m^2}{4m}\right)L = \left[\frac{1 - 0.344^2}{4 \times 0.344}\right] 159$$

$$\boxed{\left(\frac{1-m^2}{4m}\right)L = 101.9\ mH}$$

$mC = 0.344 \times 0.636\ \mu F$

$\boxed{mC = 0.219\ \mu F}$

$\dfrac{mL}{2} = 0.344 \times \dfrac{0.0795}{2}$

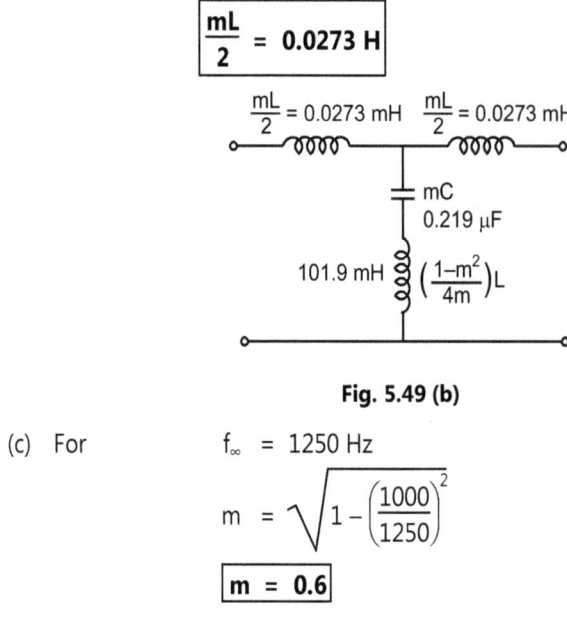

Fig. 5.49 (b)

(c) For $f_\infty = 1250$ Hz

$$m = \sqrt{1 - \left(\frac{1000}{1250}\right)^2}$$

$$\boxed{m = 0.6}$$

Now since m = 0.6, this section can be used as a terminating half-section. Therefore series and shunt arms of the terminating sections are:

$$\frac{mL}{2} = 0.6 \times 0.0785$$

$$\boxed{\frac{mL}{2} = 0.0477 \text{ H}}$$

$$= \boxed{47.7 \text{ mH}}$$

$$\frac{mC}{2} = 0.6 \times \frac{0.6366}{2}$$

$$\boxed{\frac{mC}{2} = 0.1909 \text{ }\mu\text{F}}$$

$$\left(\frac{1-m^2}{2m}\right)L = \left[\frac{1-(0.6)^2}{2(0.6)}\right] 0.1591$$

$$\boxed{\left(\frac{1-m^2}{2m}\right) = 84.8 \text{ H}}$$

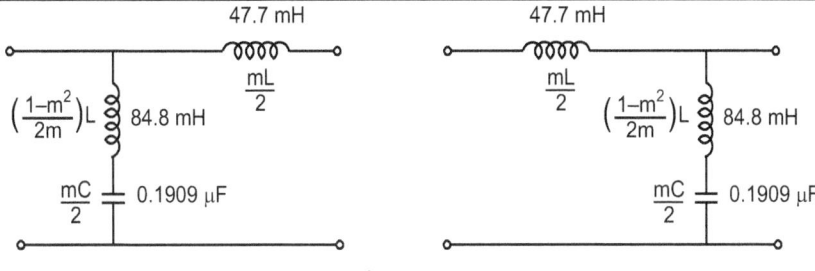

Fig. 5.49 (c)

(iii) Composite filter: The designed constant k type, n-derived filter section and terminating half-sections are all connected in cascade to form a composite low pass filter.

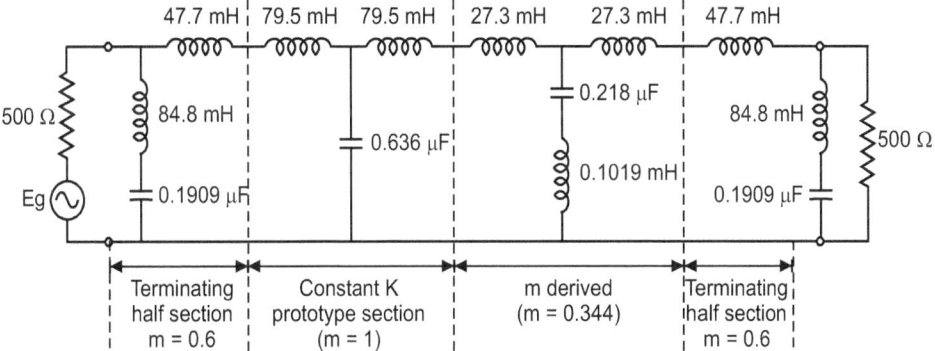

Fig. 5.49 (d)

The series inductors can be added to the circuit can be simplified to obtain equivalent composite filter as:

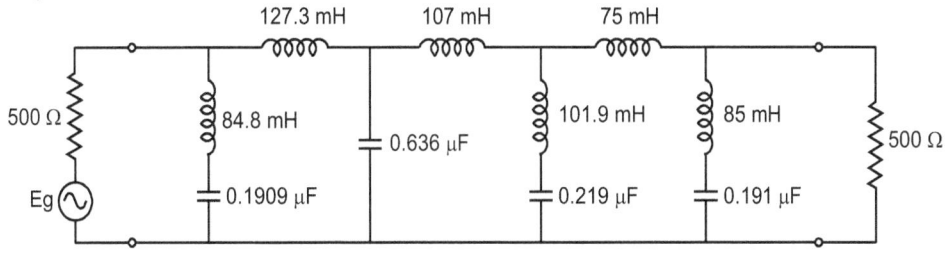

Fig. 5.49 (e)

Example 5.14 :

Design a composite high pass filter work into 1000 Ω resistance with cut-off frequency of 1000 Hz and with high attenuation of 800 Hz and 950 Hz.

Given:
$R_K = 1000\ \Omega$
$f_C = 1\ kHz$
$f_{\infty 1} = 800\ Hz$
$f_{\infty 2} = 950\ Hz$

Solution : (i) Design of prototype section

$$L = \frac{R_K}{4\pi f_C}$$

$$= \frac{1000}{4\pi \times 1000}$$

$$\boxed{L = 79 \text{ mH}}$$

$$C = \frac{1}{4\pi R_K f_C}$$

$$= \frac{1}{4\pi \times 1000 \times 1000}$$

$$\boxed{C = 0.0795 \ \mu F}$$

$$\boxed{2C = 0.159 \ \mu F}$$

Fig. 5.50 (a)

(ii) Design of m derived section

We have $\quad m = \sqrt{1 - \left(\frac{f_\infty}{f_C}\right)^2}$

(a) $f_\infty = 800$ Hz

$$m = \sqrt{1 - \left(\frac{800}{1000}\right)^2}$$

$$\boxed{m = 0.6}$$

Thus, this can be used as a terminating half section. Therefore, the series and the shunt elements are:

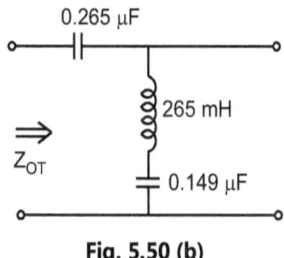

Fig. 5.50 (b)

$$\frac{2C}{m} = \frac{0.159}{0.6}$$
$$= 0.265 \, \mu F$$
$$\frac{2L}{m} = \frac{79.5 \times 2}{0.6}$$
$$= 265.0 \, mH$$
$$\left(\frac{2m}{1-m^2}\right) C = \frac{2 \times 0.6}{(1-0.36)} \times 0.0795$$
$$= 0.149 \, \mu F$$

(b) $f_\infty = 950 \, Hz$

$$m = \sqrt{1-\left(\frac{f_\infty}{f_c}\right)^2}$$
$$= \sqrt{1-\left(\frac{950}{1000}\right)^2}$$

$\boxed{m = 0.312}$

Components are:

$$\frac{2C}{m} = \frac{2 \times 0.0795}{0.312}$$
$$= \frac{0.159}{0.3} = 0.51 \, \mu F$$
$$\frac{L}{m} = \frac{0.0795}{0.312} = 25.5 \, mH$$
$$\left(\frac{4m}{1-m^2}\right) C = \left[\frac{4 \times 0.312}{1-0.097}\right] \times 0.0795 = 0.11 \, \mu F$$

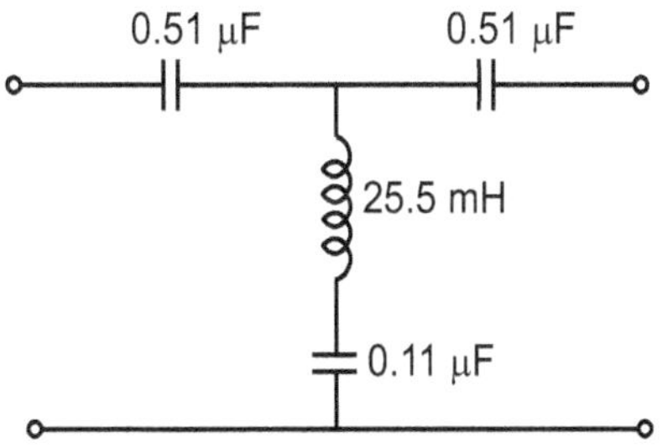

m derived filter (m = 0.312)

Fig. 5.50 (c)

(iii) Composite HPF is as shown in Fig. 5.73 (c).

The designed constant k type, m derived filter section and terminating half sections are all connected in cascade to form a composite high pass filter.

Capacitors in series can be combined and the simplified composite filter is as shown in Fig. 5.50 (e)

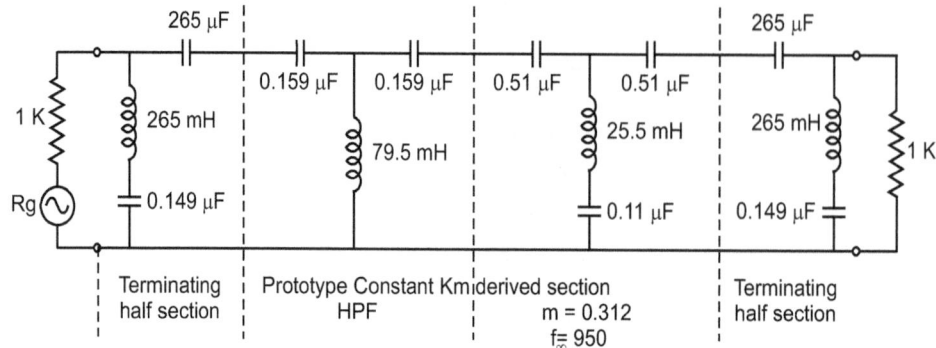

Fig. 5.50 (d)

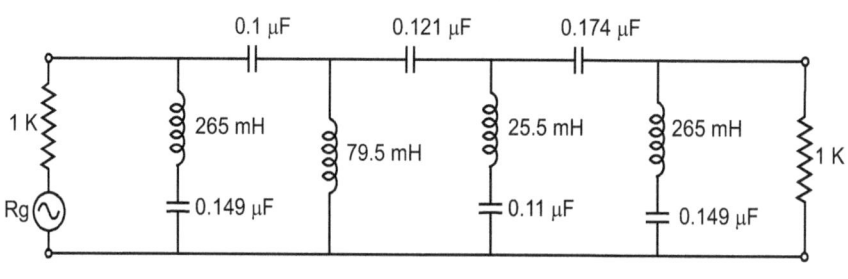

Fig. 5.50 (e)

5.20 ATTENUATORS

5.20.1 Relation in between Neper and Decibel

The attenuation is expressed either in decibels (dBs) or neper units.

Consider several four terminal (two port) networks in cascade as shown in Fig. 5.51.

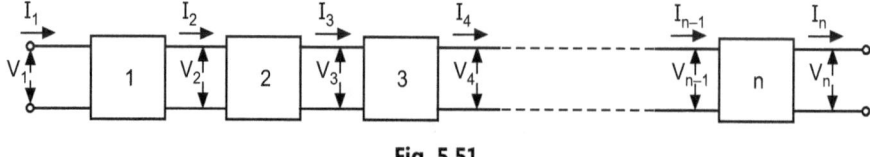

Fig. 5.51

Let the input and output image impedances or the ratios of voltage to current at input and output of the network are equal.

Then the magnitude ratios of the input to output currents or input to output voltages may be written as:

$$\left|\frac{I_1}{I_2}\right| = \left|\frac{V_1}{V_2}\right|$$

For the cascaded n networks,

$$\left|\frac{V_1}{V_n}\right| = e^a, \left|\frac{V_1}{V_2}\right| \times \left|\frac{V_2}{V_3}\right| \times \ldots \times \left|\frac{V_{n-1}}{V_n}\right|$$

Let,

$$\left|\frac{V_1}{V_2}\right| = e^a, \left|\frac{V_2}{V_3}\right|$$

$$= e^b, \ldots \times \left|\frac{V_{n-1}}{V_n}\right| = e^n$$

Hence,

$$\left|\frac{V_1}{V_2}\right| = e^a \times e^b \times \ldots \times e^n$$

$$= e^{a+b\ldots\ldots+n}$$

i.e.

$$\ln\left|\frac{V_1}{V_n}\right| = a + b + \ldots + n$$

The logarithm of the current and voltage ratio for all the networks in cascade is sum of various exponents.

Let,

$$\left|\frac{V_1}{V_2}\right| = \left|\frac{I_1}{I_2}\right| = e^\alpha$$

∴ $\quad \alpha \text{ nepers } = \ln\left|\frac{V_1}{V_2}\right| = \ln\left|\frac{I_1}{I_2}\right|$

Two voltages or currents differ by one neper when one of them is e times as large as other.

Ratio of input to output power may also be expressed as

$$\frac{P_1}{P_2} = e^{2N} \qquad \ldots \text{(a)}$$

The bel is defined as the logarithm of a power ratio,

$$\text{Number of bels } = \log\frac{P_1}{P_2}$$

$$\text{Attenuation in dB } = 10\log\frac{P_1}{P_2} = 20\log\frac{V_1}{V_2} = 20\log\frac{I_1}{I_2}$$

$$\therefore \quad \frac{P_1}{P_2} = \text{Antilog}_{10}\left|\frac{d}{10}\right| \quad \ldots (2)$$

Equating equations (a) and (b)

$$e^{2N} = \text{Antilog}\left|\frac{d}{10}\right|$$

Taking logarithm of both sides,

$$\log e^{2N} = \log \text{Antilog}\left|\frac{d}{10}\right|$$

$$\therefore \quad 2N = \frac{dB}{10}\log_e 10$$

$$\therefore \quad N = \frac{dB}{20}(2.3025)$$

$$dB = \frac{20}{2.3025}N$$

$$= 8.686\ N$$

$$\therefore \quad \boxed{1\ \text{Neper} = 8.686\ dB} \quad \ldots(5.39)$$

and

$$1\ dB = \frac{1}{8.686}\ \text{neper}$$

$$\boxed{1\ dB = 0.115\ \text{neper}} \quad \ldots(5.40)$$

In general, attenuation is expressed in decibel as

$$D = 10\log_{10}\left|\frac{P_{in}}{P_{out}}\right|$$

Attenuation can also be expressed in terms of Nepers as

$$D = 20\log_{10}\sqrt{\frac{P_{in}}{P_{out}}}$$

$$D = 20\log_{10} N$$

$$\boxed{N = \text{Antilog}_{10}\left|\frac{D}{20}\right|} \quad \ldots (5.41)$$

EXERCISE

1. Sketch the reactance curves for a constant k T section and a π section of a F low and a high pass filter.
2. In a band pass filter resonating and an antiresonating frequency must be same. Justify with the help of reactance curves.
3. Prove that resonant frequency f_0 is the geometric mean of two cut-off frequencies f_1 and f_2.
4. What are the disadvantages of a prototype filter? How are they corrected in the m derived filter?
5. Why is a m derived half section used as terminating section in a filter? Explain why is m = 0.6 used in terminating half sections.
6. Define characteristic impedance and propagation constant of a symmetrical network.
7. Define and explain the properties of an asymmetrical network.
8. For an symmetrical T and π network derive the expression for Z_{oT} and also show that $Z_{oT} = \sqrt{Z_{oC} \cdot Z_{SC}}$.
    4. Define, explain and derive the formula for image and iterative impedances as applied to L section and Half sections.
9. Define: Cut-off frequency
            Pass band
            Stop band
            Transition band
            Design impedance
   of a filter.
10. What are the desirable characteristics of ideal filter?
11. A filter circuit must have Z_1 and Z_2 as the opposite type of reactances. Justify.
12. Sketch reactance verses frequency curves of a low pass and a high pass constant k filter and obtain the expression for the cut-off frequency.
13. Sketch the reactance curves for a constant k T section and a π section of a F low and a high pass filter.
14. In a band pass filter resonating and an antiresonating frequency must be same. Justify with the help of reactance curves.

15. Prove that resonant frequency f_0 is the geometric mean of two cut-off frequencies f_1 and f_2.

16. What are the disadvantages of a prototype filter ? How are they corrected in the m derived filter ?

17. Why is a m derived half section used as terminating section in a filter ? Explain why is m = 0.6 used in terminating half sections.

18. Explain the disadvantages of a m derived filter. How are they corrected in a composite filter.

19. Define decibel and neper units. Derive the relation between these units.

Unit - VI

TRANSIENT RESPONSE

6.1 NETWORK SOLUTION USING LAPLACE TRANSFORM

Laplace Transformation method for solving differential equations offers a number of advantages over classical methods. The differential equations specifying performance of complicated networks are rather complExample The solution to such problems is time consuming. Laplace Transformation helps to get solution in a systematic way. This method gives total solution the particular integral and complementary function in one operation. The initial conditions are automatically specified in the transformed equations.

In the classical methods for solving differential equations, solutions are obtained directly in the time domain. Application of Laplace Transform transforms the differential equations to the frequency domain where the independent variable is complex frequency 's'. Differentiation and integration in the time domain are transformed into algebraic operations. Thus, the solution is obtained by simple algebraic operations in the frequency domain.

6.1.1 Method of Transformation

Fig. 6.1 shows the philosophy of transform methods. It shows the procedure to obtain Sol. of differential equation.

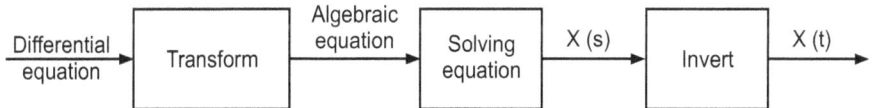

Fig. 6.1 : Transform method to solve integro-differential equation

Step I: Consider the linear differential equation

$$y(x(t)) = f(t) \quad \ldots (a)$$

where
$f(t)$ = Forcing function
$x(t)$ = Unknown variable
$y(x(t))$ = Differential equation

Step II : Transforming both sides of equation (a),

$$T[y(x(t))] = T[f(t)] \quad \ldots (b)$$
$$Y(X(s), s) = F(s) \quad \ldots (c)$$

where,
$X(s) = T[x(t)]$
$F(s) = T[f(t)]$
$Y(X(s), s)$ = Algebraic equation in s.

Thus, by process of transformation differential equation in time domain are changed to algebraic equations in frequency domain.

Step III: Solve equation (c) algebraically to obtain X (s).

Step IV: Take inverse transformation to obtain

$$x(t) = T^{-1}[X(s)] \quad \ldots (d)$$

6.1.3 Definition of Laplace Transform

The Laplace Transform of a function of time f (t) is defined as,

$$L[f(t)] = F(s) = \int_0^\infty f(t) e^{-st} dt \quad \ldots (6.1)$$

where, s is the complex frequency variable $s = \sigma + j\omega$

Thus, Laplace Transform converts general time domain function f (t) into a corresponding frequency domain representation F (s).

Example 6.1 : Find Laplace Transform of unit step function defined as,

$$u(t) = 1; \; t \geq 0$$
$$= 0; \; t < 0$$

Solution : $\quad f(t) = u(t)$

∴ By definition of Laplace Transform,

$$F(s) = \int_0^\infty u(t) e^{-st} dt$$

$$= \int_0^\infty 1 \cdot e^{-st} dt = \left. \frac{e^{-st}}{-s} \right|_0^\infty = 0 - \left(-\frac{1}{s}\right)$$

$$= \frac{1}{s}$$

∴ $\quad L\, u(t) = \frac{1}{s}$

Example 6.2 : Find Laplace Transform of $f(t) = e^{at}$.

Solution : $\quad f(t) = e^{at} u(t)$

By definition of Laplace Transform,

$$F(s) = \int_0^\infty e^{at} e^{-st} dt$$

$$= -\left. \frac{e^{-(s-a)t}}{s-a} \right|_0^\infty = \frac{1}{s-a}$$

∴ $\quad L\, e^{at} u(t) = \frac{1}{s-a}$

6.1.3 The Initial-Value and Final-Value Theorems

The initial value theorem states that the initial value of the time domain function f (t) can be obtained from its Laplace transform F (s) by first multiplying the transform by s and then letting s approach infinity.

$$f(0+) = \lim_{t \to 0+} f(t) = \lim_{s \to \infty} s F(s) \qquad \ldots (6.2)$$

The above equation is valid for continuous function or at most having a step discontinuity at t = 0.

The final value theorem states that

$$\lim_{t \to \infty} f(t) = \lim_{s \to 0} s F(s) \qquad \ldots (6.3)$$

provided the poles of F (s) must not be in right half of complex frequency plane.

Table 6.1 : Properties of Laplace Transform

Operation	Property
Addition	$L [a f_1(t) + b f_2(t)] = a F_1(s) + b F_2(s)$
Scalar multiplication	$L [k f(t)] = k F(s)$
Time differentiation	$L \left\{ \dfrac{d f(t)}{dt} \right\} = s F(s) - f(0-)$
	$L \left\{ \dfrac{d^2 f(t)}{dt^2} \right\} = s^2 F(s) - s f(0-) - f'(0-)$
	$L \left\{ \dfrac{d^n f(t)}{dt^n} \right\} = s^n F(s) - s^{n-1} f(0-) - s^{n-2} f'(0-) \ldots - f^{n-1}(0-)$
Time integration	$\displaystyle\int_{0-}^{t} f(u) \, du = \dfrac{F(s)}{s}$
Complex translation	$L e^{at} f(t) = F(s - a)$
Shifting theorem	$L [f(t-a) u(t-a)] = e^{-as} F(s)$
Convolution theorem	$L f_1(t) * f_2(t) = F_1(s) F_2(s)$
Initial value theorem	$f(0+) = \lim_{s \to \infty} s F(s)$
Final value theorem	$F(\infty) = \lim_{s \to 0} s F(s)$

6.1.4 Inverse Laplace Transform

If $\{f(t)\} = F(s)$, then $f(t)$ is called the inverse Laplace Transform of $F(s)$. This relation is denoted by

$$L^{-1}\{F(s)\} = f(t) \qquad \ldots (6.4)$$

Following are some of the methods to find inverse Laplace Transform by using known Laplace transforms of elementary functions.

1. Shifting Theorem

If $\qquad L^{-1}[F(s)] = f(t)$

then, $\qquad L^{-1}\{F(s-a)\} = e^{at} f(t) \qquad \ldots (6.5)$

2. Frequency Multiplication Theorem

If standard transform $F(s)$ is multiplied by s, then the inverse transform is the differentiation of $f(t)$.

If $\qquad L^{-1}\{F(s)\} = f(t)$ and $f(0) = 0$,

Then, $\qquad L^{-1}\{s F(s)\} = \dfrac{d}{dt} f(t) \qquad \ldots (6.6)$

This can be generalized as,

$$L^{-1}\{s^n F(s)\} = \dfrac{d^n}{dt^n} \{f(t)\} \qquad \ldots (6.7)$$

with conditions $f(0) = f'(0) = \ldots\ldots = f^{n-1}(0) = 0$.

6.1.5 Laplace Transform of Basic R.L.C. Components

(A) Resistance: Voltage and current through the resistor are related in time domain by expression

$$v_R(t) = R\, i_R(t) \qquad \ldots (a)$$
or $\qquad i_R(t) = G\, v_R(t) \qquad \ldots (b)$

The corresponding transform equations are,

$$V_R(s) = R\, I_R(s) \qquad \ldots (c)$$
$$I_R(s) = G\, V_R(s) \qquad \ldots (d)$$

Thus, $\qquad \dfrac{V_R(s)}{I_R(s)} = Z_R(s) = R \qquad \ldots (6.8)$

is the transformed impedance of resistor.

$$\dfrac{I_R(s)}{V_R(s)} = Y_R(s) = G \qquad \ldots (6.9)$$

is the transformed admittance of resistor.

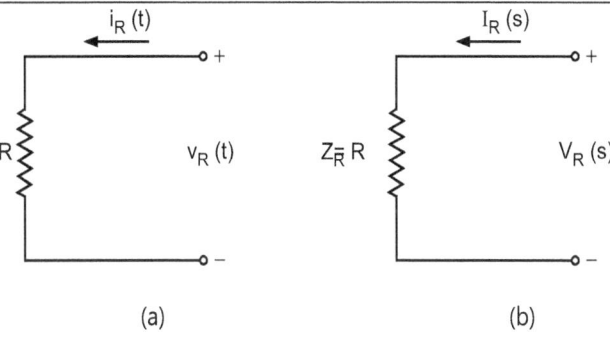

(a) (b)

Fig. 6.2: The resistor and its transformed impedance

(B) Inductance: The time domain relationship between voltage and current in an inductor is expressed as,

$$v_L(t) = L \frac{di_L(t)}{dt} \qquad \ldots (6.10)$$

Transforming equation (6.10) in s domain,

$$V_L(s) = L\left[s\,I_L(s) - i_L(0-)\right] \qquad \ldots (6.11)$$

where, $i_L(0-)$ is the initial current in the inductor.

Therefore,
$$I_L(s) = \frac{1}{sL} V(s) + \frac{i_L(0-)}{s} \qquad \ldots (6.12)$$

$$I_L(s) - \frac{i_L(0-)}{s} = I_1(s) = \frac{1}{sL} V(s)$$

$$\therefore \quad \frac{I_1(s)}{V(s)} = \frac{1}{sL} = \text{Transformed admittance}$$

$$= Y_L(s) \qquad \ldots (6.13)$$

and transformed impedance is

$$Z_L(s) = \frac{1}{Y_L(s)} = sL \qquad \ldots (6.14)$$

(a) Impedance

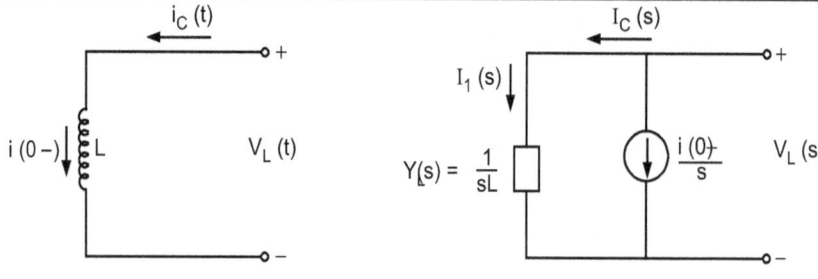

(b) Admittance

Fig. 6.3 : The inductor with initial current and its transform impedance and admittance

(C) Capacitance: The time domain relationship between voltage and current for a capacitor is given by,

$$i_C(t) = C \frac{dV_C(t)}{dt}$$

$$V_C(t) = \frac{1}{C} \int_{-\infty}^{t} i_C(t)\, dt \qquad \text{... (6.15)}$$

The equivalent transform equation for voltage is

$$V_C(s) = \frac{1}{C}\left[\frac{I_C(s)}{s} - \frac{q(0-)}{s}\right] \qquad \text{... (6.16)}$$

where, $\dfrac{q(0-)}{C}$ (Initial voltage on the capacitor)

∴ $\dfrac{1}{sC} I_C(s) = V_C(s) + \dfrac{V_C(0-)}{s}$ ... (e)

Let $V_C(s) + \dfrac{V_C(0-)}{s} = V_1(s)$

∴ $Z_C(s) = \dfrac{V_1(s)}{I_1(s)} = \dfrac{1}{sC}$ ... (6.17)

Thus, capacitor with an initial charge has an equivalent transform circuit with an impedance $\dfrac{1}{sC}$ in series with a voltage source having transform $\dfrac{-V_C(0-)}{s}$.

Similarly from equation (6.6),

$$I_C(s) = C\left[s V_C(s) - V_C(0-)\right]$$

$$sC V_C(s) = I_C(s) + C V_C(0-) \qquad \text{... (f)}$$

Let transform current in $Y_C(s)$ be,

$$I_1(s) = I_C(s) - C V_C(0-)$$

NETWORK ANALYSIS (S.E. SEM III E & TC. SU) — TRANSIENT RESPONSE

$$\therefore \quad Y_C(s) = \frac{I_1(s)}{V_C(s)} = sC \qquad \ldots (6.18)$$

Thus, capacitor with an initial charge has an equivalent transform representation as an admittance sC in parallel with transform current source of value $C\, v_C(0-)$.

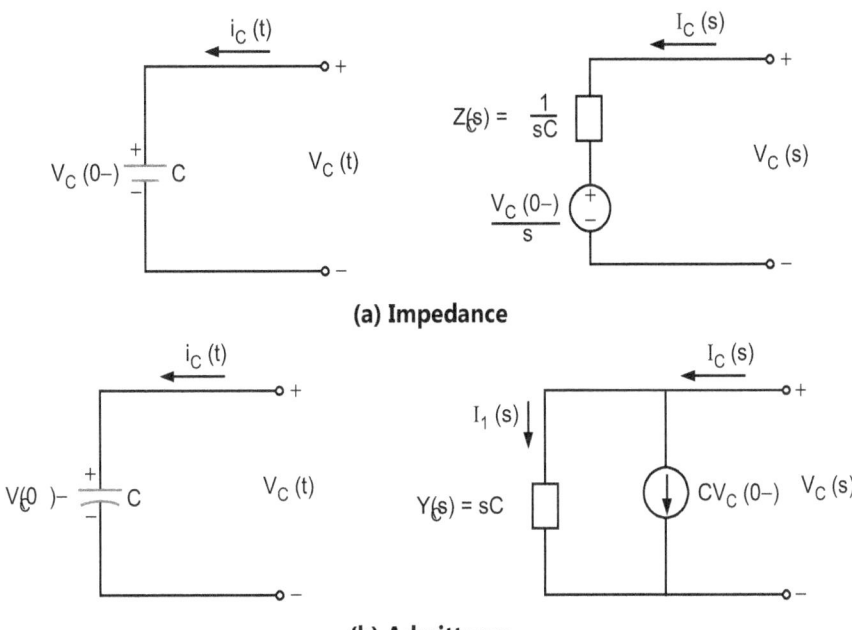

(a) Impedance

(b) Admittance

Fig. 6.4 : The capacitor with initial voltage and its transform impedance and admittance

Example 6.3 : In the network shown in the Fig. 6.5, the switch K is moved from position a to position b at t = 0, a steady state having previously been established at position a. Solve for the current i (t) using the Laplace transformation method.

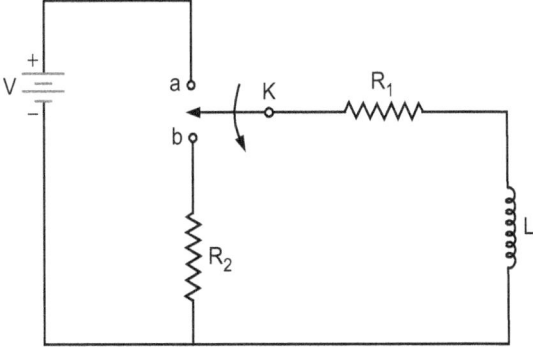

Fig. 6.5

Solution : When switch is in position 'a', steady state is achieved and inductor L acts as S.C. in the steady state as shown in Fig. 6.5 (a).

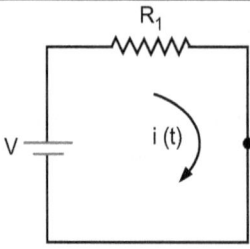

Fig. 6.5 (a)

When the switch is moved to position 'b', the circuit takes the form as shown in Fig. 6.5 (b).

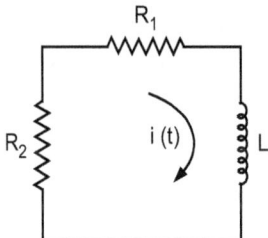   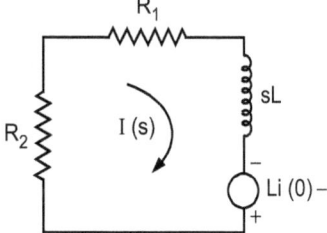

Fig. 6.5 (b): Circuit in position 'b'   **Fig. 6.5 (c): Transformed circuit**

Applying KVL to circuit in Fig. 6.5 (b),

$$(R_1 + R_2)\, i(t) + L\frac{d}{dt} i(t) = 0$$

Taking Laplace Transform,

$$L\,[s\, I(s) - i_L(0-)] + (R_1 + R_2)\, I(s) = 0$$

$$\therefore \quad L\left[s\, I(s) - \frac{V}{R_1}\right] + (R_1 + R_2)\, I(s) = 0$$

Collecting terms of $I(s)$,

$$[sL + R_1 + R_2]\, I(s) = \frac{LV}{R_1}$$

$$\therefore \quad I(s) = \frac{LV}{R_1}\left(\frac{1}{sL + R_1 + R_2}\right)$$

$$= \frac{V}{R_1}\left[\frac{1}{s + \frac{(R_1 + R_2)}{L}}\right]$$

Taking Inverse Laplace Transform,

$$i(t) = \frac{V}{R_1}\, e^{-\left(\frac{R_1 + R_2}{L}\right)t} \quad \text{for } t \geq 0$$

Example 6.4 : In the network shown as in Fig. 6.6 the switch K is moved from position a to position b at t = 0. A steady state current being previously established, derive the expression for current i (t).

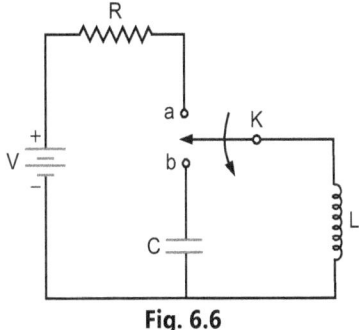

Fig. 6.6

Solution : When switch is in position 'a', steady state is established. The inductor L acts as S.C. in the steady state.

$$i_a(t) = \frac{V}{R}$$

$$i_L(0-) = \frac{V}{R} \text{ Amp.}$$

$$V_C(0-) = 0 \text{ volts}$$

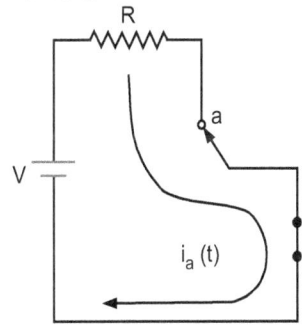

Fig. 6.6 (a)

In position 'b' circuit becomes as shown in Fig. 6.6(b).

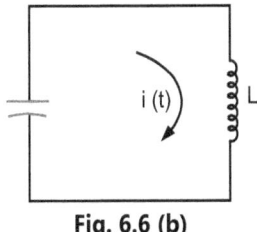

Fig. 6.6 (b)

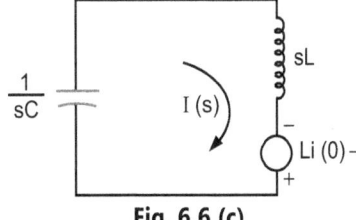

Fig. 6.6 (c)

Applying KVL to circuit in Fig. 6.6 (b),

$$L\frac{di(t)}{dt} + \frac{1}{C}\int_{-\infty}^{t} i(t)\, dt = 0$$

But
$$V_C(0-) = \frac{1}{C}\int_{-\infty}^{0} i(t)\,dt = 0$$

∴
$$L\frac{di(t)}{dt} + \frac{1}{C}\int_{0}^{t} i(t)\,dt = 0$$

Taking Laplace Transform,

$$L[sI(s) - i_L(0-)] + \frac{1}{sC} I(s) = 0$$

$$I(s)\left[sL + \frac{1}{sC}\right] - L\frac{V}{R} = 0$$

$$I(s)\left(\frac{1 + s^2 LC}{sC}\right) = \frac{VL}{R}$$

∴
$$I(s) = \frac{VL}{R} \cdot \frac{sC}{1 + s^2 LC}$$

$$= \left(\frac{V}{R}\right) \cdot \frac{s}{s^2 + \frac{1}{LC}}$$

Taking Inverse Laplace Transform,

$$i(t) = \left(\frac{V}{R}\right) \cos\left(\frac{t}{\sqrt{LC}}\right) \text{ Amp}$$

6.2 RESISTOR-CAPACITOR (R-C) CIRCUITS

In this section we shall discuss the properties of R-C network with capacitor initially having a voltage (V_0), and then the R-C network driven by a d-c voltage source (V), and capacitor again having a initial voltage (V_0). Before that, we shall discuss the construction and properties of the capacitor.

6.2.1 Capacitor and its Properties

Capacitor is a circuit element which stores energy in electric field. In case of the resistor voltage-current relationship (V = R. I.) is linear and instantaneous. Voltage and current will exists simultaneously in resistor. But in the case of capacitor voltage is proportional to charge and not the currents. As capacitor has ability to store the charge, hence there may be voltage across it even when current is not flowing through it. Capacitor does not dissipate energy and hence called as reactive element.

Ideal capacitor (or condenser) consists of two parallel conducting plates seperated by a ideal insulator as shown in Fig. 3.7.

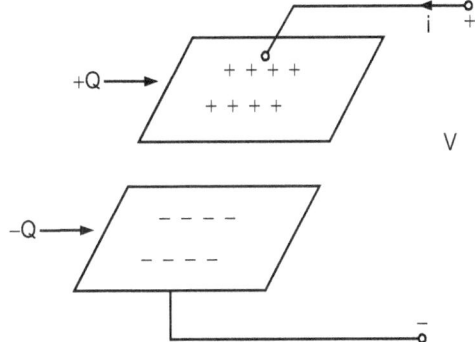

Fig. 6.7: Construction of a capacitor

As mentioned above "voltage across capacitor is proportional to charge Q on the plate".

Thus $\quad Q = C \cdot V$

Constant of proportionality is called capacitance. Unit of the capacitor is Farad (F). Value of C depends upon geometry of conducting plates and physical properties of the insulating material. Circuit symbol of a capacitor is as shown in Fig. 3.8.

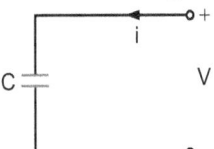

Fig. 6.8: Circuit symbol of capacitor with voltage and current conventions

Current in the capacitor (i) is time rate of change of charge. Thus

$$i = \frac{dQ}{dt} = C\frac{dV}{dt} \qquad \ldots(6.19)$$

Above equation gives voltage-current relationship in a capacitor.

"Current in a capacitor is present only when the voltage across it is changing with time". No current will flow if voltage derivative is zero. Thus "For d.c. or constant voltage $\frac{dv}{dt}$ is zero. Hence current is zero and capacitor behaves like an open circuit.

Buildup of the voltage on capacitor due to current flowing through it is given by

$$v(t) = \frac{1}{C}\int_{-\infty}^{t} i(t)\, dt \qquad \ldots(6.20)$$

$$= \frac{1}{C}\int_{-\infty}^{0} i(t)\, dt + \frac{1}{C}\int_{0}^{1} i(t)\, dt$$

$$= \frac{1}{C} \int_{-\infty}^{0} i(t).dt = \frac{Q_0}{C} = V_0 \text{ is known as initial voltage on}$$

capacitor which is due to initial charge (Q_0) on capacitor.

Thus $\quad v(t) = V_0 + \frac{1}{C} \int_0^t I(t).dt \qquad \ldots (6.21)$

This gives capacitor charging equation.

If a capacitor with initial voltage (V_0) is discharged by a current flowing in opposite direction as shown besides in Fig. 6.9 then the discharge equation is given by

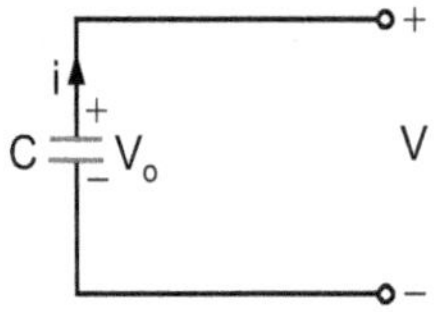

Fig. 6.9: Capacitor discharging

$$v(t) = V_0 - \frac{1}{C} \int_0^t i(t)\,dt \qquad \ldots(6.22)$$

Energy and power Relationship in a capacitor: "As capacitor is able to store charge and hence voltage in this form of storage represents storage of energy".

We have $\quad p(t) = v(t)\, i(t) \text{ watts}$

$$= V(t) . C\, d\frac{v(t)}{dt}$$

$$= \frac{d}{dt} \left[\frac{1}{2} C.v^2 \right]$$

Since power is the time rate of change of energy, energy stored in capacitor at any instant of time is given by

$$W_e(t) = \frac{1}{2} Cv^2 \qquad \ldots(6.23)$$

Positive value of power represents power delivered to capacitor due to charging and −ve value of the power represents power delivered by the capacitor to rest of the circuits due to discharging.

Example 6.5 : If the current waveform shown below is applied to 2µF capacitor, Find capacitor voltage $V_c(t)$ and sketch the waveform. Assume initial capacitor voltage is zero.

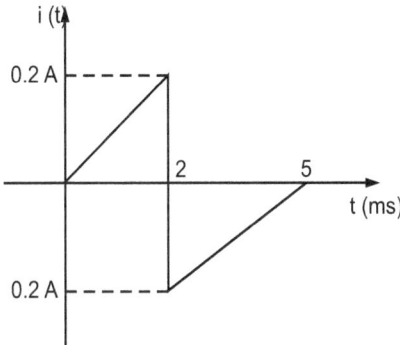

Fig. 6.10

Solution : Given that $V_0 = 0$. Hence for $t > 0$ the voltage on capacitor is given by equation (6.12) as

$$V_C(t) = \frac{1}{C} \int_0^1 i(t) \, dt$$

For $0 < t < 2ms$, $\quad i(t) = \frac{0.2}{2} \times 10^3 t = 100t$

For $2.0 \, ms < t < 5.0 \, ms \quad i(t) = -0.2 + \frac{200}{3}(t-2)$

Thus for $0 < t < 2$ ms, the voltage is

$$V_c(t) = \frac{1}{2 \times 10^{-6}} \int_0^{2ms} 100 \, t \, dt = 50 \left[\frac{t^2}{2}\right]_0^{2ms}$$

At $\quad t = 2ms, \quad V_c(2ms) = 50 \times \frac{4 \times 10^{-6}}{2} = 100$ volts.

Also at t = 2 ms current changes from + 0.2 A to −0.2 A. Thus current changes instantaneously but the voltage on capacitor will not change at this instant and will remain at 100 V only. At t = 5 ms the voltage on capacitor is given as.

$$v(t) = 100.0 + \frac{1}{C}\int_{2ms}^{5ms} -0.2 \, dt + \frac{1}{C}\int_{2ms}^{5ms} \frac{200}{3}(t-2)$$

$$= 100 - 10^5 \, [t]_{2ms}^{5ms} + \frac{200 \times 10^6}{3 \times 2 \times 2} \times [t-2]_{2ms}^{5ms}$$

$$= 100 - 300 + 150 = -50 \text{ volts}$$

Thus required voltage waveform is as shown in below.

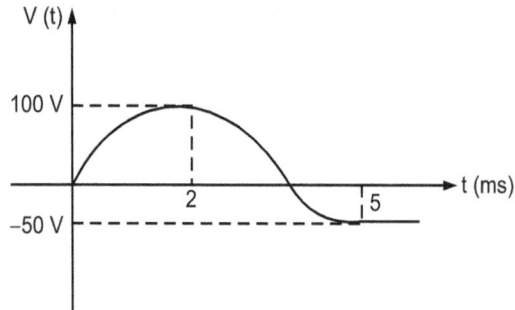

Fig. 6.11: Capacitor voltage waveform

Linearity and Superposition: An element is said to be linear if and only if superposition theorem is valid for them and vice versa.

It can be shown that superposition theorem is valid for the capacitor if and only if initial voltage (V_o) on the capacitor is zero. Other wise superposition theorem can not be applied to the capacitor. Thus for charged capacitor (For which $V_o \neq 0$) superposition theorem is not valid.

Hence capacitor is a linear element if and only if it is not charged (Initial voltage on capacitor is zero).

Series and Parallel Connection of Capacitor: Consider two capacitor C_1 and C_2 connected in parallel as shown in Fig. 6.12 (a). Voltage across the two capacitor is some.

$$i = i_1 + i_2 = C_1 \frac{dv}{dt} + C_2 \frac{dv}{dt} = (C_1 + C_2) \frac{dv}{dt}$$

If the two capacitor are to be replaced by a single capacitor of value C as shown in Fig. 6.12 (b) then

$$C = C_1 + C_2 \qquad \ldots(6.24)$$

Thus "Equivalent Capacitance of a parallel combination is given by the sum of individual capacitance" Any initial voltage on parallel capacitor will also be present on equivalent capacitor.

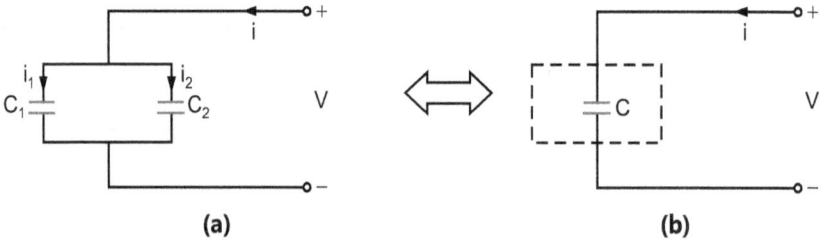

Fig. 6.12: Parallel connection of capacitor

Now consider capacitor C_1 with initial voltage V_{o1} and capacitor C_2 with initial voltage V_{o2} connected in series as shown in Fig. 6.13 (a).

We have
$$v = v_1 + v_2$$
$$= \left[\frac{1}{C_1}\int_0^t i\,dt + V_{o1}\right] + \left[\frac{1}{C_2}\int_0^t i\,dt + V_{o2}\right]$$

OR
$$= \left\{\left(\frac{1}{C_1} + \frac{1}{C_2}\right)\int_0^t i\,dt\right\} + (V_{o1} + V_{o2})$$

$$= \frac{1}{C}\int_0^t i\,dt + V_o$$

Thus equivalent capacitance (c) is given by
$$\frac{1}{C} = \frac{1}{C_1} + \frac{1}{C_2} \qquad \text{... (6.25)}$$

and also
$$V_o = V_{o1} + V_{o2} \qquad \text{...(6.26)}$$

Thus, "For series connection of capacitors, the reciprocal of equivalent capacitance is the sum of reciprocal of individual capacitance".

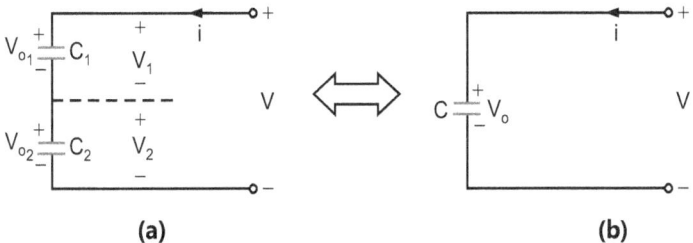

(a) (b)

Fig. 6.13: Capacitors in parallel

6.2.2 Undriven R-C Circuit

Consider the circuit shown in Fig. 6.14. The switch in initially on the position "a" for a long time.

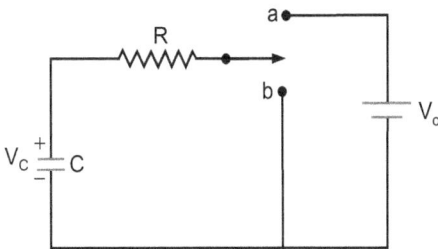

Fig. 6.14: R-C network with capacitor voltage $V_c = V_o$ at time t = 0

The capacitor voltage is $v_c = v_o$ volts. At t = 0 the switch is thrown to position "b", and circuit will be as shown below in Fig. 6.15.

Now, capacitor will discharge into resistor. Because of this discharge voltage on capacitor will reduce until it reaches to zero. We are interested to find rate at which capacitor will fall.

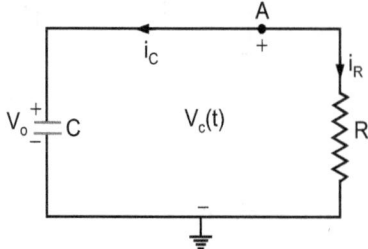

Fig. 6.15: R.C. circuit for t > 0

KCL at node 'A' gives

$$i_C + i_R = 0.$$

$$C\frac{dv_c}{dt} + \frac{v_c}{R} = 0$$

This is a first order homogeneous linear differential equation with constant coefficients. [A linear differential equation is homogeneous if its R. H. side is zero. If R. H. side is not zero then it is a non-homogeneous LDE].

Rearranging above equation gives, $\frac{dv_c}{v_c} = -\frac{1}{RC}dt$. Integrating this equation on both sides gives.

$$\int \frac{dv_c}{v_c} = \int -\frac{1}{RC} dt$$

OR

$$\ln v_c = -\frac{t}{RC} + K \text{ (constant)}$$

Hence
$$v_c(t) = e^{-\frac{1}{RC} + K} = e^K e^{-\frac{1}{RC}} = A e^{-\frac{1}{RC}} \qquad ...(b)$$

Where A is a arbitrary constant whose value can be determined if we know value of v at any instant of time.

We know that at t 0, v = v_c = V_0 volts.

Hence $v_{c(0)}$ = A = V_0 volts

Hence voltage across capacitor at any instant of time (t) > 0 given by

$$v_c(t) = V_0 e^{-\frac{1}{RC}} \qquad ...(6.27)$$

Current $i_c(t)$ through capacitor at any instant of time (t) > 0 is given by

$$i_c(t) = C\frac{dv_c(t)}{dt}$$

$$= -\frac{CV_0 e^{-\frac{t}{RC}}}{RC}$$

Thus
$$i_c(t) = -\frac{V_o}{R} e^{-\frac{t}{RC}} \qquad \ldots(6.28)$$

Minus sign on t (i.e., –t) indicates that the capacitor is discharging.

Waveforms for capacitor voltage [v_c (t)] and the current [v_c (t)] as given by equations (6.29) and (6.28) is as shown below in Fig. 6.16.

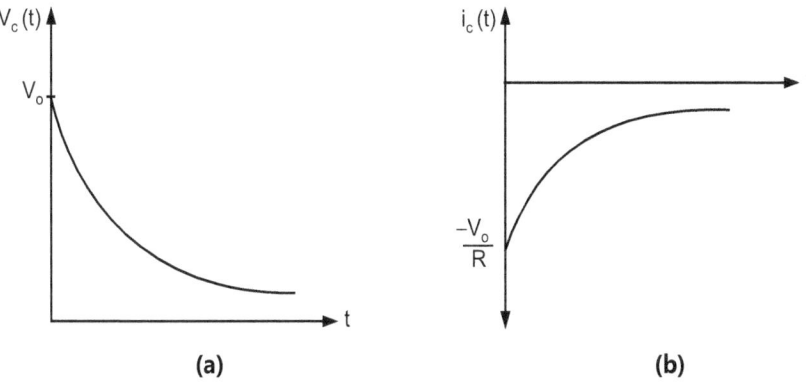

(a) (b)

Fig. 6.16: Capacitor voltage and current waveforms

By graph it is obvious that capacitor voltage v_c (t) decays exponentially becomes zero as t → ∞. Rate of decays depends upon RC. Simile discharging current is maximum at t = 0 and decays exponentially to become zero at t → ∞.

Physical explanation for this can be given as below. Initially energy stored is capacitor is $\frac{CV^2}{2}$. As the charge flows through resistor from one plate capacitor to other plate, energy is dissipated in the resistor at the rate of R_i^2. Due to this dissipation of the energy, energy stored in the capacitor is reduced hence voltage on capacitor and the current also reduces.

Time Constant (T): The product RC = T is called as Time constant c of RC circuit, and indicates how fast circuit settles down to its quiescent (steady state) value. For example when t = T then by the equation (a) we have,

$$v_c(T) = \frac{V_o}{e} = 0.37 \, V_o \qquad \ldots(a)$$

Thus "Time constant (T) indicates the. time R-C circuit take in order to reduce initial voltage on capacitor (V_o) by a factor of $\frac{1}{e} = 0.37$".

Also for t = 2T, $\qquad v_c(2T) = \frac{V_o}{e^2}$

For t = 3T, $v_c(3T) = \dfrac{V_o}{e^3}$ and

For t = 4T, We have $v_c(4T) = \dfrac{V_o}{e^4} = 0.02\, V_o$

Thus after a time t = 4T, the voltage on capacitor reduces to 2% of initial value, hence capacitor can be assumed to be discharged completely. The waveform is as shown below in Fig. 6.17.

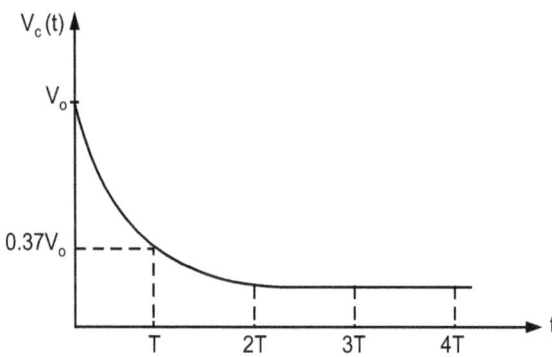

Fig. 6.17: Capacitor discharge

Example 6.6 : In the circuit shown below find the expression for $v_2(t)$ if the switch is closed at t = 0. Find $v_2(t)$ and i(t) when t = 3.33 ms.

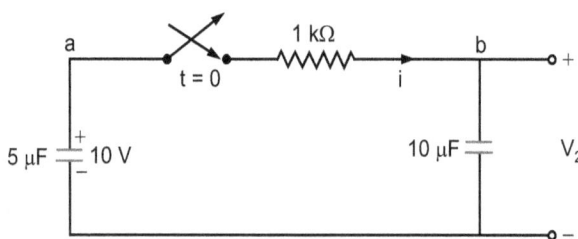

Fig. 6.18

Solution : At t = 0 switch is closed. Then two capacitors are in series. Hence the equivalent capacitance is

$$C_{eq} = \dfrac{10 \times 5}{15} = \dfrac{10}{3}\, \mu F$$

Hence the circuit will be as shown below in Fig. 6.19.

Current i is given by $i(t) = \dfrac{10}{1} \times e^{-\dfrac{t}{3.33\, ms}}\, mA.$

Returning to original circuit of Fig. 6.19 we have

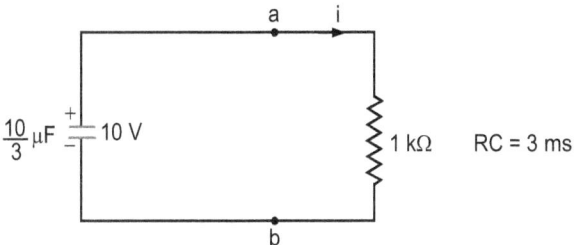

Fig. 6.19: Equivalent circuit for t > 0

$$v_2(t) = v_2(0) + \frac{1}{10\,\mu F}\int_0^t i\,dt$$

$$= 0 + \frac{1}{10^{-5}}\int_0^t 10\,e^{-\frac{t}{3.3ms}} \times 10^{-3}\,dt$$

$$= 1000\left[e^{-\frac{t}{3.33\,mm}}\right]_0^t \times \frac{-1}{1} \times 3.33 \times 10^{-3}$$

Thus $\qquad v_2(t) = 3.3\left[1 - e^{-\frac{t}{3.33\,ms}}\right]$ volts $\qquad\qquad$ ...(a)

This is the required expression for voltage $v_2(t)$

$$i(t) = 10 \times 10^{-6} \frac{dv_2(t)}{dt}$$

$$= 10^{-5} \times 3.3\left(-e^{-\frac{t}{3.3\,ms}}\right) \times \frac{-1}{3.3 \times 10^{-3}}$$

$$= 10^{-2}\,e^{-\frac{t}{3.3ms}}$$

$$= 10\,e^{-\frac{t}{3.3ms}}\ mA$$

Thus required expression for current is

$$i(t) = 10\,e^{-\frac{t}{3.3ms}}\ mA \qquad\qquad ...(b)$$

At $\qquad$ t = 3.3 ms, we have

$v_2(t) = 3.3\,[1 - e^{-1}] = 0.67 \times 3.3$

$\qquad\quad = 2.211$ volts

$i(t) = 10e^{-1}\ 0.37 \times 10$ mA

$\qquad = 3.7$ mA

Unit VI | 6.19

6.2.3 Driven R-C Circuit (Step Response of a R-C Circuit)

Consider a capacitor with initial voltage V_o and is connected to a battery of voltage V volts through a resistor R and in series with switch as shown below in Fig. 6.20(a).

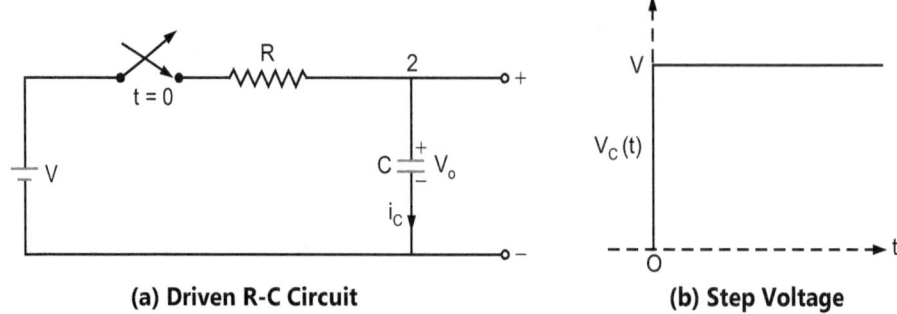

(a) Driven R-C Circuit (b) Step Voltage

Fig. 6.20: Step response of a R-C circuit.

When switch is opened voltage applied to the R-C circuit is zero. When switch is closed at t = 0 then voltage of V volts is suddenly applied to R-C circuit. This is known as step voltage and is shown in Fig. 6.20 (b).

As long as switch is opened capacitor, will not discharge and retains its voltage V_o.

Let switch be closed at t = 0.

It $V = V_o$, then voltage across resistor is zero, which means no current will flow through R-C circuit and the capacitor maintain its voltage at Vo.

It $V > V_o$, then capacitor will be charging and capacitor voltage will increase until it reaches battery voltage V after which charging will be stopped. Thus under steady state (quiescent condition) voltage across the capacitor is the battery voltage (V). If $V < V_o$, then capacitor will be discharging until the voltage across capacitor again reaches to battery voltage.

Thus for any value of voltage V, the capacitor may charge or discharge depending upon V_o and V. For example if V_o = 5V and V = 10V, then the capacitor will go on charging until its voltage attains 10V. Alternatively V_o = 10V, V = 5V, then the capacitor will discharge until its voltage reches volts.

Thus, at any instant of time, voltage across the capacitor v_c (t) consists c a steady state component of value V and a component of delaying exponential with time constant RC.

Hence $v_c(t) = V + A e^{-\frac{1}{RC}}$

Where A is the magnitude of decaying exponential, value of which can be determined from the knowledge of initial value of v_c (t).

At t = 0 we know that $v_c(0) = V_o$

Hence $V_o = V + A e^{-0} = V + A$

OR $A = V_o - V$

Thus capacitor voltage at any time $t > 0$ is given

$$v_c(t) = V + (V_0 - V)\, e^{-\frac{1}{RC}} \qquad \ldots(6.30)$$

$$= \text{(steady state value)} + \text{(Transient value)}$$

The validity of above equation can be checked as below. At $t = 0$ voltage on capacitor is $v_c(0) = V + (V_0 - V) = V_0$, (Initial voltage). And at $t \to \infty$ value of the capacitor voltage is V which is the steady state value.

Steady state component (Response) is also called as forced OR driven response since its value will depends upon driving force (Excitations).

Transient response will vanishes as $t \to \infty$. But in practice, we can say that transient response vanishes after a time of $T = 4\tau$.

Alternative Proof: Alternatively equation (6.30) can be derived by considering KCL at node in Fig. 6.20(a).

We have
$$i_c - i_R = 0$$

$$C\frac{dv_c}{dt} - \left(\frac{V - V_c}{R}\right) = 0$$

OR $$C\frac{dv_c}{dt} + \frac{v_c}{R} = \frac{V}{R} \qquad \ldots(a)$$

This is a non-homogeneous linear differential equation with a constant forcing function. The solution of this equation consists of two parts. (1) Complimentary solution which is obtained by making forcing function zero (Homogeneous solution) (2) Particular solution which is obtained by considering forcing function.

Homogeneous solution is obtained by making right-hand side zero. Thus we have

$$C\frac{dv_c}{dt} + \frac{v_c}{R} = 0$$

OR $$\left(C.s. + \frac{1}{R}\right)v_c = 0$$

Hence roof of equation is $\quad s = \dfrac{1}{-Rc}$

Hence transient solution is

$$v_c(tr) = A\, e^{-\frac{1}{RC}}$$

Particular solution is obtain by considering the forcing function. Since forcing function is a constant, we assume a constant for forced solution.

i.e. $\quad v_c(ss) = K$

By (a) $\quad 0 + \dfrac{K}{R} = \dfrac{V}{R}$

Hence $\quad \boxed{K = V}$

Therefore, complete solution is given by

$$v_c(t) = v_c(tr) + v_c(ss) = Ae^{-\frac{1}{RC}} + V \qquad ...(6.31)$$

At $\quad t = 0, V(0) = V_o = A + V$

Hence $\quad A = V_o - V$

Therefore, complete solution is given by,

$$v_c(t) = V + (V_o - V) e^{-\frac{1}{RC}} \qquad ...(6.32)$$

Thus equation (6.32) is same as that of equation (6.33). Capacitor voltage as given by equation (6.30) or (6.32) is shown in Fig. 6.21 below.

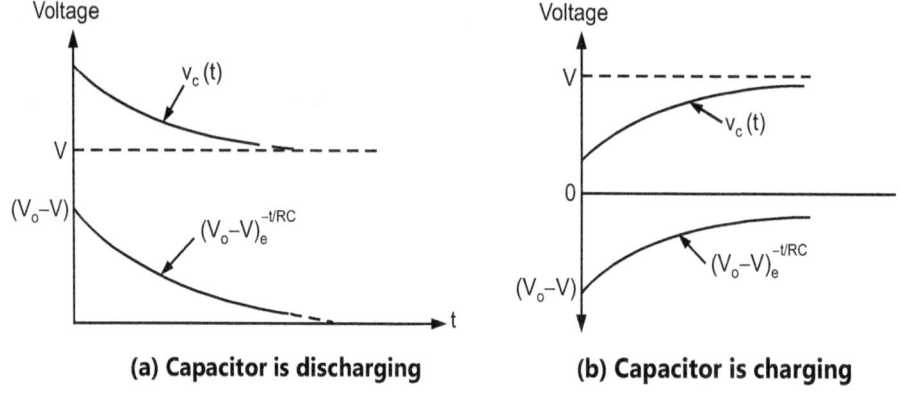

(a) Capacitor is discharging   (b) Capacitor is charging

Fig. 6.21 Capacitor voltage waveforms

If $V_o > V$, then $(V_o - V)$ is positive, capacitor will discharges from V_o to V and then remain constant at V volts as shown in 6.21 (a).

If $V_o < V$, then $(V_o - V)$ is negative. Now the capacitor actually charges and its voltage increases from initial voltage (V_o) exponetially until it will reaches battery voltage V and then it will remain constant at V volts as shown in Fig. 6.21 (b).

The current through capacitor can be obtained by following expression.

$$i_c(t) = C\frac{dv_c(t)}{dt} = C \times (V_o - V) e^{-\frac{t}{RC}} \times -\frac{1}{RC}$$

OR

$$i_c(t) = \left(\frac{V - V_o}{R}\right) e^{-\frac{1}{RC}} \qquad ...(6.33)$$

Current as given by above expression is plotted in the waveform shown below.

If $V > V_o$ then current $i_c(t)$ is positive indicating it as a charging current as shown in Fig. 6.22 (a).

If $V_o > V$ then current $i_c(t)$ is negative indicating it as a discharging current as shown in Fig. 6.22 (b).

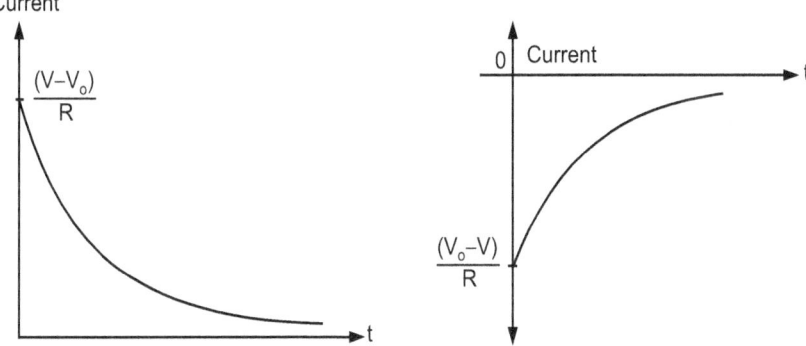

(a) V > V₀ (charging current) (b) V₀ > V (Discharging current)

Fig. 6.22 : Capacitor current waveforms

Note: By voltage waveform it is obvious that voltage across capacitor cannot charge instantaneously. A capacitor which is charged initially will behave like a voltage source. A uncharged capacitor will initially behave like a short circuit.

Example 6.7 : In the circuit shown below switch is closed at t = 0. Find $V_2(t)$ and $i(t)$.

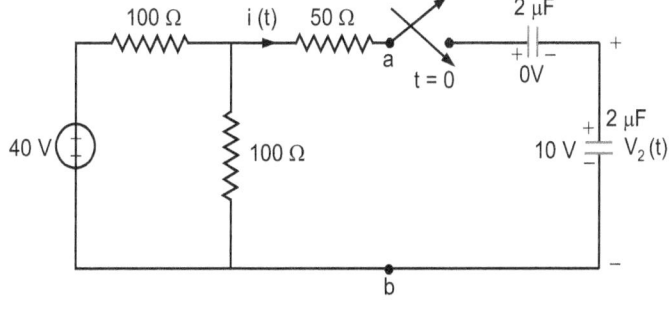

Fig. 6.23

Solution : For t > 0 when switch is closed then thevenin equivalent at left of a –b is given by

$$V_{ab} = \frac{100 \times 40}{200} = 20 \text{ V}$$

$$R_{ab} = 50 + 100 || 100 = 50 + 50 = 100 \text{ }\Omega$$

Also 2µF and 2 µF are in series to give the equivalent capacitance of 1µF. The equivalent circuit for t > 0 is as shown below.

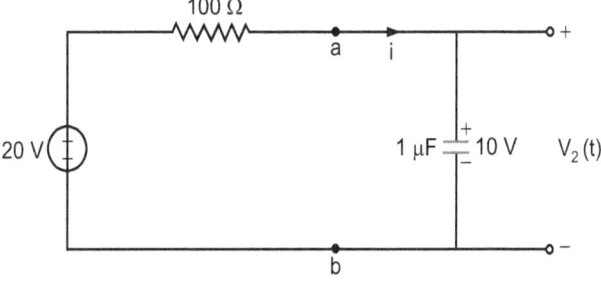

Fig. 6.23 (a) : Thevenin equivalent circuit

Current i is given by
$$i = \left(\frac{V - V_o}{R}\right) e^{-\frac{t}{RC}}$$

OR
$$i = \left(\frac{20 - 10}{100}\right) e^{-\frac{t}{10^{-4}}} = 0.1 \, e^{-10^4 t} \text{ Amps.}$$

Now returning to original circuit of Fig. 6.23. We have

$$v_2(t) = V_o + \frac{1}{C} \int i \, dt = 10 + \frac{10^6}{2} \int_0^t 0.1 \, e^{-10^4 t} \, dt$$

$$= 10 + \frac{10^5}{2} \left[\frac{e^{-10^4 t}}{-10^4}\right]_0^t = 10 + 5[1 - e^{-10^4 t}] \text{ volts}$$

Example 6.8 : The switch of the circuit shown in the Fig. has been open for a long time. At t = 0 it is closed. (a) Calculate v_c at 2m sec after the switch is closed. (b) If the switch is now kept closed for a long time find v_c two milliseconds after it is suddenly opened.

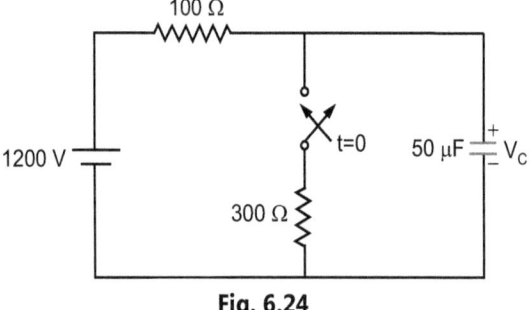

Fig. 6.24

Solution : When switch was opened for a long time then voltage on capacitor = V_o = 1200V.
For t > 0 the Thevenin equivalent circuit, will be as shown below.

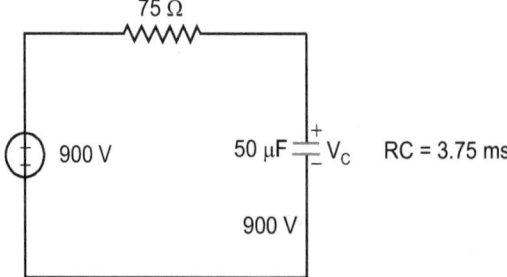

Fig. 6.25: Thevenin equivalent circuit for t > 0

where
$$V_{oc} = V_{eq} = \frac{300 \times 1200}{400} = 900 \text{ V}$$

and
$$R_{eq} = 300 \parallel 100 = 75 \, \Omega$$

The circuit is driven R.C. circuit, with initial voltage on capacitor as 1200 volts.

Using equation (6.30) we have,

$$V_c(t) = 900 + (1200 - 900) e^{-\frac{t}{3.75 \text{ ms}}}$$

$$= 900 + 300 e^{-\frac{t}{3.75 \text{ ms}}}$$

Voltage on capacitor after t = 2 ms is given by

$$V_c(2\text{ms}) = 900 + 300 e^{-\frac{2}{3.75}} - 900 + 176$$

$$= 1076 \text{ volts}$$

6.3 RESISTOR – INDUCTOR (R-L) CIRCUITS

In this section we shall discuss properties of the inductor first. Then properties of a R-L network with inductor having initial current (I_0) is discussed. Then R-L network driven by a d.c. voltage source (V) and inductor having initial current (I_0) is discussed.

6.3.1 Inductor and its Properties

Physical construction of a inductor consists of a coil of pure conducting wire, around a medium or core as shown in Fig. 6.26 below.

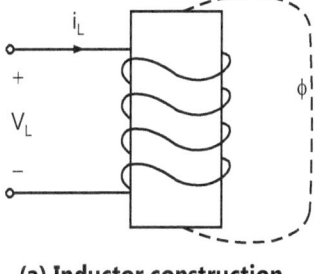
(a) Inductor construction

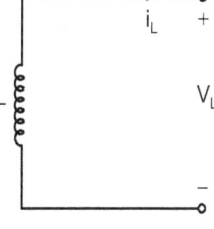
(b) Symbol of inductor

Fig. 6.26

Whenever a current passes through any wire then magnetic field will be established around the wire. Magnetic flux (ϕ) is proportional to the current (i_L) flowing through it. If the wire is wound in the form of coil, then the flux due to each turn is reinforced. Hence, total magnetic flux is proportional to current and also number of turns (N).

Thus $\phi \propto N i_L$ OR $\phi = K N i_L$ ...(6.34)

As this flux links all the N turns, Total flux linkage

$$(\lambda) = N\phi = K N^2 i_L \qquad ...(6.35)$$

Ideally flux linkage (λ) is proportional to the current.

i.e.
$$\lambda = Li_L \quad \ldots(6.36)$$

The proportionality constant (L) is called as the inductance more precisely *self inductance*,

Thus
$$L = KN^2 \quad \ldots(6.37)$$

Value of inductance [Unit is Henry (H)] is proportional to N^2.

Voltage (V_L) and Current (i_L) Relation in Inductor

V_L – i_L relationship in inductor can be derived by making use of Faraday's Law of the magnetic induction. This law states that "Induced voltage in wire is equal to time rate of change of the flux linkages".

Thus, induced voltage at terminal
$$(v_L) = \frac{d\lambda}{dt} = L\frac{di_L}{dt} \quad \ldots(6.38)$$

Symbol for induced voltage (v_L) and the terminal current (i_L) is as shown in Fig. 6.26 (b).

Voltage on the inductor is present only when current through it is changing with time. Thus "under constant (or d.c.) excitation voltage across inductor is zero because current is constant. Thus for d.c. inductor acts as a short circuit".

Integrating above equation we have.

$$i_L(t) = \frac{1}{L}\int_{-\infty}^{t} v_L(t)\,dt \quad \ldots(6.39)$$

$$= \frac{1}{L}\int_{-\infty}^{0} v_L(t)\,dt + \frac{1}{L}\int_{0}^{t} v_L(t)\,dt$$

Hence
$$i_L(t) = I_0 + \frac{1}{L}\int_{0}^{t} V_L(t)\,dt \quad \ldots(6.40)$$

I_o is called as initial current which corresponds to initial stored energy of $\frac{1}{2}LI_0^2$. By the equation (6.40) it is obvious that in inductor it takes some time to build up the current. In the inductor, current is proportional to the magnetic field and not voltage across it.

If we compare equation equations (6.38) and (6.40) with these equations of R-C circuit i.e. equations (6.19) and (6.21), then two equations are identicle if L replaces C and i and v are interchanged.

Energy and Power Relationship in Inductor

Instantaneous power in inductor $p(t) = v(t) i(t)$ W

OR
$$p(t) = I(t) \cdot L\frac{di(t)}{dT} = L \cdot i\frac{d}{dt} = \frac{d}{dt}\left[\frac{1}{2}Li^2\right]$$

Since, energy is obtained by integrating power.

i.e. $\omega = \int p \, dt$

Energy stored in the inductor = $\omega_m(t) = \dfrac{1}{2} Li^2$ ...(6.41)

Positive value of $\omega(t)$ implies energy stored in inductor and negative value of $\omega m(t)$ represents energy supplied by the inductor.

Example 6.9 : Figure shows voltage waveform applied across 100 mh inductor. As a result there is a current in the inductor. Assume initial current zero, determine expression for the current and sketch its waveform.

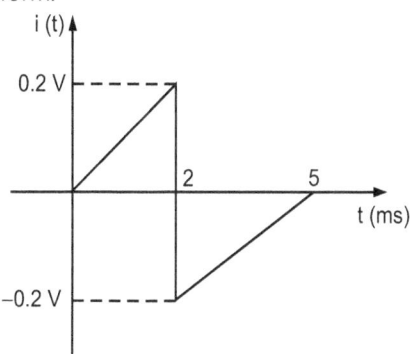

Fig. 6.27

Solution : Current in the inductor is given by relation.

$$i_L(t) = I_o + \dfrac{1}{L}\int_0^t v_L \, dt$$

OR $$i_L(t) = \dfrac{10^3}{100}\int_0^t v_L \, dt = 10\int_0^t v_L \, dt$$

For $0 < t < 2$ sec, $$v_L(t) = \dfrac{0.2}{2} t = 0.1 t$$

Hence $$i_L(t) = 10\int_0^2 0.1 t$$

$$= \left[\dfrac{t^2}{2}\right]_0^2$$

At $t = 2$ sec, $i_L(t) = \dfrac{4}{2} = 2$ Amp.

At $t = 2$ sec, the voltage changes from 0.2 V to -0.2 V but current cannot change at the instant.

For 2 < t < 5 sec we have $v_L(t) = -0.2 + \dfrac{0.2}{3}[t-2]$ and hence we have

$$i_L(t) = 2 - \dfrac{0.2}{L}\int_2^5 dt + \dfrac{0.2}{3L}\int_2^5 (t-2)\,dt$$

$$= 2 - 2\,[t]_2^5 + \dfrac{2}{3}\left[\dfrac{(t-2)^2}{2}\right]_2^t$$

At t = 5 sec $\quad i_L(t) = 2 - 2[5-2] + \dfrac{2}{3} \times \dfrac{9}{2}$

$$= 2 - 6 + 3 = -1 \text{ Amp.}$$

The waveform is as shown below.

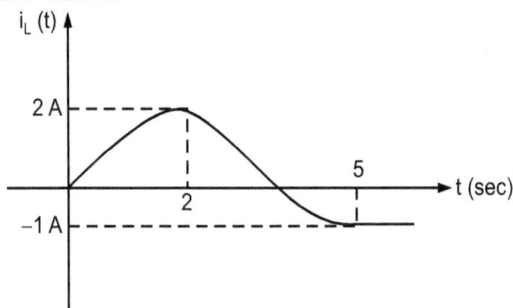

Fig. 6.28

Example 6.10: A current source $i_o(t)$ of waveform shown below is connected to a $\dfrac{1}{3}$ H inductor. Sketch the voltage $V_L(t)$ using the same co-ordinate.

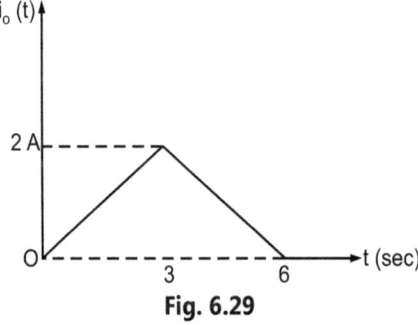

Fig. 6.29

Solution : We have voltage across inductor is given by

$$v_L(t) = L\dfrac{di_L}{dt} = \dfrac{1}{3}\dfrac{d}{dt}i_L(t)$$

For 0 < t < 3, $\qquad \dfrac{di_L}{dt} = \dfrac{2}{3}$ A/sec,

Hence in this range we have

$$v_L(t) = \dfrac{1}{3} \times \dfrac{2}{3} = \dfrac{2}{9} \text{ volts}$$

for 3 < t < 6, we have

$$\frac{di_L}{dt} = \frac{2-0}{3-6} = \frac{-2}{3} \text{ A/sec}$$

Hence we have

$$v_L(t) = \frac{1}{3} \times \frac{-2}{3} = \frac{-2}{9} \text{ volts}$$

The voltage waveform is as shown below.

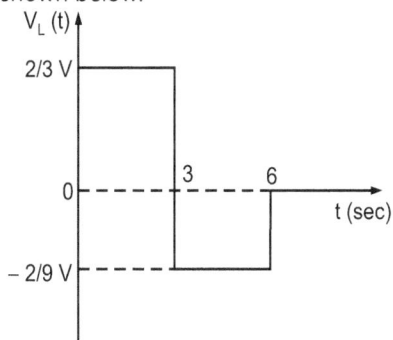

Fig. 6.30: Voltage waveforms

Linearity and Superposition: An element is said to be linear if and only if superposition theorem is valid for them and vice versa.

It can be shown that superposition theorem is valid for inductor if and only if initial current in the inductor (I_o) is zero. Otherwise superposition theorem cannot be applied. Thus, for energized inductor we cannot apply superposition theorem.

Thus, inductor acts as linear element if and only if it is not energized (Initial current in the inductor is zero).

Series and Parallel Connection of Inductors: Consider the inductor L_1 and L_2 connected in series as shown in Fig. 6.31. Current through two inductors are same.

Also
$$v = v_1 + v_2 = L_1 \frac{di}{dt} + L_2 \frac{di}{dt}$$
$$= (L_1 + L_2) \frac{di}{dt} = L_{eq} \frac{di}{dt}$$

where
$$L_{eq} = L_1 + L_2 \qquad \qquad ...(6.42)$$

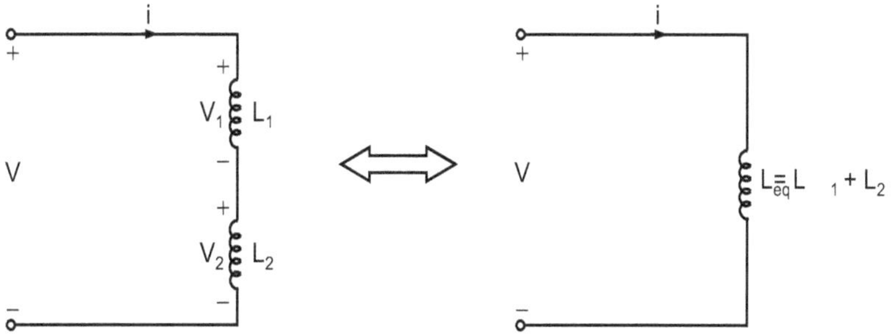

Fig. 6.31: Inductors in series

Thus, in series connection equivalent inductance is addition of two inductance. Also any initial current present in the two inductors will also be present on equivalent inductors also. Now consider two inductors connected in parallel as shown in Fig. 3.32. Here both the inductors are having same voltage.

Now,
$$i = i_1 + i_2 = \frac{1}{L_1}\int_0^t v\,dt + \frac{1}{L_2}\int_0^t v\,dt$$
$$= \left(\frac{1}{L_1} + \frac{1}{L_2}\right)\int_0^t v\,dt = \frac{1}{L_L}\int_0^t v\,dt$$

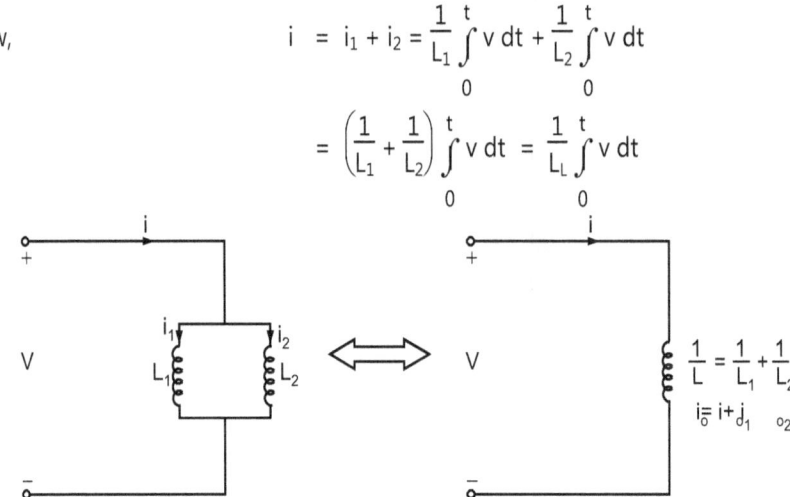

Fig. 6.32 : Inductor in parallel

Thus, equivalent inductance of a parallel connected inductors is given by,
$$\frac{1}{L} = \frac{1}{L_1} + \frac{1}{L_2} \qquad \ldots(6.43)$$

If any initial current is present in individual inductor, then sum of these initial currents will be present on equivalent inductor.

6.3.2 Undriven R-L Circuit

Consider circuit shown below in Fig. 6.33 (a).

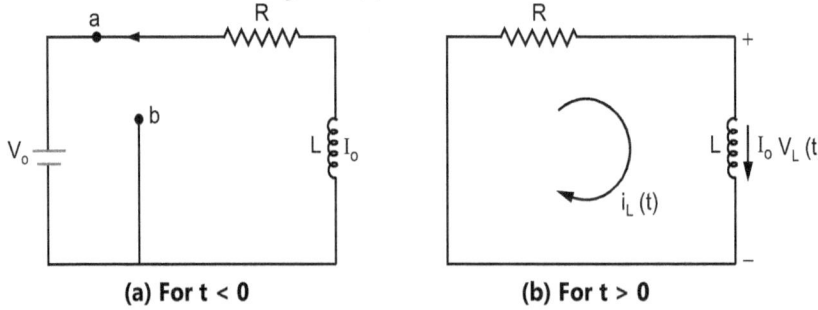

(a) For t < 0   (b) For t > 0

Fig. 6.33: Undriven circuit

Initially switch was on position 'a' for a long time. Inductor then acts as a short circuit and current through inductor = $I_o = \dfrac{V_o}{R}$. This is known as initial current. It the switch is thrown on position 'b' at t = 0, for t > 0, the circuit will be as shown in Fig. 6.33 (b).

Now inductor current (I_o) will flow through resistor R. Hence energy stored in the inductor $\left(\frac{1}{2} L I_o^2\right)$ will be dissipated as a heat in the resistor. Because of this the initial current (I_o) will reduce. We are interested to find the rate at which inductor current reduces to zero.

KVL across the circuit of Fig. 6.33 (b) gives

$$R \cdot i_L + L \frac{di_L}{dt} = 0 \qquad \ldots(a)$$

This is a homogeneous linear differential equation. We can use *variable separable* method to solve this differential equation. Thus,

$$L \frac{di_L}{dt} = -R\, i_L \quad \text{OR} \quad \frac{di_L}{i_L} = -\frac{R}{L} dt \qquad \ldots(b)$$

Integrating equation (b) gives

$$\log_e (i_L) = -\frac{R}{L} t + K$$

Hence
$$i_L = e^{-\frac{R}{L}t + K} = e^{-K} e^{-\frac{R}{L}t} = A e^{-\frac{R}{L}t}$$

Thus
$$i_L(t) = A e^{-\frac{R}{L}t} \qquad \ldots(c)$$

Value of A can be found using initial value of $i_L(t)$.

Thus at = 0, $\qquad i_L(0) = I_o = A$

Hence
$$i_L(t) = I_o e^{-\frac{R}{L}t} \qquad \ldots(6.48)$$

Time constant of R-L circuit: $T = \frac{L}{R}$ is known as time constant of a R-L circuit. Time constant is defined as the rate at which current (i_L) drops to $\frac{1}{e}$ or 0.37 times initial current (I_o).

Current waveform is as shown below in Fig. 6.34.

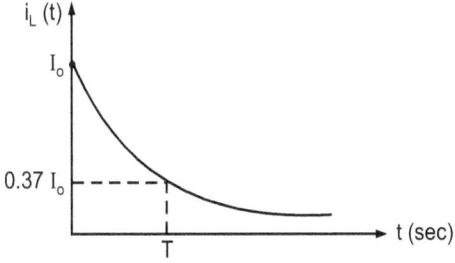

Fig. 6.34: Current waveform of undriven R-L

Voltage across inductor can be found as below.

$$v_L(t) = L\frac{di_L}{dt} = L\frac{di}{dt} = L I_0 e^{-t/T} \times -\frac{1}{T} = -L I_0 e^{-t/T} \times \frac{R}{L} = -R I_0 e^{-t/T}$$

Thus $\quad v_L(t) = -R I_0 e^{-\frac{R}{L}t}$ ...(6.45)

Negative sign of $v_L(t)$ indicates that current through inductor is decreasing. Also voltage induced is maximum at $t = 0$ and is equal to $-R.\ I_0$. The waveform for voltage $v_L(t)$ is as shown blow in Fig. 6.35.

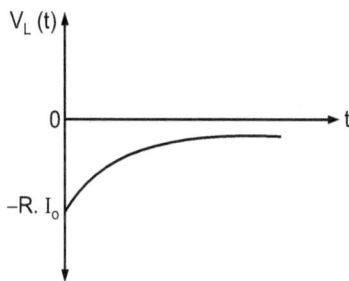

Fig. 6.35: Voltage waveform of R-L circuit

Example 6.11: In the circuit shown inductor is fluxed such that current i : 2 Amp. At the time $t = 0$, this inductor is connected to a resistor. If the resistor has a value of 1 kΩ and inductor a value of 50 mH. Determine the time at which current in inductor will have a value of 1 Amp.

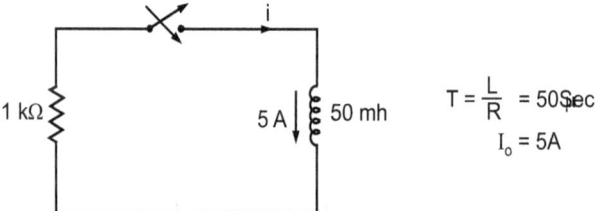

Fig. 3.36

Solution : Given that for $t < 0$, inductor current is 5 Amp. for $t > 0$ current through inductor is given by

$$i_L(t) = I(t) = 5e^{-\frac{t_1}{T}} = 5e^{-20000\,t}$$

Let t_1 be the time after which switch is closed at $t = 0$ at which current $i(t)$ reduces to 1 Amp.

Thus $\quad 1 = 5e^{-\frac{t_1}{T}}$

OR $\quad e^{-\frac{t_1}{T}} = 0.2$

Hence $\quad \frac{t_1}{T} = -1.61$

Thus $\quad t_1 = 1.61\,T = 1.61 \times 50\,\mu\,\text{sec} = 80.5\,\mu\text{sec}.$

Thus after a time of 80.5 μ sec, the current through the inductor reduces to 1 Amp.

6.3.3 Driven R-L Circuit (Step response of R-L Circuit)

Consider a inductor with initial current I_o and is connected to a battery of v volts through a switch and a resistor (R) as shown below.

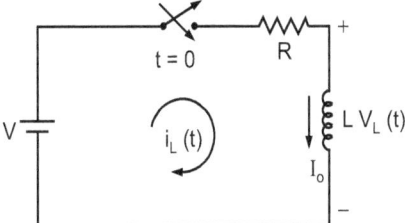

Fig. 6.37: Step response of a R-L circuit

As long as switch is opened inductor will retain its stored energy $\left[\frac{1}{2}LI_o^2\right]$. Let at t= 0 the switch is closed. Current i_L (t) at any instant of time constants or two parts. (a) i_{ss}: Steady state component , (b) i_{tr}: Transient component.

If the switch is closed for a long time, then under steady state inductor is acting as a short circuit (Because current is constant).

Thus $\quad i_{ss} = \frac{V}{R}$ = Steady state component

The transient condition is given by

$$i_{tr} = A\,e^{-t/T}$$

Thus circuit current i (t) at any time is given by

$$i_L(t) = \frac{V}{R} + A e^{-\frac{R}{L}t} \qquad \ldots(a)$$

Constant 'A' is determined by initial value of current. At t = 0 we have

$$i_L(0) = I_o$$

Hence by (a) $\quad I_o = \frac{V}{R} + A$

OR $\quad A = \left(I_o - \frac{V}{R}\right) \qquad \ldots(6.46)$

Thus complete solution for $i_L(t)$ is

$$i_L(t) = \frac{V}{R} + \left(I_o - \frac{V}{R}\right) e^{-\frac{R}{L}t} \qquad \ldots(6.47)$$

= Steady state components + Transient component

Current wave form is as shown below in Fig. 6.38.

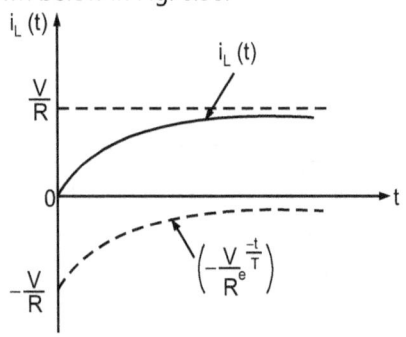

Fig. 6.38: Current waveform with $I_o = 0A$

Note: If $\frac{V}{R} > I_o$ then $i_L(t)$ is positive indicating that inductor energy is increasing.

Voltage across inductor at any instant of time is given by:

$$v_L(t) = L\frac{di_L}{dt} = L\left[\left(I_o - \frac{V}{R}\right) e^{-t/T} \times -\frac{R}{L}\right]$$

$$= -R\left(I_o - \frac{V}{R}\right) e^{-t/T}$$

Thus $\qquad v_L(t) = (V - RI_o) e^{-Rt/L} \qquad \ldots(6.48)$

Voltage waveform when $I_o = 0$ is as shown below.

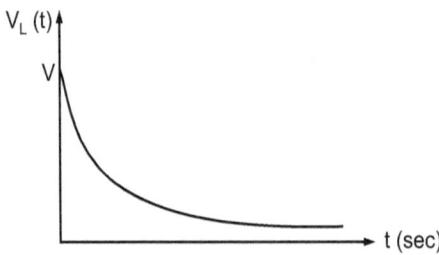

Fig. 6.39: Inductor voltage waveform with $t_o = 0$

By this waveform, it is obvious that under steady state ($t = \infty$), inductor voltage is zero. Thus inductor acts as a short circuit.

Example 6.12: In the circuit shown below switch is closed at t = 0, Determine and sketch i_L (T) and v_L (t) for t > 0.

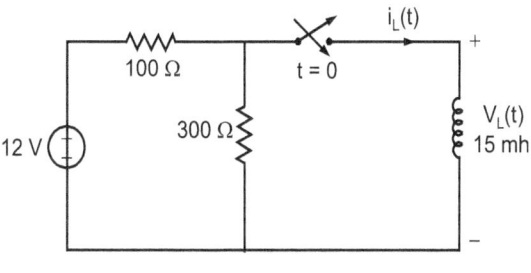

Fig. 6.40

Solution : Switch was closed at t = 0, this means it was initially opened. Hence initial current on inductor is I_o = 0 Amp.

When switch was closed, for t > 0, replace the circuit by Thevenin equivalent circuit as shown below.

where
$$V_{oc} = \frac{300 \times 12}{400}$$
$$= 9 \text{ volts}$$

and
$$R = 300 \parallel 100$$
$$= 75 \, \Omega$$

Hence
$$T = \frac{L}{R} = \frac{15 \times 10^{-3}}{75}$$
$$= 0.2 \text{ ms}$$

This is a driven R-L circuit, with initial current (I_o) is zero. Thus we have by equations (6.47) and (6.47).

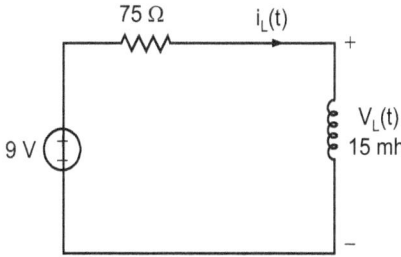

Fig. 6.41: Thevenin equivalent circuit for t > 0

$$i_L(t) = \frac{9}{75} + \left(0 - \frac{9}{75}\right) e^{-t/T}$$

$$= \frac{9}{75} [1 - e^{-5000 \, t}] \text{ Amp}$$

$$v_L(t) = (9 - 0) \, e^{-t/T}$$
$$= 9 e^{-5000 \, t} \text{ volts}$$

Waveforms for voltage and currents are as shown below.

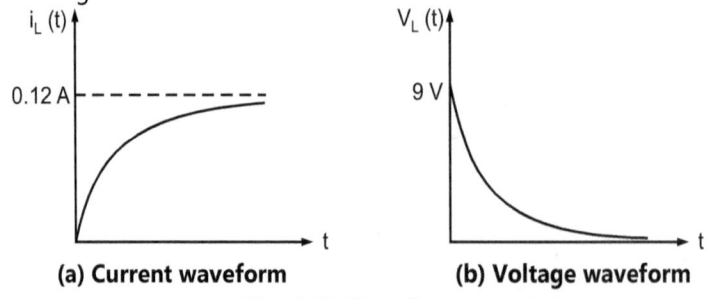

(a) Current waveform (b) Voltage waveform

Fig. 6.42: Waveforms

Example 6.13 : Calculate rate of change of current at
1. The instant of closing the switch.
2. When $t = T = \dfrac{L}{R}$
3. Find final steady state value of current. Circuit is switched to 200 V d.c. at t = 0.

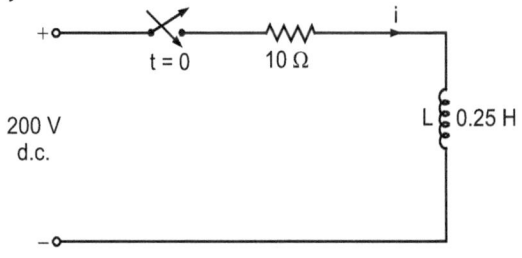

Fig. 6.43

Solution : (a) When switch is closed at t = 0, the circuit acts as driven R-L circuit with initial current (I_o) as zero.

Thus
$$i(t) = \frac{V}{R} + \left(0 - \frac{V}{R}\right) e^{-\frac{R}{L}t} = \frac{V}{R}\left[1 - e^{-\frac{R}{L}t}\right]$$

Rate of change of current = $\dfrac{di}{dt} = -\dfrac{V}{R} + e^{-\frac{R}{L}t} \times \dfrac{-R}{L} = +\dfrac{V}{L} e^{-\frac{R}{L}t}$

at t = 0, $\quad \dfrac{di}{dt}(0^+) = \dfrac{V}{L} = \dfrac{200}{0.25} = 100$ A/sec.

(b) at $\quad t = T = \dfrac{L}{T} = 0.025$ sec, the rate of change of current is

$$= \frac{di}{dt}(t = T) = \frac{V}{L} e^{-1} = 100 \times \frac{1}{e} \text{ A/sec} = 26.8 \text{ Amp/sec.}$$

(c) Under steady state inductor acts as short circuit. Thus steady state value of current i

$$(t = \infty) = \frac{V}{R} = \frac{200}{10} = 20 \text{ Amp.}$$

Example 6.14: Determine as a function of time the voltage across 3.2 Ω resistor and across inductor, if switch is closed at t = 0 and hence calculate voltage at t = 5 ms.

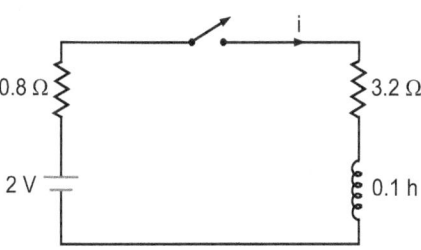

Fig. 6.44

Solution : Assume initial current on inductor (I_o) be zero. When switch is closed at t = 0, the circuit acts as a driven R-C circuit.

Hence Loop current $= i(t) = \frac{V}{R}\left[1 - e^{-\frac{R}{L}t}\right]$

$$T = \frac{L}{R} = \frac{0.1}{4.0} = \frac{1}{40} \text{ sec.}$$

Thus $i(t) = \frac{20}{4}[1 - e^{-40t}] = 5[1 - e^{-40t}]$ Amp

1. Voltage across 3.2 Ω resistor $= V_R = 3.2 \times 5[1 - e^{-40t}]$ volts
$= 16[1 - e^{-40t}]$ volts

This is the required expression for voltage across resistor

at t = 5 ms
We have $V_R (5 \text{ ms}) = 16[1 - e^{-40 \times 5 \times 10^{-3}}]$
$= 16[1 - e^{-0.2}] = 16[1 - 0.818]$
Thus we have $V_R \, 5 \text{ ms} = 2.9$ volts

2. Voltage across inductor $= V_L = L\frac{di_L}{dt} = L \times \frac{V}{R} e^{-\frac{R}{L}t} \times \frac{R}{L}$

Thus $V_L(t) = Ve^{-\frac{R}{L}t} = 20 \, e^{-40 t}$ volts

This is the required expression for voltage across inductor. At t = 5 ms we have v_L (5ms) = 20 $e^{-0.2}$ = 16.37 volts

Example 6.15: The switch shown below has been closed for a long time. Find i_L for all 't' after switch is opened at t = 0.

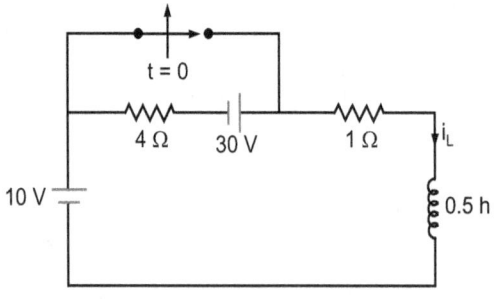

Fig. 6.45

Solution : When switch is closed for a long time then inductor acts as a short circuit. And initial current in the inductor = $I_0 = \frac{10}{1}$ = 10 Amp. When switch is opened at t = 0, Then for t > 0 the circuit will be as shown below in Fig. 6.46 (a).

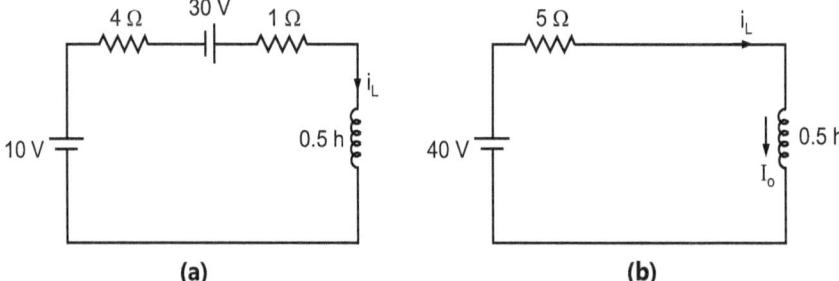

(a)   (b)

Fig. 6.46

The circuit can be simplified as shown in Fig. 6.46 (b). This is a driven R-L circuit with initial current I_0 = 10A and is driven by a battery of 40V.

$$i_L(t) = \frac{40}{5} + \left(10 - \frac{40}{5}\right) e^{-t/T} \text{ where } T = \frac{L}{R} = 0.1 \text{ sec}$$

OR $i_L(t) = 8 + 2e^{-10t}$

This is the required expression for current.

6.3.4 Step Response of First Order Circuit

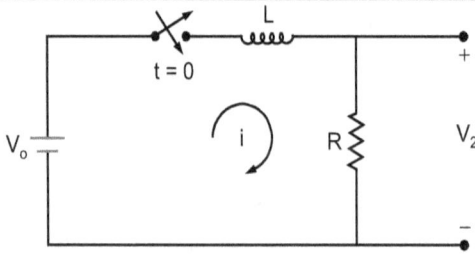

Fig. 6.47 : Consider circuit

Consider circuit shown above. If at t = 0 the switch is closed, then voltage V_o is applied to the R-L circuit. V_o is the step voltage because the voltage suddenly jumps from zero to V_o.
For $t \geq 0$, KVL across the loop gives:

$$Ri + L\frac{di}{dt} = V_o \ (t \geq 0)$$

As discussed earlier, this is a driven R-L circuit, hence current i (t) is given by

$$i(t) = \frac{V_o}{R}\left(1 - e^{-\frac{R}{L}t}\right)$$

Thus, output voltage v_2 (t) is given by

$$v_2(t) = V_o(1 - e^{-\sigma_1 t}) \qquad ...(6.49)$$

Output response is as shown below in Fig. 6.48.

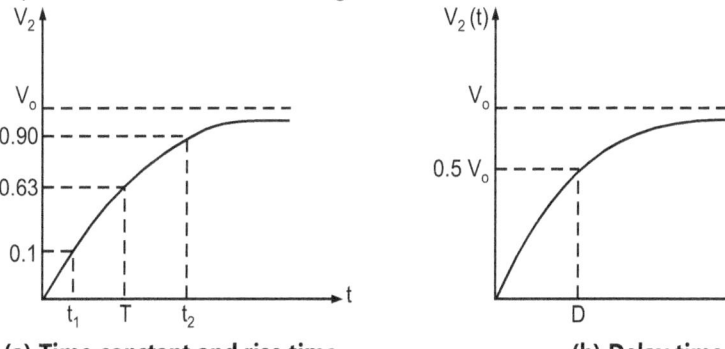

(a) Time constant and rise time (b) Delay time

Fig. 6.48: Step response of first order circuit

(a) Time constant (T): It is the time after t > 0 at which voltage reches 63% of the final value (V_o).

Thus at $\qquad T = \frac{L}{R} = \frac{1}{\sigma}, \ v_2 = V_o(1 - e^{-1}) = 0.63 \ V_o$

(b) Rise Time (t_r): It is the time in which output voltage v_2 (t) takes to rise from 10% to the 90% of the final value (V_o).

If t_1 is the time in which output voltage v_2 (t) takes to reaches 10% of final value and t_2 is the time required for response to reach 90% of final value (V_o),

Then $\qquad t_r = t_2 - t_1 \qquad ...(6.50)$

Now at $\qquad t = t_1, \ 0.1 \ V_0 = V_o\left(1 - e^{-\sigma_1 t_1}\right)$

OR $\qquad t_1 = \frac{1}{\sigma_1} \ln\left[\frac{10}{9}\right]$

at $\qquad t = t_2 \ 0.9 \ V_o = V_o\left(1 - e^{-\sigma_1 t_2}\right)$

OR $\quad t_2 = \dfrac{1}{\sigma_1} \ln(10)$

Thus $\quad t_r = t_2 - t_1 = \dfrac{1}{\sigma_1} \ln 9 = \dfrac{2.2}{\sigma_1} = 2.2\,T$

Thus $\quad t_r = 2.2\,T$ ...(6.51)

(c) Delay Time (t_D): It is the time required for the output response to reach 50% of its final value.

Thus at $\quad t = t_D$,

$$v_2(t_D) = V_o \left[1 - e^{-\sigma_1 t_D}\right] = 0.5\,V_o$$

Or $\quad t_D = \dfrac{\ln 2}{\sigma_1} = \dfrac{0.692}{\sigma_1}$

$\quad\quad\quad\quad = 0.692\,T$

Thus $\quad t_D = 0.7\,T$ ...(6.52)

Thus for a first order circuit delay time is 0.7 times the time constant.

6.4 RESISTOR - CAPACITOR - INDUCTOR (R-L-C) CIRCUITS

Consider general form of a second order linear differential equations with constant coefficient as shown below.

$$a_0 \dfrac{d^2 i}{dt^2} + a_1 \dfrac{di}{dt} + a_2 i = 0 \qquad \text{...(6.53)}$$

Solution $i(t)$ of this equation should be such that addition of $i(t)$, its first derivative, and second derivative when multiplied by constants will give zero. Hence solution of the $i(t)$ is in the form.

$$i(t) = k\,e^{st}$$

Where k is a constant and root 's' may be real, imaginary or complExample

Thus $a_0 s^2 k\,e^{st} + a_1 k\,e^{st} + a_2 k\,e^{st} = 0$

OR $\quad\quad a_0 S^2 + a_1 s + a_2 = 0$ ...(6.54)

This equation is known as characteristic (or auxiliary) equation. Two roots equations are given by.

$$S_1, S_2 = -\dfrac{a_1}{2a_c} \pm \dfrac{1}{2a_0}\sqrt{a_1^2 - 4\,a_1\,a_0} \qquad \text{...(6.55)}$$

Two form of solution of equation is:

$$i_1 = k_1\,e^{s_1 t} \quad \text{and} \quad i_2 = k_2\,e^{s_2 t}$$

Then $i = i_1 + i_2$ is also solution of equation (6.54). The general form of solution of given differential equation (6.53) is:

$$i(t) = k_1\,e^{s_1 t} + k_2\,e^{s_2 t} \qquad \text{...(6.56)}$$

Roots s_1, s_2 are determined by coefficients a_0, a_1, a_2. The radical $\pm\sqrt{a_1^2 - 4a_0 a_2}$ may be zero, real, real and complex or imaginary depending upon a_0, a_1 and a_2.

Step response of a R-L-C circuit gives a second order linear differential equations with the constant coefficient solution for all four cases will be discussed.

6.4.1 Step Response R-L-C circuit

When a step (d.c.) voltage is given to a R-L-C circuit, then the second order differential equations are formed. The solution of this equation depends upon the type of the roots of the equation.

Case I: When roots of equation are real and unequal consider the circuit shown below in Fig. 6.49.

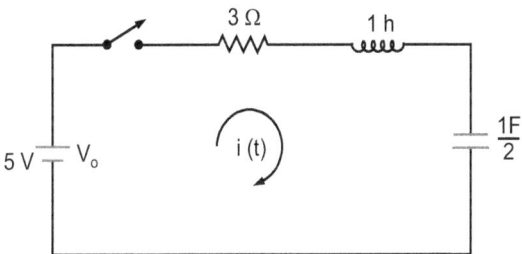

Fig. 6.49: Over damped circuit

Let switches be Open for $t < 0$. Capacitors and inductors are not energised. At $t = 0$, the switch is closed. For $t > 0$ the loop equation will becomes.

$$\frac{1}{C}\int i\, dt + L\frac{di}{dt} + Ri = V_o$$

OR $\quad 2\int i\, dt + \frac{di}{dt} + 3i = 5 \quad\quad\quad …(1)$

Differentiating this equation gives

$$\frac{d^2i}{dt^2} + 3\frac{di}{dt} + 2i = 0 \quad\quad\quad …(6.57)$$

This is a homogeneous linear differential equation (L.D.E.) of form of equation (6.61). This is also known as characteristic equation.

As before if $i(t) = e^{st}$ is the trial solution, then equation (6.61) becomes

$$S^2 + 3.5 + 2 = 0$$

The roots of this equation are

$$S_1, S_2 = \frac{-3 \pm \sqrt{9 - 4 \times 2}}{2} = \frac{-3}{2} \pm \frac{1}{2}$$

$$= -\frac{1}{2} \text{ or } -2.$$

Thus $\boxed{S_1 = -0.5}$ and $\boxed{S_2 = -2}$

Thus two roots are *real, negative and unequal.* Hence solution will become
$$i(t) = k_1 e^{-t} + k_2 e^{-2t} \qquad \ldots(6.58)$$
Constant k_1 and k_2 are found by knowledge of the initial conditions.

At $t = 0$, $i(t) = 0$ (Because of the inductor, current cannot flow instantaneously).

Thus $\qquad\qquad 0 = k_1 + k_2 \qquad \ldots(a)$

Also by equation (a) we have at $t = 0$
$$0 + \frac{di}{dt} + 0 = 5$$

Hence $\qquad \left.\dfrac{di}{dt}\right|_{t=0} = 5 \text{ A/sec}$

Differentiating equation (6.58) we have
$$\frac{di}{dt} = -k_1 e^{-t} - 2k_2 e^{-2t}$$

Also by equation (1) we have at $t = -0$

At $\quad t = 0, \qquad \left.\dfrac{di}{dt}\right|_{t=0} = k_1 - 2k_2 = 5$

Thus $\qquad -k_1 - 2k_2 = 5 \qquad \ldots(b)$

adding (a) and (b) we have $\boxed{k_2 = -5}$

Hence $\qquad\qquad k_1 = -k_2$
$$= +5 \text{ hence } \boxed{k_1 = 5}$$

Hence $\qquad i(t) = 5e^{-t} - 5e^{-2t} \qquad \ldots(6.59)$

This is particular solution for the current.

Plot of the current waveform is as shown below.

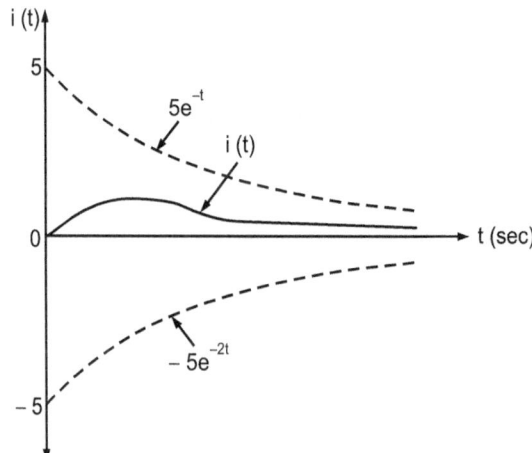

Fig. 6.50: Plot of total current and components currents waveforms

Case II: When roots of the equation are real and repeated:

Here $(a_1^2 - 4 a_0 a_2) = 0$ OR $a_1^2 = 4 a_0 a_2$

For this consider circuit shown below.

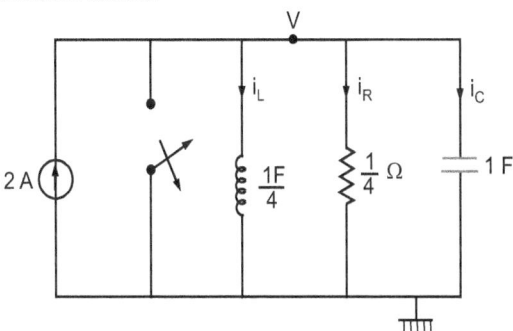

Fig. 6.51: Critically damped circuit

For t < 0, switch was closed. Hence, inductor and capacitor are unenergised. At t = 0, the switch is opened. KCL at node v gives

$$i_R + i_C + i_L = 2$$

$$4v + 1\frac{dv}{dt} + 4 \int v \, dt = 2 \qquad \ldots(1)$$

Differentiating this equation gives

$$\frac{d^2v}{dt^2} + 4\frac{dv}{dt} + 4v = 0 \qquad \ldots(6.60)$$

Characteristic equation will become

$$S^2 + 4S + 4 = 0$$

Roots of the equation are

$$S_1, S_2 = \frac{-4 \pm \sqrt{16 - 4 \times 1 \times 4}}{2} = \frac{-4}{2} \pm -2$$

Thus $\boxed{S_1 = -2}$ and $\boxed{S_2 = 2}$

Thus two roots are real, negative and equal. The general solution of the equation (6.60) becomes.

$$v(t) = k_1 e^{-2t} + k_2 t e^{-2t} \qquad \ldots(6.61)$$

k_1 and k_2 are constant, which can be found by using initial conditions.

at t = 0, v(0)   = 0 + k_1

Thus $k_1 = 0$

also by (1), $\left.\frac{dv}{dt}\right|_{t=0}$ = 2 volts/sec.

Now differentiating equation (6.62), we get

$$\frac{dv}{dt} = -2k_1 e^{-2t} + k_2 [-2t e^{-2t} + e^{-2t}]$$

Thus at $t = 0$,

$$\left.\frac{dv}{dt}\right|_{t=0} = 0 + k_2 [0 + 1] = 2$$

Thus $k_2 = 2$

Hence desired particular solution for $v(t)$ is

$$v(t) = 2t\, e^{-2t} \qquad \ldots(6.62)$$

Plot of the voltage waveform corresponding to equation (6.62) is as shown below

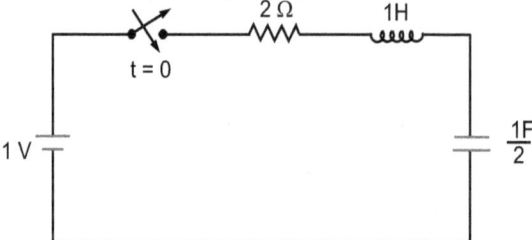

Fig. 6.52: Plot of voltage waveform for the critically damped circuit

Case III: When roots of the equation are complex: Here $(a_1^2 - 4 a_0 a_2) < 0$ OR $a_1^2 = 4a_0 a_2$.

For this consider circuit shown below in Fig. 6.53.

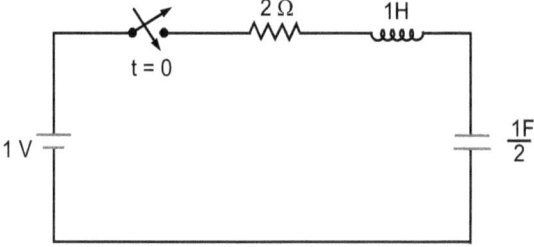

Fig. 6.53: Under-damped circuit

For $t > 0$, loop equation will be

$$2 \int i(t)\, dt + 1 \frac{di}{dt} + 2i(t) = 1 \qquad \ldots(1)$$

Differentiating this equation gives

$$\frac{d^2 i}{dt^2} + 2 \frac{di}{dt} + 2i = 0$$

The characteristic equation becomes

$$S^2 + 2S + 2 = 0 \qquad \ldots(6.63)$$

Roots of this equation are

$$S_1, S_2 = \frac{-2 \pm \sqrt{4 - 4 \times 1 \times 2}}{2 \times 1} = \frac{-2 \pm \sqrt{-4}}{2}$$

$$= -1 + J1$$

Thus $\quad S_1 = -1 + J1 \text{ and } S_2 = -1 - J1$

With these roots, the general solution of the equation becomes

$$i(t) = k_1 e^{-S_1 t} + k_2 e^{-S_2 t}$$

$$= k_1 e^{(-1+J1)t} + k_2 e^{(-1-J1)t}$$

Thus $\quad i(t) = e^{-t}[k_1 e^{Jt} + k_2 e^{-Jt}] \quad \ldots(6.64)$

By using "Eulers identity" which is given as

$$e^{\pm J\omega t} = \cos \omega t \pm J \sin \omega t$$

We have $\quad e^{\pm Jt} = \cos t \pm J \sin t$

Hence equation (6.64) becomes,

$$i(t) = e^{-t}[k_1(\cos t + J \sin t) + k_2(\cos t - J \sin t)]$$

$$= e^{-t}[(k_1 + k_2)\cos t + J(k_1 - k_2)\sin t]$$

Thus $\quad i(t) = e^{-t}[k_3 \cos t + k_4 \sin t] \quad \ldots(6.65)$

where $\quad k_3 = k_1 + k_2 \text{ and } k_4$

$$= J(k_1 - k_2)$$

Value of the constant k_3 and k_4 can be using initial conditions.

At $t = 0$, we know that $i(t) = i(0) = 0 = k_3$

Also by equation (1) we have

at $t = 0$, $\quad \left.\dfrac{di}{dt}\right|_{t=0} = \dfrac{1}{1}$

$$= 1 \text{ A/sec}$$

Now, differentiating equation (6.65) we have

$$\dfrac{di(t)}{dt} = \dfrac{d}{dt}[e^{-t} k_4 \sin t]$$

$$= k_4[e^{-t}\cos t - e^{-t}\sin t]$$

At $t = 0$, $\quad \dfrac{di(t)}{dt} = k_4 = 1$

Thus $\quad \boxed{k_4 = 1}$

Hence, particular solution of the current is

$$i(t) = e^{-t} \sin t \quad \ldots(6.66)$$

Current waveform $i(t)$ as given by above equation is known as 'Damped sinusoidal' and is as n below

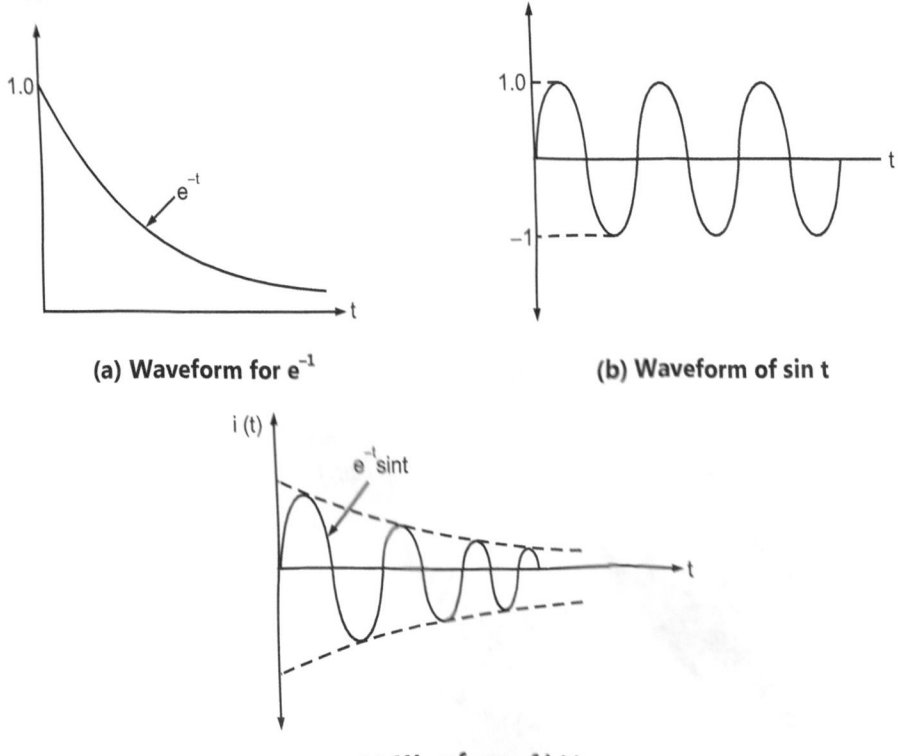

(a) Waveform for e^{-1}

(b) Waveform of sin t

(c) Waveform of i (t)

Fig. 6.54: Waveform of I (t) is a product of two waveform shown in (a) and (b)

Case IV: When roots of the equation are imaginary: This is a special case of complex root in which a_1 is zero. This corresponds to the zero resistance (R = 0) in the R-L-C circuit. Consider the circuit as shown in Fig. 6.56 below.

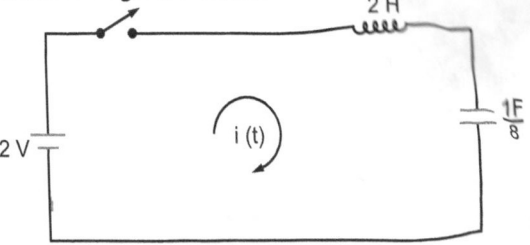

Fig. 6.55: Oscillatory circuit

When switch is closed at t = 0, then KVL across the loop gives

$$8 \int i \, dt + 2 \frac{di}{dt} = 2 \qquad \ldots(1)$$

Differentiating

$$8i + 2 \frac{d^2 i}{dt^2} = 0$$

Characteristic equation becomes

$$2S^2 + 8 = 0$$

OR $\quad S^2 + 4 = 0$

Roots of equation are $\quad S_1, S_2 = \sqrt{-4} = \pm J2$

Thus $\quad \boxed{S_1 = -S_2 = J2}$

Thus roots *are equal, and imaginary*. The solution will be

$$i(t) = k_1 e^{J2t} + k_2 e^{-J2t}$$
$$= k_1 [\cos 2t + j \sin 2t] + k [\cos 2t - J \sin 2t]$$

Thus $\quad i(t) = (k_1 + k_2) \cos 2t + J(k_1 - k_2) \sin 2t$

OR $\quad i(t) = k_3 \cos 2t + k_4 \sin 2t \quad\quad …(6.67)$

where $\quad k_3 = k_1 + k_2$

and $\quad k_4 = J(k_1 - k_2)$

Constants k_3, k_4 are fond using the initial conditions.

At $t = 0$, $\quad i(0) = 0 = k_3$ thus $k_3 = 0$

Also by (1) we have $\quad \left.\dfrac{di}{dt}\right|_{t=0} = \dfrac{2}{2} = 1$ Amp/sec

Differentiating $\quad \left.\dfrac{di}{dt}\right|_{t=0} = k_4 . 2 \cos 2t \Big|_{t=0} = 2k_4 = 1$

Hence equation (6.67) we have

$$k_4 = \dfrac{1}{2}$$

Thus the particular solution for the current $i(t)$ is

$$i(t) = \dfrac{1}{2} \sin 2t \quad\quad …(6.68)$$

Current waveform as given by (6.68) is purely sinusoidal and is given as shown in Fig. 6.56.

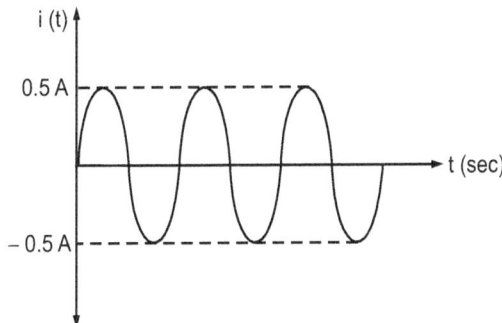

Fig. 6.56: Sinusoidal (oscillatory) waveform as represented by i (t)

Table 6.1 shown (on next page) will summerises four possible cases of the characteristic equation $a_0 S^2 + a_1 S + a_2 = 0$ where a_0 a_1 and a_2 are real and non-negative.

NETWORK ANALYSIS (S.E. SEM III E & TC. SU) — TRANSIENT RESPONSE

Example 6.16: In the network shown switch k is closed and steady state is reached. At t = 0, switch is opened. Find an expression for the current in the inductor $i_2(t)$.

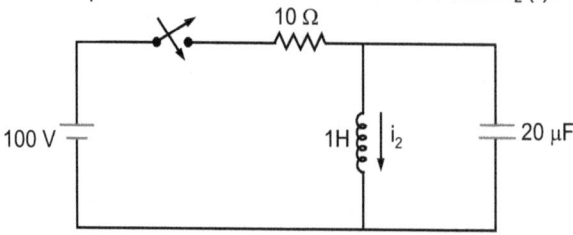

Fig. 6.57

Solution: When switch is closed and steady state is reached (For t < 0) then inductor acts as a short circuit. Hence current through inductor is

Table 6.2: Characteristic equation is $a_0 S^2 + a_1 S + a_2 = 0$

Case	Coefficient condition	Nature of Roots	Type of circuit	Form of solution	Response
I	$a_1^2 > 4 a_0 a_2$	Negative, Real and unequal	Over damped circuit	$i = k_1 e^{S_1 t} + k_2 e^{S_2 t}$	i(t) curve
II	$a_1^2 = 4 a_0 a_2$	Negative, real and equal	Critical damped circuit	$i = k_1 e^{S_1 t} + k_2 t e^{S_1 t}$	i(t) curve
III	$a_1^2 < 4 a_0 a_2$	Complex and conjugate (Real part is negative)	Under damped circuit	$i = e^{-6t} [k_3 \cos \omega t + k_4 \sin \omega t]$	i(t) curve
IV	$a_1 = 0$, $a_2 \neq 0$, $a_0 \neq 0$	Conjugate imaginary	Oscillatory circuit	$i = i_2 \cos \omega t + k_2 \sin \omega t$ $S_1, S_2 = \pm J\omega$	i(t) curve

$$i_L(0) = I_0 \frac{100}{10} = 10 \text{ Amp.}$$

For t ≥ 0 the circuit will be as shown below

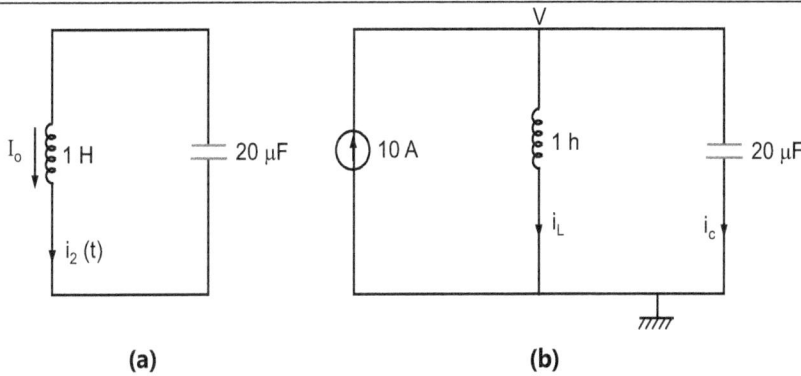

(a) (b)

Fig. 6.58

KCL at 'v' gives $\quad i_L + i_C = -10$

$$C\frac{dv}{dt} + \frac{1}{L}\int v\, dt = -10$$

$$20 \times 10^{-6} \times \frac{dv}{dt} + \frac{1}{1}\int v\, dt = -10 \qquad \ldots(a)$$

OR $\quad 20 \times 10^{-6} \frac{d^2v}{dt^2} + v = 0 \qquad \ldots(b)$

Hence characteristic equation is $S^2 + \dfrac{1}{20 \times 10^{-6}} = 0$

Hence $\quad S_1, S_2 = J\, 223.6$

Thus roots are *imaginary*. Hence solution will be

$$v(t) = k_1 e^{-J\,223.6\,t} + k_2 e^{-J\,223.6t}$$
$$= (k_1 + k_2)\cos(223.6)\,t + J[k_2 - k_1]\sin(223.6)\,t$$

Hence $\quad v(t) = k_3 \cos 223.6\,t + k_4 \sin 223.6\,t$

at $t = 0$, $\quad v(0) = 0 = k_3$

Also at $t = 0$, $\quad \left.\dfrac{dv}{dt}\right|_{t=0} = \dfrac{-10}{C} = -0.5 \times 10^6$ V/sec

Hence $\quad -0.5 \times 10^6 = [k_4\, 223.6 \cos(223.6)\,t]_{t=0}$

Hence $\quad k_4 = -2236.14$

Thus solution of $v(t)$ is given by $v(t) = -2236.14 \sin(223.6)\,t$

Hence current through inductor for $t > 0$ is

$$i_2(t) = \frac{1}{L}\int v(t)\, dt = \frac{-2236.1}{1}\int \sin(223.6)\,t$$

$$= \frac{-2236.1}{223.6}[-\cos(223.6)\,t] = 10\cos(223.6)\,t$$

EXERCISE

1. Explain various properties of a capacitor.
2. An capacitor with initial voltage V_0 is connected to a resistor of value R ohms at t = 0. Derive the expression for the voltage across capacitor and current through capacitor at any time t > 0.
3. Explain various properties of an inductor.
4. An inductor with initial current I_0 is connected to a resistor of R ohms at t = 0. Derive the expression for the current through inductor and voltage across inductor at any time t > 0.
5. The network shown attains steady state initially. At t = 0, switch is closed. Find $v_2(t)$ for t > 0.

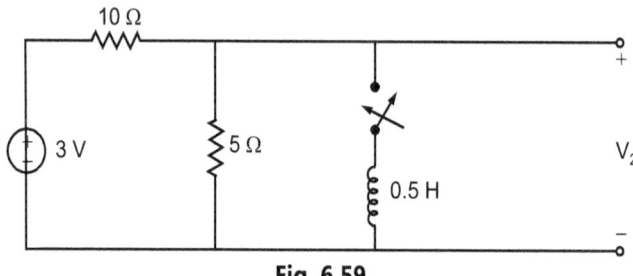

Fig. 6.59

6. Explain time constant in general. Determine the time constant of a source free R–L circuit in which the power output from inductance is 100 W at specific instant of time, and changes by 30 W after 1 sec.
7. Derive the expression for the current i(t) flowing in the circuit shown. i(0) = 0A, when the switch is closed at t = 0. Show the behaviour of i(t) graphically.

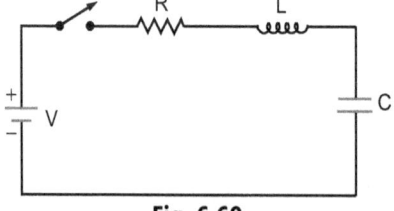

Fig. 6.60

8. In the circuit shown below, assume that the ammeter is ideal. If the initial values of voltage v_c and current i_L are 10V and 4A respectively. Determine the range of the ammeter.

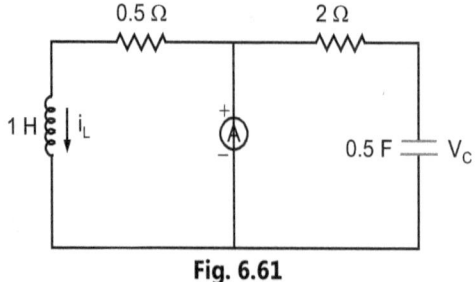

Fig. 6.61

9. A switch is closed at t = 0 connecting a Battery of V voltage with a series R-C circuit.
   (a) Determine the ratio of energy delivered to the capacitor to the total energy supplied by the source as a function of time.
   (b) Show that this ratio approaches 0.5 as t → ∞.

9. Find inverse L.T. of the following functions :

   (a) $\dfrac{3}{s(s^2 + 6s + 9)}$

   (b) $\dfrac{2s}{(s^2 + 4)(s + 5)}$

   (c) $\dfrac{1}{s(s^2 - a^2)}$

   (d) $\dfrac{s^2 + 7s^2 + 14s + 11}{s^3 + 6s^2 + 11s + 16}$

   (e) $\dfrac{s^2 + 3s^2 + 3s + 2}{s^2 + 2s + 2}$

   (f) $\dfrac{(s + 1)}{s^2(s^2 + 4s + 4)}$

   (g) $\dfrac{s^4 + 10s^2 + 9}{s^3 + 4s}$

   (h) $\dfrac{2(s^2 + 4s + 3)}{(s^2 + 8s + 12)}$

10. In the circuit switch 'K' is closed and steady state conditions reached. At t = 0 switch opened obtain expression for current through inductor and plot it.

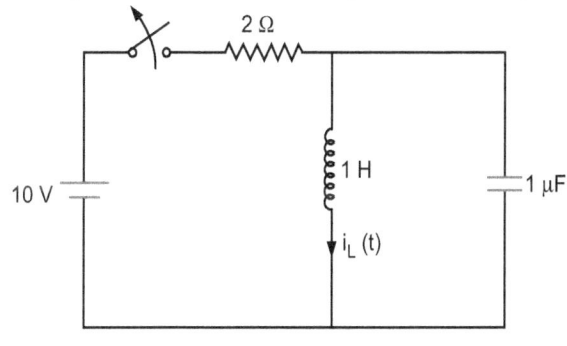

Fig. 6.62

(**Ans.** 5 cos 1000 t)

11. In the circuit shown find current through inductor if V(t) = 5 U(t).

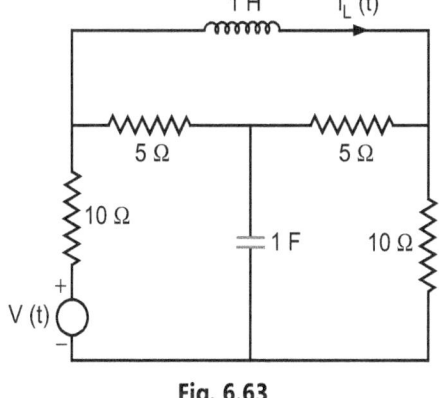

Fig. 6.63

12. Initially circuit is not energised at t = 0 both switches closed using superposition theorem find current in inductor use L.T.

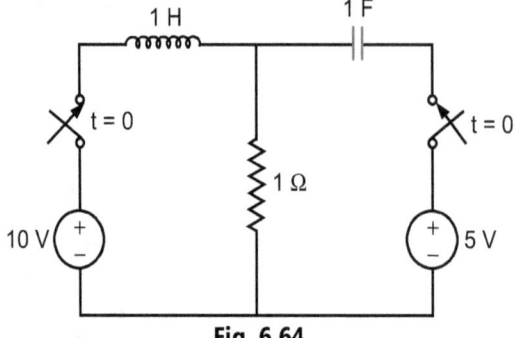

Fig. 6.64

14. For the circuit shown determine response V(t) when input i(t) is (1) impulse function, (2) unit step function.

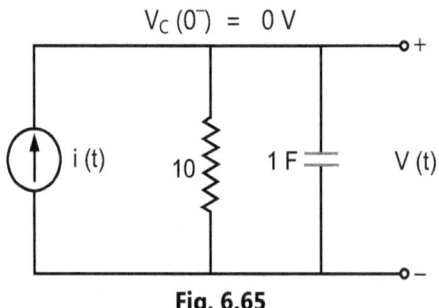

Fig. 6.65

(**Ans.** (1) e^{-t}, (2) $1 - e^{-t}$)

15. Assume unit impulse current find differential equation relating v(t) and i(t).

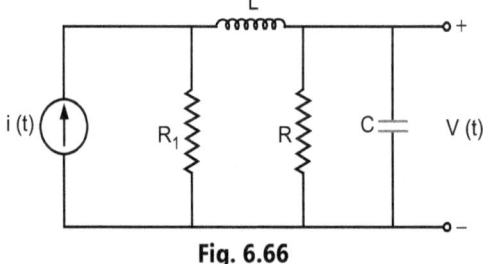

Fig. 6.66

www.ingramcontent.com/pod-product-compliance
Lightning Source LLC
Chambersburg PA
CBHW081413230426
43668CB00016B/2226